PSYCHOLOGY: A STUDY OF A SCIENCE

THE SERIES

STUDY I. CONCEPTUAL AND SYSTEMATIC

Volume 1. **Sensory, Perceptual, and Physiological Formulations**

CONTRIBUTORS: *Albert A. Blank, James J. Gibson, C. H. Graham, D. O. Hebb, Harry Helson, J. C. R. Licklider, Clifford T. Morgan, Kenneth N. Ogle, M. H. Pirenne and F. H. C. Marriott, Leo Postman and Edward C. Tolman, W. C. H. Prentice*

Volume 2. **General Systematic Formulations, Learning, and Special Processes**

CONTRIBUTORS: *Dorwin Cartwright, Douglas G. Ellson, W. K. Estes, F. C. Frick, Edwin R. Guthrie, Harry F. Harlow, R. A. Hinde, Arthur L. Irion, Frank A. Logan, Neal E. Miller, B. F. Skinner, Edward C. Tolman*

Volume 3. **Formulations of the Person and the Social Context**

CONTRIBUTORS: *Solomon E. Asch, Raymond B. Cattell, Franz J. Kallmann, Daniel Katz and Ezra Stotland, Paul F. Lazarsfeld, Henry A. Murray, Theodore M. Newcomb, Talcott Parsons, David Rapaport, Carl R. Rogers, Herbert A. Thelen*

STUDY II. EMPIRICAL SUBSTRUCTURE AND RELATIONS WITH OTHER SCIENCES

Volume 4. **Biologically Oriented Fields: Their Place in Psychology and in Biological Science**

> CONTRIBUTORS: *Fred Attneave, Paul R. David and Laurence H. Snyder, R. C. Davis, I. T. Diamond and K. L. Chow, C. H. Graham and Philburn Ratoosh, William H. Ittelson, Robert B. Livingston, Carl Pfaffmann, Karl H. Pribram, Floyd Ratliff, W. A. Rosenblith and Eda B. Vidale, Burton S. Rosner, Gerhardt von Bonin, Karl Zener and Mercedes Gaffron*

Volume 5. **The Process Areas, the Person, and Some Applied Fields: Their Place in Psychology and in Science**

> CONTRIBUTORS: *D. E. Berlyne, Irvin L. Child, Paul M. Fitts, Norman Guttman, Ernest R. Hilgard, Douglas H. Lawrence, Robert W. Leeper, Daniel R. Miller, Leo Postman, Eliot H. Rodnick, Julian B. Rotter, Nevitt Sanford, W. N. Schoenfeld and W. W. Cumming, Franklin V. Taylor*

Volume 6. **Investigations of Man as Socius: Their Place in Psychology and the Social Sciences**

> CONTRIBUTORS: *Kenneth J. Arrow, Donald T. Campbell, David French, A. Irving Hallowell, Alex Inkeles, George Katona, William W. Lambert, Robert E. Lane, F. G. Lounsbury, Charles E. Osgood, Muzafer Sherif, Herbert A. Simon, George and Louise Spindler, James Tobin and F. Trenery Dolbear, Jr.*

POSTSCRIPT TO THE STUDY
(This title in preparation)

Volume 7. Psychology and the Human Agent *(by Sigmund Koch)*

Psychology: A Study of a Science

STUDY I. CONCEPTUAL AND SYSTEMATIC

Volume 2. General Systematic Formulations, Learning, and Special Processes

Edited by Sigmund Koch

DUKE UNIVERSITY

McGRAW-HILL BOOK COMPANY

New York   Toronto   London

1959

PSYCHOLOGY: A STUDY OF A SCIENCE was made possible by funds granted by the National Science Foundation to the American Psychological Association, and carried out under the sponsorship of the latter organization. Neither agency, however, is to be construed as endorsing any of the published findings or conclusions of the Study.

9 10 11 12 13 14 15 16 – MAMM – 7 5 4 3 2 1 0

35271

PREFACE

When one looks back over the history of science, the successes are likely to be stressed and the failures forgotten. Thus one tends to see science as starting with a sure sense of direction and progressing neatly to its present form. Or so it is for the older and well established branches of science; but not for psychology. Psychology has not one sure sense of direction but several quite unsure directions. Growth is erratic and there is much casting about for the most crucial problems and the most powerful methods. These apparent differences between psychology and the older branches of science may result from the difficulty of developing a science of man; it is perhaps significant that many of the problems of psychology were not attacked by the methods of science until so late a date in history. Or the differences may be an illusion resulting from the much closer view we have of the beginning struggles to develop a science of psychology than we now have of the beginning efforts in the older sciences.

Certainly psychology has its problems, and they are not easy. Nevertheless, knowledge has grown rapidly in the short history of man's efforts to develop a science of behavior, and the time seems appropriate for a major effort to examine the progress that has been made in attempting to find a way, or ways, to the attainment of the explanatory power that we like to think of as characteristic of science. A growing body of empirical information, a serious concern over methodological issues, and a variety of efforts to bring a selected body of fact into the organizing framework of theory all emphasize the need for that line of questioning—always going on in science—which explores the shape of knowledge, the range and inner connections of the ideas through which it has been developed and organized, the changing substructures of empirical data, and their emerging relations to each other and to the findings of other sciences. The seven volumes of *Psychology: A Study of a Science* are a response to this need.

The first three volumes, which bear the collective title *Study I. Conceptual and Systematic*, are concerned with many of the systematic formulations of recent and current influence which psychologists have developed to account for the phenomena in which they are interested.

Each systematic position is analyzed by its originator, or a person connected with its development, in a way which gives attention to the problems it seeks to solve, the empirical basis on which it rests, its degree of success, and its relations to other formulations.

A second set of three volumes, collectively called *Study II. Empirical Substructure and Relations with Other Sciences*, inquires, again through the efforts of creatively active investigators, into the organization of various fields of empirical knowledge, the relations of one to another, and to work going forward in other sciences. It also examines such problems in reverse through the participation of social and biological scientists who consider the relations of their own special fields to various parts of psychology. The three volumes of Study II, now in preparation, will be published at a later date.

Volume 7—*Psychology and the Human Agent*—will present the Study Director's view of certain problems of psychological inquiry in the light of the findings of the project.

Primary credit for the initiation of these studies goes to the Association's Policy and Planning Board, which decided in 1952 that the time had come for a thorough and critical examination of the status and development of psychology. The National Science Foundation agreed upon the desirability of such an undertaking and has generously supported the effort. When funds from the National Science Foundation were found to be insufficient for all of the expenses of the studies, the American Psychological Association provided the supplementary funds necessary to complete the work.

From the beginning, the study was divided into two parts. One part dealt with the education of psychologists and the factors conducive to research productivity in psychology. That part was directed by Professor Kenneth Clark of the University of Minnesota, who has reported the findings in *America's Psychologists: A Survey of a Growing Profession*, published by the American Psychological Association in 1957.

The other part, the part with which the present series of volumes is concerned, has dealt with the substance of psychological thought and data. Professor Sigmund Koch of Duke University has been responsible for this part of the study. Working closely with him has been a panel of consultants consisting of Lyle H. Lanier, Howard H. Kendler, Conrad G. Mueller, and Karl E. Zener. These men, but chiefly Dr. Koch, have planned, organized, interpreted and edited the work, and successfully enlisted the cooperation of the approximately 80 authors whose original papers will constitute the basic material of the series.

In the background, at a safe distance from the labors that have sometimes engulfed Dr. Koch, his panel of consultants, and the primary authors, has been a steering committee on which I had the pleasure of serving as chairman, and having as colleagues Clarence H. Graham, Lyle H. Lanier, Robert B. MacLeod, Eliot H. Rodnick, M. Brewster Smith, and Robert L. Thorndike. The steering committee helped to make administrative arrangements and helped to decide on the scope of the studies, but takes no credit for their successful completion.

In the preface to *America's Psychologists* we have already acknowledged our gratitude to Kenneth Clark and his collaborators who helped to produce that volume. It is our final pleasant duty to express our thanks to Duke University for making Dr. Koch's time available; to the National Science Foundation for its necessary and generous financial support and for the counsel and support of John T. Wilson, Assistant Director for the Biological Sciences; to Lyle H. Lanier, Howard H. Kendler, Conrad G. Mueller, and Karl E. Zener for their critical and devoted help; to all of the authors whose names appear on the title pages for their original contributions; and—most of all—to Sigmund Koch for directing and driving through to completion what we hope will be an oft-consulted aid to the scholars and research workers who are striving to increase the rigor and further the development of scientific psychology.

Dael Wolfle, CHAIRMAN
STEERING COMMITTEE
POLICY AND PLANNING BOARD

CONTENTS

INTRODUCTION TO VOLUME 2

Psychology: A Study of a Science is a report of inquiries into the status and tendency of psychological science. Some eighty distinguished authors have contributed sustained essays which consider: (Study I) major theoretical formulations of recent importance; and (Study II) the structure, mutual interrelations, and associations with other sciences of the main empirical areas in which psychological research is pursued. The findings of *Study I   Conceptual and Systematic* comprise the initial three volumes of the series; *Study II   Empirical Substructure and Relations with Other Sciences* is reported in the following three volumes. A final volume by the Study Director—*Psychology and the Human Agent* —includes commentary on the significance of the findings.

The present volume is the second in the series and is part of Study I. Each of the twelve essays in this book is a self-contained presentation which may be read with profit independently of the others, or of the contents of other volumes. Yet the reader must bear in mind that the present volume is only a fragment of Study I, and that Study I is part of a larger enterprise having certain unifying values, aims, and methods. For a conception of these latter, the reader is referred to Dael Wolfle's Preface and to the two introductory sections in Volume I—one for the series, the other specifically for Study I.

As an immediate aid to the reader, a resumé of the Study's design is given.

Study I   Conceptual and Systematic. This study involved the intensive analysis of thirty-four "systematic formulations" of widely varying type and subject-matter reference and all of established influence in recent psychology. A "systematic formulation" was defined quite generally as "any set of sentences formulated as a tool for ordering knowledge with respect to some specified domain of events, or furthering the discovery of such knowledge": in applying this definition, care was taken that no formulation be precluded by nonconformity to standardized conceptions of the nature of "theory." Since each systematic formulation is the end-product of a human effort to see and state order in a given domain, each analysis was made either by the originator(s) of the formulation in question or (in a few cases) by individuals creatively associated

1

with the *development* of formulations of which they were not the primary authors.

Each systematist was invited to approach his work with certain common *themes of analysis* in mind. These were designed to invite a convergence of insight on those problems of systematization which had emerged from the practice of the past three decades, more or less. Some of the suggested problems had been conspicuous in previous "meta-systematic" discussion, but required in our opinion exposure to a wider range of systematically schooled sensibilities. Others were problems that seemed critically posed by recent systematic work, yet ones which had received little or no explicit attention.

The dominating hope was for analyses that might illumine the relations between the creative *processes* of systematizing and their publicly expressed *products*. It was thus hoped that the atmosphere of the study might encourage as much concern with background influences, orienting presuppositions, and working methods, as with conceptual content, research achievements, and prospects. It was felt that analysis of this order could itself have creative consequences; reflective scrutiny of the extent and depth envisaged means *re*thinking. The primary intent of the discussion themes (and indeed the constant aim of all editorial effort) was to realize an atmosphere that might invite such emphases. Authors were requested to make explicit reference to the themes in their writing only to an extent they deemed appropriate or congenial. The use of the themes for facilitating the collation of findings was thus a secondary, if still important, aim. As matters turned out, most authors adhered to them sufficiently to give the reader an excellent purchase for the detection of similarities and differences on key issues.

The grounds for the selection of the thirty-four formulations included in Study I are given in Volume 1 (pp. 21–27). The aim was a reasonably balanced diversification of formulations (as judged by many consultants) with respect to (*a*) subject-matter reference, and (*b*) conceptual and methodological "type." Many significant formulations that we would have wished to represent in the original list were excluded by spatial and other arbitrary restrictions. Nor are all formulations originally chosen included in the present volumes. Though the proportion of inclusions is remarkable, there were some individuals who could not participate. We do not, then, claim "representativeness" even in an informal and impressionistic sense. We do, however, claim sufficient diversity to extend markedly the range of formulations which in recent years have been given sustained analytic attention.

Study II   Empirical Substructure and Relations with Other Sciences. This study seeks increased understanding of the internal structure of psychological science and its place in the matrix of scientific activity. Over forty contributors, having distinguished research backgrounds in psychology, or in related biological and social sciences, were invited to write papers which examine the organization of empirical knowledge within subareas of these disciplines, and which chart their cross connections. Psychologist contributors consider the relations between their own fields of special competence and the rest of psychology, and inquire also into relations with relevant segments of other sciences. Social and biological science contributors examine the relations between their own fields and psychology.

All authors are individuals whose research interests have bridged conventionally discriminated fields of knowledge. Each was asked to place special emphasis on those "bridging problems" which had been central in his own research experience. As in the case of Study I, an attempt was made to encourage differentiated and stratified analysis, and to invite a convergence of visions on significant cross-cutting issues, by proposing certain common themes of analysis. The "themes" for Study II comprise a detailed breakdown of the senses in which questions of "mapping" subject-matter structure and exploring field interrelations might be entertained.

Though the topography of a science is too vast and labile for comprehensive or final mapping, this very fact makes it more important to assay the contours of knowledge as best we can. Study II exploits the only resource available for such problems—individual vision—but in a novel way. It assumes that a *pooling* of expert, specialized sensibilities can give insight into the emerging structure of a science of a sort not ordinarily available.

A fuller statement of the plan for Study II appears in the General Introduction to the Series (Vol. I, pp. 1–18). An adequate account of working methods must await publication of the completed study.

Psychology and the Human Agent. This volume is a postscript to the Study, representing certain views formed by the Director in its course. The book (*a*) records those attitudes towards *a* science and science which necessarily color the spirit of the Study, (*b*) constructs trends from the massive findings of the two group studies, and (*c*) considers, in the light of the Study's premises and apparent trends, certain problems of psychological inquiry suggested by the practice of the past several decades.

In this day in which "self studies" and reductions of enigma by seminar are becoming commonplace in social science, it may be helpful to mention a few of the special features of *Psychology: A Study of a Science.* May we stress (in random order) the following points:

1. Both group studies are "collaborative" but only in the special sense that many creative men agreed to pursue, within the climate of the Study, *individual* tasks of vital interest to themselves. The Study is not collaborative or "groupish" in any sense implying an intention to relinquish individuality or even idiosyncrasy to some prissy conception of the common weal.

2. The Study aims for *no* grand "integration" of knowledge. If a "Summa Psychologica" or even a "Synopticon" had seemed even remotely within reach, our inclination would have been to abstain on principle. The Study seeks to reflect the diversity of thought that actually exists and is premised on the values of widespread diversification of approach as a condition to the health of a science. It conceives of its contributor groups as *pluralities* of creative individuals who view those areas which they know best through the screen of their own expert sensibilities. The discussion outlines invite the play of individual sensibilities on commensurable themes, thus helping the reader to collate positions.

3. The Study's aims are neither legislative nor evaluative. It rejects all monolithic codes for the generation and processing of knowledge, or for virtuous scientific conduct. If there is a central bias, it is for the loosening of those constraints which can keep men from significant problems or thoughts through fear of the unorthodox.

The Study by no means devalues the insights of recent "science of science" but would wish them set in a perspective better adjusted to a field barely beginning to test established methods of science on an illimitably diverse and intricate collection of subject matters. Such a perspective can emerge by seeing the end-products of science as everywhere conditioned by human decision, value, creative option; by freeing from staleness that truism which holds scientific inquiry to be continuous with other human activities. Analysis in science, then, becomes more than a succession of routine tasks in the "logic" of science; it becomes an enterprise which can uncover the significance of its objects only by holding in view the relations between creative process and sentential product, strategic gamble and cognitive outcome.

For those connected with psychological science, neither the contributors to the present volume nor the topics will require special introduction. Six of the formulations herein discussed—those of Lewin (treated by Cartwright), Tolman, Guthrie, Miller, Hull-Spence (treated by Logan), and Skinner—have long represented major systematic reference points in fundamental psychology. Estes' formulation is perhaps outstanding in the recent class of efforts towards a statistical systematization of learning. Harlow and Irion consider the systematic import of relatively limited domains of learning data, one of them ("learning sets") a field of investigation only recently opened up, and the other (rote learning) the oldest area of learning experimentation. Hinde presents what to date must be a unique analytico-systematic appraisal of the work on animal behavior by European ethologists. Finally, Frick and Ellson present general analyses of two of the mathematical formulations (information theory and linear frequency theory) which have been most heavily drawn upon in recent attempts to achieve "mathematical models" of psychological and behavioral processes. Be it noted that the two latter formulations are of *methodic* import in that they are relational analyses applicable (at least in principle) to *classes* of possible event-systems; all other formulations considered herein have, in the first instance, *substantive* reference.

The twelve formulations included have a loose family relationship, though one difficult to specify. It is possible to say that, by and large, they are "behavioral" formulations, that most give primary or strong emphasis to problems of learning (and would be called instances of "learning theory"), that most have explanatory intentions of some generality. But these are "by and larges" and "mosts." It can assuredly be said that the formulations represented in this volume have (in their respective ways) powerfully determined the horizons of thought in what might be called "behavior theory" by some, "basic psychological theory" by others.

Mention of certain editorial provisions is in order. Readers will find the complete statement of discussion themes, as sent to contributors, reproduced in the Appendix. There is, of course, variation in the extent to which the different presentations adhere to the discussion themes. As an aid to readers interested in the detection of key convergences and divergences of positions, index numbers corresponding to the principal thematic items have been inserted, where relevant, in the individual tables of contents appearing before each paper. The system of index numbers is explained in the Appendix.

A statement of a few trends of Study I, based on the essays in all three volumes, appears as an editorial epilogue in Volume 3. The statement is brief, being restricted to those generalizations which seem so obvious as to be almost self-defining. Further discussion of trends will be offered in the final volume of the series, *Psychology and the Human Agent*. There is, however, no standard "theory" of the meaning of this study. If there were, we would consider the main aim compromised. That aim has been to develop materials of unique comprehensiveness and depth in terms of which each reader may enrich his *own* view of systematic psychology. The thirty-four essays of Study I can reward efforts towards secondary analysis and synthesis—whether by student, specialized scholar, or general reader—for a long time to come. Let there be as many theories of this study as there are readers.

Psychology: A Study of a Science is the result of a project sponsored by the American Psychological Association and subsidized by the National Science Foundation. The project was known as "Project A" of the "APA Study of the Status and Development of Psychology." The work profited from the counsel of an Advisory Committee consisting of Dael Wolfle, Chairman, and Clarence H. Graham, Lyle H. Lanier, Robert B. MacLeod, Eliot H. Rodnick, M. Brewster Smith, and Robert L. Thorndike. Howard H. Kendler, Lyle H. Lanier, Conrad G. Mueller, and Karl E. Zener composed a Panel of Consultants to the Director. The generous part played by the members of both groups is described in the introductory sections of Volume 1.

LEWINIAN THEORY AS A CONTEMPORARY SYSTEMATIC FRAMEWORK

DORWIN CARTWRIGHT
Research Center for Group Dynamics and Department of Psychology, University of Michigan

   *The bracketed numbers, when they occur in the tables of contents of the essays in this volume, indicate items in the Suggested Discussion Topics relevant to the headings which they follow. See Note on the Use of Discussion Topic Index Numbers in Appendix.

This paper examines the significance of Lewinian theory for psychologists of today. The theory, as embodied in the publications of Lewin, was developed during a period of about thirty years which ended with his death in 1947. Its influence has been strong and pervasive, not confined to any single branch of psychology nor to those psychologists who were personally associated with him. For this reason, my task here is a difficult one. I cannot "speak for" those who have been influenced by Lewin's work nor can I presume to guess how Lewin would have modified or extended his thought in the light of recent developments. This paper, therefore, must be a personal one in which I give my own diagnosis of the present condition of psychology and my own view of the significance of the general Lewinian approach for the tasks that lie ahead.[1] Since Lewin's influence has permeated psychological thinking for more than a quarter-century and since his own thought was developed in a widely shared intellectual climate, it is natural that the point of view advocated here will contain many features acceptable to a great variety of psychologists. I shall try, however, to emphasize those aspects of Lewinian thought which in my opinion represent a distinctive orientation.

It will be useful to begin with a general characterization of the nature of Lewin's contribution to psychology. He referred to his work by various names, "dynamic theory," "topological psychology," "vector psychology," and "field theory," but his final preference seems to have been "field theory." What, then, is field theory? Lewin [95, p. 45] answered this question most concisely when he asserted that "field theory is probably best characterized as a method: namely, a method of analyzing causal relations and of building scientific constructs." In other words, it is a set of beliefs about the proper way to build empirical theories; it is, in current terminology, a metatheory. But this is not the entire story, for Lewin's impact on psychology derives from more than his metatheoretical contributions. His influence has been exerted also through certain constructs which he introduced. The current language of psychologists contains many terms due to Lewin: life space, psychological force, valence, tension, level of aspiration, time perspective, and others. In this paper we shall be concerned with field theory both as a theory

---

[1] The reader is referred to three other critical expositions of Lewinian theory. The first, by Leeper [85], is a detailed analysis of Lewin's topological and vector concepts. The second, by Deutsch [40], discusses the significance of Lewinian theory for social psychology. The third, by Escalona [44], reports especially certain recent developments in work with children. Although I cannot agree with every detail of these three treatments, I can recommend them highly to anyone wishing to understand the nature of Lewin's contribution to psychology. Because these three discussions together provide a comprehensive treatment, this paper will necessarily cover many of the points contained in them.

about theorizing and as a set of constructs for describing psychological phenomena.

Because of the relatively heavy emphasis in Lewinian theory on meta-theoretical and programmatic problems, I have not found it possible in this chapter to conform strictly to the outline provided by the editorial committee. Where it has seemed necessary to deviate, a footnote indicates the relation of the outline followed here to that recommended by the committee.

BACKGROUND FACTORS AND ORIENTING ATTITUDES

What is the task of psychology? Most psychologists would agree that the task of psychology, stated in general terms, is to understand, explain, or predict human behavior. If one does not press too hard concerning the precise meaning of such terms as "behavior," "understand," or "predict," there appears to be good agreement as to the goals of psychology. If, however, one examines how particular psychologists go about their work and attempts to infer from this what the actual goals are, then agreement is not so evident.

Contemporary psychological thought is heavily determined by the fact that psychology gained its independence from philosophy only in the last half of the nineteenth century. The right to independence, the justification for separate status, was the psychologist's ability to employ experimentation and measurement. These two marks of "science" served as indicators of respectability among psychologists. "If you can't manipulate it experimentally or at least measure it, you shouldn't talk about it" became the psychologist's creed. Sensation, perception, learning (as a modification of observed behavior), and ability (defined as a test score), by meeting these requirements reasonably well, threatened for a time to become *the* field psychology. Such a narrow designation did not achieve full acceptance only because of the persistence of a "lunatic fringe" who insisted that human experience and behavior are "richer" than this list of topics would suggest, that man loves, hates, is driven by anxiety, holds doggedly to prejudices, fights and dies for abstract ideas, creates art, writes poetry, and responds deeply to religion. Although respectable psychologists have come more and more over the years to recognize the possibility of measuring such "fuzzy" phenomena and of doing experiments upon them, conflict still exists between those who would be true to human experience and those who would be "scientific" above all else, and tension remains within those who attempt both. This tension is symptomatic of some of the most basic issues of present-day psychology concerning its task in the immediate future.

For Lewin, and those who accept his orientation, the most important task of psychology is to devise ways of treating the full empirical reality of human experience and behavior in a scientific manner without doing violence to them. If "hope" or "frustration" cannot now be measured precisely, they should not for this reason be exiled to the world of the novelist. Nor should they be tortuously "explained" in terms of some inappropriate theory simply because the theory is quantitative or formally elegant. Rather, research tools and concepts appropriate to the degree of available knowledge should be employed, and any step toward extending the legitimate domain of psychology should be cause for gratification. The major contributions of a Freud or a Lewin consist in making psychology better able to deal with such things as dreams, aspirations, frustration, social climates, and other undeniable, though "messy," facts of life.

This preference for what Robert MacLeod once called "sloppy validity over neat reliability" is not, of course, held only by field theorists, nor does it characterize the essential features of field theory, but it may help account for the complaint of Estes [45] that field theorists have contributed little to the limited domain of psychological activity referred to as "behavior theory." Field theory, together with gestalt psychology more generally, developed as a revolt against the prevailing tendency to prejudge the nature of psychological phenomena by imposing a priori dicta concerning the properties they must have. Neither commitment to a theoretical belief (e.g., that perception must be composed of elements of sensation) nor allegiance to a methodological principle (e.g., that all data must be scalable) should become so important to the psychologist that he blinds himself to the proper subject matter of psychology. It is the full understanding of this rich, complicated, and often baffling subject matter that is the ultimate goal of psychology. Every theoretical formulation and every method of research must be evaluated in terms of its contribution toward achieving this goal. The ideal that psychology as a science should consist of precisely quantified data organized into a completely coherent and logically rigorous system of theory is indeed attractive. But one may seriously question whether this ideal will best be realized by insisting at every stage of research that rigor and precision be accorded the highest priority.

Open-minded observation. Discussions of psychological theory tend to concentrate nowadays on the logical and semantic aspects of the symbols that constitute a theory. And, for some reason, the derivation of Boyle's law from the molecular theory of gases inevitably enters as the ideal to which all psychologists should aspire. I do not wish to disparage concern for the logical properties of conceptual systems (field theorists are greatly interested in such matters) nor to depreciate the elegance or practical utility of the molecular theory of gases, but I am greatly afraid that the contemporary interest of psychologists in formal theory has tended too much to minimize the important task of observation. Barker and Wright [13] have recently voiced this same fear when they assert that psychology is less interested than other sciences in the painstaking observation of phenomena in their natural state.

Although we have daily records of the behavior of volcanoes, of the tides, of sun spots, and of rats and monkeys, there have been few scientific records of how a human mother cared for her young, how a particular teacher behaved in the classroom and how the children responded, what a family actually did and said during a mealtime, or how any boy lived his life from the time he awoke in the morning until he went to sleep at night [13, p. 2].

The approach to psychological research advocated here is hardly debatable in principle; everyone favors empirical data. And yet it is remarkable what low status is given, by American psychologists at least, to a "merely phenomenological analysis" and how great a pressure there is to reject "clinical insight" as a proper aid to *scientific* psychology. The high status accorded formal rigor, experimental control, and precise measurement threatens to blind psychology to reality as it actually exists. The great activity of recent years, to cite one example, devoted to measuring "empathic ability" has produced indecisive conclusions not merely because of the logical flaws of measurement pointed out so ably by Gage and Cronbach [64] but perhaps more importantly because of the neglect of such careful phenomenological analyses as that of Scheler [121] concerning the nature of sympathy. One reason that so much of psychological theory is "impractical," and thus one source of the unfortunate gulf between pure and applied psychology, is the tendency of psychological theorists to select for investigation only those variables which lend themselves immediately to the niceties of formal and methodological manipulation. Psychological theorists must not forget the importance of maintaining an open-minded look at what people actually think, feel, and do and at the settings or situations in which events take place. Any theory will be judged ultimately by how well it copes with descriptive data of this sort.

In order to gain a balanced view of Lewin's basic orientation, it is important to recall not only his concern for mathematical models and formal systems in such works as *Principles of Topological Psychology* and *The Conceptual Representation and Measurement of Psychological Forces* but also the great value he placed upon the movies he took of a single child trying to sit on a stone or to walk up stairs for the first time and upon such richly descriptive studies as that of Dembo [37] on anger. It is significant that, although Lewin was disturbed by the dominance of "dust-bowl empiricism" in American psychology during much of his life, he felt constrained time after time, in presenting his topological concepts, to point out that these were intended to be *aids to description*. "In presenting them we are not promulgating a new 'system' limited to a specific content, but rather we are describing a 'tool,' a set of concepts by means of which one can represent psychological reality" [91, p. 6]. In discussing how his objectives compared to those of Hull he developed this point further. "Psychology needs stressing the formalistic. Yet, it would soon prove most unfortunate if one should lose sight of the fact that the main purpose of psychological theories is, after all, to explain reality. In psychology, for a long time to come, the richness and fruitfulness of theories should not be judged by their formalistic perfection alone" [91, p. 22].

Description and explanation. One could easily caricature the position advanced here by saying that it would have psychologists act like a court reporter whose assignment is simply to get down on paper everything that is said or done. This would be a caricature of the intended point of view because the essential argument is not that the psychologist's task *consists of* observation but that psychological theory should *begin* with observations of naturally occurring behavior and should be *evaluated* in terms of how adequately they help us understand such behavior. *For observation to be of any use to the psychologist it must be converted into a description.* And the essential difference between a psychologist and a reporter or novelist lies in the kind of description provided.

One of the basic paradoxes of science is that, whereas observation provides the ultimate test of a scientific theory, the language of description employed by the scientist influences his observations. The very fact of having a descriptive concept available serves to sensitize the observer to certain phenomena; it helps him to see what is there. At the same time, an "incorrect" concept may lead him to give a distorted picture of actual events. For this reason, many advances in psychology consist of the creation of new concepts, and much of the difficulty in making progress stems from an uncritical acceptance of the language generally employed by psychologists.

The psychologist, then, is properly concerned with the language of descriptions that he uses. To him any description should be "two-faced," looking simultaneously to the world of data and to that of concepts. It is this double-directedness of description that allows concepts both to describe and to explain. A "mere description" consists of a set of concepts which refer primarily to data and only loosely to a system of concepts. If, however, it can be shown that certain events "must" occur because the corresponding concepts are related in a particular way, then these events have been explained.

14 DORWIN CARTWRIGHT

Lewin stated this point of view as follows:

> The task of dynamic psychology is to find the psychological laws and to represent the situation in such a way that the actual events can be derived from it in a conceptually univocal manner. If the objection is raised that it is self-evident that the events follow from these representations of situations, one has to answer that this is exactly the purpose. What we are trying to do is to represent situations in such a way that the events follow from them "self-evidently," namely as purely logical consequences.

> If one wants to call this "description," it is not worth while to quibble over words. But if one considers conceptual derivation and the transition from phenomenal to dynamic facts as the characteristics of an explanation, then what we have here is in fact explanation [91, p. 82].

In this connection it may be helpful to consider briefly the accusation that field theorists cannot predict but can only account for psychological events after they have happened. This criticism may have two different meanings. The criticism may mean that field theoretical explanations are "contained in" the description of particular situations. The answer then consists of maintaining that it is not necessary to invoke causes outside the situation to explain it. An adequate description of a situation together with a knowledge of the relevant psychological laws permits one to *derive* the events immediately brought about by the situation. Thus, to give an oversimplified example, if one knows that the need tension of an individual is at a certain level and if one knows the law relating tension to tendencies to action, then it is possible to derive (in this sense, predict) that certain action will occur. The criticism may, on the other hand, imply that the laws of psychology are not sufficiently developed and the techniques of measurement and observation are not now adequate to allow absolutely certain derivations from the description of one concrete situation to the properties of a subsequent one. The answer to this form of the criticism can only be that field theorists are in no different status, in principle, than other theorists.

Language of description. Since the description of any concrete situation consists of a symbolic representation of it, one must be concerned with the choice and manipulation of symbols. What language should psychologists employ? The answer to this question is a point at which field theorists part company with many other psychologists. To the field theorist it appears that psychology should describe events in a psychological, rather than physical or physiological, language. Without denying the possibility of an eventual unification of science so that a single language may be used, the field theorist asserts that insistence upon using the language of physics or physiology at this time imposes harmful restrictions upon accurate description of psychological events.

Lewin believed that use of the language of physics or of physiology consists actually of employing an inappropriate model for representing psychological events. His discussion of this problem may seem strange to those who have categorized Lewin as a "model builder."

We have intentionally avoided the use of any model of a physical or of a nonphysical nature for the explanation of psychological dynamics.

Like an illustration the working out of a model can have a certain value. On the other hand it can, especially in psychology, involve serious dangers: a model usually contains much that is purely arbitrary. One usually uses it like an illustration only in so far as the analogy holds, i.e., really only as long as it is convenient. As soon as consequences ensue which do not agree with the real facts, one evades the difficulty by asserting that it is after all only a model or an illustration. . . . In this respect model and illustration are sharply distinguished from the mathematical representation which we are trying to attain. If one decides to represent a real fact by a mathematical concept then one is forced to acknowledge all the consequences which are involved in this concept. . . .

One must welcome every attempt to go beyond vague ideas to concrete formulations in psychological dynamics. Often the psychologists who take this task seriously have been driven to attempt to make "physiological" theories. I do not consider that tendency fortunate. Certainly one cannot object in the least to applying physiological methods and to including in the theory material so obtained. . . . But the so-called physiological theories which are based on psychological facts have almost always the character of a physiological or rather physical model of which the same is to be said as of the other models. With a physiological model, too, the relationships with which one is concerned are not expressed directly in concepts but only indirectly in illustration, and these often include superfluous specializations. The task of scientific research is, however, to determine the dynamic characteristics of the facts themselves [91, pp. 77–80].

A much more recent analysis of hypothetical constructs by Rozeboom [119] places this point of view in the context of current discussions of "mediation variables."

Neurophysiological content is not only at present inadequate for behavioral HCs (hypothetical constructs), but also basically irrelevant. Presuming the switchboard theory of neural action to be true, we could in principle replace each neurone with a mechanical or electronic device with the same connections and input-output characteristics as the replaced cell without affecting the validity of any behavioral law. Since neurophysiological attributes are thus not essential for a physical behavior system, a set of HCs need possess no nuerophysiological content in order to describe the necessary properties of the causal mediators underlying behavior. . . . I suggest, therefore, (*a*) that despite the complexity of the central nervous system, those of its properties which are essentially involved in the causal determination of the dependent variables of behavioral psychology may possibly be reflected by a relatively small number of HCs without neurophysiological reference; and (b) that the necessary ontological content of such HCs need consist only of existential quantification (the logical operator "∃x") and relational predicates [119, p. 262].

Even in describing the environment of a person a physical description is not sufficient. Although no one would deny that the environment is mediated by physical processes, there is real question as to the present possibility of describing this environment in the language of physics, employing only such terms as electromagnetic field, molecule, ion, or centimeter, gram, and second. Cassirer has stated the problem in the following terms:

No longer in a merely physical universe, man lives in a symbolic universe. Language, myth, art, and religion are parts of this universe. They are the varied threads which weave the symbolic net, the tangled web of human experience. All human progress in thought and experience refines upon and strengthens this net. No longer can man confront reality immediately; he cannot see it, as it were, face to face. Physical reality seems to recede in proportion as man's symbolic activity advances. Instead of dealing with things themselves man is in a sense constantly conversing with himself. He has so enveloped himself in linguistic forms, in artistic images, in mythical symbols or religious rites that he cannot see or know anything except by the inter-position of this artificial medium. His situation is the same in the theoretical as in the practical sphere. Even here man does not live in a world of hard facts, or according to immediate needs and desires. He lives rather in the midst of imaginary emotions, in hopes and fears, in illusions and disillusions, in his fantasies and dreams. "What disturbs and alarms man," said Epictetus, "are not the things, but his opinions and fancies about the things" [31, p. 43].

A proper respect for the nature of psychological phenomena places upon psychologists the task of constructing a language adequate to represent these phenomena. Presuppositions about the ultimate unity of science or about the biological nature of man should not be allowed to force an arbitrary descriptive language upon psychology.

Concreteness. One final orienting attitude of field theorists deserves careful examination here. An important value to be gained from insistence on a painstaking observation of natural events is the stress it continually places upon concreteness. As Lewin has pointed out:

Only what is concrete can have effects. This proposition may seem obvious. But one often ignores it in explaining an event by development, by adaptation . . . by an abstract drive, and in treating these principles as concrete causes. . . . These fallacies arise in part from a confusion between the law that governs the effects of certain concrete events and these events themselves. Effects can be produced only by what is "concrete," i.e., by something that has the position of an individual fact which exists at a certain moment [91, pp. 32–33].

Once this principle is accepted, Lewin believed, four important consequences follow. (1) Every specific instance of behavior must be viewed as the result of the interaction of several features of a given concrete situation. (2) The description of human behavior cannot, without peril, concentrate exclusively on cognition, or learning, or motivation, or personality, or social influences, or economics, or politics, or culture. (3) A distinction must be made between the concrete field, or life space, in which behavior takes place and the phase space, or property space, which may be employed to represent quantitative relations among properties. (4) Causation must be viewed as contemporary with the event caused; "since neither the past nor the future exists at the present moment it cannot have effects at the present" [91, p. 35].

1. Lewinian field theory and gestalt psychology both emphasize the importance of recognizing the interdependence of parts of any concrete situation. The classical demonstrations of gestalt phenomena in perception illustrate the point adequately. A sensitive analysis of how a given child learns in a classroom will also reveal the interdependence of such aspects of the situation as state of tension, level of aspiration, time perspective, relations with teacher and other students, social pressures from family, and even the family's relations with other families within the community. Stating the point as an abstract principle, Lewin said, "only by the concrete whole which comprises the object and the situation are the vectors which determine the dynamics of the event defined" [90, p. 29].

2. If behavior is determined by the concrete total situation in which it exists, then any theory which attempts to account for behavior solely in terms of learning, or motivation, or any other limited aspect of the total complex of determinants cannot be adequate. It is true that no comprehensive theory of human behavior has yet been developed by field theorists (or anyone else), but field theorists attempt to formulate their theories in such a way that a representation of the total situation is possible in principle.

Lewin's own professional career illustrates how a commitment to represent faithfully the concrete situation requires one to cross the boundaries of the traditionally designated "fields of psychology" and even of the academic "disciplines." Lewin's early research dealt with learning and perception [87, 88, 89, 99] but this led him to see the inevitable interplay between these processes and motivation, as illustrated for example in the Zeigarnik effect [142]. Investigation of these motivational influences led in turn to an analysis of reward and punishment

[90, pp. 114–170] and of conflict [90, pp. 66–113], both of which required inclusion of motivational forces "induced" by other people. Once the importance of these social influences was recognized, it became appropriate to examine how one person, e.g., a group leader, uses his ability to induce forces on another person to help or restrict him. Closer scrutiny of these aspects of the situation then led to the studies of "types" of leadership and of social atmospheres [94, pp. 71–83, 98]. It led also to studies of the constellation of forces determined by group membership [94, pp. 84–102, 145–158], and by the values of groups [94, pp. 56–68]. Finally, it led to an examination of the restraints and compulsions exerted by technology, economics, laws, and social "channels" and "gatekeepers" [95, pp. 170–187]. The important feature of this whole development is that the desire to represent faithfully the full complexity of concrete situations resulted in a continual crossing of the traditional boundaries of the social sciences rather than a progressive narrowing of attention to a limited number of variables. This insistence upon the complexity of the determinants of any concrete instance of behavior makes the task of building a true "behavior theory" extremely difficult. The field theorist believes, however, that theories which do not take these complexities into account are bound to be not merely limited, or miniature systems, but actually incorrect.

3. The third consequence of the principle that "only what is concrete can have effects" is that a distinction must be made between "life space" and "phase space." Although this distinction was never extensively discussed by Lewin and the full ramifications of it for psychology have never been worked out, I believe that in it lies a clarification of the field theorist's treatment of *interdependence*. Lewin's brief discussion of the problem may be illuminating.

Success in a certain sport may depend upon a combination of muscular strength, velocity of movement, ability to make quick decisions, and precise perception of direction and distance. A change in any one of these five variables might alter the result to a certain degree. One can represent these variables as five dimensions of a diagram. The resultant of any possible constellation of these factors for the amount of success can be marked as a point in the diagram. The totality of these points then is a diagrammatic representation of this dependence, in other words, of an empirical law.

Physics frequently makes use of such representation of a multitude of factors influencing an event. To each of certain properties, such as temperature, pressure, time, spatial position, one dimension is coordinated. Such a representation in physics is called "phase space." Such a phase space may have twenty dimensions if twenty factors have to be considered. A phase space is something definitely different from that three-dimensional "physical space" within which physical objects are moving. In the same way the psychological space, the life space or psychological field, in which psychological locomotion or structural changes take place, is something different from those diagrams where dimensions mean merely gradations of properties [95, p. 44].

The life space is intended to represent the concrete situation whose interdependent properties determine a specific psychological event. A phase space may be constructed to express the laws governing the properties of life spaces. Thus, in an experiment like that of Zeigarnik [142] a given act of recall is conceived as being determined by the resultant of the psychological forces acting on the person at a given time. The law suggested by Zeigarnik's findings asserts that the magnitude of the psychological force toward recalling a particular activity is some positive function of the magnitude of inner-personal tension associated with the activity. This law may be represented by means of a two-dimensional phase space; the concrete situation in which a specific subject exists is represented by the subject's life space. The precise form of the law will depend upon the nature of interdependence among properties of concrete life spaces. Field theorists are completely in favor of such laws and in the use of phase spaces for their representation, but they believe that the close dependence of such laws upon the properties of the life space has been insufficiently recognized.

4. The principle of contemporaneity of causation raises basic issues concerning the meaning of "cause" and the way in which "time" is to be treated in science. No attempt will be made here to present a comprehensive analysis of these thorny problems; the reader is referred to the extended discussion given by Lewin [95, pp. 43–59]. It is sufficient to note that field theorists are content, in attempting to account for the occurrence of a concrete event, to describe the "here and now" and to show how the occurrence of the event is required by the nature of the situation. Asked to account for "why" an individual does something at a particular time, the field theorist describes the situation in which the individual exists at that time. He does not describe some state of affairs in the individual's past. This is not to deny that "residues" of the past may exist at a later time and combine, together with other contemporary influences, to make up the complex of determinants of behavior. But it is these residues, rather than the original events, which exert influence on later behavior.

One fact has persistently added confusion to the psychologist's thinking about the proper treatment of time in psychological theory: human beings are aware of time. As Lewin noted, the cognitive structure of an individual has a time dimension, extending from the "psychological past" into the "psychological future." An individual's behavior is oriented to both the future and the past *as they exist for him at any given time.* He remembers, for example, that he failed at some undertaking in the past and expects to succeed when he tries the next time. The principle of contemporaneity of causation asserts that both the "expectation" and the "memory" exist at the moment they exert their influence on behavior and that the exertion of such an influence demonstrates neither causation from the future nor from the past.

An illustration of the practical importance of this distinction between "ahistorical" and "genetic" explanations of behavior is provided by Ezriel [46] in his discussion of experimentation and psychoanalysis. It has commonly been assumed, he points out, that psychoanalysis employs only genetic explanations of behavior; Freud compared the analyst with an archaeologist who "digs up" the patient's past. But Freud's treatment of two basic phenomena, "psychical reality" and "transference," actually requires use, as Ezriel shows, of ahistorical causation.

By psychical reality Freud meant the fact that an apparent "memory" uncovered in psycho-analysis often turned out to be a phantasy, but one which was nevertheless psychologically as effective as if it had been a memory of a real event. This meant that what the analyst was uncovering was not a replica of actual events in the patient's past life, but *unconscious structures active in the present* though formed in the past out of both phantasies and correct or distorted memories of actual events [46, p. 32].

Ezriel's discussion of transference develops the same general point.

While patient and analyst had ostensibly started their work like two friendly archaeologists trying to dig up the patient's past, they were in fact two human beings interacting with one another, and the patient attributed to the analyst various roles—friend or foe, victim or persecutor, and many other things—according to his temporarily dominant unconscious phantasies in the particular session.

There is thus no difference between analysing the content of the material produced by the patient, and eliciting new material by analysing the content of the patient's resistance against communicating it. Both consist in analysing his "here and now" relations with the analyst in which the patient's unconscious structures (the precipitates of unresolved conflicts with persons of his childhood environment) manifest themselves [46, p. 32].

Ezriel concludes that the traditional adherence by psychoanalysts to genetic, rather than ahistorical, explanations of behavior has had a deleterious effect on research.

I think the main reason that no systematic experimental work has been attempted in the psycho-analytic situation is that analysts have not yet accepted the full implications of transference and psychical reality. This seems to be largely due to a belief that only genetic propositions can explain

differences between personalities and hence why various people respond differently to the same external situation [46, pp. 34–35].

Summary. In this section I have tried to indicate the major basic assumptions which have guided the work of field theorists along the paths that give it a distinctive character. Although the differences between field theorists and others are concerned largely with matters of emphasis, priority, and tactics, these basic assumptions exert a profound influence upon the ways in which the work of psychologists proceeds.

For field theorists the most important task of psychology is to devise ways of treating the full empirical reality of human experience and behavior in a scientific manner without doing violence to them. Acceptance of this task places a responsibility on the psychologist to keep in constant touch with human behavior as it is found in natural situations. Open-minded observation should guide theorizing and serve as a check upon theory. But observations must be converted into descriptions, and the development of an adequate language of description poses one of the most difficult problems for psychology. The concepts employed must have a double-directedness, to phenomena and to other concepts. An "explanation" consists of describing concrete situations in such a way that it can be shown from the system of concepts that certain events "must" occur.

The language of psychologists should be psychological. Although there may ultimately develop a way to describe the physical world, physiological processes, and psychological events in a single language, psychology will be deterred in fulfilling its basic task if it assumes that it must describe human experience in physical or physiological terms.

The principle that "only what is concrete can have effects" leads to four important consequences for the student of human behavior. (1) Every instance of behavior is the result of the interaction of several features of a given concrete situation. (2) The description of human behavior requires inclusion of phenomena traditionally classified into various fields of psychology and academic disciplines. (3) A clear distinction must be made between the concrete life space in which behavior takes place and the phase space employed to represent quantitative relations among properties. (4) Causation must be viewed as contemporary with the event caused.

STRUCTURE OF SYSTEM, AN OVERVIEW

An adequate description of any concrete psychological situation requires use of a language composed of constructs having both clear operational definitions and unambiguous conceptual properties. Lewin contributed much to the building of such a language for psychology. He believed that the difficult task of achieving satisfactory concepts lies at the very center of the scientific enterprise (as we shall see in the later discussion of the "method of construction"). He did not believe, however, that it is wise to create a single, formally elegant *system* of concepts apart from the slow accumulation of empirical data. In the earlier stages of a science, before the formal structure of its theory is highly developed, it is important to use as aids to description many "quasi constructs" having suggestive, rather than rigorous, relations to other concepts. As progress is made, these terms will be gradually replaced by ones more tightly tied together into a formal system. Lewin both introduced quasi constructs and attempted to reduce the need for them by evolving a coherent system of constructs.

In this section we shall consider some of the more fundamental of these constructs, examine briefly how they are used by field theorists, and explore some of their interrelations. This treatment must necessarily be only an overview.

Life space. The most fundamental, as well as the most widely known, of the Lewinian concepts is that of life space. It refers to the totality of facts which determine the behavior of an individual at a certain moment. The essential features of this concept are described by Lewin in the following statements.

One can say that behavior and development depend on the state of the person and his environment, $B = F(P,E)$. In this equation the person (P) and his environment (E) have to be viewed as variables which are mutually dependent upon each other. In other words, to understand or to predict behavior, the person and his environment have to be considered as *one* constellation of interdependent factors. We call the totality of these factors the life space (LSp) of that individual, and write $B = F(P,E) = F(LSp)$. The life space, therefore, includes both the person and his psychological environment. The task of explaining behavior then becomes identical with (1) finding a scientific representation of the life space (LSp) and (2) determining the function (F) which links the behavior to the life space. The function (F) is what one usually calls a *law* [95, pp. 239–240].

In this discussion it is important to note that the term "environment" is not strictly an "independent" variable; it both influences the "person" and is influenced by it. It is "psychological" and represents the world as it exists for the individual in question. It is important, too, to realize that Lewin used the term "behavior" in a very broad way to refer to changes in the life space. Thus, behavior might be a change of location of the person in his environment, a cognitive reorganization of the environment, or a restructuring of the person.[2]

Two aspects of the life space need to be distinguished, though they are empirically interdependent. These refer to its structural and dynamic properties. *Structure* is the arrangement of the parts of the life space. The basic concepts of structure are region and boundary. With these it is possible to build up more complex concepts to describe such structural properties as degree of differentiation, centrality, path, and distance. *Dynamic* concepts deal with the tendencies of the life space to change, or to resist change. The principal dynamic concepts are interdependence, tension, force, field of forces, equilibrium, and power. Both the structural and the dynamic properties of the concrete situation must be represented in order to understand any specific behavior.

One further feature of the life space requires consideration, although its formal treatment was not extensively developed by Lewin. As noted above, the life space refers to the totality of facts which determine the behavior of an individual at a certain point in time. In one sense these facts are "real" and exist only at the specified time. It must be noted, however, that distinctions may be made among them according to their degree of psychological reality-irreality (for example, facts vs. phantasies or wishes vs. expectations) and according to their psychological time-location (one's view of the future, present, and past). These properties of the life space are called "level of reality" and "time perspective." Lewin suggested that they could ultimately be treated as *dimensions* of the life space.

Several of the early empirical studies initiated by Lewin were concerned with levels of reality. From this work he drew the following generalizations:

> One of the most important dynamic differences between different degrees of reality is the greater fluidity of the more irreal levels. This greater fluidity shows itself in different facts: (1) Barriers in the environment offer relatively little resistance (one can do what one wants to do in irreality); (2) the boundaries of environmental regions can be shifted more easily and are less definitely determined . . . ; (3) a diffuse discharge of an inner-personal tension system occurs more quickly . . . ; (4) the boundaries between person and environment are less clear and the structure of the environment depends to a greater extent on the needs of the person [91, pp. 199–200].

[2] In this section I am attempting to present the major concepts as they are generally used, without considering at this point any ambiguities or difficulties they may have. A more critical evaluation of the concepts life space, person, environment, and behavior is presented in the later section concerning the formal organization of the system.

The way in which time perspective was treated by Lewin may be indicated in the following quotation:

The time perspective existing at a given time has been shown to be very important for many problems such as the level of aspiration, the mood, the constructiveness, and the initiative of the individual. Farber [48] has shown, for instance, that the amount of suffering of a prisoner depends more on his expectation in regard to his release, which may be five years ahead, than on the pleasantness or unpleasantness of his present occupation [95, pp. 53–54].

Practically everyone of consequence in the history of humanity—in religion, politics, or science—has been dominated by a time perspective which has reached out far into future generations, and which frequently was based on an awareness of an equally long past. But a large time perspective is not peculiar to great men. A hundred and thirty billion dollars of life insurance in force in the United States offer an impressive bit of evidence for the degree to which a relatively distant psychological future, not connected with the well-being of one's own person, affects the everyday life of the average citizen [94, p. 105].

Lewin believed that some of the most significant features of the development of an individual have to do with both time perspective and levels of reality.

During development, an enlargement of the time perspective takes place. The small child lives in the present; his time perspective includes only the immediate past and the immediate future. This smallness of time perspective is characteristic of what is usually called "primitive behavior." The time dimension of the life space of the child grows with increasing age; more and more distant future and past events affect present behavior.

Normal development brings with it, in addition, an increased differentiation in the reality-irreality dimensions of the life space. The young child does not clearly distinguish wishes from facts, hopes from expectations. The older person is said to be better able to distinguish between daydream wishes and reality, although wishful thinking is certainly very common in adults, too [95, p. 75].

Psychological environment. *Region.* The psychological environment of the life space is composed of regions surrounded by boundaries.[3] If two regions have a boundary arc in common, they are said to be neighboring. If two regions have a common part, they are said to be overlapping. The subparts or subregions of a region are regions lying entirely within that region. The degree of differentiation of a region refers to the

---

[3] In this discussion I shall not attempt to give the formal topological definitions of such terms as boundary and region. The "definitions" stated here are intended, rather, to indicate the intuitive meaning of these concepts.

number of its subparts. The position of a subregion is characterized by the region which includes it.

The concept of region is coordinated to (1) activity, such as "eating," "going to the movies," "making a decision," or "working on a task"; (2) passive state, such as "being fired from a job," "being admired," or "being rewarded"; (3) social entities, including such groups as "family," "church," "company," such subparts of groups as the role of "father," "bishop," or "foreman," and individual people; (4) the person whose life space is being represented. This list is not exhaustive. For certain purposes Lewin spoke of the "quasi-physical environment" which corresponds to the individual's perception of the physical world. This environment is composed of parts of the geographical world, such as "room," "street," or "town," and objects, such as "toy," "candy," or "car." It seems promising also to deal in a similar fashion with an individual's concepts so that a region is coordinated to such things as "democracy," "contemporary painting," or "equal length" [22, 141]. However, the exact way in which the quasi-physical environment and an individual's concepts are to be related to the other meanings of region has not been satisfactorily worked out.

For each type of coordination it is possible to specify a meaning for the representation of the person as being located in a region. Thus, if the person is located in the region "going to the movies," this means that the person is engaging in this activity. Similarly, if he is located in a passive state region, this state characterizes him. And, if he is located in the region "church," he has membership in that church, or if he is located in the region "bishop," he occupies that office. Needless to say, a person may be located in more than one region at a time; he may go to the movies while being admired and occupying the office of bishop. In any given empirical situation it may be actually impossible, of course, to be located simultaneously in certain combinations of regions, such as occupying the office of bishop and being a member of a gang of thieves.

Locomotion. Locomotion is said to occur if the person changes his location. It should be apparent that locomotion is not identical with physical movement of a biological organism; an individual may change his group memberships, for example, without changing his geographical location.

Cognitive structure. The arrangement of the regions of an individual's psychological environment is called his cognitive structure. If two regions are neighboring, it is possible for locomotion to take place so that the person goes from one to the other without passing through a third region. A change of structure takes place if the arrangement of regions changes or if the environment changes its degree of differentiation. Such restructuring of the psychological environment occurs during learning (e.g., when a new insight occurs) and during development or regression.

Path. A path between regions *A* and *E* is a collection of pairs of neighboring regions of the form, *AB, BC, . . . , DE*, where all the regions *A, B, C, . . . , D, E* are different from each other.[4] If there is a path from *A* to *E* in the environment of the life space and if the person is located at *A*, then it is possible for the person to reach *E* (assuming a proper constellation of forces), otherwise not. It is permissible, of course, for there to be more than one path between any pair of regions. If the regions constituting a path are coordinated to activities, then the existence of a path indicates that it is possible to get from a starting activity to a terminal one by engaging in the specified sequence of intermediate activities. If an individual wants to engage in some activity but there is no path from his current location to that activity, then he cannot reach the desired activity without a restructuring of the environment.

The length of a path may be specified as the number of boundaries which must be crossed in any locomotion from one end of the path to the other. The distance between two regions is the length of the shortest path between them.

Force. The basic concept for describing the dynamic features of the life space is that of force. It is used to characterize the direction and strength of the tendency to change or to resist change. The conceptual properties of force are direction, strength, and point of application. The direction and strength of a force can be treated mathematically as a vector. The combination of the forces acting at a given point at the same time is the *resultant* force. The most fundamental proposition concerning force is: "whenever a resultant force (different from zero) exists, there is either a locomotion in the direction of that force or a change in cognitive structure equivalent to this locomotion" [95, p. 256]. A major part of the work of field theorists has been concerned with the analysis of component forces, their determinants, and the effects of their combination.

In this analysis it has proved useful to distinguish certain types of force. A *driving force* is coordinated to a tendency to change, usually to a locomotion of the person. A *restraining force* corresponds to a barrier or obstacle to locomotion and is effective only when some driving force opposes it. Both driving and restraining forces may arise from the needs and abilities of an individual, from the actions of another individual, or

---

[4] The definitions of path, length of path, and distance given here are not identical with those provided by Lewin [92, p. 25]. They conform more closely to the definitions given by graph theory [67]. The definitions which I have given here conform, I believe, rather closely to the meanings intended by Lewin in his less formalized discussions of these terms.

from impersonal aspects of the situation. These forces are called *own,* *induced,* and *impersonal,* respectively.

Force field. One must usually assume that many forces exist simultaneously at different regions of the life space. A force field specifies for each region the strength and direction of the force which would act on the person if he were located at that region. A region is said to have a *positive valence* if it is attractive to the person and to have a *negative valence* if it is repulsive. These terms can be defined more precisely by stating that a positive valence corresponds to a field of driving forces where all forces are directed toward the same region and that a negative valence corresponds to such a field where all forces are directed away from the same region. It should be noted that force fields may be composed of own, induced, or impersonal forces and of driving or restraining forces.

Conflict of forces. A conflict situation may be defined as one where forces acting on the person are opposite in direction and about equal in strength. Any of the different types of forces may enter into a conflict situation. Although all conflicts have certain properties in common, important differences in behavior arise from different combinations of conflicting forces. These differences have been analyzed extensively by Lewin [90, pp. 66–170; 92, pp. 175–200; 95, pp. 256–269]. It will be possible here only to suggest the major features of this analysis.

Conflicts involving driving forces are the familiar "choice" situations. The simultaneous presence of two or more valences in the life space may generate conflicts of various sorts, depending upon the signs of the valences, the structure of the psychological environment, the gradients of the force fields as distributed spatially, and the locations of the person and the valences. It can be shown, for example, that if a person is located between two mutually exclusive positive valences, he will tend to remain at a region between them which minimizes the distance to each. If, on the other hand, he is located between two negative valences, he will tend to try to increase the distance from both and will tend to "leave the field." For this reason, the use of threat of punishment to get someone to do a disagreeable task can succeed only if all passable paths leading away from the area of conflict go through one of the negatively valent regions. Conflicts may also arise from the simultaneous presence of positive and negative valences in the same direction from the person. When these two valences are located in the same region, we have the familiar cases of "ambivalence." If the two valences are not in the same region as, for example, when a reward is promised for doing a disagreeable task, there will be a tendency to seek a path to the region of positive valence which does not pass through the one of negative valence. It is assumed that the magnitude of driving forces decreases with increasing distance from the valence (the familiar concept of goal gradient), and field theoretical derivations concerning the points of equilibrium in overlapping force fields are essentially the same as those described by Miller [113].

Conflicts between driving and restraining forces produce "frustration" situations. It often happens that a person is surrounded by a field of restraining forces (barrier) such that he cannot go beyond the area bounded by this field. The area within such a field has been termed "space of free movement," a concept of considerable use in Lewin's analysis [95, pp. 130–154] of problems of adolescence and in Lippitt's treatment [103] of the social-emotional consequences of different styles of leadership. An important difference exists between the situation in which the barrier surrounds the person with a positive valence outside and the one in which the person is outside with the valence within. In all cases of conflict between driving and restraining forces there arises a tendency to find a way to circumvent the barrier or to remove it. Under certain circumstances attempts to remove a frustrating barrier will take the form of "aggression," thus producing phenomena of the sort described by Dembo [37] and by Dollard et al. [42]. Field theorists do not believe, however, that it is correct to assert that frustration always sets up tendencies toward aggression.

The analysis of conflict is further complicated by the fact that each of the types of conflict discussed thus far can involve own, induced, or impersonal forces in all possible combinations. Of considerable interest to social psychology are the situations in which own and induced forces are in conflict. If another person O has power over the person P he can induce driving or restraining forces in P's life space. Thus, if a person's own needs make "going to a party" have positive valence and if the person's boss asks him "to work at the office," a conflict of driving forces is set up. Since O's ability to set up induced forces in P's life space depends upon O's power over P, one resolution of such a conflict is for P to attempt to change O's power over him or to get O to exercise his power in certain ways. Some of the most interesting problems of interpersonal relations arise from the conflict of own and induced forces [26]. Perhaps of equal interest are the situations in which the person is subjected to conflicting induced forces set up by different people. Meyers [112] has studied situations in which two adults give conflicting commands to the same child. One of the classic problems of social organization is how to minimize the conflicts which result when the same individual has more than one boss. Through the concepts of power and induced force, it is possible to treat within one set of concepts the effects of social organizations upon individual motivation.

Overlapping situations. In order to describe the full complexity of the determinants of a given instance of behavior, it is often necessary to recognize that an individual may be involved simultaneously in more than one situation. He may, for example, sit in a classroom and both listen to the teacher and plan a fishing expedition. Or, he may be influenced at the same time by his membership in two different groups. The relative effect of each of several overlapping situations upon behavior is indicated by the relative *potency* of each. In particular, the effect a force has on behavior is proportional to the potency of the related situation.

The concepts of overlapping situations and potency have been used by Barker, Dembo, and Lewin [12] in their study of the constructiveness of primary and secondary play, by Cartwright and Festinger [22, 27] in their theory of decision making, by Lewin [95, pp. 143–44] in his discussion of social marginality as reflected in adolescence or in membership in minority groups, and by Watson and Lippitt [131] in their investigation of the problems of maintaining identification with both the home culture and the host culture in programs of cross-cultural education.

Person. Up to this point we have treated the person as an undifferentiated region which has a location within regions of the psychological environment and whose locomotion is determined by forces acting upon it. In field theory, however, the person is also treated as a differentiated entity, having both structural and dynamic properties. The structural elements of the person are the same as those of the environment, namely, region and boundary, but they are coordinated to different empirical data. The fundamental dynamic concept applicable to the person is that of interdependence of the states of regions. Lewin's treatment of the person as a differentiated entity was mainly programmatic, except for the analysis of *tension* which was carried out in considerable detail.

Simple and organizational interdependence. Lewin distinguished two basic types of interdependence which may exist among regions.

1. One type of dependence, which has been called *simple dependence,* has the following characteristics. First, it is based on a process which has the character of "spreading" from one part to neighboring regions according to proximity. Second, the change of the dependent part usually occurs in the direction of equalizing its state and the state of the influencing part. For instance, spreading of tension means that neighboring parts tend to change so that a state of equal tension is approached in all parts. Third, the dependence of part *a* on part *b* is essentially of the same type (although not necessarily of the same degree) as the dependence of part *b* on part *a*.

2. The dependence which has been called *organizational interdependence* shows rather different characteristics. First, it is a type of dependence between *a* and *b* similar to that between leader and led, or between someone using a tool and the tool. In such a case, the way *a* depends upon *b* is

obviously rather different from the way *b* depends on *a*. Second, the organizational dependence usually does not work from neighbor to neighbor like the spreading of tension. It is a selective process: sometimes one part, sometimes another part of the system is used as a tool in a specific way. For instance, the same need may produce an organized activity in different parts of the muscular system. Third, the kind of change resulting from the organized interdependence of *a* and *b* usually does not tend to equalize the state of *a* and *b*. The subordinate part *b* (i.e., the part which is led, the tool) changes in a way which helps *a* (the leading part) to reach its objective, but it does not lead to greater final equality between the two [95, pp. 117–118].

The concept of oraganizational interdependence is required for handling problems of hierarchical ordering of needs, sentiments, values, those problems associated with the phenomena of "integration," and those involving the steering of behavior. Lewin was able merely to indicate in broad terms the way in which such an analysis might proceed, and a more thorough treatment of these problems is still awaited. The concept of a simple dependence has proved to be most useful in dealing with the spread of need tensions.

Inner-personal tension systems. Tension is defined as a state of an inner-personal region which may vary in magnitude and which displays a tendency to spread. More specifically, if the magnitudes of tension of two neighboring regions are unequal, there is a tendency for them to become equal. The concept of tension is coordinated to the existence of a need: if a need or "quasi need" (i.e., an intention) is activated, then the magnitude of tension of a corresponding inner-personal region is greater than zero. The stronger the need, the greater is the magnitude of tension and, according to the principle of the spread of tension, the larger is the number of regions under tension. Consumption, or the realization of an intention, reduces the level of tension. Overconsumption (satiation) results in a state that may be thought of as "negative tension," which also may spread.

The boundary of a region may vary with respect to its permeability. If the boundary between two neighboring regions is not completely permeable, some minimal difference in the magnitudes of tension of the two regions will be maintained. Generally speaking, the permeability of the boundaries of a person decreases with increasing age. Thus, a high state of tension in a region of a child has more widespread effects than does the same state of tension in a region of an adult.

Structure of the person. One of the most important of the structural properties of the person is its degree of differentiation, or the number of distinguishable parts contained in it. Many factors influence the degree of differentiation of a person, but in general it may be said that there is a tendency for the degree of differentiation to increase with the development of the individual.

Consideration of the arrangement of regions within the person leads to two additional structural concepts: *central-peripheral* and *inner-outer*. The degree of centrality of a region is inversely related to the maximal distance of that region from any other region within the person. Thus, the more central a region, the more readily will it influence all other regions of the person through spread of tension (assuming a constant value for the permeability of all boundaries) and the more readily, on the average, will it be influenced by other regions of the person. The inner-outer distinction refers to how readily a region can be affected by influences spreading to it from outside the person. The outermost region of the person has a common boundary with the outer boundary of the person. The innermost region lies at the greatest distance from the outside of the person.[5] Lewin showed that the most central region and the innermost region are not necessarily the same, though in some of his earlier writings he did not draw a sharp distinction between the two concepts. They are used more or less interchangeably, for example, in his insightful description [94, pp. 18–30] of differences between personality types in Germany and the United States. He also used the concept of centrality in a more suggestive than formal way to account for certain differences in speed of satiation reported by Karsten [78]. Recently, Sanford [120] has employed the concepts central-peripheral, inner-outer, along with that of temporal stability, to bring about considerable clarification of the meaning of "surface" and "depth" as found in many discussions of personality theory.

For completeness, a final distinction advanced by Lewin deserves brief mention here. In his various writings one encounters a number of references to the belief that the person should be conceived as being composed of "inner-personal" regions which have to do mainly with motivational tensions and a "motor-perceptual" stratum which, much like Freud's ego, keeps the person in touch with the environment through perception and action. This distinction points to a basic problem in Lewinian field theory which I shall discuss at greater length in a subsequent section (Formal organization of the system).

Relations between person and environment. In order to comprehend the essential nature of Lewinian theory it is necessary to understand that properties of the person and of the psychological environment are conceived as existing in one interdependent field. The state of the person influences the properties of the environment, and vice versa. Specific

---

[5] It should be noted that there is a technical difference between the definition of inner region advanced by Lewin and that suggested by Bavelas [16]. Further empirical work will be required in order to choose between the two.

instances of this general proposition can be found in virtually all areas of psychological investigation: motivational tensions influence cognitive structure and certain cognitive states may generate tensions; the activation of a tension system produces tendencies toward locomotion of the person in his environment and obstacles to this locomotion may result in a dedifferentiation of the person—to mention but two examples. Lewin [92, pp. 95–108; 95, pp. 9–20, 87–128] has discussed in detail certain aspects of the interdependence of person and environment. I shall merely outline here some of the more important features of this treatment.

Tension, valence, and force. The most basic assumption concerning relations between person and environment asserts a functional relation between tension in the person and valence (force field) in the environment. When an inner-personal region is in a state of tension, an "appropriate" environmental region acquires positive valence (i.e., becomes the center of a force field). The environmental region "selected" depends upon the qualitative nature of the region under tension and the qualitative nature of the environmental region. The magnitude of valence is some positive function of tension. Lewin stated this assumption in the following formula: $Va(G) = F(t,G)$. Thus, if a tension system corresponding to hunger is activated, an environmental region concerned with eating acquires positive valence. The exact way in which "objects" become selected has not been worked out within field theory.

It follows from this assumption, from the definition of valence as a force field, and from the assumption of a goal gradient, that the magnitude of force operating on the person toward some goal region is a positive function of the magnitude of tension and a negative function of the distance of the person from the goal. Given a constant level of tension, as the person approaches a goal region the magnitude of force toward the goal increases. When the person actually reaches the goal, and "consumption" takes place, the corresponding tension system is released so that the level of tension approaches zero.

Zeigarnik effect. A most fruitful program of experimentation to document this conception of tension and force became possible by assuming that the intention to complete an activity generates a corresponding tension system. As Lewin sometimes stated it, an intention may be treated as a "quasi need." The validity of this assumption was established by Ovsiankina [116] who found a marked tendency for people to resume an interrupted task when left in a "free" situation. Zeigarnik [142], by assuming that a tension system sets up not only forces to complete the activity but also to think about it, was able to test a number of derivations from this theory by measuring tendencies to recall completed and interrupted tasks.

The fundamental fact established by Zeigarnik is that interrupted tasks are better recalled than completed ones. This follows immediately from the relation between tension and force and from the assumption that a tension is released upon completion of the task. It should be noted in this connection that the tendency to recall derives from the tension set up by the quasi need and not from the mere fact that the task is interrupted. Marrow [109] demonstrated that if interruption is made equivalent to reaching the goal and completion to not reaching it, then more completed than interrupted tasks are recalled. A closely related derivation asserts that the difference in recall between interrupted and completed tasks should increase with increasing motivation to complete the tasks (greater motivation being reflected in a higher level of tension). This derivation was confirmed by Zeigarnik [142] and by Marrow [109].

More complicated derivations are possible if one assumes that tension systems tend to equilibrate over time and that the rate of equilibration increases with increasing fluidity of the boundaries separating regions under tension. The first assumption was tested by Zeigarnik [142] who showed that the difference between recall for interrupted and for completed tasks decreases if the test is made at increasing intervals after the initial experiment. She tested the second assumption by making the further assumption that fluidity of boundaries increases when an individual becomes more tired. Her experiment showed a small difference in recall for interrupted and completed tasks among subjects who were tired. A closely related finding is that if the tasks are presented initially in such a way that each is seen as merely another instance of the same total activity, there is virtually no difference in recall between interrupted and completed tasks. This finding is consistent with the general theory if it is assumed that the boundaries between such tasks are highly fluid.

Other derivations which can be made from the same general theory will not be discussed here. A summary is provided by Lewin [95, p. 18]. It should be added at this point that a large number of studies have been undertaken to replicate and to extend the original Zeigarnik work. When Zeigarnik's original conditions have been exactly reproduced the same findings have been obtained. Certain reported failures to replicate the findings appear to be due to the fact that the experimenter did not actually create the conditions specified by the theory (e.g., the requirement that the boundaries between the tension systems be of sufficient impermeability). One important clarification has come from several studies which introduced "success" and "failure" as variables in addition to those of "interruption" and "completion," sometimes unintentionally and sometimes in a systematic fashion. It should come as no surprise that if "interruption" has the meaning of "failure" to the subject, the tendency to recall is different from when it means "success" or has no relation to the ego. Lewis [100] and Lewis and Franklin [101] have provided a way of reconciling many of the apparently conflicting findings through their systematic comparison of ego-orientation and task-orientation. More recently Atkinson [8] has shown how individual measures of n-achievement can be used to account for differences among subjects in reactions to the possibility of failure. All of these developments are consistent, in my opinion, with the Lewinian theory, though they indicate needed extensions and elaborations (in particular, they point to the desirability of integrating the theories of tension and level of aspiration). These developments illustrate a basic tenet of field theory that "objectively" the same stimulus conditions will produce widely different behaviors when brought to bear on differently constituted life spaces.

Spread of tension and valence. One can derive certain interesting consequences from the theory of tension and valence outlined here by examining more closely the tendency of tension to spread. It should be evident that the exact course of the spread of tension (how far it spreads, to what regions, and how rapidly) depends upon the level of tension, the arrangement of regions, and the permeability of boundaries. Since it is also assumed that whenever a region is in a state of tension there will be a positive valence in a corresponding region of the environment (provided that an "appropriate" one exists), the spread of tension will increase the number of regions having positive valence. Moreover, the structural and dynamic properties of the person will affect the way in which new valences arise.

A consequence of this theory is that the stronger the state of need, the wider, on the average, will be the realm of environmental regions having positive valence. This conclusion appears to be consistent with commonly observed facts. An individual long deprived of food, for example, finds many things attractive which he would ordinarily not eat, and an individual long isolated from social interaction may be pleased to spend time in the company of a boor.

The theory also provides a basis for dealing with the phenomena of substitution. If a barrier in the environment prevents the person from reaching a region of positive valence, then by means of the spread of tension new environmental regions will acquire positive valence. Exactly which regions acquire *substitute valence* will depend, of course, on the structure of the person. It has been suggested that one of the determinants of the arrangement of inner-personal regions is the relation of similarity among the activities or objects to which the regions refer. Cartwright [23] obtained ratings of the attractiveness of a number of activities before and after interrupting the subject on one of them. Following interruption tasks similar to the interrupted one gained in attractiveness much more than did dissimilar ones. The attractiveness of similar activities was also more affected by completion and failure. In this experiment, at least, it appears that similarity does affect the distance between regions of the person and thus the interdependence of valences of environmental regions.

It would be expected from the same line of reasoning that completing an activity similar to the one originally having positive valence should reduce the tension in the regions corresponding to both activities. In other words, the similar activity should have *substitute value* for the original one. While experimental evidence provided by Lissner [106], Mahler [108], Sliosberg [123], and Adler [2] supports this general approach, they make it clear that many factors in addition to similarity affect the interdependence among levels of tension in personal regions. It is clear, for example, that an activity may acquire substitute valence but provide little substitute value. In such a case it seems that the boundary between the two inner-personal regions is dynamically unidirectional, permitting an increase of tension in the first to raise the tension of the second but not permitting a reduction of the tension of the second to affect the level of the first. Further work on the interdependence of tension systems should lead rather easily to a clarification of these problems.

Social relations. For an adequate description of human behavior it is essential, of course, to recognize that man lives primarily in a social world. In constructing the life space of a given individual this social world is treated in the same way as the physical world: those aspects which influence the individual at a given time are included in the life space and are represented in the form that they have for the individual. If an individual believes, for example, that he is a member of a group, this fact is contained in his life space regardless of the opinions of other members of the group. The task of relating different life spaces to one another (i.e., of constructing a social field) is important, but it is too complex and underdeveloped for discussion here.

Group membership. In discussing the kinds of empirical entities that may be coordinated to regions of the life space, we saw that groups and subparts of groups may exist as regions of the environment of a person. All the structural and dynamic properties of environmental regions discussed above may be attributes of these social regions. Thus, a group or subpart of a group may have positive or negative valence, or both, and a person may experience conflict because of the operation of such force fields. Similarly, all the phenomena of frustration and substitution can be observed with respect to a person's position in social regions.

The valence, or attractiveness, of membership in a group may have profound effects upon an individual. The special case of enforced membership in a group with negative valence has been analyzed in great detail by Lewin [94, pp. 145–158, 186–200]. The more general implications of attraction-to-group for the theory of group dynamics are discussed by Cartwright and Zander [29, pp. 73–91], and various techniques of measurement are described by Libo [102].

As noted above, forces which originate in groups or other people rather than in the needs of the person are called induced forces. The ability of a group, or individual, to induce forces in the person's life space reflects the power of these social entities over the person. Ordinarily, membership within a group means that the group and representative members of the group have power to induce forces on the person. Such forces usually steer the locomotion of the person into activities which are instrumental to the achievement of group goals or are "required" by the norms and values of the group. If an individual "accepts" (or internalizes) the norms or goals of a group, these set up own forces and tension systems within the person. Horwitz [74] has documented this last proposition in an experiment in which he employed the Zeigarnik technique with group, rather than individual, activities.

Power. The concept of power (or power field) entered into Lewin's writing almost from the beginning, although he did not give it precise definition until much later. He noted in his early discussion of reward and punishment that such situations must necessarily involve the ability of one individual or group to set up driving and restraining forces in the life space of another individual. He also employed the concept of power in analyzing such diverse phenomena as the reactions of children to a strange adult, the resistance of children to eating certain foods, the developmental stage of "negativity," and the nature of various styles of group leadership. As field theorists have turned their efforts to developing a theory of group dynamics the concept of power has become of central importance—see, for example, Cartwright et al. [26].

Lewin's formal definition of power was stated as a relationship between two entities, a and b, which were conceived of quite generally so as to include the possibility of dealing with power relations between individuals, groups, and subparts of the life space. He defined the power of b over a "as the quotient of the maximum force which b can induce on a, and the maximum resistance which a can offer" [95, p. 336].[6] It

[6] More recent work with the concept of power leads me to believe that the formal definition of power should be revised somewhat in order to eliminate certain mathematical difficulties. It would be better, I believe, to define power as a *difference* rather than as a *quotient*. Also, it would be preferable to relate power to the maximum difference that can occur between the induced force and the resisting force rather than to the difference between the maximum induced

should be noted, in addition, that in the elaboration of this definition he made it clear that the power of *b* over *a* must always be specified with respect to the regions of the life space in which the power exists. Individual *a* may be subjected to strong induced forces from *b* in certain regions but not others, and he may be able to set up stronger resisting forces in some than others. The distribution of power throughout the life space is one of its most important features.

A considerable amount of research has been conducted to discover the determinants of power. One of the best established generalizations was originally proposed by Festinger [49] on the basis of the findings of Festinger, Schachter, and Back [53] and Back [9]. Festinger states "the maximum force which the group can successfully induce on a member counter to his own forces cannot be greater than the sum of the forces acting on that member to remain in the group. The greater the resultant force to remain in the group, the more effective will be the attempts to influence the member" [49, p. 277]. In other words, the more an individual is attracted to group membership or to another individual the greater the power that group or individual will have. It is also clear that there are many other "bases" of power. These are discussed in some detail by French and Raven [61]. Finally, it should be noted that, given a constant social relationship (such as attraction or institutional authority), the magnitude of induced forces which *b* can set up on *a* will depend upon *b*'s skills of exerting influence. A pioneering study of this problem was conducted by Frank [58].

Some of the most important consequences of the power relations among people have to do with emotional security. The fact that *b* has great power over *a* means that *b* is able to influence *a*'s satisfaction of his needs: power gives ability to help or hinder. Arsenian [6], Wright [138], and Cartwright [25] have suggested that the security of an individual might be defined as a ratio in whose numerator is put the person's perception of the magnitude of his own power plus all friendly or supportive power he can count upon from other sources, and in whose denominator is put the person's perception of the magnitude of all hostile power that may be mobilized against him. Empirical documentation of the many symptoms of insecurity deriving from power relations has been presented by Cartwright et al. [26], Pepitone [117], Hurwitz, Zander, and Hymovitch [75], and Zander, Cohen, and Stotland [140].

Summary. The above discussion of Lewin's system of constructs has been confined to those constructs which have both received formal treat-

---

force and the maximum resisting force. These revisions would lead to a definition of the power of *b* over *a* (with respect to a given matter) as the maximum difference that can occur between the induced force on *a* set up on *b* and the force which *a* can mobilize in opposition to it.

ment and been subjected to empirical testing. There are many additional "quasi constructs" which have played an important role in Lewinian work (e.g., level of aspiration, social atmosphere, social channels, values, morale, and interdependence of fate). Space has not permitted an examination of these. As field theorists have extended their research activities to new phenomena they have usually employed such "quasi constructs" rather than attempting to extend the formal system immediately. Nevertheless, it is the belief of field theorists that as work proceeds it will be increasingly possible to replace the "quasi constructs" with other constructs, mainly those enumerated above, which will fit rigorously into a formal system. A more detailed discussion of how the transition from "quasi constructs" to a formal system of genuine constructs should proceed is given in subsequent sections.

INITIAL EVIDENTIAL GROUNDS FOR ASSUMPTIONS OF SYSTEM[7]

Throughout Lewin's professional career there was a continuous interaction between empirical research and formal theorizing. It would be entirely incorrect to say either that he first developed a "system" and then submitted it to empirical testing or that he took a body of empirical data and built a "system" to fit. A more correct statement would be that, although he adopted a theoretical orientation very early in his career and maintained it throughout his life, he viewed the construction of a formal system as a gradual process to be carried out over the years in the most intimate association with empirical work. In this section I shall attempt to extract the empirical aspects from the theoretical and to describe in the "language of data" the principal kinds of empirical phenomena which have been investigated by field theorists. It will be necessary to limit the discussion of specific studies to those which were originated rather directly under Lewin's influence. The main purpose of

[7] Since Lewinian field theory does not consist of a "completed" set of constructs all of which are now related to one another in a rigorously systematic fashion, I find it difficult to make the distinctions, suggested by the editorial committee, between this section on "Initial evidential grounds for assumptions of system" and the later one on "Evidence for the system." For this reason, I have attempted to cover both topics in this section. Because of the impossibility of making any indisputable distinction between field theorists and many other psychologists whose work is congenial to the field theoretical approach and because of the tremendous volume of such work, I have found it necessary to restrict the bibliographic references to a sampling of those investigations which were closely associated with Lewin or more recently with the Research Center for Group Dynamics. This is grievously arbitrary and results in a most limited picture of the empirical work related to field theory. I can only apologize to the reader and to those whose work is not specifically cited.

this section is to convey some impression of the great range of empirical content deemed to be relevant to field theory.

The research described here may be put in proper historical perspective by noting that Lewin's doctoral dissertation [87] was published in 1917 and that his career was terminated by his death in 1947. For approximately the first half of this period of thirty years, his work was centered in Berlin and was carried out in close association with those who were then developing the gestalt point of view. The most important publications of this era appeared in the *Psychologische Forschung*. During the second half of his career, Lewin's research was done in the United States, primarily at Cornell University, the State University of Iowa, and the Massachusetts Institute of Technology, where he established the Research Center for Group Dynamics. After his death, this center was moved to the University of Michigan. Lewin's theoretical orientation has continued to influence the research of the Michigan group.

Associative bonds and dynamic processes. The earliest work of Lewin [87, 88, 89] consisted of an experimental and theoretical critique of earlier research of Ach [1] in which it had been assumed that "associative bonds" set up dynamic tendencies to reproduce a second item when a first item is stimulated. The general conclusions drawn from this critique were that mere connections are never causes of events. Energy must be set free and this derives from mental systems under tension (originated by needs and intentions). In these experiments the major variables manipulated were frequency of association, intention to recall, and expectations created by the sequence of items presented in the test series. Lewin drew upon the more dynamic emphasis of the Würzburg school and attempted to disentangle the structural and dynamic aspects of memory.

Dynamic studies of memory. The natural development of this work led to the investigations, cited above, of the influences of tension systems upon recall. The principal consequence of this research was to place heavy emphasis upon motivational variables, and thus also structural properties of the person, as determinants of memory and thinking. These studies helped to shape the theoretical constructs of need tension, force, and interdependence among parts of the person and demonstrated the feasibility of conducting laboratory experiments upon motivational variables.

Interruption and resumption. One of the most useful of the new techniques was to set up in the subject a "quasi need" or intention to complete some task and then to interrupt him before completion. Ovsiankina [116] demonstrated a marked tendency for subjects to resume the interrupted activity if left free. She also examined how the tendency to resume is affected by the particular nature of the task and the point of interruption in the sequence of work. Katz [80] later repeated Ovsiankina's experiment, introducing several controls and methodological refinements, and confirmed the earlier findings except for those concerning the effect of the point of interruption upon resumption. Katz found the frequency of resumption to decline steadily as the task was interrupted closer to completion, while Ovsiankina observed an increase when the task was interrupted very close to completion. Since the technique of interruption has been used mainly as a means of testing broad theoretical propositions, little research has been directed toward reconciling such detailed quantitative contradictions that have emerged from this line of work. As the theory of tension becomes stated more quantitatively, more detailed research will be required.

There has arisen one important theoretical issue concerning the origin of tendencies to resume. Ovsiankina originally raised the question where these tendencies derive from a tension system set up when the subject begins to work on the task or from the mere perception of an incompleted task. She undertook an experiment in which a subject could complete either a task which he himself had started or another one which had been partially completed by someone else. Ovsiankina found an overwhelming preference to complete the one which the subject himself had started. Adler and Kounin [3] later reached the same conclusion from an experiment which avoided some methodological shortcomings of the earlier work. Recently, however, the issue has been opened again by Henle and Aull [72]. Although they obtained the same quantitative results as Adler and Kounin, they conclude from a careful analysis of the subjects' reports that the meanings of the two tasks are so different to the subjects that a perceptual explanation of the results is still possible. They correctly point out that Lewin maintained that behavior is a function of both the person and the psychological environment and that the person should not be viewed as operating on a passive environment. The issue, then, should be stated as a problem of determining under what conditions a perceptual constellation does set up a tendency toward action. It is quite possible, of course, that such a tendency is also accompanied by a tension system.

Substitution. The research on resumption of interrupted tasks led directly to a related question: can the completion of a task different from the interrupted one reduce the tendency to resume the interrupted one? In other words, can one task have substitute value for another? Lissner [106] conducted an experiment in which subjects completed a second task after being interrupted on a first and measured tendencies to resume the first. She found that the more similar the second to the first and the more difficult the second, the less the tendency to resume the first. Mahler [108] investigated whether an "irreal" substitute action can lead to satisfaction of the need. She also used the technique of interruption but forced the subject to complete the original task in one of four ways: (1) by an action different from the natural one, (2) by talking rather than doing, (3) by thinking out the completion, and (4) by an "act of magic." She found, in general, that less real actions have less substitute value, but she also found many exceptions to this generalization. The critical question seems to be whether the intrinsic goal of the task has been reached. Thus, a "problem" task can be solved by talking or thinking just as well as by writing. If, however, the success of such a task requires telling the answer to the experimenter, thinking has little substitute value. Magic solutions have no substitute value in a realistic setting, but they do have substitute value if the whole setting is magical. Adler [2] varied experimentally the attitude of the subject toward working on the task, creating in one group of subjects a "concrete" and in one group an "abstract" attitude. In the former situation, subjects were "building a particular house" while in the latter they were "building houses." When the concrete attitude was established, little substitute value resulted from completion of a second house. When the setting called for an abstract attitude, there was considerable substitute value, provided that the subjects were old enough to maintain an abstract attitude.

A different approach to substitution was initiated by Dembo [37] who found substitute actions arising spontaneously in a frustrating situation. She observed, however, that such substitutes usually have little lasting substitute value. Sliosberg [123] systematically attempted to get young children to accept make-believe substitutes (for example, a piece of cardboard candy). When the total situation was "serious" these substitutes were rejected, but if the situation was one of make-believe the substitutes were more readily accepted. And Cartwright [23] attempted to measure the spread of valence to similar activities when the original task was interrupted.

All of these studies, it should be noted, are dealing in an experimental fashion with a concept originally advanced by Freud. The earliest experimental investigations of Freudian concepts were undertaken by field theorists.

Satiation. What happens if the same activity is repeated over and over again? Karsten [78] investigated this question in an experiment involving the extensive repetition of such tasks as drawing figures, reading a poem, or writing letters. As repetition is continued there usually occur first small variations in the manner of executing the task, then much larger variations, then a breaking up of the activity into smaller units of action with a concomitant reduction of "meaning," then the making of mistakes, and finally fatigue and the appearance of "bodily" symptoms. Interestingly enough, if the meaning of the same activity is modified by embedding it in a different context, the bodily symptoms and fatigue often disappear. Karsten found that the speed of satiation depends upon the "size" of the activity being satiated (whether, for example, the task is to "draw a cat" or "to draw pictures"), the "centrality" or "ego-involvement" of the activity, and the state of the person (whether generally tired, for instance). Pursuing this last point further, Freund [63] found an increase in the speed of satiation during menstruation. Seashore and Bavelas [122] report results generally similar to those of Karsten.

Kounin [84] made use of a technique of "co-satiation" in which the effects of satiating one activity upon the speed of satiating a second activity are measured. In experiments on satiation and co-satiation with individuals of the same mental age but varying chronological age he found that both the speed of satiation and the degree of co-satiation decrease with increasing chronological age. These results are interpreted in terms of the degree of differentiation of inner-personal regions and the permeability of boundaries. Kounin advanced the concept of rigidity to account for these and other results.

Frustration. One of the important earlier studies at Berlin was that of Dembo [37] on the effects of frustration. She gave subjects impossible tasks to perform and carefully observed the various symptoms of emotional tension that emerged. These included such things as anger, aggression, regression, substitution, and flights into irreality. A carefully controlled and quantitative study of frustration and regression was later conducted by Barker, Dembo, and Lewin [12] who found marked reductions in the constructiveness of play among children in a situation of frustration.

The interaction of social factors and frustration was experimentally investigated by Wright [138, 139] who found, among other things, that when pairs of strong friends are subjected to frustration they display less reduction in constructiveness of play, less negative emotionality, more cooperation between themselves, and more aggression against the experimenter than do pairs of weak friends. French [59] subjected groups to frustration by giving them insoluble group problems. He compared previously organized groups to groups created in the laboratory and found a greater expression of interpersonal aggression and more tendencies to leave the field in the organized groups but a greater tendency to group disintegration in the newly created groups.

Level of aspiration. Among all the research topics investigated by the Lewinian group in Berlin, level of aspiration seems to have generated the largest amount of research in America. The term, level of aspiration, was introduced by Dembo [37]. Hoppe [73] conducted the first experimental investigation of the phenomena. This was followed by a study carried out by Jucknat [76]. The important facts produced by this early work were that the experience of success or failure does not depend simply upon some "objective" standard of performance but upon the aspiration that the subject sets for himself. Performance falling too far above or below this level of aspiration does not result in feelings of success or failure. Furthermore, an experience of success tends to raise the level of aspiration for future performance, and failure tends to lower it. The results of this line of work also raised important questions concerning any simple application of the hedonistic principle because people tend not to set a level of aspiration which will "guarantee" success.

In 1935 there appeared in English three articles by Frank [54, 55, 56] which served to introduce the topic to American psychologists. In the years immediately following a whole flood of studies appeared. These were reviewed by Frank [57] in 1941. The most comprehensive survey of research findings and theoretical exposition of the topic was presented by Lewin, Dembo, Festinger, and Sears [97]. It is not possible here to describe this large body of literature. We merely note that it includes investigations of specific situational factors, personality traits, socioeconomic influences, reference groups, and processes of development. Festinger [50] has advanced a theory of social comparison processes in which aspiration, self-evaluation, and social communication are treated together. Much of the more recent research on discrepancies between ideal self and actual self has been influenced by the earlier work on level of aspiration.

Decision. The emphasis in field theory upon psychological forces and their interaction has stimulated various investigations of conflict, choice, and decision. Despite the obvious differences in terminology much of this work has dealt with the same phenomena as those reported by Miller [113] in his discussion of types of conflict and those treated by Tolman [128] under the label of vicarious trial and error. Several studies have been directed toward investigating the determinants of decision-time. Escalona [43] tested certain theoretical derivations concerning decision-making among manic-depressive patients. Wright [137] found that children who were inconsistently altruistic or egoistic took longer to make decisions involving these values. Jucknat [76] and Barker [10, 11] demonstrated greater indecision the stronger the valences of the alternatives, the greater the reality level of the choice, and in choices between negative (as compared to positive) alternatives. Cartwright [22] and Cartwright and Festinger [27] showed how decision-time depends upon the differentiation of the cognitive field and upon an attitude of cautiousness.

The term, group decision, was employed by Lewin [96] to describe the situation where individuals make a decision in a group situation concerning their own future behavior. In a number of experiments it was shown that making such a decision appears to "freeze" the intention so that the behavior is more likely to occur than if no such decision takes place. Bennett [18] has recently investigated some of the many variables simultaneously manipulated in a "group decision" and concludes that the act of making a decision and the perception that a majority of other people are also making the same decision account for the effect.

Social perception. The term, social perception, has come to refer to two rather different sorts of phenomena: the influence of social variables upon perception and the perception of social objects. Although field theorists have not conducted much research upon the social determinants of perception, the basic proposition that the person and psychological environment constitute an interdependent field has predisposed them to accept readily the so-called new look in perception advanced by Bruner and others [19]. Lewin's various discussions of the determinants of the "meaning" of perceived objects and events always stressed the importance of social variables.

Considerably more research has been done on the perception of social objects. This work has been greatly influenced by Heider [70, 71] and by Asch [7]. Kelley [81], for instance, demonstrated how an expectation that an individual will be "warm" or "cold" influences the actual perception of the individual and the readiness to interact with him. Pepitone [117] constructed an experiment to examine some of the determinants of the perception of social power and approval. Thibaut and Riecken [126] studied a situation in which the subject is confronted with a person having relatively high or relatively low power who complies to an influence attempt made by the subject. They found that the perceived causal locus for compliance is "internal" to high-power and "external" to low-power individuals. And Festinger, Pepitone, and Newcomb [52] investigated a group phenomenon which they call deindividuation in which members of a group do not pay attention to other individuals qua individuals. Under such conditions individuals do not relate events taking place in the group to specific individuals.

Values. When Lewin moved from Germany to the United States one of the things that impressed him most was the extreme difference between the two countries in certain of the values held by residents of each. Lewin [94, pp. 3–68] wrote several articles outlining the nature of these differences and developing a theory of how to change cultural values. The problem of developing techniques for doing quantitative research on cultural values has proved to be most difficult. Bavelas [14] and Kalhorn [77] devised an ingenious technique for discovering the content of values and the social surrogates among school children. White [133, 134] developed a scheme for analyzing the content of documents in order to reveal the values expressed in them. And Wright [137] studied the ontogenetic development of the value of "fairness" by means of an experiment with children in which the allocation of desirable toys between themselves and others had to be made.

Phenomena related to the concepts of group standard or group norm have been studied rather intensively. Lewin [95, pp. 188–237] showed how a wide variety of such phenomena could be analyzed as quasi-stationary equilibria. Coch and French [35] employed this approach in a field experiment in which group standards concerning work output in a factory were changed. A large number of studies were stimulated by a field study of Festinger, Schachter, and Back [53] in which the development of group standards in a housing project was documented. Summaries of this work may be found in Festinger [49] and Kelley and Thibaut [83, pp. 765–770].

Authority and social influence. Among the many differences which Lewin noted between Germany and the United States he was particularly interested in styles of leadership and the social-emotional atmosphere of groups. In a characteristic fashion this interest was converted into experiments contrasting the effects of different styles of leadership. The results, reported by Lewin, Lippitt, and White [98] and Lippitt [103], have had a deep influence both upon social psychological research and upon practices in education, social group work, and administration. One of the first repercussions of this research was increased acceptance of the view that leadership consists of behaviors that may be developed and taught. Bavelas [15] reported dramatic improvements in the functioning of groups as a result of training leaders in the skills of democratic leadership. Interest in leadership training rapidly developed in many directions. Of these I can only mention the experimental workshop established for training community leaders which was evaluated by Lippitt [104]. The techniques of training and the philosophy of combining training with research which characterized this workshop were then employed in establishing the National Training Laboratories in Group Development which holds annual programs at Bethel, Maine.

Research on the determinants of leadership in children's groups has been carried out in summer camps, classrooms, and the laboratory by Lippitt, Polansky, Redl, and Rosen [105] and Grosser, Polansky, and Lippitt [66]. This work has been able to distinguish acts of leadership which are deliberate attempts to influence others from those which exert their effects through a process of emotional contagion.

Leadership and social influence more generally usually occur in some social setting possessing a structure. Individuals have positions within such structures and much of their behavior is influenced by the relations among these positions. Several studies have been conducted by field theorists to examine how these "sociological" variables interact with more traditional "psychological" ones in determining the actions and feelings of individuals. French and Snyder [62] explored the ways in which the opinions and attitudes of enlisted men affect the ability of noncommissioned officers to influence their behavior. Zander, Cohen, and Stotland [140] studied the working relations among psychiatrists, clinical psychologists, and psychiatric social workers in order to discover how legal and institutional relations among the professions affect the attitudes and behavior of individual members of these groups. Cohen [36] conducted an experiment in a business office in which the supervisor's behavior toward subordinates was systematically varied so as to provide a well-structured or poorly structured environment for the subordinates. The dependent variables in this study were many symptoms which may be taken as reactions to threat. Kelley [82] created a status hierarchy in the laboratory and investigated the ways in which this influences the direction of the flow and the content of communication. And Bavelas [17] stimulated a large number of experiments in which the communication channels within a group are systematically controlled and varied while various aspects of group functioning are observed.

Cooperation and competition. As field theorists have turned their attention to interpersonal relations they have become interested in the ways in which various institutional arrangements influence the motivational interdependence of people. Deutsch [39, 38] compared the consequences of organizing college classes so that the students were cooperatively or competitively related to one another. He found marked differences in such things as interpersonal liking, readiness to be influenced, coordination of efforts, productivity, and comprehension of communications. Lewin, in discussing the consequences of membership in minority groups, often pointed out that group membership can result in the members' sharing a common fate. Thibaut [125] set up an experiment in which some of the consequences of such a state of affairs could be recorded.

Intergroup relations. The rise of Hitler and the existence of prejudice and discrimination against minority groups in the United States stimulated Lewin to become deeply concerned with such phenomena. He wrote extensively on the problem [94] and took steps which led to the establishment of the Commission on Community Interrelations of the American Jewish Congress. This research organization conducted a number of basic studies of the dynamics of prejudice and techniques for improving intergroup relations. One of the most imaginative approaches to these problems was a series of experiments, conducted by Citron, Chein, and Harding [33] and by Citron and Harding [34], in which techniques were developed for handling antiminority remarks and for training citizens to use these techniques. This organization also made extensive use of the technique known as "action research," one of the best illustrations being that of the community self survey as described by Wormser and Selltiz [136]. When the Research Center for Human Relations was established at New York University, this line of work was continued there. Among the many important studies conducted by this group special mention should be made of the investigations of attitudes in interracial housing reported by Deutsch and Collins [41] and Wilner, Walkley, and Cook [135].

Food habits. As field theorists have broadened their interests in attempting to account for the total field of determinants of behavior, their research has become increasingly interdisciplinary. A good example of this trend may be seen in the research of Lewin [93] on the question of why people eat what they do. On the basis of this work he constructed a theory of social channels and gatekeepers in which he analyzed the ecological processes by which food gets onto the table. From this analysis it was possible to designate certain individuals as gatekeepers whose decisions are crucial in determining what other people eat. A number of cultural, economic, and technological variables were shown to influence these decisions.

Summary. From this sketchy survey of research conducted by Lewin and those closely associated with him, it should be apparent that field theorists aspire to deal with a very large range of psychological phenomena. The settings in which research occurs and the kinds of people studied are, moreover, extremely heterogeneous. Such a breadth of research activity reflects the field theorist's commitment to attempt to understand the total life space or field of determinants of behavior and an unwillingness to restrict his interests to some limited kind of behavior. He cannot accept in principle any view of psychology that would create a categorical separation, or discontinuity, between theories of learning, perception, motivation, personality, childhood, adolescence, maturity, social relations, or any other classification of human behavior and experience. He believes that psychological theory should resist the development of any such separations and should contribute to the understanding of people of all ages and in all possible states and circumstances.

A minimal prerequisite for the achievement of such a theory is the creation of a language of description applicable to the entire domain of psychology.

METHOD OF CONSTRUCTION[8]

How is psychology to acquire an adequate language? The proposal that psychological theory be stated in the language of physics or physiology has been rejected by field theorists, as noted above. Psychology, then, confronts the critical task of building for itself an adequate set of concepts, and psychologists are deeply divided on how to proceed. Lewin, in seeking guides for his own development of concepts, relied heavily upon the conclusions reached by Cassirer [30] from his extensive analysis of the history of science. The implications of this analysis for psychology were elaborated by Lewin in his paper on the conflict between Aristotelian and Galileian modes of thought in psychology [90, pp. 1–42].

Cassirer maintains that the crucial feature of the advance of natural science has been a change in the kind of concepts used. Scientific progress has consisted, in large measure, of moving from "thing-concepts" to "relation-concepts," or from the method of "abstraction" to that of "construction." This diagnosis of the source of scientific progress has had a fundamental influence on the thinking of psychological field theorists.

Abstraction and construction. The essence of the distinction advanced by Cassirer can be stated most concisely by a quotation from Weyl's discussion of the philosophy of mathematics and natural science.

Aristotle ascends from the single object to the concept by isolating individual features of the object and by "abstracting" from everything else. Thus every other object which exhibits those same features falls under the same concept, or into the same class. In this procedure (as in descriptive botany or zoology) only the *really existing* objects are concerned, and classes are formed preferably in such manner that, according to the testimony of experience, the concepts entail as many "connotations" as possible. In the mathematical-physical or "functional" formation of concepts, on the other hand, no abstraction takes place, but we make certain individual features variable that are capable of continuous gradation, and the concept does not extend to all actual, but all *possible* objects thus obtainable . . . [132, p. 150].

The method of abstraction, as Cassirer points out, has appealed to those who are empirically oriented because it has the apparent advantage of making very few assumptions about empirical reality.

[8] At this point I find it necessary to depart rather markedly from the outline provided by the editorial committee. The material presented here is most closely related, I believe, to the committee's section on "Construction of function forms." Before functional relations among variables can be treated productively, it is necessary to achieve a satisfactory designation of the variables. Since field theory is greatly interested in the prior question of how to construct concepts, I have taken the liberty of substituting a discussion of the construction of concepts in place of one concerning the construction of functions.

Nothing is presupposed save the existence of things in their inexhaustible multiplicity, and the power of the mind to select from this wealth of particular existences those features that are *common* to several of them. When we thus collect objects characterized by possession of some common property into classes, and when we repeat this process upon higher levels, there gradually arises an ever firmer order and division of being, according to the series of factual similarities running through the particular things. The essential functions of thought, in this connection, are merely those of comparing and differentiating a sensuously given manifold [30, pp. 4–5].

Although this policy of nonintervention on the part of the scientist has undoubtedly made the method of abstraction attractive to those who highly regard empirical data, it entails certain unfortunate consequences. We quote Cassirer again.

If we merely follow the traditional rule for passing from the particular to the universal, we reach the paradoxial result that thought, in so far as it mounts from lower to higher and more inclusive concepts, moves in mere *negations*. The essential act here presupposed is that we drop certain determinations, which we had hitherto held; that we abstract from them and exclude them from consideration as irrelevant. What enables the mind to form concepts is just its fortunate gift of forgetfulness, its inability to grasp the individual differences everywhere present in the particular cases. . . . If we adhere strictly to this conception, we reach the strange result that all the logical labor which we apply to a given sensuous intuition serves only to separate us more and more from it. Instead of reaching a deeper comprehension of its import and structure, we reach only a superficial schema from which all peculiar traits of the particular case have vanished [30, pp. 18–19].

The basic difficulty with the method of abstraction, Cassirer concludes, lies in an error it makes in its very attempt to stay close to empirical data.

It is only owing to the fact that science abandons the attempt to give a direct, sensuous copy of reality, that science is able to represent this reality as a necessary connection of grounds and consequents [30, p. 164].

As soon as we take one step beyond the first naïve observation of isolated facts, as soon as we ask about the *connection* and *law* of the real, we have transcended the strict limits prescribed by the positivistic demand. In order even to indicate this connection and law clearly and adequately, we must go back to a system that develops only universal hypothetical connections of grounds and consequences, and which renounces in principle the "reality" of its elements [30, p. 117].

Inertia is for Galileo—as empty space was for Democritus—a postulate that we cannot do without in the scientific exposition of phenomena, but which is not itself a concrete sensible process of external reality. It denotes an idea, conceived for the purpose of ordering the phenomena, yet not standing on the same plane methodologically with these phenomena [30, p. 169].

A fundamental issue, then, lies at the basis of the distinction between abstraction and construction. The elements of abstraction are phenomena or objects of the scientist's experience; the elements of construction are ideas. The method of construction rests on an apparent paradox: in order to develop concepts adequate to describe empirical reality we must construct them by an act of thought. The ideal concepts of natural science "go beyond the given, in order to grasp more sharply the systematic structural relations of the given" [30, p. 128]. Viewed from this perspective, the so-called conceptual properties of constructs carry an essential rather than any "surplus" meaning. Operational definitions serve to coordinate constructs to specific empirical data, but conceptual definitions place them in a system of ideas so that they may be manipulated in accordance with the laws of logic and so that the necessary connections of grounds and consequents displayed in the empirical data can be grasped. The operational and conceptual definitions of a construct, moreover, cannot be successfully developed independently of each other because the operations, or measurements, used in any particular definition must fit the requirements of the conceptual properties of the construct. Only when both operational and conceptual definitions are given is it possible for a construct to represent the particularities of individual cases and to show the necessity of the occurrence of these particularities. A test score on an intelligence test, for instance, may provide some actuarial information about an individual through knowledge of empirical correlations between test scores and other characteristics of people, but unless the test score can be related to a construct (or set of constructs) with conceptual properties and thus to a logical system it is not possible to understand why variations in intelligence must be related to other characteristics of the individual.

Two important consequences flow from an adequate understanding of the utility of conceptual definitions. Both have to do with the place of statistics in the psychologist's methodological armament. It is more than an interesting historical fact that Galileo and Newton did not proceed according to approved statistical procedures; they employed neither a representative sample nor a factor analysis. Indeed, it may be argued that it is fortunate that modern statistics was not available to them, for the classical branches of natural science have rarely used statistics except as a tool for estimating "errors of measurement." The first big advance in physics came when it was recognized that laws do not "summarize" the distribution of observed events but state necessary relations among all "possible" events. Applied to the contemporary psychological scene this experience shows, I believe, that one can "account for" variance among data in only a limited sense so long as one employs exclusively operational definitions. If one wants to "explain" variance, he must use terms having conceptual as well as operational definitions. I believe, too, that it is at least an intuitive awareness of the difference between "frequency of association" and "law" (and not merely pragmatic considerations) that has kept even the most "scientific" psychologists from adopting representative sampling as a *sine qua non* of experimentation.[9] Once a law has been proposed, the psychologist is interested in testing it against all conditions included under the law whether these occur frequently or not.

In recent years psychologists have discussed with considerable heat the distinction advanced by Allport [5] between ideographic and nomothetic approaches [47] or between clinical and statistical prediction [111]. To the field theorist the issue is not properly stated. He agrees with the ideographic or clinical approach in stressing the necessity for representing the full complexity of individual cases and accepts the proposition that no two people are exactly alike. He agrees, too, that the frequent occurrence of an event is a poor guide to predicting its occurrence in the future. But he does not accept the view that unique or infrequent events are unlawful. He believes that by employing concepts defined through the method of construction and by establishing functional relations as laws it is possible to demonstrate the necessity of "unique" events. Lewin stated the situation in the following way:

If one represents behavior or any kind of mental event by B and the whole situation including the person by S, then B may be treated as a function of S: $B = f(S)$. In this equation the function f, or better its general form, represents what one ordinarily calls a law. If one substitutes for the variables in this formula the constants which are characteristic for the individual case one gets the application to the concrete situation.

The determination of the laws is therefore only one side of the task of explaining mental life. The other side, which is of equal importance and inseparably connected with the determination of the laws, involves the task of representing concrete situations in such a way that the actual event can be derived from them according to the principles which are given in the general laws [91, p. 11].

Field theorists hold, then, that the development of adequate concepts in psychology will be accomplished by use of the method of construction. A limited number of "elements of construction" are needed

---

[9] This comment about representative sampling does not, of course, reflect any lack of appreciation for the importance of proper sampling as a technique for estimating the incidence of properties or events in a parent population. What is at issue is the proper use of information about the distribution of data in the population.

which, together with laws governing their relations, can serve to represent all of the individual phenomena of interest to the psychologist. This is the task to which Lewin devoted himself and which remains to be completed.

In psychology, one can use psychological "position," psychological "forces," and similar concepts as elements. The general laws of psychology are statements of the empirical relations between these constructive elements or certain properties of them. It is possible to construct an infinite number of constellations in line with those laws; each of these constellations corresponds to an individual case at a given time. In this way, the gap between generalities and specificities, between laws and individual differences, can be bridged [95, p. 61].

A good example of the method advocated here is Lewin's classical analysis of "types of conflict" in which he was able to show how the various types could be constructed from certain constellations of psychological forces [90, pp. 114–170]. Miller's treatment of the same problem, although using different elements of construction, also illustrates the procedure [113].

In this connection, it may be useful to note that the "elements of construction" are essentially the "primitives" of a mathematical system. It must be added, however, that a term like "psychological force" may serve as an element of construction, or primitive, in constructing higher-order concepts like those of "equilibrium" or "central force field," whereas from another point of view it may itself be constructed from other primitives like "magnitude," "direction," and "point of application." The ideal of the formal theorist is to achieve a small number of primitives from which it is possible to build up a large system of higher-order constructs. In the construction of a system of concepts to be used in empirical research, however, it is perfectly proper to employ as elements of construction terms which may at a later stage of development be constructed from other elements.

Commensurability. A major advantage of employing the method of construction is that it provides, in principle, a commensurate *system* of concepts. The empirical psychologist is overwhelmed by the multiplicity of psychological phenomena and by their apparent qualitative diversity. The theorist, moreover, is confronted with a heterogeneous collection of descriptive terms which have no clear relationship to one another. Field theorists hope through the use of proper procedures in the building of constructs to reduce this chaos and to achieve a commensurate system of concepts. Leeper has stated this point clearly in his critique of Lewin's work.

It is easy to say that we need always to recognize that behavior is a product not only of motives and habits, but also of the complex structure of the particular present situation. But it is a difficult thing, practically, to conceive this total assortment of causal factors in such a fashion that we can really relate behavior to all of these different elements. We have meant to do so. But we have lacked the intellectual tools required to secure effective command over such complex materials. Part of the difficulty comes because the various factors in motivational situations seem to be qualitatively different, incommensurable in nature. It is as if we were asked to add together three quarts of milk, six pounds of rice, four yards of silk, and ten amperes of electric current. It is the contention of Lewin, however, that the factors are not really incommensurable. There is actually an interaction between them in a human life. He has tried, therefore, to develop constructs that would put all the factors into commensurate terms so that we might effectively take into account the situational elements as well as the factors of motive, habit, and response [85, pp. 29–30].

The achievement of a coherent system of concepts requires, field theorists believe, utilization of the method of construction. Concepts must be constructed from a limited number of undefined terms (primitives) and a few postulates concerning their "properties." The concepts are to be *defined* in terms of the primitives. By allowing only such constructs in the language of theory, one achieves a coherent conceptual system in which it is clear how each concept relates logically to each other one and of what "conceptual type" each concept is. Until this is achieved there can be little hope of obtaining quantitative laws. It has always been remarkable to me how many apparently different phenomena Lewin was able to describe by means of a limited number of elements of construction. Some impression of how this feat was accomplished may be gained from his interesting discussion of the conceptual dimensions of his various constructs.

1. *Position* is a "spatial relation of regions. . . ." Examples of psychological concepts which have the conceptual dimension of position are: group belongingness of an individual, his occupational position, involvement in an activity.

2. *Locomotion* has a different dimension from position. It refers to a "relation of positions at different times." Any psychological phenomenon that can be represented as a locomotion—and that holds for most "behavior" —would have the same conceptual dimension.

3. *Cognitive structure* might be regarded as having the same dimension as position because it refers to the relative position of different parts of a field. Structure does not refer, however, to the position of one point but to the position of a multitude of points or regions.

4. *Force* or "tendency to locomotion" has conceptually a different character from actual locomotion, although locomotion is one of the symptoms (operational definition) for a constellation of forces where the resultant force is greater than zero. . . .

5. A *goal* has the conceptual dimension of a "force field"—that is, of a

distribution of forces in space. Goal (or in field-theoretical terminology, a positive valence) is a force field of a special structure, namely, a force field where all forces point toward the same region. To conceive of a goal in this way gives it a definite place within the totality of possible patterns of force fields. The counterpart of a distribution of forces toward one region is the distribution away from one region. This is equivalent to the concept of "aversion." Other types of force fields are equivalent to what is called a "difficulty" or "barrier." The transformation of such everyday concepts as goals, difficulties, aversions into force fields of different types makes it possible to link these qualitatively very different entities in a way which lays open their functional similarity and differences.

6. *Conflict* refers not to one force field but to the *overlapping of at least two force fields.* "Frustration" has the same dimension as conflict. A systematic survey of the possible types of frustration or conflict should, therefore, inquire how force fields can overlap in such a way that equally strong but opposite forces result at some points of the field. Such analysis permits a systematic treatment of the conditions and the effects of conflicts. The concept *equilibrium* has the same dimension as conflict; it refers to certain constellations of overlapping force fields.

7. *Fear* may seem to have the same dimension as aversion. However, in most cases fear is related to the psychological future. It has to deal with some aspect of "time perspective." In this respect it is similar to concepts like hope, plan, expectation. *Expectation* refers to the psychological structure and the distribution of forces on the reality level of the psychological future. *Hope* refers to a relation between the structure of the reality level and of the wish level of the psychological future. *Guilt* refers to the relation between the structure of the reality and wish level of the psychological past.

8. The concept of *power* refers to a "possibility of inducing forces" of a certain magnitude on another person. The concept of *power field,* therefore, does not have the same conceptual dimension as that of a force field. In using concepts like attack, defense, aggression, friendship, one has to be aware of the different dimensions of the concepts: power field, force field, force and behavior.

9. *Values* influence behavior but do not have the character of a goal (that is, of a force field). For example, the individual does not try to "reach" the value of fairness but fairness is "guiding" his behavior. . . . Values are not force fields but they "induce" force fields. That means values are constructs which have the same psychological dimension as *power fields.* It is interesting to consider from this point of view the psychoanalytical theory that values are "internalized" parents. Independent of whether this statement in regard to the genesis of values is or is not correct we can at least say that values and persons are equivalent in so far as both can be represented by power fields [95, pp. 39–41].

Constructs and quasi constructs. At this point a question of tactics is in order. It is very well, one may say, to assert the need for a system of concepts, defined in terms of a limited number of elements of construction and clearly ordered according to conceptual type, but how does psychology go about achieving this? Is it not necessary to engage in a great deal of pure description before we know enough to invent the correct system of constructs? The Lewinian answer is a qualified "yes." Even though Lewin felt confident of the value of the system of concepts he built up from such elements of construction as force and region, he found it necessary to employ a number of quasi constructs, like level of aspiration, social atmosphere, or gatekeeper, which could not be defined, when introduced, in terms commensurate with the more formal system.[10] But it is clear that he considered these only as starting points. His discussion of the "frustration-aggression" research of Dollard et al. [42] is illuminating in this respect.

In SR theory "frustration" is treated as a "concept," as an "element of construction." The attempt is made to define this concept operationally and to proceed from there to a quantitative theory, for instance, about the relation between frustration and aggression. When the psychologist who follows field-theoretical lines speaks about frustration, learning, hope, friendship, aggression he is conscious of the fact that he is using "popular terms." These terms are quite helpful, even necessary, in the beginning. However, they are not considered, within field theory, as psychological concepts in the sense of scientific "elements of construction." The reason for this is that a term like "frustration" (*a*) lacks a conceptual definition through coordination to mathematical concepts, (*b*) refers in a vague way to a multitude of different settings rather than to *one* conceptually definable type of situation.

If this is correct, it would be scientifically meaningless to attempt, for instance, to link the intensity of frustration lawfully with any specific effect (such as aggression); for one would have to know the type of frustration and the detailed setting in order to make any definite derivations. Indeed, the experiments show that it is as correct to say "frustration leads to increased friendship and nonaggression" as it is to say "frustration leads to aggression." It is correct to say that frustration leads to increased as well as to decreased productivity, that it leads to new efforts as well as to passivity.

The field-theoretical approach in this point is more radical. Its higher demands on concepts can be formulated in the following way: Psychology should be as much concerned with the question of what frustration "is" psychologically, as with the effect of frustration. In fact, field theory considers it impossible to investigate the laws of frustration, hope, friendship, or autocracy without investigating at the same time what frustration, hope, friendship, or autocracy "is" psychologically.

I am well aware that questions about the "nature" of objects or events

---

[10] It is interesting in this connection to recall that when Lewin first introduced the term "valence" it had reference only to the "demand character" of objects and activities. Only after several years did he define valence in terms of forces (i.e., as a central force field) and thus place it unambiguously in a system of concepts.

have been much abused and have been asked in a scientifically meaningless, metaphysical way. . . . There is one meaning behind the question about the "nature" of things which is as essential for psychology as it is for science in general. If a chemist finds a certain material he may be able to define it operationally by pointing out where it can be found and by specifying its color and weight. In studying this material, the first question will be: "What is this material chemically?" He might find that it is an element or a compound, or he might find that the chemical constitution of this material varied from piece to piece (as much as the psychological nature of frustration varied from occasion to occasion). In this case, the material, in spite of its being well-defined operationally, does not represent "*one* type" from the point of view of the chemist. The criterion for this oneness is the possibility of representing it by *one* chemical formula, through one combination of "elements of conceptual construction" (such as ions, atoms). What an object is is now determined by the possibility of characterizing it by one combination of conceptual constructs [95, pp. 34–36].

At any given stage, then, the complete body of psychological theory will necessarily contain quasi constructs which do not yet fit rigorously into the more formally developed parts of the theory. The admissibility of such terms is essential if psychology is to avoid the danger, referred to above, of allowing formal systems to define the field of psychology. It should be recognized, however, that such quasi constructs serve as programmatic guides for next steps in conceptualizing. Quasi constructs, like "need," "ego," "attitude," "ability," or "learning," should be welcomed by psychological theorists, for they are important way stations along the route to rigorous theory, but they should also provide a challenge because they cannot be included in rigorous derivations.

Method of successive approximation. The psychologist is not interested only in conceptually rigorous constructs; he is also concerned with the empirical relations among them. In implementing this concern he may proceed, however, in various ways. One line of procedure is to select two or three properties, hold constant or randomize all others, and then concentrate on determining precisely the equation specifying their functional relations. The emphasis placed on exact quantification makes this procedure attractive to many "scientifically" minded psychologists, but the procedure contains some difficulties which make the field theorist doubt its desirability. The crux of the problem lies in the selection of properties. Which ones are to be chosen? Surely they are not selected at random. A general map is needed to show the full array of interdependencies before undertaking a precise quantitative determination of the relations among a limited number of properties. Research should proceed by a series of successive approximations, beginning with a gross determination of "what goes with what" and moving progressively to a more and more exact specification of the form of the functional relations. The first approximation is a simplification of the empirical situation in that it ignores the quantitative details, but it is acceptable in that "the representation given in the first approximation will not be destroyed but only made more articulated by the second approximation since the whole situation is taken into account from the beginning" [91, p. 17]. Lewin points out that the early experiments on tension systems deliberately attempted such a first approximation and he credits this procedure for the fact that more precisely quantitative experiments carried out subsequently have not forced any basic change of the original theory.

Either one tries to determine the actual percentage of resumption as accurately as possible, or one is mainly interested in the question whether the effect of an intention can be adequately understood as the creation of a tension system. For the latter question it is at present of minor importance whether the percentage of resumption is 75, 80, or 85, because any of these figures would be in line with the general assumption. To prove or disprove the theory of tension systems, it seems much more important to find a variety of derivations from this theory which should be as different as possible from each other, and to test as many as possible of these derivations, even if this test should be rather crude quantitatively at the beginning [95, pp. 8–9].

The fact that it is possible to employ this method of successive approximation while using concepts which are built up rigorously from elements of construction sheds some light on the distinction between intervening variables and hypothetical constructs advanced by Mac-Corquodale and Meehl [107]. Without entering into a detailed discussion of this problem, I should like to suggest that Lewinian concepts are more properly classed as hypothetical constructs than as intervening variables. The existence of "tension," for example, is assumed and its general properties specified long before quantitative equations can be determined. The elaboration of this point of view has been developed by Rozeboom, who reaches the following conclusion:

Once we realize, in fact, that the structure of a system of HC (hypothetical constructs) is in itself a predicate sufficient to carry a set of existential operators, we become aware that it is not even necessary for the hypothesis to specify in quantitative detail the functional relations by which the variables are connected. It is sufficient that the hypothesis merely designates for each construct the other variables of which it is an immediate function and those which, in turn, the construct immediately helps determine. . . . Recognition that the structure of causal linkages among a set of mediation variables is independent of the specific quantitative nature of the relations frees us from preoccupation with excessive quantification of empirical relations during the early phases of a science, enabling us to identify the major immanent determinants of behavior prior to discovery of their exact relations to their causal antecedents and observable consequences [119, p. 263].

Summary. In order to understand the essential approach of field theory it is necessary to understand what has been called here the method of construction. This method, originated in the field of mathematics, has been employed throughout recent centuries in the natural sciences. It is currently being used in psychology by field theorists and by many theorists who differ from Lewinians in other respects. The method of construction replaces the method of abstraction and puts upon the scientist the responsibility to create a system of constructs which will relate to one another in a logical system (through conceptual definitions) and will refer unambiguously to empirical data (through operational definitions). The successful construction of such a system will produce concepts which are commensurate and which can be located according to their "type" or "dimension." The tactical problem of how to achieve such a system requires at any given stage of development the use of quasi constructs and the method of approximation.

MENSURATIONAL AND QUANTIFICATIONAL PROCEDURES

Use of mathematics. One of the most significant features of Lewin's work lies in the use he made of mathematics. Since his approach to mathematics stressed its nonquantitative aspects, one may question whether it should be discussed under the heading of "mensuration and quantification." Lewin rejected the implicit assumption made by psychologists of his day that the use of mathematics is equivalent to treating things quantitatively. For this reason, it seems to me to be appropriate to discuss here the broader question of the role of mathematics in psychological theory.

Mathematics has, of course, been employed in psychology ever since its earliest attempts to become an empirical science. The famous "laws" of psychophysics, advanced by men like Weber or Fechner, were stated as mathematical equations, and the whole movement of psychological testing was based upon statistical techniques. Mathematical statistics continues to contribute to psychology by making it possible to quantify variables, by providing satisfactory techniques for sampling large universes, and by developing methods for assessing the dependability of measuring instruments and of generalizations about data. If, however, one were to characterize the essential nature of the use of mathematics by psychologists, one would have to say that until recent years it consisted almost entirely of providing techniques for the processing of data.

Lewin, on the other hand, saw the possibility of using mathematics as an aid in constructing psychological theory. He was impressed by the fact that the natural sciences had employed mathematics not merely to process data but as a means of representing essential properties of physical events. The fundamental concept of "physical space," for example, was defined in terms of geometry, and all theoretical manipulations of the concept were carried out according to the requirements of geometry as a logical-mathematical system. Geometry was an indispensable part of physical theory. Psychological theory too, Lewin believed, will have to contain concepts whose elements of construction are mathematically described empirical entities (such as psychological space and psychological forces).

Topology. The idea that psychology will have to make use of the concept of space occurred to Lewin early in his career. In 1912, while still a student, he defended the thesis that "psychology, dealing with manifolds of coexisting facts, would be finally forced to use not only the concept of time but that of space, too" [91, p. vii]. Thus from the very beginning of his theoretical work the concept of "life space" was fundamental, and a search for an appropriate mathematics for representing this space occupied a large portion of his energy for many years. In order to understand how Lewin arrived at the conclusion that topology can best represent the life space, it is important to remember that the scientific world at that time was in a ferment, just beginning to realize the full implications of the view that physical space need not necessarily be represented in terms of euclidean geometry. The freedom thus given to physicists to seek a better mathematical system for representing physical space encouraged Lewin to believe that psychological space, too, might be represented in terms of a noneuclidean geometry.

After considering carefully the empirical properties of psychological space, Lewin concluded that topology is best suited for the task. It is a branch of geometry dealing with the most general properties of space, being concerned with transformations which preserve certain properties and invariants. Thus, for example, a circle, triangle, and a polygon with any number of sides are topologically equivalent being Jordan curves (i.e., a closed curve which does not intersect itself). Topology is a rigorous mathematical system, permitting logical derivations, and yet it does not require the making of assumptions about quantitative properties of psychological phenomena—assumptions which do not seem to be justified by the nature of these phenomena. It provides, moreover, the promise of allowing "first approximations" which will not have to be abandoned later when more precise quantification becomes possible.[11]

---

[11] This feature of topology makes it quite different from many of the current "mathematical models" which make quantitative assumptions of questionable empirical validity.

A full discussion of the topological concepts employed by Lewin would not be appropriate here; the reader is referred instead to the primary sources [91; 92; 95, pp. 305–338]. But in order to clarify some of the issues involved in any use of mathematics for theory, it may be well at this point to consider one criticism often raised against Lewin's use of topology. This criticism holds that Lewin did not employ any *theorems* of topology to derive psychological events and, therefore, that he did not use topology as a mathematical model. It is correct, I believe, that Lewin did not explicitly employ any topological theorems in his theoretical derivations, but I would question the conclusion often drawn from this fact: that Lewin's interest in topology led him up a blind alley. Certain considerations point to the contrary conclusion.

1. The use of topology made it possible to take seriously the notion of psychological space. The elementary concepts of topology, such as region, boundary, and path, allow the representation of such basic psychological phenomena as "approach" or "avoidance" without implying that these terms have meaning in a physical space (for example, it is possible to represent the fact that a man is approaching "occupancy of the White House" or "marriage" without specifying his geographical location). The use of topological concepts for this purpose was intended to be more than "mere pictures"; if any theorems of topology led to incorrect psychological derivations, then the use of topology would have to be abandoned or modified. A field theorist would certainly accept the proposition that when the primitives of topology are mapped onto psychological phenomena all the theorems of topology must produce true statements about psychological properties. It is in this sense that field theorists take topology seriously. It should be noted, however, that this does not imply that theorems of topology, by themselves, will necessarily produce particularly interesting psychological derivations. In fact it was in part a conviction that topological concepts are insufficient to represent the full richness of psychological phenomena that diverted Lewin's attention away from the theorems of topology as a potential source of significant psychological derivations.

2. Topological concepts, although essential for representing psychological space and the structural properties of person and environment, do not in themselves permit the representation of the dynamic aspects of psychological phenomena. Lewin was quite explicit about this matter:

Among psychological constructs one may distinguish geometrical and dynamical constructs. Examples of dynamical constructs in psychology are instinct, libido, force, tension. Dynamical constructs deal with causation, with the conditions of change. They are the main objects of interest in psychology. Examples of geometrical constructs are direction, distance, and position.

The geometrical constructs might be called "constructs of the first order" as compared with dynamical concepts as "constructs of the second order." The dynamical constructs are based partly upon the geometrical ones [92, p. 20].

Lewin's concept of "psychological force" illustrates the interrelations between geometrical and dynamic constructs. Its purpose is to represent "tendencies to change." Such tendencies, having location, direction, and magnitude, can be represented by the formal properties of force, which are direction, magnitude, and point of application. A psychological force can be expressed mathematically as a vector whose direction and point of application are stated in terms of the geometrical concepts of position and direction.

A complete formal system which will provide theorems of real interest to psychology will consist not only of geometrical (topological) concepts but also of dynamic ones.

3. Lewin believed, however, that topology, particularly as presented by Veblen [129], was in a sense too general and that certain developments of it would be required before it would be entirely satisfactory for representing the geometrical aspects of psychological phenomena. He was especially concerned about the inability to deal with concepts of "distance" and "direction." For this reason, he devoted considerable energy to the task of inventing a "hodological" space which could better deal with these. Rather than assuming that topology was fully developed in those aspects of importance to psychology and testing the applicability of all its formal properties, he attempted to develop those aspects which together with dynamic concepts would provide theorems of value to psychology. This extension of topology would, presumably, not violate any formal properties of the already developed system.

Linear graphs. In recent years the University of Michigan's Research Center for Group Dynamics has had a program of work involving the collaboration of mathematicians and psychologists and devoted to exploring further the possibilities of employing mathematics in the construction of psychological theory. From this work certain conclusions can be drawn.

1. Although Lewin discussed the possibility of representing the life space by a multidimensional topological space, his diagrams were almost always two-dimensional planar maps. As Harary and Norman [67] show, if one ignores the points within regions of this map, it is possible to construct a linear graph which will correspond exactly to any planar map. The correspondence between planar maps and certain linear graphs is accomplished by mapping each region of the planar map onto

a point of the graph and each boundary between regions onto a line joining these points. An illustration of this procedure is given in Fig. 1. The planar map in Fig. 1a consists of four regions, each of which has a common boundary arc with each other region. The linear graph in Fig. 1b corresponds to this map since each region of the map has a corresponding point in the graph and each boundary has a corresponding line. Bavelas [16] was the first psychologist to attempt this "translation" in his restatement (in terms of points and lines) of such concepts as "centrality" and "distance" (which Lewin had treated by regions and boundaries). I believe that eventually it will be possible to express the major properties of Lewin's hodological space in terms of linear graphs since graph theory makes explicit use of the concept "path." A graphical

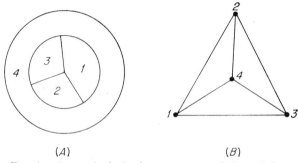

(A)   (B)

Fig. 1a. A topological planar map consisting of four regions each of which has a common boundary arc with each other.
Fig. 1b. A linear graph corresponding to the planar map in which each point corresponds to a region of the map and each line to a common boundary arc.

representation of psychological phenomena has several advantages, though it must be noted that linear graphs do not permit one to distinguish parts within points (like points within regions of the planar map).

2. One advantage of linear graphs over planar maps derives from the famous "four color" property of such maps. Although topologists have never been able to construct a formal proof, they are agreed that it is possible to color every map drawn on a sphere or a plane with no more than four colors in such a way that no two regions, having a common boundary arc, have the same color. Stated in terms more directly relevant to psychology, this property of maps makes it impossible to add a region to the map in Fig. 1a in such a way that all five regions will have a common boundary arc with one another. It is obvious, however, that one can add a point to the graph of Fig. 1b and join it by a line to

each of the other points by the simple procedure of allowing lines to cross. Since it is almost certain that more than four "parts" of the life space may all be directly touching one another, linear graphs would appear to be more appropriate than planar maps for representing the life space.[12]

3. Leeper [85, pp. 109–110] has pointed out that Lewin did not entirely succeed in representing the type of situation that contains an "irrevocable path," in which a person can move freely from *A* to *B* but once having reached *B* cannot return to *A*. It could be noted also that in Lewin's treatment of inner-personal regions the boundaries were "not directed" in the sense that influences could pass equally in either direction. This inability to treat asymmetrical relations imposes a serious limitation on Lewin's use of topology. It now appears, however, that the mathematical theory of linear graphs is ideally equipped to handle such situations by use of the general concept of "directed graph." As shown

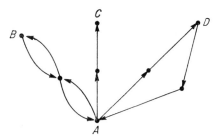

Fig. 2. A linear graph showing "revocable" and "irrevocable" paths. The path from *A* to *B* can be retraced after each step; the path from *A* to *C* cannot be retraced; and one can return to *A* after reaching *D* but without retracing.

in Harary, Norman, and Cartwright [68], it is possible to treat in a completely rigorous fashion structures made up of points and *directed* lines. Figure 2 illustrates a situation in which it is possible to retrace one's steps along the path from *A* to *B*, not possible to retrace along the path from *A* to *C*, but possible to return to *A* after reaching *D* without retracing. Other more complicated situations could be represented with the same concepts. Furthermore, it is possible to characterize rigorously such properties of total structures as "degree of connectedness." French [60] has recently employed certain structural properties of directed graphs together with certain dynamic properties to derive several features of social influence processes.

4. A recent development in the utilization of linear graphs for repre-

---

[12] It should be noted that there are other ways in which this difficulty can be overcome. For example, it can be shown that one can color a map drawn on a torus with seven or fewer colors. Or, if one allows regions of a planar map to have a boundary point (rather than arc) in common, then an infinite number of regions can touch one another. Neither of these solutions, however, seems as satisfactory as employing linear graphs.

senting psychological situations has been to designate the "sign" of each line of a graph as either plus or minus. Thus, the fact that A likes B is represented by a directed line from A to B of positive sign, that A dislikes C by a directed line from A to C of negative sign, and that A is indifferent to D by the absence of any line from A to D. Although the full ramifications of signed graphs for representing psychological phenomena have not yet been explored, it does seem that by designating the sign of lines one will be better able to handle such polarities as likedislike or facilitation-inhibition. Cartwright and Harary [28] have recently been able to state Heider's theory of balance [71] in terms of signed graphs and to show how the theory can thereby be generalized to situations not originally encompassed in the theory.

5. In discussing how to determine whether two environmental regions of the life space have a common boundary, Lewin employed the criterion of "possibility of direct locomotion from one to the other." If it is possible to go directly from A to B, then regions A and B have a common boundary (or, in graph theory, points A and B are joined by a line). If it is impossible to go directly from the one to the other, then there is no common boundary. It would appear, in the light of current psychological thought, that a better conception might envisage a continuous gradation from the "impossible" to the "certainly possible." The connectedness of two parts of the psychological environment would not then be viewed dichotomously but as a continuous variable which could be stated in terms of probability. The graph theoretical concept of "strength," outlined by Harary and Norman [67, pp. 31–32], would seem to lend itself to representing such probabilities. A complete assessment of this approach, however, has not yet been completed.

Summary. The field theorist believes that the question of how to design techniques of measurement and quantification must be answered in accordance with the nature of the theoretical concepts employed. In particular, it should not be assumed on a priori grounds that all psychological phenomena can be coordinated to continuous variables. Lewin maintained that many constructs in psychology would have to be nonquantitative and that their corresponding operational indicators would also be nonquantitative. This view does not hold that psychology should not employ mathematics in dealing with such phenomena. On the contrary, Lewin was one of the first to show that psychologists might fruitfully use branches of mathematics other than the calculus, algebra, and probability theory in order to deal rigorously with psychological data.

The idea that psychological data can be related, in part, to a finitely structured space has been a basic assumption of field theorists. The concepts of topology, and more recently those of linear graphs, have been employed in constructing the basic concepts of field theory. These, it should be noted, do not preclude the use of quantitative concepts, like those of distance or strength of force, in the same system. In fact, both kinds should be used but they should be carefully distinguished, especially in designing operational indicators of the concepts. Scientific rigor will be more readily achieved in this way than by attempting to force all data to fit such assumptions as those of infinite divisibility and continuous gradation.

FORMAL ORGANIZATION OF THE SYSTEM

Since Lewinian field theory does not consist of a single formalized system of concepts and hypothesis, it will not be possible in this section to discuss the formal organization of field theory as if it were such a system. It should be noted that several "miniature" formalized systems have been developed by field theorists to deal with some limited set of phenomena. Among the more explicitly formulated of these are the derivations of Lewin [95, pp. 9–20] concerning the concept of tension, the quantitative theory of decision-time proposed by Cartwright and Festinger [27], the formulation of Heider's concept of balance advanced by Cartwright and Harary [28], and the formal theory of social power developed by French [60]. In addition there are, of course, many less formalized theoretical treatments of specific empirical data which employ Lewinian concepts. Although it would be instructive to examine the formal organization of any of these systems, no one of them can be taken as "the" statement of field theory. And while it is likely that these various "miniature" systems can eventually be combined into a more inclusive one, such an integration has not yet been accomplished.

For these reasons I have decided in this section to discuss certain problems involved in a rigorous formalization of Lewin's most basic constructs. In doing so I shall concentrate on the constructs: life space, person, environment, and behavior.

The concept of life space. To the historian of psychology Lewin's use of the concept, life space, should pose some interesting problems concerning the relations between rigorous and creative thinking. The idea of life space, as noted above, was fundamental to all of Lewin's theorizing; without it the other parts of his conceptual system would be virtually meaningless. By using it he was able to proceed in a most creative way to conduct a psychological analysis of a vast array of phenomena which had previously defied any sort of effective analysis. Even his most intuitive, or least formal, thinking proceeded with the life space as a basic assumption. But in spite of the central significance of this concept, a close scrutiny of its properties reveals many ambiguities. These are, as might be expected, more pronounced in Lewin's earlier discussions but they were never completely eliminated. In a sense the life space was a "programmatic" concept; it served to indicate an approach, to designate a way of thinking about psychological phenomena.

Although the term, life space, appears throughout Lewin's writing, it is rarely given explicit definition. The essential idea can be grasped, however, from the following concise statements.

Life space. Totality of facts which determine the behavior (B) of an individual at a certain moment. The life space (L) represents the totality of possible events. The life space includes the person (P) and the environment (E). $B = f(L) = f(P,E)$. It can be represented by a finitely structured space [91, p. 216].

The critical terms in grasping the meaning of life space, then, are *person, environment,* and *behavior.* And much of the difficulty in understanding Lewin's use of life space lies in the meaning to be attributed to these concepts. An examination of Lewin's formal definitions will reveal that each is defined in terms of the others. This procedure is essential for the construction of a coherent, logical system, but it leaves unsettled the question of how these concepts are related to empirical data. Can one, for instance, coordinate "person" to "biological organism," "environment" to "patterns of physical stimuli," and "behavior" to "patterns of motor responses"? The answer is obviously "no" in each of these cases, but there is difficulty in arriving at a satisfactory positive answer.

Person. Terms like "person," "ego," or "self" have been among the most troublesome for psychologists. Lewin, like others, did not always maintain a single meaning for the word "person" in his various writings over the years. Sometimes he appeared to speak of the person as the entity whose behavior is to be studied. In the quotation cited immediately above, the word "individual" was used in this sense. Some such term is needed to denote the specific point of reference being used in constructing any given life space, to indicate whose life space is under consideration. There can be little doubt, however, that Lewin intended to restrict the term "person" to refer to certain parts of the life space, i.e., to certain parts of the totality of facts which determine the behavior of a given individual. For some purposes it is convenient to represent the person as an undifferentiated point and merely to deal with its position in the environment of the life space. For other purposes, it is necessary to treat the person as differentiated into parts. In either case, the person and environment are in interaction, together determining events in the life space. As noted in an earlier section, the state of tension associated with particular regions within the person and certain properties of regions of the environment jointly determine the distribution of forces in the environment, and distance of the person from the goal region partially determines the magnitude of forces acting on the person.

Environment. It is clear that Lewin did not intend for the term, environment, to refer to the physical world in which an organism is situated nor even to the proximal stimuli which may impinge upon the organism's receptors. The environment, or the psychological environment as Lewin sometimes called it, refers to the world *as it exists for the individual being studied.*

Objectivity in psychology demands representing the field correctly as it exists for the individual in question at that particular time. For this field the child's friendships, conscious and "unconscious" goals, dreams, ideals, and fears are at least as essential as any physical setting. Since this field is different for every age and for every individual, the situation as characterized by physics or sociology, which is the same for everybody, cannot be substituted for it [95, p. 240].

The food that lies behind doors at the end of a maze so that neither smell nor sight can reach it is not part of the life space of the animal. If the individual knows that food lies there this *knowledge,* of course, has to be represented in his life space, because this knowledge affects behavior. It is also necessary to take into account the subjective probability with which the individual views the present or future state of affairs because the degree of certainty of expectation also influences his behavior.

The principle of representing within the life space all that affects behavior at that time, but nothing else, prevents the inclusion of physical food which is not perceived. This food cannot possibly influence his behavior at that time under the conditions mentioned. Indeed, the individual will start his journey if he thinks the food is there even if it is actually not there, and he will not move toward the food which actually is at the end of the maze if he does not know it is there [95, pp. 57–58].

The insistence that a person's psychological environment contains only those facts which *exist for him* led Lewin sometimes to speak as if he equated the psychological environment with the phenomenal field, and there are those who have classified Lewin as a phenomenologist. Such an interpretation is given by F. H. Allport as shown in the following quotations:

It was the original intent of Lewin, or so it seems to the present writer, to develop a field theory of a consistently phenomenological sort. . . .

It must also be remembered that it is only the individual's *phenomenological experience* of objects and of himself among them that make up the content of the field. . . . The field can be described only in subjective terms [4, pp. 149–150].

A similar impression might be created by the discussion of Spence [124] in which he equates the approach of Lewin with those of Köhler,

Koffka, and Snygg. More specifically, Spence makes the following statement.

The methods of determining the structure and properties of these fields whether "brain field," "behavioral environment" or "life space" are, however, essentially the same, and . . . involve extensive use of the phenomenological type of introspection [124, p. 54].

Such characterizations of Lewin's point of view are, in my opinion, not strictly correct. Although Lewin held that phenomenal properties must be included in the psychological environment and although he favored use of subjects' accounts of the world as they experience it, he did not *equate* the psychological environment with the phenomenal world. His basic criterion was whether any given fact had an effect on behavior, not whether it appeared in conscious awareness. He explicitly asserted that the life space should include within it "unconscious" determinants of behavior. Leeper [86] has presented a point of view entirely consistent with that of Lewin, it seems to me, in his excellent discussion of cognitive processes.

The question is, therefore, whether we should define cognitive processes, perception, thinking, concept formation and the like in terms of *conscious* processes exclusively, or whether we should say that consciousness may be present or absent, as the case may be, and that all these processes are to be defined in terms of their other functional relations [86, p. 735].

It seems better, therefore, to avoid narrow definitions and to say that cognitive processes include all the means whereby the individual represents anything to himself or uses these representations as a means of guiding his behavior [86, p. 736].

Behavior. Just what empirical data Lewin intended to coordinate to the term, behavior, is more difficult to determine. The problem here is not a methodological one, for in the conduct of empirical research there is no doubt that Lewin employed all of the standard behavioral indicators. He "tested" his theories with such data as number of items recalled, reaction time, verbal statements of expectations, frequency of aggressive actions, speed of performance, and compliance with requests. And yet the exact way in which these indicators were related to the theoretical concept, behavior, was never entirely clear. At first glance, Lewin seems to provide a quite definite linkage by asserting that behavior is coordinated to locomotion of the person in the life space. Thus, if in a decision situation the person is subjected to conflicting forces directed toward two different regions of the environment (e.g., "going to the movies" and "going to a concert") and if the resultant force is in the direction of one of these, then the person will engage in the corresponding activity. But as Leeper [85, p. 116] has noted, since the position of the person in the psychological environment both before and after locomotion is defined "as it exists for the individual," all that can be derived strictly from a locomotion in the psychological environment is a change of the situation as it exists for the individual. Whether or not there will be a particular *motor performance* is another matter. Since there is ordinarily a fairly close correspondence (at least in the typical laboratory experiment) between the subject's cognitive representation of any action he takes and the experimenter's description of it, Lewin's failure to make an explicit logical step from locomotion to motor performance caused little practical difficulty. Nevertheless, Lewin acknowledged the cogency of Leeper's criticism, believed it to be quite important, and made several attempts to modify his system (see below).

With this interpretation of the component terms of the concept, life space, it may be instructive to consider the statement made by Brunswik [20] that the life space is "post-perceptual and pre-behavioral." It seems to me that Brunswik pointed here to an important issue concerning Lewin's use of the term, life space. This statement can be accepted, however, only by ignoring certain features of Lewin's theorizing, the modifications he suggested in response to Brunswik's characterization, and the actual procedures he employed in conducting research. Nevertheless, I believe that Brunswik was correct in so far as he referred to the more explicitly developed parts of Lewin's treatment. Considering only these parts, it appears that the life space is a *resultant* of certain processes (perceptual) and behavior is a change of the life space (rather than motor responses). The formula, $B = f(L)$, relates changes in the life space to properties of the life space; B is not to be equated with motor response, and L is not the same as stimulus or pattern of stimuli.

It is perfectly clear, however, that Lewin could not accept this characterization of the life space as a satisfactory one. It is clear, too, that contemporary field theorists reject it. Although a rigorous formulation of an alternative conceptualization of the life space has not been achieved, the outlines can be indicated. Even in Lewin's earliest writings there are terms which served to indicate the problem, though they did little to solve it. Some of these were: alien factors, foreign hull of the life space, and motor-perceptual stratum. In responding to Brunswik, Lewin attempted to outline the way in which he would treat the life space, the physical and social world, and the relations between these.

Within the realm of facts existing at a given time one can distinguish three areas in which changes are or might be of interest to psychology:
1. The "life space"; i.e., the person and the psychological environment as it exists for him. We usually have this field in mind if we refer to needs, motivation, mood, goals, anxiety, ideals.

2. A multitude of processes in the physical or social world, which do not affect the life space of the individual at that time.

3. A "boundary zone" of the life space: certain parts of the physical or social world do affect the state of the life space at that time. The process of perception, for instance, is intimately linked with this boundary zone because what is perceived is partly determined by the physical "stimuli"; i.e., that part of the physical world which affects the sensory organs at that time. Another process located in the boundary zone is the "execution" of an action [95, p. 57].

The boundary zone of the life space, then, is the locus of perceptual (psychophysical) processes and of motor performances. These are located in a boundary zone because both perception and motor performance are influenced both by the life space and by the physical (and social) world external to the life space, and because influences originating inside the life space must pass through this boundary to affect the outside, and vice versa.[13] This conception is obviously only a first step toward stating the problems involved in relating the life space to the physical and social world, yet it does provide a basis for integrating the many diverse fields of investigation to which psychologists have addressed themselves.

A suggested formulation. In my own thinking about these problems I have found it helpful to employ a schematic diagram of the various classes of facts and functional relations with which the psychologist is concerned.[14] This diagram is presented in Fig. 3. Each circle stands for a given class of events, and each line stands for a given kind of interdependence. The various circles have the following meanings: P stands for those facts which Lewin represented in the person; E refers to the psychological environment; S indicates the sensorium, or that part of the boundary zone of the life space which receives "information" or "stimulation" from the physical-social world; M symbolizes the motorium, also a part of the boundary zone, which "acts upon" the physical-social world; H represents the foreign hull of the life space, defined by Lewin as those facts "which are not subject to psychological laws but which influence the state of the life space" [91, p. 216]; A denotes those alien facts making up the

[13] Originally, Lewin placed the "motor-perceptual stratum" at the boundary of the person rather than the life space. When Leeper pointed out the inconsistency of this treatment, Lewin adopted the procedure outlined here.

[14] A somewhat different schematic diagram is proposed by Escalona [44, p. 979] to deal with the same problem. The diagram which I describe here, while more detailed, is essentially consistent with Escalona's. It should be clear that the diagram of Fig. 3 is not intended as a representation of a concrete situation or a particular individual but rather as a chart for sorting out the various problems of psychology. Even for this latter purpose a complete analysis would require an indication of the temporal dimension, a task which we shall not undertake here. Physical time and psychological time would have to be distinguished in the same way as other properties.

physical-social world which have no influence upon the life space at a
given time.

P and E (person and environment) make up the core, or the
"classical parts" of the life space, but it is clear that the boundary zone,
containing S and M (sensorium and motorium), should also be considered a part of the life space. The solid lines connecting these circles
to one another are intended to indicate that all these facts are interdependent and can be handled by a single system of commensurate concepts. Perceptual processes, for example, are located in S and are both influenced by and influence motivational states of P and cognitive states
of E.

The dotted lines connecting H (the hull) with S and M refer to
those processes by which the physical-social world affect the sensorium

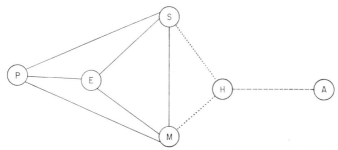

Fig. 3. A schematic diagram of the facts and relations involved
in the life space, the boundary zone, and the physical and social
world. For a detailed explanation of the symbols see text.

of the life space and by which the motorium exerts effects upon the
physical-social world. H and A (alien facts) together make up the
"objective" world of physical and social facts, and the dashed line
connecting them indicates that nonpsychological laws govern their relations. It should be apparent, however, that this representation of the "objective" world is an oversimplification in that it treats physical and social
facts homogeneously.

In order to illustrate the way in which the diagram may be used,
let us consider the theory of decision-time advanced by Cartwright and
Festinger [27]. This theory attempts to account for certain observed
relations between (1) the degree of similarity of pairs of stimuli, measured
in physical terms, and (2) decision-time, defined as the number of
milliseconds elapsing between presentation of the stimuli and the recording of a response. In terms of Fig. 3, the experimental manipulations
and the measurement of responses occur in H. The sounds produced by
the experimenter in reading the instructions also occur in H, but the

processes of "listening to the instructions," "understanding them," and "abiding by them" take place in the parts of the diagram labeled S, M, P, and E. Such factors as a "set toward speed or accuracy" are also located in these parts of the diagram and are represented in the theory as forces acting in the environment upon the person. The theory asserts, in essence, that when a properly prepared subject confronts a given pair of stimuli a certain constellation of forces is set up in the environment, that the time required for the "resolution" of the conflicting forces depends upon the nature of the constellation of forces, and that an observable "decision" will not occur until the conflict has been resolved. It is of particular interest here to note that the quantitative expression of this theory requires the specification of two constants, unique for each subject, one indicating the subject's basic "reaction time" (a property of the system H, S, M) and the other providing a conversion from "psychological time" (a property of the system P, E) to "physical time" (a property of H). Although the "heart" of the theory is concerned with processes occurring in the life space, a complete account of the experiment must describe events occurring in the entire system consisting of H, S, P, E, and M. It is only by taking for granted a whole host of things —that the subject is not blind or deaf, that he can understand the instructions, that he is cooperative, that he is capable of verbal responses, etc.—that the theory can account for the findings.

The diagram of Fig. 3 can be employed in a similar fashion to reveal the conceptual locus of the variables contained in any of the field theoretical investigations. I am convinced that such an analysis helps greatly to reveal where conceptual clarification is needed and to point to fruitful problems for further investigations. Without attempting a detailed analysis of any single study, let us now examine some of the general problems which are suggested by this diagram.

Psychological ecology. Toward the end of his life, Lewin was greatly interested in a set of problems which he referred to as "psychological ecology." The task of psychological ecology is, according to Lewin, to discover "what part of the physical or social world will determine during a given period the 'boundary zone' of the life space" [95, p. 59]. In terms of our diagram this task is one of describing H. Lewin's own work in this area was confined largely to his "channel theory of food habits." This "theory" consists of an analysis of how a given item of food happens to arrive on the dinner table and involves consideration of such factors as agricultural technology, the economics of food, the culture of the population, and the behavior of "gatekeepers." Lewin was forced to develop such a theory when he realized that the answer to the question, "Why do people eat what they eat?" is "Because that particular food is placed on the table in front of them." We shall not consider the details of this theory here, but it is important to recognize that a proper description of the *H,* the foreign hull of the life space, is an essential task of psychology.

This task is a difficult one, without established procedures or concepts, and one to which psychologists are not particularly accustomed. It involves the thorniest problems of psychophysics, in so far as one is dealing with the physical world, as Brunswik [21] has so brilliantly shown. And, related to the social world, it raises the most perplexing problems of linking psychology to sociology, economics, and political science. The description of the physical world given by psychological ecology cannot be identical with that given by a physicist (even though this world obeys the laws of physics). Lewin's analysis of "how food gets on the table" is obviously not that of a physicist. An ecological analysis must extract those features of the "objective" world which are significant as determiners of psychological events. (This is the meaning of the lines connecting *H* to *S* and *M.*)

One suggestive approach toward solving the problem of how to describe the psychologically relevant aspects of the physical and social world has been advanced by Chein [32]. As a general starting point he suggests classifying these features under five headings: (1) stimuli—anything capable of initiating a change of activity, (2) goal objects and noxicants—anything which can provide satisfaction or produce pain, (3) supports and constraints—anything which makes particular behaviors easier or more difficult, (4) directors—anything which tends to induce particular directions of behavior, and (5) global features—such properties as stability or degree of organization.

The whole field of "social perception" is, of course, inextricably involved in this problem. How does one define the "stimulus properties" of a social object? Surely not in the language of physics. The most common technique is to compare test responses of the stimulus person with attributions made by the perceiver [64], but this methodological finesse hardly solves the problem. There have been several clever experimental attempts to produce social variables in the laboratory and to treat these as "stimuli" for social perception. Notable among these are the studies of social power conducted by Pepitone [117] and Thibaut and Riecken [126]. Although these manipulations are intuitively convincing, they are not derived from any clear system of descriptive concepts.

In many ways, the most impressive attack on the general problem of psychological ecology is that carried out by Barker and Wright [13] in their extensive study of the behavior of children in the town of Midwest. Basic to their analysis are two extra-individual, ecological behavior units: *behavior setting* and *behavior objects.*

A behavior setting is a standing behavior pattern together with the context of this behavior, including the part of the milieu to which the behavior is attached and with which it has a synomorphic relationship . . . [i.e., one of perceived fittingness. Behavior settings have the following properties]:

1. *Visibility.* Behavior settings are prominent units of extra-individual behavior identified with a high degree of agreement by independent observers. They are obvious empirical facts about behavior in Midwest.

2. *Phenomenal character.* They are features of the phenomenal worlds of both laymen and scientists, and a description of the community in terms of behavior settings corresponds to common experience.

3. *Internal dynamics.* Behavior settings involve persons, nonpsychological milieu, and behavior in an interacting field of forces. Behavior settings coerce behavior and vice versa.

4. *Comprehensiveness.* Behavior settings blanket the community. We estimate that in Midwest 95 per cent of all behavior occurs within the behavior settings we have identified.

5. *Variety of attributes.* Behavior settings have many discriminable behavioral and nonbehavioral characteristics. They are rich material for analysis.

6. *External dynamics.* Behavior settings are not independent community units, and in fact, the pattern of one setting is often radically changed by the behavior occurring in another behavior setting.

7. *Theoretical position.* Behavior settings are present empirical facts. They can be demonstrated to the hardest empiricist. However, they are theoretically promising. Their internal structure and dynamics and their external relations suggest that they can be profitably conceptualized and incorporated into productive theory [13, pp. 9–10].

Behavior objects are such things as dolls, books, ladders, and toothbrushes. They are differentiated from behavior settings on two grounds.

First, the pattern of behavior associated with a behavior object is circumjacent to the milieu rather than the reverse, as with behavior settings. A person does not enter and behave within the boundaries of a doll or a book as he does in the case of a store and a picnic. . . . Second, behavior objects are, themselves, located within behavior settings [13, p. 10].

It is not possible here to indicate the rich empirical data which Barker and Wright have collected by use of these and other conceptual tools. It should be apparent, however, that the conceptual locus of these concepts is at the foreign hull of the life space. Work of this sort will rapidly clarify the many theoretical and methodological problems involved in psychological ecology and will help prevent field theory from becoming "encapsulated" in the sense that Brunswik feared it might.

Influencing the motorium. One of the early studies done under Lewin's supervision was an experiment by Voight [130] concerning the way in which the structure of the perceptual field influences the shooting at targets. In this little-known study, Voigt had subjects shoot a light-pistol, without taking aim, at targets of various kinds and at varying distances. He found, among other things, that the angular precision of shooting is related to distance in a way indicating that steering is guided by perceived size of target (influenced by size constancy) rather than by retinal size of the image. He was also able to show that steering of the motorium is a joint function of the perceptual field and properties of the motorium. The conceptual locus of this investigation, in terms of our diagram, is in the area containing S, P, E, and M. More specifically, the problem under investigation is one of determining how the motorium is steered by the sensorium through the intervention of the person and environment.[15] Though this investigation was concerned with the problem of how the individual produces events in the physical world, it may serve as a paradigm for stating the problem for any type of "overt" behavior.

Lewin's discussion of how the person and psychological environment influence the motorium was essentially preliminary and programmatic. The following quotation summarizes his general view of the nature of the problem.

There seem to be at least two rather different relations between the motoric and the inner-personal region of the person. The one is characterized by the interrelation between the tensions of these regions (such as spreading of tension). This type of interrelation can be logically derived from the concept of tension. Besides, the motoric can have the position of a tool for the inner-personal systems. In other words, between the inner-personal region and the motoric there exists the relation of an inducing thing to an induced field, or of thing and medium. The second type of interrelation seems to increase in importance from infancy to adulthood [92, pp. 105–106].

This general statement of the relations between the motorium and the rest of the life space focuses attention on three theoretical problems requiring further investigation.

1. What properties does the motorium have? Lewin's own thinking about this question was greatly influenced by the distinction made by Heider [69] between "thing" and "medium." The motorium is a medium through which influences from the person or psychological environment are exerted upon the physical or social world. For certain

---

[15] The relations between M and H in this experiment were rather rigidly fixed by use of a light-pistol, thus producing a one-to-one correspondence between the aiming of the pistol and the effect produced on the target. Had the experiment been concerned with something like dart-throwing or bombing, the results as measured at the target would also have been influenced by physical conditions intervening between "aiming" and "hitting."

purposes, in dealing with transactions with the physical world (walking, performing a motor task, driving a car, etc.), the motorium may be considered to be the muscular apparatus of the organism. Even in such cases, however, it may prove to be useful to consider tools as a part of the motorium. The psychological significance of certain physical handicaps can be properly understood only by examining the way in which the motorium serves or fails to serve the individual in the execution of his needs. The problem of how to characterize the motorium when dealing with social actions is even more difficult. It is clear, however, that properties of the person and his psychological environment do somehow get converted into events in the social world and that individuals vary greatly in their social skills. An individual's social behavior may be flexible or rigid in much the same sense that his physical behavior may.

The formal properties of the motorium have not been systematically specified. Lewin, thinking of the motorium as a medium, suggested that it be considered as consisting of differentiated parts. To be effective the motorium needs to be highly differentiated into parts which can "act" independently of one another. The difference, for example, between a clumsy and a dexterous performance may lie partially in the capacity of fine parts of the motorium to be steered independently of one another. Other properties of the motorium, obviously, need to be specified.

2. How do tensions in the person affect the motorium? It appears from research like that of Dembo [37] on anger and Barker, Dembo, and Lewin [12] on frustration and regression that a high level of tension "spreads" to the motorium with the result that its degree of differentiation is reduced and its parts become "rigidly" interconnected. Too high a level of motivation in a sport requiring a delicate muscular coordination may produce deteriorated performance through a "freezing." On the other hand, moderate levels of tension appear to result in a more differentiated steering of behavior in a goal-directed fashion. Such goal-directed behavior (in contrast to the simple spread of tension) is accomplished, according to Lewin, by a complicated process originating in the tension systems of the person which set up force fields within the psychological environment which, in turn, induce changes in the motorium. This distinction between the two ways in which tension systems may affect the motorium involves the theoretical distinction, referred to in an earlier section, between simple dependence and organizational dependence.

3. How are changes induced in the motorium? Lewin's answer to this question was very sketchy; he simply noted that the process of induction belongs to the general problem of organizational dependence. In other words, events occurring in the person and environment stand

in a "head-tool" relation to the motorium. An exploitation of this approach to the problem should illuminate such matters as the "integration" or "hierarchial organization" of overt behavior.

Concentration on the relations among person, environment, and motorium bring certain psychological problems into greater prominence. In my own research [24] on the purchase of government bonds during World War II, for example, it became clear that a specification of the cognitions and motivations of people was not sufficient to predict with much success whether or not they would buy bonds during a given period of time. If, however, these data were considered in conjunction with two other kinds of information, rather good predictions could be made. The additional information needed concerned: (1) whether or not the individual was placed in a situation where he had to make a *decision* to buy or not to buy, and (2) how much money he possessed. The first factor, that of forcing a decision, served to place the motorium under the control of a motivational system (*P* and *E*). The second factor, possessing money, is more difficult to conceptualize, but it points to the fact that the motorium requires resources of particular kinds for the execution of particular overt actions.

Problems of "skill" are also brought to the fore by considering the motorium. Schools of psychotherapy which concentrate exclusively upon problems of motivation seem to be overlooking an important aspect of the ways in which individuals cope with the physical and social world. Just as older notions of "retraining" were one-sided, so too are modern views that therapy consists of "straightening out motivation." Freudian proponents of "ego" functions, like Redl [118], would seem to have a more balanced view of the total problem. Similar comments are appropriate concerning the field of "human relations training." Here such techniques of "skill training" as represented in certain uses of role playing [104] are just as important as efforts at modifying the motivation or values of those being trained.

Circular processes involving the system: P, E-M-H-S-P, E. A careful examination of Lewin's theories of motivation makes it clear that he could not escape the problem of how processes within the life space relate to the foreign hull of the life space. This conclusion is perhaps dramatized most vividly in his treatment of the distinction between substitute valence and substitute value which was forced by the experimental findings of Dembo [37], Lissner [106], and Mahler [108]. Here it was found that when the achievement of a goal is blocked certain "substitute activities" acquired valence. Not all of these substitutes, however, served to reduce the original tension system (i.e., to have substitute value). It would appear that the phenomenon of "substitute valence" can be handled adequately within the system made up of *P* and *E*. Ordinarily, however, a tension system will not be released unless certain events take place in M which, in turn, produce certain changes in H. Furthermore, tension will still not be released unless these changes in H produce effects in S and consequently in E. It is possible, of course, for there to be "autistic" need satisfaction, but such instances must be distinguished from "realistic" gratification. It is only through the operation of such a circular system involving the life space, the boundary zone, and the foreign hull that an individual can "keep in touch with reality."

Lewin's concept of barrier, or restraining force, can be refined, too, by a careful analysis of all of the factors represented in Fig. 3. The formal definition of barrier as that which offers resistance to locomotion appears to refer exclusively to the psychological environment since these resistances exert influences opposite to the driving forces which clearly exist in E. But Leeper has pointed out certain ambiguities in Lewin's various discussions of barriers, ambiguities incidentally which Lewin readily acknowledged.

Lewin's concept of barriers has been confusing because it has not been made to conform consistently to one or the other of two types of factors, both of which must be recognized but distinguished. His basic concept of barriers, as factors that give rise to restraining forces that operate only to impede actual locomotion through the region, is suited only for the description of what might better be called objective obstructions (regardless of whether they are outside the person or obstructions of the type of imperfect skills, poor vision, or other limitations of the motoric regions). Such objective obstructions operate regardless of whether the person psychologically appreciates their existence. Their operation must be discounted before data on speed of locomotion, for example, may be taken as indicating the strengths of driving forces. But, in addition to this concept of objective obstructions we need also a concept of barriers as regions of the psychological environment. Barriers in this sense may operate by affecting valences, by giving rise to restraining forces that can operate at a distance, and by screening out the driving forces related to more remote regions. In determining the behavior of the moment, what chiefly must be considered is barrier-regions as defined in this second sense [85, pp. 107–108].

With the aid of the diagram of Fig. 3, it seems to me that the import of Leeper's criticism can be better appreciated and that a slightly different solution to the problem may be advanced. It is clear that obstacles to the objective achievement of some goal may reside in S (e.g., perceptual insensitivities), in M (e.g., inadequate skills), or in H (e.g., an object is too heavy to lift or a law prohibits a foreigner from becoming President of the United States). It is clear, too, that these obstacles may prevent an individual from reaching his goal even though he did not know that they were present (i.e., they were not present in the psychological environment). It is also clear that barriers may exist in *E* which have no valid counterpart in *S, M,* or *H* (e.g., the person believes erroneously that he cannot do something). But it is more usually the case that the individual makes use of the entire circular system composed of *P, E, S, M,* and *H* to keep in touch with reality with respect to barriers just as he does regarding sources of gratification. Barriers, it seems to me, can be best conceived as restraining forces, and the various distinctions required can best be represented by designating in each instance the "source" of the force and its point of application. Depending on the circumstances of the particular case, restraining forces may exist in *E* with sources in *S, M,* or *H,* and the way in which they can be overcome will depend upon the nature of the source. Restraining forces may also exist in *S, M,* or *H* and will have different effects in each instance.

There are a host of social psychological theories which refer at least implicitly to the circular system made up of life space, boundary zone, and social world. Most of these theories invoke a general notion of "equilibrium" to refer to the fact that certain states of *P* and *E* are in some sense preferred and from this fact they derive various tendencies toward cognitive distortion, toward selective contact with the social world, and toward certain kinds of social communication. Thus, Newcomb [115] postulates a strain toward symmetry in the attitudes of two or more people in social interaction and derives from this various predictions concerning selective communication and pressures to change opinions. The theory of social communication advanced by Festinger [49] specifies how the need for "social reality" leads to pressures to change one's own opinions or those of others. His forthcoming theory of "cognitive dissonance" will indicate further how certain cognitive properties lead an individual to seek out social interactions of a certain kind. Newcomb [114] has also developed a theory of "autistic hostility" to account for the tendency of people to avoid interaction with others toward whom they have hostile feelings, a tendency documented by Festinger and Kelley [51] and by others. All these theories are concerned, in one way or another, with the way in which properties of *P* and *E* influence *M,* the way in which *M* influences *H,* and the way in which changes produced in *H* influence *S* and eventually *P* and *E*. Most of these theories, however, "short-circuit" one or more of the steps involved by assuming one-to-one correspondence between each end of the link (e.g., by assuming veridicality of perception). Perhaps their future elaboration will examine more closely the processes involved at each step in the circular system.

Lewin's emphasis upon the person and psychological environment has helped to counteract a tendency among some theorists to speak as if behavior were determined entirely by the system made up of *H-S-M-H*.

Although it is apparent that some processes do involve primarily this system, such "reflexes," which depend only slightly upon properties of P or E (i.e., upon motivational states and cognitive structures), constitute only a small part of the phenomena of interest to psychologists. Studies like those on the influence of needs and values on perception [19] and those pursuing such distinctions as that drawn by Gelb and Goldstein [65] between abstract and concrete "mindedness" are concerned with the intervention of properties of P and E in processes taking place in H-S-M-H. The task of research is, of course, to determine under what conditions P and E do or do not enter into the total process and to describe the nature of such interventions.

CONCLUSIONS[16]

This rather general account of Lewinian theory suggests certain conclusions about the needs of psychology. If other theoretical orientations also point to the same needs, so much the better. It may be hoped that field theorists and theorists of other schools will work in future years to satisfy these needs.

Empiricism and formal theory. Contemporary psychological theory is in danger of losing touch with empirical reality. The placing of too great a value upon formal elegance in the construction of theory may well create an insurmountable chasm between the theorist and the psychologist who is interested in the naturally occurring behavior of people. Unless future interest in "model building" is closely guided by an unbiased reference to empirical facts, formal elegance will be purchased at the cost of empirical applicability. Psychology requires a balanced respect for both empirical facts and rigorous theory. Open-minded description is needed to keep psychology continually concerned with its proper subject matter, but adequate description cannot be accomplished without formal theory. While the traditional emphasis of Lewinian psychologists upon the hypothetico-deductive method is still appropriate, one should not forget that formal theory is useful in an empirical science only in so far as it serves as an aid to description.

The need for a proper balance between naïve empiricism and

[16] At this point I omit the following sections contained in the outline of the editorial committee: "Scope or range of application of system," "History of system to date in mediating research," "Evidence for the system," and "Specific methods, concepts or principles of the system believed valuable outside the context of the system." These topics have been included in the previous sections to such an extent that further discussion would be excessively repetitious. In this final section, I have tried to combine the two suggested topics: "Degree of programmaticity" and "Intermediate and long range strategy for the development of the system."

formalization has implications for the collection of data as well as for the building of theory. It might be well for psychologists to take another look at their use of the experimental method, which has long been one of psychology's most powerful tools. An experiment, especially when coupled with the hypothetico-deductive method, seldom provides information other than that "called for" by the experimenter, and its results are rarely more significant than the theory which guides the experimenter. Too much of current psychological research, I fear, is designed not so much to discover new facts as to confirm some derivation from a limited formal theory. It is in the formulation of research problems that the major advances of psychology take place. Careful observation, recording, and measurement of naturally occurring events and of "experiments of nature" will for a long time to come be the most important *source* of the significant problems of psychology. For this reason, it would seem wise for psychologists to avoid any premature judgment that painstaking observation is inferior or antithetical to rigorous theory. Methods of research, like those employed by such ethologists as Tinbergen [127], could well be developed and refined in other branches of psychology.

Generality of theories. Psychology, like other disciplines, has in recent years been subjected to strong pressures toward specialization. Efforts to develop rigorous theory have often resulted in a sharp restriction of the range of empirical phenomena treated by a given theory. One result has been that the boundaries around various fields of psychology have tended to become impermeable barriers so that the theoretical constructs of one domain have no clear relation to those of another. Field theory, by focusing attention upon the concrete manifold of interdependent facts influencing behavior, attempts to resist this theoretical narrowness. It is the goal of field theorists to develop constructs which will be equally applicable to perception, learning, motivation, personality, development, social, normal, and abnormal psychology. While it is undoubtedly true that attention has been directed to some aspects more than others, field theorists still believe that it is possible, in principle, to employ a single system of commensurate constructs for dealing with all the facts of psychology. This is not to say that the task has been accomplished; efforts directed toward the integration of psychological theory are badly needed.

The importance to field theory of the concept, life space, as the total situation in which individuals exist has tended progressively to broaden interest from problems of motivation and learning to those of social psychology. It has become increasingly clear that social relations must be taken into account in any open-minded description of the way in which behavior is generated and modified. The work of Lewin, Lippitt, and White [98] demonstrated that a personal characteristic like "aggressiveness" can be basically modified by the nature of groups to which the individual belongs. Lewis [100], Deutsch [39], and Horwitz [74] have shown how the quality of relations among individuals affects the satisfaction of needs and the release of tension. And many of the studies on level of aspiration reported by Lewin, Dembo, Festinger, and Sears [97] have made it clear how goal setting and the experience of success or failure depend upon the social groups to which individuals refer themselves. Significant progress is also being made in putting to empirical test theoretical notions like those of Mead [110] concerning social influences on the formation of the self. These and other trends all indicate how essential it is that social psychology be encompassed in a single theory of human behavior.

A theoretical problem of high priority, if psychology is to deal with social phenomena, is how to conceptualize the interdependence and interaction of several individuals. One might state this problem as one of determining how to "combine" individual life spaces, though I fear that this may be a misleading way of putting the matter. In one of his last publications Lewin [95, pp. 188–237] undertook to formulate the nature of the problem, but he did little more than indicate its major features. It is interesting that he employed such terms as "social field," "social space," and "group life space." He suggested that such notions cannot be avoided and pointed out the necessity of developing concepts for linking properties and states of the individual to those of the social field. A fundamental difficulty, he noted, arises in going from the individual life space, which is constructed to represent the world as it exists for the individual, to the social field, which must encompass the "subjective" situations of many individuals. In my own opinion, the most promising approach to this problem will be one which focuses on ecology, that is, on the conceptualization of the hull of the life space.

As soon as one goes out of the laboratory into "life" and attempts open-mindedly to observe what people do it becomes apparent that economic and political phenomena play a much more important part than would be expected from reading psychological theory. Relatively little work has yet been undertaken by psychologists in these areas. The pioneering work of Katona [79], however, shows how economic facts can be incorporated into a coherent psychological theory, and research on power [26] provides a clue as to the way in which variables traditionally allocated to political science can be treated in field theoretical concepts. Major advances in psychological theory may be expected from intensive work on such untraditional problems.

Future developments in field theory. As noted in our discussion of Lewinian theory, the most elaborated parts of the theory have to do with those motivational and cognitive processes treated by the concepts of person and psychological environment. It would appear that the important extensions of field theory in the foreseeable future will consist of working out a detailed way for treating the sensorium, motorium, and foreign hull of the life space with concepts commensurate to those now employed for dealing with the person and psychological environment. A good beginning has been made in the work of psychological ecology, where it is realized that the "objective" environment must be described in terms having psychological rather than physical meaning. If current efforts, such as those of Zajonc [141], to describe "messages" and "cognitive structure" in the same set of concepts prove successful, another bridge between the inner core of the life space and its foreign hull will be established.

Demonstrations of the influence of needs and values upon perceptual processes serve to underscore the necessity for treating the person, psychological environment, and the sensorium as an interdependent system. Such demonstrations in and of themselves do not, however, contribute a great deal to the unified conceptualization of all these processes. Motivation, cognition, and perception have to be described in commensurate terms before a real understanding of these phenomena will be attained. Much the same difficulties exist in dealing with the motorium. A conceptual analysis of the motorium, of what skill "is," of how steering takes place, and of how the motorium acts on both the social and physical world should improve greatly our understanding of human behavior.

The conceptual representation of "value" especially deserves attention. Although the study of values has at last attained a modicum of respectability among scientific psychologists, research efforts thus far have been confined mainly to problems of measurement. From a field theoretical point of view, however, the most urgent task is to determine the conceptual properties to be attributed to the construct "value." Lewin suggested that "value" and "goal" are of different conceptual types, that "goal" is a central force field while "value" induces force fields. This observation led him to conclude that values and individuals are similar in that both are capable of inducing forces, a conclusion which is congruent with much of psychoanalytic thinking. This insight is quite important because it links problems of value to those of interpersonal relations and social power, but it provides only a beginning. An urgent task of psychology is to obtain answers to questions like these: How do values become established in an individual's life space? How does a value become activated? How do values relate to one another? What effects do values have? In what ways do values differ from needs or motives? Answers to questions such as these will help specify the conceptual properties of "value" and put psychology in a position to provide a conceptually integrated treatment of the rapidly growing research on such topics as self-esteem, attitudes, authoritarianism, social motives (like those for achievement and affiliation), and national character.

The interest of field theorists in showing how cognitive structure affects behavior has diverted attention, perhaps too much, away from the determinants of cognitive structure itself. It is true that Lewin set up the general principle that psychological forces may result either in a locomotion of the person or a restructuring of the psychological environment, but the conditions under which one or the other will take place were never clearly specified nor was it ever entirely clear exactly how restructuring takes place. The recent work of Zajonc [141] on "cognitive tuning" suggests one promising approach toward a better treatment of these problems.

To the critic of Lewinian theory it is especially interesting that Lewin's absorption in dynamics and in problems of ontogenetic development did not result in richer specification of the laws of development and change. Some might be inclined to attribute this fact to his insistence upon the principle of contemporaneity; his dynamics always referred to a relatively small time differential. I am inclined to believe, however, that the reason lies in the intrinsic difficulty in formulating such laws and especially in the necessity of conceiving of the entire causal system made up of person, psychological environment, sensorium, motorium, and foreign hull of the life space. The most concerted attack on this problem undertaken by Lewin [95, pp. 170–237] led him into an analysis of psychological ecology and into the construction of a circular causal system involving the life space and its foreign hull. As work proceeds on the sensorium, motorium, psychological ecology, and on the determinants of cognition, motivation, and action, field theory will be better able to deal with problems of change and development.

REFERENCES

1. Ach, N. *Über den Willensakt und das Temperament: Ein experimentelle Untersuchung.* Leipzig: Quelle und Meyer, 1910.

2. Adler, D. L. Types of similarity and the substitute value of activities at different age levels. Unpublished doctoral dissertation, State Univer. of Iowa, 1939.

3. Adler, D. L., & Kounin, J. S. Some factors operating at the moment of resumption of interrupted tasks. *J. Psychol.,* 1939, **7**, 255–267.

4. Allport, F. H. *Theories of perception and the concept of structure.* New York: Wiley, 1955.

5. Allport, G. W. *Personality: a psychological interpretation.* New York: Holt, 1937.

6. Arsenian, J. M. Young children in an insecure situation. *J. abnorm. soc. Psychol.*, 1943, **38**, 225–249.

7. Asch, S. E. Forming impressions of personality. *J. abnorm. soc. Psychol.*, 1946, **41**, 258–290.

8. Atkinson, J. W. The achievement motive and recall of interrupted and completed tasks. *J. exp. Psychol.*, 1953, **46**, 381–390.

9. Back, K. Influence through social communication. *J. abnorm. soc. Psychol.*, 1951, **46**, 9–23.

10. Barker, R. G. An experimental study of the resolution of conflict in children. In A. McNemar, & M. A. Merrill (Eds.), *Studies in personality.* New York: McGraw-Hill, 1942.

11. Barker, R. G. An experimental study of the relationship between certainty of choice and the relative valence of the alternatives. *J. Person.*, 1946, **15**, 41–52.

12. Barker, R., Dembo, T., & Lewin, K. Frustration and regression. *Univer. Iowa Stud. Child Welf.*, 1941, **18**, No. 1.

13. Barker, R. G., & Wright, H. F. *Midwest and its children.* Evanston, Ill.: Row, Peterson, 1954.

14. Bavelas, A. A method for investigating individual and group ideology. *Sociometry*, 1942, **5**, 371–377.

15. Bavelas, A. Morale and the training of leaders. In G. Watson (Ed.), *Civilian morale.* Boston: Houghton Mifflin, 1942. Pp. 143–165.

16. Bavelas, A. A mathematical model for group structures. *Applied Anthrop.*, 1948, **7**, No. 3, 16–30.

17. Bavelas, A. Communication patterns in task-oriented groups. In D. Cartwright, & A. Zander (Eds.), *Group dynamics: research and theory.* Evanston, Ill.: Row, Peterson, 1953. Pp. 493–506.

18. Bennett, E. B. Discussion, decision, commitment, and consensus in "group decision." *Hum. Relat.*, 1955, **8**, 251–273.

19. Bruner, J. S., & Krech, D. (Eds.), *Perception and personality, a symposium.* Durham, N.C.: Duke Univer. Press, 1950.

20. Brunswik, E. Organismic achievement and environmental probability. *Psychol. Rev.*, 1943, **50**, 255–272.

21. Brunswik, E. *Perception and the representative design of psychological experiments.* Berkeley, Calif.: Univer. California Press, 1956.

22. Cartwright, D. Decision-time in relation to the differentiation of the phenomenal field. *Psychol. Rev.*, 1941, **48**, 425–442.

23. Cartwright, D. The effect of interruption, completion, and failure upon the attractiveness of activities. *J. exp. Psychol.*, 1942, **31**, 1–16.

24. Cartwright, D. Some principles of mass persuasion. *Hum. Relat.*, 1949, **2**, 253–267.

25. Cartwright, D. Emotional dimensions of group life. In M. L. Reymert (Ed.), *Feelings and emotions.* New York: McGraw-Hill, 1950. Pp. 439–447.

26. Cartwright, D. (Ed.), *Studies in social power.* Ann Arbor, Mich.: Institute for Social Research, 1959.

27. Cartwright, D., & Festinger, L. A quantitative theory of decision. *Psychol. Rev.,* 1943, **50**, 595–621.

28. Cartwright, D., & Harary, F. Structural balance: a generalization of Heider's theory. *Psychol. Rev.,* 1956, **63**, 277–293.

29. Cartwright, D., & Zander, A. *Group dynamics: research and theory.* Evanston, Ill.: Row, Peterson, 1953.

30. Cassirer, E. *Substance and function, and Einstein's theory of relativity.* New York: Dover, 1953. (Reprint of 1923 translation of publications originally appearing in 1910 and 1921.)

31. Cassirer, E. *An essay on man.* Garden City, N.Y.: Doubleday, 1953. (Original publication in 1944.)

32. Chein, I. Environment as a determinant of behavior. *J. soc. Psychol.,* 1954, **39**, 115–127.

33. Citron, A. F., Chein, I., & Harding, J. Anti-minority remarks: a problem for action research. *J. abnorm. soc. Psychol.,* 1950, **45**, 99–126.

34. Citron, A. F., & Harding, J. An experiment in training volunteers to answer anti-minority remarks. *J. abnorm. soc. Psychol.,* 1950, **45**, 310–328.

35. Coch, L., & French, J. R. P., Jr. Overcoming resistance to change. *Hum. Relat.,* 1948, **1**, 512–532.

36. Cohen, A. R. Situational structure, self-esteem, and threat-oriented reactions to power. In Cartwright, D. (Ed.), *Studies in social power.* Ann Arbor, Mich.: Institute for Social Research, 1959.

37. Dembo, T. Der Ärger als dynamisches Problem. *Psychol. Forsch.,* 1931, **15**, 1–144.

38. Deutsch, M. An experimental study of the effects of cooperation and competition upon group process. *Hum. Relat.,* 1949, **2**, 199–232.

39. Deutsch, M. A theory of cooperation and competition. *Hum. Relat.,* 1949, **2**, 129–152.

40. Deutsch, M. Field theory in social psychology. In G. Lindzey (Ed.), *Handbook of social psychology.* Cambridge, Mass.: Addison-Wesley, 1954. Pp. 181–222.

41. Deutsch, M., & Collins, M. E. *Interracial housing.* Minneapolis, Minn.: Univer. Minnesota Press, 1951.

42. Dollard, J., et al. *Frustration and aggression.* New Haven, Conn.: Yale Univer. Press, 1939.

43. Escalona, S. K. The effect of success and failure upon the level of aspiration and behavior in manic-depressive psychoses. *Univer. Iowa Stud. Child Welf.,* 1940, **16**, 199–307.

44. Escalona, S. K. The influence of topological and vector psychology upon current research in child development: an addendum. In L. Carmichael (Ed.), *Manual of child psychology.* (2d ed.) New York: Wiley, 1954. Pp. 971–983.

45. Estes, W. K. Kurt Lewin. In Estes, W. K., et al., *Modern learning theory.* New York: Appleton-Century-Crofts, 1954. Pp. 317–344.

46. Ezriel, H. Experimentation within the psycho-analytic session. *Brit. J. Phil. Sci.,* 1956, **7**, 29–48.

47. Falk, J. L. Issues distinguishing ideographic from nomothetic approaches to personality theory. *Psychol. Rev.*, 1956, **63**, 53–62.

48. Farber, M. L. Suffering and time perspective of the prisoner. *Univer. Iowa Stud. Child Welf.*, 1944, **20**, 155–227.

49. Festinger, L. Informal social communication. *Psychol. Rev.*, 1950, **57**, 271–292.

50. Festinger, L. A theory of social comparison processes. *Hum. Relat.*, 1954, **7**, 117–140.

51. Festinger, L., & Kelley, H. H. *Changing attitudes through social contact.* Ann Arbor, Mich.: Institute for Social Research, 1951.

52. Festinger, L., Pepitone, A., & Newcomb, T. Some consequences of de-individuation in a group. *J. abnorm. soc. Psychol.*, 1952, **47**, 382–389.

53. Festinger, L., Schachter, S., & Back, K. *Social pressures in informal groups.* New York: Harper, 1950.

54. Frank, J. D. Individual differences in certain aspects of the level of aspiration. *Amer. J. Psychol.*, 1935, **47**, 119–128.

55. Frank, J. D. The influence of the level of performance in one task on the level of aspiration in another. *J. exper. Psychol.*, 1935, **18**, 159–171.

56. Frank, J. D. Some psychological determinants of the level of aspiration. *Amer. J. Psychol.*, 1935, **47**, 285–293.

57. Frank, J. D. Recent studies of the level of aspiration. *Psychol. Bull.*, 1941, **38**, 218–225.

58. Frank, J. D. Experimental studies of personal pressure and resistance: II. Methods of overcoming resistance. *J. gen. Psychol.*, 1944, **30**, 43–56.

59. French, J. R. P., Jr. The disruption and cohesion of groups. *J. abnorm. soc. Psychol.*, 1941, **36**, 361–377.

60. French, J. R. P., Jr. A formal theory of social power. *Psychol. Rev.*, 1956, **63**, 181–194.

61. French, J. R. P., Jr., & Raven, B. The bases of social power. In Cartwright, D. (Ed.), *Studies in social power.* Ann Arbor, Mich.: Institute for Social Research, 1959.

62. French, J. R. P., Jr., & Snyder, R. Leadership and interpersonal power. In Cartwright, D. (Ed.), *Studies in social power.* Ann Arbor, Mich.: Institute for Social Research, 1959.

63. Freund, A. Psychische Sättigung in Menstruum und Intermenstruum. *Psychol. Forsch.*, 1930, **13**, 198–217.

64. Gage, N. L., & Cronbach, L. J. Conceptual and methodological problems in interpersonal perception. *Psychol. Rev.*, 1955, **62**, 411–422.

65. Gelb, A., & Goldstein, K. Über Farbennamenamnesie nebst Bemerkungen über das Wesen der amnestischen Aphasie überhaupt und die Beziehung zwischen Sprache und dem Berhalten zur Umwelt. *Psychol. Forsch.*, 1924, **6**, 127–186.

66. Grosser, D., Polansky, N., & Lippitt, R. A laboratory study of behavioral contagion. *Hum. Relat.*, 1951, **4**, 115–142.

67. Harary, F., & Norman, R. Z. *Graph theory as a mathematical model in the social sciences.* Ann Arbor, Mich.: Institute for Social Research, 1953.

68. Harary, F., Norman, R. Z., & Cartwright, D. *Introduction to digraph theory for social scientists.* Ann Arbor, Mich.: Institute for Social Research, in press.

69. Heider, F. Ding und Medium. *Symposium,* 1927, **1**, 109–157.

70. Heider, F. Social perception and phenomenal causality. *Psychol. Rev.,* 1944, **51**, 358–374.

71. Heider, F. Attitudes and cognitive organization. *J. Psychol.,* 1946, **21**, 107 112.

72. Henle, M., & Aull, G. Factors decisive for resumption of interrupted activities: the question reopened. *Psychol. Rev.,* 1953, **60**, 81–88.

73. Hoppe, F. Erfolg und Misserfolg. *Psychol. Forsch.,* 1930, **14**, 1–62.

74. Horwitz, M. The recall of interrupted group tasks: an experimental study of individual motivation in relation to group goals. *Hum. Relat.,* 1954, **7**, 3–38.

75. Hurwitz, J. I., Zander, A. F., & Hymovitch, B. Some effects of power on the relations among group members. In D. Cartwright, & A. Zander, (Eds.), *Group dynamics: research and theory.* Evanston, Ill.: Row, Peterson, 1953. Pp. 483–492.

76. Jucknat, M. Leistung, Anspruchsniveau und Selbstbewusstsein. *Psychol. Forsch.,* 1937, **22**, 89–179.

77. Kalhorn, J. Values and sources of authority among rural children. *Univer. Iowa Stud. Child Welf.,* 1944, **20**, 99–152.

78. Karsten, A. Psychische Sättigung. *Psychol. Forsch.,* 1928, **10**, 142–254.

79. Katona, G. *Psychological analysis of economic behavior.* New York: McGraw-Hill, 1951.

80. Katz, E. *Some factors affecting resumption of interrupted activities by preschool children.* Minneapolis, Minn.: Univer. Minnesota Press, 1938.

81. Kelley, H. H. The warm-cold variable in first impressions of persons. *J. Pers.,* 1950, **18**, 431–439.

82. Kelley, H. H. Communication in experimentally created hierarchies. *Hum. Relat.,* 1951, **4**, 39–56.

83. Kelley, H. H., & Thibaut, J. W. Experimental studies of group problem solving and process. In G. Lindzey (Ed.), *Handbook of social psychology.* Cambridge, Mass.: Addison-Wesley, 1954. Pp. 735–785.

84. Kounin, J. Experimental studies of rigidity. I & II. *Charact. & Pers.,* 1941, **9**, 251–282.

85. Leeper, R. W. *Lewin's topological and vector psychology.* Eugene, Ore.: Univer. of Oregon, 1943.

86. Leeper, R. W. Cognitive processes. In S. S. Stevens (Ed.), *Handbook of experimental psychology.* New York: Wiley, 1951.

87. Lewin, K. Die psychische Tatigkeit bei der Hemmung von Willensvorganger und das Grundgesetz der Assoziation. *Zeit. Psychol.,* 1917, **77**, 212–247.

88. Lewin, K. Das Problem der Willensmessung und das Grundgesetz der Assoziation. I & II. *Psychol. Forsch.,* 1922, **1**, 191–302; **2**, 65–140.

89. Lewin, K. Vorbemerkungen über die psychischen Kräfte und Energien und über die Struktur der Seele. *Psychol. Forsch.*, 1926, **7**, 294–329.

90. Lewin, K. *A dynamic theory of personality*. New York: McGraw-Hill, 1935.

91. Lewin, K. *Principles of topological psychology*. New York: McGraw-Hill, 1936.

92. Lewin, K. *The conceptual representation and the measurement of psychological forces*. Durham, N C · Duke Univer. Press, 1938.

93. Lewin, K. Forces behind food habits and methods of change. *Bull. Nat. Research Council*, 1943, **108**, 35–65.

94. Lewin, K. *Resolving social conflicts*. New York: Harper, 1948.

95. Lewin, K. *Field theory in social science*. New York: Harper, 1951.

96. Lewin, K. Studies in group decision. In D. Cartwright, & A. Zander (Eds.), *Group dynamics: research and theory*. Evanston, Ill.: Row, Peterson, 1953. Pp. 287–301.

97. Lewin, K., Dembo, T., Festinger, L., & Sears, P. S. Level of aspiration. In J. McV. Hunt (Ed.), *Personality and the behavior disorders*. New York: Ronald, 1944. Pp. 333–378.

98. Lewin, K., Lippitt, R., & White, R. K. Patterns of aggressive behavior in experimentally created "social climates." *J. soc. Psychol.*, 1939, **10**, 271–279.

99. Lewin, K., & Sakuma, K. Die Sehrichtung monokularer und binocularer Objecte bei Bewegung und das Zustendekommen des Tiefeneffekts. *Psychol. Forsch.*, 1925, **6**, 298–357.

100. Lewis, H. B. An experimental study of the role of the ego in work: I. The role of the ego in cooperative work. *J. exp. Psychol.*, 1944, **34**, 113–126.

101. Lewis, H. B., & Franklin, M. An experimental study of the role of the ego in work: II. The significance of task orientation in work. *J. exp. Psychol.*, 1944, **34**, 195–215.

102. Libo, L. *Measuring group cohesiveness*. Ann Arbor, Mich.: Institute for Social Research, 1953.

103. Lippitt, R. An experimental study of authoritarian and democratic group atmospheres. *Univer. Iowa Stud. Child Welf.*, 1940, **16**, No. 3, 43–195.

104. Lippitt, R. *Training in community relations*. New York: Harper, 1949.

105. Lippitt, R., Polansky, N., Redl, F., & Rosen, S. The dynamics of power. *Hum. Relat.*, 1952, **5**, 37–64.

106. Lissner, K. Die Entspannung von Bedürfnissen durch Ersatzhandlungen. *Psychol. Forsch.*, 1933, **18**, 218–250.

107. MacCorquodale, K., & Meehl, P. E. On a distinction between hypothetical constructs and intervening variables. *Psychol. Rev.*, 1948, **55**, 95–107.

108. Mahler, V. Ersatzhandlungen verschiedenen Realitätsgrades. *Psychol. Forsch.*, 1933, **18**, 26–89.

109. Marrow, A. J. Goal tensions and recall (I & II). *J. gen. Psychol.*, 1938, **19**, 3–35, 37–64.

110. Mead, G. H. *Mind, self and society.* (Posthumous; C. M. Morris, Ed.) Chicago: Univer. Chicago Press, 1934.

111. Meehl, P. E. *Clinical versus statistical prediction.* Minneapolis, Minn.: Univer. of Minnesota Press, 1954.

112. Meyers, C. E. The effect of conflicting authority on the child. *Univer. Iowa Stud. Child Welf.*, 1944, **20**, 31–98.

113. Miller, N. E. Experimental studies of conflict. In J. McV. Hunt (Ed.), *Personality and the behavior disorders.* Vol. 1. New York: Ronald, 1944. Pp. 431–465.

114. Newcomb, T. M. Autistic hostility and social reality. *Hum. Relat.*, 1947, **1**, 69–86.

115. Newcomb, T. An approach to the study of communicative acts. *Psychol. Rev.*, 1953, **60**, 393–404.

116. Ovsiankina, M. Die Wiederaufnahme von unterbrochenen Handlungen. *Psychol. Forsch.*, 1928, **11**, 302–389.

117. Pepitone, A. Motivational effects in social perception. *Hum. Relat.*, 1950, **3**, 57–76.

118. Redl, F., & Wineman, D. *Children who hate.* Glencoe, Ill.: Free Press, 1951.

119. Rozeboom, W. W. Mediation variables in scientific theory. *Psychol. Rev.*, 1956, **63**, 249–264.

120. Sanford, N. Surface and depth in the individual personality. *Psychol. Rev.*, 1956, **63**, 349–359.

121. Scheler, M. F. *The nature of sympathy.* Peter Heath (Trans.) London: Routledge, 1954.

122. Seashore, H. E., & Bavelas, A. A study of frustration in children. *J. genet. Psychol.*, 1942, **61**, 279–314.

123. Sliosberg, S. Zur Dynamik des Ersatzes in Spiel- und Ernstsituationen. *Psychol. Forsch*, 1934, **19**, 122–181.

124. Spence, K. W. The nature of theory construction in contemporary psychology. *Psychol. Rev.*, 1944, **51**, 47–68.

125. Thibaut, J. W. An experimental study of the cohesiveness of underprivileged groups. *Hum. Relat.*, 1950, **3**, 251–278.

126. Thibaut, J. W., & Riecken, H. W. Some determinants and consequences of the perception of social causality. *J. Pers.*, 1955, **24**, 113–133.

127. Tinbergen, N. *The study of instinct.* London: Oxford Univer. Press, 1951.

128. Tolman, E. C. The determiners of behavior at a choice point. *Psychol. Rev.*, 1938, **45**, 1–41.

129. Veblen, O. *Analysis situs.* (2d ed.) New York: Amer. Math. Soc., 1931.

130. Voigt, G. Über die Richtungspräzision einer Fernhandlung. *Psychol. Forsch.*, 1932, **16**, 70–113.

131. Watson, J., & Lippitt, R. *Learning across cultures.* Ann Arbor, Mich.: Institute for Social Research, 1955.

132. Weyl, H. *Philosophy of mathematics and natural science.* Princeton, N.J.: Princeton Univer. Press, 1949.

133. White, R. K. Hitler, Roosevelt, and the nature of war propaganda. *J. abnorm. soc. Psychol.,* 1949, **44,** 157–174.

134. White, R. K. *Value-analysis: the nature and use of the method.* New York: Society for the Psychological Study of Social Issues, 1951.

135. Wilner, D. M., Walkley, R. P., & Cook, S. W. *Human relations in interracial housing.* Minneapolis, Minn.: Univer. Minnesota Press, 1955.

136. Wormser, M. H., & Selltiz, C. *How to conduct a community self-survey of civil rights.* New York: Association Press, 1951.

137. Wright, B. A. Altruism in children and the perceived conduct of others. *J. abnorm. soc. Psychol.,* 1942, **37,** 218–233.

138. Wright, M. E. Constructiveness of play as affected by group organization and frustration. *Charact. & Pers.,* 1942, **11,** 40–49.

139. Wright, M. E. The influence of frustration upon the social relations of young children. *Charact. & Pers.,* 1943, **12,** 111–122.

140. Zander, A., Cohen, A. R., & Stotland, E. *Role relations in the mental health professions.* Ann Arbor, Mich.: Institute for Social Research, 1957.

141. Zajonc, R. B. Cognitive structure and cognitive tuning. Unpublished doctoral dissertation, Univer. of Michigan, 1954.

142. Zeigarnik, B. Über das Behalten von erledigten und unerledigten Handlungen. *Psychol. Forsch.,* 1927, **9,** 1–85.

PRINCIPLES OF PURPOSIVE BEHAVIOR

EDWARD C. TOLMAN
University of California

INTRODUCTION

I would like to begin by letting off steam. If in what follows I have not done a very clear or useful job, I would plead some half-dozen reasons. First, I think the days of such grandiose, all-covering systems in psychology as mine attempted to be are, at least for the present, pretty much passé. I feel, therefore, that it might have been more decent and more dignified to let such an instance of the relatively immediate dead past bury its dead. Secondly, I don't enjoy trying to use my mind in too analytical a way. Hence, I have found it frustrating and difficult to try to subject my system to the required sorts of analyses. Thirdly, I suppose I am personally antipathetic to the notion that science progresses through intense, self-conscious analysis of where one has got and where one is going. Such analyses are obviously a proper function for the philosopher of science and they may be valuable for many individual scientists. But I myself become frightened and restricted when I begin to worry too much as to what particular logical and methodological canons I should or should not obey. It seems to me that very often major new scientific insights have come when the scientist, like the ape, has been shaken out of his up-until-then approved scientific rules such as that food can be reached only by the hand and discovers "out of the blue," and perhaps purely by analogy, [66] the new rule of using a stick (or a sign-gestalt). Fourthly, I have

an inveterate tendency to make my ideas too complicated and too
high-flown so that they become less and less susceptible to empirical
test. Fifthly, because of increasing laziness, I have not of late kept up,
as I should have, with the more recent theoretical and empirical
discussions which bear upon my argument. If I had, the argument
would have been different and better and also I would have given
more credit to those to whom credit is due. Finally, to talk about one's
own ideas and to resort frequently to the use of the first person singular,
as one tends to do in such an analysis, brings about a conflict, at least
in me, between enjoying my exhibitionism and being made to feel
guilty by my superego. However, I am probably merely giving vent to
spleen and had better turn to the argument itself.

BACKGROUND FACTORS AND ORIENTING ATTITUDES

Rather against my will and because of parental pressure, I
graduated from the Massachusetts Institute of Technology. I had been
good in science and mathematics in high school and there seemed no
good reason why I should not go on to be an engineer. And, presumably, I picked up some sort of a feeling for scientific method as a result
of this training at M.I.T. But I knew I did not want to be an engineer,
so when I had graduated I went to Harvard as a graduate student in
philosophy, but I soon discovered that psychology was what I wanted.
But those were the days of introspectionistic structuralism which by
definition seemed to me unscientific and incommunicable. Hence
when I was first exposed to Watson's behaviorism [96] in 1914, in a
course given by Yerkes, I was "sold." However, although I was sold
on objectivism and behaviorism as *the* method in psychology, the
only categorizing rubrics which I had at hand were mentalistic ones.
So when I began to try to develop a behavioristic system of my own,
what I really was doing was trying to rewrite a common-sense mentalistic psychology—or what the gestalt psychologists have called a
phenomenology—in operational behavioristic terms. Köhler has
called me a "cryptophenomenologist."[1] He is probably right. What I
wanted was a behavioristic psychology which would be able to deal
with real organisms in terms of their inner psychological dynamics.
That is, I rejected the extreme peripheralism and muscle-twitch-ism of
Watson. And I was tremendously influenced by Perry [68], who demonstrated that both cognition and motivation could be treated as perfectly objective facts, without taint of teleology or of subjectivism. The
problem was to get these central processes which I came to call
"intervening variables" [79] out into objective pointer readings. I

[1] In his Hitchcock Lectures at the University of California, Berkeley, 1955.

suppose I also had some yen to deal with the more embracing problem of personality structure. But there was not much in the way of Freudian or other notions (save intelligence tests) concerning personality structure available in those days, at least in America.

In any event, what happened with me—as happened, I expect, with many another beginning psychologist of that era—was that having been attracted to psychology in the first place by personal and social needs, I proceeded, once I got in, to retreat to such "safe" subjects as learning and memory with occasional forays into motivation, usually at a "safe" biological level.

When I got to California, I more or less accidentally started a rat laboratory. And I became tremendously interested in trial-and-error learning as previously investigated by Thorndike. I wanted to defend Thorndike on the importance of motivation as against Watson's claims of mere frequency and recency as the determiners of the gradual (or relatively sudden) increase in the correct response. However, I did not like the Law of Effect. I felt the need for the construct of a driving motive, relative to which, and only relative to which, the goal (or the punishment) constituted an "effect." I also felt that a response could not be defined as a specific muscle contraction but must in some way be defined as a directed, goal-oriented manipulation or "performance." I still feel that "response" is one of the most slippery and unanalyzed of our current concepts.[2] We all gaily use the term to mean anything from a secretion of 10 drops of saliva to entering a given alley, to running an entire maze, to the slope of a Skinner box curve, to achieving a Ph.D., or to a symbolic act of hostility against one's father by attacking some authority figure. Now, I ask you!

Finally, of course, I was much influenced by gestalt psychology. Köhler's studies of problem solving in apes [38] were terribly illuminating to me and reinforced my "centralist" notions. However, I remained at heart an associationist and, although I became convinced that the whole in some degree governs its parts, these wholes, I felt, were acquired by learning and were not autochthonously given. That is, I talked about acquired sign-gestalten rather than about innately ready, pure perceptual gestalten. As for perception, I have always been about as sleazy about it as I have been about responses. The "stimulus" as we use it today seems to be just as slippery a term as that of response. But I am afraid I haven't been able to do much about clarifying it.

I turn now to some of the specific rubrics which have been suggested under "orienting attitudes."

[2] For this reason I have been much stimulated by Barker and Wright's recent attempt [3] to specify more significant units of behavior, though I have not yet been able to incorporate their suggestions into my own thinking.

The nature and limits of psychological prediction. I have, on the one hand, tended to assume that, if we knew enough, all responses (performances), great or small, could be predicted—meaning individual performances on individual occasions. And, on the other hand, I have also been aware that what I actually do as a rat psychologist is to try to predict merely the average responses of a specifically defined group of rats under a specific set of conditions. This would mean that I could expect to predict the response of the individual rat only with a certain degree of probability. To a large extent this circumstance that one can predict the individual's response only as having a certain probability is, I think, a part of what Brunswik argued for [10, 89].

Level of analysis. Further, I have been interested primarily in getting "behavioral" laws at their own level. It seemed that psychology, when I started, was being handicapped by trying to take over the inadequate reflex notions of the neurology of the time. Later, of course, I also became more aware of the social determiners of behavior. And, having a penchant for the vague and the confused, I was once led [81] to suggest a position opposite to the standard "reductionism." The reductionist point of view would hold that social behaviors and individual psychological behaviors are to be explained by neurophysiological processes. I suggested that, in a certain sense, this could be turned upside down and that we might assert rather that the laws of sociology come first, since they determine the response ranges and the nature of the stimulus settings actually available to the individual; and that the laws of individual behavior come next, for these determine the range of neurophysiological process that can occur. Thus, while not denying that in one sense physiology "explains" psychology and psychology "explains" sociology, I did then, and I do now, assert that, in another equally important and perhaps more pragmatically useful sense, sociological phenomena control (explain) psychological phenomena and psychological phenomena control (explain) neurophysiological ones. But this was all relatively aside from my main experimental interests and I have not made use of these ideas in any of my theorizing on learning.

Utility and role of "models." Although I myself have sometimes used the term "model," it has come to mean so many different things from, say, an equation-form, a sociometric diagram, a mechanico-electrical rat, a stochastic model of learning, to a chart for the interrelationships between independent, intervening, and dependent variables, that the word has lost for me any specific meaning. As I see it, the word "model" is merely a sloppy synonym used, when one gets tired of some more specific term, to designate the specific type of theoretical organization that one is proposing.

Comprehensiveness of empirical reference. I have always wanted my psychology to be as wide as the study of a life career and as narrow as the study of a rat's entrance into a specific blind. But, actually, I have for the most part studied only average numbers of entrances into specific blinds, or jumps to a particular type of door, and have hoped that the principles found there would have something to do with a really interesting piece of behavior—say, the choice and pursuit of a life career.

Degree and mode of quantitative and mensurational specificity toward which it is desirable and/or feasible to aim. I am very relaxed about this. Be as fine in your measurement as you can. But, under those overcontrolled artificial conditions in which you can be very fine and get great specificity and fineness of measurement, the relations or "laws" which you uncover are probably going to have very little generality. Psychology today seems *to me* to be suffering from a flight into too high-powered a statistics and into too over-mathematized a fitting of curves. The experimental situations for which one can achieve such overrefinement probably do not obey the canons of "representative design"—see Brunswik [10]. But I am obviously again here venting my spleen. I did learn quite a lot of mathematics once, but I have forgotten it and have not kept it up; and so I tend to minimize the importance of too refined measurements and too developed a mathematical treatment until we really know a great deal more about the general qualitative lists and patterns of the determiners of behavior than we as yet do.

Type of formal organization. I believe that my various forays into theory vary all the way from "informal exposition" to a few minor attempts at relatively "explicit hypothetico-deductive axiomization." For the most part my assumed variables and my assumed functions connecting them to one another have been in the form of mere loose qualitative hunches though sometimes they have been stated in would-be more precise quantitative and mathematical terms, e.g., see the discussions of VTE [82, 83, 88]. Apparently, I have no scientific superego which urges me to be mathematical, deductive, and axiomatic. My intervening variables are generally speaking mere temporarily believed-in, inductive, more or less qualitative generalizations which categorize and sum up for me (act as mnemonic symbols for) various empirically found relationships. They do not lead to any then-and-there precise further quantitative predictions. They do, however (when mixed with a healthy brew of intuition, common sense, and phenomenology), lead to suggestions for further types of empirical relations to be tested. That is, they are loosely defined *"hypothetical constructs"*—see MacCorquodale and Meehl [48] on hypothetical constructs vs. intervening variables—which lead to hypotheses through intuition, common sense, phenomenology, and very general notions about neurophysiology. Psychology, given all its many parts, is today still such a vast continent of unknowns that it has always seemed to me rather silly to try to be too precise, too quantitative, too deductive and axiomatic, save in very experimentally overcontrolled and over-limited areas.

STRUCTURE OF THE SYSTEM AS THUS FAR DEVELOPED

1. Exhaustive itemization of systematic independent, intervening, and dependent variables.

2. Mode of definition of representative variables of each category.

3. Major interrelations among constructs.

4. Discussion of order of determining and other characteristics of construct linkages.

The above four rubrics are suggested in the outline. But I shall consider them together by presenting and discussing a series of figures in which I shall try to indicate the major independent, intervening, and dependent variables postulated by me.[3] But I shall not attempt to be "exhaustive" as suggested in rubric {1}. That is, I shall not now attempt to revive all the flights of fancy that I may have indulged in at one time or another in the past. Rather, I shall restrict myself to a consideration of what I consider to have been my major theoretical constructs, reformulating and elaborating some of them for the purposes of what I now believe to be a more coherent and more empirically useful set of statements. I shall also limit my discussion to a consideration of the variables and interconnecting functions to be assumed in the explanation of the behavior in a few of the basic experiments on the instrumental learning and performance of rats. For, as I indicated above, I believe that, if these can be clearly envisaged, some fundamental principles will be found which can eventually be expanded and built upon so as to become helpful for the explanation of human behavior. Here and there I shall suggest such further human implications.

In Figs. 1, 2, and 3, I have presented the variables—independent variables, intervening variables (hypothetical constructs), and the

[3] And intervening variables, as I conceive them, will have in part the properties of *hypothetical constructs* and not merely be intervening mathematical quantities. However, the "surplus meanings" of my intervening variables which make them into hypothetical constructs are not at this stage primarily neurophysiological, as it is suggested by MacCorquodale and Meehl [48] that they should be, but are derived rather from intuition, common experience, a little sophomoric neurology, and my own phenomenology.

dependent variables—and the interconnecting causal connections (the latter represented by arrows) which I conceive to be involved in the learning and performance of (1) a simple approach to and eating of food, (2) a case of simple escape from an electric shock, and (3) a case of simple avoidance of an electric shock. In subsequent charts, I shall consider two more complicated setups, viz., choice-point learning, and latent or incidental learning.

A case of approach. *Independent variables.* Look at Fig. 1. Look first at the independent variables. These have been separated into two

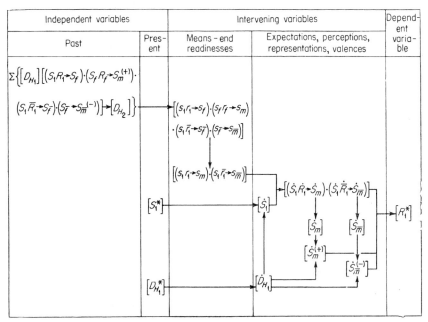

Fig. 1. Approach

columns labeled "past" and "present." In the "past" column is a complex symbol which stands for a complicated interconnected array of independent variables which have occurred in the trials preceding the one in question, or in other somewhat similar previous situations. In the second, "present," column are the symbols which stand for the specific and particular variables which are presented to the animal at the beginning of the given trial, that is, on the trial the results of which are to be predicted.

Before, however, examining these symbols for the independent variables in more detail, let us look briefly at the other parts of the figure.

Intervening variables and the dependent variable. It will be noted that the intervening variables also are divided into two columns: means-end readinesses in the first column; and perceptions, representations, expectancies, and valences in the second column. Finally, the last column in the chart contains the dependent variable: namely, in this case, the to-be-predicted strength of the tendency on the given trial to approach the food. This latter is symbolized as R_1*.[4]

It should be emphasized that because of common practice, I have throughout symbolized the manipulatory organism-environment rearrangements (i.e., performances) which I am concerned with, by the letters R or r. And, for literary convenience, I have often called them "responses" rather than "performances." It is to be stressed again, however, that for me the type of response I am interested in is always to be identified as a pattern of *organism-environment rearrangements* and not as a detailed set of muscular or glandular activities. These latter may vary from trial to trial and yet the total "performance" remain the same. Thus, for example, "going towards a light" is a *performance* in my sense of the term and is not properly a response (a set of muscular contractions). That is, it does not fit into the original Hullian definition of a response, although the Hullians often seem to forget this fact and tend to talk of "going toward the light" as if it were specified by a specific set of muscular contractions. In so doing they seem to me to cheat themselves and to make confusion for the rest of us.

Independent variables (past). Return now and look in more detail at the complex symbol for the past independent variables—those involved in previous trials, or in any previous training relatively similar to the trial in question.[5] This symbol is $\Sigma\{[D_{H_1}][(S_1R_1 \rightarrow S_f) \cdot (S_fR_f \rightarrow S_m{}^+) \cdot (S_1\bar{R}_1 \rightarrow S_{\bar{f}}) \cdot (S_{\bar{f}} \rightarrow S_{\bar{m}}{}^-)] \rightarrow [D_{H_2}]\}$.[6] Σ is the symbol for the frequencies, recencies, and distribution of such previous trials or previous training. D_{H_1} represents the *hunger drive-stimulation* (the hungriness and its magnitude) which was present and operative throughout each of these preceding trials. (I have therefore placed this D_{H_1} in a bracket coordinate with the bracket containing the parentheses representing the successive stimulus − response → stimulus events involved in each trial.) And D_{H_2} represents the hunger drive-stimulation and its magnitude present at the termination of each such previous trial. D_{H_2} has usually been assumed by both experimenters

---

[4] The independent and dependent variables have been symbolized by capital letters. And a single then-and-there immediately present instance of one of these independent or dependent variables is symbolized by adding an asterisk to the letter.

[5] The trial in question may, of course, be the first one in the given setup.

[6] The dots between the parentheses symbolize "and."

and theoreticians to be less in magnitude than D_{H_1}. But we need more evidence than we now have to be certain that this is always the case. There are certainly some findings, e.g., Bruce [9], which suggest that the result of the reaching of a small amount of food (or, in the case of thirst, a small amount of water) following an early trial is actually to enhance rather than to decrease the drive-stimulation.[7]

Let us consider further for a moment the nature of the D_{H_1}'s and D_{H_2}'s. I have called them "drive-stimulations" rather than simply "drives" or simply "stimuli" to distinguish them as internal conditions which have properties both similar to and different from those of ordinary stimuli and also different from those of drives as often conceived. In fact, such *stimulations* have, I believe, three kinds of property, viz., they can be discriminated by the organism (at least to some extent) one from another; they have energizing properties; and they have value-giving properties.

First, they can be discriminated. Drives can, at least to some extent, be discriminated by organisms, even by rats. Thus it appears that rats can be trained to do one performance for one degree of initial hunger D_{H_1} and to do another performance for another degree of hunger D_{H_1}' [7, 36]. And also rats are able to distinguish between two different drives such as hunger and thirst in the sense that they can make one performance for thirst D_{T_1} and another for hunger D_{H_1} [2, 8, 29, 43]. And certainly human beings, if not rats, can to some extent actually rate the degrees of their immediate hungers (their D_{H_1}'s) and also probably their terminal hungers (their D_{H_2}'s).

Second, drive-stimulations have energizing properties. In saying that a drive-stimulation (for example, a D_{H_1}) energizes, I refer to two different types of fact: (1) an initial hunger drive-stimulation tends to lower thresholds for both foodlike objects and for to-be-explored objects and for eating responses to the former and for exploring responses to the latter; (2) the second fact is that these explorations and eatings will exhibit trial and error until success is reached.[8] This matter of "success" leads us to the third property of drive-stimulations.

---

[7] This seeming fact raises doubt concerning the doctrine of drive-reduction as the basis of reinforcement. However, the doctrine of drive-reduction is not one which I shall argue for or against here. I shall come back to it later.

[8] Trial-and-error exploratoriness I conceive to be a function of any drive, e.g., hunger, thirst, sex, or what not. I also assume, however, that in addition to such major biological drives there also often appears a pure curiosity drive. The goal of this latter is the experience of distant stimuli merely per se and it also is accompanied by its own exploratory trial and error. For exciting experimental evidence for such a curiosity drive, see Berlyne [5] and the investigations of Montgomery and Harlow and of their associates [22, 54, 55, 56, 57].

Finally, it may be noted that there is perhaps a curvilinear relationship between

Third, drive-stimulations have value-giving properties. A drive-stimulation sets up both positive and negative goals. That is to say, a drive-stimulation such as hunger lends positive value to one specific type of terminal stimulus or stimuli and also it may (at least temporarily) lend negative value to any stimuli which are not the final goal stimuli.[9] This presence of positive and negative values is symbolized in Fig. 1 by the plus superscript on the positive terminal stimulus $S_m{}^+$ and the minus superscript on the stimulus[10] of $S_{\bar{m}}{}^-$. If it would not have confused the diagram, I would have drawn arrows directly from D_{H_1} to these positive and negative goal stimuli ($S_m{}^+$ and $S_{\bar{m}}{}^-$) to indicate that the positive and negative values on them are the direct product of the governing drive-stimulation D_{H_1}.

Finally, before leaving this consideration of the drive-stimulations, I must introduce my notion that there is also always in any case of behavior still another drive (in addition to that of curiosity) also operating. This last I have not indicated in the diagram because it would have made the drawing too complicated. It would be a drive against effort or work and/or uncertainty and it would mean that the performances (the R's) would have negative values in proportion to the amounts of work they involve. For when it comes to a selection among alternative ($SR \rightarrow S$) routes the organism will, generally speaking, come to select the *easiest* and/or most *probable* route. Although most psychologists have, it seems to me, either explicitly or implicitly recognized this phenomenon (Hull by his concepts of reactive and conditioned inhibition), no one has perhaps given any altogether agreed-upon theoretical analysis of it. As I have said, my own present solution—and I have indicated this either implicitly or explicitly in the past, see especially [88]—is to postulate that, along with each major governing drive-stimulation, there is also involved an additional drive

---

the strength of any main basic drive-stimulation and such an accompanying pure curiosity drive. If a main biological drive be either too weak or too strong, there tends, it seems, to be a lower magnitude of pure curiosity. Or to put it in common sense terms, if the major drive-stimulation is too weak, the animal is not sufficiently "interested" to examine widely and, if the major drive-stimulation is too strong, he tends to be too "tense" to examine widely [15].

[9] As we shall see below, in the case of a so-called negative drive such as fear, the drive-stimulation lends, first of all, negative value to certain types of presented stimuli (e.g., pain), and it seems probable that it may also lend positive value to any type of stimulus which is not a pain stimulus itself and is not followed by a pain stimulus.

[10] S_m is a symbol for all the "mouth," stomach, and nutritional stimuli resulting from eating and $S_{\bar{m}}$ is a symbol for any stimuli which are *not* such final consummatory stimuli.

to be called that *against effort and uncertainty* and/or that *for little effort and for certainty.*[11]

But let us turn now to the meaning of the four parentheses within the second bracket, viz.,

$$[(S_1R_1 \rightarrow S_f) \cdot (S_fR_f \rightarrow S_m{}^+) \cdot (S_1\bar{R}_1 \rightarrow S_{\bar{f}}) \cdot (S_{\bar{f}} \rightarrow S_{\bar{m}}{}^-)]$$

The parenthesis $(S_1R_1 \rightarrow S_f)$ symbolizes, as an independent variable, the fact that the manipulatory response R_1 of responding to the given alley S_1[12] by going down it resulted on each trial in a consequent reaching of the further stimulus of food S_f. It is important to emphasize once more that this performance R_1 of going down the alley is to be identified as a discriminable general organism-environment rearrangement. It gets the animal to the end of the alley and may maintain its identity over a range of different sets of muscle contractions on different occasions.

Furthermore, it is to be emphasized that S_1 (the alley as stimulus) is to be specified, not in terms of a single atomlike stimulus or in terms of simple relatively "proximal" effects, see Brunswik [10, 89], upon the sensory surfaces but rather as a complicated "distal" stimulus-object which also includes a set of associated behavior-support stimuli.[13] That is, S_1 symbolizes the alley as a pattern of potential-releasing stimuli *plus* a pattern of immediate "behavior-support" or *feedback* stimuli.

In other words (whatever I may have said earlier) I am now suggesting that behavior-support properties are also to be conceived as stimulus patterns, i.e., as some characteristic *pattern* of *feedback* stimuli (from distance receptors and/or tactile and proprioceptive receptors) which result as the animal makes a given performance and which are *necessary supports* if this performance is to be carried out successfully.

[11] Another type of argument advanced by Hull [28] for explaining the choosing of a shorter route was the assumption that the shorter route would as such be more rapidly *learned*. My own bias as a result of some of the latent learning experiments, especially that of Blodgett [6], *in which he used a simple two-way maze*, is to believe that the longer route may be equally rapidly learned, but that when a goal is introduced the longer route by virtue of its length becomes less preferred simply because of the drive-stimulation against work. (Brunswik, at least in private conversations, has contended that the preference for a shorter route may perhaps really be subsumed under the heading of choosing the more *certain* route.) In any event, it appears that such a doctrine as I am here proposing involves the assumption that work or uncertainty comes, as such, to be discriminated by the organism and to be accompanied by negative values.

[12] I am here assuming the case of a single alley with food at the end of it.

[13] For an initial discussion of behavior-supports see Tolman [78].

Turn now to the parenthesis $(S_fR_f \rightarrow S_m{}^+)$. This symbolizes the further fact that R_f (the response of eating the food S_f) results in the reaching of a set of final goal stimuli $S_m{}^+$. These goal stimuli $S_m{}^+$ are to be conceived as stimuli in the *mouth*, the stomach, and to some extent in the underlying nutritional system.[14] And the plus superscript accompanying this $S_m{}^+$ symbolizes the fact, already discussed above, that there will be persistence and trial and error until this $S_m{}^+$ is reached, that in other words $S_m{}^+$ is to be conceived as having "positive value."

The parenthesis $(S_1\bar{R}_1 \rightarrow S_{\bar{f}})$ symbolizes the fact that, when the rat does not run down the alley $\bar{R}_1$, he stays in the presence of, or reaches, nonfood stimuli $S_{\bar{f}}$. And the parenthesis $(S_{\bar{f}} \rightarrow S_{\bar{m}}{}^-)$ symbolizes the further fact that a stimulus of nonfood $S_{\bar{f}}$ leads to (is accompanied by) stimuli which are nongustatory stimuli $S_{\bar{m}}{}^-$. And these nongustatory stimuli have, as such, a negative value.

Including now also the bracketed D_{H_1} and the bracketed D_{H_2}, the total brace represents the fact that in the preceding trials each of the following things has happened. There has been a hunger drive-stimulation D_{H_1}. Further, in the presence of this hunger drive-stimulation the rats have made the response R_1 of going down the alley S_1 and this response has got them to the food stimuli S_f. *And* they have made the further response of eating R_f in the presence of these food stimuli S_f and this latter response has got them to the internal goal stimuli $S_m{}^+$, where these goal stimuli have been positive in the sense that the rats have shown exploration tendencies and persistence on each trial until these goal stimuli $S_m{}^+$ were reached. *And* in the course of their explorations they have made *other* responses than R_1 (i.e., they have made $\bar{R}_1$) and these $\bar{R}_1$ responses have led to nonfood stimuli $S_{\bar{f}}$. *And* these nonfood stimuli $S_{\bar{f}}$ have led to, or been accompanied by, nongoal stimuli $S_{\bar{m}}{}^-$, where these latter have been negative in the sense that as long as the $S_{\bar{m}}{}^-$ stimuli were present the rats have continued to make exploratory responses. Finally, each trial has ended with the rats

---

[14] See the work of Neal Miller and his associates [4, 39, 53]. These workers made fistulas in the stomachs of their rats by which actual food or saline solutions or balloons (which could be blown up) could be introduced and the results of these procedures could be compared with those of normal eating through the mouth. By various permutations and combinations of these procedures Miller and his associates discovered that mouth stimuli, stomach stimuli, and nutritional stimuli were all involved in the goal of eating. Sheffield and Roby [74] also found that saccharin, a nonnutritive taste, merely as such, constitutes a goal stimulus. P. T. Young's [97, 98] findings also suggest the fact that mere mouth stimuli likewise constitute a significant part of the total goal. For convenience I have used the subscript m to cover all these resultant *mouth*, stomach, and nutritional system stimuli.

reaching $S_m{}^+$ which has then presumably produced some new value of the hunger drive-stimulation D_{H_2}—equal to, greater than, or less than D_{H_1}.

Means-end readinesses. Before considering the other, "present," independent variables, let us look now at the first column of intervening variables, labeled "means-end readinesses." As the causal arrow indicates, I have assumed that the frequencies, recencies, and distributions Σ of the previous trials under such and such drive-stimulation conditions D_{H_1}'s have produced directly a corresponding set of means-end readinesses. It will be noted that, whereas the independent variables were symbolized by capitals, these means-end readinesses have been symbolized by lower-case letters. Further, these means-end readinesses[15] are to be thought of as acquired cognitive dispositions resulting directly from preceding trials or from other, related, previous training. And, as such acquired dispositions, they are conceived to be one of the major determiners of the final performance. These acquired dispositions or readinesses can be thought of as dispositional sets for certain types of (stimulus − response → stimulus)-sequences or for certain types of (stimulus − stimulus)-sequence. In other words, when an *instance* of an s_1 is presented, there tends to be released an expectancy (see next column in the chart) that an instance of the kind of performance symbolized by r_1 will lead to an instance of s_2 (or else simply that the presentation of an instance of an s_1 will by itself lead to, or be accompanied by, an instance of an s_2).[16]

But let us examine now in more detail the symbolic expression for the total series of means-end readinesses, viz.,

$$[(s_1r_1 \rightarrow s_f) \cdot (s_f r_f \rightarrow s_m) \cdot (s_1 \bar{r}_1 \rightarrow s_{\bar{f}}) \cdot (s_{\bar{f}} \rightarrow s_{\bar{m}})]$$

This stands for the fact that the animal has acquired a disposition or set to the effect that an s_1 *type* of stimulus, when manipulated by an r_1 *type* of response, will lead to a food stimulus of *type* s_f; and that he has also acquired a set to the effect that food stimuli of the *type* s_f, when manipulated by the eating *type* of response r_f, will lead to mouth, stomach, and nutritional goal stimuli of *type* s_m; and that he has acquired a set to the effect that not performing an r_1 (i.e., $\bar{r}_1$) will lead to, or leave him in the presence of, nonfood stimuli of type $s_{\bar{f}}$; and that finally he has acquired a set to the effect that nonfood stimuli $s_{\bar{f}}$ will, simply as such, be accompanied by nongustatory stimuli $s_{\bar{m}}$. He has learned all this and these dispositions or sets remain present in him (or, if you prefer, in his nervous system) *whether or not he is hungry at the*

---

[15] I also call them "beliefs."

[16] Means-end readinesses or beliefs are symbolized by lower-case letters.

moment[17] and *whether or not any instances of the type of stimuli and responses in question are present at the moment.*

Further, it is to be emphasized that separate items in this total set of means-end readinesses can be present and be ready to function without the others. Thus, the animal can have the readiness $(s_f r_f \rightarrow s_m)$ without then having the readiness that $(s_1 r_1 \rightarrow s_f)$. That is, he can have learned that eating the given type of food leads to certain types of gustatory (mouth, etc.) stimuli without having yet learned that going down the given type of alley leads to this type of food. And he can have the readiness $(s_{\bar{f}} \rightarrow s_{\bar{m}})$, i.e., no food leads to nongustatory stimuli, without yet having the readiness $(s_1 \bar{r}_1 \rightarrow s_{\bar{f}})$. Indeed the fact that animals are usually trained to eat the given food, before the experiment proper has begun, means that they are extremely likely to have the readinesses $(s_f r_f \rightarrow s_m)$ before they have the one $(s_1 r_1 \rightarrow s_f)$. And, owing to all their past experiences, they are also likely to have the readiness $(s_{\bar{f}} \rightarrow s_{\bar{m}})$ before they have acquired the one relative to the specific alley that $(s_1 \bar{r}_1 \rightarrow s_{\bar{f}})$.

Finally, it is my assumption (see Fig. 1 again) that all these readinesses expressed in the total bracket

$$[(s_1 r_1 \rightarrow s_f) \cdot (s_f r_f \rightarrow s_m) \cdot (s_1 \bar{r}_1 \rightarrow s_{\bar{f}}) \cdot (s_{\bar{f}} \rightarrow s_{\bar{m}})]$$

can telescope into the two more comprehensive ones:

$$[(s_1 r_1 \rightarrow s_m) \cdot (s_1 \bar{r}_1 \rightarrow s_{\bar{m}})]$$

This latter symbol represents the over-all readinesses to the effect that "going down" r_1 the specific type of alley s_1 will lead to a gustatory goal stimulus s_m and that not going down $\bar{r}_1$ such an alley s_1 will lead to (or be accompanied by) a nongustatory stimulus $s_{\bar{m}}$.

Further, I would like to suggest that such a telescoping is only a simple case of what is probably a general property of all readinesses. I would suggest, namely, that readinesses (beliefs) can combine and interact not only in this fashion of telescoping but in other ways as well. I would argue, in short, that the experiments on insight, reasoning, and short-cutting suggest that readinesses can be added and multiplied as well as telescoped. And when so added or multiplied, they may lead to new responses, never before exhibited.

[17] This is the reason that there are no plus or minus superscripts on the items in these means-end readinesses. The means-end readinesses are to be conceived as pure *cognitive* dispositions. This does not mean, however, that the motivational and value items in the independent variables (i.e., D_{H_1} and D_{H_2} and the positive value on $S_{\bar{m}}^+$ and the negative value on $S_{\bar{m}}^-$) may not have some influence on the acquisition of such means-end readinesses. But this question of the effect of "effect" upon learning will be postponed until we turn in our resumé to the Laws of learning.

Finally, it must be pointed out that means-end readinesses (beliefs) have two kinds of magnitudes. An organism may *hold strongly* that a given type of s_1r_1 leads to a given type of s_2 (or that a given s_1 leads directly to a given s_2). In this sense, his readiness has a high magnitude. (His "belief" is strong.) On the other hand, such a belief *though held strongly* may be to the effect that only in a certain (and it may be low) proportion of instances will the s_2 consequence follow. In this latter sense, the magnitude of the readiness will be low. How, empirically, we are to distinguish between these two types of cases in rats is not altogether clear. But certainly with human beings we can ask them to state both their beliefs as to *probability* of the outcome (the second type of magnitude) and their degree of *confidence*[18] in this belief as to the outcome (the first type of magnitude).

Independent variables (present). Let us now turn back to the two independent variables in the column labeled "present." These are symbolized as S_1^* and $D_{H_1}^*$. They are to be conceived as the characters and magnitudes of the alley stimulus S_1 and of the drive-stimulation D_{H_1} specifically present on the given trial. The asterisks are to indicate that each has a specific, particular, *then-and-there* value which may or may not be different from the characters and magnitudes of these two variables in the preceding trials summarized by the symbol Σ.

Intervening variables (perceptions, expectancies, representations, and valences).[19] Turn next to the second column under "Intervening variables." It will be noted that all the letters in this column are capitalized and have dots over them. The dots are to indicate that these symbols refer to intervening variables rather than to independent or dependent variables. And the symbols are capitalized to indicate that, like the independent and dependent variables, they are particular events, which are conceived to be present only on the individual occasion. To sum up, they are capitalized to distinguish them from the means-end readinesses (symbolized by lower-case letters); but they have dots over them to distinguish them from the independent and dependent variables (i.e., the physically or physiologically defined stimuli, responses, and drive-stimulations).

Let us examine them one by one. Consider $\dot{S}_1$. Whereas the symbol S_1^* (in the column for independent variables) stands for the pattern of stimuli produced by the actual physical presence of the alley, the symbol $\dot{S}_1$ stands for the resulting discrimination ("perception")[20]

---

[18] For the possibility of getting good confidence ratings in human subjects, see Irwin et al. [33].

[19] Perceptions, expectancies, and representations are symbolized by capital letters with dots over them.

[20] By a "perception" I do not, of course, mean a necessarily conscious event.

of this complex stimulus. (For the method of measuring or estimating such "perceptions" see below.)

Similarly, whereas the symbol $D_{H_1}{}^*$ in the column for the independent variables stood for the specific hunger drive-stimulation on the particular occasion, as determined by what has actually been done to the animal (usually in the way of such and such a degree of deprivation), the symbol $\dot{D}_{H_1}$ stands for the actual discriminated and effective (or, if you will permit me, "perceived") drive-stimulation on that occasion. (This latter may be greater or less than objectively, biochemically, it should be.) Further, it will be observed that $\dot{S}_1$ is conceived to be caused by both $S_1{}^*$ and $\dot{D}_{H_1}$.[21]

Look next at the symbol $[(\dot{S}_1\dot{R}_1 \rightarrow \dot{S}_m) \cdot (\dot{S}_1\ddot{R}_1 \rightarrow \dot{S}_{\bar{m}})]$. This stands for two concrete expectancies: (1) that $\dot{R}_1$ (a "represented" response of going down the perceived alley $\dot{S}_1$) will result in a "represented" (and expected) pattern of gustatory stimuli $\dot{S}_m$, and (2) that a "represented" response of not-going-down $\ddot{R}$ the perceived alley $\dot{S}_1$ will result in a represented (and expected) pattern of nongoal stimuli $\dot{S}_{\bar{m}}$. And as shown by the causal arrows, these two expectancies are conceived to be caused by the combined action of the means-end readiness $(s_1r_1 \rightarrow s_m)$ and $(s_1\bar{r}_1 \rightarrow s_{\bar{m}})$ and the here-and-now aroused perception of the presence of the alley $(\dot{S}_1)$.

Note also that I have repeated $\dot{S}_m$ and $\dot{S}_{\bar{m}}$ in boxes below. This bringing them down is partly for convenience in diagraming. But it is also meant to suggest that as "representations" such "expected" entities can be perhaps in some degree separated from, and function independently of, the specific expectancies in which they are embodied.

Finally, note that, when the "represented" $\dot{S}_m$ and $\dot{S}_{\bar{m}}$ are combined with the action of the "effective" hunger $\dot{D}_{H_1}$, they become endowed with positive and negative valences.[22] The fact that they acquire such valences is symbolized in the still lower boxes by the addition of the plus and minus superscripts.

It is to be noted that I here speak of "valences" rather than of "values." The term "values" was used for the independent variables, symbolized by $S_m{}^+$ and $S_{\bar{m}}{}^-$. And such values are specified by the objective degree to which the animals, having reached an actual instance of an S_m, would tend on the further occasions to persist and to show trial and error in reaching it again; or, similarly, having got

---

[21] This allows for the effects, such as they may be, of motives on perception. The *hungry* animal may well be more ready to perceive certain types of external stimulus situations than others. But, as we all know, the facts as to such effects, if any, are still perhaps dubious and certainly unclear.

[22] Valences are symbolized by the symbols for the expected good or bad goal stimuli with a $^+$ or a $^-$ superscript added.

away from an actual $S_{\bar{m}}$, to what extent they would tend on subsequent occasions to show restlessness until they got away from this $S_{\bar{m}}$ again. "Valences," on the other hand, are conceived as the intervening variables, symbolized by $\acute{S}_m{}^+$ and $\acute{S}_{\bar{m}}{}^-$ which function as such only on the individual occasion. They correspond to what the animal then and there "expects" in the way of "goodness" or "badness" (which may or may not correspond to the actual values as determined by the animal's behavior when he has got to the corresponding actual S_m or $S_{\bar{m}}$). Thus, for example, an experimenter may in fact alter the situation during or before the given trial so that the expected values, i.e., the valences built up as a result of the preceding trials, will no longer correspond to the actual values. The experimenter may, for example, make the true consummatory value of the food $S_m{}^+$ either greater or less than it was on the preceding trials. The consummatory consequence (the value) of the food, when got to, may thus be greater or less than expected, i.e., than "its valence $(\acute{S}_m{}^+)$ during the trial." And *pari passu* the internal consequences of nonfood (value) may be made more or less than its expected value (valence). To use Lewin's terminology, the valences are in the animal's "life space," whereas the values are in the effects of the actual environment upon the organism.

Finally, I assume that it is the magnitudes (in both senses, see above) of the expectancies $(\acute{S}_1\acute{R}_1 \rightarrow \acute{S}_m)$ and $(\acute{S}_1\acute{R}_1 \rightarrow \acute{S}_{\bar{m}})$ and the magnitudes of the valences $\acute{S}_m{}^+$ and $\acute{S}_{\bar{m}}{}^-$ which act together to determine the magnitude of the resulting dependent response $(\dot{R}_1{}^*)$ rather than its opposite $\check{R}_1{}^*.$[23]

So much for a survey of the symbols in Fig. 1 and of the constructs for which they stand. Thus far I have merely stated these constructs and indicated the assumed causal interactions between them. That is, I have presented these constructs in what the outline for Project A would call my "system" language. How far can I now also state them in an "empirical language"? How far, in short, can I suggest empirical pointer readings for them?

Pointer readings. Let us look first at the independent variables. Begin with Σ. The symbol Σ stands for the frequency, recency, and distribution of previous trials. This construct of frequency, recency, and distribution presents no great difficulty. The pointer readings for it are obtained by timepieces and counting. And these timings and countings give us relatively undisputed measures of what all of us would mean by frequencies, recencies, and distributions.

---

[23] The expected, represented, and valenced $\acute{S}_m{}^+$'s and $\acute{S}_m{}^-$'s are handled in a Hullian analysis by the constructs of r_g and s_g. But I find that these hypothetical, relatively peripheral, constructs do not help me in my own thinking.

Look next at D_{H_1} and D_{H_2}, the hunger drive-stimulations present at the beginning and end of each trial. As defined above, a hungriness (a D_{H_1} or a D_{H_2}) is a disposition to approach and to eat. My suggested pointer reading for either a D_{H_1} or a D_{H_2} will be some measure of a general tendency in the given state of the animal to approach and/or eat foods *in general*. This measure would have to be obtained in some agreed-upon *standard situation* (say, a Skinner box) and not in the apparatus used in the specific experiment under consideration. That is, before the beginning of each trial (in the case of a D_{H_1}) a group of rats, comparable to those which *had had the same number of preceding trials* in the experiment proper, would have to be tested with a variety of foods in the Skinner box and average rates of pressing and/or eating measured.[24] These measures would then be taken as the empirical pointer readings for the then-and-there D_{H_1}. Such a procedure would, of course, mean that the rats thus tested would then have to be sacrificed in the sense that they then could not be used further in the experiment proper. For the experience of pressing the lever and eating in a Skinner box just before the given trial would presumably to some degree distort the animals' D_{H_1} for the given trial. The total procedure would thus be a tremendous task and would involve the use of a great number of rats. Something like it, however, seems to me to be called for until some day we can perhaps get some direct biochemical measure of a D_{H_1}.

It may be argued, however, that there is another less costly method for empirically estimating magnitudes of D_{H_1}. Indeed, it has been assumed by most experimenters that hunger drive-stimulations D_{H_1}'s are directly related to hours of food-deprivation or to maintained percentages of decrease in body weight. Thus it is assumed that if at the beginning of a given trial the deprivation has been for 22 hr—or if the body weight has been kept at 80 per cent of normal—then the hunger drive-stimulation, the D_{H_1}, will have a constant value for this trial.

It also seems to be assumed—at least in the case of hours of deprivation—that relatively known curves have been established [95] between different hours of deprivation and different strengths of D_{H_1}. That is, it is assumed, for example, that the D_{H_1}'s vary from 6 hr deprivation to 12 hr deprivation to 24 hr deprivation, or even to 48 hr according to some relatively known curve.

But there are, I believe, certain assumptions underlying all these thoughts and procedures about D_{H_1}'s which need to be brought to light. We assume, I believe, that a drive-stimulation, such as hungriness, is fundamentally a biochemical-physiological state. But it has

---

[24] It would be necessary that the rats had had plenty of previous training in the Skinner box beforehand so that there would be no problem of their having to learn what to do

further been assumed that the actual magnitudes of this state are reflected rather directly by the number of crossings in the Columbia Obstruction Box, or by rates of pressing in the Skinner box. But these last assumptions seem shaky. It appears, therefore, that ultimately the desired measure for initial (or terminal) hungriness, or for any other basic drive-stimulation, must be some direct physiological or biochemical one—see Ritchie [72]. However, I shall nevertheless conclude that today, in default of any such direct measures, the best that we can do is to use, as has been suggested, some measure of general readiness to approach and/or consume a standard goal in a standard situation.

Consider further the D_{H_2} after each trial. For this also we must obtain an empirical pointer reading. Such a reading would have to be obtained *after* each trial. And again this may perhaps be done by some measure of the then-and-there new (posttrial) readinesses to approach and/or eat the standard food in a standard setup. These D_{H_2} measures would perhaps be even more troublesome to make than those for the D_{H_1}. But it seems important to make them to discover whether actually the hungriness goes up or down after a given trial. As I have suggested above, my hunch is that it probably goes up after each of the first few trials, but that it probably goes down after later trials.

Turn next to empirical measures of the qualitative natures of S_m and $S_{\bar{m}}$. The only empirical attacks that we have on these to date are those of Miller and his coworkers already referred to. But what about the positive and negative values? Whereas D_{H_1} and D_{H_2} were conceived as the readinesses for food in general, S_m^+ is to be conceived rather as the readiness for the specific internal (mouth, stomach, and nutritional) stimuli resulting from the eating of the *specific food* in the *specific situation*. And $S_{\bar{m}}^-$ is to be conceived as the unreadiness (the "discomfort") in the presence of any stimuli other than S_m^+ in this specific situation. That is, both these "values" are to be measured directly in the specific situation. S_m^+ might be obtained by some measure of actual rate of eating of the specific food in the goal-end of the specific approach box at the termination of each trial. And $S_{\bar{m}}^-$ might be obtained by some measure of something like restlessness in the other parts of the box on the given trial. These will be difficult measures to obtain but perhaps they can be arrived at.

Pointer readings for intervening variables. Turn first to the means-end readinesses. The basic empirical setup, according to me, for obtaining pointer readings for means-end readinesses would be transfer experiments. Such experiments would involve either a transfer from preceding trials to the trial in question in the same apparatus, or they might involve a transfer from a series of trials in some different situations to the trial in question in the given situation. It is from such transfer experiments, with their favorable or negative effects upon the test trial, that we would infer the kinds and strengths of the means-end readinesses which were established by the training previous to the test trial and which are, therefore, to be assumed to explain the positive or negative transfer to that test trial. If the success and smoothness of the performance in the transferred-to test trial proves enhanced by the preceding training (or preceding trials in the same specific setup), then we must infer that the means-end readinesses (the beliefs) established by the preceding training were very similar to those which we assume as leading to the expectancy producing the given behavior in the given trial. Whereas, if the performance in the test trial is less correct than it would be without this preceding training, then we must infer that the means-end readinesses (beliefs) established by the preceding training (or trials) were relatively incompatible with those required for the correct expectancy and correct performance. And by different sorts of such transfer experiments we could become more and more precise in our specifications. That is, we could learn more and more about the means-end readinesses which the animal brings with him as well as of the one operative in the test trial itself.[25]

To test such a contention will, of course, require tremendous labor. And much ingenuity and insight will be required to devise and to carry out the needed experiments. Nevertheless, the notion I am arguing for does not seem altogether new. Learning psychologists have always assumed, I believe, that "habits" established in prior learning have an effect upon subsequent learning. And they have also assumed, I think, that the effect of such previous "habits" on the present learning will help to specify both the nature of those previous habits and the nature of the present habit being developed. The only really new gimmick I am introducing is the assumption that a habit, as a generalized disposition, is to be conceived, not as a simple s-r connection, but rather as an $s_1 r_1 \rightarrow s_2$ connection or an $s_1 \rightarrow s_2$ connection. And it is these $s_1 r_1 \rightarrow s_2$ and $s_1 \rightarrow s_2$ connections which transfer and combine with one another in complex ways. But the laws of these transfers and

[25] At this point it may be well to emphasize again that what I am calling means-end readiness or beliefs are really of two types. On the one hand, they have the general form $(s_1 r_1 \rightarrow s_2)$ and, on the other, they have the general form $(s_1 \rightarrow s_2)$. Perhaps the term "means-end readiness" is really appropriate only to the first type. But certainly the term "belief" is appropriate to both types. Given the first type of belief, the organism is ready to expect that, if an instance of s_1 is presented, a response of the r_1 type will lead to an instance of s_2. Given the second type of belief, the organism is ready to expect that, if an instance of s_1 be presented, then an instance of s_2 will either be simultaneous with the instances of s_1 or follow it relatively immediately.

interactions and their generalization are, I must admit, still very hazy.[26]

Let me sum up. A means-end readiness, as I conceive it, is a condition in the organism which is equivalent to what in ordinary parlance we call a "belief" (a readiness or disposition) to the effect that an instance of this *sort* of stimulus situation, if reacted to by an instance of this *sort* of response, will lead to an instance of that *sort* of further stimulus situation, or else, that an instance of this *sort* of stimulus situation will simply by itself be accompanied, or followed, by an instance of that *sort* of stimulus situation. Further, I assume that the different readinesses or beliefs (dispositions) are stored up together (in the nervous system). When they are concretely activated in the form of expectancies they tend to interact and/or consolidate with one another. And I would also assert that "thinking," as we know it in human beings, is in essence no more than an activated interplay among

[26] The difficulty of devising any really good or easy empirical pointer readings for means-end readinesses (beliefs) has, however, made me wonder at times whether this concept should not be abandoned. And actually in various recent discussions [87, 88] I have got along without it. The concept did, however, appear at some length in my original book [78]. If it were to be omitted, one could still perhaps get by with the concept of more general expectancies—these more general expectancies being a substitute for the concept of means-end readinesses—and this is what was actually done some years ago in a joint article with Krechevsky [90]. There is, however, a second feature in the original concept of the means-end readiness (belief), as contrasted with the concept of the expectancy, that I would like to preserve, namely, the notion that the means-end readiness (belief) is an enduring disposition, whereas the expectancy is a specific then-and-there activation (usually more specific though not necessarily so) of this disposition.

Furthermore, as a "cryptophenomenologist" it seems to me that a means-end readiness or a belief is phenomenologically a rather different thing from an expectancy. A belief is an "*if* this sort of thing, then that sort of thing." An expectancy, on the other hand, is a "*now* this concrete thing, therefore, that concrete thing." And this difference I would like to preserve and I would like to hope that eventually we can find really good and different sorts of pointer readings to parallel this difference.

Finally, it will be recalled that it was suggested above that means-end readinesses interact by telescoping or multiplying with one another, thus producing new ones which result in new expectancies and hence new performances. And it was also suggested that such interactions among means-end readinesses explain short-cutting, *Umweg,* insight, and reasoning. I would now like to modify these suggestions merely to the extent of emphasizing that it was also said that such interactions take place among *"activated means-end readinesses"* and it has now been emphasized that activated means-end readinesses are really expectancies. "Thinking," in short, is probably to be thought of as an interaction among expectancies which produce new expectancies. And then these new expectancies leave, as a deposit, corresponding new means-end readinesses. And it is these latter which are then in the organism's equipment for future occasions.

expectancies resulting from such previously acquired readinesses which result in new expectancies and resultant new means-end readinesses.[27]

Perceptions, expectancies, representations, and valences. Turn first to $\acute{S}_1$. This is the symbol for the "perception" of S_1*. What are the empirical pointer readings for such a perception? Apparently what in practice we actually do is to substitute, one by one, changes in the given stimulus situation to discover which of such changes do and which ones do not disrupt an established response. In this way we discover the precise range of physical S_1*'s which will be equivalent in the sense that any one within this given range will tend to produce the given behavior. The $\acute{S}_1$ is thus defined by this range of objectively defined S_1*'s which do not cause *disruption*. An $\acute{S}_1$ is, in short, a reevaluation by the experimenter of the physical S_1's in terms of what variations the latter can have and still produce the same response. In essence, it would seem that what we do is to perform the equivalent of a psychophysical experiment (save that instead of using verbal judgments we use the going off, or not going off, of some overt response as our indicator). A couple of concrete examples would be the experiments of Honzik [25, 26] with the 14-unit elevated **T** maze and an experiment of Ritchie's [71] with the elevated single **T** maze. Many more experiments of such types are, however, needed.

Further, we shall also need pointer readings for the additional feedback stimuli (behavior-supports) involved in an $\acute{S}_1$. Although **I** believe such feedback stimuli to be a most important feature of an $\acute{S}_1$, neither I nor anybody else seems to have done any good experiments

---

[27] In order to draw the teeth of possible critics I am ready to admit that this matter of pointer readings for intervening variables—the means-end readinesses (beliefs) and also the expectancies, the representations, the perceptions, and the valences to be discussed below—is the weakest part of my theory. I would like to suggest again, however, that the hypothetical little r_g's and s_g's of the Hullians are almost equally difficult of empirical verification. The experiment of Seward [73] which showed that a white box at the end of the maze must produce a little r_g and resultant proprioceptive s_g different from those produced by a black box seems to indicate that the hypothetical r_g's and resultant s_g's can no longer be thought of as peripheral motor and sensory processes but rather as more central processes. And, if this latter has to be admitted, why not stick to common sense and phenomenology and talk directly about "believed," "expected," "represented," and "perceived" entities for which, by using many behavioral experiments, we may hope eventually to get pointer readings. If we can't ever get adequate behavioral pointer readings, then, it seems to me, we shall have to give up and wait (and it may be a good long time) for our biochemical and neurophysiological friends to catch up and help us out. But I don't think that in the meantime "fake" peripheral constructs such as little r_g's and s_g's are going to help very much. (But this, no doubt, is a special prejudice of mine.)

with rats on this problem. They would have to be experiments in which the maze or other apparatus "looked" as if it would support such and such behaviors (provide appropriate feedback stimuli for) but in fact would not. It is to be noted that the experiments on visual illusions with human subjects initiated by Ames and expanded by Cantril and his associates [34] come closest to what I have in mind. What we want to do is to vary the actual geographical, mechanical, and gravitational features with their resultant feedback stimuli connected with a given "appearing" setup and see which variations in these resultant feedback stimuli would and which ones would not cause disruption of (make impossible) the initial response produced by $\acute{S}_1$.

Consider next $\acute{D}_{H_1}$. This, it will be remembered, is the symbol for the discriminative perception (not necessarily, or usually, conscious) of the hunger drive-stimulation. That is, it is the symbol for that range of drive-stimulations D_{H_1}'s (probably specifiable today only in terms of degrees of deprivation, see above) over which variations can be made without causing a disruption of the behavior. That is, there will be a range of the actual D_{H_1}'s which will all be reacted to as alike (i.e., not cause disruption) in the character and magnitude of the behavior. This range of D_{H_1}'s will define the $\acute{D}_{H_1}$.

With human beings we can do this perhaps fairly easily. We can discover those ranges of actual drive-stimulations (measured by hours of deprivation or what not) which will be reported as alike by the subject and those which will not. Again this would be like a psychophysical experiment.

I say here nothing about (and the chart does not include) $\acute{D}_{H_2}$'s. For, according to my analysis, the D_{H_2}'s, the terminal drive-stimulations, are not perceived, represented, or valenced. A better and more complete analysis, might someday have to include them. But I shall leave that for the future.

Next turn to the expectancies $[(\acute{S}_1\acute{R}_1 \rightarrow \acute{S}_m) \cdot (\acute{S}_1\acute{R}_1 \rightarrow \acute{S}_{\bar{m}})]$. Such expectancies, it is to be remembered, are not more than activated readinesses from the storehouse of readinesses plus the perception ($\acute{S}_1$) of the presence of an initial sign stimulus which fits into the category, s_1.

The question as to the empirical pointer readings for such expectancies can be answered, I believe, by varying the actual $(S_1R_1 \rightarrow S_m)$-type sequences in the physical and physiological worlds and discovering which ranges do and which do not allow the given behavior to go off undisrupted. Again we need psychophysical sorts of experiments. But this time ones re external and internal environmental *sequences* and not merely re the individual items in these sequences.

Finally, we have to consider the problem of pointer readings for the represented and valenced $\acute{S}_m{}^+$ and $\acute{S}_{\bar{m}}{}^-$. The discriminated (effective) $\dot{D}_{H_1}$ leads to a positive valence on the "represented" $\dot{S}_m$ and a negative valence on the "represented" $\dot{S}_{\bar{m}}$. How do we get pointer readings for these expected stimuli with their "expected" values (i.e., their valences)?

Miller and his associates, as we saw above, indicated a way of specifying both the characters and the positive valences by determining how much more milk rats of a given deprivation (D_{H_1}) would drink when a given $\dot{S}_m$ has been artificially provided (by blowing up the stomach, by putting actual milk into the stomach, or by putting it into the mouth). And in this way it was discovered in a rough way what internal stimuli served as goals and how strong their respective positive valences were.

But many more experiments need to be done with different values of D_{H_1}. (Miller and associates used only one value of D_{H_1}—very carefully controlled in terms of time of test since previous feeding or since preceding injection and also by careful control of daily caloric intake.)

Finally, the pointer reading for the dependent variable $(R_1{}^*)$ is merely some agreed-upon objective observation of whether the rat actually goes down the alley, crosses a certain mark with his tail, or what not.

Summary re pointer readings. Let me briefly sum up what has been said concerning empirical definitions (pointer readings). Most of the independent and the dependent variables are to be specified by agreed-upon statements as to what external or internal environmental events (i.e., Σs, S_1s, R_1s, S_2s, S_ms, etc.) are or are not, have or have not been, present. In the case of drive states (D_{H_1}s and D_{H_2}s) the pointer readings are less clear. At present we have to satisfy ourselves with such measures as hours of deprivation, percentage losses in body weight, or approach and/or eating tendencies to food in general in some agreed-upon "standard situation" such as the Skinner box.

Means-end readinesses (beliefs) are to be got at by *transfer experiments*. But it must be admitted that precise pointer readings for them have not yet been achieved.

Perceptions, expectancies, and representations are to be got at by *disruption experiments* carried out relative to each specific concrete setup. In essence these disruption experiments would be psychophysical types of experiments. But again it must be admitted that the ground has only been scratched as far as getting precise pointer readings is concerned. Positive and negative valences are also measured by disruption experiments in which goal stimuli with various "values" are provided artificially to see to what extent these do or do not modify the original behavior. Again only a beginning in the direction of the necessary studies has been made.

In the above discussion of pointer readings I have slid over the problem of rs and Rs. The rs and $\bar{r}$s in the means-end readinesses and the $\dot{R}$s and the $\check{R}$s in the expectancies must also be got at by pointer readings. We must know what r_1s or $\bar{r}_1$s the organism brings, as readinesses, to the given situation and what concrete instances of these rs and $\bar{r}$s (i.e., $\dot{R}$s and not $\check{R}$s) are activated by the concrete presentation of $\dot{S}_1$.

Also it must be noted that the rs and $\bar{r}$s and the $\dot{R}$s and $\check{R}$s have a further aspect, in addition to their mere qualitative identifying characteristics. This further aspect is their *work* or *uncertainty* characteristics (see above). The organism brings not only a belief that a given type of r or $\bar{r}$ will get him to a given type of s_2 and has not only an expectancy that a concrete instance ($\dot{R}$ or $\check{R}$) of such an r or $\bar{r}$ will in the given situation get him to a concrete $\dot{S}_2$, but he also believes and expects that given specific amounts of work or effort will be involved. For, as has been indicated, I further assume that accompanying any major drive-stimulation there is always also a drive-stimulation against work. As a result of this drive-stimulation against work there will be negative valences on the $\dot{R}$s and $\check{R}$s contained in the expectancies. For the chart really to have been complete a $D_{W_1}{}^*$ and a $\dot{D}_{W_1}$ (drive against work) should have been added and negative valences should also have been added to these represented $\dot{R}$s and $\check{R}$s. I have left all these out because it would have made the chart too complicated. I have also left them out, I expect, because I do not know how to get good pointer readings for these work features and their accompanying valences and have not really thought the problem through.

So much for the discussion of a case of simple approach to food when the animal is hungry. Let us turn now to a case of simple escape.

A case of escape. Figure 2 represents the case for a simple instance of escape. The complex symbol

$$\Sigma\{[D_{F_1}][(S_1 \to S_p{}^-) \cdot (S_1 R_1 \to S_2) \cdot (S_2 \to S_{\bar{p}}{}^+)] \to [D_{F_2}]\}$$

stands for the frequencies, recencies, and distribution of previous trials in the given situation (or in some similar situation) in which, under an initial fear drive-stimulation, i.e., a degree of "fearfulness" or "timidity," D_{F_1}, a stimulus situation S_1 has led to, or been accompanied by, a negatively valued pain stimulus $S_p{}^-$; and a manipulatory response R_1 to this S_1 has led to a new stimulus situation S_2; and this new stimulus situation S_2 has led to (or been accompanied by) a positively valued nonpain stimulus $S_{\bar{p}}{}^+$; and the whole experience has resulted in some new degree of fearfulness D_{F_2}, which may have been greater than, less than, or equal to the original fearfulness D_{F_1}.

In the usual rat experiment the S_1 is, of course, a box with an electrified grid on the floor. The S_p^- is the resulting pain stimulus from the grid. The R_1 is the response (performance) of jumping off, running off, pressing a treadle, or whatever. And the S_2 is another adjacent box or another part of the same box with no grid in it, or, in the case of the treadle, it may be the same box and grid but now with the treadle down.

Look next at the symbols for the means-end readinesses (beliefs) which I assume to have got established as a result of such previous trials. These means-end readinesses or beliefs are represented by the

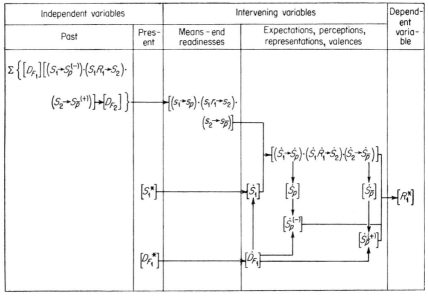

Independent variables		Intervening variables		Dependent variable
Past	Present	Means–end readinesses	Expectations, perceptions, representations, valences	

FIG. 2. Escape

symbol $[(s_1 \rightarrow s_p) \cdot (s_1 r_1 \rightarrow s_2) \cdot (s_2 \rightarrow s_{\bar{p}})]$. They are acquired generalized readinesses to the effect that a given type of situation s_1, if presented, leads to (is accompanied by) a pain type of situation s_p; and that an r_1 type of response to this s_1 will lead to a new external type of stimulus situation s_2; and that this latter will lead to (or be accompanied by) a nonpain type of stimulus situation $s_{\bar{p}}$.

Look back now at the independent variables (in the second column)—those assumed to be "present" at the beginning of the given trial. These are represented by the symbols $S_1{}^*$ and $D_{F_1}{}^* \cdot S_1{}^*$ stands for the box with the grid as it is presented to the rat on the given trial. And $D_{F_1}{}^*$ stands for the degree of timidity (fearfulness) which the animal brings to this trial.

Consider next the second column of intervening variables. We see that the external stimulus of the box and grid S_1^* is conceived to lead to a perception of itself $\acute{S}_1$, and that the independently measured fearfulness, or timidity, is conceived to lead to a discriminated ("perceived") effective fearfulness $\acute{D}_{F_1}$. The diagram also indicated that $\acute{D}_{F_1}$ may affect the perception $\acute{S}_1$. Again we see that $\acute{S}_1$, combined with the readinesses produced by the preceding trials, is assumed to produce, on the given trial, a set of concrete expectancies as follows: that the perceived $\acute{S}_1$ will lead to, or be accompanied by, an expected pain stimulus $\acute{S}_p$; and that the response $\acute{R}_1$ to the perceived stimulus $\acute{S}_1$ is expected to lead to a different stimulus situation $\acute{S}_2$; and that this latter will be accompanied by a nonpain stimulus situation $\acute{S}_{\bar{p}}$. Finally, it appears that the represented $\acute{S}_p$ combined with the perceived timidity $\acute{D}_{F_1}$ on the given trial will cause a negative valence on $\acute{S}_p$ (that is, $\acute{S}_p^-$); and that this $\acute{D}_{F_1}$ combined with the represented $\acute{S}_{\bar{p}}$ will also cause a positive valence on $\acute{S}_{\bar{p}}$ (that is, $\acute{S}_{\bar{p}}^+$).

Finally, we see that the expectancy complex (with its included representations and their attached valences) is assumed to determine the strength of the independent variable R_1^*—the actual tendency to jump off, to press the lever, or whatever it may be.[28]

Empirical pointer readings. The methods of getting empirical pointer readings for these variables will be much the same as it was in the approach case.

Independent and dependent variables. Σ will be measured by timings and countings. D_{F_1} and D_{F_2} will be determined by some measure of the standard fear response in a standard situation. And the various Ss and Rs will be specified by common-sense physics or, in the case of S_p, by some as yet perhaps very largely hypothetical physiology.

Intervening variables. The readinesses caused by the previous trials or other previous training $(s_1 \rightarrow s_p)$ and $(s_1 r_1 \rightarrow s_2)$ and $(s_2 \rightarrow s_{\bar{p}})$ will be determined by transfer experiments. And the expectancies, perceptions, representations, and valences on the given trial will be determined by disruption experiments in the given apparatus for the given trial. All this will certainly be a difficult job. But this does not, I believe, invalidate the conceptual and experimental suggestiveness of such constructs.

A case of avoidance. Let us turn now to a case of simple avoidance learning, as diagrammed in Fig. 3. In the column for "past" independent variables we find the complex symbol:

$$\Sigma\{[D_{F_1}][(S_1 R_1 \rightarrow S_2) \cdot (S_2 \rightarrow S_p{}^-) \cdot (S_1 \bar{R}_1 \rightarrow S_{\bar{p}}{}^+)] \rightarrow [D_{F_2}]\}$$

This differs from that for the setup for escape in that here the animal is not presented with pain S_p in the presence of S_1. But, if he makes a

---

[28] Again a negative work valence on $\acute{R}_1$ should have been included.

response R_1 to S_1 this leads him to S_2 and then this S_2 will bring about, willy nilly, a negative pain stimulus S_p^{-}. Or, concretely, in the usual experiment the rat is placed in a box or alley in which he does not get a shock *unless* he makes some specified response R_1, unless, that is, he steps into another compartment, or presses a lever or goes in a certain direction, or the like. Such an R_1 leads to S_2 (a new stimulus situation). But getting to this S_2 means that a shock is encountered, that is, a pain stimulus, S_p. If the rat does *not do* R_1 (i.e., if he does anything which may be labeled $\bar{R}_1$), then he remains in the presence of nonpain $S_{\bar{p}}$.

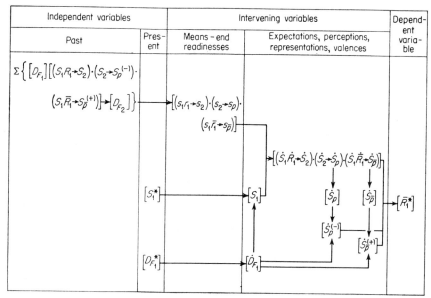

Fig. 3. Avoidance

The rest of the diagram follows in the same manner as in Figs. 1 and 2 and needs no special comment. The one distinctive feature of this avoidance case is that the dependent variable measured now is the degree to which the animal does *not* do R_1—in other words, the magnitude of $\bar{R}_1{}^*$.[29]

Empirical pointer readings will present similar and equally difficult problems as in the cases of approach and escape. But I will not attempt to spell them out.

Choice-point learning. Let us consider now the very common type of setup, that of a maze or discrimination box, in which the rats are faced, not with the alternative of *merely doing something* or *not doing it*,

[29] Here, also, there will be negative valences on the amounts of work involved in $\dot{R}_1$ or $\dot{\bar{R}}_1$.

but rather with the alternative of doing one or another of two different things. The single **T** maze or **Y** maze or the simple discrimination box are examples. The analysis for such cases is presented in Fig. 4.

The really distinctive difference between this figure and the three previous ones is that here, in Fig. 4, the alternative character of the two responses R_1 and R_1' is emphasized and also the fact that these two responses lead to two alternative consequences (S_2 and S_2'), one of which then leads to a positive goal stimulus ($S_m{}^+$) and the other to a

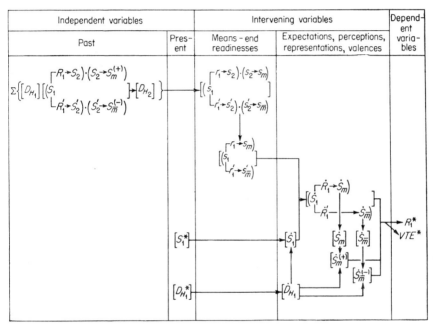

FIG. 4. Choice-point learning

negative nongoal stimulus $S_{\bar{m}}{}^-$. This has the further consequence that in observing the final behavior the experimenter records not only the proportion of R_1 responses but also the gradually decreasing proportion of R_1' responses. And at certain definite stages of learning the experimenter may also observe and record tentative oscillations between the two (i.e., vicarious trial and error, VTE).

Of course, it might have been equally appropriate in the three previous figures to have indicated the alternativeness between R_1 and $\bar{R}_1$. But such experiments are usually set up so that $\bar{R}_1$ is not a clearly identifiable entity. It may be anything different from R_1 such as running to the other end of the box, cleaning the whiskers, or it may be merely sitting still. Therefore, the three previous charts seem a more appropriate depiction of the facts as we now have them. In the future, however, experiments may perhaps be carried out in which the $\bar{R}$'s can be given more precise experimental specification. If this latter proves the case, figures more similar to Fig. 4 will also become appropriate for the three previous cases.

Figure 4 as a whole follows the same principles as the previous ones and needs no new special comment. And the problems of the empirical pointer readings will also be much the same.

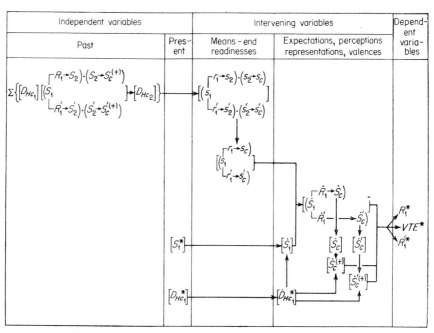

FIG. 5. Early in learning—first period in latent learning

Early in learning and latent and incidental learning. I shall turn now to an analysis of the situation in which again two alternative responses occur but in which either one, at the time in question, is equally "good." This would be the situation early in learning of a **T** maze or in the "first phase" of the Blodgett type of latent learning experiment [6]. This situation is represented in Fig. 5.

The essential difference between this case and that diagramed in Fig. 4 must be made clear. In Fig. 4 the situation was one in which there had been a sufficient number of trials so that the respective good and bad consequences (valences) resulting from the two alternative responses had had a chance to develop and to combine with the expectancies to make the one response more probable than the other. In

Fig. 5 the situation is one in which both alternative consequences are, to all intents and purposes, equally good. Either the rats have not yet learned that there is a difference between the two outcomes or, as in the first phase of the latent or incidental learning experiment, actually there is no difference between the two outcomes.

The distinctive new assumption which now has to be added and which is represented in Fig. 5 is the assumption that any main drive such as hunger will also have associated with it an auxiliary cognitive or curiosity drive (see footnote 8), represented by symbolizing the initial drive-stimulation as $D_{H_{c_1}}$ where the "c" indicates the curiosity drive. And also in line with this same assumption I have symbolized the goal stimuli as S_c^+. I have assumed, in short, that any drive-stimulation such as hungriness (or fearfulness) has to some degree a pure cognitive or "curiosity" drive-stimulation associated with it. This latter has its own goal—namely, some characteristic pattern of external and/or internal stimuli, whatever it may be, which results from examining. And as long as the presence of the specific goal for the main drive is not present (as in the first phase of the Blodgett type of latent learning experiment) or is not "remembered" as in the early trials of the usual maze, then the animals get "rewarded" curiosity-wise by all the alternative paths, and the animals take them approximately 50:50.

In later trials (or after food has been introduced as in the Blodgett-type experiment) then the valences S_m^+ and the $S_{\overline{m}}^-$ corresponding to hunger far outweigh the mere curiosity valences S_c^+. And hence the response of going in the food direction comes to dominate. That is to say, then Fig. 4 will again more truly depict the situation.

Summary of the five learning paradigms. This ends my analysis of the common types of setup in rat learning experiments. I have presented five paradigms for such experiments and I have indicated the variables which seem to be involved according to my system in each paradigm. And I have suggested procedures for obtaining pointer readings. There are, however, a number of very basic questions raised by my system which have not yet been answered. The most obvious question is: What do I conceive to be the quantitative laws of learning; what are the relative importances of frequency, recency, and distribution, on the one hand, and of "effect" (reinforcement) on the other; what, then, do I consider to be the laws of learning?[30]

---

[30] This may be as good a place as any to emphasize my very real indebtedness to MacCorquodale and Meehl [50] for their analysis of my expectancy theory of learning. I have borrowed a number of their concepts, although they may well not recognize them as such. For example, I believe that my present introduction of the $(s_1 \rightarrow s_2)$ type of means-end readiness and of the $(\dot{S}_1 \rightarrow \dot{S}_2)$ type of expectancy is

Laws of learning. Learning, as has been indicated, is conceived by me as the acquisition of $(s_1r_1 \rightarrow s_2)$ connections or of $(s_1 \rightarrow s_2)$ connections. Such connections I have called means-end readinesses or beliefs. It is the nature of the laws determining the acquisition of such readinesses or beliefs which we are now to consider.[31]

What are the conditions under which such beliefs are formed and strengthened? For the purposes of this discussion I shall consider only cases of 100 per cent original reinforcement (see footnote 31). This seems to be the type of case which most theorists have had in mind when they constructed their theories of learning. And it certainly was the one I had in mind when I constructed mine.[32]

In general there are two main classes of conditions which have been advanced. These may be roughly identified with Thorndike's

closely related to their Postulate 4 [50, p. 242]. And previous to their discussion I had never clearly seen that when, for example, I talked about "equivalence beliefs" I was really talking about $(S_1 \rightarrow S_2)$ learning.

It was they also, I believe, who revivified my belief that mine is *mostly* an $(S_1R_1 \rightarrow S_2)$ type of theory and not, as Spence [75] suggested, primarily an $(S_1 \rightarrow S_2)$ type of theory. However, as I have just said, I do now also include purely $(S_1 \rightarrow S_2)$ types of learning.

[31] It must be noted again in passing that beliefs or readinesses seem to have two kinds of strengths. Thus, a belief may have strength because it holds that the s_2 type of stimulus will follow the s_1 type of stimulus in a high percentage of instances. Or a belief may have strength (even though the expected frequency of the s_2 consequence is low), in the sense that it is held to very strongly. This latter is, I suspect, the type of strength of belief we usually think of.

It should be noted further that there may be some form of interaction between these two types of strengths. Thus, if we measure strength by a number of trials to extinction (the usual procedure), then in a setup in which, during learning, the S_2 has followed in less than 100 per cent of the trials (i.e., partial reinforcement) we know that a weak belief in the first sense (i.e., a lowish probability of s_2) would seem to produce a strong belief in the second sense. For it will take more trials to extinguish than will a belief established in a setup in which during learning there had been 100 per cent reinforcement. But it may well be that a fairer procedure would be to take as our measuring unit, in extinction, not single trials but the number of trials which constituted a cycle in the original learning. If, for example, S_2 followed in the original learning in 25 per cent of the trials in every cycle of four trials, whereas in a comparable group it followed on every trial, then perhaps a fairer comparison would be between the number of four-trial blocks necessary for extinction in the partial reinforcement case as against the number of single-trial blocks necessary for extinction in the 100 per cent reinforcement case.

[32] Actually, however, I believe our theories and our experimental designs for testing our theories of learning will need many revisions when we have allowed ourselves really to go to town on all the implications of partial reinforcement situations or, as Brunswik would have phrased it, when we have really accepted the essentially "probabilistic" character [10, 89] of the environmental relations relative to which the organism usually learns.

laws of "Exercise" and of "Effect." Under "Exercise" I should put all the factors of frequency, recency, and distributions of trials summarized by the symbol Σ in the charts. And under "Effect" I should put such factors as the magnitudes and characters of the final values (e.g., the $S_m{}^+$'s and the $S_p{}^-$'s and the $S_c{}^+$'s) and/or the terminal drive-stimulations (the D_2's).

We now all agree in a general way as to how "exercise" (i.e., frequency, recency, and distribution of trials) affect learning. But there still seems to be considerable disagreement as to the nature and importance of "effects." My own position in the past was that exercise factors determine the results almost exclusively. And it was, of course, the latent learning experiments [77] (in those cases in which latent learning was demonstrated) which gave me this bias. Recently, however, the findings of Postman and Adams [69, 70] on incidental learning in human subjects, together with further thinking about those negative cases with rats in which latent learning has not been found, have led me now to believe that "effect," in the sense of final positive or negative values attached to the terminal stimuli, does also always play some part in favoring the acquisition of beliefs.

It will be recalled that in Fig. 5, and in the discussion following it, I had to assume that during the latent (or incidental) learning periods there must be invoked a subsidiary curiosity (examining) drive which gives positive valences to all parts of the maze and especially to the terminal goal boxes and blind ends (even though no biological goal objects were then to be found in these latter).[33] Thus, even though in the latent learning period of a latent learning experiment the rat finds no positive biological goal in the goal box, he does find positive goals for curiosity $S_c{}^+$'s in both goal boxes and blind ends. Thus I would now tend to accept the Law of Effect in so far as I now believe that these positive goals for curiosity at the ends of both true path segments and blind ends do aid the acquisition of the beliefs as to the $(s_1 r_1 \rightarrow s_2)$ or $(s_1 \rightarrow s_2)$ connections leading to such goal boxes and blind ends. Note, however, that these effects, according to me, favor the learning of what leads to the blind ends just as truly as they favor the learning of what leads to the goal box.[34]

Further, my contention would be that a biologically bad effect (e.g., a shock or $S_p{}^-$) will be just as good and probably in some cases a more favorable condition for learning an $(s_1 r_1 \rightarrow s_p)$ or an $(s_1 \rightarrow s_p)$

[33] A recent article by Desiderato [14] has demonstrated that maintenance conditions, which may be thought to favor the strength of a sort of exploratory (curiosity) drive, do increase latent learning.

[34] Herb's latent learning experiment [24] seemed to bear out this notion that in the latent period the rats also learn which responses lead to the blind ends.

than will be a biologically good effect (e.g., an $S_m{}^+$) for learning an $(s_1 r_1 \rightarrow s_m)$ or an $(s_1 \rightarrow s_m)$.

A related question also arises. When there is a strong biological goal (positive or negative) at one end of a choice, how much do the rats learn, not only where this positive (or negative) goal is, but also what is at the end of the other choice? In all the figures, I have allowed for both types of beliefs becoming established. But was this right? I know of no adequate experiments which answer the question. The Hullians seem to hold that rats learn only the one response, that leading to a positive goal, because it is the latter which is followed by "need reduction." Thus Mowrer [58] and Miller [52] and now many others seem to assume that in escape and avoidance learning the only thing which is learned is the response which leads to nonshock (or security) because this is followed by need-reduction of the "conditioned anxiety." But in my terms rats may learn not only what to get to but also what to get from. My hunch, nevertheless, would be that in most escape or avoidance learning the rat may well learn primarily how to get away from or avoid an $S_p{}^-$, and only in some special setups and under special conditions will he also be learning how to get a specific complementary $S_{\bar{p}}{}^+$.

Finally, however, in any case I do not believe that the rat (or the man) learns because *after each trial* the need (be it conditioned anxiety, a hunger, a thirst, a sex drive, a curiosity drive, or whatever) is reduced. An animal is not learning to get to need-reduction. The "effects" which favor learning (in so far as they do) are not those of need-reduction, because a need may often not be reduced but enhanced. These effects are rather the mere positive or negative values of the terminal goal stimuli, simply as such.[35]

We must note now another quite obvious determiner of the acquisition of beliefs, viz., that of the time intervals involved in $(S_1 R_1 \rightarrow S_2)$ or in $(S_1 \rightarrow S_2)$ setups. These time factors might perhaps have been included under "Exercise." In any event, it is now usually accepted that, generally speaking, the shorter the time intervals involved in $(S_1 R_1 \rightarrow S_2)$ or in $(S_1 \rightarrow S_2)$ setups, the faster the learning.

Still another feature about learning, as I conceive the latter, should perhaps again be emphasized. In asserting that learning is primarily the acquisition of connections of the type $(s_1 r_1 \rightarrow s_2)$ and/or $(s_1 \rightarrow s_2)$ I have asserted that these s's and r's are generalized entities. An s_1, an s_2, an s_3, an s_f, an s_p, an $s_{\bar{p}}$, and an s_m, an $s_{\bar{m}}$, or an s_c each has some spread along its own dimension of generalization. The presentation of a cor-

[35] Or, as suggested by the recent exciting work of Olds and associates [63, 64, 65] and of Delgado and Miller and associates [12, 13], the final "effects" may be specific resultant neural excitations in specific parts of the brain.

responding S within such a spread will, to varying degrees depending upon the shape of the corresponding generalization curve, be accepted by the organism as an instance of the given type of s. Also, when the organism has acquired a means-end readiness of the type $(s_1r_1 \rightarrow s_2)$ there will also be some spread of specific R's any one of which will, to some degree, be accepted as instance of the learned r. These problems of generalization are, as we all know, among the most difficult and yet most important of the empirical problems which we still have before us. And I shall have nothing very final to say about them.

Such generalizations have been investigated perhaps most often in setups for classical conditioning. (Classical conditioning—along with the learning of nonsense syllable pairs—falls for me as the reader will, I hope, have guessed under the rubric of $(s_1 \rightarrow s_2)$ learning.)[36] But even here no simple laws have been found. Early in conditioning the generalization spread of s_1 seems to be broad. But later it becomes more narrow. And in some stages of learning even a stimulus along a totally different physical dimension will sometimes evoke the conditioned response. Thus, if the animal has been conditioned to salivate to a sudden bright light, it may be found that at some stages of the learning he will also salivate to a sudden buzzer.

Also, in the case of instrumental $(s_1r_1 \rightarrow s_2)$ learning, cases of spread from one physical dimension to a stimulus in quite another physical dimension were demonstrated in monkeys by the early and important experiments of Klüver [37].

Work has also been done on generalization in discrimination experiments with rats. Rats which have been taught to discriminate white and black (i.e., have learned to accept white as the s_1 which, when jumped to r_1, leads to getting to the food platform s_2 and to accept black as the s_1' which, when jumped to r_1', leads to a locked door s_2', will sometimes with practically no further training discriminate a light gray door from a dark gray door—see, for example, [91]. But here, also, much more work needs to be done to arrive at truly general principles.[37]

[36] Thus, for example, in simple salivary conditioning, S_1 is the conditioned stimulus (light, buzzer, or whatever) and S_2 is the unconditioned stimulus, food. Or in nonsense learning an S_1 is the first syllable of any pair and S_2 is the subsequent syllable.

[37] Haire [21] has recently done some human experiments which seem to indicate that the continua along which perceptual discriminations generalize eventually have to be defined in "phenomenological" terms if any real sense is to be made out of the results.

Further, it is to be noted that below, under the heading of "Principles of performance," what I have really done is to suggest a specific theoretical concept as to the laws of S_1 generalizations.

Again, almost no work has been done on the generalization of responses (performances) (i.e., what range of R's will, to a greater or lesser extent, be accepted as instances of r_1). If the rats have been taught, for example, the response r_1 of "going towards the light," how far will this "going towards the light" spread to going slightly to one side of the light? Or, if they have learned to make a right-angled right-hand turn r_1, what range of other right turns (acute or obtuse) will this spread to? We really don't know. And, finally, practically nothing seems to have been done on s_2 generalizations.

To sum up: I believe that in the learning of connections of the type $(s_1r_1 \rightarrow s_2)$ or $(s_1 \rightarrow s_2)$, exercise is more important than effect. I do believe, however, that effect, in the sense of final positively or negatively valued goal stimuli and not in the sense of need-reduction, always does play some part (even if these positive goal stimuli are only those that result from cognitive exploration). Finally, however, the influence of effect is perhaps especially important in simple $(s_1 \rightarrow s_2)$ learning, where s_1 is, say, a shock-box and s_2 is the resulting pain stimulus.[38] I also believe that the time relationships are very important. And finally, I assert that the s's and r's involved represent generalization gradients and not single values.

There are still a few other points to be considered. In various earlier writings [78, 84, 85] I have invoked a phenomenon of "fixation."[39] What I referred to by this term was the fact that under some conditions —such as those of extreme overlearning, damaged brain, overintense motivation or a conflict situation—the beliefs acquired seem to become *unduly* resistant to extinction. That is, even though the goal, the S_2, was removed, the animals kept on responding, as if it were present, for an unduly long time. In short, what the rats ended up with seemed relatively automatic and not much like a "belief." So I called them fixations, rigid "cognitive maps" [85]. At the present time, however, I feel that this sharp distinction between a supposed means-end readiness or belief, on the one hand, and a supposed fixation, on the other, was probably a mistake. Some means-end readinesses (beliefs) of either the type $(s_1r_1 \rightarrow s_2)$ or $(s_1 \rightarrow s_2)$ can be thought of as becoming unduly resistant to extinction and as taking a lot of negative evidence (extinction trials) to break them down. But there seems to be no sharp line between such overfixated beliefs and the more easily changeable

---

[38] This type of $s_1 \rightarrow s_2$ learning I have in another place [84] called the acquisition of "equivalence beliefs." Recently Spence [76] has also agreed that "effect" may perhaps be primarily important in this latter $(s_1 \rightarrow s_2)$ type of learning.

[39] For an early experiment on overlearning as a cause of fixation see Krechevsky and Honzik [40].

ones. The differences should, therefore, I believe, be thought of as ones of degree and not ones of kind.

Still another point. It must be noted that I have proposed no quantitative laws of learning other than "more" and "less." I have not attempted to write equations, draw curves, or establish constants. It has seemed to me obvious that the precise equations, the shapes of the curves, the constants, would all be influenced by the specific features of the given apparatus and the specific training procedures from which they were obtained. Hence they will have little generality. I do, of course, however, subscribe to the now well-substantiated fact that, in general, learning curves are negatively accelerated and that they tend to reach asymptotes.

Let us turn now to the problem of "secondary reinforcement." My feeling is that this at present *ad hoc* concept is pointing towards some set of facts which is very important but about which we have as yet very little real empirical understanding. A "secondary reinforcement" I would think of as merely a "subgoal" on the way toward some more final goal. And this subgoal has acquired, at least temporarily, a positive goal value. Thus, if a chain such as $(S_1R_1 \rightarrow S_2) \cdot (S_2R_2 \rightarrow S_3) \cdot (S_3R_3 \rightarrow S_f) \cdot (S_fR_f \rightarrow S_m^+)$ has often been repeated, then under certain conditions (which no one has yet clearly specified) one or more of the subterminal S's seem to take on, at least temporarily, positive value. For example, S_f (the food) may acquire such temporary value; or S_3 (the goal box) may acquire it; or S_2 (a poker chip) as in the Cowles experiments [11] or in the Lambert, Solomon, and Watson experiment [41] may acquire it. Then the sequence of behavior would read $(S_1R_1 \rightarrow S_2^+) \cdot (S_2R_2 \rightarrow S_3^+) \cdot S_3R_3 \rightarrow S_f^+) \cdot (S_fR_f \rightarrow S_m^+)$, with positive values on S_2, S_3, and S_f as well as on S_m—such values decreasing in magnitude from right to left. But, if I am not mistaken, this has been demonstrated only when the initial hunger stimulation D_{H_1} continues to be present. The rat or chimpanzee (or child) will, provided it is hungry, continue for some time to go to food S_f, even though prevented from eating, or to the goal box or vending machine S_3, even though food no longer be present in it. And the chimpanzee or the child will continue to pick up poker chip tokens S_2's and do things to get the latter, provided it is still hungry, even though it can no longer use them in the vending machine for food or candy. But there is no clear evidence as yet that the animals will do these things when hunger is no longer present. That is, as yet there seems to be no good evidence that such subgoals get set up in their own right. Or, in other words, there is no good evidence that there develop real independent second-order drives relative to these types of subgoals. We have no certain proof that rats or chimpanzees or children come permanently to love poker chips when they are no longer subgoals to food or candy.[40]

Yet, it still seems probable that at least adult human beings have developed second-order drives. It does seem as if Allport's concept of "functional autonomy" [1] does hold for them. For most of the good present-day work on the psychology of human motivation has had to assume and seems more or less successfully to have demonstrated that human beings do have second-order drives.[41] So I am strongly in favor of further experimentation along these lines. But at present I am rather troubled at the loose and *ad hoc* invocation of "secondary reinforcement" (or, in my own language, of "subgoals") whenever one finds it convenient to do so.

So much for a review of my notions of learning. Let me turn now to a brief analysis of the notions as to motivation which are involved in the system.

Motivation. In introducing D_1s into the figures I was influenced by two considerations. The first was my belief that animals respond only when energized. Only when hungry or fearful or sexually aroused or curious (exploratorily inclined) or whatever, do animals and human beings *perceive* and *behave* and hence have a chance to learn. The second was my belief that only if animals are thus energized (motivated) in some specific way, do the goal stimuli such as $S_m{}^+$, $S_{\bar{m}}{}^-$, $S_p{}^-$, $S_{\bar{p}}{}^+$, and $S_c{}^+$ have positive or negative values and hence lead to expected valences and bring about actual performances. Thus, as I pointed out earlier, the diagrams really ought to have included causal arrows from the D_1s to the pluses and minuses on the goal stimuli. (I left these arrows out simply in order to make the drawings less complicated.)

In introducing D_2s I also wanted to allow for the fact of need-reductions or of possible need-enhancements as a result of reaching the final positive or negative goal stimuli. However, as has been indicated, I hold to the view that, in so far as "effect" does favor learning, this "effect" is not the changes in the drive-stimulation per se but rather the mere final presences or absences of certain types of terminal stimuli. It is the positive or negative values on these stimuli (e.g., taste, stomach, and nutritional stimuli in the case of hungriness, pain stimuli in the case of fearfulness, and some sort of as yet unspecifiable stimuli in the case of cognitive exploration or curiosity) which

---

[40] There is, however, a little evidence in one experiment by MacCorquodale and Meehl [49] that rats tend to go more to a food and water box than to an empty box even when satiated for both food and water. This could, however, be explained by me by the greater exploratory (curiosity) opportunities provided by a baited box.

[41] Consider, for example, McClelland's need "achievement" [46].

are the ultimately positive or negative goals or "reinforcers." And, motivationally speaking, it is these which the animal wants or does not want. He runs the maze to get to them and escapes or avoids the electric grid to get from them.[42] He does not, I am asserting, run the maze to lower his hungriness or his curiosity nor jump off the grid to lower his fearfulness.

It must be pointed out also, however, that in the cases of positive appetites (e.g., hunger, thirst, sex, etc.) it may well be that when these become intense there undoubtedly arise simultaneous pains. To get away from these pains may then be added to the drive to get to the positive goal stimuli. For example, in the case of food hunger the animal may be not merely seeking the "pleasant" mouth, stomach, and nutritional stimuli but also seeking to escape the "pain" of the hunger pangs. To discover operationally how much he is seeking the positive goal stimuli and how much he is avoiding the negative pain stimuli will undoubtedly prove a difficult task. It may be that at the behavioral level we can discover no distinguishing criteria, although I would not be sure of this. But eventually with increasing neurophysiological techniques one ought to be able in the end to specify how much he is doing the one and how much the other. Furthermore, it must be pointed out that, in so far as there be such an initiating pain, the symbol for the complex of independent variables in, say, the case of hunger would have to be expanded to read as follows:

$$\Sigma\{[D_{H_1}][(S_p{}^-) \cdot (S_1 R_1 \rightarrow S_f) \cdot (S_f R_{\bar{f}} \rightarrow S_m{}^+) \cdot (S_1 \bar{R}_1 \rightarrow S_{\bar{f}}) \cdot (S_{\bar{f}} \rightarrow S_{\bar{m}}) \cdot$$
$$(S_m{}^+ \rightarrow S_{\bar{p}}{}^+)] \rightarrow [D_{H_2}]\}$$

And similar expansions would also have to be made in the expressions for the intervening variables in the means-end readinesses column and in the column for expectancies, perceptions, representations, and valences.

Finally, it must be pointed out that I have taken no stand on the number and types of drive-stimulations. I assume some basic biological drives, such as hunger, thirst, sex, and fear, and I have added curiosity or exploratoriness. These are the ones I have used in the figures. But there may be "higher" drives such as, say, the drive for "self-realization" which Maslow [51] and others have argued for, and there may be acquired second-order and third-order drives, such as the drive for wealth, the drive for achievement, the drive for prestige, the drive for a particular bit of property, etc., etc. Assuming that there be such higher- and second-order (and perhaps even third-order) drives, I would have to assert that two features must hold for each of them.

[42] Or, as suggested in footnote 35, he runs to get to or to escape from or to avoid certain correlated and resultant neural excitations in the brain.

First, there must be certain defining (and ultimately characterizable) patterns of external and/or internal stimuli which constitute the defining positive and/or negative goals for each of them. And, secondly, there must also be assumed that for each such drive there must be an ultimately discoverable correlated neurophysiological condition—see again [72]. Thus the question of the kinds and numbers of such drives will ultimately require both further behavioral and further neurophysiological investigations.

Furthermore, it may be pointed out, however, that in the meantime psychologists do seem to have arrived already at a good many humanly important facts by assuming such secondary drives, even though these latter cannot be rigidly identified. For, given the postulation of these drives, psychologists have studied with fruitfulness and success such processes as: satiation and aspiration-level [44]; the relative weights of such secondary drives in different personality structures [62, 45]; and the differences between the hidden and manifest strengths of these drives in different personality types [16].

Let me turn now in conclusion to a last feature of my system which has not yet been adequately touched upon and which must be explicated if the system is to hold water. It has to do with what I would call the "principles of performance."

Principles of performance. There are three questions to be asked: (1) what are the laws or principles governing the intersubstitutability of motor skills; (2) what is the nature of the function by which the magnitude of the performance of a single approach, escape, or avoidance is to be predicted; (3) how do two or more simultaneously aroused performances interact to produce some new or compromise performance?

1. The first question, that of motor skills, has already been touched upon. And I am capable of no proper answer to it. Concrete instances of the question would be as follows: why is it that a rat which has learned to run a maze can then, with practically no upset, swim it or vice versa [47]? Or why is it that a rat which has learned to jump over a gap to choose a correct door will then, with very little upset, run across this gap correctly (if connecting paths be introduced)? (Actually, I believe, this latter experiment has not been done but we can be relatively certain of its outcome.) Or why is it that a rat in a Skinner box can interchangeably press the lever with left paw, right paw, or head?[43] Or why is it that those of the Guthrie and Horton [20] cats, which did show variability in their methods of tipping the "barber pole" to get out, could interchangeably use such variations as snout, rump, or

---

[43] Perhaps the first and most striking experiment which emphasized this type of variation was Muenzinger's with the guinea pigs [59, 61].

paw? We have as yet no clear answers. Hull proposed the concept of "response generalization" [31]. But this is hardly more than a phrase to cover our ignorance.

Let me present my own position on this point. It is that in any of the learning situations which we usually set up, what the subject essentially learns is primarily a type of organism-environment rearrangement. For example, he learns to make "this sort of turn" in the maze—either in terms of his own body or in terms of the position of light or noise cues in the room; he learns to get himself to "this sort of door" rather than to "that sort of door"; he learns to push "this type of lever" down; he learns to bump into "this sort of barber pole"; he learns to wait (i.e., to hold himself) until the next stimulus (be it the unconditioned stimulus in a classical conditioning experiment or the next syllable in a series of nonsense syllables) appears.[44] And he already has the motor skill equipment to accomplish these organism-environment rearrangements whether by walking, swimming, running, using this leg or that leg, his snout, or whatever. What he learns is, in short, a *performance* and each such performance can usually be carried out by a number of different motor skills.[45] That is, in most of our animal and human experiments the skills are already present and the so-called "response" we are predicting is a *performance* which may be carried out by any one of a number of skills. But the laws which govern the degrees of interchangeability of, or the hierarchies among, these skills or how the skills are originally learned we, or at any rate I, do not as yet know.

Furthermore, whereas many psychologists, especially Guthrie and Horton [20] feel that the learning of performances (they call them "acts") will eventually be understood and explained only after we have already learned about the acquisition of skills (they call them "movements"), I would hold that it is more true that an adequate understanding of skills will come only after we have an adequate understanding of the acquisition of performances within which these skills function.

2. Turn now to the second question. What is the nature of the function by which the magnitude of a simple single approach, escape, or avoidance can be predicted?

[44] I am suggesting that what I have above called $(S_1 \rightarrow S_2)$ learning may really be always an $(S_1R_1 \rightarrow S_2)$ type of learning in which the R_1 is "waiting." This indeed was the position I took in my original book, *Purposive behavior in animals and men* [78]. But I no longer wish to insist on this interpretation as against the other.

[45] In this connection we all remember Lashley's early experiment with the monkey [42] in which the animal learned to open the puzzle box by one hand and when this hand was paralyzed could open it equally well with the other hand.

It may be noted that Hull raises practically the same question (in his terms) when he presents his function for the strength of a reaction potential (an $_sE_R$) [32]. He conceives of four intervening variables: D (drive strength); V_1 (the stimulus intensity dynamism of S_1); K (the incentive motivation); and $_sH_R$ (the already acquired habit strength). And he writes the function:

$$_sE_R = f(D \times V_1 \times K \times {}_sH_R)$$

That is, he assumes that the strength of the drive D, the effect of the dynamic intensity V_1 of the S_1 stimulus, the goodness of the goal object K, and the strength of the habit bond already established between S_1 and R_1 (i.e., $_sH_R$) simply multiply together to determine the degree to which the given response will tend to go off, i.e., the strength of $_sE_R$ on the given occasion as a result of the presentation of S_1.

It is to be pointed out now that I too assume a rather similar function [88]. My function for a case of simple approach would read:

$$\dot{P}v = f_x(\dot{D}_1, \dot{Exp}_{S_2}, \dot{V}_{S_2}) - f_y(\dot{D}_w, \dot{Exp}_w, \dot{V}_w)$$

The f_x part of this function is similar to Hull's. $\dot{P}v$ is the symbol for the magnitude of the performance tendency,[46] i.e., the tendency for the performance ($S_1R_1 \rightarrow S_2$) to go off. This is analogous to Hull's $_sE_R$. D_1 is a symbol for the magnitude of the initiating drive-stimulation (be it a $\dot{D}_{H_1}$, a $\dot{D}_{F_1}$, or a $\dot{D}_{c_1}$). This is analogous to Hull's D. $\dot{Exp}_{S_2}$ is a symbol for the expectancy that the $\dot{S}_2$ will follow $\dot{S}_1\dot{R}_1$. This is analogous to Hull's $_sH_R$. And $\dot{V}_{S_2}$ is a symbol for the strength of the valence (positive or negative, primary or secondary) which is attached to the representation of $\dot{S}_2$. This is analogous to Hull's K.

It will be observed, however, that I do not include any term corresponding to Hull's V_1—stimulus intensity dynamism. If there be such a factor as a stimulus intensity dynamism, it would be taken care of in my system either by the generalization gradient around s_1 which would determine the degree to which the given $\dot{S}_1$ would be accepted as an instance of s_1, or it would be taken care of by the degree to which the given $\dot{D}_1$ operates to make S_1 "attended to" and hence determines the potency of the resulting $\dot{S}_1$.

Again, it will be observed that, whereas Hull assumes that D, V_1, K, and $_sH_R$ simply multiply to produce $_sE_R$, I shall not now attempt to make any assumption as to the exact ways in which my variables of

---

[46] "$\dot{P}v$" is an abbreviation for "performance vector." As will be seen in my answer to question (3) above concerning the interaction between performances, I consider that a performance has both magnitude and direction; hence the tendency toward it may be appropriately treated as a vector.

$\dot{D}_1$, $\dot{Exp}_{S_2}$, and $\dot{V}_{S_2}$ interact, other than to assume that, in general, increases in any one of their respective magnitudes will tend to increase the magnitude of $\dot{Pv}$. Further, it is to be noted that, since a valence $\dot{V}_{S_2}$ is for me either positive or negative, the resultant $\dot{Pv}$ may be either positive or negative. That is, the resultant performance tendency may be either one of doing R or one of not doing $R(\bar{R})$. The latter occurs in the case of avoidances.

Turn now to the f_y part of the equation. (This, as such, is lacking from Hull's equation.) This f_y part of my equation is to allow for the assumption that the performance vector will be decreased in magnitude in so far as the organism has a drive against work $\dot{D}_w$, expects $\dot{R}$ or $\dot{\bar{R}}$ to involve work, and this expected work has negative valence. The more the organism has, at the time, a general dislike of work (a drive-stimulation against work) and the more strongly he expects that the particular performance will involve work and the more arduous this work is expected to be, the weaker will be his performance vector $\dot{Pv}$.[47]

It may be noted, however, that while Hull does not introduce any such work factor as such into his equation for $_sE_R$ he does talk about "conditioned inhibition." And he apparently does subtract $_sI_R$ (conditioned inhibition) from $_sE_R$ just as I subtract the f_y function. This is not to say that Hull's notion of conditioned inhibition and my notion of expected and negatively valenced work are synonymous. But they are undoubtedly somewhat related. So much for my notions as to how the magnitude of a single performance vector for approach, escape, or avoidance R or $\bar{R}$ can be written as a function of the causally preceding variables.

3. Turn now to the third question. How do two or more different, simultaneously aroused performances tend to interact to produce a new performance different from either one of these separate performances by itself? In seeking to answer this question let us consider first, more specifically, the notion of a performance vector, a $\dot{Pv}$. A performance vector is to be conceived as a force having both magnitude and direction which, so to speak, "pushes" the organism either toward or away from the $\dot{R}_1$ involved in a given $(\dot{S}_1\dot{R}_1 \rightarrow \dot{S}_2)$ expectancy. This means that when two or more performances (vector forces) are aroused simultaneously it is the vector addition of these forces (these $\dot{Pv}$'s)

---

[47] It must also be recalled that above I suggested that along with a drive against work there must be conceived to be a related or perhaps an independent drive against uncertainty of outcome, i.e., low probability of the S_2 consequence. In other words, it may be that there should also be a third term in the equation $f_z(\dot{D}_u, \dot{Exp}_u, \dot{V}_u)$ which should also be subtracted. The u subscripts here would stand for uncertainty.

which should (if this conceptualization is valid) produce the magnitude and the direction of the actual performance which will go off.

It must be noted further that the introduction of this concept of performance vectors and their addition means that in the original Figs. 1 to 5 an additional column (under the general heading of "Intervening variables") should have been included. This column, if it had been introduced, would have been labeled "Performance vectors and their addition" and it would have been inserted between the "Expectation-perception-representation-valence" column and that for the final "Dependent variable" (i.e., the final dependent performance). It was not included, partly because I did not fully appreciate the need for it at the time I constructed the figures and partly because it would have made them even more complicated.

What I shall do from here on, after a little further elaboration of the nature of performance and of performance vectors, is merely to consider a few concrete examples of behavior experiments which obviously involve the arousal of two or more performance tendencies (performance vectors) and I will indicate what in each case I think the vectors would be and how they would add to produce the final actual performance.[48]

The admittedly greatest difficulty with this notion of performance vectors lies in the concept of direction. Lewin[49] [44] defined the direction of a psychological force in terms of the first "step" (in "hodological space" as he conceived the latter) of the psychological response brought about by that psychological force. For me, on the other hand, the direction of a performance vector is defined by the position of the S_2 relative to the position of the S_1 in the given perceptual-expectational field (or space). That is to say, the direction of a performance vector is to be specified by the direction running from the "posi-

---

[48] And in doing so I shall make use of my own no doubt somewhat over-simplified and distorted notion of a vector analysis.

[49] It will be obvious throughout this discussion of performances and performance vectors that I have been tremendously influenced by Lewin. It was from him that I got my original notions. However, as I have worked these notions over, I am now no longer clear as to how much I have retained of his ideas and how much I have altered them. And it would take a more analytical and industrious mind than mine now to make a careful exegesis and to cite specific references. I wish, nonetheless, to emphasize my overwhelming indebtedness to him.

I would like also to suggest that there may turn out to be a close relationship between my notion of performance vectors, and hence of a performance space, and Osgood's concept of a multidimensional meaning space [67]. Further, I believe that Osgood's experimental and statistical methods of identifying the dimensions of the meaning space, using human subjects, are far superior to any of the types of analyses I have yet been able to think up for specifying rat-performance spaces.

tion" of an $\acute{S}_1$ to the "position" of an $\acute{S}_2$. And this means, of course, that the positions of the $\acute{S}_1$ and $\acute{S}_2$ are, or become, part of the discriminable perceptual or representational characteristics of such $\acute{S}_1$'s and $\acute{S}_2$'s.

In the case of an approach performance I would symbolize the performance vector as $\rightarrow O - (\acute{S}_1 \dot{R}_1 \rightarrow S_2{}^+)$. In the case of an escape performance I would symbolize it as $\rightarrow O - (S_1 R_1 \rightarrow S_{\bar{2}}{}^+)$. And in the case of an avoidance performance I would symbolize it as $\leftarrow O - (\acute{S}_1 \dot{R}_1 \rightarrow \acute{S}_2{}^-)$.[50] In these symbols the O's stand for the organism. The vector arrows push the organism toward a given $\dot{R}_1$ which is expected to lead to a given $\acute{S}_2$, or pull it away from this $\dot{R}_1$ and resultant $\acute{S}_2$.

Do these three, approach, escape, and avoidance, complete the list of possible types of performance as far as their formal characters go? I believe they do. I must point out, however, that in a previous publication [87] I listed two additional formal types of performances: consummatory performances and exploratory scanning performances. It now seems to me that these two are but subtypes of approach.

A consummatory performance is simply an approach performance in which the $\acute{S}_1$ is a perceived, immediately present goal object which is then responded to by the given consummatory response, and $\acute{S}_2$ is the resultant pattern of external and/or internal stimuli which is approached and reached by such a consummatory response. Thus, for example, in the case of consummatory eating, the performance vector would be represented as $\rightarrow O - (\acute{S}_f \dot{R}_f \rightarrow \acute{S}_m{}^+)$.

Turn to exploratory scanning performances. I would now change the name to "identification performances." These identification performances constitute a very special type of approach. In fact they are, as we shall see in a moment, such a unique type that from now on I shall find it useful to classify them in a separate class even though they still are, I believe, types of approach. I shall, that is, group all other performances (whether simple approach, consummatory approach, escape, or avoidance) under the heading of "pragmatic performances" and keep "identification performances" as a separate class. From here on, then, I shall be concerned with these two main classes: identification performances and pragmatic performances. It may be noted that there will be setups in which we shall have to consider both types of performance vector as going off simultaneously or successively and thus affecting the total behavior.

But, first, we must examine in more detail the exact nature of an identification performance. An identification is, I shall hold, an ap-

[50] In the previous discussion and in the figure for avoidance I introduced the symbols $\bar{r}$ and $\dot{\bar{R}}$. I indicate the same meaning here by introducing an arrow (performance vector) pointing in the opposite direction from the performance of the given $\dot{R}_1$.

proach from a relatively grossly perceived immediate stimulus S_1, to the same stimulus perceived and discriminated more precisely, S_1'. My symbol for such an identification approach vector would be $\to O - (S_1 \dot{R}_1 \to S_1'^+)$. The S_1 would be the stimulus perceived at first as immediately present and relatively undiscriminated. The $\dot{R}_1$ would be an examining and identifying response. And as a result of this examining and identifying the organism would move into the presence of S_1', the same stimulus but perceived in some more precise way.[51]

Concretely what seems to happen is that, on occasion, when presented with an S_1, the organism before making any pragmatic performance to the immediately resultant S_1 stops and identifies it more closely and in so doing "moves himself," so to speak, from the initial relatively undiscriminated perception S_1 to a more precise perception S_1'. A pretty example can often be observed in a visual discrimination experiment with rats. A rat, as all rat runners know, usually starts with a spatial position habit (i.e., he discriminates the two S_1's primarily in terms of their spatial positions). But then he is apt, after a certain number of trials, to stop and begin to look back and forth, to make "vicarious trials and errors" or VTEs, to use Muenzinger's [60] term, before he jumps. And shortly after such VTEs have begun he begins jumping by more than chance to the correct visual stimulus, whichever side it is on. That is, he changes from undifferentiated discriminations of the visual properties of the two cards to relatively precise visual differentiations. The initial S_1's have become S_1''s as far as the visual properties are concerned. And it would appear that these examinings and lookings-at, these VTEs, constitute the pointer readings for the identification approach of the organism from the poorly discriminated visual properties to the more precisely discriminated ones.

In order, however, to make this clearer, I shall now have to introduce the concept of "perceptual discrimination spaces."[52] A perceptual discrimination space is a discriminable perceptual dimension conceived as radiating in a circular arc in front of the perceiving end of the organism. If, for example, we take the dimension of brightnesses, then the series from white to black can be considered as constituting an arc arrayed around the "perceiving nose" of the organism with the lightest perceivable white at one end and the darkest perceivable black

[51] The drive behind these identification performances is of course the curiosity drive already discussed.

[52] This concept has not, I am sure, been completely worked out. In fact, I myself am still somewhat hazy about it. Yet, intuitively I feel that the concept points to something important and that eventually something really useful may come out. I have already presented previous attempted expositions of this concept in connection with what I called the "schematic sowbug" [82, 83, 88]. See also footnote 49.

at the other. Any brightness stimulus which, to begin with, is relatively undiscriminated visually is to be thought of as lying straight ahead, i.e., as an equivalent to a medium gray or whatever the adaptation level [23] tends at that moment to be. When, as in the example of the jumping stand, the rat, however, passes from not perceiving the whiteness or the blackness of a card to perceiving it, he moves from pointing at a perceived stimulus (an $\acute{S}_1$) straight ahead to pointing towards and

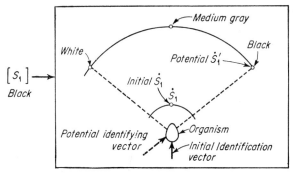

FIG. 6. Before precise identification

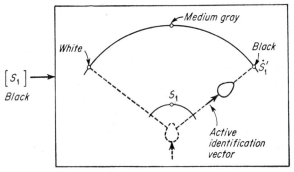

FIG. 7. During precise identification

getting to the corresponding perceived "white" or "black" stimulus which is angularly displaced from the medium gray. Probably, however, to make this clear I shall have to present a couple of figures.

In Fig. 6 the organism is represented as presented with an objectively black stimulus S_1. But, since he does not yet discriminate this, he points toward his adaptation level of medium gray (see nearer arc). However, since the stimulus is really black and he is potentially capable of discriminating black there is a potential angular vector (represented by the dashed arrow) tending to turn him towards the black end of the arc. And, as shown in Fig. 7, he sooner or later will tend to turn and to "move" (identificationally speaking) toward this S_1' of black.

Consider now that he has two cards in front of him, one white and one black. When he looks at the black card he will "move" towards the S_1' of black and when he looks at the white card he will "move" toward the S_1' of white. But why will he VTE? To understand this, I shall have to introduce a further concept, namely, that after he has "moved" in the direction of either identification, he becomes temporarily satiated for it. This concept of temporary perceptual satiation I have borrowed in part from Glanzer [18, 19]. After the rat has looked at black, the vector turning him and then moving him in the direction of black now disappears temporarily (or at least becomes weaker) owing to momentary satiation. This leaves the vector to turn and move (identificationally speaking) towards white in control. He, therefore, now looks at the white and identifies it. But the white identification process in its turn satiates. And, in the meantime, the black vector is assumed to recover. And so he looks back again at the black. Thus he continues to VTE until both identification vectors have become more permanently satiated. Finally, when this has happened the pragmatic jumping-toward vectors take over. And in so far as he has already begun to acquire the appropriate pragmatic means-end readinesses and resultant expectations as to which card leads to the food and which to the net, he also begins to jump correctly more than by chance.

One further experimental point. It was found by me [82] that in the usual visual discrimination setup in which the trials are continued only for, relatively speaking, a short period, the rats VTE more for a white vs. black discrimination than for a white vs. medium gray discrimination, and more for this latter than for a white vs. light gray discrimination. This seems contrary to what would be expected. For, if the discrimination is more difficult, one would on a common-sense, human, basis have expected the VTE-ing to have been greater rather than less. Certainly we would expect in, say, a lifted weight experiment with human subjects that, if the subjects were allowed (using the constant method) to lift each weight of a pair as many times as they wanted before giving a judgment, they would do more such lifting, more VTE-ing, when the two weights are near together in heaviness than when they are farther apart.[53] Yet the rats did more VTE-ing for the easy discrimination than for the difficult one. This led me to the notion that, in the first part of a visual discrimination experiment, the rats are really primarily discovering the stimulus dimension to be paid attention to. They are primarily making *visual* identification responses.

[53] Recent experiments by Mrs. Laura W. Phillips in the Berkeley laboratory bear this out most beautifully.

Whereas, if the usual discrimination training experiment were carried further so that the pragmatic jumping vectors would take over, the reverse results would be obtained. This led Minium and myself to a follow-up experiment [91]. The same group of rats was first trained on black vs. white and continued for a long time. The animals were then switched to medium gray vs. white and again continued on this for many days. Finally, they were switched to light gray vs. white and continued for numerous trials. It turned out that in the first few trials with each setup they did do more VTE-ing for black vs. white than for medium gray vs. white and more for this than for light gray vs. white. But it also appeared that after these initial periods the VTE-ing for black vs. white sank to practically nothing, whereas for black vs. medium gray it stayed at an appreciable level and for the black vs. dark gray it stayed at a high level.

To explain these contrasting results as to VTEs between the first trials and the later ones, let me return to the concept of the visual identification space. My hypothesis is that in the first periods of the discrimination period, since the white vs. black ends of the arc are, say, 90° apart, the *satiation* of the identification vector towards one of them does not generalize to (has no projection on) the other. Hence, when the animal has looked at white or black, he still has a strong tendency to look at the other. He will thus VTE for a relatively long time. But when the two stimuli are nearer together on the discrimination arc the *satiation* of the vector for identifying one of them will generalize in some degree to the other. That is, in this latter case, since the arrows are less than 90° apart, the shortening stemming from satiation of one of these vectors will project on the other vector. This will result in less VTE. And the nearer together angularly the two vectors are the more this will be so, and hence the less the VTE.

Later, however, as appeared in the Tolman and Minium experiment [91], when the identifications have been established, the pragmatic jumping vectors take over. The VTE-ing now becomes an expression of the degree to which the vector to jump to one of the two stimuli tends to generalize to a jumping towards the other. In this later stage, the nearer the two perceived stimuli are together on the discrimination arc the more a vector to jump to one will have a positive projection upon the other. Here, in other words, VTE-ing becomes then a case of "partial errors." And there will be more partial errors the more difficult the discrimination.

Finally, however much the reader may object to the details of the above interpretation, I hope he will at least have been convinced that some such vector interpretation, even though it may have to be considerably modified, is intriguing and has empirical suggestiveness.

It must be admitted, however, that one feature of this concept of identification spaces and identification performance vectors which has not been touched upon is that of distance. What are the distances which the organism has to overcome in passing from the immediately presented and relatively undiscriminated $\dot{S}_1$'s to the finally more discriminated $\dot{S}_1'$s? Are these distances (as I have depicted them) the same for all discriminations on a given dimension? And do such distances, even if the same for one dimension, differ as between dimensions? And, corresponding to such differences, if there be such, between distances does this mean related differences of expected work which will act as vectors in the opposite direction which will thus tend to weaken the identification process? This whole question of distances is a feature of the theory, as it is at present, which suggests, at least to my mind, certain further questions which might perhaps be empirically answered.

Another series of investigations is suggested by the problem of what conditions, other than actual ease of discrimination, tend to determine the amounts of VTE (VTE being for the present our only good pointer reading for the fact that identification performances are taking place). We do already have some answers. Thus, a wide gap to be jumped [27] or an electric grid to be passed over in front of the choice doors [60] both tend to increase VTEs. And conversely we also have some incidental but unpublished evidence from the Berkeley laboratory that, if the animals are too highly motivated for the goal, VTE-ing will be decreased. These facts require further experiments as to the interrelation between identification vectors and pragmatic vectors.[54]

Let us turn now to the question of *pragmatic performance* vectors. Let us consider a few concrete experiments where the perceptual-representational directions are apparently closely parallel to those of geographical space.

First consider performances on a single **T** maze. On such a maze there would appear to be two pragmatic performance vectors which get established at the choice point. One would correspond to an expected valence to be reached by going down the one arm; and the other would correspond to an expected valence to be reached by going

---

[54] Finally, any complete account would also raise the question of identification vectors relative to the $\dot{S}_2$s and $\dot{R}_1$s as well as relative to the $\dot{S}_1$s. Just how to get at these others, how to get pointer readings for them, I am not at all clear. Finally, it is to be stressed, whether or not the above interpretations be correct, there was pretty clear evidence obtained by Geier, Levin, and me [17] that early VTE in a discrimination setup is correlated with the individual's cognitive speed in acquiring the given type of discrimination.

down the other arm. And it would appear that these two vectors are probably to be conceived as 180° apart, thus ←0→. Or, in other words, the two vectors subtract from one another so that in so far as one at any given moment is stronger, the resultant in the other direction is weaker. And this would seem to be true even though rats differ—as demonstrated by Tolman, Ritchie, and Kalish [93]; see also, Walker et al [94]—in that the "space" on a simple **T** maze for some of the animals seems to be based upon extramaze cues, such as orienting lights or sounds, and the "space" for other animals is based rather upon some sort of internal bodily right-hand vs. left-hand cues.

Further, however, to be quite sure to what extent the two perceptual-expectational directions on a **T** maze are really 180° apart, further experiments must be done in which **Y** mazes of different angular dispersions are also tried. It might well turn out that all **Y** mazes with an angle greater than 90° give results as to speed of learning and as to VTEs which are indistinguishable from those of **T** mazes. I should expect, however, that, as the angle between the **Y** arms became less than 90°, there would, with increasing narrowness of the angle, be more VTEs and slower learning. In other words, I would assume that in these primarily spatial maze problems, VTE-ing in rats is due not to alternation between identification vectors but rather to alternation between pragmatic approach vectors. Thus it has been demonstrated that in a maze [35] VTEs correlate positively with errors rather than negatively and that there is no correlation of VTEs made by individual rats on a maze with the VTEs made in a discrimination setup [92]. In a word, the data so far suggest that, in actual geographically spatial setups, rats come already equipped with spatial identifications and their VTE-ing is an expression of the conflict between their pragmatic vectors rather than between their identification vectors.

Consider now another experiment in which geographically spatial relations were involved. This is an unpublished experiment by Crutchfield done in the Berkeley laboratory, briefly described in [80]. One group of rats was trained on a **Y** maze with food at both ends and was forced by doors, manipulated by the experimenter, to go an equal number of times to each side. A second group was similarly trained on a **T** maze, while a third group was on a ↑-shaped maze.

After equal amounts of such preliminary training with all three groups, the experimenter then opened up for each group a third path running straight ahead. Crutchfield found that the straight-ahead path was now entered most frequently in the case of the **Y**, less frequently in the case of the **T**, and still less frequently in the case of the ↑. I interpret these results to mean that the "directions" of the two pragmatic performance vectors acquired during the original training and corresponding to the entering of each of the two arms corresponded more or less exactly to the actual geographical directions. Thus the vectors pushing the rats down the two arms of the **Y** each had a resultant in the direction of the straight-ahead path. The vectors corresponding to the two arms of the **T** had no such resultant. And, finally, the vectors corresponding to the two arms of the ↑ had resultants which were opposite in direction to that of the straight ahead. The fact that even in this last case a small proportion of the rats entered the straight ahead I would attribute to an additional propensity to explore any newly opened path. This increased by a constant amount the tendency to go down the straight ahead for all three groups.

This experiment of Crutchfield's should undoubtedly be repeated. We do not know what spatial axes (those provided by the rats' own bodies or those provided by room cues) the animals were using.[55] There could be a variety of experimental variations to uncover what this space was, in terms of which the directions of the pragmatic performance vectors were specified. But, in any event, it seems clear that there was a "performance space" and that this space was in considerable correspondence with the actual geographical space.

Finally, there is one further type of experiment which I would like to propose—an experiment in which again the concept of pragmatic performance vectors would be predictive.[56] It would be a discrimination experiment in which the subjects already knew what they should pay attention to. And the difference between the cues for right and for wrong would be well above threshold. The experiment might be done with either human subjects or rat subjects. In describing it, however, let us assume that it is done with rats. The apparatus would be the usual jumping stand save that there would be landing platforms in front of each card with grids on them which could be electrified.[57]

The essence of the experimental design would consist in a comparison of immediate and delayed recall for right vs. wrong responses learned under two conditions. In the one condition, the approach responses would not involve any obstacles (other than the gaps). The grids on the landing platforms would never be electrified. In the other condition (in the original learning), the grid on the landing platform

[55] Crutchfield used an alley maze, not an elevated one.

[56] A preliminary unpublished and somewhat inconclusive pilot study of the sort of experiment I have in mind has already been performed. It was done by Mr. Robert Schweers in the Berkeley laboratory. A brief mention of it has already appeared in the literature [87].

[57] Discrimination stands with landing platforms have been frequently used in the Berkeley laboratory [82] and have proved more than satisfactory.

in front of the correct card would in each trial be electrified. Thus, in this latter condition there would be built up, according to my hypothesis, not only a forward-pointing vector toward the correct card and a backward-pointing one away from the incorrect card, but also an additional backward-pointing vector away from the correct card (because of the shock).

What now are the to-be-expected results for immediate recall (i.e., immediate relearning) vs. delayed recall (i.e., delayed relearning) as a result of these two conditions of original learning? My prediction would be that the rats which had learned under the punished (or shock) condition would do approximately the same as those which had learned under the conventional group in the immediate recall test; but in the delayed recall test they would do appreciably more poorly.[58]

Why do I expect such results? The answer lies in my assumptions as to what sort of pragmatic performance vectors would get set up in the original learnings and in my further assumptions as to what would happen to these vectors with the passage of time. In the conventional, nonshock, condition a forward-pointing approach vector toward the correct card would be built up and a backward-pointing vector away from the incorrect card would also be built up. In the shock condition (in which in the original learning there was always a shock just in front of the correct card) there would be built up in addition a backward-pointing vector away from the correct card (because of the shock). Furthermore, in order to reach the same criterion of correct performance in the original learning, the forward-pointing vector toward the correct card would have to be built up to a somewhat greater length (to compensate for the backward-pointing vector due to the shock). In a test for *immediate* recall we may assume that all these vectors would retain approximately their original magnitudes and hence again there would be approximately no difference in this immediate recall test between the two groups. When, however, it came to the tests for delayed recall (i.e., after a considerable passage of time), I would assume (since there is evidence that the conditioning of a negative response persists longer in time than the conditioning of a positive response) that the pointing-away vector from the correct card would still retain considerable magnitude. This would mean that in this delayed recall test, the group which originally had had shocks in front of the correct card would do more poorly. That is, its choices of the correct card would, because of the persistence of this negative vector, be, relatively speaking, somewhat reduced in number. This group should, in short, make more errors in the delayed recall test.

And now I will indulge in a bit of phantasy. I shall suggest that,

[58] And I think Mr. Schweers's results presented some evidence in this direction.

if the above assumptions be correct, they provide an explanation of something very like what the psychoanalysts call "repression." For the shocked group the correct card became in the original learning both positive and negative. That is, it came to evoke a *conflict* between an approach-toward vector and a going-away-from (avoidance) vector. And, if it be further assumed that a going-away-from vector retains its strength longer over time than does an approach-toward vector, then at a later date there will be more going away from this item that was thus conflictful, than there will be a going toward it. It and what it led to will, in short, tend to be "forgotten," *as far as performance is concerned*, or in other words, "repressed." But finally, whether my guesses as to the experimental results are correct, and whether, if obtained, my further assumptions suggest a valid interpretation of repression, it does seem to me that experiments of this sort should be carried out.

Before concluding this section, a general question concerning this whole concept of identification and pragmatic performance vectors is in order. For the critic may well ask whether such performance vectors can have any real applicability or usefulness for problem situations which involve other than truly spatial (i.e., truly geographical) situations. By way of answer I can as of now merely assert my faith. I believe and insist that, since all instrumental performances can be conceived as forms of approach, escape, or avoidance (three essentially spatial concepts), I also insist that all such performances must be analyzable by vectorial concepts. Mechanical and even ideational problems [67] are "gettings-to" or "gettings-from" by more "direct" or by more "indirect" routes. Furthermore, our language is full of spatial terms: e.g., "this when *approached* is seen to be that," "this is the *opposite* of that," "this is a more *direct* solution than that," "this is a more clumsy, more *roundabout, longer* way to do it than that," "this *leads* to that." The spatial concepts of distance and direction seem to me of the very warp and woof of all our thinking about performances whether these performances involve actual space or mere mechanics or mere logic. However, I must admit that the reason I feel this so strongly is perhaps because I personally like geometry better than algebra and I have better spatial (visual-kinesthetic) imagery than I have verbal imagery. Hence, it may be merely that I personally need to translate all performances and problem solving into spatial terms.

METHODOLOGICAL CONSIDERATIONS

Before concluding, let me turn again briefly to some omitted, or partially omitted, logical and methodological questions posed by the outline.

Systematic and empirical definitions of independent, intervening, and dependent variables. I have already indicated fairly clearly, I hope, how I would conceive systematically and identify empirically the independent and dependent variables. I pointed out some of the unclearnesses which we all suffer from in our systematic definitions of stimuli and of responses. But I could not clear up the matter to any great extent. I did, however, emphasize that responses are for me to be conceived as "performances" rather than as specific muscle responses or gland secretions. A performance, as seen by me, is a specific type of achievement manipulation of an environmental object or situation. It is an entering of an alley, a going to the right, a going toward a light, going away from a light, or to or from a specific place, etc. Empirical pointer readings for such performances are set up relatively easily, probably without much error, by arbitrary stipulations such as that such and such part of a rat shall or shall not have crossed a particular line. To sum up, the systematic and empirical specifications of independent variables and of the dependent variable, though still open to many questions, do not seem to lead to much confusion or lack of communication between investigators (even those from different schools). Common-sense notions and a little macroscopic physics seem, for the most part, to suffice and to allow for adequate objectivity and communication.

When it comes to the question of intervening variables, on the other hand, this is where the schools differ. My own particular brand of intervening variables were admitted to come primarily from my own phenomenology. Thus Köhler's designation of me as a cryptophenomenologist was probably correct. I do, however, attempt to objectify my intervening variables and to suggest standard defining experiments for getting empirical pointer readings for them.

Actually, however, it should be admitted that I really have considerable doubts not only about the practical feasibility of such experiments (since they would involve a tremendous amount of time and labor) but also about the validity of the results which would be obtained.

My proposal was that one should set up standard defining experiments in each of which the obtained response or responses (i.e., performances) could be conceived as depending primarily upon, as being a direct pointer reading for, the variations of one particular intervening variable as this latter is dependent upon the controlled and prescribed manipulations of one or two independent variables. It was assumed that one could thus acquire a sort of table showing just what the values of each intervening variable would be as the result of such and such values of the correlated and controlling independent variable or variables. And it was assumed, further, that these relations of the values of each intervening variable to one or two independent variables would hold in new, nonstandard, nondefining situations as well—so that the values of the intervening variables could be predicted from the values of the independent variables in the new situation. But I wish now to emphasize that this last assumption might well prove invalid. For there may be all sorts of interactions between the variables (independent as well as intervening), in the new nonstandard situations, interactions which could not have been predicted from the results obtained in the standard defining situations by themselves. For, in these latter, rigid controls of all but one or one small set of independent variables would have been imposed. Hence, I have considerable doubt concerning not only the practical feasibility but also the validity of the proposal.

It might be said, however, that there is another possible way of conceiving my intervening variables. This would be to admit that they are merely an aid to thinking ("my thinking," if you will). All anyone really sees are the empirically stipulated independent and dependent variables. In developing notions of what happens in between—such as beliefs, expectancies, representations, and valences and finally what I call performance vectors and their interactions—all I really am doing is setting up a tentative logic (or psychologic) of my own, for predicting what the dependent behavior should be and how it should be affected by variations in such and such sets of independent variables.

Actually, it seems to me that this is no worse (begging the pardon of the Hullians), and perhaps no better, than the assumption of little r's and little s's where these latter intervening variables (though sounding more physiological and concrete) are at the present stage of our physiological knowledge just as untestable as my beliefs, perceptions, expectancies, valences, and vectors. There is, however, I would admit, probably one greater defect in my cryptophenomenological position. My intervening variables seem to be less communicable to others and are probably colored by special peculiarities of my own phenomenology. To which, I answer that I like my own phenomenology and I believe it to be as good as and probably more fruitful than that of those who think in terms of little atomic r's and little atomic s's.

Initial evidential grounds for assumptions of system. Obviously, the chief evidential grounds for my system are the experiments on the instrumental learning of rats and particularly experiments in mazes. And I suppose that for the fundamental distinction between "learning" and "performance" which appears in the system as the difference between means-end readiness and expectancies, on the one hand (as purely cognitive functions), and performance vectors, as the result of cognitions plus motivations, on the other, I am indebted primarily to Blodgett. This distinction was forced upon me by his original "latent learning experiments." I owe Blodgett a great debt. Of course, actually Lashley was the first one to make the distinction between learning and performance. But we did not realize this until later.

The notion that performance readinesses or dispositions may be conceived as vectors grew out of my many associations with Lewin and my great indebtedness to him. However, my notion concerning the "performance or vector field" differs in certain ways from Lewin's and it is still in a somewhat inchoate state. My ideas concerning vectors were also much affected by my experiments on discrimination learning and my development of the somewhat bizarre concept of "the schematic sowbug" and by my observations of the phenomenon of VTE. Here in connection with VTE I borrowed much from Muenzinger and his students (especially Evelyn Gentry). And I also was much affected in my notion of a "performance" as contrasted with a mere response by Donald Macfarlane's early experiment on swimming vs. running a maze (done in our laboratory) and also by Muenzinger's early experiment on the way in which guinea pigs may alternate their specific skills from trial to trial in getting out of a puzzle box.

As I have already stressed, my original impetus to the study of the learning of rats came from Watson, Thorndike, and Perry. And it was from the last that the notion that cognition and motivation are perfectly objective components of behavior was borrowed.

But any attempt to list sources soon becomes invidious because one is bound to omit important influences. So it had better be left for an historian to reconstruct, assuming that any historian would be interested (which seems doubtful).

Generally speaking, it may be said that it is the ideas of my own students which have influenced me most. (I wish I could list them all.) And that the S-R schools of Pavlov, Guthrie, Hull, Spence, Mowrer, and Skinner have served rather as challenges than as sources of initial ideas. However, as was seen above, the beautiful work of Neal Miller and his cohorts I have taken to myself with a bang as a way of specifying the ultimate goal stimuli.

Under the suggested subheadings which contrast immediate *data language* with *construct language*, I have nothing to say other than that they may perhaps be inferred by somebody else from the body of this paper. But I myself can neither get very interested in nor completely understand such more refined logical distinctions.

Construction of function forms. My "function forms" are, I suspect, merely "general adumbrations" of what I assume to be the functional relationships between the independent, intervening, and dependent variables. They are merely of the sort: "the more of this, the more of that"; "the more of this, the less of that"; and the like. I would not attempt to fit curves or to specify the values of parameters. As I have already indicated above, such attempted precision seems to me for the most part premature. Wherever one can do it, the experimental conditions are so overcontrolled, restricted, and specific that any valid generalizations from such attempts seem to me impossible.

Mensurational and quantificational procedures. Obviously, my mensurational procedures reduce pretty much to mere statements of "more" or "less." I am not greatly concerned about equality of units, absolute zeros, or the like at this stage of the game.

Psychology today seems to me to be carried away (because, perhaps, of feelings of "insecurity") into a flight into too much statistics and too great a mathematization. This may well be my personal bias and stem from the fact that I have not kept up in my mathematics. But to me, the journals seem to be full of oversophisticated mathematical treatments of data which are in themselves of little intrinsic interest and of silly little findings which, by a high-powered statistics, can be proved to contradict the null hypothesis.

A great lack in my system is, of course, that it contains no real consideration of individual differences in spite of the fact that I owe to Tryon an original interest in this direction. I suppose I feel that, ultimately, individual differences will be found to be most usefully treated as variations along the dimensions specified by the intervening variables of the system rather than by dimensions blindly got at by factor analyses.

Formal organization of the system. All I can say here is that my system is based on hunches and on common-sense knowledge. It is certainly not "hypothetico-deductive." I have not the type of mind that can remember which were my axioms and which were my deductions. In any event, if a system were a SYSTEM, which I do not believe psychology to be, it would be largely arbitrary which one took as axioms and which one took as derivations. To attempt to build psychology on the analogy of a closed mathematical or logical system seems to me a "bad error."

I shall not say anything about "implicit" definition, "explicit" definition, "empirical or operational" definition, nor "coordinating" definition since my knowledge of these logical distinctions is too slight.

Scope or range of application of system. As indicated in the body of this essay, the system as actually developed was based primarily on experiments dealing with the instrumental learning of rats. The basic problems of learning and motivation seemed, however, also to be involved in this more restricted area, so that it has always been my hope that the relations found in these simple problems with rats could be extrapolated to the behavior of the higher animals (including man) in more complicated situations. And on occasion I have loosely made such applications [84]. I have, however, no programmatic plans for extensions of the system to such wider areas.

It is interesting to note that in many ways my system proves not too different from Hull's save in two assumptions: (1) that it is not S-R habits but $(sr \rightarrow s)$ means-end readinesses which are stored up as a result of practice, and (2) that the final propensity to behave resulting from both learning and motivation is best conceived as a performance vector and not as a reaction potential [87].

History of system to date in mediating research. Just which particular researches done in the Berkeley laboratory or elsewhere have been "mediated" (or perhaps better put) "influenced" by my system, I have no way of estimating. In general, what I hope I have done is to develop a general attitude and point of view, and that from this point of view stimulation for further research, either within or without the specificities of my system, has resulted.

I certainly have not "derived" specific deductions to be tested. Rather I have worked by hunches and, I hope, have thereby stimulated their own hunches in other persons.

Evidence for the system. I am incapable of any good answer. The evidence, such as it is, I find throughout all the experiments on instrumental learning, wherever done. At least I am almost always capable of translating, or if you will, distorting, this evidence so as to use it as support for my system (my way of looking at things). One body of data which, however, I cannot do much with is that on the acquisition of sensorimotor skills in adults or with the way in which performance vectors govern and select from among such skills. Neither have I actually been able to do much with the higher processes of thinking, verbal communication, and the like in human beings, though I do feel that these latter processes will some day lend themselves more readily to a formulation of the $(SR \rightarrow S)$ type than to a simple S-R formulation.

Specific methods, concepts, or principles of the system believed valuable outside the context of the system. I have nothing to say here.

Degree of programmaticity. Again I have nothing to say except to report that I am apt to be accused of being too programmatic and of not getting down to actual work.

Intermediate and long-range strategy for the development of the system. At my time of life, I have no real strategy for the future. I do, however, hope to carry out some experiments soon on the memory for decisions or choices in human subjects (based theoretically on the sort of performance vector analysis which I adumbrated above) and in these experiments the variables of difficulty, length of delay, and the presence or absence of special rewards and punishments upon recall will be tested. Such experiments may even prove to have some bearing upon the psychoanalytical concept of "repression."

CONCLUSION

I started out, as I indicated in the introduction, with considerable uneasiness. I felt that my so-called system was outdated and that it was a waste of time to try to rehash it and that it would be pretentious now to seek to make it fit any accepted set of prescriptions laid down by the philosophy of science. I have to confess, however, that as I have gone along I have become again more and more involved in it, though I still realize its many weak points. The system may well not stand up to any final canons of scientific procedure. But I do not much care. I have liked to think about psychology in ways that have proved congenial to me. Since all the sciences, and especially psychology, are still immersed in such tremendous realms of the uncertain and the unknown, the best that any individual scientist, especially any psychologist, can do seems to be to follow his own gleam and his own bent, however inadequate they may be. In fact, I suppose that actually this is what we all do. In the end, the only sure criterion is to have fun. And I have had fun.

REFERENCES

1. Allport, G. W. *Personality: a psychological interpretation.* New York: Holt, 1937.

2. Bailey, C. J., & Porter, L. W. Relevant cues in drive discrimination in cats. *J. comp. physiol. Psychol.,* 1955, **48,** 180–182.

3. Barker, R. G., & Wright, H. F. *Midwest and its children (the psychological ecology of an American town).* Evanston, Ill.: Row, Peterson & Company, 1954.

4. Berkun, M. M., Kesson, M. L., & Miller, N. E. Hunger-reducing effects of food by stomach fistula versus food by mouth measured by a consummatory response. *J. comp. physiol. Psychol.,* 1952, **45,** 550–554.

5. Berlyne, D. E. The arousal and satiation of perceptual curiosity in the rat. *J. comp. physiol. Psychol.,* 1955, **48,** 238–246.

6. Blodgett, H. C. The effect of the introduction of reward upon the maze performance of rats. *Univer. Calif. Pub. Psychol.,* 1924, **4,** 113–134.

7. Bloomberg, R., & Webb, W. B. Various degrees within a single drive as cues for spatial response learning in the white rat. *J. exp. Psychol.,* 1949, **39,** 628–636.

8. Bowles, R., & Pentrinovich, L. A technique for obtaining rapid drive discrimination in the rat. *J. comp. physiol. Psychol.*, 1954, **47**, 378–380.

9. Bruce, R. H. An experimental investigation of the thirst drive in rats with especial reference to the goal gradient hypothesis. *J. gen. Psychol.*, 1937, **17**, 49–62.

10. Brunswik, E. *Perception and the representative design of psychological experiments.* Berkeley, Calif.: Univer. California Press, 1956.

11. Cowles, J. T. Food tokens as incentives for learning by chimpanzees. *Comp. Psychol. Monogr.*, 1937, **14**, No. 5.

12. Delgado, J. M. R., Roberts, W. W., & Miller, N. E. Learning motivated by electrical stimulation of the brain. *Amer. J. Physiol.*, 1954, **179**, 587–593.

13. Delgado, J. M. R., Rosvold, H. E., & Looney, E. Evoking conditioned fear by electrical stimulation of the subcortical structures in the monkey brain. *J. comp. physiol.*, 1956, **49**, 373–380.

14. Desiderato, O. The interaction of several variables in latent learning. *J. exp. Psychol.*, 1956, **52**, 244–250.

15. Elliott, M. H. The effect of hunger on variability of performance. *Amer. J. Psychol.*, 1934, **46**, 10–112.

16. Frenkel-Brunswik, Else. Motivation and behavior. *Genet. Psychol. Monogr.*, 1942, **26**, 123–265.

17. Geier, F. M., Levin, M., & Tolman, E. C. Individual differences in emotionality, hypothesis formation, vicarious trial and error and visual discrimination learning in rats. *Comp. Psychol. Monogr.*, 1941, **17**, No. 3.

18. Glanzer, M. Stimulus satiation: an explanation of spontaneous alternation and related phenomena. *Psychol. Rev.*, 1953, **60**, 257–268.

19. Glanzer, M. The role of stimulus satiation in spontaneous alternation. *J. exp. Psychol.*, 1953, **45**, 387–393.

20: Guthrie, E. R., & Horton, G. P. *Cats in a puzzle box.* New York: Rinehart, 1946.

21. Haire, M. Stimulus generalization along phenomenal continua (in press).

22. Harlow, H. F. Motivation as a factor in the acquisition of new responses. In M. R. Jones (Ed.), *Current theory and research in motivation: a symposium.* Lincoln, Neb.: Univer. Nebraska Press, 1953.

23. Helson, H. Adaptation level as frame of reference for prediction of psychophysical data. *Amer. J. Psychol.*, 1947, **60**, 1–29.

24. Herb, F. H. Latent learning—non-reward followed by food in blinds. *J. comp. Pschol.*, 1940, **29**, 247–255.

25. Honzik, C. H. Maze learning in rats in the absence of specific intra- and extra-maze stimuli. *Univer. Calif. Publ. Psychol.*, 1933, **6**, 99–144.

26. Honzik, C. H. The sensory basis of maze learning in rats. *Comp. Psychol. Monog.*, 1936, **13**, No. 64.

27. Honzik, C. H., & Tolman, E. C. The action of punishment in accelerating learning. *J. comp. Psychol.*, 1938, **26**, 187–200.

28. Hull, C. L. The goal gradient hypotheses and maze learning. *Psychol. Rev.*, 1932, **39**, 25–43.

29. Hull, C. L. Differential habituation to internal stimuli in the albino rat. *J. comp. Psychol.*, 1933, **16**, 255–273.

30. Hull, C. L. The concept of the habit-family hierarchy and maze learning. *Psychol. Rev.*, 1934, **41**, 33–52, 134–152.

31. Hull, C. L. *Principles of behavior—an introduction to behavior theory.* New York: Appleton-Century, 1943.

32. Hull, C. L. *A behavior system—an introduction to behavior theory concerning the individual organism.* New Haven, Conn.: Yale Univer. Press, 1952.

33. Irwin, F. W., Smith, W. A. S., & Mayfield, J. F. Tests of two theories of decision in an "expanded judgment" situation. *J. exp. Psychol.*, 1956, **51**, 261–268.

34. Ittelson, W. H., & Cantril, H. *Perception, a transactional approach.* Garden City, N.Y.: Doubleday, 1954.

35. Jackson, L. L. VTE on an elevated maze. *J. comp. Psychol.*, 1943, **36**, 99–107.

36. Jenkins, J. J., & Hanratty, J. A. Drive intensity discrimination in the albino rat. *J. comp. physiol. Psychol.*, 1949, **42**, 228–232.

37. Klüver, H. *Behavior mechanisms in monkeys.* Chicago: Univer. Chicago Press, 1933.

38. Köhler, W. *The mentality of apes.* New York: Harcourt, Brace, 1925.

39. Kohn, M. Satiation of hunger from food injected directly into the stomach versus food ingested by mouth. *J. comp. physiol. Psychol.*, 1951, **44**, 412–422.

40. Krechevsky, I., & Honzik, C. H. Fixation in the rat. *Univer. Calif. Publ. Psychol.*, 1932, **6**, 13–26.

41. Lambert, W. W., Solomon, R. L., & Watson, P. D. Reinforcement and extinction as factors in size estimation. *J. exp. Psychol.*, 1949, **37**, 637–641.

42. Lashley, K. S. Studies of cerebral function in learning. V. The retention of motor habits after the destruction of the so-called motor areas in primates. *Arch. neurol. and psychiat.*, 1924, **12**, 249–276.

43. Leeper, R. The role of motivation in learning. A study of the phenomenon of differential motivational control of the utilization of habits. *J. exp. Psychol.*, 1937, **46**, 3–40.

44. Lewin, K. The conceptual representation and the measurement of psychological forces. *Contr. psychol. Theory*, 1938, **1**, No. 4. Durham, N.C.: Duke Univer. Press, 1938.

45. McClelland, D. C. *Personality.* New York: Sloane, 1951.

46. McClelland, D. C., Atkinson, J. W., Clark, R. A., & Lowell, E. L. *The achievement motive.* New York: Appleton-Century-Crofts, 1953.

47. Macfarlane, D. A. The rôle of kinesthesis in maze learning. *Univer. Calif. Publ. Psychol.*, 1930, **4**, 277–305.

48. MacCorquodale, K., & Meehl, P. E. On a distinction between hypothetical constructs and intervening variables. *Psychol. Rev.*, 1948, **55**, 95–107.

49. MacCorquodale, K., & Meehl, P. E. "Cognitive" learning in the

absence of competition of incentive. *J. comp. physiol. Psychol.*, 1949, 42, 383–390.

50. MacCorquodale, K., & Meehl, P. E. Edward C. Tolman. In W. K. Estes et al., *Modern learning theory.* New York: Appleton-Century-Crofts, 1954.

51. Maslow, A. Deficiency motivation and growth motivation. In M. R. Jones (Ed.), *Nebraska symposium on motivation—1955.* Lincoln, Neb.: Univer. Nebraska Press, 1955.

52. Miller, N. E. Studies of fear as an acquirable drive: I. Fear as motivation and fear-reduction as reinforcement in the learning of new responses. *J. exp. Psychol.*, 1943, 38, 89–101.

53. Miller, N. E., & Kesson, M. L. Reward effects of food via stomach fistula compared with those of food via mouth. *J. comp. physiol. Psychol.*, 1952, 45, 555–564.

54. Montgomery, K. C. The effect of the hunger and thirst drives upon exploratory behavior. *J. comp. physiol. Psychol.*, 1953, 46, 315–319.

55. Montgomery, K. C. The effect of activity deprivation upon exploratory behavior. *J. comp. physiol. Psychol.*, 1953, 46, 438–441.

56. Montgomery, K. C. The role of the exploratory drive in learning. *J. comp. physiol. Psychol.*, 1954, 47, 60–64.

57. Montgomery, K. C., & Segall, M. Discrimination learning based upon the exploratory drive. *J. comp. physiol. Psychol.*, 1955, 48, 225–228.

58. Mowrer, O. H. On the dual nature of learning—a reinterpretation of "conditioning" and "problem-solving." *Harvard educ. Rev.*, 1947, 17, 102–148.

59. Muenzinger, K. F. Plasticity and mechanization of the problem box habit in guinea pigs. *J. comp. Psychol.*, 1928, 8, 45–69.

60. Muenzinger, K. F. Vicarious trial and error at a point of choice: I. A general survey of its relation to learning efficiency. *J. genet. Psychol.*, 1938, 53, 75–86.

61. Muenzinger, K. F., Koerner, L., & Irey, E. Variability of an habitual movement in guinea pigs. *J. comp. Psychol.*, 1929, 9, 425–436.

62. Murray, H. A. *Explorations in personality.* New York: Oxford Univer. Press, 1938.

63. Olds, J. A preliminary mapping of electrical reinforcing effects in the rat brain. *J. comp. physiol. Psychol.*, 1956, 49, 419–427.

64. Olds, J. Runway and maze behavior controlled by basomedial forebrain stimulation in the rat. *J. comp. physiol. Psychol.*, 1956, 49, 507–512.

65. Olds, J., & Milner, P. Positive reinforcement produced by electrical stimulation of septal area or other regions of rat brain. *J. comp. physiol. Psychol.*, 1954, 47, 419–427.

66. Oppenheimer, R. Analogy in science. *Amer. Psychologist*, 1956, 11, 127–135.

67. Osgood, C. E., Suci, G. J., & Tannenbaum, P. H. *The measurement of meaning.* Urbana, Ill.: Univer. Illinois Press, 1957.

68. Perry, R. B. Docility and purposiveness. *Psychol. Rev.*, 1918, 25, 1–21.

69. Postman, L., & Adams, P. A. Performance variables in the experimental analyses of the law of effect. *Amer. J. Psychol.*, 1954, 67, 612–631.

70. Postman, L., & Adams, P. A. "Isolation" and the law of effect. *Amer. J. Psychol.*, 1955, 68, 96–105.

71. Ritchie, B. F. Studies in spatial learning. III. Two paths to the same location and two paths to two different locations. *J. exp. Psychol.*, 1947, 37, 25–38.

72. Ritchie, B. F. A logical and experimental analysis of the laws of motivation. In M. R. Jones (Ed.), *Nebraska symposium on motivation.* Lincoln, Neb.: Univer. Nebraska Press, 1954.

73. Seward, J. P. An experimental analysis of latent learning. *J. exp. Psychol.*, 1949, 39, 177–186.

74. Sheffield, F. D., & Roby, T. B. Reward value of non-nutritive sweet taste. *J. comp. physiol. Psychol.*, 1950, 43, 471–481.

75. Spence, K. W. Theoretical interpretations of learning. In F. A. Moss (Ed.), *Comparative psychology.* (Rev. ed.) Englewood Cliffs, N.J.: Prentice-Hall, 1942.

76. Spence, K. W. *Behavior theory and conditioning.* New Haven, Conn.: Yale Univer. Press, 1956. P. 152.

77. Thistlethwaite, D. L. A critical review of latent learning and related experiments. *Psychol. Bull.*, 1951, 48, 97–129.

78. Tolman, E. C. *Purposive behavior in animals and men.* New York: Century, 1932.

79. Tolman, E. C. Psychology versus immediate experience. *Philos. Sci.*, 1935, 2, 356–380.

80. Tolman, E. C. The determiners of behavior at a choice point. *Psychol. Rev.*, 1938, 45, 1–41.

81. Tolman, E. C. Physiology, psychology and sociology. *Psychol. Rev.*, 1938, 45, 228–241.

82. Tolman, E. C. Prediction of vicarious trial and error by means of the schematic sowbug. *Psychol. Rev.*, 1939, 46, 318–336.

83. Tolman, E. C. Discrimination vs. learning and the schematic sowbug. *Psychol. Rev.*, 1941, 48, 367–382.

84. Tolman, E. C. *Drives toward war.* New York: Appleton-Century, 1942.

85. Tolman, E. C. Cognitive maps in rats and men. *Psychol. Rev.*, 1948, 55, 189–208.

86. Tolman, E. C. There is more than one kind of learning. *Psychol. Rev.*, 1949, 56, 144–155.

87. Tolman, E. C. Performance vectors and the unconscious. *Proc. 14th Int. Cong. Psychol.* Amsterdam: North-Holland Publishing Company, 1954. Pp. 31–40.

88. Tolman, E. C. Principles of performance. *Psychol. Rev.*, 1955, 62, 315–326.

89. Tolman, E. C. Egon Brunswik: 1903–1955. *Amer. J. Psychol.*, 1956, 69, 315–324.

90. Tolman, E. C., & Krechevsky, I. Means-end-readiness and hypoth-

esis—a contribution to comparative psychology. *Psychol. Rev.,* 1933, **40,** 60–70.

91. Tolman, E. C., & Minium, E. VTE in rats: overlearning and difficulty of discrimination. *J. comp. Psychol.,* 1943, **36,** 91–98.

92. Tolman, E. C., & Ritchie, B. F. Correlation between VTE's on a maze and on a visual discrimination apparatus. *J. comp. Psychol.,* 1943, **36,** 91–98.

93. Tolman, E. C., Ritchie, B. F., & Kalish, D. Studies in spatial learning. II: Place learning versus response learning. *J. exp. Psychol.,* 1946, **36,** 221–229.

94. Walker, E. L., Dember, W. N., Earl, R. W., & Karoly, A. J. Choice alternation: I. Stimulus vs. place vs. response. *J. comp. physiol. Psychol.,* 1955, **48,** 19–23.

95. Warden, C. J. *Animal motivation: experimental studies on the albino rat.* New York: Columbia Univer. Press, 1931.

96. Watson, J. B. *Behavior* (an introduction to comparative psychology). New York: Holt, 1914.

97. Young, P. T. Food-seeking drive, affective process and learning. *Psychol. Rev.,* 1949, **50,** 98–121.

98. Young, P. T. The role of hedonic processes in the organization of behavior. *Psychol. Rev.,* 1952, **59,** 249–262.

ASSOCIATION BY CONTIGUITY

EDWIN R. GUTHRIE

University of Washington

INTRODUCTION

The volume, *Modern Learning Theory* [3], published in 1954, is a remarkable enterprise. In it the authors have achieved a penetrating and objective analysis of the distinguishable lines of attack on the problem of human and animal learning, and the effect of the volume on current psychological theory cannot fail to be far reaching. The field is for the first time in print shown up in an aerial perspective that displays the wandering trails on which we have been traveling, some of them possibly leading nowhere, and the whole system failing to reach much agreement even on direction. The clear picture of the flounderings of present-day theory will surely reduce confusion and lead to new formulations.

The present chapter is part of what might turn out to be a companion venture—a statement by men who for the purpose of the task **are** writing as systematists rather than as critics. The writer of the present chapter undertakes this venture with a certain humility and definite misgivings, being well aware, when the invitation to participate mentioned that a systematic formulation might vary "from one or a few orienting ideas . . . toward the organization of extant knowledge within a given empirical domain . . . to an explicit, elegant, and quantified systematization," that what is to be outlined in this chapter is definitely to be placed at the first extreme of the distribution. The editor has suggested an introduction covering background factors and orienting attitudes, the structure of the system in so far as one has been developed, and the evidential grounds for the adoption of the system. The rubrics that will follow these are only a crude approximation of the headings suggested by the editor, which were designed for the exposition of a developed system. The present account is better described as an orientation than as a system.

The background factors are to include a short account of the writer's education and some brief mention of the men and books that established his perspective.

BACKGROUND FACTORS

At the turn of the century, although the University of Nebraska had one of the first psychological laboratories in the United States, psychology was still, as in nearly all American universities, in a department of philosophy, though the staffs were distinct. At the time the writer entered in 1903, the university had none of the present apparatus of required courses and set curricula. The only requirement for the bachelor's degree was credit in a number of courses extending normally over a period of four years, to include one 2-hr course in English composition, taught largely by the lecture method. This freedom made possible the inclusion of courses in both Latin and Greek which had been begun in high school; mathematics through calculus and including, as the nearest approach to modern statistics, a course on the theory of errors using a text by a professor of gunnery at West Point; several courses in philosophy; but in psychology only the general course before the bachelor's degree. There followed three years of teaching mathematics in a local high school and a master's degree in philosophy that included graduate courses in mathematics and in psychology under Thaddeus Bolton and H. K. Wolfe. H. B. Alexander, whose courses were listed as philosophy, took much interest in issues that would now be recognized as psychological. H. K. Wolfe had taken his Ph.D. degree under Wundt and had returned to the university after a brief absence because there had been debate over his orthodoxy. The interlude was, fortunately for me, timed so that he was my high-school principal at the time of graduation and was teaching psychology at the university (in the Department of Education) by the time I began graduate work. In one graduate course it was my good fortune to be his only student, and although the course and our conversations dealt very little with the body of facts that a modern graduate student in psychology must be prepared to face in his examinations, his views on the philosophy of science were of great interest. A research course under Bolton devoted a winter to observations with an aesthesiometer on the limen of twoness, and served to quench interest in psychophysics, which was the chief preoccupation of psychological laboratories in those years.

The books still remembered from my Nebraska studies are all philosophical: Büsse on the mind-body problem, read in German in a seminar of Hinman's; Bosanquet's *Logic,* with its conclusion that the ground of every judgment is the whole body of knowledge; Bradley's *Appearance and Reality,* which developed the paradoxes involved in all the traditional metaphysical concepts. Ernst Mach and Avenarius were later read with that same conviction that had accompanied reading Darwin's *Origin of Species* and his *Expression of the Emotions* with a companion while in the eighth grade. The later appeal of Dewey's humanism and his views on the nature of truth might be interpreted as influences, but that interpretation is put in some question by the fact that a high-school graduation thesis written for Wolfe had taken the position that both science and religion, being dependent on words, and words being symbols dependent for their meanings on the experience of their users and auditors, would have no chance at expressing Absolute Truth. It is possible that a resigned acceptance of this conclusion, which Wolfe called curious, was the reason for the enthusiasm over Bradley, and, later on, Dewey. Acquaintance with Freud began in 1913 when as a fellow in the philosophy department at the University of Pennsylvania and as factotum of the department seminar I invited Alexander Goldenweiser down from Columbia to address us.

At Pennsylvania in 1910, the first year was spent chiefly in ancient philosophy. Newbold's seminars in Aristotle and Plato used Greek texts. During that year my enthusiasm turned to E. A. Singer who, like many philosophers of his day, extended his interest into psychology, though the only psychological paper I remember of his was on Fechner's law. It was his paper on *Mind as an Observable Object,* delivered at a meeting of the American Philosophical Association in 1910, that began to turn attention again to psychology, but this interest was confined to journal reading and arguments with several graduate students majoring in psychology. My thesis was in the area of symbolic logic and dealt with Russell's paradoxes, those propositions whose truth appears to imply their falsity, and whose falsity to imply their truth. "This proposition is false," is an illustration. The solution suggested was that when such terms as "this" were defined, the paradox disappeared.

This excursion into logic and Singer's exposition of the dependence of axioms on definitions had a lasting effect on my attitude toward logic. My second published paper [5] after the thesis was an argument that the laws of logic are conventions and not laws of thought. The fact that it had taken Russell and Whitchead some 400 pages to establish the conclusion that one plus one equals two, and that every intervening step could be challenged and would require more proof, and that the steps of these added proofs would require still more, has made me impatient with the notion that there can be any completely rigorous deduction, or ultimate validity in an argument. This scepticism colors my notions of the nature of scientific facts and scientific theory.

This account of personal background is already too long, but may bear the addition of several possible determiners. My first university teaching was at the University of Washington in 1914, a position held until retirement in 1956. A too brief acquaintance with the economist Carleton Parker who, as dean of a just started College of Business Administration, persuaded me to undertake in 1917 a mission to interview loggers in the state's camps for the Secretary of War, and a very brief career in both an infantry and an artillery OTS in 1918 served to turn attention from books to men. A year's collaboration with the late Stevenson Smith on an elementary text entitled *General Psychology in Terms of Behavior* [14] proved to be invaluable training because it represented from four to five hours of argument and writing usually seven evenings a week over a period of a year. Smith had had far more training in psychology and the experience of clinical work with children for six years. Our diverse backgrounds, one with a degree in philosophy and mathematics, and the other with a degree in psychology and neurology, made almost every paragraph of the book being written the occasion for argument. Smith's clinical interest in the problems of child psychology tended to keep our attention on the practical applications of theory, whereas my chief interest lay in undergraduate teaching, a fact that probably accounts for a strong bent toward simplification which, with some justification, has been described as oversimplification.

ORIENTING ATTITUDES

Certain strongly held beliefs concerning the nature of human communication and language, the nature of facts and explanations, and the nature of scientific truth have undoubtedly colored my excursions into learning theory. When we say "Let's get down to the facts," we do not mean that we shall merely look or taste or feel, but that we shall seek in a situation or event what description in words we can agree on and expect others to agree on. Men, therefore, help to make facts, and human purposes and motives enter into their selection and formulation. Before there were men and before language existed, the world got on well enough without being described. There were no facts in such a world. Facts involve men and discourse and common understanding and shared purposes. There is no such thing as purely inductive reasoning. No amount of repetition of events will produce a generalization. The mere repetition of events will not even result in their being numbered. Numbering is a device developed by men. Nature does no counting.

One critical test of fact and of the truth of propositions is in terms of their acceptability among men. A lone man in a world could do as well as a cat without speech and, therefore, without statements or propositions, and there would be available no test of the truth or falsity of such noises as he might make. These might frighten birds, but they would not be true or false.

Scientific explanations are made in public. They are human acts and have their own motives and their effects on men. Scientific truths must meet these conditions of general understanding, though in their case the public is a special one. It is made up of men with a common interest in a special field and with experience in that field. There are special conventions to be met, and an explanation that is unintelligible to scientists working in the field is no explanation in a scientific sense. The concepts used must have been established in common usage.

The explanation of an event or class of events must take the form of the statement of a rule of which the event or class is an instance. The pursuit of science is a search for a body of rules which will serve a number of purposes. One of these purposes is to enable men to share knowledge and thus to share the prediction and control of events. Another purpose of great importance is so to systematize and codify the rules that they can be taught to an oncoming generation.

It is the requirement that rules be communicable and teachable that makes simplicity desirable. During the eighteenth century, the impressive beginnings of the reduction of physical science to rules had led to a notion that nature was set in a pattern of simple laws, the "Laws of Nature." We have only slowly discovered that the requirement of simplicity is a human requirement. It is men that are simple, not nature. The simplification of nature that is achieved by scientific laws is achieved at the expense of prediction—by limiting prediction to classes of events.

Scientific prediction is always in terms of a rule—if an event of class A, then an event of class B. A and B are both abstract classes, not concrete events, and the prediction is contingent upon a number of assumptions. One of these is that the actual instance is an instance of A, which is always a matter of judgment. Another assumption is that the general situation does not include "interference" from circumstances that have effects inconsistent with B. When a scientific law is used for the prediction of a specific event, these disturbing contingencies are controlled if possible; if not possible, they are allowed for by granting a certain leeway of error. When physics undertakes to interfere with the actual world we call it engineering, and the engineer uses safety factors of up to 1,000 per cent in order to be reasonably sure of the outcome. A physical law like Boyle's law is stated without this allowance for error; but the error is always there and the points are never exactly on the curve.

There is no question that human behavior is highly predictable. Our lives would be intolerable if we could not depend on this predictability. Clinical practice is built upon the extreme predictability of annoying or embarrassing behavior. Clinicians are asked to suggest measures that will be followed by changed behavior. Their first responsibility is to the patient and they must take advantage of predictability on any available ground.

Most of the predictability of human behavior is in an area which is not covered by science. It derives from acquaintance with the individual, the familiarity that enables wives to anticipate the behavior of husbands or mothers to know what to expect of children, children to take advantage of the habits of parents, the police to recognize the work of known offenders, politicians to be wise in the ways of voters, credit bureaus to collect profitable estimates of the debt-paying habits of merchants. Such information is highly specific and depends on acquaintance with the individuals concerned. It is not science because it is not reduced to general rules; it can be learned, but it cannot be taught as a formal body of rules. It will not be found in textbooks because textbooks cannot be burdened with individual biographies.

Considering the fact that the lives of all of us are guided by such information, it is rather remarkable how unsuccessful we have been in formulating general rules of behavior, in describing the general circumstances under which behavior is changed by experience—the laws of learning. Learning is illustrated in every movement we make and we are continuously engaged in altering the behavior of our fellow men, but we have not been able to agree on any set of rules that such changes follow.

The knowledge by acquaintance that enables us to anticipate the ways of friends and family, the anthropological collections of descriptions of the specific ways of groups, the skills that enable a paleontologist to recognize the place of a skull in evolution, or an ethnologist to recognize the folkways of a group, or a physician to name and describe the probable course of a disease are not science. Knowledge becomes science only when it can be stated in general terms and in rules that are independent of time and place. Scientific knowledge can be put into print and read and understood by strangers at a distance.

What, then, will be the terms in which general rules of behavior are stated? What will constitute the antecedents and what the consequents? What can we look for as stimuli and what as responses? These words mean much the same as antecedent and consequent, except for the slightly misleading implication of causality which does not enter into scientific rules. Causality is a practical aspect of specific events and takes all contingencies into account. Scientific rules do not cause events; events are caused by the actual state of the world.

In the physical sciences, this problem has been solved by minimizing the role of the observer and by the use of conventional instruments of measurement with the attainment of a high degree of objectivity, or as the authors of *Modern Learning Theory* have expressed it, a high degree of intersubjective agreement. The part of a human observer is eventually reduced, by using accepted calibrated devices, to such elementary features as the noting of position on a scale which often can be recorded and made open to reading at any time, or duplicated and so made public. Many subatomic phenomena are recorded by lines on a photographic plate which can be submitted to the perception of many observers. It is worth notice that the role of the human observer is minimized, not abolished.

In psychological observation it would, of course, be a great advantage to reduce both stimuli and responses to this point of high agreement. But there is reason to believe that this reduction cannot ordinarily be obtained in psychology. The phenomena in which the psychologist is interested are not specified in terms of mass, length, and time. They involve categories not reducible to position on a scale. In fact, they normally involve patterns of situation and movement that require recognition by a human observer, and this recognition is of an order indefinitely more complex than the recognition of relative position involved in comparing a length with a scale.

However, the fact remains that such recognition can satisfy the requirements of science. Take, for instance, a case in which the categories are very far removed indeed from scale measurements. The writer recently heard Dr. Edgar A. Doll describe a measure of social competence which he and his associates had developed primarily for conveying information about the degree of impairment of social competence in cerebral palsy patients. The test included a series of items adjusted to ages from one to twenty-five years. The items included such behavior categories as *able to clothe himself* and *able to make simple wants known through speech*. Observers could reach a very high degree of agreement on whether or not these response categories were illustrated in the behavior of individuals observed. In fact, Doll reported, this agreement could reach across cultural boundaries and apply to children of different cultures. I have no doubt that the items could be translated into other languages and agreement reached between observers who could not understand each other's speech. Skills named in these items are a far cry from the scale positions to which physics reduces its observations, but the fact that we must use human observers as instruments does not alter the fact that the agreement they reach makes the data profitable material for behavioral science. Data obtained in this manner can enter into general rules and serve either as the data from which predictions are to be made or as the data which we wish to predict.

During the first century of the development of psychology, we have made great efforts to be objective. We hoped to achieve this by limiting ourselves to the categories of physics and using as the weather signs of behavior only the physical or chemical events normally activating sense organs. The determinations of absolute thresholds in the various senses, the hope that response could be treated just as movement in space which was the crude interpretation of behaviorism, failed to carry us very far toward the understanding of behavior. The reason for this is that we cannot reduce the classes of psychological facts which make up the data we must deal with to component movements in space. Patterns of stimuli and patterns of response have their psychological significance and usefulness tied to their patterning—pattern as pattern must be recognized and dealt with. Machines can be devised to respond to pattern, but the human observer remains the only practical tool we have for the recognition of patterns in their variety and multiplicity. The more simple data are not to be despised. Like the Berger rhythms there is always a chance of relating them to important psychological events or to the underlying mechanisms of behavior. Fechner's law, for instance, has some noteworthy applications to psychological behavior.

The history of our effort to use as the weather signs of behavior simple physical or chemical changes involving sense organs is an interesting one. One difficulty it encountered was that these stimuli did not always stimulate. Anesthesias or the more complex phenomena of attention could be invoked to explain failure. But the real failure goes deeper. The patterns of physical change that occasion response, we find ourselves inevitably describing in perceptual terms. It is not enough that they be available in the physical situation nor is it enough that the organism's attention orient sense organs to receive them; it is further necessary that they have meaning for the responding organism. In describing the behavior of animals we speak of such stimuli as "the sight of the box," "the sound of the food pellet," "confinement in the goal box." "Confinement" is a complex relation that is not just a matter of physical barriers. With human beings, such stimuli as "hearing a word," "viewing a printed syllable" are necessarily used as stimuli. We do not specify the type style in which the syllable is printed except when we are overscrupulous, because it is the syllable *as legible* rather than as a physical pattern that is significant. In other words, the observing of stimuli must include noting that they stimulate. That is ordinarily open to observation. We judge it in terms of the (usually) immediate alteration of response. Having observed that a given pattern does this, we assume that it will be effective on certain other occasions. Only physical patterns that are stimuli in this sense can serve as associative signals. Psychologists, without having ever recognized this explicitly, always choose their signals in the light of their experience that they do get responded to by the organism.

It is worth noting that a strong reinforcement of the tendency to reduce both stimuli and responses to elementary physical changes at sense organs or to muscular contraction and secretion followed the work of Pavlov, who was a physiologist, and not a psychologist. Pavlov [12] was not consistent in this, and "presentation of food" was assumed to be a simple physical stimulus although it was essential that the dog perceive it as food. Similarly the registration of drops of saliva emphasized one small feature of a complicated response.

To object to treating a simple physical change as a stimulus or a muscular contraction as a response is not to deny that all stimuli are analyzable into such physical changes or to deny that any specific response is analyzable into muscular contractions and glandular secretions. That should be assumed. It is, however, a denial that the psychological description of behavior can be made in physical terms. It requires psychological terms which will name recurring patterns of physical change usually requiring identification by an observer which will include recognition of their stimulus value usually judged by time relation to the response. A CS is not a stimulus for a CR until the association has taken place. It is an accident of our manner of speaking that we refer to the sound of a buzzer as the CS whether it is a stimulus or not. We should have a symbol to indicate a physical pattern we expect to act as a CS.

What has been said about the factual data in terms of which we describe behavior changes implies that it is primarily the presence or absence of specific stimuli and specific responses that is observed, not their intensity or degree. Simple physical stimuli like noise, pressure, light can be noted in terms of degree. A few responses, like the dog's reaction to Pavlov's "presentation of food," can be measured in some detail by counting number of drops of saliva secreted or the range of a leg retraction. But most responses, as observed, occur or do not occur. We note their presence or absence. The efforts to abstract measurable attributes of response like latency, vigor, time required to extinguish fail to agree with each other and so can not be regarded as measures of response strength. Only one measure shows promise. William Estes [2] has suggested a statistical description of response strength in terms of response certainty. This is, of course, dependent on the observation of presence or absence and does not imply degrees in the response but a calculus of the probabilities of the occurrence of the physical events that may serve as stimuli. He makes, however, two assumptions that may violate the nature of the actual process. One is that the elements that make up a situation have independent probabilities. The world does not present itself to men in that fashion. Physical stimuli (if we may by that term refer to the physical events that can serve as stimuli) come organized in objects and recurring sequences. We encounter the same object again and again. Our classification of objects into kinds and into genera and species, our names for recurring events, are not just our own responses to the world but a recognition of the way the world is. The physical structure of man is an adaptation to this repetitiousness in nature. Our brain and nervous system is an elaborate machine for recognizing objects and situations and for the evocation of appropriate response. The development of visual perception would seem to lend force to Estes' assumption, it is true. We may start out completely naïve and it is only experience that gives rise to the phenomena of visual perception. But some data from instinctive responses to vision, like the behavior of Thorndike's chicks which jumped or did not jump from a box according to its height, and some of the gestalt observations on general features of perception at least raise a question. The second assumption is more doubtful than the first, namely, the assumption that the effect of elements is additive. Patterning, rather than summation, appears to be the effective determiner of response. We may eventually conclude that patterning itself may be treated in Estes' terms and that the presence of a certain proportion of the elements of a pattern determines the response. George Boguslavsky, in an unpublished doctoral thesis, is attempting to deal with the phenomenon of increasing certainty of response with additional pairings of signal and original stimulus by assuming a limited group of stimulus patterns associated with the general situation in which the learning occurs and also assuming that the possible patterns (such as the possible postures or activity open to Pavlov's dog in the experimental harness) being equally probable are all gradually "conditioned" to the response, so that the response to the signal is then highly probable.

Where the description of learning shall start is a moot point. Tolman's suggestion [16] that the behavior of a rat at a choice point is a key event is well taken. Watching Dr. Paul E. Fields' motion pictures of what Tolman has called "vicarious trial and error" one is struck with the obvious and active scanning of the row of potential cues, one of which indicates the openable door, and the others punishment. The learning has occurred on previous occasions, because now the VTE is so often followed by the "right" choice. The scanning is obviously for familiar features, and it is tempting to say that the recognition of some of the patterns provokes cautionary behavior that is essentially the behavior of avoidance called out by punishment, but now associated with the pattern. The recognition during the scanning of a pattern to which the last response was jumping is followed by a jump.

But the last response to one of the "wrong" figures may also have been followed by a jump. The jump was followed by impact on the door and falling into a net. I see no way to avoid the description of this in Tolman's terms as vicarious trial and error in the sense that the sight of the wrong picture evokes, though not the prompt execution, at least some "running through" of the previous catastrophe with results that inhibit jumping. Tolman calls this "expectancy" and the term is acceptable, though I would think of expectancy in terms of the actual evocation of avoidance movements. These movements are not ordinarily overt and complete. That would require an actual jump and impact; but they are sufficient to interfere with jumping.

The law of association by contiguity is perhaps a feeble description of this, and it would have to be supplemented by further description of the nature of minimal rehearsals of previous behavior and the circumstances under which they occur. Thurstone [15] identified the capacity for such minimal rehearsal with intelligence. The law of association by contiguity is an attempt to describe the essential event. The situation is scanned for familiar features. When a familiar pattern is discovered, the response last following that pattern will be evoked.

This, of course, has pathetically little resemblance to such a law as the law of gravitation. It contains the ambiguity over minimal and overt response which must be faced with some such device as just described. The fact that the last response associated with the stimulus may not occur because other stimuli are also present and may interfere does not differentiate it from gravitation, however. All physical objects are supposed to be following the law of gravitation; but this gives little information about psychological behavior or the difference between Republicans and Democrats, though no one would deny they are at all times gravitating objects. No one has ever found any object to do more than approximate the course that the law of gravitation would predict, and we do not even know what the gravitational course of any object would be in a universe that contained more than two objects. The law yields only approximations of the courses of masses in which other forces are at a minimum. The disadvantage of the law of association is that its terms are not quantified, and in the prediction of the presence or absence of a response from the presence or absence of a stimulus (assuming no interference from the general situation—no conflicting responses) our stimulus datum cannot be easily isolated, and it is harder than physical movement to specify, to name, to observe.

We may well ask how much advance learning theory in terms of association by contiguity has made since Aristotle. I am not convinced that the advance has been substantial and I do not believe that it has advanced through the multitude of laboratory studies of the last generation. The direction of real advance may be in the direction that Estes is exploring—in the development of statistical methods of assigning probabilities to events in the light of experience. What Estes is proposing will, if it can meet the problem of natural patterns, give us quantified predictions that can be compared with actualities and enable us to add enlightening specifications to the description of stimuli that will put us in a better position for prediction. Statistical methods are also giving us a sound basis for measuring the objectivity of our human observer as a scientific instrument.

Stimuli are, of course, not the only data needed for prediction. Past associations, which Hull embodies in the concept of habit strength, must be supplemented by information of the state of the organism, which Hull covers with his concept of drive. I have tended to think of drive as covered by the stimulus situation, but the fact that in a few drives the interval of deprivation can be used as a rough indication of effect may justify the concept. In any case, the notion that we have in drive a variable measured in units and entering into the prediction of response as a multiplier of habit strength is probably an illusion.

There was another concept that Janet proposed. It has failed to interest psychologists. Janet, as a result of a lifetime dealing with mental patients, used the notion of *force mentale* [9] as a predictor of behavior. He believed that the capacity for facing decisions and for meeting new situations could be related to such a dimension. With fatigue, for instance, decisions become difficult and imposed choices lead to functional disorder. Janet proposed no explanation of this *force mentale* in physiological terms, but his use of it would suggest that it could be taken to include any form of impairment of the physiological mechanisms reinforcing action, breathing rate, pulse strength, glandular irregularities, defects in metabolism, which would interfere with the action of muscles by depriving them of oxygen, blood sugar, or the removal of fatigue products. Such defects modify profoundly the nature of psychological adjustments. Extreme fatigue is often responsible for aphasia and a sharp reduction in the scanning processes of the normal organism which are behind the solutions of difficult situations. Current psychological theory takes almost no account of man as an energy system or of the alterations in behavior that interested Janet.

Man is an energy system and it may be assumed that, lacking the atomic events that involve the conversion of mass into energy, he illustrates the principle of the conservation of energy. But he is not a closed system, and the psychological significance of behavior is not in the end describable in terms of energy. Flight and attack, approach and avoidance, correct and incorrect response may all involve the same energy output. It is only when, through malnutrition or excessive energy output, physical distress intervenes to act as a drive or as a stimulus component to modify response, that psychological categories are involved. Janet uses to good effect the description of situations which arouse the phenomena of emotional reinforcement of action, increased breathing, pulse, blood sugar supply, lactic acid elimination, and other factors affecting muscle contraction, though he does not catalogue these physical effects. H. M. Johnson once called attention to the behavior symptoms common to the effects of alcohol and the effects of fatigue. Fatigue has been notably difficult to measure in action though the changes it involves in the chemistry of muscle are definite. The psychological use of fatigue or of physiological impairment of the action system will remain open only to treatment involving general correlations between symptoms or categories of physical condition and classes of behavior effects. It will not approach the prediction of specific acts except in connection with other information. Its predictions will resemble the recently popular fad for linking frustration and aggression. These are both "fuzzy" categories, hard to define and not productive of close agreement in cases. And their use by psychologists has been rather more as ethical justification than objective description. But they are not without meaning or use. An attempt to use the psychological observers systematically would probably show that frustration has often other consequences and aggression other causes.

Janet's use of *force mentale* illustrates a field of behavior prediction in which the predicting categories are basically physiological, whereas the predicted behavior patterns are psychological. He explains, for instance, cases in which neurotic symptoms like indecision, extreme fatigue not the effect of ordinary exertion, phobias, and many other symptoms disappear during a period in which the individual discovers new sources of self-stimulation, like quarreling, stealing, dangerous sport, arson, as based on the evocation of normal emotional reinforcement which restores the normal process of adjustment.

The General Nature of Theory

A scientific explanation of a class of events states the rule of the event. Theory goes further than that. Theory arranges the rules in a hierarchy of generalizations. Specific laws are in their turn explained (or reduced) by showing that they are instances of more general rules. The explained rules are not discarded, because they are more readily applied in their specific forms.

An illustration of reduction is the attempt to reduce the law of extinction of conditioned response following repeated elicitation to a more general statement of association by contiguity, or in other words, to show that the phenomenon of extinction and also the failures to obtain extinction are both explainable by the law of association. Another example would be the attempts to explain associative inhibition as always a case of the association of an inhibiting response rather than as an independent rule.

The reasons for such attempted reductions are that they condense and simplify the rules that must be learned and at the same time cover the phenomena more adequately. The writer has made efforts to show that the phenomena of conditioned inhibition, extinction, reinforcement by effect, improvement by practice, the increase of certainty of a CR to a given CS with repetition are more adequately dealt with by the general principle. As stated, they all have exceptions and their failures to predict can be understood as cases of simple association.

Hull adopted and made his primary law a modification of Thorndike's Law of Effect which had been developed by C. Lloyd Morgan [10] and by Hobhouse [8]. A signal originally not eliciting a particular response becomes a signal for that response if the association is "confirmed" or "rewarded" or "reinforced" by the stimuli that it brings about or by the reduction of drive that it causes.

This can be illustrated over and over. But there are many ambiguities about what constitutes reward or reinforcement. As Skinner uses the term "reinforcement," any consequent that increases the certainty of the response is a reinforcement.

The sequence of CS, CR, and reinforcement can be viewed from an entirely different point of view. When a signal has been followed by a response that prevents the signal from recurring, there is no opportunity, *on any theory of learning,* for the attachment of that signal to other responses. If an association is established, it is secure from alienation until the signal is again present. This alienation will not occur, on any theory, until the CS is again present and a different R is introduced. The association is protected from unlearning, whereas if the signal remains present there is opportunity for new behavior to replace the response to the cue and the action may be unlearned. This makes specific the nature of a reward or reinforcement. They are defined in terms of straight association by contiguity. They protect learning that has occurred by making unlearning impossible. The only theory that would allow the association to be destroyed in the absence of the signal is the rather discredited theory that forgetting is a function of pure time, and that would operate against a rewarded association as well as an unrewarded one.

The writer has no adequate models to suggest. We can always ask whether a machine could be constructed to do what the human organism does and such a question has great value. Most of us accept the notion that animals and man are both physical structures and that they operate in some sense as machines. Motion pictures of the journey of phagocytes through the interstices of a blood vessel wall to the area of a bruise and their subsequent return, engorged with the debris of the escaped blood, through the walls of the blood vessel to the blood stream give a new impression of the marvelous economy of the physical body. Hints from the records of the electrical activity of the brain and new developments in electronic physics have thoroughly done away with the conception of the brain as like a telephone exchange. Even the modern telephone exchange no longer resembles much the earlier form that was familiar in the textbooks as a model of brain action.

Models serve to help us conceive the relations between stimuli and responses, but they follow theory and do not lead. Not many of us understand the intricacies of a modern analogue computer, but there are striking analogies between human thinking and the new machines which will probably be exploited in the explanation of behavior.

Scope of Theory

A great deal of psychological information will continue to have little relation to theory, as is the case in medicine. Specific devices and measures that have good effects in practice are scientific only in the sense that the methods and the effects are described in objective terms and their relation verified by the use of accepted statistical analysis. It is in the great advances in this field that psychologists have made their chief contributions during the last generation. Methods begun by workers in psychophysics have contributed a large share to this development, in spite of the fact that the interest of psychologists is no longer devoted to the analysis of sensation. Although psychologists have contributed to their development, statistical methods are not limited to psychology in their application and in that sense are not psychological. Some of them were developed in agricultural research, some in medicine, and some in sociology.

What is properly called psychological theory is made up not of models, and not of the isolated practical generalizations which guide practice, but of a body of more general statements which make up a hierarchy of rules in which more general rules form the explanatory basis for the more specific and serve as the conceptual structure which is a mnemonic device for teaching a science and as a guide for research. It was Hull's ambition to construct such a system.

Since axioms are really definitions and the rules of deductive reasoning are the folkways of human discourse and not absolute or cosmic, a system is not ultimately right or wrong but useful or not useful in the public in which it is used. One very great danger is inherent in the adoption of any system. Once it is agreed upon, the future development of a science is given direction by it. The writer's chief objection to any hypothetico-deductive system is not so much to the use of systems as to the danger of a premature restriction on the search for facts. Postulating a Thorndikean Law of Effect discourages research into the nature of the effect and into the problem of how specific effects influence the development of learning. A system may be productive of research, but research has no value in itself. It is knowledge that we are after rather than research and the test of a system is the light it throws on an area, and in psychology, not just the amount of prediction it makes possible, but the ability to predict what is worth prediction. Practically all research results in prediction, but if it is merely the prediction of how rats will behave under certain complicated conditions found only in a number of psychological laboratories, we have not furthered knowledge or science.

On the other hand, without a point of view, without some system there is no science. It was the restriction of physics to description in terms of mass, length, and time that made physics a science. In the writer's opinion, the restriction of psychology to objectively describable behavior is necessary for the establishment of a science of psychology. The psychoanalytical account of man will not be scientific until that restriction is observed. Janet remarked that the concept of the unconscious could be used scientifically only if it were used to name certain types of observable behavior. Explanations of animal behavior in such terms as "The animal sees that . . . " or "The cat thinks that . . . " or "The rat expects that . . . " are allowable only when specific, recognizable actions are indicated. As stated, they use language categories. What follows the word "that" is a statement. Animals do not have language and the description of their actions implying language is metaphorical and not scientific. We can observe action which is legitimately described as "The cat sees the mouse," or "The cat hesitates and then . . . " or "The cat responds to the sight of the release mechanism with posture and movements appropriate to escape." If we use the word "expects" to indicate a type of observable action we are on safe ground. The dog that cringes at the sight of an upraised hand may be described as expecting a blow.

If our interest is in system we may disregard the long-distance predictions of behavior that can be made from a knowledge of the species, from a knowledge of the culture, from a knowledge of the past of the individual, and give our attention to the moving event, the immediate weather signs of the next action. The data here include certain states of the organism: fatigue, excitement, depression, physiological drives in hunger, thirst, sex, oxygen–carbon dioxide imbalance.

We have, in addition to these, the present stimuli to which the animal is responding. Such a prediction basis would make a physicist despair. Despair, however, is not in order because there is open to the psychologist the same chance to minimize the complexity of his generalizations by keeping some of the data relatively constant or partialling out their effects by statistical devices or by resigning himself to high error valences.

As psychologists, our chief concern is with the phenomenon of learning. This process is what we usually mean by the word "mind." The possession of a mind means the ability to learn. The word "learning" has a variety of meanings. The Russians use the same word for "learn" and for "teach," as does an occasional American. A great source of confusion has been the tendency to use the word with a value sense as meaning "improvement." It is probably this use which accounts for the strong appeal of reward theory and for the misuse of Pavlov's term "reinforcement" for "reward."

It has been mentioned that the advance of physics dated from its convention to neglect most aspects of the world and to abstract from the world's complexity, for purposes of description, certain of its features most easily agreed upon. Man is a complex physical system, but physics can describe him only in terms of mass, length, and time.

A like abstraction must precede the development of a science of mind. The first abstraction, now a matter of general agreement, is to limit the account to behavior and neglect the phenomena of inner experience except as they can be translated into action.

Within the limits set by a restriction to behavior, there is a deepseated difficulty that psychologists still confront. This difficulty, in the opinion of the writer, will always prevent the development in psychology of a systematic basis resembling that of physics. It means that the life sciences cannot be reduced to the same predictive basis as the physical sciences. The difference is a matter of degree, not of kind. It centers about the description of behavior in terms of purpose. The quintessence of living behavior, and particularly that area of living behavior we call mind, lies in its purposiveness.

The growth of the language tools we use to describe the world is by extension of symbolic meanings from the recurring experiences which give rise to nouns and verbs based on those shared experiences. The notion of the atom—the uncuttable, the irreducible bit out of which matter is made—had its start in noting that changes in the shape of objects could be rearrangements of particles which themselves did not change shape. The Greek atomists were close to this primitive meaning. But even modern science, which has found it no longer necessary to think of the atom as "uncuttable," tends, at least for the sake of communication, to speak of "particles" which make up the atom, though sophisticated physicists, who confront the conversion of matter into energy, are well aware that this word is inadequate.

In like fashion, the notion of purpose, which had much the same linguistic history as "propose" in that both were made of words meaning "set forth," was descriptive of a behavior category of great importance in predicting behavior. What men propose can be used profitably in predicting what they will do. Biological science has been forced to use the word "purpose" to describe events and structures which are no longer assumed to have a "proposer." The concept is extended to cover those events in which the outcome can be predicted although the means by which the outcome is achieved exhibit variety and cannot be predicted. A seed of corn will germinate in a wide variety of circumstances. It is not the seed that proposed this, but the observer who now predicts the outcome even when he has no notion of the physical process by which it will be achieved. We can predict certain acts of men without asking what they purpose or propose. In the case of our own acts we are seldom aware of the movements by which they will be carried out. We may not even be aware that we possess a repertoire of movements leading to the end achievement. But every attainment of the result is carried out by a specific set of movements, depending on the situation and on the past learning of the individual.

Purposive behavior is defined in terms of its end results, not in terms of process or in terms of its antecedents. Purposive descriptions specify the outcome of action but do not specify its course. We do not need purposive terms for describing invariable sequences. In fact, invariable sequences are what constitute mechanism. A mechanism like an automatic pilot may achieve a definite end result through an indefinitely large number of ways, but each of the sequences by which the result is achieved we assume to be definitely predictable once the initial situation is given. The practically infinite number of different sequences by which the automatic pilot brings the ship back on its course from any deviation form a class of sequences whose general law is known. A body in stable equilibrium is a similar case. Any of an infinite number of disturbances of that equilibrium will end in a restoration of the original position.

Human behavior has a strong resemblance to the body in stable equilibrium or to the automatic pilot. The physiologist's conception of homeostasis describes certain end states, like body temperature or the concentration of mineral salts in the blood stream, which can be predicted while the body is in working order. They can be predicted without knowing the specific mechanisms involved—predicted merely on the basis of observation. But the physiologist assumes that there are the necessary mechanisms which form the basic explanation for the maintenance of the constant states.

When we reach to grasp an object, the course of the hand is subject to correction through vision much as the automatic pilot corrects the course of the vessel when the ship veers right or left. Purposive behavior that is predictable in terms of end result in a variety of initial circumstances and a consequent variety of sequences does resemble the operation of an automatic pilot. A human pilot is dependent on the movements of his compass. Both pilots respond to compass changes by appropriate movements which turn the wheel. In one case, the course is set by adjusting the position of an indicator on a scale of degrees. In the other case, the course is set by a phrase spoken by the mate. We assume that the movements of both and their effects are describable in terms of physics. The energy of one is furnished by the ship's cook and of the other by fuel, through engine and battery and motor.

But the analogy cannot be pushed too far. We assume that the steersman is a machine but not a machine whose behavior is describable in mechanistic terms. It requires a psychological description. One reason for this is that the responses of the automatic pilot form a simple class of mechanistic sequences whose law is known, but the steersman is subject to determiners of many sorts. His attention wanders. The attention of the automatic pilot is superhumanly concentrated on the compass. The steersman is influenced by his public relations, his employer relations, his personal relations, his state of health and digestion, his number of hours without sleep, his training, his religion. The automatic device has some faint analogies to these determiners, such as corrosion and lubrication. But these are more controllable and less complex. The outcome is, therefore, more predictable.

The predictions of science have a peculiar characteristic. They are never made in absolute terms, but only as contingent predictions. This is illustrated if one tries to press a meteorologist to make an absolute and unqualified prediction of the weather, which, like human behavior, has many determiners, hard to combine. All the meteorologist's rules are contingent. If A, then B. But if A', then B'. If A' and A are both present and B and B' differ and are incompatible, the event is not covered by our knowledge and we require another generalization in which AA' is the antecedent. Combining all possible contingencies into an absolute prediction is not meteorology. Absolute prediction can be done only on an *ad hoc* basis by searching for a state of the world as like the present combination of circumstances which confronts us, and predicting what followed on this previous occasion. That is weather prediction, but it is not a science of weather.

Several recent efforts to introduce absolute prediction into psychology have been made. Hull's effective reaction potential attempted to combine all known determiners into an unqualified prediction. That requires not only a set of generalizations about particular determiners on a contingent basis, but a rule for combining them. All that could be suggested for their combination was logical multiplication, and the effort was probably very premature.

The more or less successful efforts of psychologists to make predictions without qualification and so meet the problem of multiple determiners are in the fields of testing, which require no psychological theory and are attacked by the methods of statistics. How the results come about is a matter of indifference.

A complete reduction of behavior to statements of how effects are achieved would carry the analysis to physiological mechanisms. There are certain difficulties in the way of this reduction. The mechanisms we discover in the human body include the response of sense organs to stimulation, the initiation and conduction of nervous impulses, the initiation of muscular contraction. There are hints at other mechanisms, which we do not understand, in the brain waves. "Understanding" them would involve discovering the rule of their operation. We assume these physiological events are all mechanisms in the sense that they are describable in terms of fixed sequences of physical and chemical change.

That assumption will not work for the behavior of the steersman on a psychological level. The reason it will not work is that all our linguistic apparatus for describing behavior is developed in purposive and not in mechanistic terms. It is the end results of action that are of importance to us and for which we have developed words. The specific movements by which these end results are accomplished vary and have no names. We do note occasionally that an individual exhibits his own characteristic style of execution, but names for individual styles are not available. Human acts and animal acts are all named in terms of their end results. Signing a paper, uttering a word, turning on a light, pressing a lever, going to bed, adding two numbers, all name end results which are open to observation, can be objectively recognized. But they are names for classes of movement—responses infinite in variety. Our movements determine our signature and its genuineness can be established in court by agreement of expert witnesses. Movements peculiar to the individual result in the accent he gives a word. There are a few class names for dialects but the features that enable us to recognize a friend's voice will never have names. Nouns and verbs apply only to classes of events or objects. Proper names are not material for science except a possible science interested in their general features.

The attempt of psychologists and physiologists to isolate the basic mechanisms which explain learning is a laudable one. We must assume these explanations exist. We shall probably continue to search for the mechanistic sequences that change the effect of physical stimuli and so form the basis of learning. Pavlov's work represents such an attempt. Pavlov tried to use simple physical change at sense organs as stimuli and to record salivary flow as response. The handicap we face in such efforts lies in the fact that in an intact animal the functioning of physical changes as stimuli depends on the previous organization of these into discriminated patterns, and on the fact that responses likewise are so organized. Pavlov believed he was avoiding this difficulty by dealing with a reflex, but it must be granted that he did not succeed in getting down to a reflex level. His talk of such things as a "defense reflex" betrays his dependence on description in terms of end result, and his stimuli involve complicated organization into perceived patterns. My colleague Roger Loucks has attacked the problem of the basic mechanism by placing minute coils within the central nervous system and studying the operation of induced electrical shock as eliciting stimulus and as the signal in associative learning.

SUGGESTIONS TOWARD A SYSTEMATIC THEORY

This section is being written in response to a request that its writer attempt to take the role of a systematist and state in orderly form the outlines of a systematic account of learning. What has preceded is in response to a suggestion that the system be introduced by an account of the orienting attitudes that have "determined the aims, inductive basis, conceptual content, or formal organization of the system." At this point a confession is in order. The system will not go beyond orienting attitudes. Perhaps the rudiments of a system will appear as an attempt is made to follow the rubrics of the suggested outline.

The independent variables. From what has been already said it is evident that the prediction of immediate behavior (passing over such long-term predictions as can be made from species, culture, life history, and like data) is made from observed stimuli. The ambiguities current in the use of this word are serious and they have been fully realized by many psychologists. For the purposes of this chapter we may make use of a convenient Aristotelian device and define *stimuli* as the physical changes which are *potential* occasions for the initiation of sense organ activity and consequent afferent activity leading to response. In the absence of a number of conditions, the physical stimuli S, though present, may not be effective. A failure of attention, for instance, may prevent response. This prevention is not merely a question of the control of the actual impact of the change on sense organ, but involves adjustments within the sense organ (like the adjustment of the lens in the eye, or the tympanum of the ear) and also involves central coordination which prevents response through inhibition. We need not only a word for the potential physical stimuli S but for the potential physical stimuli that stimulate. We might call these functional stimuli. The most common use of the word "stimulus" by psychologists assumes far more than the presence of physical stimuli. It assumes that, by innate structure or experience of the individual, certain patternings of physical stimuli will be effective *as patterned*. Only observation can determine this effectiveness. In observing the behavior of an animal or of a person, what we note is not the mere availability of the physical complex but its effectiveness as an occasion for response. The term "functional stimulus" might be used to indicate that our datum is more than the physical stimulus, but the use of the same word would lead to confusion. It is here proposed that a word already in common use might be adopted and the functional stimulus be referred to as a *cue* or as a *signal*. A *cue* C might be defined as a physical stimulus which is (or has been in a similar situation) observed to alter response. We speak of animals as responding "to the sight of the lever," "to the sound of the food pellet," or of a person as responding "to the hearing of his name," or "to the sight of a nonsense syllable." We are assuming in both animals and man a previous experience that has made a class of physical stimulus patterns, often with great diversity in its members, serve as the effective occasion for response. We assume that the pattern of physical stimuli is discriminated, normally as the result of previous experience. In human learning, and there is reason to believe that the same applies to animal learning, this means that the pattern be perceived in its own right. The gestalt psychologists emphasized perceptual response, but they avoided any speculation as to how this came about. We must agree that any account of going behavior must recognize this state of affairs.

The limitation of functional stimuli C to those patterns that are observed to be effective in initiating response does not mean that this effectiveness must be verified on each occasion. It is possible to establish agreement on general effectiveness and to assume that a given physical stimulus will be a functional stimulus. In Pavlov's experiments he used bell, buzzer, touch, presentation of food, all of which could be thus assumed to be cues or signals. The observer's role in establishing a stimulus S as functional does not need confirmation on each occasion. After this definition, it is perhaps needless to point out that it is presence or absence that is the item of observation, and not intensity.

In my *Psychology of Learning* it was suggested that we must recognize the role of pattern *as such* in stimuli and also that patterns must be responded to in their own right to act as associative cues [6]. They must not only be discriminable, but discriminated. Nonreaders, for instance, are generally found not to see the letters or words that they are presumably looking at. Fernald had remarkable success in bringing about the necessary discrimination by compelling the child to trace with a finger the pattern of a word written in large characters. The association was then established, usually without requiring a repetition. Tracing compelled notice. Notice made possible the association with the utterance of the word.

Intervening variables. By this time it has become clear that the term "variable" is, except in a very limited sense, foreign to the line of thought here expressed. The essential feature of both independent and dependent "variables" is their presence or absence. The same is true of such intervening variables as may by others be demonstrated to be involved in this exposition. As variables they are capable of assuming only the values one or zero. In the application of the present "system" to complex problems of the acquisition of skills, the variable N, representing a count of repetitions of an event or members of a class of events, is clearly involved. The other variables are not established by counting but by recognition of presence or absence.

Others have maintained that the writer's use of *movement-produced stimuli* is as an intervening variable, though there is some tendency to classify this as a hypothetical construct. Another hypothetical construct could be added, the *serial response*. Both of these are often used for the explanation of such phenomena as generalization, remote association, the elaboration of the notion of "successful" movement, and in other ways.

Movement-produced stimuli are not regarded as differing in any essential from other stimuli either in their sensory modes or their role in constituting cues or signals. They may be the objects of attention and therefore dominate action. They enter into a feature of behavior to which modern psychologists devote no research, although it must eventually be studied and explained. This is the familiar phenomenon of responses (both specific movement- and act-responses) which appear to be maintained without attention—which become self-sustaining. These are involved in all skills and in all habits. We are forced to recognize a certain character of independence in them which throws some doubt on the adequacy of the language which makes integral response the final basis of an analysis. Henry Rutgers Marshall in his book *Consciousness* [11] observed that a mark of consciousness was the close relation between what we were conscious of and what will here be called integral response. We judge a cat to be conscious of an object when its integral behavior has reference to that object and is a response to it. This is a close approximation of the point of view here being stated in terms of attention and total response. But in view of the relative independence of certain local systems of serial response, such as the repetitive movements all of us make without noting them or remembering them, it is tempting to add a category of detached movement responses which are evident throughout a varied succession of actions. These movement details become conspicuous when they bring disaster, when we do not "look where we are going." It is possible that the linguistic solution is to recognize that responses of *attention* form a special category of responses. These are subject to a system of change (continuous ranging or scanning) that is relatively independent of movement routines of other systems. They are also subject to elicitation by intense stimulation of any sort and to the simultaneous presence of cues which are signals for incompatible integral responses. Reaching for one's keys is a serial response which can be executed without attention and not later remembered (no new associations formed), but if the keys are not in the usual pocket, the interruption of the automatic movement elicits attention.

Serial responses have been used in explaining rewarded behavior. If we assume that a series of movements once executed establishes each movement phase (and its results in exteroceptive and interoceptive stimulation as well as proprioceptive) as the cue for the succeeding movement, the series may be treated as one response. Skinner suggests that such series are formed in respondent conditioning, and only the first movement remains to be explained in terms of operant conditioning. My own suggestion is that the first movement has its signal if we look for it and the assumption of this will lead to its discovery.

The strong interest in automatic recording instead of observation has led psychologists of the present generation to overlook the complications involved in learning. I believe that advances in understanding what takes place in learning can be made only by patient observation of the details of the behavior involved. Movement-produced stimuli and serial movement responses are open to observation as are the encountered stimuli which originate in the environmental situation, but their observation requires more than recording the instant of a bell or a pin prick, or a shock, or a light flash. They require looking at the animal. They are not, however, as open to the experimenter's control as are the sounds and lights so much used as signals in current research.

In the present use of movement-produced stimuli and serial response, these concepts are perhaps more to be described as hypothetical constructs than as intervening variables as these terms are used by the authors of *Modern Learning Theory*. In the writer's view they are neither "intervening," in the Tolmanian sense of potential reduction to independent variables, nor are they hypothetical. Both are open to observation if observation is directed at them, but both, in most experiments on association, would be assumed rather than used as data for practical reasons.

The use made of *attention* assigns that to the same equivocal position as intervening variable or hypothetical construct. Like movement-produced stimuli and serial response, attention intervenes in the causal chain between stimulus and response, but is not reducible to the contiguity formula but ancillary to it.

It would be very gratifying, from a systematist's point of view, if attention would behave as a simple entity, reducible in some manner to a number and so capable of entering into a formula. We make an assumption that is very dangerous when we go so far as to speak of what attention can do. In the strictest sense, "attention" names a variegated class of responses which have in common only the fact that they involve movements of orientation, changes of posture, the inhibition of movements that interfere with orientation of sense organs, and minimize distraction. All that we can safely assert is that there are such responses and that they represent a high degree of integration or coordination. Some of them are native responses to certain classes of physical stimuli and can break in upon going behavior. The tendency of an infant's eyes to follow a moving light, or the general behavior of listening when a sound "stands out" from the general background of noise, is an illustration.

Attention-value can surely be acquired through learning, and this does not need demonstration. Many of the movements of attention are comparatively independent of going behavior. The chief characteristic of the general class of responses we call attention is a tendency to be centered upon some restricted area, though some division of attention is possible. We may be listening for an absent noise or watching for an object or movement not yet visible. Another characteristic is the behavior of scanning, sharply reduced and centered when some learned or unlearned cue results in fixation. Arne Towe, in an unpublished doctoral thesis, has some evidence that on successive exposures to a visual pattern which has been made a signal for pecking in pigeons, a bird varies the "aspects" of the visual pattern to which it is responding.

The importance of attention in determining response by the control of the signal has been well stated by Broadbent [1]. The importance of attention for learning theory lies in the fact that all theories which use stimuli as the predictive antecedents of response represent the response as occasioned by the signal, whether the connection is established by associative contiguity or through reinforcement. Attention, involving the nonreception of a signal, can, for S-R theories, prevent response. Strong connection, if we believe we have a measure of associative strength other than probability of occurrence, would not produce any more response than weak connections.

Responses to signals which take the actor's attention away from the signal prevent, for the time being at least, the attachment of new responses to the signal. It is possible that this describes the essential nature of reward and reinforcement. They shut off the signal so that its last association is the response which produced the diversion. A response which removed a drive, if we speak in terms of drive, would operate to the same effect, by rendering the actor inattentive to the classes of stimuli to which the actor's condition contributed attention-value. Broadbent suggests that the role of association in learning is in a sense subordinate to the role of stimulus selection. Both are involved in any acquisition of skill or learning of an act. It is possible that when an animal's response to a continuing stimulus pattern is interrupted by an attention-getting stimulus outside the one being responded to, this might leave the response to that stimulus unaffected; whereas the interruption of response by such a cause as fatigue while still attending to the pattern would make the pattern a signal for avoidance.

The distraction or interruption of attention is, of course, not the only way in which a signal may be removed. Action may directly remove the signal, or remove the actor from the signal.

Dependent variables. What we attempt to predict in going behavior is action—response. All response is made up of movement brought about by effectors or of glandular secretion. The muscles and glands are the organs of response. Every instance of response is analyzable in terms of movement; but the classes of response on a psychological level, as distinct from the reflex movements which are in the domain of physiology, are defined and most easily observed in terms of their end results. We recognize the writing, but if there had been no ink in the pen we could not without extraordinary measures specify the response or recognize the movements of hand and arm that produced it. A description of the action of the individual muscles concerned would be hopeless confusion.

There is here the ground of a separation between psychology and the natural sciences. The chains of cause and effect, the chains of connection between stimuli and responses, have an area not open to observation by known methods. End results are attainable by a variety of movement sequences, a variety that does not appear in the definition of the act, which is made in terms of outcome. Our description is on a level different from movement. What we need to know is how to predict acts. Man, viewed as a machine, learns movements, not acts. The occasion for muscular contraction is the arrival of nerve impulses at the muscle end plates of motor nerves. These impulses are transmitted from the central nervous system: their ultimate occasion is the stimulation of sense organs, though the brain and central system have complex and unexplored functions in the coordination of neural activity and may actually serve to originate, in some sense, the outgoing impulses. The chain of cause and effect therefore ends in muscular contraction. The performance of an act on any one occasion represents one chain of events in sequence. But successive performances of an act may involve sequences very different in nature.

Whatever the mechanism of learning, it must establish a causal chain of connections between stimuli and movement patterns. But psychological observation does not apply to movements as a rule. Horton and I, in an observation of cats escaping from a puzzle box, concluded that each cat accomplished the act of escape by a limited repertoire of movement series, of alternative series in which the specific series used could be clearly related, in a few instances, to differences in the stimulus situation [7]. We were tempted to generalize this observation and conclude that the movement pattern of escape was initiated by the specific pattern of stimuli encountered. No two cats used any very similar movement series, but any one cat used at least one series over and over. There were many repeated movement series that did not lead to escape.

Psychologists, in general, have not been interested in movement in observing learning. They record the end effects—escape, arrival at a goal box, number (but not nature) of "errors." They may go as far as to put an animal into an opaque box which hides the movement series from the observer as effectively as would a blindfold. Our conclusion was that the causal chain leads from physical stimulus to Rmt, meaning by Rmt the integral movement response of the animal.

Just as with practice new partial stimulus patterns S come to be discriminated and to attain status as cues C, a similar process is observable in response. I have in the past suggested that partial or local features of response may become independent of the total pattern. I would now state the matter somewhat differently.

It is these local features that we observe and record. Recurring features of response, for which we have names, are usually all that is noticed. For the total complex we have no names. Muscle groups like those involved in speech or in manipulation can develop patterns that are consistent with a variety of total behavior. We can learn to talk while driving, though the notices often placed above the driver's seat in the bus cautioning the public not to engage the driver in conversation point to limitations in this local independence. Speaking one series of numbers and writing another at the same time is impossible without interference. Most animal studies in learning note one feature only, although it is only one small aspect of a response of the whole organism. Men can learn to add numbers sitting or standing. Few men could extract the square root of 2 while dodging traffic at an intersection. As a rule our absorbed interest in noting one detail of the situation keeps us from noting others.

The partial or subresponse should probably be acknowledged as a part of a total response, and such a performance as uttering the same word sitting and standing acknowledged as two distinct Rmts or integral movement responses. We might distinguish between the Rmt and the detail of such a response in which we happen to be interested, the Rmd. The detail may be the same or equivalent in two different integral responses, Rmd and R'md, as in pronouncing the same word in two different postures. It is probable that learning this independence of local response involves learning a class of integral responses which have the detail or subresponse in common. Learning an act Ra is a very different matter and involves establishing a class of movements Rmt, R'mt, R"mt . . . which all achieve the same end. An act is a class of movements having as their defining feature the attainment of the same end result. The learning of an act involves the presumptive association of a class of cues, C, C', C" . . . with the members of the series, Rmt, R'mt, R"mt . . . . It is the essential feature of acts that they are adapted to the variations in situation.

Association by contiguity. The writer is well aware of his failure to lay down specifications for the data of learning which are sufficiently precise to meet the requirements of laboratory experiment. The present section does not offer a solution. The point of view taken is nevertheless felt to be in some sense compelling.

The sense of the word "cue" here described represents almost universal practice among psychologists. An apparent exception is Skinner's limitation of the meaning of "stimulus" to measures taken by the experimenter. Since Skinner obviously chooses his measures for their tried effects on the reading of a mechanical counter or steps in a kymograph record, and since he assumes, as we would, that the animal made movements leading to these effects, his use of the word "stimulus" proves only an apparent exception. Another exception is the current practice of assuming that the behavior to be conditioned in instrumental conditioning or operant conditioning has no cues because none are in the record, and to infer from this that instrumental conditioning involves a separate kind of learning.

As defined, Ra (act) and Rm (movement) represent uses of the word "response" in current ambiguous use. Skinner notes some detail of the end result, Rad, whereas Pavlov noted a detail of the response, Rmd.

The principle of association by contiguity does not offer as great a chance for agreement as could be reached in specifying the nature of stimulus or cue and response. The principle has taken many forms after the adoption of the restriction to behavior made the older statement in terms of the association of ideas unsatisfactory. In the tradition of C. Lloyd Morgan and Hobhouse and Thorndike it became a principle of association of cue and action resulting in the combination of contiguity and reinforcement. Hull wrote in that tradition. With Pavlov, the principle became a statement of association by contiguity only. Pavlov believed that the repetition of CS and US together strengthened the association, and he had no reference to a need for confirmation through effect. Razran is dealing with this confusion in the use of the term "reinforcement" in a manuscript in preparation.

There has also been disagreement on what it is that is associated. In C. Lloyd Morgan and Hobhouse it was a stimulus, but whether S or C not made clear, and a response, which sometimes would be characterized as a perception, sometimes as a movement, and sometimes as an act. Skinner is the first behaviorist to face the issue of the nature of the stimulus squarely and decide in favor of S in the form of an experimenter's manipulation of the environment; but having faced the issue he might be said to have walked away without solving it from the point of view of theory. The gestalt psychologists recognized association only in the disguised form of a tendency of insights once formed to be repeatable. It is here suggested that a possible statement for use would be: *A cue C previously followed by an integral movement response Rmt which does not include the detail d in which we are interested, will, after it has occurred immediately before an integral movement response R'mt which does involve d, be on the next occasion followed by R'mt and not by Rmt.*

An alternative formulation has, in my opinion, a number of advantages in intelligibility and still embodies the essential features. This alternative is: *what is being noticed becomes a signal for what is being done.*

The first phrase, "what is being noticed," conveys an adequate recognition of the active part that the organism's own activity plays in the selection of physical stimuli through attention. The word "signal" is used as a synonym for "cue" and probably reflects the increasing use of "signal" in communication theory. "What is being done" is to be taken in the primary sense of integral response. The practical use of the rule can be extended to cover acts (with a great loss of predictive specificity) when the act response is understood to include movement responses which serve to restrict attention to a limited field (and thus to restrict response) until some end movement is accomplished, and when previous learning has established a class of integral movement responses all leading to the removal of the maintaining cues.

Hull has packed as much as this into his S (stimulus) when he defines it as the stimulus energy which evokes a response on the basis of a previously formed habit, but this emphasizes the energy of the physical stimulus, whereas I believe the energy to be of minor significance as compared with the role of pattern. If the pattern operates at all or is above the threshold, energy can vary extensively without altering the essential effect. We respond to the sight of a friend in a wide range of illumination, for instance.

Attention becomes, in the present account, the point at which learning occurs. Through attention-getting stimuli, the routinized movement established in past learning can be broken into and new series established. Attention becomes routinized along with the integral response series. We think of the behavior as mechanized or routinized. But attention is open to distraction from intense stimuli or stimuli not part of the learned series. The omission of stimuli that are part of the series may serve to interrupt. An anesthetized finger would in all probability seriously interfere with playing a well-memorized piece on the piano, as would also a burned finger tip. In writing by hand, if attention is diverted from the script to the moving fingers, writing becomes difficult or impossible. Attending to the script is a part of the routine. We tend to think, when we use the word "attention," not of its role in behavior already learned, but of its conspicuous role when routine is interrupted.

The statement of the rule of association given above involves some formidable assumptions, some concerning the nature of cues, some concerning the nature of responses, and some concerning the role of attention in behavior. It will be evident that the writer is engaged in clearing up his own difficulties rather than in expounding a theory. The rule that what is being noticed becomes a signal for what is being done is even more of an oversimplification than the rules which physics offers as applying to its system of ideal solids, liquids, and gases, which are only models for use in understanding the complexity of physical events.

The following is an attempted listing of the more conspicuous of these assumptions. They are not formal postulates.

1. Patterning of physical stimuli is effective as such, as distinct from the effects of degrees of intensity or the summation of the effects of stimulus elements. *This is not to be confused with the gestalt notion that patterns have effects independent of the specific stimuli involved.*

2. The acceptance by an observer of a given pattern of physical stimuli as a cue for the observed organism will depend on data from the past history of the organism or on present observation of the perceptual response to the cue.

3. In the higher animals, the effectiveness of physical stimuli is governed by a class of responses called attention, which may restrict

effect by avoiding the orientation and sense organ adjustment required for effectiveness, or by involving postures allowing or excluding particular responses to the stimuli. Attention has certain natural occasions including intense stimuli, sudden change in situation, movement, and others.

Attention, being part of the integral response, is conditionable as are other detailed features of response. The physical stimuli present in attention become cues for the action elicited.

With intense stimuli or abrupt changes in stimulation, attention may take the form of fixation, and behavior be limited to response to a very restricted area of the physical situation.

4. When two cues that have been associated with integral responses which have incompatible movement patterns are both present, action is withheld and the movements involved in attention become pronounced. Attention includes behavior which may be called scanning and takes the form of rapid changes in sense organ orientation.

5. At any moment the class of integral movement responses possible is limited by the going action. Not only the act of running but the patterns of muscular contraction involved in running are made impossible by sitting in a chair. Running movements are dependent on "feedback" from their own results.

Breaking in upon present action requires normally a diversion of attention by natural or learned cues, and the assumption of a state of readiness or transition. Such a response as stopping running, which is a complicated achievement, cannot be elicited unless an animal is running. Sheffield [13] found that the animal's going behavior at the time a physical stimulus was introduced when added to the record made possible a greatly improved prediction. No cue for stopping can be made effective when an animal is standing or crouching. This holds as well for reinforcement theory as for contiguity theory. There is no response present to reinforce.

The class of movement responses included in the general term "attention" involves changes of stance and of readiness. Practical training recognizes this. The military use of commands to get attention, preparatory commands, and commands of execution is based on the fact that going behavior imposes strict limitations on the movement responses elicitable at any one moment.

6. It is, therefore, assumed that rules which do not take into account what the animal is doing when stimulated will not be descriptive of the phenomenon of association. Present behavior is assumed to be determined in part by movement-produced stimuli which include exteroceptive, interoceptive, and proprioceptive stimuli. These the observer infers from the seen behavior. Even the judgment of an observer that certain visual patterns are acting is an interpretation of the observed orientation of the

animal. It cannot be inferred from the availability of the patterns in the environment.

7. The complexity of the nexus of determiners of action requires that prediction allow for high degrees of error. Most instances of associative learning are cited after the fact, and do not constitute prediction. I believe that it was Wickens who remarked many years ago that the presence of an associative cue appeared to be a necessary but not a sufficient condition of the appearance of the associated response. If we are considering absolute and not contingent prediction this is of course true. But even in this sense the rule of association would have a high practical value because it would lead to the discovery of effective cues by limiting our area of search.

8. An assumption that involves stimuli, responses, and the nature of attention may be added. It may be phrased in common terms: what is being noticed, as a response is elicited, becomes a potential cue for that response. This involves assuming that the central nervous system in some fashion achieves the integration of a specific pattern of physical stimuli as a cue and that this cue selects the response associated with it from then on until the cue has been associated with another response.

INITIAL EVIDENTIAL GROUNDS FOR THESE SUGGESTIONS

It has by this time been made evident that the general position taken here has grown out of common knowledge and a restricted class of experiments in learning. Most of the experimentation on learning has, particularly since Pavlov, attempted to relate physical stimuli directly to acts. These are ideal data for the laboratory in the sense that they minimize the role of an observer's judgment and can be made to record themselves. They deal with the rules of immediate sequence in behavior and, therefore, promise to furnish generalizations that are in some sense basic for the understanding of more complicated behavior. My first reduction in enthusiasm over this approach came in failures to condition certain elementary response details like the knee jerk, and in the mixed results that Yacorzynski and I found in the conditioning of an arm flexion evoked by shock. A winter's research attempted to discover whether visual patterns could be associated with nonsense syllables, when exposed in the periphery of one quadrant of the field of vision, and the response be evoked by the figures in another quadrant. I found that an exposure too brief to allow fixation to travel from the fixation point to the figure did not establish the association in the original quadrant and that the figure could not be named unless visually explored. Recognition when exploration was possible was contingent on noticing "features" such as a sharp angle "like a nose" and features usually describable in words.

Experiments in such areas as maze learning or problem solving had followed the lead of Morgan, Hobhouse, and Thorndike and had been built around the general conception of learning as improvement. The attainment of a goal by means unspecified and unrecorded appeared to involve much more than the strengthening of a response, and did not answer the question of how the specific movements are achieved. On re-reading Thorndike, it occurred to me that every goal achievement is accomplished by specific means and that the real problem is how the organism learns, not general goal achievement, *but its own goal achievement.* In our puzzle-box watching, Horton and I found that cats in general learn to escape and that curves of learning, both for all the cats and for individual cats, could be plotted from the data by overlooking what individual cats did and paying attention only to such data as elapsed times. By our observation sessions and by an examination of our photographs, both still and motion pictures, our opinion was strengthened that what each cat learned was specific series of movements which are altered by many repetitions, very often radically altered, and by new movements which might or might not reduce the time for escape.

Another source of subjective satisfaction with the concepts of associative learning by contiguity was their apparent adequacy for describing the successful cases of interference with children's habits in some hundreds of cases in Smith's clinic. The profitable rule for interference appeared to be to attempt to name and specify the cues responsible for the embarrassing behavior and by any available device seek to produce other and unobjectionable behavior *in the presence of the cues.* This was an astonishingly useful rule in the hands of a skilled clinician wise in the ways of children. The principal topic in the department for many years was the analysis of habit changes in these terms, of course, usually after the fact.

An early concern with learning curves (Ebbinghaus) which were so popular in the 1920s had resulted in the conviction that they were functions of the material to be learned rather than the descriptions of any basic phenomenon. The realization that even nonsense syllables involve previously acquired perception, and that associations are enormously facilitated by perception, led to thinking in terms of cues rather than stimuli. A strong behavioristic bias, dating from Singer's paper, guided thinking toward the explanation of movement as the direction to pursue. The question can always be asked: *how did this movement pattern reach the muscles?* Büsse's *Geist und Köerper* compared the popular notions of interaction of mind and body with a train in which front and rear are joined not by a coupling but by feelings of amity between the conductor in the rear and the engine driver in the front. The search for the coupling has not yet been entirely successful, but there is a strong bias toward a physical chain of connection that is not satisfied with "reward" explanations.

As data, cue and response are not comparable to the instrumented data of physics. They are subject to more errors of observation and their connection is subject to interference, over which control is limited. Every good lecturer, however, can establish on one occasion firm associations in students between the lecturer's own spoken words (physical stimuli which experience shows will operate as cues) and implicit verbal responses in his audience which will be testable in a later examination, and with enough certainty to offer a strong presumption that the student who does not have the answer was absent from the lecture. Paul Fields's rats [4] acquire series of correct choices among successive rows of pictures that might tax the lecturer. The experiment in which a pairing of a stimulus (not verified as a cue) and a response detail is repeated 150 times does not appeal to me as an observation of any basic type of learning.

FORMULATION OF METHOD

The suggested rule of learning, that what is being noticed becomes a signal for whatever is being done, has little resemblance to the predictive equations of physics. In actual use, or in any attempt to verify it or to assess its predictive error in specific classes of instances, it involves data from the past history of the actor as well as data open to present observation. "What is being noticed" cannot be represented by a number and is the object of a consensus of observers. Conventional learning experiments avoid this issue by using stimuli that experience has shown to be uniformly effective in procuring the actor's attention: signals such as shock, sudden noise, tapping a rat's tail, a sudden bright light. These are "built-in" eliciters of attention, and their use enables the experimenter to forget that, in the course of ordinary learning, attention depends on past experience with the patterns of stimuli and on the perceptual reaction that has resulted. The experimenter is also enabled to forget that even these extraordinary stimuli are probably reacted to as perceptual cues and that this reaction may mediate the final response. In generalization, for instance, the fact that a touch at a spot on the left side may evoke a conditioned response, although never previously associated with feeding, may depend on the association of touches in that area with the perception of "an object on the left" and with learned movements of attention or defense that are practically identical for nearby stimuli. The confused and irregular results of experiments on generalization may be explainable in terms of past association and not in terms of a uniform function for which a general equation could be written. The confirmation of this point of view would demand far more elaborate observation than current research provides.

The tenses of the verbs "is being noticed" and "is being done" involve a certain vagueness about the exact instant of the word "becomes." Behavior does not consist of a series of disparate moments; it is a flow of change. Both stimuli and movement responses may be extended over periods of time and the moments we choose for observation, the cross sections of the time series of events, lose much of the significance of what is going on. All responses are responsible for series of stimuli. We pick out certain distinguishable features for observation and record. The observer's judgment and practical convenience set the nature of the data. The exact time relations are thus hard to establish. The experiments in remote association, which in some areas establish an optimum effective period of the order of a half-second between cue and response, probably represent not cause and effect in the sense of immediate succession, but an interval that allows time for attention, perceptual response to the cue (appropriate movement or minimal adjustment), and the cessation of interfering activities. Longer periods allow distraction and the introduction of interfering behavior. They may not at all weaken the "connection" between cue and response but render less probable the occurrence of the cue. Perceptual cues take time to "mature," as is indicated by certain lines of experimentation on reaction times. Such hypothetical links in the chain of causation are open to experiment, but will require arduous and detailed observation.

QUANTITATIVE PROCEDURES

The consistency of observer judgments is measurable in terms of statistical methods. On this basis we can assume that many types of physical stimuli can be used as data because experience has demonstrated that all observers will admit that they are noticed. The intense stimuli in current use fall into this class. Certain other classes of physical stimuli which are potential cues assume in different subjects a common experience (e.g., printed nonsense syllables) or assume that an individual will, on successive occasions, react to the same aspect of the physical pattern. For any pattern or class of patterns this also is open to measure in terms of past observations.

Patterning itself can be measured, in certain classes of patterns, in terms of number of identical elements necessary for equivalence as cues, or in terms of the effective proportion of elements (e.g., the analysis of closure), but in most experiments, if the physical stimuli are above the threshhold as a pattern, the significance of the physical pattern for the experimenter interested in learning is exhausted in noting the presence or absence of the general pattern. There is, of course, an upper limit as well as a lower. Both require observer judgment, and psychological significance is restricted to the range between threshold intensity and the point where other factors change the cue value. Between these points it is a matter of presence or absence.

FORMAL ORGANIZATION

The writer many years ago published an article entitled *Formal Logic and Logical Form* [5] in which the rules of logic and deductive reasoning were held to be practical conventions. This view would contraindicate an interest in formal organization of a system except in those fields in which long experience has gradually established wide areas of general agreement on method and fact, as was true of geometry in Euclid's time and, centuries later, in the fields of astronomy and physics. Psychology has large undigested aggregates like psychoanalysis and the data on public opinion, in which basic agreements have not been worked out. Present day clinical psychology has a strong admixture of ethics and folkways. Even the writers on learning theory are still using definitions of learning which are in different universes of discourse and interest. The use of the laboratory rat almost exclusively as a subject escapes the complications of human learning, not because rat learning is essentially simpler, but because we are protected from many aspects of it since the subjects cannot contribute their own suggestions. It will be a very long time before we are prepared to formalize our account. The problem of reinforcement vs. contiguity should be settled before embarking on a system. When the choice is made too early, and the fundamental definitions and categories become official and items that all graduate students must master for the purpose of nationwide examinations, we may find ourselves committed to unproductive efforts. The scholastics systematized a world of unripe knowledge and may thereby have protected it from its enemies, but at the same time they denied it the chance for progress.

AFTERTHOUGHTS ON THE PREDICTABILITY OF BEHAVIOR

Dr. W. F. Thompson of the Fisheries Research Institute of the University of Washington has pointed out that the runs of salmon in the Columbia River extend over a period of about seven months; in the Frazer River, three hundred miles north, the season is approximately five months, and in the northern salmon streams in Alaska the season is limited to four or five weeks. The runs reflect the climatic conditions under which the eggs can hatch and the young fry survive their first year in fresh water. The severe limits of survival in northern waters are responded to by the development of inherited mechanisms which bring the great majority of the run to the mouth of the home stream during the weeks when propagation and survival are possible, usually after three years in the sea. The frequency curve of return resembles a normal probability curve with the mean a characteristic of the "race" adapted to the stream. The bulk of the run returns not only to the main stream left years before but to the same tributary, even if that is an artificial pond.

If either the date of return or the point of return were narrowly fixed by inheritance, in the rare case of a very early or very late summer the whole race would perish. In such seasons, only the deviants would have offspring. It is Thompson's opinion that the viability of a race depends not only on the development of an inherited return mechanism but on provision for inaccuracy which ensures that there will be a few individuals to take advantage of the changed conditions of climate and locale.

There is in sexual reproduction a natural provision for the introduction of variety through the "shuffling" of chromosomes. Mendelian inheritance can be predicted for the distribution of traits among large numbers but not individual cases in more than a few instances of single dominant traits.

It is possible that natural provision for variability, and so for a limitation on the prediction of individual instances, is made in behavior. On efforts to subject laboratory animals to repeated exposures to the same situation over and over, we are foiled not only by incomplete control of the situation but also by the fact that on each occasion the animal is changed by virtue of its previous experience and by certain characteristics of attention, which has, as in the case of the continuous irregular movements of the eyes, its own "reshuffling" mechanism which alters beyond our complete control the features of the physical stimulus situation available as cues. Hull covered this by allowing for a factor he called "oscillation," but this term does not give full recognition to the introduction of the unpredictable in behavior which is not covered by assuming a normal distribution of error in results. Hull's treatment is based on the fundamental assumption that response is a variable measured in units; but it is rather the occurrence or nonoccurrence that is of importance to psychology. "Oscillation" is not about a point on a dimension but from presence to absence of the response presumably dependent on the presence or absence of the cue, assuming all else the same.

The attainment of high prediction in the case of a single association should be possible following the lead of Pavlov's experience that better control of extraneous stimuli in his new soundproof laboratory with the experimenter not visible reduced the number of pairings required for uniform response from about fifty to the order of ten. If we take precautions to have the subject in the same posture or movement and to ensure attention at the proper moment, it is possible that we will reach a practical certainty of response with one association. This cannot be achieved in maze learning which leaves both factors uncontrolled. It was not attainable by Pavlov's methods which used physical stimuli extended over long periods during which changes in attention were inevitable.

The high predictability of human behavior referred to earlier in this chapter attaches not to the elementary event of the formation of an association but to the complex results of associative learning that has already taken place. Habits involve associations by the score or by the thousand. Once they have been established they are extremely stable. The making and breaking of habits involves reassociation and new associations. It is these elements that are so hard to deal with in the laboratory; but it is quite possible that if we undertake a line of careful observation and control we shall be in a position to accept or reject or to reformulate the rule of learning.

REFERENCES

1. Broadbent, D. E. Classical conditioning and human watch-keeping. *Psychol. Rev.,* 1953, **60,** 331–339.

2. Estes, W. K. Toward a statistical theory of learning. *Psychol. Rev.,* 1950, **57,** 94–107.

3. Estes, W. K., et al. Modern learning theory. New York: Appleton-Century-Crofts, 1954.

4. Fields, P. E. Multiple discrimination learning by white rats. *J. comp. physiol. Psychol.,* 1954, **47,** 472–476.

5. Guthrie, E. R. Formal logic and logical form. *Midwest Quart.,* January, 1914.

6. Guthrie, E. R. *The psychology of learning.* New York: Harper, 1935.

7. Guthrie, E. R., & Horton, G. P. *Cats in a puzzle box.* New York: Rinehart, 1946.

8. Hobhouse, L. T. *Mind in evolution.* London: Macmillan, 1901.

9. Janet, P. *Principles of psychotherapy.* H. M. Guthrie & E. R. Guthrie (Trans.) New York: Macmillan, 1924.

10. Lloyd Morgan, C. *Animal behavior.* London: E. Arnold, 1900.

11. Marshall, H. R. *Consciousness.* London: Macmillan, 1909.

12. Pavlov, I. P. *Conditioned reflexes.* G. V. Anrep (Trans.) London: Oxford Univer. Press, 1927.

13. Sheffield, F. D. Avoidance training and the contiguity principle. *J. comp. physiol. Psychol.,* 1948, **41,** 165–167.

14. Smith, S., & Guthrie, E. R. *General psychology in terms of behavior.* New York: Appleton, 1921.

15. Thurstone, L. L. *The nature of intelligence.* New York: Harcourt, Brace, 1924.

16. Tolman, E. C. The determiners of behavior at a choice point. *Psychol. Rev.,* 1938, **45,** 1–41.

LIBERALIZATION OF BASIC S-R CONCEPTS: EXTENSIONS TO CONFLICT BEHAVIOR, MOTIVATION, AND SOCIAL LEARNING[1]

NEAL E. MILLER
Yale University

[1] Work on this paper was supported by a research grant, M647, from the National Institute of Mental Health, of the National Institutes of Health, Public Health Service.

INTRODUCTION

The plan of this paper is to begin with a rather detailed consideration of some hypotheses about approach-avoidance conflict behavior as a concrete example of theory construction. I believe that the main problems of theory construction are more meaningful if discussed in the context of a real example. This more formal section of Part I will be followed by some informal remarks on the strategy for investigating significant aspects of conflict behavior not covered by the hypotheses.

In Part II I shall comment freely on a potpourri of topics that have especially interested me. First I shall direct attention to a number of changes in conventional S-R concepts which considerably increase their power and range. Then I shall consider certain controversial problems which need additional theoretical and experimental analysis—e.g., creative thought, flexible cybernetic behavior, new trails for research on motivation, and theories of reinforcement. I shall touch briefly on a few of the main points of my collaborative work with John Dollard on social learning, personality, and psychotherapy. Working toward the ultimate goal of a basic science of human behavior, we have tried to integrate certain contributions of the laboratory, the clinic, and the socio-anthropological field study. Finally, I shall deal with the experimental design required but seldom used to justify intervening variables, with implications for psychopharmacology and brain stimulation, and with the strategy of a rigorous though qualitative approach to problems of quantification.

Part I. Approach-Avoidance Conflict Behavior[2]

BACKGROUND FACTORS

My attitudes towards psychological theory have grown out of an early interest and training in physics, chemistry, and biology. These attitudes were further molded by study with Smith and Guthrie at the University of Washington, and especially, by extensive work with Hull at Yale. The general method of analysis of approach-avoidance conflict and the contents of the assumptions involved come directly from Hull.

The interest in the topic of conflict behavior is part of a general line of development started by courses in personality with Terman at Stanford, encouraged by the general atmosphere of the Institute of Human Relations under Mark May at Yale, greatly facilitated by a brief psychoanalysis with Heinz Hartman in Vienna, and sharpened and implemented by intensive collaborative work with John Dollard at Yale.

At present the systematization is at the purely behavioral level, but there is no reason why variables at the physiological and sociological levels should not be introduced. I believe that, in general, the most profitable level of analysis will vary with the specific phenomena being studied and also with the particular contemporary state of development

---

[2] Another exposition of a similar topic has been presented elsewhere [63]. Rather than try to paraphrase certain statements which I have already labored to clarify, I have taken the liberty of plagiarizing a few sentences and even paragraphs from this earlier article of mine.

of the disciplines involved. In other words, it is unsafe to make sweeping generalizations about the most desirable level of analysis since a technological or theoretical breakthrough can completely change the picture.

Specific attitudes toward theory. Pure empiricism is a delusion. A theorylike process is inevitably involved in drawing boundaries around certain parts of the flux of experience to define observable events and in the selection of the events that are observed. Since multitudinous events could be observed and an enormous number of relationships could be determined among all of these events, gathering all the facts with no bias from theory is utterly impossible. Scientists are forced to make a drastic selection, either unconsciously on the basis of perceptual habits and the folklore and linguistic categories of the culture, or consciously on the basis of explicitly formulated theory.

Nature of scientific theory. Scientific theory is only an elaboration and formalization of common-sense processes of perception and communication. Theory is trying to make sense out of observations—to abstract and generalize. The goal of theory construction is to produce a parsimonious system of symbols (in either verbal or other forms) that can be used to make rigorous deductions about some of the consequences of different sets of conditions.

As I see it, there is a continuum from extremely simple to complex examples of theory construction. A simple example is a smooth curve which summarizes a set of empirically determined values. In this case the deduction consists of following certain simple rules to read the curve in order to predict that a given value on the abscissa will yield a certain value on the ordinate. If an empirical equation is fitted to the curve, the solution of that equation constitutes the deduction. At a considerably higher level of development, the equation may be rational instead of empirical. High-school geometry is another familiar example. It consists of a set of definitions and axioms, or in other words, terms and rules for manipulating the terms. This relatively limited number of basic terms and rules can be used to deduce the consequences of the great number of different conditions. Every one who has mastered the system will agree, for example, on the deduction of the Pythagorean theorem. Such agreement is the goal of rigor.

Being able to state any orderly relationship, or in other words, to summarize a set of data parsimoniously by any method is quite an achievement which leads the scientist to believe that he is on a good track. The greater the parsimony (e.g., ratio of facts to assumptions), the greater the achievement and the more likely the scientist is to conclude intuitively that he is on the track of a fundamental regularity in nature.

The principles of lower-level theories may often be deduced from the higher-level ones until finally we reach something like the Maxwell electromagnetic wave theory or the General Theory of Relativity. There is obviously an enormous difference between these higher-level theories and the simple empirical curve, but in at least certain respects, the difference seems to be more one of degree than of kind.

Function of definitions. For example, in order for any of the foregoing types of abstract statements to be useful, the scientist must have some relatively unambiguous way of relating the terms in the theory to the phenomena that interest him. In order to use the simplest empirical curve, he must have some way of relating the values on the abscissa and on the ordinate to relevant observables. This process is not nearly as simple as it seems, since many assumptions may be implicit in the process of observing and defining events and ordering them into even primitive scales. The orderliness of the curves and the generality of their application may depend upon the particular type of measurement used—for example, whether one uses the expansion of a column of water or of hydrogen as the measure on the base line against which to plot other observations. The water will yield complex discontinuities at its boiling and freezing points. The hydrogen will yield simpler, more orderly curves over a much wider range, and hence, is selected as a better measure of temperature.

The linking of the antecedent conditions and consequent deductions of the theory to observable phenomena is accomplished by definitions. Carnap [19] has called such definitions *reduction sentences* because they reduce the terms of the theory to observables. An operational definition is a special kind of reduction sentence. Often psychological theories fail to be useful because there is no practical way of relating both the antecedent conditions and the deduced consequences of the theory with events that can be identified unambiguously and publicly.

Carnap [19] has pointed out that many of the definitions which scientists use to connect theoretical terms with observables are incomplete. They may be called *partial definitions*. The advantage of the partial definition is that it does not completely limit the meaning of the term once and for all but allows room for expanding the meaning, step by step, on the basis of accumulated knowledge. For example, temperature may be defined by the expansion of a column of mercury. This definition is rigorous in that the appropriate use of a mercury thermometer is sufficient to determine the temperature of a body; it is partial in that many other effects, in addition to the expansion of mercury, may be linked with temperature and either used as measures of it or deduced as consequences of it. Examples of other phenomena linked with temperature are changes in the electrical resistance of a wire, the voltage produced by a thermocouple, and the spectrum of emitted light. As long as any room is left for adding such other effects as may be usefully related to temperature, the definition is not complete but partial.

In short, the use of a scientific theory involves three steps: (1) the unambiguous connection of a series of observable antecedent conditions with the terms of the theory by means of definitions, (2) the rigorous derivation of deductions by manipulating the terms according to specific rules, and (3) linking the terms in the deductions with observable phenomena by means of definitions.[3] When an observable consequence of a certain set of conditions is deduced in advance, it is called a *prediction;* when it is derived after the fact, it is called an *explanation* [35].

The foregoing three steps are involved in all the examples of theory from the simple use of empirically fitted curves to the most advanced theories of modern physics. It is to emphasize this similarity that these diverse levels of theory have been placed together.

Limitations of scientific theory. Usually laws formulated by specifying one observable phenomenon directly as a function of other observable conditions are found to have less generality than formulations involving a higher level of theoretical abstraction. The great power of good theoretical constructs comes from their generality. Though science strives towards generality, it is not necessary to have one all-embracing theory. Physics made a great deal of progress while it was still divided into separate, more limited theories such as those of mechanics, hydrostatics, heat, electricity, and optics.

Although different theories should not be scrambled illogically together in one grand eclectic hash, there is nothing to prevent the scientist from using entirely different models to deal with different aspects of his theoretical and practical problems. In short, rigorous but limited models can be extremely useful.

All scientific formulations are highly selective and relatively limited. Thus the laws of falling bodies deal only with masses and forces and have nothing to say about the socially important facts of whether the falling body is a hydrogen bomb that will wipe out a city or a package of supplies that will mean survival to a stranded party. Although the latter distinctions are enormously important, they are not dealt with by that particular set of scientific principles. Similarly, the following hypothesis about approach-avoidance conflict behavior will be limited to only a few aspects of the conflict behavior.

Science is limited in another respect. In order to make predictions,

---

[3] It should be noted that the same term may appear in both the antecedent conditions and the consequent deductions. Thus, in the example of the Pythagorean theorem, the hypotenuse and the base are both measured in the same units of length. Furthermore, the length of the hypotenuse may be predicted in one situation but used as an antecedent condition in a different situation.

one must not only know the *principles* but also the specific *conditions*. Thus an engineer might have a complete knowledge of all of the relevant principles of physics but be unable to predict how much it would cost to build a bridge until he knew all the relevant conditions—the load to be borne, the length of the span, the velocity of winds, and whether the foundation was bedrock or quicksand. Most of the physicist's exact predictions deal with quite specific and precisely defined conditions, such as a freely falling body in a vacuum with accurate instruments available to measure distance and time. No physicist will even attempt to predict where a given snowflake will fall in a blizzard, although snowflakes are much more common and of much greater practical importance than freely falling bodies in a vacuum. Often the engineer applying physical science allows himself factors of safety of more than 200 per cent to take care of uncontrolled variations in the conditions. He may also have to supplement theory with those less precisely verbalized but highly significant results of experience which may be described as art or skill.

Nevertheless, these relatively limited activities of the scientist are of enormous practical value. They have been the essential basis for giving the average man of today medical care, access to the world's greatest music, swift travel, the ability to talk to loved ones at a distance, and myriads of other advantages beyond the dreams of the most powerful princes of the past.

Sophistication of theory and simplification of experiments. In line with the need to control conditions as well as to know principles, it is my impression that, as our theories of learning and behavior are becoming more complex and sophisticated, we are being driven to simpler experimental situations. As Spence [103] has so well illustrated, the old labyrinthian mazes and complex problem-boxes have been found to be hopelessly complex and confusing; we are forced into simpler situations such as the straight runway and the Skinner box. The classical conditioning experiments are one such simplified pure case and the principles derived from them are believed to be a good first approximation to certain useful laws of behavior. The formulation to follow is an example of extending these laws to a new situation and testing deductions derived from such an extension.

Plan of the work on conflict. In a modest way, the example to follow will illustrate a type of experimental-theoretical work which I believe is desirable. Principles which have been abstracted from the results of simple, controlled experimental situations, and which have been found to have a considerable degree of generality, are applied to a new aspect of behavior. As needed, additional assumptions are made. First, very simple deductions from these principles are tested in very simple experimental situations. Then, attempts are made to apply the joint action of a greater number of principles to more complex situations, with additional checks at each successive stage of development.

Role of experiments on animals. It is assumed that the basic mechanisms of learning and conflict are similar enough in man and the other mammals so that work on the latter will often generalize to man. More specifically, the assumption is that all the psychological processes found in other mammals are likely also to be present in man. It should be noted that this assumption does not deny the possibility that man may have additional capacities which are much less well developed or absent in the lower mammals. All that is assumed is that what is found in lower mammals will probably be found also in man.

For certain (but not all) problems it may be desirable to work out the laws first in more rigorously controlled experimental situations with animals. Although these laws will have to be checked later at the human level, it will be easier to check them once they have been precisely formulated so that one knows exactly what to look for than it would to discover them in the complex human situations which are less subject to experimental simplification and control. Furthermore, one's confidence in the conclusions from the less-controlled clinical situation is increased if the same relationship is found also in the better-controlled animal experiments.

Animal experiments seem to be an especially strategic way to investigate certain simple aspects of conflict behavior. On the one hand, the variables that appear to be involved (approach, avoidance, pain, fear, appetitive drives) seem to be common to both species. On the other hand, it is especially hard to subject human subjects in the laboratory to carefully controlled, deliberately elicited, strong conflicts of a vital nature, but relatively easy to do this with experimental animals.

FIRST STAGES OF DEVELOPMENT OF SYSTEM

In the course of an experiment on reaction formation [56], hungry albino rats were first trained to run down a short alley for food, then given electric shocks at the goal. Such animals showed obvious conflict behavior—they would start, go part way toward the goal, stop, and vacillate. The vacillations were characterized by increasingly slower approaches interrupted by sudden withdrawals.

The behavior of these animals seemed worthy of systematic study for the following reasons:

1. The behavior in this experimental situation appeared to be typical of conflict behavior in a wide variety of other situations: squirrels in conflict about taking a nut from a child's hand, children in conflict about

petting strange animals, bashful boys in love with a girl but afraid to ask for a date, and various phenomena observed in the clinic.

2. Evidence from both clinical observations and so-called experimental neuroses indicated the importance of conflict in producing abnormal behavior.

3. The experimental situation allowed a high degree of control of relevant variables in a conflict that was vitally serious to the subject animals.

4. It seemed feasible to devise a little harness device to record in detail an important aspect of the behavior, namely, the responses of approach and avoidance.

5. It was possible to deduce a number of facts about the conflict behavior in terms of assumptions, such as Hull's [36] goal gradient, which had already been found useful in dealing with other aspects of learned behavior. The fact that the observations seemed likely to fit into a meaningful pattern was particularly attractive.

For the foregoing reasons, it seemed desirable to initiate a program of theoretical and experimental analysis of conflict behavior. The new approach of trying to analyse the *laws* of conflict behavior instead of attempting to produce allegedly neurotic behavior, seemed likely to lead to increased scientific understanding, and to help to bridge the gap between the laboratory and the clinic.

The postulates. It seemed possible to account for a number (but not all) of the significant aspects of the conflict behavior in terms of the following assumptions:

(A) *The tendency to approach a goal is stronger the nearer the subject is to it.* This is an application of Hull's [36] principle of the goal gradient and will be called the *Gradient of Approach.*

(B) *The tendency to avoid a feared stimulus is stronger the nearer the subject is to it.* This was an extension of the general idea of the gradient of reinforcement [80] to avoidance learning. It will be called the *Gradient of Avoidance.*

(C) *The strength of avoidance increases more rapidly with nearness than does that of approach.* In other words, the gradient of avoidance is *steeper* than that of approach. This was a new assumption necessary to account for the behavior of going part way and then stopping.

(D) *The strength of tendencies to approach or avoid varies directly with the strength of the drive upon which they are based.* In other words, an increase in drive raises the *height* of the entire gradient. This assumption was necessary to explain the fact that stronger shocks stopped the animals whereas weaker shocks did not and also to explain the intuitively expected result that stronger shocks would be necessary to stop hungrier animals. This assumption was a specific application of the general notion that response strength varies with relevant drive.

(E) *Below the asymptote of learning, increasing the number of reinforced trials will increase the strength of the response tendency that is reinforced.*

(F) *When two incompatible responses are in conflict, the stronger one will occur.*

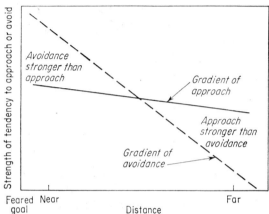

Fɪɢ. 1. Simple graphic representation of an approach-avoidance conflict. The tendency to approach is the stronger of the two tendencies far from the goal, whereas the tendency to avoid is the stronger of the two near to the goal. Therefore, when far from the goal, the subject should tend to approach part way and then stop. In short, he should tend to remain in the region where the two gradients intersect.

It is only for the sake of simplicity that the gradients are represented by straight lines in these diagrams. Similar deductions could be made on the basis of any curves that have a continuous negative slope that is steeper for avoidance than for approach at each point above the abscissa. *From Miller* [59].

The last two assumptions also are ones which have been found useful in accounting for other types of data. Therefore only one of the assumptions, namely, C, is new.

Some deductions. The first deductions following from these assumptions are illustrated in Figs. 1-3. It should be noted that the gradients cross each other in all these figures. All of the following deductions hold only within the range of conditions which allow the gradients to intersect.

It is also assumed that the subject is free to move, is started away from the goal, and has had enough time to reach his point of equilibrium.

In the first figure, it can be seen that the approach is stronger than the avoidance at a distance from the goal, so that the subject should start out by approaching, but when he goes beyond the point at which the gradients intersect, avoidance is stronger than approach so he should stop. The first deduction is:

1. *The subject should approach part way and then stop.* It should be noted that this behavior of going part way and then stopping can be deduced only from the particular assumptions used. If the gradients are

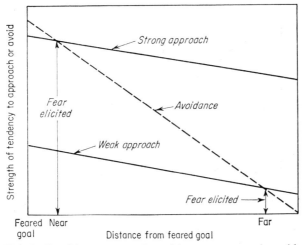

Fig. 2. Graphic representation of how an approach-avoidance conflict is affected by increasing the strength of approach. *From Miller* [59].

parallel, the subject will be expected either to go all the way up to the goal or to retreat completely away from it, depending on which tendency is stronger. If the approach is steeper than the avoidance, subjects started near to the goal will be expected to go all the way up to it; subjects started farther from the goal will be expected to retreat until the strength of avoidance becomes negligible.

Figure 2 shows that raising the height of the approach gradient should move the point of intersection nearer to the goal. The height of the approach gradient can be raised by increasing the strength of hunger (D) or by increasing the number of reinforced training trials (E). The next two deductions follow:

2. *Increasing the strength of hunger should cause subjects to approach nearer to the goal.*

3. *Increasing the number of reinforced training trials (below the asymptote) should cause subjects to approach nearer to the goal.*

Similarly, as Fig. 3 shows, raising the height of the gradient of avoidance should cause the subject to remain farther away from the goal. The height of the gradient of avoidance can be raised by increasing the strength of fear (D) or by increasing the number of reinforced avoidance trials (E). Hence, the next two deductions follow:

4. *Increasing the strength of fear should cause the subjects to remain farther away from the goal.*

5. *Increasing the number of reinforced avoidance trials (below the*

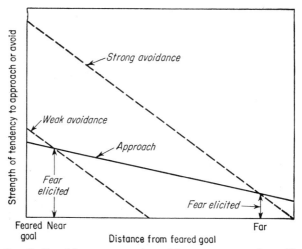

Fig. 3. Graphic representation of how an approach-avoidance conflict is affected by increasing the strength of avoidance. *From Miller* [59].

asymptote) should cause the subjects to remain farther away from the goal.

It should be noted that, for convenience of exposition, the gradients of approach and avoidance are drawn as straight lines. Exactly the same deductions, however, would follow from any types of curves that have a negative slope throughout that is steeper for avoidance than approach at each value on the abscissa.

The advantage of the graphic type of exposition and deduction that we have employed is that it is simple and readily understood. The disadvantage is that one must draw some particular type of curve, thus implying a more specific assumption concerning the exact shape of the function than is necessary for immediate purposes or desirable on the basis of available evidence. Then, this implication has to be denied by a somewhat awkward disclaimer. It would be possible to make more rigorous and elegant deductions using either the algebra of inequalities or symbolic logic. Such a deduction, however, would consume more space and be harder for the average reader to follow.

Some partial definitions. In order to test the deductions, it was necessary to relate the terms of the theory to specific experimental conditions by partial definitions. Actually, these definitions were intuitively assumed at first; the following formal statement was made much later. Note that whereas the postulates are labeled by capital letters, the partial definitions are labeled by small ones.

a. Nearness can be measured by spatial distance in the experimental alley.

b. The animals running to food are being trained to approach under the motivation of hunger.

c. Each trial running to food when hungry is a reinforced training trial for approach.

d. Greater amounts of food deprivation, up to a limit of at least 48 hr under the particular conditions used, produce greater strengths of hunger drive.

e. Animals running away from electric shock are being trained to avoid under the motivation of fear.

f. Each trial on which the animals receive electric shock is a reinforced trial for avoidance.

g. Greater strengths of electric shock, within the limits used, produce greater strength of fear drive.

h. Within the limits of the animal's capacity, the strength of the response tendency is positively related to the speed with which the subject will start to run.

i. Within the limits of the animal's capacity to pull, the strength of the response tendency is positively related to the strength of pull exerted by an animal temporarily restrained.

Verification of deductions about separate effects. The first experiments actually performed had to do with developing the recording technique and confirming deductions concerning the effects of strength of shock and of hunger on conflict behavior [55]. It was only after these experiments were under way that we thought of studying the avoidance and the approach tendencies separately in still simpler experimental situations. It often happens that the simplest ideas are not the ones that occur first.

For clarity of exposition, we shall first describe the experiments studying approach and avoidance separately in very simple situations. In the first of these, Bugelski and Miller [14] trained albino rats to run away from a brief electric shock received at the distinctive end of a straight alley. On test trials without shock, they confirmed a simple deduction from the gradient of avoidance (B) and the partial definition (h) relating strength of tendency to starting speed:

6. *Subjects placed nearer the end of the alley at which they had received shocks started running faster than those placed farther from the shock end.*

Meanwhile, our group was casting about for better ways to study separately the effects of the gradients of approach and avoidance. Eventually, we evolved the strength-of-pull technique which involved another

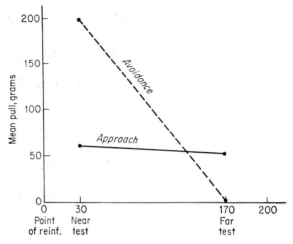

Fig. 4. Gradients of approach and avoidance. The approach gradient represents the force with which rats under a 48-hr hunger drive pulled against a restraining harness at different distances from the point at which they had been fed. The avoidance gradient shows the force with which rats pulled away from the point at which they had received a strong shock on the previous trial. *From Brown* [12].

partial definition (i). Using this technique, Judson Brown [12] secured evidence summarized in Figs. 4 and 5, verifying the following simple deductions:

7. *Approach animals pulled harder when stopped near to the goal than they did when stopped far from the goal.*

8. *Avoidance animals pulled harder when stopped near to the goal than when stopped farther from the goal.*

9. *Distance from the goal reduced the strength of pull of the avoidance animals more than that of the approach ones.* It should be noted that, on the basis of exploratory work, the experimental conditions were

arranged so that the strength of pull for the avoidance animals was stronger than that of the approach animals in the test near the goal and weaker than that of the approach animals in the test far from the goal. Since this kind of reversal (i.e., crossing of the gradients) could not possibly be produced by any distortion in the units at different levels of the scale on the ordinate, the demonstration of greater steepness of avoidance did not involve any assumptions about the equality of the units on

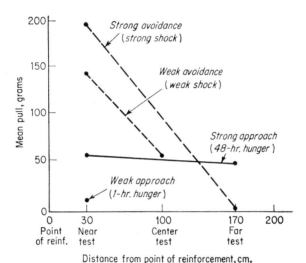

FIG. 5. Effect of strength of drive upon height of gradient. The two avoidance gradients represent the strength of pull on near and far nonshock tests of two groups of rats that had received shocks of different strengths. The approach gradient represents the strength of pull at near and far points of animals tested after 48 hr of food deprivation; weak approach represents a single test at the near point of another group of animals with 1 hr of food deprivation. *From Brown* [12].

the ordinate. I believe that it is very important clearly to recognize that at present most of our measurements are made with scales that do not necessarily involve psychologically equal units. Therefore, we should try to design tests that do not depend on the dubious assumption of equal interval scales.

10. *Increasing the number of hours of food deprivation increased the strength of pull of the approach animals.*

11. *Increasing the strength of electric shock increased the height of the gradient of avoidance measured by strength of pull.*

It should be noted that even in these simple experiments, the assumptions were not tested directly. Each test involved the partial definitions of experimental conditions, such as nearness and strength of hunger. Each test also involved the assumption contained in the partial definition (h or i) on which the technique of measurement was based.

Verification of deductions about joint effects. Having seen that the simple deductions, involving the separate effects of approach and avoidance were verified, let us now turn to the deductions involving the joint effect of approach and avoidance in a conflict situation. In order to test these deductions, Miller, Brown, and Lewis [75] trained albino rats to run down a short alley to food while wearing a harness attached to a device which traced on moving paper a record of their runs. Then they were given electric shocks at the goal. Different groups were tested after different strengths of shock and with different degrees of hunger. Deductions 1, 2, and 4 were confirmed. The rats tended to go part way to the goal and then stop. As can be seen in Fig. 6, either decreasing the strength of hunger or increasing the strength of electric shock caused the rats to stop farther from the goal.

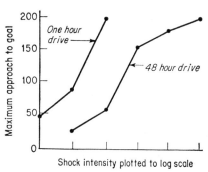

Shock intensity plotted to log scale

Fig. 6. Effect of strength of shock and of hunger on farthest run toward goal in an approach-avoidance conflict.

At a considerably later time, Kaufman and Miller [42] confirmed deduction 3 by showing that in groups given progressively more approach-training trials, progressively more of the animals reached the goal in spite of having received electric shock. Incidental observations appear to confirm the analogous deduction 5 with respect to the effect of increased number of avoidance trials reinforced by shock, but that deduction has never been systematically tested.

In short, 10 out of 11 deductions have been confirmed, and incidental evidence suggests that the eleventh is probably correct. The ratio of 10 deductions to 6 assumptions (and 9 partial definitions) would not be impressive if each assumption and definition were made *post hoc* to fit the data from these particular experiments. Since only one assumption was new, and the partial definitions were determined (although not explicitly stated) before the experiments on the basis of other experience, the ratio of new facts to new assumptions is high and the verification is quite convincing.

Deduction of greater steepness of avoidance gradient. While testing the foregoing deductions, Judson Brown and I had been speculating on the basis for the greater steepness of the gradient of avoidance. It did not seem reasonable that this was a function merely of the difference between going toward and away. Although we realized that the slope of such gradients could be modified by special discrimination training [59], such training did not seem to be involved in our experiments. Finally, we agreed on an explanation based on the following two additional assumptions which are commonly made in stimulus-response learning theory:

(G) *In the conflict situation (anticipatory to shock) fear is a learned drive elicited primarily by situational cues but hunger is more dependent on internal physiological factors.*
(H) *The strength of learned drives, like that of other learned responses, varies inversely with distance from the point of reinforcement.*

The essence of the deduction is as follows. Since fear is a learned drive, it will be most strongly aroused by the cues originally most closely associated with reinforcement. Therefore, when the subject is confronted with cues at a distance, the gradient of reinforcement will have a double effect—it will weaken not only the specific responses involved in withdrawal, but also the fear motivating these responses. This double effect will cause the avoidance to fall off rapidly. On the other hand, since the hunger motivating approach is more dependent on internal physiological factors, it will be less influenced by distance from the point of reinforcement so that its strength will remain relatively constant. The gradient of reinforcement will operate only on the responses involved in approach; it will not also affect the drive. Therefore, one can deduce:

12. *The gradient of approach should fall off less steeply than that of avoidance.*

As far as the current experiments on conflict were concerned, adding the two new assumptions (G and H) in order to replace assumption C by deducing it from them, reduced rather than increased the parsimony of the system. However, these assumptions had been found to be extremely useful in dealing with a considerable amount of experimental data in other areas of learning and behavior theory [64] and, as will subsequently be seen, suggested new deductions which were experimentally confirmed.

SUMMARY OF VARIABLES IN FIRST STAGES OF SYSTEM

The variables used to account for the results of the experiments in the conflict alley may now be listed and discussed according to the categories suggested in the outline of Project A. A diagrammatic summary of these variables is presented in Fig. 7.

Variables I through IV are the intervening variables. It will be noticed that, on the antecedent side, each of these is the point of convergence of more than two arrows, and on the consequent side, the source of several arrows either directly (in the case of III and IV) or via another variable (in the case of I and II). I believe that there is no justification for using an intervening variable unless there is reason to expect the variable to be affected by at least two antecedent conditions

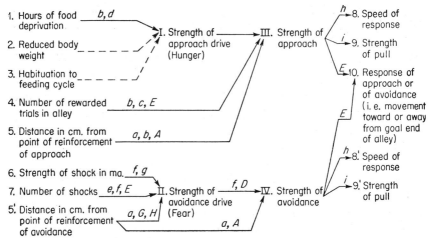

Fig. 7. Simplest formulation to account for results of experiments completed in the conflict alley. The arrows representing the functional relationship assumed between the terms are labeled with letters indicating the definitions or assumptions involved. There are a considerable number of additional unspecified variables, such as amount of food used as a reward, size of bars in shock grid, and individual differences among rats, which are either held constant or randomized by the experimental design and hence may be omitted for the present purpose. The response of approach (or avoidance), 10 on the consequent side, changes the distances 5 and 5' on the antecedent side. Thus, there is an effect, like that of negative feedback, which tends to produce movement toward a point of equilibrium. See the text for further discussion.

and have at least two consequents. A later section will discuss the experimental design needed, but seldom employed, to make intervening variables useful.

Relativity of systematic vs. empirical distinction.[4] Variables 1 through 7 are independent; 8, 9, and 10 are dependent. Although these variables are closely related to specific experimental operations, it should be noted

[4] The discussion in this section takes off from a distinction made by Koch in the original outline of these volumes and further specified in a personal communication from him.

that they are stated in somewhat general terms. Therefore, according to the usage of this book, they should probably be called *systematic* independent and dependent variables.

For example, "hours of food deprivation" does not specify the exact proportion of various elements in the diet used to maintain the animal. It is assumed that the same general qualitative type of relationship— namely, that, within limits, greater number of hours of deprivation produces stronger hunger and stronger pull—will hold for different kinds of diets. This assumption could turn out to be false. Therefore, one should call "hours of deprivation" a systematic independent variable. The more complete specifications of the maintenance schedule would be the empirical independent variable.

The distinction between systematic and empirical variables, however, is relative. Suppose one were to specify the proportion of carbohydrates, fats, and proteins in the diet. These might turn out to be satisfactory empirical independent variables, or it might turn out that various carbohydrates were not interchangeable so that one would have to descend to a still lower level. One might even specify flour made of wheat from a given source, only to find that an as yet unknown vitamin was essential so that the particular vintage or conditions of storage of the wheat were crucial.

It is possible to proceed down the scale to an almost infinite number of possible empirical independent variables; even the most detailed operational description of procedure involves assumptions about the general applicability of the terms used. It is impossible for a theorist to be completely certain in advance whether or not these assumptions are justifiable. It is equally impossible for a person who believes himself to be a pure empiricist to avoid such assumptions. For example, some of the early quantitative work on the combustion of gases was confused by the fact that the chemists of those days did not know that hydrogen and carbon monoxide were two different gases [21].

Dynamic relationships. Returning to Fig. 7, it will be noted that 5′ (Distance from Point of Reinforcement for Avoidance) has arrows indicating that it affects both II (Strength of Fear) and IV (Strength of Avoidance). This dual effect for avoidance, compared with the single effect for approach, is the basis for the greater effect of distance on avoidance than on approach. But it can also be seen that the Response of Approach or Avoidance on the consequent side of the diagram will change the Distance in centimeters from the Point of Reinforcement on the antecedent side. Because such changes in distance affect the strength of avoidance more than that of approach, the response of approaching tends to increase the relative strength of avoidance until approach is stopped, whereas the response of avoidance tends to decrease the relative strength of avoidance until it is stopped. It is this phenomenon (analogous to negative feedback) which leads to the deduction of a point of stable equilibrium represented diagrammatically by the point at which the two gradients cross.

We have just pointed out that Distance from the Point of Reinforcement for Avoidance has arrows indicating that it affects both Strength of Fear and Strength of Avoidance. It would be consistent with general S-R learning theory to assume similar dual effects (indicated by similar double arrows) also for 6 (Strength of Shock) and 7 (Number of Shocks). Such assumptions have not been made specific, however, since they are not involved in any of the experiments to date. Indeed, it would be difficult to devise an appropriate test comparing the effect of strength of shock with that of strength of hunger until we can discover some independent means of equating the strength of these two drives in the same way that a meter stick can be used to equate the distances of approach and avoidance.

In Fig. 7, each of the arrows representing functional connections between terms is labeled with letters designating the partial definitions or assumptions involved in the relationship. It will be noticed that some terms are linked only by definitions (represented by small letters), some are linked only by assumptions (represented by capital letters), and others are linked by both. This emphasizes the fact that the distinction between a major assumption (postulate or law) and a partial definition is often a relative and somewhat arbitrary one. For example, the laws of physics involve definitions and the usefulness of the definitions is dependent on the particular uniformities in nature expressed in certain laws. Thus, various laws, such as Ohm's law, are involved in the construction of the meters commonly used to measure volts and amperes.

Sample of General Issues in Behavior Theory Not Included in System

The arrows from two of the independent variables, Reduced Body Weight and Habituation to Feeding Cycle, are only dotted lines and are not labeled by any letters. In this particular series of experiments, these variables were merely held constant; therefore no special assumptions were made about their effects. It would be easy to make such assumptions, however, and to test the deductions resulting from them. These particular variables were put into the diagram to illustrate the belief that strength of hunger depends on a number of factors. A considerable number of other variables, such as amount and palatability of food used as a reward, size of bars in the grid, and method of controlling electric current, are omitted from the diagram because these variables were either held constant or randomized by the design of the present series of experiments. It is frequently desirable to restrict one's problem in this way, but one cannot be certain in advance whether the particular restrictions will increase or decrease the fruitfulness of the work.

The present formulation deals with strength of hunger during performance, or in other words, at the time the test is made. One could also ask: "What is the effect of strength of hunger during training?" In other words, one could transpose to the conflict situation the problem of the effect of drive on learning vs. on performance. Going to the logical extreme of running animals to food when not hungry and testing them when hungry raises the problem of latent learning. Similarly, an investigation of the effects of changing either the strength or the type of drive between training and testing would get one into the problem of drive generalization. One could also try to determine whether the effects of drive and of number of reinforced approach trials combine multiplicatively or in some other fashion. Massed vs. distributed trials could be studied or forgetting curves plotted, or one might start off from an early experiment of mine [53] and analyze the conditions under which a rat placed directly into the goal box, which was concealed by a curtain, and shocked there would, without any further training, show *foresight* by not running down an alley leading to that goal box. Work of this kind would enter the realm of the higher mental processes. In short, most of the manifold problems of learning and behavior theory are potentially involved in this miniature system.

As a point of departure, it would be simplest to assume that all the variables involved in these problems have effects on conflict behavior similar to those observed in other experimental situations. But that assumption is by no means certain. Ultimately, the effect of all these variables could and should be investigated in a conflict situation. If these variables function in the same way in the conflict and in other situations, this finding will increase our faith that we are "carving nature to the joint." If they function in different ways, we shall be faced with new and interesting problems.

With such a large number of possibilities available, and only limited resources, the investigation of all these variables was deferred and no specific assumptions were made concerning their effects. The decision, then, was to hold such variables constant in the studies while expanding the theoretical and experimental program in a different direction.

INCLUSION OF STIMULUS SIMILARITY AND EXTENSION TO DISPLACEMENT

Now that the early stages of the development of the miniature system have been described, some of its extensions may be briefly sketched.

From almost the beginning, we thought of distance in space as a special case of the stimulus similarity. According to this hypothesis, the spatial gradients of approach and avoidance could be derived from the more general principle of a gradient of stimulus generalization. Furthermore, the notion of a gradient of stimulus generalization allowed us to incorporate into the system conflicts induced by difficult discriminations. The theoretical analysis and experimental verification have been described elsewhere [10, 59].

Tests of simple deductions. We shall only mention here an experiment in which Brown [11] trained animals to approach an illuminated ground-glass panel to secure food. Then he measured the rat's strength of pull when temporarily restrained as a function of the similarity of the test illumination to that during training. The effects of absolute brightness were balanced out by groups originally trained to approach either dim or bright panels, respectively.

He found that the animals tested with stimuli more similar to those used in training pulled harder and thus verified a simple deduction from the assumption that there is a gradient of stimulus generalization of the approach responses. Furthermore, animals tested with food deprivation pulled harder on both the similiar and dissimilar tests, thus verifying a simple deduction from the assumption that increases in drive raise the height of the entire gradient. (See Fig. 16.) Incidentally, I believe that this latter assumption may account for a considerable range of phenomena outside the realm of conflict behavior—for example, apparent reductions in S-R thresholds under increased drive, effect of drive on responses in certain projective test situations, and certain aspects of hallucinatory behavior.

More complex deductions. If one assumes that gradients in space and in other dimensions of stimulus similarity are basically the same, one will expect the gradient of stimulus generalization of avoidance motivated by a learned drive, such as fear, to be steeper than that of approach motivated by a primary drive such as hunger. This assumption, along with the preceding ones, allows us to extend the miniature system to include phenomena of the type that have been described clinically as displacement. In an analysis presented elsewhere [61], I have used this extension to derive the following eight deductions describing specific ways in which the phenomena of displacement should be affected by various conditions:

1. *When the direct response to the original stimulus is prevented by the absence of that stimulus, displaced responses will occur to other similar stimuli, and the strongest displaced response will occur to the most similar stimulus present.* For example, a girl who is prevented from marrying her sweetheart by his death, and who is completely recovered from her grief and other possibly negative factors, will be expected to prefer the suitor who is most similar to him.

2. *When the direct response to the original stimulus is prevented by conflict, the strongest displaced response will occur to stimuli which have an intermediate degree of similarity to the original one.* Thus a girl who is prevented from marrying her sweetheart by a violent quarrel would be expected to prefer someone not completely similar, but not completely different.

3. *If the relative strength of the inhibitory response is increased, the point of strongest displacement, and hence object choice, will shift in the direction of stimuli which are less similar to the original one eliciting the direct response.* In other words, the more unhappy the girl's experience with her previous sweetheart, the less similar should be her choice of a second love object.

4. *If the strength of the drive motivating the direct response to the original stimulus is held constant, the strength of a displaced response will be weaker than the direct response to the original stimulus would have been.*

5. *If the strength of the drive motivating the direct response to the original stimulus is held constant, the strength of the displaced response will be greater when the direct response to the original stimulus is prevented by the absence of that stimulus (provided other very similar stimulus objects are present), and progressively weaker the stronger the inhibition involved.*

Corollary: If the inhibition is strong enough so that the two gradients do not cross, no displaced response will occur.

6. *If the drive motivating the direct response to the original stimulus is increased, the strength of all displaced responses will be increased.*

7. *If the strength of the drive motivating the direct response to the original stimulus is increased, it will be possible for increasingly dissimilar stimuli to elicit displaced responses.* This might give the appearance of lowering the threshold of response to such stimuli.

8. *In situations in which the direct response to the original stimulus is prevented by conflict, increasing the strength of the drive to the inhibited response will shift the point of strongest displacement, and hence object choice, in the direction of stimuli which are more similar to the original one eliciting the direct response.*

General clinical evidence seems to confirm these deductions. Furthermore, other investigators have extended this system to predictions of behavior in projective doll-play situations and have secured verifications of a number of deductions [109, 97].

Additional experimental tests. After seeing that the more general assumptions would help to explain clinical phenomena of displacement, an attempt was made to test deductions in experimental situations. Murray and Miller [89] used the strength-of-pull technique to study separately the generalization of approach and avoidance to new stimulus situations, e.g., from a narrow black to a wide white alley. They confirmed the simple deductions, by showing (1) that there is a gradient of generalization for both habits, and (2) that the avoidance habit is weakened more by generalization than the approach one.

Miller and Kraeling [79] verified the deduction from the joint action of the two types of generalization by showing that when an approach-avoidance habit is established in one situation and generalized to another somewhat similar one, albino rats are more likely to approach the goal in the new situation than in the original one.

Murray and Berkun [88] applied the model to a situation involving both the dimensions of distance and similarity and confirmed the following deductions: After an approach-avoidance conflict had been established in an original alley, rats left it and entered other somewhat different ones. The more different the new alley, the nearer they approached to the food end. The second of these two deductions has been confirmed in a somewhat different experimental situation by Berkun [6] who also confirmed a number of additional deductions concerning the "therapeutic" effects of various types of trials in the original and in the displacement situation.

Implications for projective tests. The extension of conflict theory to displacement has certain implications for projective tests. When a response to an original stimulus is inhibited by conflict, we might expect it to be more likely to occur to a somewhat similar but somewhat different stimulus than to a more direct question about, or picture of, the original situation. Furthermore, the stronger the subject's motivation, and the weaker his inhibition, the more likely the inhibited response should be to occur.

But other factors must be considered also. One of these is the nearness (or similarity along a variety of culturally modified dimensions) of the response elicited by the test situation to the primary tabooed one. Combining this dimension with the one of stimulus similarity, one might expect pictures depicting a violent form of aggression against an insect to be roughly equivalent to those depicting a mild form of aggression against a man.

Other dimensions are the ambiguity of the eliciting stimulus which will determine the range of responses that are not in too direct conflict with it, and the generally permissive or prohibitive context of the test situation. To these we must add the subject's responses to certain thoughts which may be elicited but not reported. For example, the lower avoidance in the projective situation might release a sexual or aggressive thought that would be frightening enough to cause the subject to "retreat" and fail to express even relatively innocent thoughts.

From the foregoing incomplete analysis we can see why the method of the projective test should have certain advantages, but we can also see that the factors determining the net outcome of the conflicting tendencies are by no means simple.

Why avoidance gradient is steeper. The extension of the assumptions about spatial distance to include all dimensions of stimulus generalization made it easier to test a crucial prediction from the assumptions used in deducing the greater steepness of the gradient of avoidance. Applied to the situation of stimulus generalization, the essence of the original deduction runs as follows. When the subject is tested for avoidance in a stimulus situation different from the one used in training, the gradient of stimulus generalization has a double effect—it will weaken not only the specific responses involved in avoidance, but also the fear motivating these responses. When a similar test is given to other subjects who have been trained to approach, the gradient of stimulus generalization will not affect the hunger, which is primarily dependent on internal physiological factors, but only the responses involved in approach. Therefore, the gradient of approach should fall off less steeply than that of avoidance.

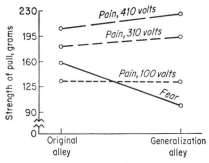

This line of reasoning leads also to the following deduction. If one group of avoidance animals is taught to run down an alley in order to escape from a strong electric shock and then is tested

FIG. 8. The generalization of responses motivated by the learned drive of fear and by the primary drive of pain. *From Miller and Murray* [82].

without shock in both the original and a different alley, that group should show a steep gradient of stimulus generalization because both the fear motivating their behavior and the habit of running will be weakened by the change to the new alley. If another group of animals is trained in exactly the same way but tested in both alleys *with the shock on,* the change in the stimulus situation will not be expected to affect the drive (pain and fear from shock) but only the habit of running. Therefore, this group should show a less steep gradient of stimulus generalization.

The results of an experiment by Miller and Murray [82] testing this deduction are shown in Fig. 8. It can be seen that, exactly as predicted, the group trained and tested with a 310-volt shock showed a relatively flat gradient of stimulus generalization (actually sloping up, but not reliably so), while the fear group, trained with a 310-volt shock and tested without shock, showed a gradient that sloped downward. The difference in slope is highly reliable in the direction confirming the deduction.

It can be seen also that administering the tests with the shock on not only greatly flattened the gradient of stimulus generalization but also raised the height of the entire gradient. Therefore, one could say that the gradient was flatter merely because the animals in the different alley were pulling as hard as they could so that further increases in strength of avoidance could not increase the strength of pull. This would be the same thing as saying that the units of measurement were greatly compressed toward the top of the ordinate so that the upper curves were spuriously flattened. One check on this was further to increase the strength of shock. As can be seen, this increased the height of the gradient, indicating that we were not running entirely off the scale.

Another much more convincing check was running another group trained and tested with a weaker shock (100 volts). As can be seen, the gradient of this group actually crossed that of the one trained with the stronger shock but tested without shock. Since the relationship of crossing can not be an artifact of the units of measurement, our confirmation did not depend on any assumptions concerning the equality of the units on the ordinate.

Can the approach gradient ever be steeper than that for avoidance? We have just seen evidence supporting the deduction that the greater steepness of the gradient of avoidance in our experimental situations was produced by the fact that distance (or stimulus dissimilarity) had a double effect on that gradient—weakening not only the strength of the avoidance habit, but also that of the learned fear motivating that habit. This type of analysis raises an interesting question: what would happen if the drive motivating avoidance were elicited chiefly by internal cues, which remained relatively constant in different external stimulus contexts, whereas the drive motivating approach was primarily aroused by external cues which changed with the stimulus context?

In such a case, the gradient of approach should be steeper than that of avoidance. Then, as has already been explained, we would expect the subject either (a) not to approach at all, if the intersection of the gradients was between him and the goal, or (b) to go completely up to the goal, if he was between it and the point of intersection. The subject's behavior might vary markedly from situation to situation, but we would not see that pattern of approaching part way and then stopping and vacillating which is so easy to identify as a symptom of conflict. It is conceivable that such behavior occurs under certain circumstances, but has been generally unreported because it is less perspicuous than the other pattern.

Summary of Variables in the System Expanded to Include Displacement and Additional Independent and Dependent Variables

A somewhat expanded formulation to account for experiments performed on conflict and displacement and for future experiments involving certain additional variables is summarized in Fig. 9. The intervening variables are I through IX; the systematic independent variables are 1 through 21; the systematic dependent variables are 22 through 28. Because the distinctions among such variables are not absolute, we see again that some of the variables that are described as systematic independent might, on some interpretations of the theory, be classified as empirical independent. Distance in centimeters from point of reinforcement of approach is a case in point. Similarly, a few variables that have been classified as intervening might be considered to be systematic independent, examples being amount of reinforcement for approach, stimulus similarity, and strength of noxious stimulus. In any event, the exact classification of the variables is not nearly as important as the way they are assumed to function.

One of the most important changes in the diagram is that the intervening variables are made the focus of more arrows. For example, hunger is assumed to be affected by six different independent variables and to affect the rate of bar pressing reinforced on a variable-interval schedule as well as the strength of approach measured by speed of response and strength of pull. These assumptions suggest a large amount of additional experimental work. To give a single example, any combination of factors 1 through 6 which produces an increase in rate of bar pressing will be expected also to produce an increase in speed of response, strength of pull, and distance of approach toward the goal. If the results of a variety of experiments testing such expectations show the type of consistent interrelations demanded by the assumptions, the status of hunger as a useful unitary intervening variable will be greatly increased. But there is a very real possibility, indeed a probability, that such experiments will show that this simple formulation has to be modified. This general topic will be pursued further in a later section on the type of experimental design required, but seldom used, to make intervening variables useful.

Many additional experimental problems are implicit in this expanded formulation. We shall discuss only a few examples. The dotted arrow with the circled minus sign between hours of water deprivation and strength of hunger is meant to raise the problem of the possible interactions between hunger and thirst. After the various interactions have been studied, will the results fall into a simple pattern so that a given strength of thirst, no matter how it is produced, has a certain effect on

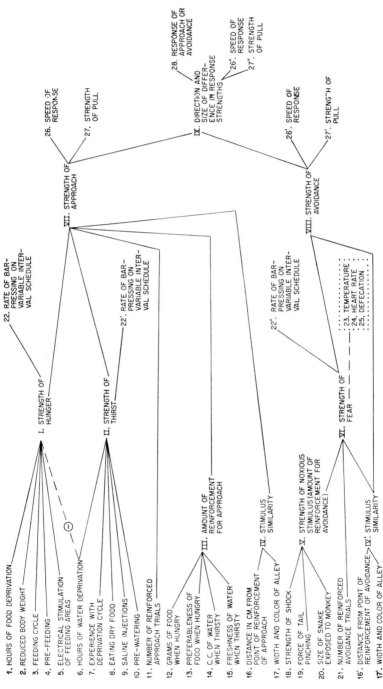

FIG. 9. Somewhat expanded formulation to account for experiments performed on conflict and displacement and future experiments involving certain additional variables.

224

the strength of hunger? Or will it be simpler to assume that specific operations such as water deprivation, or eating dry food, have effects on both hunger and thirst?

Turning our attention for the moment to IX on the right-hand side of the diagram, the representation there is meant to imply that speed of response and strength of pull are a function of the *algebraic* difference between the two response strengths. This assumption, however, is by no means certain. It is entirely possible that administering at the goal shocks that are too weak to stop the animal from approaching and eating will be found to have the dynamogenic effect of increasing speed of running or strength of pull instead of reducing them as would be expected from algebraic summation.

It can be seen that in this expanded formulation of the system, there is a relative decrease in the proportion of instances in which the theorist is assuming that a relationship which has already been found useful in integrating a large number of observations in other situations will also be applicable to a new situation. There is a corresponding increase in the proportion of instances in which the theorist is simply making a more or less plausible guess in order to pose a problem clearly. This change is largely the result of attempting to tie down the intervening variables by a greater number of experimental operations on the antecedent side and measures on the consequent side. The attempt to extend the system to the types of experimental situations that will really test the general utility of the intervening variables spotlights difficult problems which are latent in many of our efforts to construct psychological theories.

Effects of Alcohol and Barbiturates

Conger [22] has extended the theory in a different direction by adding the assumption that alcohol produces a greater reduction in fear motivating avoidance than in hunger (and presumably other primary drives) motivating approach. He has confirmed the simplest deductions from this extension by measuring approach and avoidance separately in a controlled experimental situation and showing that the alcohol produces a greater reduction in the strength of pull of frightened rats avoiding the place where they had previously received electric shocks than that of hungry rats approaching food.

He has tested also the more complex situation in which approach and avoidance are operating simultaneously. He trained hungry rats to approach food and then threw them into an approach-avoidance conflict by giving them electric shocks at the goal. He verified the deduction by finding that they were more likely to go back to the food after receiving injections of alcohol than of normal saline.

He also verified another deduction, namely, that it was easier to train rats to avoid food (and electric shock) on the trials on which they were sober, and to go to food (without shock) whenever they were drunk, than it was to teach them the opposite discrimination of going to food when they were sober and avoiding it when drunk. Thus, Conger's assumption was verified by deductions involving three relatively different techniques: strength of pull, conflict behavior, and the learning of a discrimination.

This extension of the theory has been used to explain a number of the perplexing social effects of alcohol by Conger [22], Dollard and Miller [25], and Miller [68].

Bailey and Miller [3] have extended the theory along similar lines by assuming that barbiturates, such as sodium amytal, produce a greater reduction in the strength of the fear motivating avoidance than in that of other drives motivating approach. A deduction from this assumption has been used to explain an observation reported by Masserman [50] and has been confirmed in a similar but simpler experimental situation in which Bailey and Miller [3] found that an injection of sodium amytal caused cats in a simple approach-avoidance conflict to resume eating at the place where they had received electric shocks.

EXTENSIONS TO PSYCHOTHERAPY

Miller [59] and Dollard and Miller [25] have further extended the miniature system to cover some of the phenomena commonly observed in psychotherapy. This extension involved the following additions to the partial definitions:

j. The definition of nearness is extended to apply to any situation in which the subject can be said to be coming nearer to a goal in space, time, or some dimension of qualitative or culturally defined similarity of cues.

k. The definition of avoidance is extended to apply to the responses producing inhibition and repression.

l. The definition of approach is extended to the responses that are inhibited or repressed.

The meaning of the foregoing three definitions is illustrated by the example of a patient who is trying to remember the traumatic battlefield event that has produced a functional amnesia. His goal is to remember the traumatic event. According to *l*, the chain of thoughts leading up to the inhibited memory of that event will function in the same way as approach response in the conflict alley. According to *k*, the responses producing inhibition and repression of the memory will function like the avoidance responses in the conflict alley. According to *j*, remembering events more closely associated with the traumatic memory will be analogous to coming nearer to the goal in a conflict alley. There-fore, as the subject approaches nearer to his goal of remembering the traumatic event, we will expect the strength of the repression to increase more rapidly than the strength of the memory, so that the subject will be able to remember more remotely associated events, but not the nearer ones. Similarly, we will expect barbiturates, such as sodium amytal, to reduce the gradient of strength of the repression so that the subjects will be able to remember events nearer to the traumatic ones, and if the repression is not too strong, will be able to remember the traumatic event itself.

It should be noted that the foregoing definitions are only a con-venient, first approximation; it may be necessary to modify them. For example, we have already suggested that the gradients of all responses now classified as approach may not fall off more steeply than all those now classified as avoidance. The analysis that we have made of the reasons why the gradient of avoidance is steeper than that of approach suggests that it might be better to classify responses on the basis of the way the motivation involved is aroused. Responses primarily motivated by drives that are dependent on external cues in the environment should show steeper gradients of generalization than those motivated by drives dependent on physiological factors or internal cues that the organism carries with it from situation to situation.

Need for better definition or scaling of empirical variables. It is obvious that the definitions stated above are a considerable distance from the empirical level. Therefore, it frequently will be more difficult to secure complete agreement on the application of these definitions to clinical phenomena than it has been to secure agreement on the ap-plication of the preceding ones to simple experimental situations. The chief roadblock to rigorously testing the applicability of the conflict system to clinical phenomena is the lack of more exact definitions of the empirical variables. I believe that this barrier can be overcome by creating various scales. At first, these will probably have to be very simple ordinal scales, such as the following tentative scale of distance from a young man's goal of marriage: being present at a social gathering with girls, coming near to a girl, talking to a girl about impersonal sub-jects, talking about more personal subjects, asking for a date, dancing, kissing, going steady, becoming engaged, getting married. These scales, like any others, will have to be validated by their usefulness in establishing relatively simple but general scientific laws.

The task will not be easy and the fact that we probably will be deal-ing with acquired equivalence of cues [76] leads to the distressing pos-sibility that the events may have to be ranked in a somewhat different order for different individuals. We may have to start with cases in which the cultural training is quite uniform for all individuals in our society, or group together individuals who have had similar experiences.

In a recent monograph, one of my students, Murray [87], has described some of his attempts to make and use simple scales based on a quantitative content analysis of recorded psychotherapeutic interviews. Murray and Berkun [88] have used such a content analysis in an attempt to test deductions from an application of the conflict theory to a psychotherapeutic case and have checked the results against those of an experiment on rats. Auld and Murray [1] have summarized some of the attempts at scaling by other people with different theoretical orientations. Meanwhile, Dollard, Auld, and White have been working for some time on a monumental effort to scale psychotherapeutic materials and to test the reliability and the descriptive adequacy of their categories.

Of course, the usefulness of such scales is not limited to the present miniature system. The development of any program of linking *any type of theory* more rigorously to the empirical facts of psychotherapy depends upon the innovation of better techniques for securing public agreement upon these facts, or in short, upon evolving better definitions of the empirical variables.

Tentative verification of selected deductions concerning psychotherapy. In the absence of more rigorous definitions of the empirical variables, any attempt to check deductions from our miniature system against the phenomena of psychotherapy will necessarily be somewhat informal and limited to situations which seem to be clear-cut enough so that it is hoped that one can achieve general agreement. Such selection of situations, however, makes it easier to ignore phenomena that do not clearly fit the theory. With these limitations in mind, one can say that, as a first approximation, a number of significant deductions seem to be tentatively confirmed by the clinical observations that are available. Going part way and then stopping, or in other words, being unable to achieve or leave the goal, seems to be characteristic of patients in an approach-avoidance conflict. Furthermore, weakening the strength of the drive motivating avoidance or increasing the strength of the drive motivating approach seems to cause patients to go nearer to their goals.

At this point, we come to some new deductions which may be made with the assumption H, *that fear, like other learned responses, varies inversely with distance from the point of reinforcement.* In other words, we will expect the strength of fear elicited at any given distance from a feared stimulus to be a function of the height of the avoidance gradient at that particular distance. Turning back to Figs. 2 and 3, the following relationships can be seen to hold for the range of distances within which the two gradients intersect:

1. *Increasing the strength of approach should cause the subject to go nearer to the feared goal, and at this point, stronger fear should be elicited.*

2. *Decreasing the over-all strength of avoidance should cause the subject to go nearer to the goal, and at this point stronger fear should be elicited.*

3. *The increase in fear should be greater when the same distance of approach toward the goal is produced by raising the gradient of approach than when it is produced by lowering the gradient of avoidance.* It should be noted that this deduction is dependent on the fact that the gradient of avoidance is steeper than that of approach.[5]

4. *In each of the above cases, greater distances of approach toward the goal should produce greater increases in fear.* In order not to be dependent on the assumption of linearity, this deduction must be restricted to those cases in which the greater distance of approach includes the smaller one.

5. *After the goal is reached, further increases in the strength of approach should not produce additional increases in the fear elicited, but further reductions in the strength of avoidance should produce additional reductions in the fear elicited.*

The evidence supporting these deductions has been summarized in somewhat more detail elsewhere [25]; it can only be suggested here. The first of these deductions is in line with the clinical evidence that increasing the patient's motivation to approach seems to increase his fear and conflict. As would be expected from the last two deductions, such increases are practicable without producing intolerable fear only when the patients are relatively near to the goal, either because the initial conflict is weak or because they are approaching the end of successful therapy. Attempting to force patients ahead does not seem to be practicable in the face of the strong inhibitions and repressions of the severe neurotic.

The second deduction offers an explanation for the paradoxical

[5] If we take the greater steepness of the gradient of avoidance as a postulate, and assume that the strength of fear elicited is a function of the height of the gradient, this deduction follows immediately. If we attempt to deduce the greater steepness of the gradient of avoidance, the deduction concerning the strength of fear is not so simple and unequivocal. It would be simplest to assume that the fear generalized with distance in exactly the same way as does any other habit. This would give us a gradient of fear parallel to the gradient of approach, and the greater steepness of avoidance would emerge only when the strength of the fear drive along its gradient potentiated (e.g., was multiplied by) the strength of the avoidance habit along its gradient. On the other hand, one could assume that the hunger drive would provide relevant cues for approach which would make the near and far situations more similar for that habit and hence make the gradient of approach flatter than that of fear.

negative therapeutic effect. After the therapist has succeeded in diminishing the patient's exaggerated idea of the dangerousness of the goal so that the patient moves nearer to it, one frequently observes an increase in the amount of fear and conflict elicited. Even more striking results appear where the conditions are better known and more clear-cut, namely, in the use of the barbiturates to treat amnesia produced by traumatic conditions of combat. In such cases, we have seen that the hypothesis that this drug reduces the fear motivating avoidance leads us to expect a decrease in the repression producing amnesia for the traumatic events. But, as the amnesia is lifted and the subject approaches nearer the goal of recovering his memory of the traumatic incident, one should observe an obvious increase in the amount of fear elicited. According to the vivid descriptions of Grinker and Spiegel [28, 29] this is exactly what happens.

The third deduction seems to be confirmed by the general experience of therapists that it is much better to concentrate on reducing avoidance (in other words, analyzing resistance) than on trying to increase approach. As would be expected from the last two deductions, this procedure seems to be required especially during the early treatment of severe neurotics.

It should be possible to make rigorous tests of the foregoing five deductions in simple experimental situations with animals provided one could find some measure (other than distance of approach) that will vary with fear and can be applied to the freely moving animal in the conflict alley. Our group has spent considerable effort trying to develop such measures (23 and 24 in the dotted box in Fig. 9) on rats. We have not succeeded to date and are planning to shift to dogs which we hope may be better for this purpose.

GENERAL EVALUATION

Range of application. The range of application of this miniature system is potentially quite broad; its boundaries are not sharply defined. The same assumptions that are used in it can explain a number of the characteristics of avoidance-avoidance conflict and the difference between such conflict and pure approach-approach competition; they are also useful in dealing with double approach-avoidance conflict (i.e., choice between two goals eliciting ambivalent responses), and with discrimination conflict. These additional applications have been described elsewhere [59].

The concepts in the system presumably apply wherever the relevant conditions appear, be it in a simple animal experiment, a projective test, child rearing, a neurosis, psychotherapy, combat, economics, politics, or international relations. So far, attempts at applications have been made only in the areas of experimental work on conflict and displacement with animals, effects of alcohol and barbiturates on conflicts, and conflicts occurring in child rearing, neurosis, and psychotherapy. In all these areas, except the animal experiments, rigorous testing of the application of the theory is severely limited by the difficulty in specifying the relevant conditions and in measuring the relevant responses, or in other words, defining precisely the empirical data variables. Therefore, the applications to these other areas are at present somewhat programmatic.

Evidence for the system. The main studies which this miniature system has mediated have already been described. Almost all of them have been experiments on rats running in straight alleys. These experiments were specifically designed to test deductions from the assumptions made in the system. They have involved developing new techniques, such as recording the distance of approach and the strength of pull, and have resulted in the gathering of new data.

Because of the systematic, step-by-step program of research, the evidence from the foregoing animal studies is relatively complete and convincing for the part of the system that is summarized in Fig. 7, and for the part of Fig. 9 that deals with the extension to displacement.

The extension of the system summarized in the part of Fig. 9 that is relevant to experiments designed to test the unitary character of the intervening variables remains programmatic. However, the problem of determining whether hunger, for example, functions as a single unitary intervening variable, or as a cluster of loosely associated variables, is a somewhat separate issue. Specific hungers and/or satiation variables could be substituted in the system without changing its essential character. Furthermore, it is quite possible that the unity of the intervening variables can be tested more economically in situations that do not necessarily involve approach-avoidance conflict [e.g., 68, 72]. Again we see how a theory of conflict behavior can potentially involve all the controversial issues of behavior theory. Carving out a particular miniature system is largely an arbitrary matter of expediency.

Data that do not fit. We have confined ourselves to only one aspect of conflict behavior—the maximum distance of approach toward a goal. Some other significant aspects of behavior, which are not so far included in this system, will be mentioned in the next section on plans for the future. Furthermore, we have picked experimental situations which minimize the difficulty of defining the response and the stimulus. For example, we chose stimulus situations (narrow black, intermediate gray, and wide white alleys) which were relatively easy to arrange in an ordinal series of similarity.

The most relevant single observation not accounted for by the present system is the fact that, instead of stopping and remaining at a given point as might be expected from the intersection of the gradients, the animals tend to oscillate in a general region. As has been pointed out elsewhere [59] the existence of such oscillations can be accounted for by an assumption which has already been found useful in explaining other types of behavioral data, namely, that *the initiation of a given response of either approach or avoidance produces stimuli which provide additional cues for continuing that response.* In other words, a certain amount of positive feedback is involved which functions like psychological momentum and causes the subject to overshoot. This hypothesis will account for the general shape of the most characteristic and regular oscillations, but will not by itself account for the fact that the retreat is so much more rapid than the approach. Other oscillations appear to be more random.

A second regular pattern of behavior observed in the conflict alley is a stepwise one in which an increasingly hesitant approach is terminated by a period of crouching which is followed by another approach, etc. It seems probable that this pattern can be accounted for by extinction of fear during the period of crouching. Furthermore, the assumption concerning response-produced cues allows one to deduce the conditions that should favor oscillations and those that should favor stepwise approach.

It can be seen that the response-produced cues, if indeed they produce an effect analogous to positive feedback, introduce an element of unstable equilibrium, or all-or-nothing tendency, into the behavior. This effect is exactly opposite to that of the crossing of the gradients, which functions like negative feedback and produces stable equilibrium. And indeed, the behavior of animals in approach-avoidance conflict does exhibit these two opposing attributes. The animal placed at the start of the alley may go part way up and then stop and vacillate in a reasonably narrow region as though oscillating around a point of equilibrium. Then he may retreat completely back to the start of the alley and remain there for a while, as though some other source of positive feedback, such as the anticipatory goal response, had been removed. Then he may suddenly start out on another approach episode.

This all-or-nothing aspect of the behavior is completely obscured in the process of securing the averages plotted as the curve in Fig. 6. In fact, it would be possible to secure such a curve if all the animals either remained crouching at the start or went completely to the goal, with an increasing proportion reaching the goal as the strength of hunger is increased or that of electric shock decreased. Actually, Fig. 6 represents two effects: an increasing proportion of animals shifting all the way from the start to the goal, as well as shifts toward the goal by animals that go part way and then stop.

But the shorter the alley, the greater the probability that the gradients will not intersect within its length, and also that chance fluctuations in the level of motivation and/or the effects of the mechanisms producing positive feedback will shift the point of intersection from beyond one end of the alley to beyond the other end. In such cases, the behavior will appear to be solely of the all-or-nothing type; it will be impossible to demonstrate going part way and then stopping.

In order to minimize possible artifacts produced when the point of intersection oscillates beyond the end of the alley and to secure more clear-cut effects which can be observed in single animals without artifacts of averaging, Coons, Trapold, and I have studied conflict behavior in a runway over 100 ft long. We observed that a given animal might oscillate over a considerable portion of this distance. However, we found that, when hungrier, the animals tended to advance nearer to the goal and retreat less far from it, than when they were less hungry. Since these comparisons did not include trials on which an animal either failed to start or ran completely to the goal, the general results summarized in Fig. 6 are confirmed without any possibility of the trend's being an artifact of averaging a number of all-or-nothing changes.

Comparison with competing formulations. As far as behavior in space is concerned, Hull [38, 40] has made a formulation that is so similar to the present one that it is supplementary rather than competing. Hull has focused his attention more on developing certain implications of shrewd guesses concerning the exact quantitative shape of functions. On the other hand, I have tended to feel that, for the moment, it is better to concentrate on qualitative relationships that can be tested with the ordinal scales at our disposal and to test the general applicability and functional unity of the intervening variables before devoting time to further quantification that assumes cardinal scales. Instead of choosing a single quantitative curve and exploring its consequences, I have approached quantification by approximation and correction, determining what kinds of results, obtainable with the qualitative scales that we now possess, would narrow the range of possibilities to curves with certain general characteristics [61, p. 171].

With respect to behavior in space, Lewin's [48] insightful formulation is similar in its main functional attributes, though couched in quite different language. His system has been less thoroughly worked out and is especially deficient in the attempt to formulate the partial definitions required to bridge the gap between the theoretical formulations in terms of psychological life space and the actually observed empirical independent and dependent variables. Perhaps that is one of the reasons why it has been responsible for fewer experimental studies. Because of the functional parallelism of the basic assumptions involved in the two, the choice between Lewin's formulation of conflict and mine does not hinge specifically on agreement with empirical data on conflict behavior but rather on the general advantages of a life-space vectorial system vs. a liberalized stimulus-response one.

Neither Hull nor Lewin have attempted to extend their analyses from distance in space to stimulus similarity in order to include phenomena such as displacement and discrimination conflict. Furthermore, they have not dealt with the effects of drugs, with neurosis, or psychotherapy. There is nothing inherent in their formulations, however, which obviously excludes adding the assumptions that would be necessary to include such phenomena.

The chief advantages of the present formulation are that it has been worked out in more detail, applied to a greater variety of phenomena, and accompanied by a systematic program of experimental verification.

Methodological value beyond specific context. The present miniature system introduces no innovation in general scientific method or theory construction. Outside of its specific content, its general methodological value lies only in demonstrating that certain well-known procedures of science can be used to integrate a variety of psychological data ranging from experimental results on animals to clinical observations on neurotic patients. My general strategy has been to use animal experiments to formulate and verify principles applicable to neurotic behavior rather than to attempt to duplicate in animals the spectacular aspects of neurotic symptoms. I have tried to deduce with reasonable rigor a variety of phenomena from a limited set of principles and the specific conditions involved. My tactics have been to proceed step by step, verifying simple deductions from the principles in simple situations and then attempting to apply the principles and test the deductions in more complex situations. I believe that these features of the program, which are by no means unique, can be applied successfully to a considerable number of other areas in psychology. I would caution, however, that the details of scientific strategy must vary with the current conditions of the specific problem being investigated.

INTERMEDIATE AND LONG-RANGE STRATEGY

Most of my research strategy in this area is relatively short-range, guided by the results of the immediately preceding experiments and by the interests of my students and assistants.

Development of new measures. One set of problems has to do with the development of new measures. As has already been pointed out, a variety of measures is needed to test and make meaningful the intervening variables. New measures are also required for testing deductions in those situations, such as psychotherapy, where suitable measures are not already available.

For some time, I have been interested in trying to develop some independent measure of fear, or of the general state of activation or disturbance of the animal, in the conflict situation. Such a measure would allow tests of deductions concerning the effect of strength of approach and avoidance drives on the intensity of fear and conflict elicited (the double arrows in Figs. 2 and 3); it might also reveal unexpected relationships. Furthermore, such an independent measure would be useful in experiments on avoidance learning, getting the theorist out of the awkward position of using fear in his explanation of avoidance and avoidance as his measure of fear.

So far, a number of attempts to find a convenient physiological measure, which might be used in rats with appropriate experimental controls, have been unsuccessful. Dr. Arlo Myers has spent considerable time successfully developing beautiful techniques for recording accurately a number of physiological measures in the freely moving rat—d-c potential and resistance of the kidney, internal temperature of various organs, muzzle temperature, and heart rate. To date, none of these has turned out to be promising as an index of rapid changes in fear or general activation. We shall probably shift to the muzzle temperature and heart rate of the dog since other investigators have reported encouraging results with these measures [102, 27].

I am also interested in recording the psychogalvanic response in human subjects and in the scaling of psychotherapeutic interviews, but have not yet participated directly in such activities. As has already been pointed out, the development of better scales is a necessary part of long-range strategy.

Some applications or extensions of present concepts. Another set of problems involves rather straightforward extensions of the present system. Conflict behavior should be studied in two-dimensional space to determine whether the subjects would circle as one would predict, and whether or not the opportunities for lateral movement would reduce the extent of oscillations back and forth from the goal. Will the gradient of avoidance be steeper than that of approach in time as it is in space? For example, when asked to write a paper for a symposium at some distant date, the advantages seem to outweigh the disadvantages so that one often accepts, but as the date draws nearer, the effect of the disadvantages increases more rapidly than does the prospect of reward, so that one often regrets having accepted. Can such temporal factors be studied by rigorous empirical methods?

The possible therapeutic effect of displacement, or in other words, stimulus change, has been opened up by Berkun [6] but needs further investigation. All the types of "therapy" described by Masserman [50] involve changing the stimulus situation. According to our displacement theory, such stimulus changes would be expected to produce some therapeutic effect because the gradient of generalization of avoidance is steeper than that of approach. A concrete example of the effects of such stimulus change comes from a recent experiment by Myers [90]. In the course of demonstrating that unpredictable electric shock produces more generalized fear than does predictable shock, he used the suppression of drinking as his measure of fear. He found that, if drinking had been suppressed by unpredictable shocks in an apparatus, changing the stimulus situation by introducing a strong flashing light would tend to cause the animals to resume drinking. Another experiment [79] has shown that a change from a narrow black to a wide white alley (or vice versa) will cause animals inhibited by an approach-avoidance conflict to resume eating at the goal. Are the therapeutic effects in Masserman's experiments the results of similar types of stimulus change? When this effect of stimulus change is controlled by a suitable experimental design, does any additional therapeutic effect remain to be explained? To what extent is the variable of stimulus change involved in the effect of drugs or of electroconvulsive shocks on fear and conflict?

Is the effect of alcohol which has been studied by Conger [22] partly or wholly a function of the fact that the habits of approach were older than those of avoidance? How can experimental techniques be devised for studying approach-avoidance conflict with children or adult human subjects? How well can the concepts be applied to new areas such as installment buying in economics and appeasement in international relations?

Significant conflict phenomena not covered by present hypotheses. In addition to relatively straightforward extensions of the system, some of the foregoing problems are likely to involve a natural-history type of observation and data collection in the new types of conflict situations, the addition of new assumptions to explain the new phenomena observed, and the development of new techniques to measure the phenomena and to test the deductions from the new assumptions. The investigation of other problems will lead to more radical alterations in the assumptions.

We have already mentioned the attempt to check on the deductions of oscillation from the assumption of a positive feedback created by response-produced stimuli. We have also designed experiments to compare the role in approach-avoidance conflict behavior of cues produced by different drives with those of cues produced by different anticipatory goal-responses.

In my opinion [59], an important area to investigate is the possible role of conflict in inducing drives over and above the original ones motivating the conflict behavior, or in producing more stress and disruption than would be predicted from the mere sum of the drives involved. I am attempting to study conflict-induced drives by building up difficult discriminations, similar to those involved in the experimental neurosis described by Pavlov [93]. But the apparatus is designed so that a specific response, such as pulling back on a leash or pressing a bar, will remove the discrimination problem from the subject. The advantage of this technique is that it allows other conditions, such as degree of monotonous confinement, to remain constant.

The goal of the initial study is to demonstrate conflict-induced drive by comparing the learning and performance of the "escape from discrimination" response under the experimental condition of difficult discrimination with that under the control condition of an easy discrimination arranged so that the animal is rewarded at exactly the same rate. No electric shock or other punishment will be used in these discriminations and we are starting with a technique analogous to Pavlov's classical conditioning.

If a phenomenon of "escape from discrimination conflict" can be demonstrated, it will be important to determine its laws. In order to determine these laws, we plan to try to put the response that removes the discrimination problem on a variable-interval schedule. Using the rate of responding as a measure of drive induced by discrimination conflict, we shall try to find whether this rate is a function of variables such as the degree of restraint, monotony, strength of hunger, rate of presentation of stimuli, rate of increase in difficulty of discrimination, or drugs. Though guided by theoretical hunches, the first stage of such an investigation will necessarily involve a considerable amount of systematic, empirical exploration.

Other families of problems have been suggested at the end of a previous paper [59]. Can ways be found to study the various types of incompatibility: mechanical, neural, chemical, perceptual, and acquired? How do complex habits interact? Specifically, when competing patterns of response have some subunits that are obviously mutually exclusive and others that are identical, how do these subunits interact in the production of compromise responses? What is the role of symbolic mediation in determining whether or not the complex response occurs all-or-none as a whole, or is fractionated by conflict into subunits some of which are inhibited while others are not?

General policy. In surveying the foregoing types of problems, it seems to me that the best strategy is to attack first those problems which are most likely to open up new areas of investigation. Two such problems are the development of an independent measure of fear or activation and the attempt to demonstrate conflict-induced drive. But if these problems turn out to be too difficult with the means currently at our disposal, it will be prudent to turn to other problems. A large number of alternatives, all of reasonably equal a priori fruitfulness, are possible. My preference is to mix studies verifying more complex deductions of the present assumptions with those aimed at testing such new assumptions as are indicated by the unexplained behavior observed in the experiments on conflict. The choice of such assumptions will depend on the degree to which they have already been found useful in integrating data from other types of experiments and the degree to which they seem likely to integrate new realms of data.

It will be noted that my description of strategy is clearer and more logical when I am looking backward at the work that has already been accomplished than it is when I am attempting to peer into the future.

Part II. Liberalization of S-R Theory

The preceding analysis of conflict behavior represents a concrete example of a type of activity in which I have been deeply involved—trying to cast the first slender rope of a bridge across the chasm separating the laboratory from the clinic and other sources of examples of complex social behavior. Such work, which is fortunately becoming much more conventional, has been greatly facilitated by the general context of the Institute of Human Relations under Mark May and owes a unique debt to intensive collaboration with John Dollard.

As a result of trying to take the conventional S-R concepts out of the laboratory and apply them to concrete examples of social behavior, a number of changes have evolved which significantly increase their range and power. This part of the paper will briefly describe the liberalization of certain S-R concepts; it will consider certain controversial problems which require additional theoretical and experimental analysis, recapitulate a few key points deriving from collaborative work with John Dollard on problems of social learning, personality, and psychotherapy, and analyze some methodological issues of critical importance to the development of behavior theory.

CHANGES IN CERTAIN BASIC S-R CONCEPTS

Functional behavioral definitions. Hull [39, 40] and many other stimulus-response psychologists have either omitted definitions of basic concepts or emphasized physical energy and anatomical location. I have been one of those who have believed that it is more useful, and also more in accord with our actual practice, to begin with functional behavioral definitions of basic concepts, and then subsequently to try to correlate the phenomena so defined with physical energies, geometric patterns, anatomical locations, or other events that can be independently specified.

The general method is illustrated by the following quotation from Miller and Dollard [76, p. 59]:

> It is obvious that "response," as here used, is not restricted to the conventional usage, in which a response is defined as a muscular contraction or a glandular secretion. It is also obvious that "stimulation" is not restricted to the conventional usage, in which a stimulus is defined as an energy change activating receptors. According to the present usage, a response is any activity by or within the individual which can become functionally connected with an antecedent event through learning; a stimulus is any event to which a response can be so connected. This definition is not circular for cases in which the events referred to have been empirically identified. Thus, "sitting up" in dogs is known to be a response because it can be functionally connected by reward with the antecedent command, "Sit up!"; the command is thereby known to be a stimulus. Stimulus a may be used to determine that 1, 2, 3, and 4 are responses; response 1 may be used to determine that a, b, c, d are stimuli. Then a prediction may be made that the connections b-2, c-3, d-4, etc., are learnable.

In the procedure just illustrated it is obvious that the first step, identifying a specifiable condition as a stimulus because a specific response can be connected to it by learning, is purely empirical, circular, and safe. The second step, however, is a prediction from the assumption that an event which is the stimulus for the learning of one kind of response can also serve as a stimulus for other responses. This second step is not circular because the assumption could, in principle, be disproved. In fact, the second step is far from safe; the assumption may actually turn out to be wrong.

The foregoing type of definition has the advantage that "Any specifiable attribute of the environment, which the gestalt psychologists or other students of perception discover as a consistent basis for discriminations, can be used in the stimulus, or cue, position of a stimulus-response formula" [25, p. 34]. Additional advantages will become apparent in our discussion of thinking, drive-producing, and cue-producing responses.

Furthermore, I believe that a definition in this general form is the only type feasible at present. For example, suppose we want to know whether polarized light or radio waves can be stimuli for bees. There is no way to decide the matter from a priori considerations of the physical energies involved. The only thing that we can do is to set up a discrimination experiment to determine whether or not physically specified changes in the polarization of light, or the onset of radio waves, can be correlated with changes in the animal's behavior. It is conceivable that electrical recordings from end organs, sensory nerves, or sensory projection areas could be substituted for the learned response. But I doubt whether most of us would want to accept such results if they were consistently contradicted by discrimination experiments. Similarly, as a first approximation, we might substitute for the learned response an innate reaction, but I doubt if we would want to call the event a stimulus if, in an exhaustive series of experiments, we found it impossible to make any learned response contingent on it. In the latter case, we would be forced at the very least to designate this as a special subclass of stimuli.

Stimulus similarity is defined in the same general way. If, in a test experiment, a response learned to stimulus A generalizes more to I than to 1, we say that I is more similar to A than is 1. Thus far, the procedure is perfectly circular. Then, we predict that if we use a new response, the same stimuli will order themselves in the same sequence on the new gradient of stimulus generalization. This is not a world-shaking prediction, but it could be wrong. Then we go on to other predictions about these stimuli, e.g., that it will be easier to learn a discrimination between A and 1 than between A and I. We also predict that certain results will be secured in experiments on displacement or on paired-associates learning of nonsense syllables, etc.

If we wanted to start differently, we could use the results of the discrimination experiment or of verbal ratings of similarity as the initial basis for the definition. But the general pattern of a functional definition would remain essentially the same.

In the same way, I have defined rewards as events empirically found to have the effect of strengthening cue-response connections, and have pointed out that this definition is not circular as long as the fact that an event that has been found to strengthen one connection is used to predict that it will strengthen others [76, p. 30]. This kind of definition of reward has been discussed in illuminating detail by Meehl [51].

Following the same pattern, I would tentatively say that any specifiable conditions may be defined as increasing a drive when they specifically increase the performance of responses rewarded by the offset of those conditions, or by the goal objects that produce satiation. In using the word "specific," I do not mean to imply that the increase in drive cannot also increase the performance of other responses, but that it should produce a greater increase in the responses that have been specifically rewarded by the reduction in, or the goal objects of, that drive. Again the definition is circular with respect to the defining response, but the assumption is made that, if a specifiable set of conditions can be used to motivate the performance of a given response, it will motivate any other response that is reinforced in the same way.

I am more dissatisfied with the foregoing definition of drive than with the others. One of the reasons is that it is tied in too closely with a specific hypothesis of reinforcement, drive reduction. Other hypotheses, however, are independent of this definition; for example, the hypothesis that all drives have cue function and that any cue will become a drive if intense enough.

All of the foregoing definitions begin with defining the class membership in terms of a functional property and are circular with respect to the specific defining operation. Then they assume that this functional property is general so that it may be predicted in new situations. For example, if an experiment shows that a reaction of the organism can be attached to a new cue and hence is learnable, we classify it as a response. Then we assume that it will be possible to attach this reaction to other new cues. We can think of many examples in which this assumption seems to apply, but we are not certain that it is universally true. For instance, it is probably easier to attach the rat's approach responses to the odor of food, and crouching to the sound of a loud buzzer, than it is to attach crouching to the odor and approach to the buzzer. We express this by saying that approach is higher in the initial hierarchy of responses to the odor and crouching in the hierarchy of responses to the buzzer. If we can demonstrate that such differences occur in the absence of previous learning, we substitute the term "innate" for "initial." But in principle, if we work long enough and are clever enough, we should be able to attach the crouching to the odor and the approach to the buzzer. If we cannot do this, our theoretical system will have to be more complicated.

The complications may not be great provided we can show that our failure was attributable to the presence of a strong response incompatible with the one we were trying to establish. If, as actually may turn out to be the case, we find other exceptions to the generality of functional properties, so that an event may serve as a cue for some responses but not for others, our theoretical system, *or any other one*, will have to be distressingly complex, unless simple laws can be found to describe the exceptions.

We are confronted by exactly the same thing with respect to all of the other categories. That is, for example, our system becomes much more complicated if the effects of certain types of reinforcement tend to be specific to certain types of responses. The difficulty is not a major one if we can find simple laws to describe such specificities, but if they exist and we cannot find such simple laws, *any* theory of learning becomes much more complicated.

So far, we have described operations which can be used to classify a specifiable event as a member of a specific category. I believe definitions of this kind are fundamental, but it obviously will be very advantageous if we can find relationships between our lists of events in different categories and any other independently specifiable attributes of the events. For example, it would be immensely helpful if we could say that any movement of the striped muscles was learnable and hence could be described as a response, or that certain geometrical or gestalt properties defined a continuum of stimulus similarity. Nevertheless, I believe that we need our functional definitions in order to determine the laws essential for the subsequent more powerful and parsimonious definitions. We shall discuss this problem in more detail in connection with the drive reduction hypothesis of reinforcement.

Even after we get over the hurdle of the generality of our functional classification, many other problems remain. For instance, having defined response, we are confronted with the problem of response patterns or units. One aspect of this problem has been raised in Logan's [49] discussion of the micromolar approach to behavior theory. We are also confronted with the problem of determining the compatibility and incompatibility of various responses [59].

In general, stimulus-response psychologists have tended to bypass problems of the type we have just been raising. By intuition and trial and error, they have concentrated on experimental situations in which the stimulus and response were so simple and manageable that the lack of more precise definitions or laws concerning these variables was not a practical problem. Using such situations, stimulus-response psychologists have concentrated on determining the laws governing the connections of responses to stimuli. Thus, stimulus-response psychologists may be said to know and care relatively little about either stimuli or responses; they are specialists on the hyphen between the S and R and could more aptly be called "hyphen psychologists," or to use Thorndike's term, "connectionists." While admitting our ignorance, I trust it is not necessary to point out that we have made considerable progress on this basis. Unfortunately, it is also true that other theorists are not far ahead of us in solving these particular problems.

Thinking: central cue- and drive-producing responses. One of the most important advantages of functional definitions of stimulus and response is that such definitions can be applied to central as well as to peripheral events. Instead of emphasizing anatomical location, our definitions direct attention toward the more significant problem of functional laws. These definitions free the S-R theory of thinking from being restricted to proprioception, allowing the theory to exploit images, response-produced drives and rewards, perceptual responses, perceptual learning of acquired distinctiveness or similarity, and the possibility that central responses can contribute to the focusing of attention [76, pp. 54–90].[6]

[6] Recent work on the reticular formation may give us the first suggestion of the types of central response that might be involved in the focusing of attention.

Adding to the peripheral responses, the possibility of images and other central responses made possible by myriad potential connections in the brain greatly increases the number of different distinctive cue-producing responses that are available and that do not interfere with overt activity. Therefore, the new functional definitions make it easier for stimulus-response theory to handle the more complex, higher mental processes. In fact, one might deduce that the animals with a greater capacity to make central responses, and especially with a greater capacity to make a number of them simultaneously, should be superior on problems such as delayed response and reasoning.

It is obvious that the postulation of central responses, such as perception and imagery, reduces the gap between S-R and cognitive theory. But there is still a difference in that we clearly assume that these central processes follow the same laws as do peripheral stimuli and responses. By contrast, cognitive theories tend to leave the laws governing the central processes rather vague, while implying that they are different from those governing peripheral responses [106].

It is also obvious that our cue- and drive-producing responses serve much the same function as Hebb's cell assemblies and phase sequences except that we have not made specific neurological hypotheses, have applied them to somewhat different problems, and have assumed that contiguity alone, without reinforcement, is not sufficient for producing learning or maintaining performance. Though Hebb has attempted to deal with the empirical phenomena of reinforcement and experimental extinction, I have not been able to convince myself that his treatment is adequate. To cite two examples: I am skeptical of his explanation of why a cell assembly should grow to a certain size and then stop, instead of continuing to capture new neurons by contiguity until the whole brain was fired in one magnificent convulsion; nor do I see why an animal that was maintained under chronic moderate hunger should not have his sequences disturbed, and hence display motivation, when his metabolism was changed by satiation.

It is easier to determine the laws of peripheral stimuli and responses because they can be independently manipulated and objectively measured. After determining these laws, we explore the consequences of assuming that internal processes can be described in terms of "stimulus-response" sequences following exactly the same laws.[7] This assumption may turn out to be incorrect, but at least it focuses attention squarely on the problem of trying to formulate the laws governing the central processes and gives one a point of departure. It seems worthwhile to

---

[7] This is the key assumption. For example, if further experimental work should indicate that contiguity is sufficient for forming associations between external cues and responses, we would attempt to apply the same law to central processes.

begin with the parsimonious assumption that the relatively hidden central processes follow the same laws as the observable peripheral ones, see how far one can go on this basis, and then add different assumptions if necessary.

Same laws can produce different outcomes. It can be seen that I am tentatively assuming that the greater intellectual capacities of animals, such as man, which have much more highly developed central processes along with their anatomically better developed brains, are attributable to the potentialities of compounding more similarly functioning "units" rather than to a completely new type of function. To use a simple analogy, a calculating machine with many banks of keys and many dials may involve exactly the same kinds of parts and functions as one with only two banks of keys and two dials. But as a result of more replications of functionally similar units, one is able to do completely new things with the larger machine. For example, one could not use the smaller machine to apply the machine formula for computing the constants for a correlation (the sum of squares and cross products according to the formula $(A + B)^2 = A^2 + 2AB + B^2$) because one would not have enough dials to keep the two sums of squares and the cross products from running into each other. Merely because it has more units of the same kind, the larger machine can keep these different sums separated and can use this new and much more economical method which is completely beyond the capacity of the smaller machine.

From the foregoing example, it should be clear that, assuming that the principles are the same does not necessarily mean that one must predict that the outcome will be the same. The outcome is dependent upon the conditions as well as the principles. In the foregoing example, changing the conditions by adding more units to the machine enabled it to perform a completely new task. Similarly, compounding S-R links in series and parallel leads to completely new deductions.

Superiority of creative thought over symbolic trial and error. As I have pointed out [25, p. 111], instrumental acts are limited by the environment to one of the sequences leading from the start to the goal, while by contrast, an important attribute of cue-producing responses is that they are not limited in this way and can also proceed in the opposite sequence, working backward from the goal. Concretely, when one is at the office, one can get home only by walking in a given direction through all the intervening steps on one of the possible routes, but one can think of being home without thinking of all the intervening steps, and one can also think of walking in the opposite direction from home to the office. On the way home, one's behavior can be guided by thoughts of the roadblock near home.

Similarly in trying to derive the formula for the area of a triangle, one can begin near the goal by thinking: "If I can make it into a rectangle, I'll know how to get the area." Then one can be guided by this thought in trying to think of various ways of making a triangle into a rectangle.

The extreme importance of the distinction between mere symbolic trial and error and thinking guided by (or working backward from) the goal should not be underestimated. Figure 10 illustrates the situation in which there are four alternatives at the first choice point, each of which leads on to four additional alternatives, etc. By the time we reach

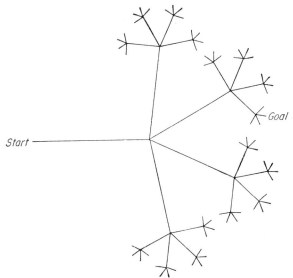

Fig. 10. Difficulty of canvassing all the alternatives by symbolic trial and error contrasted with efficiency of being guided by, or working backward from, the goal.

the third stage of choices, there are 64 alternatives, and if we carried the figure out four additional stages, there would be 16,384, i.e., 4^7. To canvass all these alternatives by symbolic trial and error would be a considerable task. However, to the extent that the behavior may be guided by the goal, the difficulty is reduced. To take the extreme case, if the goal is clearly in sight, or if one works backward from the goal, it is not necessary to canvass a single wrong alternative.

But the foregoing example is extremely simple compared with the task of canvassing all the conceivable moves in a chess game, or the successive stages of alternatives in many real-life problems. Thus, it becomes obvious that there are definite limitations to mere symbolic trial and error, and that goal-directed thinking of the type we have sketched here and analyzed elsewhere [25, pp. 110–115] is enormously more effective.

We can see that some of the earlier writers who treated thinking as mere symbolic trial and error missed its most important attribute. Its ability to be guided by the goal (the definition of the problem), so that the dice are loaded in favor of combinations of habits likely to succeed, is one of the key characteristics of creative thinking.

Do central responses require less reinforcement? Let us conclude with a far simpler example of how the same laws might produce different results with central processes. Incidental observation suggests that the learning and maintained performance of external responses require less reinforcement the less effortful they are. If we experimentally verified this principle and made the plausible assumption that central responses require minimal effort, we would predict that central responses could be learned and maintained with minimal reinforcement. Relatively weak secondary reinforcements should be much more likely to produce the incidental learning of such responses. Therefore, organisms in which central responses play a larger role should show more apparently latent learning.

Studies stemming from modern S-R analysis of higher mental processes. The foregoing type of analysis has led directly to a number of experiments on the role of cue-producing responses. I shall summarize only those with which I have been directly connected. Miller [53] showed that providing rats with a distinctive anticipatory goal-response increased their ability to show "foresight," and in another experiment [54] that human galvanic skin response could be conditioned to the cue of a word spoken aloud, would then generalize to the cue of thinking the word, and thereby, could be transferred to any new stimulus arousing the thought of that word. Grose [30] secured additional evidence demonstrating almost complete generalization of the conditioned galvanic skin response from the cue of saying a word aloud to the cue of thinking it, and also from the cue of thinking to that of speaking the word. In experiments on children, Birge [9] showed that a distinctive label could mediate the transfer of an instrumental response from one situation to another. She also showed that similar instrumental responses tended to mediate the transfer of similar labels. Finally, Lawrence [45, 46, 47] performed a series of experiments showing how training animals to pay attention to certain classes of cues can influence subsequent learning.

The same type of analysis has led to an understanding of the important role of learned drives and rewards, or in other words, emotional factors in thinking. It has indicated that in order to be creative one needs a nice balance between the courage to rebel against conventional formulations and the discipline to submit to the restraints of logic and evidence.

This type of analysis has suggested the advantages of alternating between phases of uncritical production of ideas and critical selection of them. It has led to an explanation of why repression should make behavior more primitive, childlike, and stupid. It has also shown why psychotherapy should meet resistance, but if successful, lead to more intelligent, farsighted, adaptive behavior [25].

Finally, the notion of response-produced strong stimulation has been applied to studies of learnable drives and rewards [64].

Some unsolved problems. Many problems remain, however. Most theories of intelligent behavior have surprisingly little to say about the difference in *capacity* responsible for different levels of intellectual performance in animals or man. There is a striking contrast between the success of psychologists in devising tests to measure intelligence and their failure to devise adequate theories of the capacities responsible for differences in intelligence. To date, most theorists have largely ignored the problem of capacity, merely listing traits or assuming differences in such things as verbal responses, unspecified parameters of equations, emergent levels of learning, or an ability to reorganize bad gestalts into good ones. Although such hunches are all right as a point of departure, they do not constitute a useful theory of the obvious intellectual differences between toads and men. For example, although verbal responses certainly are involved in thinking, other capacities are also required, as I predict anyone will discover who tries to teach a talking bird to solve problems in algebra.

In the foregoing discussion and elsewhere [76, pp. 72, 89], I have suggested a few factors which might be involved. One of the factors which make the mental processes of man so much "higher" than those of animals may be a greater capacity to respond selectively to more subtle aspects of the environment as cues—especially to aspects such as triangularity, numerosity, and other relations and patterns which are commonly referred to as "abstract." Another factor may be a capacity to make a greater variety of distinctive central cue-producing responses, and especially a greater capacity to respond with a number of different cue-producing responses simultaneously so that further responses may be elicited on the basis of a pattern of cues representing several different units of experience. But many of the most interesting problems remain untouched.

For instance, what is the "filing system" of the brain? To take a simple example, one might ask the question: "What mammal flies at night?" The answer, "Bat," comes immediately. One does not have to canvass either a mental list of all mammals to see which ones fly (or search a list of all flying creatures to see which ones are mammals) and then eliminate the creatures that are not nocturnal. The prompt elicitation of thoughts on the basis of such multiple requirements (i.e., cues) is obviously an enormous aid to efficient problem solving. How does the brain accomplish this? To what extent is it a matter of mere algebraic summation? How much patterning is involved? Under what conditions is some sort of scanning required? What kinds of training are necessary? I venture the hypothesis that such a response to multiple cues (i.e., requirements) originally is a somewhat inefficient matter of simple summation, but that with specific training in responding only to correct combinations, patterning leads to more precisely selective behavior. Such problems could be analyzed experimentally.

Relational responses to relational cues: flexible cybernetic behavior. Stimulus-response psychologists, who tended to use the old definition of the stimulus as a specific energy (or energy change) and of the response as a specific muscular contraction or glandular secretion, had difficulty in explaining the flexibility of behavior exemplified by the appropriate modification of adaptive responses in new situations—a serious difficulty because no two situations are completely identical. Critics such as Lashley [44] and Tolman [105] have long since emphasized these difficulties. Furthermore, the emphasis of the gestalt psychologists on total patterns did not solve the problem of how the stimulus pattern was translated into the response one. Hull's [37] habit-family hierarchy was an attempt to solve this problem. But Hull, rightly, was dissatisfied with his deduction of this mechanism and, hence, also advanced the habit-family hierarchy as an independent postulate, a procedure which takes account of, but does nothing to explain, the flexibility of behavior. It seems probable that a mechanism of the type Hull tried to deduce in this paper does operate in certain cases and that the assumption of central perceptual and imageal cue-producing responses would greatly increase the power of the mechanism. However, I believe that there also is a simpler and more radical solution to at least part of the problem.

The essentials of a new approach are contained in an analysis of copying [76] which turns out to be functionally similar to the engineering developments recently highlighted by Wiener under the name "cybernetics." This type of analysis depends on guidance by feedback and on the assumption of relational responses to relational stimuli. These "new" types of stimuli and responses fit easily into our functional definitions. There is considerable evidence for their existence.

In the original example [76], a novice struggling to master singing on key first learned to respond to the cue of his own note being below that of the model's by tensing his vocal chords to raise the pitch of his voice—i.e., he responded to the direction of a difference with a direction of adjustment. Similarly, he learned to slide the pitch down when he was singing too high. With practice, he learned to respond to larger discrepancies with larger adjustments and smaller discrepancies with smaller ones. Concurrently, the cue of difference of pitch was becoming a learned drive and the cue of sameness a learned reward so that subsequent behavior could be shaped by response-produced drive induction and reduction.

The assumption of certain elements of similarity among different instances of being flat (as contrasted with being sharp or on key) allowed these responses of approximation and correction to generalize to new pitches. In these new situations, the same relational response, e.g., tensing, produced the appropriate correction even though the absolute level of pitch was different.

In the same way, a person might learn to respond to the cue of seeing his hand to the left of a pencil by moving to the right until his path of approach was directly lined up with the pencil. On different occasions, the same relational response, moving to the right, might be made to the same relational cue, too far to the left, although the specific patterns of absolute stimulation and movement might be quite different.

The same type of analysis might be applied to the general orienting responses of the head and eyes, with the subject learning to turn until his eyes were lined up correctly, and then to approach or avoid. It is easy to design a simple mechanism that will approach a light in this manner, always following the light although never repeating the exact pattern of specific movements. In fact, a simple phototropic organism, such as the single-celled Euglena, can respond only in this way. It is obvious that cybernetic responses of this type are much more flexible than specific ballistic responses to specific push-button cues, and that an S-R analysis does not need to be limited to the latter.

In other publications [25, p. 87; 64, p. 466], we have pointed out how such responses might function to produce goal-oriented learned drives.

A more rigorous and comprehensive attempt to apply this cybernetic type of analysis should involve an experimental program determining what types of difference, direction of difference or magnitude of difference, can serve as cues, and how a response learned to such a cue at one level of a continuum such as pitch, will generalize to other different levels and even conceivably to other continua. For example, Miller [52] found that children readily use "the box-of-a-different-color" as a cue and that a response to this cue will generalize to new combinations of colors; similarly, Harlow et al. [33] have found that monkeys can be taught to respond to the cue of "oddity," or in other words "the one object that is different in any group of three."

The addition of other features, such as the habit of responding to a barrier by backing up and moving at a tangent, would be needed to round out the analysis. If such a detailed analysis were made and experimentally tested, we might be able to account for the goal-oriented, flexible quality of behavior rather than merely assuming it. We might also account for failures to adjust immediately to certain changes. There is no reason why such an analysis cannot be made in modern stimulus-response terms.

Role of proprioceptive feedback. There are many additional problems which could be the basis for experimental programs. Often, a response of a given absolute magnitude must be made without any chance for guidance all of the way to the goal by concurrent feedback—e.g., to sink a putt, the golf ball must be hit in the right direction with the right force. It seems highly probable, however, that such responses can be guided by proprioceptive feedback, with the subject learning to increase the force until he produces a certain proprioceptive stimulus and then to stop. In such cases, the problem of different response amplitudes will reduce to proprioceptive discrimination, and response generalization will be a special case of stimulus generalization.

Responses governed by proprioceptive feedback will necessarily be somewhat slow; in fact precise, delicate responses usually are relatively slow. But is this the sole mechanism, or is there some cruder, faster mechanism whereby responses of grossly different amplitude can be made without waiting for control by proprioceptive feedback?

Learning to correct for distortions—man's capacity as a computer. A whole different set of problems is raised by man's enormous capacity to adjust rapidly to various forms of perceptual and motor distortion. It is obvious that relational responses to relational cues, guided by continuous feedback, will not be greatly affected by distortions unless the relationships are actually reversed as in mirror drawing. However, with a response like the golf putt, that cannot be guided by continuous feedback all of the way to the goal, the correction has to be made in advance. We automatically "compute" such corrections when we adjust to a faster or sloping green, a longer or heavier club, or allow for the wind. If one looks through prisms which displace everything to the left, one does not have to practice on every separate point before one can look, close one's eyes, and then touch objects reasonably accurately. Similarly, one rapidly adjusts to various mechanical systems that magnify or reduce one's movements.

How much practice of what kinds does one need to correct for different kinds of distortion? How much transfer is there to new points in the distorted space? Are some kinds of distortion (i.e., curvilinear relationships or reversals) more difficult than others? The use of an analogue computer to introduce precisely specifiable changes into the S-R relationships in a simple psychomotor task, such as looking at a point, closing one's eyes, and then moving a pointer to touch the point, ought to enable one to analyze man's capacity as a computer to correct for various types of systematic distortion. Such experiments would give the theorist new problems and new data.

Multiple cue and response potentialities. By now it should be apparent that I believe that most stimulus objects present the organism with a multiplicity of potential cues. Thus, the organism may learn to respond to the absolute position of a stimulus object, to its relative position, to its absolute brightness, to its relative brightness, to its color, to its form, to its being the one object that is different, etc.

Some of these cues may be relatively direct products of end-organ stimulation, others may be the result of various levels of innate mechanisms for analyzing and processing such stimulation, and yet others may be the result of learned cue-producing responses. These cues may differ in innate perspicuousness, which in turn may be modified by learned factors such as end-organ orientation and the focusing of attention.

Similarly, the organism has many responses in its repertoire. For example, stimulation of the spinal cat can elicit coordinated walking, running, or hopping responses which presumably are organized on an innate basis and vastly simplify the problem of learning locomotion. As we have already pointed out, responses can probably be made either on a relational or on a more absolute, ballistic basis. Furthermore, it is conceivable that the innate wiring diagram of the organism allows for the possibility of responses which, in effect, specify a given new posture as a "balanced" or "null" position so that deviations from that posture produce feedback inducing movement in the proper direction until the posture is restored. A simple example of a mechanism of this type is a recording instrument in which a signal unbalances one arm of a bridge circuit, causes a galvanometer to be deflected from a null position, and thereby actuates a motor which continues to run in the right direction until the other arm of the bridge has been changed enough to bring the circuit back into balance.

Therefore, the same physical movement to the same physical stimulus object may in different instances be an example of a different type of response to a different part of the population of cues. The only way to determine for certain what response to what cue is the dominant one is to perform a series of critical tests in which different potential responses to different potential cues are pitted against each other. After a sufficient series of tests, one may predict the performance in additional test situations. We do not yet have the laws to enable us to make many predictions directly from the experimental conditions but there is no reason why we can not begin to discover such laws if we abandon relatively sterile either-or controversies and devote ourselves to the determination of the laws.

At present we are limited to the rather vague but general principle that differential reinforcement can cause organisms to learn to respond to a particular aspect of the population of potential cues with a particular type of potential response. In general the environment seems to reinforce responding to objects with acts that produce certain end results.

Maturation of concepts—learning sets. I have just argued that most stimulus situations confront the subject with a multiplicity of potential cues. My first publication [52] showed that the relative dominance of such cues can vary with age. Using a convenient technique, the critical-choice direct delayed reaction, which required no verbal skills, I found that position was the dominant cue for the youngest children. But with increasing age, first a simple configuration and then color became dominant over position for most children in the situations used.

The shifts in relative dominance of cues observed in these and other studies might be produced in two ways: (*a*) the mechanisms responsible for the ability to respond to these cues, and hence for their perspicuousness, may mature at different rates, and/or (*b*) the subject may be rewarded for learning to pay attention to different cues [76, p. 72]. Furthermore, it is possible that the mechanism for learning to pay attention to a specific cue is subject to maturation during childhood. Incidentally, recent studies of the functions of the reticular formation demonstrate considerable central control over afferent impulses and may supply a neurophysiological mechanism for the "focusing" of attention as well as new techniques for investigating this problem in animals.

It can be seen that learning to pay attention to specific types of cues could be the basis for the acquired distinctiveness which Lawrence [45, 46, 47] has studied in my laboratory and the learning sets which Harlow and his students have studied at Wisconsin. Furthermore, maturational (and learned) changes in the capacity to respond to cues and in the dominance of different cues should have an important effect on the concepts which children of different ages are likely to acquire. It seems reasonable to suppose that the more subtle and "abstract" cues, such as numerosity and circularity, which may depend on central mechanisms for processing information, would be especially susceptible to effects of postnatal maturation and of learning.

Similarly, the relative position of various members of a hierarchy of responses may be modified by both maturation and learning, and this relative position will be expected to affect the child's readiness to learn specific types of skill or knowledge.

It is obvious that empirical work sharpening up the definitions of functional units of cue and response would contribute to a better understanding of the foregoing problems.

COMMENTS ON SELECTED CONTROVERSIAL ISSUES

This part of the paper continues the general discussion of the way in which I differ from certain other stimulus-response psychologists by a brief discussion of a number of controversial issues.

Do Drives Fall into the Class of Stimuli?

The notion that characteristic stimuli are associated with drive states is relatively old but not completely accepted. I have explored some of the consequences of carrying this notion to its logical conclusion by assuming that all drives are strong stimuli and that any stimulus becomes a drive if intense enough [76].

One deduction from this assumption is that drive generalization should occur as a special case of stimulus generalization. This deduction has been tested in a series of experiments, first briefly summarized [57] and then reported in more detail after World War II [61]. The first of these experiments showed that, if thirsty rats are trained to run down a short alley for water and then tested without thirst, they will not only run faster but also drink more if tested with the irrelevant drive of hunger than if tested without this irrelevant drive. Since hunger and thirst are so closely related, a second experiment was performed in which hungry rats were trained to take the correct arm of a T maze to secure food. Subsequent tests without hunger showed that they would both run faster and choose more correctly if tested with the irrelevant drives of either electric shock or fear than if tested without these additional drives.

Additional evidence was subsequently secured in our laboratory by von Felsinger [107] who showed that induced estrus (presumably involving sexual motivation) increased the running speed and improved the error scores of two groups of satiated rats which had originally been trained to run a maze when hungry or thirsty respectively. Similarly, Webb [108] at Iowa found that thirst as an irrelevant drive increased the performance by food-satiated animals of a habit originally learned under hunger. Although Webb's experiment had the advantage of using more than two levels of irrelevant drive, his thirsty animals may have stopped eating dry food and thus been somewhat hungry when tested.

Hull [39], who was familiar with the results of the first experiments in this series, interpreted them in a different way. Instead of a gradient of drive-stimulus generalization, he assumed a completely general energizing effect, possibly mediated by substances in the blood. Aside from the fact that the blood-substance subhypothesis would be too slow to account for rapid response to pain, the chief difference between Hull's hypothesis and mine is that I would predict the type of relationships that would be expected from a gradient of stimulus generalization. For example, if irrelevant drive A had more effect on a habit based on drive B than drive C, then a habit based on drive A should be more affected by B as an irrelevant drive than by C. By contrast, Hull's 1943 postulate predicts completely equal effects, although his 1952 one is more guarded in this respect. The experiments required to decide between these two main alternatives have not yet been performed.

Response-produced drives and rewards. By combining the hypothesis that strong stimuli serve as drives with the notion of response-produced stimulation, one arrives at the hypothesis that learnable drives are the product of responses that produce intense stimulation. One also arrives at the hypothesis that secondary reinforcement is produced by responses that reduce strong stimulation. It should be remembered that these responses might occur within the central nervous system. These hypotheses, which have led to a considerable amount of significant work, have been presented in detail elsewhere [64, 25]. Some further thoughts will be presented in a subsequent section on learned elicitation vs. learned channeling.

Drive stimulation vs. reduction in threshold. A number of workers [96, 4, 99] have assumed that, instead of acting as strong stimuli, drives serve to reduce thresholds. One of the original points of departure was Richter's [96] observation that andrenalectomized rats would prefer saline to tap water, even with low saline concentrations that elicited no differential response from normal control rats. This better discrimination of the rats with great salt need was interpreted as a reduction in the threshold for the taste of salt, produced by the specific need or drive. Subsequent work has demonstrated that the threshold of the sense organs, measured electrophysiologically, remains the same [94], and that, if normal rats are properly motivated by electric shock, they can discriminate just as well as adrenalectomized ones [34]. Thus the original support is pulled out from under the threshold hypothesis.

Meanwhile, however, Beach and Holz-Tucker [4] were led to the threshold hypothesis by the observation that increasing the androgen level in the blood of male rats increases the range of stimulus objects to which they will exhibit copulatory responses. As we have already pointed out in the earlier part of this paper, such an observation could just as well be explained by assuming that increases in drive raise the level of the entire gradient of stimulus generalization.

It should be clear that going through the experimental operations to demonstrate a reduction in threshold of response to a stimulus does not rule out the possibility that this reduction was produced by the presence of some other source of stimulation. The traditional physiological and psychological experiments on the positive summation of stimuli demonstrate that the threshold of response to the test stimulus is reduced by the presence of the one with which it summates. Conversely, if one deals with the central rather than the peripheral effects of stimulation, it is obvious that a genuine reduction in threshold might cause a stimulus to function as though it were intensified. It is actually quite difficult to discriminate between these two hypotheses: drive as a strong stimulus, or drive as a state which reduces the threshold of peripheral end organs or central synapses.

Sheffield and Campbell [99] and Campbell and Sheffield [18] have presented evidence purporting to support the threshold hypothesis by disproving the drive-stimulus one. They show that, if a rat is kept under relatively soundproof conditions, his rate of activity does not go up when he is hungry, but that the introduction of a novel stimulus will greatly increase the activity of the hungry rat and still more increase it if the novel stimulus is regularly associated with feeding. It is assumed that, if drive were a stimulus, it would have to produce similar increases in activity. Since such an increase was not observed, it is concluded that the function of the drive must have been solely to decrease the threshold of responsiveness to the novel stimulus, an assumption functionally similar to Hull's [39] postulate that drive serves to multiply whatever habit strength is present.

Although these experiments show that drives do not inevitably goad the animal into activity, they do not rule out the possibility that drives are strong stimuli. An electric shock is a strong stimulus. Whether an animal shows increased activity by jumping or decreased activity by crouching to an electric shock depends on whether the reward of turning off the shock is administered for jumping or for crouching. It will be remembered that my definition of drive says nothing about activity, but deals rather with increasing the performance of responses *rewarded* by the offset of the drive or by the goal objects that produce its satiation.

In Fig. 1 of the article by Sheffield and Campbell [99], it will be noticed that, whereas the activity in response to a stimulus that immediately precedes daily feeding increases during a series of trials, the activity to a control stimulus that does not precede feeding progressively decreases. It seems logical to me to assume that the nonrewarded responses to the latter stimulus gradually extinguish and that the nonrewarded responses to the gradually mounting drive stimulus also extinguish in the context of the other constant cues in the Sheffield-Campbell apparatus.

To state the converse side of the argument, suppose that at unpredictable intervals, without providing any stimulation, the experimenters had introduced food alternately at opposite sides of their activity apparatus throughout the test session. Then the animals would have been reinforced for shuttling on a variable-interval schedule. We would expect their shuttling, which would be recorded as activity, to increase with increasing hunger just as does the rate of bar pressing [67]. In short, we can only predict that subjects will be active to a pattern of stimulation including strong drive when activity has been reinforced to that pattern. The situation used by Sheffield and Campbell [99] involved long periods during which activity was not reinforced to the pattern of drive stimulus plus apparatus without the sound of the food delivery mechanism.

The Nature of Reinforcement

It seems to be a fact that some stimulus situations are much more effective than others in determining whether or not the responses that lead to them will be learned and performed. Thus, all theorists are forced to assign the empirical law of effect some role in their theories. A consistent application of the empirical law of effect would result in a long list of stimulus situations that can serve as rewards and of those that are relatively neutral. In practice, most experimenters limit themselves to relatively few situations which are known to function as effective rewards.

The drive-stimulus-reduction hypothesis. Since a catalogue of rewards is so cumbersome, some theorists have looked for a simple general principle, or principles, that will allow them to determine whether an event should be listed as a reward or not. One attempt at such a principle is the drive-reduction hypothesis of reinforcement.

It is well known that turning off a strong motivational stimulus, such as an electric shock, will serve a reward to reinforce whatever response the animal was making just before he escaped from the shock. It is also known that food will serve as a reward for a hungry animal, and that this same food, if given in sufficient quantities, will reduce the strength of the hunger drive. The drive-reduction hypothesis attempts to abstract a common element from observations of this kind. In its weak form, it states that the sudden reduction in the strength of any strong motivational stimulus always serves as a reward, or in other words, is a *sufficient* condition for reinforcement. In its strong form, it states that all reward is produced in this way, or in other words, that drive reduction is not only a sufficient but also the *necessary* condition for reinforcement.

By defining drives as strong stimuli, I have sharpened the hypothesis into the assumption that it is the sudden reduction in the strength of intense stimulation that serves as a reinforcement.

Not completely committed to drive-stimulus-reduction hypothesis. Although I believe that the foregoing hypothesis has a considerably less than 50 per cent chance of being correct, especially in its strong form, I do believe it is better at the present moment than any other single hypothesis. Therefore, I feel that it is worthwhile to try out applying it consistently, if only to highlight the obstacles and infuriate others into devising superior hypotheses and the experimental programs to support them.

When one systematically explores a given hypothesis and points out the weaknesses of various theoretical and experimental attacks on this hypothesis, however, it is difficult to avoid the reputation (and after that, the fact) of being emotionally fixated on the hypothesis. Furthermore, the very controversial nature of the drive-stimulus-reduction hypothesis makes it conspicuous, so that it seems to be the cornerstone of one's whole theoretical thinking.

Let me try to destroy both illusions. The stimulus-reduction hypothesis of reinforcement could be discarded without having an appreciable effect on the rest of my theoretical formulations. I take this occasion to urge attempts to formulate and rigorously test competing hypotheses, and time permitting, may even join in that activity myself. However unsatisfactory, the drive-reduction hypothesis is not likely to be abandoned as long as it is the best thing of its kind that we have. The decisive way to kill it is with a superior alternative.

Various possible bases for correlation between reinforcement and satiation. Let us start out with the original observation that there seems to be a correlation between the operations of satiation and those of reinforcement. This is not surprising because animals that are not rewarded by substances that reduce their drives are likely to come from a long line of extinct ancestors. Furthermore, the process could also work the other way—individuals that do not eventually become satiated on a given form of pleasure may starve to death while enjoying the thrill of tickling themselves.

We should remember that a correlation does not necessarily indicate a direct causal relationship. The drive reduction could produce the reinforcement, the reinforcement could produce the drive reduction, or natural selection could have built a correlation into the organism that did not involve any direct causal relationship. For example, an increase in pleasure could be the true basis for reinforcement and animals could have evolved by natural selection so that in general only nutritious substances taste good and the pleasantness of these is some function of the strength of hunger.

Sample studies illustrating fruitfulness of hypothesis. If natural selection has produced a spurious correlation, we would expect this correlation to be more likely to disappear if we manipulated drives in unusual ways which have not been encountered in natural selection. On the other hand, if it is a true causal relationship, it should survive these unusual manipulations.

In order to test the drive-reduction hypothesis in this way, and also to learn more about the mechanism of drives, I have been involved in a series of experiments which have tried to induce and reduce drives in unusual ways [73, 7, 78]. These experiments have shown that food injected via a plastic fistula directly into the stomach of a rat promptly reduces hunger as measured either by the amount of food subsequently eaten or by the rate at which the animals will work at pressing a bar to secure food on a variable-interval schedule of reinforcement. But food taken normally by mouth has a greater effect on both of these two measures. Similar results have been secured for thirst, which has also been induced by injecting hypertonic saline into the ventricles of the brain and reduced by injecting water. In short, there seem to be a number of mechanisms—located in the mouth, stomach, and brain—for regulating drive.

Furthermore, exactly as the drive-reduction hypothesis would predict from the foregoing facts, food injected directly into the stomach will serve as a reward to cause rats to choose the correct side of a T maze, but food taken normally by mouth will serve as a stronger reward to produce more rapid learning. The rewarding effect of food injected directly into the stomach would not be expected from hypotheses that used either the pleasant taste or the consummatory response as the sole basis of reinforcement. Conversely, the saccharine solution which Sheffield and Roby [100] proved was a reward for hungry animals has been found by us to reduce hunger [67].

Effects of electrical stimulation of the brain. Another series of studies has demonstrated the possibilities of motivating learning and performance by direct electrical stimulation of the brain [83, 23, 70]. In connection with these studies, I have discussed [71] the implications for theories of reinforcement of the reward effect discovered by Olds and Milner [92] and have shown how the drive-stimulus-reduction hypothesis can suggest significant new studies of central motivation and reward—studies which ultimately may lead to a superior hypothesis. A summary of my recent physiological studies of motivation has been published elsewhere [73].

Campbell's psychophysical studies. The hypothesis that drives are strong stimuli and that sudden reductions in them produce reinforcement, has further demonstrated its usefulness by starting Byron Campbell on a series of studies which extend the psychophysical tradition to a new area by quantitatively studying the rewarding effects of sudden reductions in the strength of strong stimuli. Electric shocks and loud sounds have been used in these studies which show that, when the stimulation is reduced to zero, stronger initial strengths of stimulation produce greater learning and performance. But when the motivation is not reduced to zero, a given absolute amount of reduction is less effective the higher the initial level. Within the middle ranges, equal reinforcing effects seem to be produced by equal ratios of reduction, a relationship like Weber's law, which breaks down at the extremes. Thus, what might be described as a "reinforcement threshold" seems to show the same general type of curve as does the psychophysical threshold for a just noticeable difference, although much larger changes are required to produce a reinforcing effect [17, 15, 16].

Relationship of drive to learning. A stimulus-response analysis can clarify some of the apparent confusion about the relationship of drive to learning [66]. In the practical teaching situation, everyone knows that poorly motivated students do not learn. This is chiefly because they do not expose themselves to the proper cues or perform the correct responses, for example, open their books and study. But most experiments on this topic have concerned themselves with a somewhat different problem: the relationship of drive to reinforcement. Therefore, they have tried to control the factors of exposure to cues and number of responses by giving both groups the same number of trials in very simple situations. One must be careful in generalizing from this kind of experiment to the practical situation; a film of mine [77] yields a better analogy.

When the drive is promptly reduced to zero after the correct response, there is a perfect correlation between the strength of drive and the amount of drive reduction. Thus, according to the stimulus-reduction hypothesis, stronger drives should produce more reinforcement and better learning. These conditions are met in most experiments on escape learning and eyelid conditioning. The results of such experiments agree with the theory.[8]

In the work of Campbell and his collaborators, we have just seen that when the drive stimulus is reduced a *constant absolute value,* the amount of reinforcement follows the same Weber's law principle as other stimuli; it is less at the higher levels of drive. Under these circumstances, the intense-stimulus-reduction hypothesis would not expect a positive relationship between the strength of drive and amount of learning.

In experiments in which the correct response is reinforced by pellets of food or sips of water, it is obvious that, at the extreme low end of the continuum, there will be little possibility of drive reduction if there is almost no drive present. And indeed, experiments on so-called latent learning seem to agree that extremely low drives (whether all relevant primary and secondary drives are zero is controversial) seem to produce less learning than does higher drive.

When we start comparing moderate drives with strong ones, however, we simply do not know what the relationship is between the strength of

---

[8] It should be noted, however, that all such experiments have involved noxious stimuli so that one might claim that the positive results were produced by a learned drive, such as fear, which persisted from training to testing.

drive and the *relative* amount of drive reduction produced by a single pellet of food or sip of water. Therefore, it should not be too surprising that the results of such experiments are confusing. Even if the animal were fed to satiation at the end of a trial, the total amount of drive reduction would be confounded with considerable delay. Perhaps techniques for manipulating hunger and thirst by electrical stimulation of the brain (or measuring them by central recording) will develop to the point where we can conduct decisive experiments on such drives.

Spence [103] has clearly pointed out and documented an additional source of possible confusion, namely, that whenever an incorrect response is dominant at the beginning of learning, Hull's [39] principle that drive multiplies the strength of habits predicts that increases in drive will increase its excitatory potential more than that of the subdominant correct responses. To this and other excellent points that he makes, I would add only that one must consider (1) possible innate responses to different strengths of drive, and (2) the possibility that rates and amplitudes are specific responses as would be expected from a micromolar analysis of the type expounded by Logan [49].

Large areas in which lack of suitable measures makes hypothesis inapplicable. In experiments using extremely strong stimuli, such as electric shocks, intense lights, or sounds that are under external control, the stimulus-reduction hypothesis clearly applies and is routinely verified. But perhaps the most damning thing that can be said about this hypothesis is that there are so many situations in which, with our present techniques, we cannot tell for certain whether the net effect of a given experimental operation is to produce an increase or a decrease in the motivating stimulus. Although such limitations are not unique to this hypothesis, a clear-cut possibility of disproof would be preferable to the present ambiguity. For example, if the change from complete darkness to weak illumination is reinforcing, it can be argued that the small increase in visual stimulation is more than overbalanced by a reduction in boredom or fear. Similarly, it can be argued either that tiny pellets of food produce brief reductions in drive, or that they do not appreciably reduce hunger and may even whet the animal's appetite. Guthrie [31] can argue that a boy banging on a drum is seeking stimulation and Harlow [32] can say the same for the curiosity of his monkeys. On the other hand, a plausible case can be made that both boy and monkey are escaping from the intolerable tension of boredom. Such ambiguities have motivated me to the program of research aimed at trying to learn more about the mechanisms of drive induction and reduction. Perhaps there are physiological ways of securing independent measures of at least certain drives, or behavioral techniques for trying to extend the correlation between satiation and reinforcement to other drives such as curiosity [73, 91].

Alternative hypotheses. Guthrie's [31] version of the pure contiguity hypothesis is enormously appealing because of its simplicity and because it would be relatively easy to imagine a physiological mechanism that worked in this way. I have been unable to see, however, why it should not predict that a thoroughly learned response to a momentary stimulus will never extinguish. After a given response is learned to the point where it regularly is the first and last response to that stimulus, should not more and more of the atypical members of the population of cues be conditioned to the response so that it would become progressively more certain to occur?

There is also the problem of why the stimulus-change produced by the *onset* of a painful stimulus does not protect preceding responses from retroactive inhibition. One might modify Guthrie's hypothesis to avoid these difficulties by assuming that only the termination of a stimulus (and *not* changes produced by adding new cues) functions to protect responses from retroactive inhibition, and that such protection is proportional to the number of cue elements that are removed. Then, the effect of terminating a weak stimulus would be negligible because the change in the total population of cue elements would be so small, but the termination of a strong stimulus would be more effective because many more cue elements would be removed. With such modifications, Guthrie's application of the contiguity hypothesis would become functionally very similar to the hypothesis that reinforcement is produced by the prompt reduction in a strong stimulus.

Various two-factor theories have considerable attractiveness. It is easy to imagine a simple contiguity mechanism being evolved at an early stage and then supplemented with some sort of booster effect from reward or the escape from punishment. Indeed, it is quite possible that careful research on primitive organisms, or on more complex ones primitivized by removing higher segments of the brain, would show that it is possible for them to learn several responses by simple conditioning but not to select among them by trial and error, even when the proper conditions for trial and error learning are realized.

Actually, the shift from a single factor to a multifactor theory need not be very disruptive to the general features of such miniature systems as I have proposed as long as most of the laws—gradient of reinforcement, stimulus generalization, experimental extinction, spontaneous recovery, etc.—remain the same [25, p. 42]. These laws seem to be the same for classically conditioned autonomic responses as well as for trial-and-error somatic responses reinforced by either escape from electric shock or rewarding a hungry animal with food.

To use a simple analogy, to change the lighting in an apartment house from electricity to gas, would be a major undertaking because the two sources of energy follow completely different laws, and thus would require changes such as those from wires to pipes. A change from a-c to d-c current would involve relatively minor alterations, since these two types of current have relatively similar functional properties. A shift from alternating current delivered by a private company to alternating current delivered by a municipal one would involve only a small change in the connections to the basement (which, indeed, would be highly significant to those who sell the current from different sources), but there would be no changes in the wiring and appliances throughout the apartment house since the current from these two sources follows identical laws.

Proponents of multiple-factor theories of learning can attract more serious attention if they can rigorously specify different laws associated with supposedly different types of learning.

Cognitive theories. S-R theorists are confronted with the problem of explaining man's obviously intelligent behavior; cognitive theorists are confronted with the problem of explaining obvious stupidity. Although recognizing that much of man's behavior involves cognitions, I have preferred the strategy of trying to explain such behavior as the outgrowth of simpler, noncognitive mechanisms. It is hard for me to conceive of cognitive insight as the sole means of acquiring maladaptive neurotic symptoms or those many motor skills that seem to be almost entirely unconscious.

One obvious alternative taken by many cognitive theorists is to assume different levels of learning—a lower S-R one to explain stupid behavior and a higher cognitive one to explain intelligent behavior. This may turn out to be the most parsimonious explanation possible, but the theorist will have to be careful to specify under what conditions both occur or else he will be limited to *post hoc* explanations. Another alternative is to adopt the general pattern of Tolman's theory—using association as the basic element of learning, and the empirical law of effect as the mechanism of activation—but stating the laws in terms of automatic processes. Spence's [103] theory is tending in this direction. Variations of this general pattern certainly should be rigorously explored. But one must be careful that the theory does not predict that, if rats or earthworms show any learning with motivation and reward, they should show approximately as good latent learning.

New Trails for Research on Motivation[9]

We are still a long way from a satisfactory understanding of motivation. To take a simple example, much of our human social behavior is

[9] Throughout this section I frequently use the term motivation to include the effects of both drive and reward, using the latter terms if I want to distinguish the two effects.

overdetermined by many different sources of drive and reinforcement. Thus, money is the focus of many needs; its possession the means to many rewards. But our experimental literature has scarcely begun [95] to tackle the problems of how different sources of drive and reward summate positively or negatively in the learning and maintenance of a given habit.

Learned elicitation vs. learned channeling. Most of the motivation of adult human social behavior is either acquired by or profoundly modified by learning. I have called such motivations *learnable drives and rewards* to emphasize the fact that the basic physiological mechanism is probably innate, although the arousal or reduction in response to specific cues is a product of learning [64]. In the case of fear, it seems possible for part of the response innately elicited by pain (loud sounds and perhaps a considerable variety of other situations) to be conditioned to new cues so that it can be elicited in the complete absence of any obvious, relevant primary drive. Let us call this *learned elicitation*.

I have assumed that the elicitation of a number of social drives might be learned in the same way as fear, for example, as a result of thousands of instances in which feeding and other sources of infant gratification are associated with the appearance of an approving parent. However, I have repeatedly failed to establish experimentally any appreciable learned elicitation of drive on the basis of primary drives such as hunger or thirst [cf. 91].[10]

Although this failure has not caused me to abandon completely the attempt to apply the fear-elicitation paradigm to appetitive drives, it has caused me to shift the emphasis in a new direction. As pointed out earlier [64], even the primary drives themselves may be profoundly modified by learning, so that hunger becomes the desire for a particular kind of food prepared according to culturally determined standards of what is appetizing. Thus, one must learn to like snails or oysters. But the elicitation of the appetite for such foods never becomes completely independent of hunger, since even these delicacies have little appeal after complete satiation by a Thanksgiving dinner. Furthermore, although the taste for snails and other exotic foods is learned, it is continually reinforced by eating them when hungry. Therefore, one does not need to worry about the problem of experimental extinction vs. functional autonomy.

---

[10] It is conceivable that this failure is due to the fact that these drives are aroused so slowly that one is always dealing with delayed, or even backward, conditioning. That is one of the reasons why I have been interested in exploring possibilities of eliciting drives rapidly by techniques such as electrical or chemical stimulation of the brain [73]. On the other hand, it may be that such failures are due to the absence of any mechanism for a response-produced drive like the one involved in fear.

It should be noted, however, that hunger probably can be channeled only to certain categories of objects, namely, foods. I venture that it would be much more difficult to develop and maintain an appetite for sawdust. Are there other drives that permit more latitude in channeling? What are the defining characteristics of their potential goal objects?

The desire for a specific kind of food may be called *learned channeling of drive*. It may be contrasted with the fear of a previously neutral cue which we have just described as learned elicitation of drive.

The foregoing two examples—channeling of hunger and elicitation of fear—may not be completely different, but represent the extremes of a continuum. An intermediate case could occur if there is a latent fear of some type of situation which can be further strengthened by learning. Or there might be an innate tendency to fear some general class of situations which can be made more specific by learning. Furthermore, we might find that the reaction to a conditioned fear stimulus would vary with the general level of anxiety of the subject and be influenced by physiological factors such as endocrine changes.

Can rewards for one drive channel a different one? Another possibility is that reinforcement by the goal objects of a given drive may help to determine the direction in which a second one is channeled.[11] If such channeling occurs, it might easily be mistaken for the establishment of learned elicitation, and/or secondary reinforcement that became independent of the first drive.

A possible illustration of such a channeled drive is the Freudian hypothesis that sex begins as a dependent drive (*Anlehnungstriebe*), so that a young man's eventual object choice may be determined by earlier rewards in the nursing situation under the primary drive of hunger. If this were the case, it is clear that the young man's attraction to his bride might continue to be reinforced by adult sexual (and other) gratifications even though he discovered that she could not cook.

To take a simpler example, Scott [98] observed that two bottle-fed sheep showed no tendency whatsoever to follow the rest of the herd whereas several thousand normally nursed controls all showed strong gregarious tendencies. This observation suggests that gregariousness in sheep may be influenced by learning during the nursing situation. But some special innate susceptibility or additional source of motivation must be involved since not all mammals are as gregarious as sheep.

Similarly, a variety of obvious rewards, such as feeding, determine a dog's attachment to a particular master or family. This attachment may be strong enough to motivate the dog to learn to respond to various

---

[11] I use the more general phrase "reinforcement by goal objects" to emphasize the fact that this hypothesis is not necessarily tied to the drive-stimulus-reduction hypothesis of reinforcement.

cues by being ready to leap into the car so that he will not be left be-hind. But equally well-treated cats usually do not acquire a similar motivation. Such observations raise the possibility that, as part of the pattern of hunting in packs, evolution has produced in dogs some special motivational mechanism that can be channeled either to the pack or to the adoptive human family.

The "imprinting" of ducks to follow people and other objects may be an extreme example of channeling. We have already suggested that this "motivation to follow" probably could be used as a drive for the trial-and-error learning of whatever response produced the release per-mitting the baby duck to follow its leader [64]. But the original behavior of the newly hatched duck in the absence of any suitable moving objects to follow suggests some strong original motivation, perhaps fear. Could this motivation also be studied? Would its reduction by a suitable object prove to be the source of reinforcement for the original imprinting? What role is played by feeding and other reinforcements which often are con-founded with "imprinting"?

It is possible that the type of behavior which we have described as channeling is nothing more than an array of specific habits. Certainly the line between (or blending of) habit and motivation needs clarifica-tion as Brown [13] has ably argued.

What I would like to point out is that such habits seem to have many of the functional properties of drives. Oysters for people, or novel foods for rats, do not function as effective rewards until the subject has learned to eat them. How much of this is a function of mere delay in seizing and swallowing? I venture that at least some of the effect may be due to the elimination of aversions by counterconditioning and the acquisition of secondary reinforcement.

Furthermore, the aroma, sight, or even description of a particular delicacy seems to produce a considerable increase in the motivation of a moderately hungry person. I venture that, under appropriate circum-stances, it would also facilitate the trial-and-error learning and perform-ance of any response that circumvented a block to the direct approach to the incentive. Furthermore, Tinklepaugh's [104] observations on monkeys and my own incidental observations of people suggest that, once a learned strong anticipatory goal response for a particular food is aroused, other foods may be less effective as rewards. Again the factor of delay in consumption needs to be controlled.

Finally, we need to know the laws governing the ways in which motivation can be channeled and/or elicited by new cues. For example, what conditions can inhibit the development of intellectual curiosity in children and what conditions can enhance it? For that matter, what conditions can arrest, strengthen, or channel the curiosity of a cat?

Throughout the preceding discussion we have raised a number of theoretical possibilities. Although the animal examples cited should readily lend themselves to precise experimental analysis, such work has not been done, so that our discussion has had to be highly speculative; many different theoretical possibilities are open.

What drives may be elicited or channeled by learning? Since the conditions of social and individual learning are complex and variable, we will expect learnable drives to exist in a baffling variety of combinations in response to a baffling variety of cues. Thus, any standard list of socially learned motives will only be as simple and as stable as the conditions of learning involved. This may explain the baffling variety of such lists.

One might go on to ask, however, what kind of different physiological mechanisms may underlie learnable drives? It seems plausible that fear might be the underlying mechanism in a number of instances that seem different because different conditions of training have caused different categories of cues to arouse the fear, and other specific categories of cues to serve as the goals because they, respectively, reduce these specific fears. Thus, it is interesting to note that we speak of the fear of failure, the fear of disapproval, the fear of losing money, status, or love.

Similarly, Freudian theory presupposes that sex underlies a large number of superficially different motives.

Do certain social motives, such as curiosity, gregariousness, and jealousy, all have a common mechanism, or does each have distinctive ones? Can such motives be elicited, channeled, or both? If they are channeled, what are the characteristics defining potential goals? We have scarcely made a beginning toward answering some of these questions. If we knew more about some of these other sources of motivation, we might not be so strongly tempted to place such a heavy theoretical burden on fear. We must solve such problems before we can begin to understand the wonderfully complex web of human social motivation.

Need to study new types of drive; one way to do it. Most of the basic research on motivation to date has been confined to an extremely limited number of so-called primary drives such as hunger, thirst, sex, and pain. There is a great need to study new types of motivation in the laboratory. Our present list of experimentally studied motives is far too short. A promising break away from our old limitations has been made with studies of fear and more recent studies of "curosity" and "activity." We need to extrapolate this new trend.

A new view of fear. The old view of fear as an emotion was inferior in that it stressed innate and disrupting effects of fear and did not even give a clear picture of how these were achieved. The newer and much more powerful understanding is (a) that fear is a drive, like hunger or thirst, which may motivate either adaptive or maladaptive behavior, and (b) that a sudden reduction in the strength of fear serves as a reward to reinforce immediately preceding responses.

The point of departure for this new understanding of fear was Mowrer's [86] trenchant stimulus-response analysis of Freud's [26] insightful paper on the problem of anxiety. Mowrer's pioneering work led me to set up an experimental demonstration that fear has a crucial functional property of drive in that it can motivate the trial-and-error learning and performance of whatever response is followed by a sudden reduction in the strength of fear [58, 60]. I believe that this same experimental paradigm that I applied to fear can be used to study many other sources of motivation.

In my experiment on fear, albino rats were placed in a simple apparatus consisting of two compartments separated by a door. One was white with a grid as a floor; the other was black without a grid. Before training, the animals showed no marked preference for either compartment. Then, they were given a number of trials during which they received electric shock in the white compartment and escaped into the black compartment through the open door. After this training, the animals would run out of the white compartment, even if no shock was on the grid.

Then, during additional trials without further shocks came the critical test to demonstrate that the rats' running was not the mere persistence of a habit, but also had the crucial property of a drive, namely that it could motivate, and its reduction reinforce, the learning of a *new* habit. The door, previously always open, was closed. The only way that it could be opened was by rotating, by a fraction of a turn, a little wheel which was above the door. Under these conditions, the rats exhibited trial-and-error behavior and gradually learned to escape from the white compartment by promptly rotating the wheel.

When the conditions were changed, so that only pressing a bar would open the door, wheel turning extinguished and a second, new habit (bar pressing) was learned. Thus, the fear, presumably established by the shocks in the white compartment, was shown to have the same functional properties as a drive such as pain in that it could motivate the trial-and-error performance of response and its reduction could reinforce the immediately preceding response.

This new view that fear is a drive and that fear-reduction is a reinforcement has many consequences. These have been developed in the course of studies in which I have been involved—investigations of behavior in combat [24, 110, 65], and an analysis of neurosis and psychotherapy [25]. In going beyond the experimental studies of animals in vital fear situations, I have chosen to look for "naturally" occurring situations where people were confronted with vital dangers, rather than bringing subjects into the relatively safe laboratory and in effect merely saying "boo!" to them.[12] I shall have space to hint at only a few of the main points gleaned from such studies. Many of the ideas emerged from collaboration with John Dollard.

As soon as fear is thought of as a drive, one notices that it can motivate desirable behavior, such as being alert and resourceful, driving slowly, looking for the source of danger and planning ways to minimize it —for example, buying insurance. Of course, fear can also motivate undesirable behavior such as cowardly running and hiding, cheating, and lying. The most important thing, then, is *not how afraid a man is but what fear motivates him to do.*

Since a sudden reduction in the intensity of fear serves as a reward to strengthen responses, a frightened person will learn those responses he is making when his fear is reduced. If he eventually escapes from the fear by brave, adaptive behavior, he should learn to become more courageous and resourceful; if he temporarily reduces fear by cowardly and maladaptive behavior, he should learn to become more craven. If neurotic symptoms reduce fear, they will be learned. Other symptoms, such as ulcers, may be part of the direct physiological reaction to fear.

One way of reducing fear is to turn away from, suppress, or repress the fear-arousing stimuli. When mild fears are reduced in this way, the subject learns to avoid unpleasant topics; when intense fears are involved, complete repression may be reinforced. It is obvious that avoiding looking at and thinking about possible sources of danger may actually increase the probability of disaster or decrease the possibility of making the discrimination that no significant danger exists. Furthermore, anyone who wants to use fear as a motivation must effectively emphasize the proper escapes from fear or run the danger of having his subjects find their own escape by avoiding him and forgetting his message. In using fear as a drive it is important to remember that *the escape from fear is what reinforces learned behavior.*

Many additional practical points come out of the naturalistic study of fear, for example, the importance of knowing exactly what to expect or planning and knowing what to do to minimize the danger, of concentrating on the task at hand, of breaking seemingly impossible tasks into manageable steps and concentrating on the successful performance of each step, the value of reassurance from the group or self-administered reassurance, the effectiveness of strong positive motivation and of rewards (counterconditioning) for nonfearful behavior. Additional dis-

---

[12] My work in the Air Force during World War II convinced me of the difficulties of devising situations that would really frighten eager young aviation cadets without terrifying generals and congressmen.

cussion more oriented toward theory and experiment will be found in Miller [64].

Curiosity. In the course of a fruitless search for a learned drive based on hunger, Myers and Miller [91] applied to curiosity the same apparatus and theoretical paradigm that had been used in the study of fear. Curiosity had previously been brought into the laboratory from somewhat different points of view by the ingenious work of Berlyne [8], Harlow [32], and Montgomery [85]. In addition to applying the same operations used in the study of fear, Myers and I suggested the importance of determining whether a new drive, such as curiosity, shows the same pattern of deprivation-reinforcement-satiation as previously studied drives such as hunger. In other words, is there a correlation between the operations of reinforcement and satiation, so that an event which increases the *subsequent* performance of a response when administered immediately after that response is also found to tend to decrease the performance of responses motivated by that drive when it is administered in sufficient amount immediately before testing those responses?[13]

Finally, Kagan and Berkun [41] have used the same general paradigm for studying "activity drive" and Zimbardo and Miller [112] have used it as the point of departure for studying the effect of hunger on curiosity.

Drive elicited by perceptual mechanisms? The general approach can be further illustrated by another experiment. In an attempt to bridge the gap between gestalt theory, perceptual learning, and S-R theory, I wondered whether the vector toward a good gestalt had the properties of a drive. If it did, one might expect animals exposed to a bad gestalt to learn by trial and error a simple response that would cause it to change to a better one. The "bad gestalt" of a series of broken lines was projected in front of pigeons. Pecking on a response key caused this to change to the "good gestalt" of unbroken lines. For a control group, the same response caused a pattern of straight lines to change to one of broken lines.

To circumvent certain practical difficulties, we started with trained birds, tried to measure any reinforcing effect by a difference in resistance to extinction, and introduced a number of controls for possible stimulus generalization between the situations of training and of extinction.

[13] It should be noted that one can imagine special conditions under which the drive-stimulus-reduction hypothesis would not demand quite the same pattern as hunger seems to exhibit. Suppose pressing a bar turned off a shock which was almost immediately turned back on. There would be a correlation between the operations of reinforcement and satiation, but the period of "satiation" might be so brief that it easily could be missed. Furthermore, longer periods of "deprivation" might not produce greater amounts of recovery from "satiation."

The difference, although in the right direction, was relatively small and unreliable. Perhaps a tendency toward a good gestalt cannot function as a drive, or perhaps we used a technique that elicited it only weakly. But the experiment illustrates how the method can be applied.

With sufficiently ingenious apparatus, the same general method could be used to determine whether or not motivational effects are produced by sensory blurring, perceptual distortions, or the disruption of "phase sequences" that have been established by either perceptual experience or experimental training.

This paper has already suggested a way of applying the same general paradigm to the experimental study of motivation possibly produced by conflict.

Motivation for achievement. Observations of human and animal behavior suggest many additional possible sources of motivation for experimental study. For example, a child that has just learned to turn over from its stomach to its back may cry until it is placed on its stomach so that it can practice this fascinating act again. Can trial-and-error learning be motivated by this "drive"?

After the child has become skillful in turning over in both directions, he seems to become bored with this activity but strives persistently against many difficulties for other skills—to pull himself up, to stand, to walk, and eventually to ski. What is the drive and reward for each of these skills? Is there a separate drive for every maturing potential skill or is there some mechanism to produce in infants what might be loosely labeled as a general drive toward achievement? If so, what kind of mechanism could possibly produce this result? How much of the adult motive is attributable to rewards that channel such a drive and how much to some drive that is elicited by social punishments for failure to improve and rewards for improving?

Conceivably, the blocking of almost any response tends to induce motivation and the partial or complete occurrence of the blocked response tends to relieve the motivation and function as a reward. This hypothesis might be checked by eliciting movements, such as circling, by central stimulation and determining whether such stimulation can motivate learning without any additional rewards, if, and only if, the movements are first blocked and then released. It is just barely conceivable that such a mechanism might be one step toward the development of a motivation that would have some of the functions of a drive to achieve.

Certain ideas as motivation. Similarly, observation of infants strongly suggests that they have something like definite ideas and that these can serve as transient but strong motivations. I have observed a child under the age of nine months seem to get the idea that he wanted to get a certain tray off a low shelf, struggle vigorously this way and that until he finally succeeded, and then show a look of joy and triumph.

In the adult it is obvious that, as the definite result of social training, certain thoughts, such as "I may have cancer," can elicit strong motivation. I have described such motives as *mediated learned drives* [64]. Could this mechanism have been involved in the infant, and if so, how, or was some more basic mechanism involved, and if so, what?

Perhaps, as I have suggested in a discussion of *goal-directed drives* [64], the discrepancy between an anticipatory goal response (or certain other ideas) and the current state of affairs can be the basis for motivation. Again, we need to know far more empirical facts aimed at a penetrating analysis of the details of such behavior and its possible mechanisms.

Possible response characteristics in infant hunger. Let me conclude with one more concrete example. I have observed an infant during the first two weeks of life change within a few minutes from a state of relative quiescence to one of crying, reddening, and extreme activation so that my first reaction was to search for a jabbing pin. No such obvious source of activation was found, but when given a bottle, he drank vigorously and quieted down. If the milk in the bottle ran out, he became extremely activated, but by the time a new bottle could be heated, he sometimes had quieted down, was out of the mood, and refused it.

The suddenness of these shifts contrasts with what might be expected from the gradual accumulation (or restoration) of a physiological deficit; it suggests that hunger may have some of the properties of a response, being inhibited until it finally breaks through and then strengthens and maintains itself by positive feedback. On the other hand, perhaps it is not the hunger itself, but only the anticipatory goal responses or overt responses to the hunger, that have this characteristic.

In any event, it should be reasonably straightforward and profitable to devise objective techniques for recording the reactions of human or animal infants to hunger. Then one could systematically study the effects of a few simple controlled experimental operations of the type that frequently occur by chance in the natural environment.

Additional problems. In conclusion, let me emphasize that the foregoing examples are but a small sample of the types of naturalistic observations which point up the shortcomings of our current understanding of motivation. Each such observation could serve as the point of departure for a new line of research. I have made a number of suggestions, but these are meant more to point up the problems than to serve as definitive solutions to them. Many other problems remain to be raised. For example, some motivations in some people seem to be relatively central in that they cannot be changed without a profound effect on the entire personality; others are peripheral and can be changed with little effect. What are the principles and conditions that cause different motivations to be central with different individuals? Why are some learned drives amazingly resistant to change, whereas others change easily? How are hierarchies of learned drives and rewards built up, and how do they interact?

SOCIAL LEARNING, PERSONALITY, AND PSYCHOTHERAPY

I have already pointed out that my collaboration with John Dollard in applying learning principles to social situations outside of the laboratory has posed problems which helped to liberalize and extend the principles. One of the reasons for this is that, in dealing with social behavior, one cannot select simple cues and responses which allow one to ignore vexing problems. Another reason is that the concrete examples of real social behavior often involve new phenomena which would not be called to one's attention by work restricted to the laboratory. The attempt to analyze these new phenomena in terms of the principles derived from the laboratory often suggests new kinds of experiments to perform.

Adequate treatments of the attempts to apply learning and behavior theory to more complex social phenomena would be another major task requiring a separate paper; only a few of the main points can be indicated here. Fortunately, events have moved swiftly since the publication of our books on these topics so that many of their contributions are becoming part of the *Zeitgeist*.

The book on *Social Learning and Imitation* [76] clarified a relationship between psychology and various social sciences. In order to be able to predict any specific item of learned behavior, one must know not only the *principles*, but also the *conditions* of learning. To take a simple example, one could know everything about principles, such as the gradient of reward, but be completely unable to predict which way a rat would turn in a T maze unless one knew also the relevant conditions, namely, which arm of the maze contained the reward and which arm was wired for electric shock. With human social behavior, psychology provides the principles of learning and of innate drives, cues, rewards, and responses. The other social sciences, such as sociology and social anthropology, describe the conditions of learning—or in other words, the location of the rewards, punishments, and other conditions of the social maze. One must know *both* the psychological principles and the social conditions in order to predict human behavior.

Furthermore, the present conditions of learning are the product of prior conditions plus the principles of learning, so that a knowledge of psychological principles helps one to understand current conditions.

This book also illustrates a process of analyzing a concrete example of social behavior, the imitative behavior of children in the family setting, and of designing experiments on animals and on children to test the theoretical analysis. Then, the analysis is applied to more complex forms of behavior, such as the prestige of models. Additional experiments are performed to test this further application of the principles. Finally, applications are made to yet more complex phenomena such as crowd behavior and copying in the diffusion of cultures.

In the course of this work, it is necessary to emphasize learnable drives and rewards and the higher mental processes.

We also encounter problems and data which suggest new hypotheses. I shall mention only two, related to the learning of language. One of these is that the early vocal behavior of the infant is in part generalized from his crying behavior, which is instrumental in bringing rewarding help from the parents. The other supplementary (not alternative) hypothesis is that, through manifold association with rewards of loving care, the phonemes of the parents' language acquire secondary reinforcement value for the infant, and that this learned reward value generalizes to the sounds which the child makes when he is babbling. This generalized secondary reinforcement helps to reinforce his babbling behavior, to shape it into patterns that are more likely to approximate words in his language, and to reward the imitation of sounds. We suggest that this hypothesis could be tested by studying the babbling behavior of children after an attempt has been made to give certain phonemes special learned reward value by associating them with rewarding care of the child, while different phonemes have been presented equally frequently, but in a neutral or aversive situation. Other hypotheses about the learning and functions of language are also presented [76, pp. 80–84].

In separate papers the same type of learning-theory analysis in terms of drive, cue, response, and reward has been applied to advertising [62] and to the application of newer training methods, such as graphic communication, to the problems of education [74]. The latter publication contains a special section on *Scientific Principles for Maximum Learning from Motion Pictures,* which deals with a considerable variety of theoretical and experimental problems such as hypotheses about changing motivations and attitudes, how to secure maximum abstraction and generalization to new situations, how to teach students to discriminate and perceive better, and the superiority of logical over rote learning.

The second book, *Personality and Psychotherapy* [25] presents a closer integration of three great scientific traditions. One of these is psychoanalysis, initiated by the genius of Freud and carried on by his many able students in the art of psychotherapy. Psychotherapy has much to contribute because it represents a unique opportunity for the naturalistic observation of people responding emotionally and using their higher mental processes while struggling with problems which are vitally serious to them.

Another tradition stems from the work of Pavlov, Thorndike, Hull, and a host of other experimentalists who have applied the exactness of natural science method to the study of the principles of learning. Finally, modern social science is crucial because it describes the social conditions under which a human being learns. The ultimate goal toward which we aimed was to combine the vitality of psychoanalysis, the rigor of the natural science laboratory, and the facts of culture. A psychology of this kind eventually should occupy a fundamental position in the social sciences and humanities, making it unnecessary for each of them to invent its own special assumptions about human nature.

One of our points of departure was the assumption that, if functional symptoms of neurosis are acquired, they must be acquired either by known laws of learning or by other laws that have not yet been studied in the laboratory, but should be investigated there. Similarly, we viewed psychotherapy as a process of emotional reeducation involving the unlearning of maladaptive responses and the learning of more adaptive ones.

Starting from these premises, we attempted to show in detail how various symptoms are learned because they are reinforced by reduction in fear (guilt and other drives), just as the turning of a wheel by a rat is automatically reinforced by escape from the fear-provoking box in which he has received electric shocks. Our analysis was most clear-cut and convincing in the combat neuroses because the conditions of learning are more recent and better known in such cases. This analysis showed why the acquisition of the symptom should be accompanied by *belle indifférence,* and its interruption should produce misery which frequently results in the learning of a substitute symptom, just as the rat learns to press the bar when the apparatus is changed so that turning the wheel can no longer be used to reduce his fear.

Other symptoms may not be the direct products of learning but rather the physiological effects of chronic high drive produced by conflict. The present paper has already mentioned a few of the applications of conflict theory to neurosis and psychotherapy.

We also made a detailed analysis of repression which hinged on three main points: (1) that the higher mental processes involve cue-producing responses—many of which may be central; (2) that strong aversive drives, such as fear, can be attached to these response-produced cues; and (3) that the sudden reduction in drive when the person stops thinking these painful thoughts can reinforce the response responsible for stopping the thought. From this, it follows that there should be a tendency to suppress painful thoughts—for example, shy away from the topic of the H-bomb—and if the aversive motivation is strong enough, this automatic tendency should become overpowering and lead to complete repression. But since the repressed cue-producing responses are essential components of thought, reasoning, foresight, planning, and social control, it follows that those aspects of behavior involved in repression should become more childlike, primitive, and stupid. Similarly, the recovery of repression should meet resistance, but once the cue-producing responses are fully restored, behavior should become more adult, intelligent, and discriminating. This is the barest outline of the pattern of S-R reinforcement analysis which helps to explain psychoanalytic observations.

Although the overcoming of repression is both a sign that significant reductions in anxiety have occurred and a means to more intelligent behavior, we point out that it is a mistake to believe that the main goal of psychotherapy is to throw off all restraints. We attempt to show in detail exactly how intelligent, socially necessary suppressions and restraints are substituted for blind, unrealistic, and frequently ineffective repressions and inhibitions.

Further theoretical analysis shows the importance of experimental extinction and counterconditioning during psychotherapy, and also the importance of a process whereby the patient learns to discriminate between the conditions that had established unrealistic fears in his past and the altered conditions of his present circumstances. Thus we see why mere catharsis—as in an explosion of drunken rage—is not necessarily therapeutic. A chapter on drugs shows how we should expect them to help in therapy and what limitations we may expect them to have.

By demonstrating in detail how the acquisition of a functional neurosis is a process of learning and how psychotherapy is a process of relearning, we show that these phenomena fall within the natural realm of the psychologist both as a research scientist and as an educator, or in this case, psychotherapist.

Although we emphasize the role of learning, our formulation does not exclude the role of innate psychological mechanisms involving factors such as the innate strength of various drives, the ability to withstand various types of pain and stress, the sensitivity to different stimuli, the repertoire of innate responses which is available, the relative dominance of different responses, and native intelligence. The interactions among innate, learned, and social factors are further discussed in a separate paper [69].

We show that childhood experiences are important because of the helplessness of the child, but that neurosis can also be created in adulthood under similar conditions of helplessness in combat. We attempt to analyze the conditions of child-rearing which are especially likely to produce neurotic conflict. In this realm, however, we would like to emphasize that we do not yet have a "science" of child-rearing. We believe that, in the long run, the development of better scientific understanding of child development would be enormously more valuable than efforts at repairing the damage.

Our interest is primarily not in abnormal behavior for its own sake, but rather as a type of behavior which, by exaggeration, illustrates processes that are significant in normal behavior and the normal personality. We also believe that it would be highly profitable to try to use similar methods to study intensively the behavior of especially well-adjusted people.

Finally, we have been impressed with the fact that the normal use of the mind in solving material problems is enormously aided by the cultural and scientific heritage of techniques, such as mathematics and physical sciences, which are taught in the schools. Thus, most school boys today can readily solve "material" problems which baffled the best minds of the ancient world. By contrast, we have learned much less about special techniques for solving social and emotional problems. We look forward to the day when knowledge in this area has advanced to the point where students may be taught, in the home and in the school, techniques for solving social and emotional problems which are as effective as those man has discovered for solving the problems of his physical environment.

SOME BASIC METHODOLOGICAL QUESTIONS

Experimental design required but seldom used to justify intervening variables. Figure 11 shows that it is simpler to represent the relationship

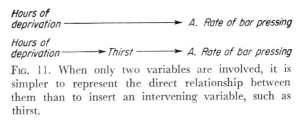

Fig. 11. When only two variables are involved, it is simpler to represent the direct relationship between them than to insert an intervening variable, such as thirst.

between the effect of a single experimental manipulation on a single measure as a direct relationship between the independent and dependent variable. An intervening variable only complicates matters by forcing one to use two functional relationships (represented by the arrows) instead of one.

If we multiply the number of experimental manipulations but use only one measure (or multiply the number of measures, but only use one experimental manipulation), the same comparison holds: inserting an intervening variable only complicates the interpretation. In this connection, it is interesting to note that one of the leading opponents of the use of intervening variables [101] has limited himself almost exclusively to a single measure, the rate of bar pressing.

In Fig. 12 we can see that the break-even point is reached when we compare the effects of two different experimental operations on two different empirical measures. In that case, either type of formulation involves the assumption of four functional relationships.

Although it is obvious that an intervening variable can always be inserted into the middle of a single relationship, we shall see that the design illustrated in Fig. 12 gives us our first chance of proving that a single

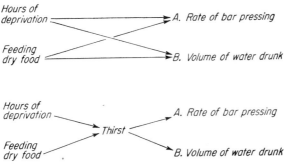

FIG. 12. In expressing all the relationships among two independent variables and two dependent variables, the use of an intervening variable, such as thirst, does not increase the number of functions that must be assumed and may have certain advantages.

intervening variable cannot account for the data. It is this possibility of disproof that makes the formulation meaningful. Although many behavior theorists have used intervening variables, there are relatively few experiments which use the design required to test and justify such variables.

Figure 13 shows that using an intervening variable produces a real gain in efficiency when one is dealing with the effects of more than two experimental manipulations on more than two empirical measures. With three of each, nine direct relationships are involved, but only six via the intervening variable.

Looking at the intervening variable in Fig. 13, it is obvious that if a given number of hours of water deprivation is more effective than eating a given amount of dry food in producing thirst as measured by the rate of bar pressing, it should also be more effective in inducing thirst as measured by the volume of water drunk. This theoretically demanded relationship does not, however, necessarily have to follow empirically. For example, it is conceivable that the deprivation would elicit less drinking than the dry food. If we got such discrepant results, we could not interpret them in terms of a single intervening variable. In other words, this type of design yields the possibility of disproving the hypothesis.

I have been interested in applying the appropriate type of experimental design to test whether some of the simplest of the situations in which we commonly assume intervening variables can actually be accounted for in terms of a single such variable. In many cases the different

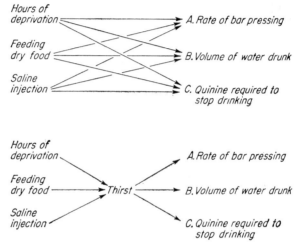

Fig. 13. In summarizing all the relationships among three independent and three dependent variables, the use of an intervening variable can, under appropriate circumstances, be considerably more efficient than stating each of the direct relationships.

measures show the type of agreement that would be expected if they were all pure measures of the same intervening variable [67]. But in other cases there is disagreement [68, 73].

For example, Fig. 14 shows one type of tentative result which one of my students, Martin Choy [20], has secured. The experimental treatment was allowing hungry animals, which had water available but had been deprived of food for 23 hrs, to eat dry food without water for 15 min and then giving them 5 cc of 13.2 per cent saline by stomach tube. It can be seen that this treatment reduced the rate of bar pressing reinforced by water on a variable-interval schedule, but increased the amount of water drunk and the amount of quinine required to stop the rats from drinking.

In this case, we might assume (1) that the combination of a stomach full of dry food plus strong salt solution produces pain, (2) that bar pressing is an impure measure which can be affected by pain as well as by thirst, and (3) that the bar pressing is affected more by the distraction of pain than are the other two measures of thirst. As long as these re-

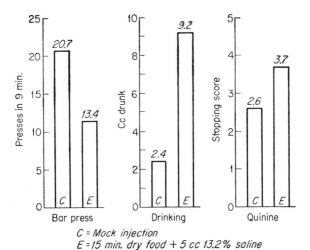

C = Mock injection
E = 15 min. dry food + 5 cc 13.2% saline

FIG. 14. How three measures of "thirst" are affected by the experimental procedure of feeding dry food without water to hungry rats and then administering 5 cc of 13.2 per cent saline via stomach tube. The effect on bar pressing is opposite to that on the other two measures. *From Choy* [20].

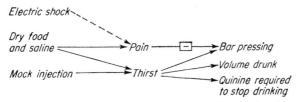

FIG. 15. Diagrammatic representation of how the discrepant results in Fig. 14 might be explained in terms of two intervening variables.

main untested assumptions introduced merely to explain the anomalous results, I shall remain dissatisfied. But it is possible to test these assumptions by using some other agent, such as an electric shock, which presumably produces pain. The assumptions will be confirmed if the other agent produces a larger reduction in the rate of bar pressing than in the other two measures of thirst. I plan to perform this experiment. The theoretical assumptions are summarized diagrammatically in Fig. 15.

Impure measures vs. specific factors. The foregoing explanation assumes that thirst is a unitary intervening variable but the measures are impure and therefore can be influenced by factors other than thirst. But it is also possible that thirst is not a single unitary variable. There could be a number of different centers for different subfunctions. For example, the center, or centers, primarily regulating volume drunk might be especially responsive to the mouth and throat factors that are eliminated when water is injected directly into the stomach. It is quite possible that the general trend toward encephalization as higher forms evolve could result in the regulation of "the same drive" by a number of centers which are at different levels in the brainstem, emphasize somewhat different functions, and may not be completely integrated into a system that always functions as a unit.

It can be seen that if behavior theorists start performing the types of experiments that will really test their intervening variables, we are likely to find ourselves following along in the footsteps of the aptitude testers who long since have run into the problem of general vs. specific factors. Perhaps we shall eventually be using a form of matrix algebra, somewhat analogous to multiple-factor analysis, but adapted to the somewhat different conditions of our experimental designs. In the meantime, my first inclination will be to try to purify the measures and experimentally isolate the variables.

Implications for psychopharmacology and for central stimulation. One of the practical implications of this line of work is that in studying the effects of drugs on motivation (or other intervening variables) it will be desirable to use a variety of measures in order to avoid being misled by side-effects that are specific to the particular indicators used [68, 72]. The same papers that make this point with additional examples also discuss the advantages and disadvantages of a number of techniques for measuring motivation and suggest some possible new techniques.

Exactly the same argument holds in the study of unusual techniques, such as direct electrical or chemical stimulation of the brain, for manipulating motivations. It is necessary to use rigorous behavioral tests to determine, point by point, whether the reaction elicited by such techniques has all the functional properties of normal drive induction or reduction [70, 73].

Some problems of quantification. Other things equal, there are many advantages to a theory that is at a high level of quantification. One of the greatest difficulties of a qualitative theory is that it is often unable to handle situations in which two or more factors are working in opposite directions. In such cases, the outcome depends on the relative strength of the two factors and a qualitative theory often has no way of predicting which of the two factors will be stronger. By contrast, a quantitative theory often can deal with the absolute magnitudes with enough precision to make a definite prediction.

Furthermore the qualitative theory is limited to predictions that a given operation will produce an increase or a decrease. Since there is a 50 per cent chance of getting one of these effects for some irrelevant reason, a single confirmation is not impressive. By contrast, when a more quantitative theory can predict that light should be bent by exactly $3°$, there are many more chances of disproof. Since exact agreement is unlikely to be produced by chance, it is extremely convincing. Quantitative discrepancies can quickly show up defects in the theory and pave the way toward correction. For these and other reasons, science has always striven for the high levels of quantification represented by cardinal scales.

Strategy of using qualitative tests first. In spite of being painfully aware of the disadvantages of a qualitative theory limited to ordinal scales and predictions of "greater than," I believe that there is some virtue in the strategy of putting one's theoretical notions through qualitative tests first before plunging into laborious attempts to quantify them. There certainly is no virtue in the misleading trappings of pseudo-quantification. I do not maintain that my strategy is necessarily the best; perhaps a more direct approach to quantification is desirable. We will never know unless someone tries it, as indeed a number of excellent people are.

My main emphasis has been on trying to be rigorous though qualitative. Remember the discussion of the relativity of the distinction between empirical independent variables, systematic independent variables, and intervening variables. There is no way of determining a priori the scientific usefulness of such variables. Therefore, I believe it is best to use the qualitative measures that are available to test the utility of one's main variables—to determine the approximate functional laws, the generality of these laws, and the unitary nature of the variables—before investing too much time in trying to quantify them. We have already discussed the design required to test the unity of intervening variables and commented on the fact that such tests are seldom made.

Effects of inequalities in scale units. Our present behavioral scales are ordinal ones; we have no assurance that the intervals in various parts of the scale are equal. A keen awareness of the effects that can be produced when the units at one end of the scale are systematically compressed generates a healthy caution.

A good example comes from Judson Brown's [11] experiment which we have already described. He studied the effect of strength of hunger on the gradient of stimulus generalization. Hungry rats were trained to run down a short path to get food in front of an illuminated panel. Then they were tested either under the same illumination used in training, or a different amount of illumination. Such tests were given either with a 46-hr or a 1-hr drive. Other factors were balanced. Two different measures were used: (a) the time taken to run from the start of the path to the middle, and (b) the force in grams with which the animals pulled against a harness which restrained them for 5 sec when they were halfway to food.

The results are presented in Fig. 16. Brown presented his results in terms of starting time (A); we are also presenting the curves for *the*

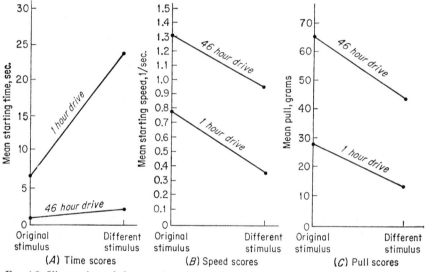

(A) Time scores   (B) Speed scores   (C) Pull scores

Fig. 16. Illustration of the way in which different scales of measurement may affect data. The gradients of stimulus generalization plotted in time scores appear to diverge widely. When the same data are replotted as speed scores, the gradients are approximately parallel, as they also are when measured by the strength-of-pull technique. *Data from Brown* [11].

same data transformed to speed scores (B). The fact that the curves seem to slope in opposite directions is not significant since increased time or decreased speed both represent weaker responses. But in another respect, the same data plotted in these two different scales seem to show quite different results. With the time scores, the two curves diverge markedly; the change in drive seems to have a much greater effect on tests with the different stimulus than on those with the original one. By contrast, with the speed scores the two curves are approximately parallel; the change in drive seems to have equal effects on the different and original stimuli. This striking difference is produced entirely by the fact that there is a curvilinear relationship between the units in these two scales.

Turning now to the strength of pull (C), it is obvious that these scores show a pattern which is quite similar to that of the speed scores. Because of this agreement, the fact that speed probably is more closely related to energy requirements than is time, and the fact that the speed scores are more normally distributed, I have long since changed from the use of time to speed scores. But it is quite possible that speed scores are far from ideal; they may distort relationships at both ends of the scale.

It is instructive to think of the upper and lower limits of various types of measures of performance. Frequency scores cannot go beyond zero or 100 per cent, which places a certain limit on probability models. There probably is an upper physiological limit for speed. Thus, a man chased by one vicious dog might be more frightened if ten more suddenly appeared, but not run any faster. At the low end, a scale of speed of running may also be extremely insensitive, but for another reason. The speed scores are so near to zero that multiplying the time by a factor of even 100 can only reduce them by a fraction of a unit. Similarly, amplitude scales reach the limit of movement of the member measured; force scales reach the limit of strength. As these latter scales approach their limits, they probably tend to become progressively more compressed.

No type of operation will assure equal-interval scale. One might think that certain types of scale-making operations will insure the equality of the units. But I see no way of deciding a priori that any given operation is the correct one. For example, we might use a beam balance to determine equal weights, reversing the position of the weights on the pan to check the balance. But if the equal weights were hydrogen atoms and we packed four of them closely enough together to form a helium atom, it would turn out to be simplest to assume that the atoms had lost something when they were packed this closely together so that four of them did not weigh four times as much as a single one.

To use another example, if one did not control temperature, a steel ruler would become somewhat shorter as one moved from the equator toward the poles. It is only the fact that rulers do not expand and contract in much more capricious ways that makes them useful in establishing equal-interval scales. If one were limited to an a priori logical analysis of the operations, one could never be sure of the relative constancy of the measuring rod which is essential to equal-interval scales of distance.

Similarly, one could not predict that water would make a poor thermometer because it would change from progressive contraction to expansion as it was cooled to near its freezing point. But how can one tell whether the reversal is in the behavior of the water or in the effects of our operations for changing temperature? As long as we are dealing with a single relationship, there is little to restrict the theoretical possibilities. It is only when one compares the expansion and contraction of a number of different substances (or cross-checks with yet other phenomena varying with temperature) that one finds that it is simpler to use hydrogen as the thermometer and assume that there are anomalies in the contraction of water. In other words, the ultimate choice of a given set of units in a scale must be based on whether or not it yields the simplest matrix of relationships, or in short, the simplest laws.

Within the behavioral field, Spence's [103] characteristically excellent program of quantification looks promising because it seems to be yielding a series of reasonably simple laws and predictions which he is beginning to cross-check with a variety of different tests.

Effect of carrying variables through entire range. It often is conceptually useful to imagine the effects of extrapolating a variable to each of its extreme limits. Similarly, it may be useful to try to determine empirically the effects at each limit. For example, one of the tentative results of Spence's [103] program, which we have already quoted with strong approval, is that in simple instrumental learning situations, drive D, incentive K, and immediacy of reward J seem to combine additively with each other but multiplicatively with the number of training trials, or in other words, habit strength H. The equation for performance E is $E = H(D + K + J)$.

Now let us see what this means if we take each of the variables down to the lower extreme limit of zero. Performance will be zero if either habit strength H or the sum of drive, plus incentive, plus immediacy of reward $(D + K + J)$ is zero. But with high values of the other variables, we might expect considerable performance with either zero drive, zero incentive, or zero immediacy of reward (infinite delay). It seems rather unlikely that such an outcome would be experimentally confirmed in a test situation that was carefully designed to minimize uncontrolled sources of drive and reward produced by motives such as curiosity. But on the other hand, the very fact that the prediction seems to go against common-sense expectations would make its possible confirmation a brilliant coup for the theory.

Turning our attention to Spence's [103] speed data, we see that the evidence for an additive combination is parallel curves, or in other words, zero interaction; the evidence for a multiplicative type of combination is diverging curves, or in other words, interaction among variables. In these experiments, it is interesting to note that none of the variables which fail to show interaction (drive, amount of incentive, immediacy of reward) is carried down to a level approaching zero. Thus, there is less opportunity for them to show diverging curves, or in other words, interaction. The one variable which shows the interaction, interpreted as a multiplicative relationship, is habit strength (i.e., number of training trials). This is the variable that is carried down to near zero, thus having the most opportunity to show interaction, especially if the speed units should be compressed at the extreme lower end of the scale.

The next step would seem to be to determine how the variables combine at the extremes, unless one wants to make the assumption that speed yields an equal-interval scale only in the middle ranges. But if one makes that assumption and therefore excludes the extreme end of the scale, one should avoid extremely low levels of performance produced by near zero habit strength as well as those produced by near-zero drive, no incentive, or long delay.

Gradually approximating the exact form of functions, although limited to qualitative tests. Acknowledging the fact that our present scales are merely ordinal does not necessarily force one into a defeatist position. It can motivate one to try to devise the types of tests that will yield definitive results within the limitations of qualitative scales.

To use an illustration which has already been discussed, suppose one is interested in determining whether one gradient of stimulus generalization is steeper than another. With an equal-interval scale, it would not make much difference if the two gradients were at different heights. But if the scale were compressed at the upper limit, the higher gradient might appear flatter merely because of this distortion in the units. That is why we chose our experimental conditions so that the two gradients actually crossed—a relationship which proves a difference in slope even if the units on the scale should be unequal.

The algebra of inequalities is another technique for making rigorous deductions that do not depend upon the equal-interval scale. One of my earlier studies [81] used this technique to make first approximations of the general forms of a function that would have to be assumed in order to allow different competing sets of assumptions to account for all of the data in some experiments.[14] Other applications might be made to other problems.

A somewhat different example comes from Hull [39, Chap. 10]. On the basis of Yoshioka's [111] work on the ease of setting up preference for the shorter of two paths in a variety of mazes, Hull concluded that a logarithmic function for the gradient of reinforcement would not work and therefore shifted to a growth function. Although each of Yoshioka's tests involved only the determination of which group was better (i.e., a qualitative relationship not demanding an equal-interval scale for excitatory tendency), Hull was able to use these tests to decide between two types of functional relationships. Actually, Hull leaped to a more specific function that the data justified. Yoshioka's tests did eliminate the

---

[14] Since I was out of the country and did not get to see the proof, two errors crept into p. 195 of the article. In its corrected form, Eq. (3) should read $E + I + X = D_x$ and footnote 12 should read $D > D_x > D_{ax}$ and $D > D_a > D_{ax}$.

logarithmic function; his tests and other data limited the type of relationship to functions with certain specifiable characteristics which are met by growth curves, but which could also be satisfied by certain deviations from exact growth curves. Nevertheless, this approximation of a general type of functional relationship, before having an equal-interval scale, is an interesting model.

Similarly, in my article on Displacement [61, p. 171] I show in some detail that some deductions will follow from any curves which have a negative slope throughout, other deductions demand somewhat more restricted classes of curves, and still other deductions demand curves with quite specific characteristics, namely curves that are concave and that are raised by increases in drive in such a way that the absolute increase at any point is some positive function of the original height of the curve at that point. All of these deductions can be tested by qualitative experiments. They seem to be confirmed by clinical data; their more rigorous verification by experimental data would be another example of specifying a considerable number of the quantitative characteristics of a functional relationship before developing an equal-interval scale. With sufficient ingenuity, it may be possible to devise theoretical analyses and experimental tests that will enable us to approximate certain functional relationships so closely that they may become a basis for equal-interval scales.

I believe that it is worthwhile to devote further attention to a rigorous though qualitative approach which first determines the general significance of the variables, and then goes on to narrow down the choice toward a more exact quantitative function.

REFERENCES

1. Auld, F., & Murray, E. J. Content-analysis studies of psychotherapy. *Psychol. Bull.*, 1955, 52:377–395.

2. Bailey, C. J. The effectiveness of drives as cues. *J. comp. physiol. Psychol.*, 1955, 48:183–187.

3. Bailey, C. J., & Miller, N. E. The effect of sodium amytal on an approach-avoidance conflict in cats. *J. comp. physiol. Psychol.*, 1952, 45:205–208.

4. Beach, F. A., & Holz-Tucker, A. M. Effects of different concentrations of androgen upon sexual behavior in castrated male rats. *J. comp. physiol. Psychol.*, 1949, 42:433–453.

5. Bergmann, G., & Spence, K. W. Operationism and theory in psychology. *Psychol. Rev.*, 1941, 48:1–14.

6. Berkun, M. M. Factors in the recovery from approach-avoidance conflict. *J. exp. Psychol.*, 1957, 54:65–73.

7. Berkun, M. M., Kessen, M. L., & Miller, N. E. Hunger-reducing

effects of food by stomach fistula versus food by mouth measured by a consummatory response. *J. comp. physiol. Psychol.*, 1952, 45:550–554.

8. Berlyne, D. E. Novelty and curiosity as determiners of exploratory behavior. *Brit. J. Psychol.*, 1950, 41:68–80.

9. Birge, Jane S. Verbal responses in transfer. Unpublished doctoral dissertation, Yale Univer., 1941.

10. Brown, J. S. Factors determining conflict reactions in difficult discriminations. *J. exp. Psychol.*, 1942, 31:272–292.

11. Brown, J. S. The generalization of approach responses as a function of stimulus intensity and strength of motivation. *J. comp. Psychol.*, 1942, 33:209–226.

12. Brown, J. S. Gradients of approach and avoidance responses and their relation to level of motivation. *J. comp. physiol. Psychol.*, 1948, 41: 450–465.

13. Brown, J. S. Problems presented by the concept of acquired drives. In M. R. Jones (Ed.), *Current theory and research in motivation: a symposium.* Lincoln, Neb.: Univer. Nebraska Press, 1953.

14. Bugelski, R., & Miller, N. E. A spatial gradient in the strength of avoidance responses. *J. exp. Psychol.*, 1938, 23:494–505.

15. Campbell, B. A. The fractional reduction in noxious stimulation required to produce "just noticeable" learning. *J. comp. physiol. Psychol.*, 1955, 48:141–148.

16. Campbell, B. A. Auditory and aversion thresholds of rats for bands of noise. *Science*, 1957, 125:596–597.

17. Campbell, B. A., & Kraeling, D. Response strength as a function of drive level and amount of drive reduction. *J. exp. Psychol.*, 1953, 45:97–101.

18. Campbell, B. A., & Sheffield, F. D. Relation of random activity to food deprivation. *J. comp. physiol. Psychol.*, 1953, 46:320–322.

19. Carnap, R. Testability and meaning. *Phil. Sci.*, 1936, 3:420–471.

20. Choy, M. Effects of unusual manipulations of "thirst" upon a variety of measures. Unpublished senior thesis, Yale Univer., 1956.

21. Conant, J. B. *On understanding science.* New Haven, Conn.: Yale Univer. Press, 1947.

22. Conger, J. J. The effects of alcohol on conflict behavior in the albino rat. *Quart. J. Stud. Alcohol*, 1951, 12:1–29.

23. Delgado, J. M. R., Roberts, W. W., & Miller, N. E. Learning motivated by electrical stimulation of the brain. *Amer. J. Physiol.*, 1954, 179: 587–593.

24. Dollard, J. *Fear in battle.* New Haven, Conn.: Yale Univer. Press, 1943.

25. Dollard, J., & Miller, N. E. *Personality and psychotherapy.* New York: McGraw-Hill, 1950.

26. Freud, S. *The problem of anxiety.* New York: Norton, 1936.

27. Fuller, J. L. Personal communication, 1956.

28. Grinker, R. R., & Spiegel, J. P. *Men under stress.* New York: McGraw-Hill–Blakiston, 1945.

29. Grinker, R. R., & Spiegel, J. P. *War neurosis.* New York: McGraw-Hill–Blakiston, 1945.

30. Grose, Robert F. A comparison of vocal and subvocal conditioning of the galvanic skin response. Unpublished doctoral dissertation, Yale Univer., 1952.

31. Guthrie, E. R. *The psychology of learning.* (Rev. ed.) New York: Harper, 1952.

32. Harlow, H. F. Motivation as a factor in the acquisition of new responses. In M. R. Jones (Ed.), *Current theory and research in motivation: a symposium.* Lincoln, Neb.: Univer. Nebraska Press, 1953.

33. Harlow, H. F., Meyer, D., & Settlage, P. H. The effects of large cortical lesions on the solution of oddity problems by monkeys. *J. comp. physiol. Psychol.,* 1951, **44**:320–326.

34. Harriman, A. E., & McLeod, R. B. Discrimination thresholds of salt for normal and adrenalectomized rats. *Amer. J. Psychol.,* 1953, **66**:465–471.

35. Hempel, C. G. The function of general laws in history. In H. Feigl & W. Sellars (Eds.), *Readings in philosophical analysis.* New York: Appleton-Century-Crofts, 1949. Pp. 459–471.

36. Hull, C. L. The goal gradient hypothesis and maze learning. *Psychol. Rev.,* 1932, **39**:25–43.

37. Hull, C. L. The concept of the habit-family hierarchy and maze learning. *Psychol. Rev.,* 1934, **41**:33–54, 134–152.

38. Hull, C. L. The goal gradient hypothesis applied to some "field-force" problems in the behavior of young children. *Psychol. Rev.,* 1938, **45**:271–299.

39. Hull, C. L. *Principles of behavior.* New York: Appleton-Century-Crofts, 1943.

40. Hull, C. L. *A behavior system.* New Haven, Conn.: Yale Univer. Press, 1952.

41. Kagan, J., & Berkun, M. The reward value of running activity. *J. comp. physiol. Psychol.,* 1954, **47**:108.

42. Kaufman, E. L., & Miller, N. E. Effect of number of reinforcements on strength of approach in an approach-avoidance conflict. *J. comp. physiol. Psychol.,* 1949, **42**:65–74.

43. Kohn, M. Satiation of hunger from food injected directly into the stomach versus food ingested by mouth. *J. comp. physiol. Psychol.,* 1951, **44**:412–422.

44. Lashley, K. S. Learning: I. Nervous mechanisms in learning. In C. Murchison (Ed.), *The foundations of experimental psychology.* Worcester, Mass.: Clark Univer. Press, 1929. Pp. 524–563.

45. Lawrence, D. H. Acquired distinctiveness of cues: I. Transfer between discriminations on the basis of familiarity with the stimulus. *J. exp. Psychol.,* 1949, **39**:770–784.

46. Lawrence, D. H. Acquired distinctiveness of cues: II. Selective association in a constant stimulus situation. *J. exp. Psychol.,* 1950, **40**:175–188.

47. Lawrence, D. H. The transfer of a discrimination along a continuum. *J. comp. physiol. Psychol.*, 1952, 45:511–516.

48. Lewin, K. Environmental forces in child behavior and development. In C. Murchison (Ed.), *A handbook of child psychology*. Worcester, Mass.: Clark Univer. Press, 1931.

49. Logan, F. A. A micromolar approach to behavior theory. *Psychol. Rev.*, 1956, 63:63–73.

50. Masserman, J. H. *Principles of dynamic psychiatry*. Philadelphia: Saunders, 1946.

51. Meehl, P. E. On the circularity of the law of effect. *Psychol. Bull.*, 1950, 47:52–75.

52. Miller, N. E. The perception of children: a genetic study employing the critical choice delayed reaction. *Ped. Sem. J. genet. Psychol.*, 1934, 44:321–339.

53. Miller, N. E. A reply to "sign-gestalt or conditioned reflex?" *Psychol. Rev.*, 1935, 42:280–292.

54. Miller, N. E. The influence of past experience upon the transfer of subsequent training. Unpublished doctoral dissertation, Yale Univer., 1935.

55. Miller, N. E. Analysis of the form of conflict reactions. *Psychol. Bull.*, 1937, 34:720.

56. Miller, N. E. Reaction formation in rats: an experimental analog for a Freudian phenomenon. *Psychol. Bull.*, 1937, 34:724.

57. Miller, N. E. Experiments relating Freudian displacement to generalization of conditioning. *Psychol. Bull.*, 1937, 36:516–517.

58. Miller, N. E. An experimental investigation of acquired drives. *Psychol. Bull.*, 1941, 38:534–535.

59. Miller, N. E. Experimental studies of conflict. In J. McV. Hunt (Ed.), *Personality and the behavior disorders*. New York: Ronald, 1944. Pp. 431–465.

60. Miller, N. E. Studies of fear as an acquirable drive: I. Fear as motivation and fear-reduction as reinforcement in the learning of new responses. *J. exp. Psychol.*, 1948, 38:89–101.

61. Miller, N. E. Theory and experiment relating psychoanalytic displacement to stimulus response generalization. *J. abnorm. soc. Psychol.*, 1948, 43:155–178.

62. Miller, N. E. Social science and the art of advertising. *J. Marketing*, 1950, 14:580–584.

63. Miller, N. E. Comments on theoretical models illustrated by the development of a theory of conflict behavior. *J. Pers.*, 1951, 20:82–100.

64. Miller, N. E. Learnable drives and rewards. In S. S. Stevens (Ed.), *Handbook of experimental psychology*. New York: Wiley, 1951. Pp. 435–472.

65. Miller, N. E. Fear. In R. H. Williams (Ed.), *Human factors in military operations*. Chevy Chase, Md.: Johns Hopkins Univer., Operations Research Office, 1954. Pp. 269–281.

66. Miller, N. E. The role of motivation in learning. Committee on Human Resources, Research and Development Board, Department of De-

fense. *Symposium on psychology of learning basic to military training problems.* Washington, D.C., GPO, May 7–8, 1953. Pp. 103–116.

67. Miller, N. E. Shortcomings of food consumption as a measure of hunger: results from other behavioral techniques. *Ann. N.Y. Acad. Sci.,* 1955, 63:141–143.

68. Miller, N. E. Effects of drugs on motivation: the value of using a variety of measures. *Ann. N.Y. Acad. Sci.,* 1956, 65:318–333.

69. Miller, N. E. A psychologist speaks In H. D. Kruse (Ed.), *Integrating the approaches to mental disease.* New York: Paul B. Hoeber, 1958. Chap. 5, pp. 43–45.

70. Miller, N. E. Learning and performance motivated by direct stimulation of the brain. In D. E. Sheer (Ed.), *Electrical stimulation of the brain: subcortical integrative systems.* Houston, Tex.: Univer. Texas Press, 1957.

71. Miller, N. E. Comments on the implications of the Olds reward effect for theories of reinforcement. In D. E. Sheer (Ed.), *Electrical stimulation of the brain: subcortical integrative systems.* Houston, Tex.: Univer. Texas Press, 1957.

72. Miller, N. E. Objective techniques for studying motivational effects of drugs on animals. In S. Garatlini & V. Ghetti (Eds.), *Psychotropic Drugs.* Amsterdam: Elsevier, 1958. Pp. 83–103.

73. Miller, N. E. Experiments on motivation: studies combining psychological, physiological, and pharmacological techniques. *Science,* 1957, 126:1271–1278.

74. Miller, N. E., et al. *Graphic communication in the crisis in education.* Audio-Visual Communication Rev., Washington, D.C.: National Education Association, 1958, 5, No. 3.

75. Miller, N. E., Brown, J. S., & Lewis, H. A theoretical and experimental analysis of conflict behavior: approach-avoidance conflict as a function of strength of drive and strength of shock. (Unpublished.)

76. Miller, N. E., & Dollard, J. *Social learning and imitation.* New Haven, Conn.: Yale Univer. Press, 1941.

77. Miller, N. E., & Hart, G. Motivation and reward in learning. 15-min Education Sound Film. University Park, Pa.: Psychological Cinema Register, 1948.

78. Miller, N. E., & Kessen, M. L. Reward effects of food via stomach fistula compared with those of food via mouth. *J. comp. physiol. Psychol.,* 1952, 45:555–564.

79. Miller, N. E., & Kraeling, D. Displacement: greater generalization of approach than avoidance in a generalized approach-avoidance conflict. *J. exp. Psychol.,* 1952, 43:217–221.

80. Miller, N. E., & Miles, W. R. Effect of caffeine on the running speed of hungry, satiated, and frustrated rats. *J. comp. Psychol.,* 1935, 20:397–412.

81. Miller, N. E., & Miles, W. R. Alcohol and removal of reward: an analytical study of rodent maze behavior. *J. comp. Psychol.,* 1936, 21:179–204.

82. Miller, N. E., & Murray, E. J. Displacement and conflict: learnable drive as a basis for the steeper gradient of avoidance than of approach. *J. exp. Psychol.*, 1952, 43:227–231.

83. Miller, N. E., Roberts, W. W., & Delgado, J. M. R. Motivation of learning by electrical stimulation in the thalamus. Motion picture presented at meetings of A.P.A. Cleveland, Ohio: Presidential Address of Experimental Division, Sept., 1953.

84. Miller, N. E., & Stevenson, S. S. Agitated behavior of rats during experimental extinction and a curve of spontaneous recovery. *J. comp. Psychol.*, 1936, 21:205–231.

85. Montgomery, K. C. Exploratory behavior as a function of "similarity" of stimulus situations. *J. comp. physiol. Psychol.*, 1953, 46:129–133.

86. Mowrer, O. H. A stimulus-response analysis of anxiety and its role as a reinforcing agent. *Psychol. Rev.*, 1939, 46:553–566.

87. Murray, E. J. A content analysis method for studying psychotherapy. *Psychol. Monog.*, 1956, 70: No. 13, Whole No. 420. Pp. 1–31.

88. Murray, E. J., & Berkun, M. M. Displacement as a function of conflict. *J. abnorm. soc. Psychol.*, 1955, 51:47–56.

89. Murray, E. J., & Miller, N. E. Displacement: steeper gradient of generalization of avoidance than of approach with age of habit controlled. *J. exp. Psychol.*, 1952, 43:222–226.

90. Myers, A. K. The effects of predictable vs. unpredictable punishment in the albino rat. Doctoral dissertation, Yale Univer., 1956. (In preparation for publication.)

91. Myers, A. K., & Miller, N. E. Failure to find a learned drive based on hunger; evidence for learning motivated by "exploration." *J. comp. physiol. Psychol.*, 1954, 47:428–436.

92. Olds, J., & Milner, P. Positive reinforcement produced by electrical stimulation of septal area and other regions of rat brain. *J. comp. physiol. Psychol.*, 1954, 47:419–427.

93. Pavlov, I. P. *Conditioned reflexes*. G. V. Anrep. (Trans.) London: Oxford Univer. Press, 1927.

94. Pfaffman, C., & Bare, J. K. Gustatory nerve discharges in normal and adrenalectomized rats. *J. comp. physiol. Psychol.*, 1950, 43:320–324.

95. Porter, L. W., & Miller, N. E. Training under two drives, alternately present, vs. training under a single drive. *J. exp. Psychol.*, 1957, 54:1–7.

96. Richter, C. P. Salt taste thresholds for normal and adrenalectomized rats. *Endocrinology*, 1939, 24:367–371.

97. Sears, R. R., Whiting, J. W. M., Nowlis, V., & Sears, P. S. Some child-rearing antecedents of aggression and dependency in young children. *Genet. Psychol. Monog.*, 1953, 47:135–234.

98. Scott, J. P. Social behavior, organization and leadership in a small flock of domestic sheep. *Comp. Psychol. Monogr.*, 1945, 18:(96) 1–29.

99. Sheffield, F. D., & Campbell, B. A. The role of experience in the "spontaneous" activity of hungry rats. *J. comp. physiol. Psychol.*, 1954, 47: 97–100.

100. Sheffield, F. D., & Roby, T. B. Reward value of a non-nutritive sweet taste. *J. comp. physiol. Psychol.*, 1950, **43**:471–481.

101. Skinner, B. F. Are theories of learning necessary? *Psychol. Rev.*, 1950, **57**:193–216.

102. Solomon, R. L., Sidd, J. J., Watson, P. D., & Black, A. H. The use of d-Tubocurrine in the extinction of fear in dogs. *Amer. Psychologist*, 1955, **10**:395. (Abstract)

103. Spence, K. W. *Behavior theory and conditioning.* New Haven, Conn.: Yale Univer. Press, 1956.

104. Tinklepaugh, O. L. An experimental study of representative factors in monkeys. *J. comp. Psychol.*, 1928, **8**:197–236.

105. Tolman, E. C. *Purposive behavior in animals and man.* New York: Appleton-Century-Crofts, 1932.

106. Tolman, E. C. There is more than one kind of learning. *Psychol. Rev.*, 1949, **56**:144–155.

107. von Felsinger, J. M. The effect of induced estrus as an irrelevant drive on the learning of a maze habit and on its persistence during satiation. Unpublished doctoral dissertation, Yale Univer., 1948.

108. Webb, W. B. The motivational aspects of an irrelevant drive in the behavior of the white rat. *J. exp. Psychol.*, 1949, **39**:1–14.

109. Whiting, J. W. M., & Child, I. L. *Child training and personality.* New Haven, Conn.: Yale Univer. Press, 1953.

110. Wickert, F. *Psychological research on problems of redistribution.* Washington, D.C.: GPO, 1947.

111. Yoshioka, J. G. Weber's law in the discrimination of maze distance by the white rat. *Univer. Calif. Publ. Psychol.*, 1929, **4**:155–184.

112. Zimbardo, P. G., & Miller, N. E. The facilitation of exploration by hunger in rats. *J. comp. physiol. Psychol.*, 1958, **51**:43–46.

THE HULL-SPENCE APPROACH

FRANK A. LOGAN
Yale University

INTRODUCTION

Clark L. Hull began publishing descriptions of his theory of learned behavior around 1930, and from then until his death in 1952, devoted his energies to the testing, modification, and extension of his theoretical ideas. During the first decade of this period, Hull worked closely in collaboration with Kenneth W. Spence, Hull concentrating on the basic principles involved in classical and instrumental conditioning and Spence concerning himself primarily with his separate but related theory of discrimination learning. Their interests expanded following publication of Hull's *Principles of Behavior* in 1943. That is, Spence turned to a more detailed and systematic study of the data underlying the basic assumptions of a theory of simple learning phenomena, the results of which have only recently been collected in *Behavior Theory and Conditioning*, while Hull began to attempt the application of the initial basic principles to more complex individual behavior as described in his posthumous work, *A Behavior System*.

A number of others, notably Neal E. Miller, have participated in the development of what has been characterized as the S-R reinforcement interpretation of learning. Miller's many contributions to the basic theory, and his important extensions of it to conflict, social behavior, and psychotherapy are largely omitted here because they are represented elsewhere in the project. Indeed, properly to identify and credit all the contributors would be an exceedingly difficult task and has simply not been attempted. Since, however, the following analyses are either descriptions of or direct outgrowths from this general approach, the writer must disclaim credit for many of the ideas while, at the same time, accepting responsibility for their presentation.

In a larger sense, most of the orienting attitudes and much of the basic methodology are not unique to the Hullian approach and are equally applicable not only to other systems in psychology but also to other sciences. The complete identification of these interrelationships is a problem for historians and philosophers of science, and the present account will offer only a minimal attempt to trace the historical antecedents of the ideas or to contrast them with alternatives. The purpose, instead, is to characterize the Hullian approach as seen by the present writer, and readers interested in a more comparative account should consult Spence [175, 176] and Hilgard [64, 65].

The approach falls within the general rubric of behaviorism as initially set forth by Watson. That is, the subject matter is the behavior of living organisms, and as Spence has pointed out, this does not differ in kind from the subject matter of other sciences. The most basic assumption is that behavior exhibits sufficient order and regularity that lawful description of it can be made. This is, of course, determinism. At least it is assumed that any "free" effects are so small or so infrequent as to make determinism a fruitful working hypothesis.

The general attitudes, techniques, and methods of the approach have been discussed by Spence [173] and are largely imitations of some of those developed by the successful physical sciences. Thus, interesting phenomena are abstracted from the natural environment and subjected to systematic and controlled study. The data from such studies are reported in objective, i.e., interpersonally reliable, terms and form the basis of behavioral laws.

The singular goal of the approach is the derivation of these behavioral laws, or particular instances of them, from an explicit set of postulates. The postulates, plus the relevant boundary conditions of any study, serve as "givens" from which the theorems are derived by the rules of logic and mathematics. The usefulness of the postulates is judged solely by the correspondence between these theorems and the appropriate empirical events.

The ability to derive theorems accurately corresponding to empirical phenomena is the sense in which the theory provides "explanation" of the phenomena. Of course, at a more molecular level, one might seek to explain (describe, deduce) the postulates themselves, but this is not necessarily a task of the theorist. Similarly, applied psychologists may utilize the predictive power of the theory for practical "control" problems, but the theorist's activities fall within the realm of pure science.

In implementing the approach, it is assumed that some of the basic principles governing learned behavior can be determined from a study of the relatively simple learning phenomena: classical and instrumental conditioning. These experimental paradigms are not thought of as trivial laboratory settings; a great deal of "everyday" behavior can be seen to be uncontrolled instances of them. However, it is not argued that the more complex phenomena can be understood solely in terms of the principles derived from the simpler situations. New variables and different specifications of old variables are most probably involved in the more complex areas, but it is assumed that the basic principles will, by and large, still apply. Should this be true, then the reasonable approach is first to isolate these principles in the simpler situations and only then turn to the more complex ones.

This hypothesis cannot be evaluated a priori; its value is entirely a matter of fact. Although one may doubt the likelihood that the hypothesis will be true [see, e.g., 61, 11], it is yet too early to make any definitive statements in this regard. There have, however, been a number of encouraging attempts to apply some of the principles to more complex areas. These have included discrimination learning [164], verbal learning [70, 47], motor learning [2, 42, 86, 194], problem solving [8], social learning [123], legal development [147], culture [124], kinship terminology [132], and most extensively, psychotherapy [37].

As mentioned earlier, Hull was willing to explore the way in which the theoretical approach would deal with more complex phenomena without fully resolving many of the specific problems in his 1943 theory. This did not reflect a failure to recognize such problems nor an underestimate of their importance. Indeed, his subsequent research was directed at the formalization and quantification of the postulates. However, no one was more aware of the tentative and illustrative nature of his work than Hull; he seldom referred in conversation to what he had done, talking instead about what could be done by those who would rebuild the theory.

In contrast to Hull's willingness to risk almost certainly being wrong about many details in order to illustrate the approach more extensively, Spence has followed a more intensive and rigorous program. He has held his theorizing close to the available data and has concentrated on a systematic empirical study of some of the more quantitative assumptions. On his part, this view has not resulted from a denial of the ultimate possibility of a comprehensive behavior theory, but rather from the belief that it must be attained gradually.

There is much to be said for both approaches. Certainly an adequate comprehensive theory should be built upon the solid foundation provided by systematic and detailed testing of the theory in the simpler situations. Yet, in Hull's day, there was a need to gain perspective on the larger goal and to show that the approach was at least potentially useful as a means toward a general theory of learned behavior. Even now, a great deal of important information can be fed back by those who encounter difficulties in attempting to apply the theory to more complex phenomena.

However, if there is any one thing that has impeded the development of better theories, it is the paucity of basic, systematic data and of repeatedly verified laws. Although these are the kinds of empirical knowledge that are most likely to stimulate useful theoretical ideas, few psychologists have been willing to undertake the painstaking labor necessary. The psychological literature contains many tentatively established findings which invite replication and systematic elaboration, and the theorist frequently finds himself not only guessing with his postulates, but also speculating about the phenomena his postulates are intended to describe.

This state of affairs is probably justified in a relatively young science where the initial identification of significant variables has put a premium on creativity and originality. Certainly the Hullian approach has contributed greatly to the advancement of empirical knowledge during the past twenty-five years of this exploratory stage. This has resulted largely from an emphasis on the value of systematic and integrated research programs, rather than the haphazard study of any variable which chanced to catch the fancy of an experimenter. Perhaps now, at mid-century, one of the major contributions of the Hullian approach will be so to affect the attitudes of psychologists that greater value will be attached to the rigorous and systematic determination, and further verification, of psychological laws.

The present description of the Hullian approach will be made in three major parts. In the first are treated several matters which are general characteristics of the approach and are not peculiar to any specific set of postulates. We shall then turn to a description of the independent, intervening, and dependent variables with which the theory has been concerned, contrasting some of the current alternative formulations. Finally, we shall discuss a variety of research areas in an attempt to illustrate the interplay between the theory and research. It should be recognized at the outset that the treatment given will not provide a completely comprehensive account of the approach since many important topics are omitted or dealt with only briefly. However, most of the problems which seem important at this juncture are raised, and the descriptions given, supplemented by extant writings on specific issues, should permit a reasonably broad characterization of the approach.

We shall consider concomitantly several formulations by Hull and by Spence. Emphasis is placed on Hull's 1943 and 1949 postulates, and on Spence's analysis of discrimination learning and the theory given in his Silliman Lectures at Yale. In addition to these, occasional reference is also made to the micromolar theory being developed by the present writer, and because this approach has not yet been widely discussed, a brief description of it here seems necessary.

The classical theories of Hull and Spence define the response in molar terms, like pressing a bar, running down an alley, etc. All the quantitative characteristics of a response are predicted from a single terminal construct, excitatory potential. That is, the independent variables, such as practice, drive, reward, etc., converge upon excitatory potential and this single number is used to determine whether the response will occur, how quickly it will occur, and what its amplitude will be. This kind of theory has several general implications. Most critically, one would expect that the different response measures would increase as training progresses, and would be highly correlated with each other.

A micromolar theory, on the other hand, identifies quantitatively different behaviors as different responses with separate excitatory potentials. Thus, running fast is a different response from running slowly, rather than being simply a stronger strength of approach. Such a theory does not imply that response measures will necessarily increase with training; they will increase only if the subject has something to gain from such increases. Response speed is a case in point, because the subject can usually get the reward sooner by responding faster. Accordingly, one would expect speed measures to increase with training, as they typically do. However, a measure such as the force a rat exerts on a bar does not continue to increase with training because it does not pay to press the bar harder than necessary to activate the feeding mechanism.

Similarly, a micromolar theory does not require that the several response measures be correlated with each other. Instead, the organism is viewed as learning whatever response pattern maximizes reward while minimizing effort, be it a slow, vigorous response, a fast, gentle one, or some other combination. Conditions in which maximum reward is given for some particular speed or amplitude are called correlated reinforcement, and data from such conditions are especially relevant to the question of whether quantitatively different behaviors should be treated as different responses.

Notwithstanding the promise which a micromolar approach seems to have, it has not yet been sufficiently developed to present in more than a general way. However, it serves as a good illustration of one of the most important features of the Hullian approach, namely, that every aspect of the theory is modifiable in the face of advancing knowledge. Small details are changed quite readily. And even more general aspects, such as the definition of the response and the assumption that reward is necessary for learning, are not irrevocably cast. Accordingly, the Hullian approach involves much more a commitment to a method of theorizing than to a particular set of theoretical ideas.

THE HULLIAN APPROACH TO THEORY IN PSYCHOLOGY

In this part are discussed a variety of methodological questions about the Hullian approach to theory in psychology. Specifically, we shall consider how the postulates are constructed and quantified, how theorems are derived from them, and how the theory is related to other disciplines. In doing so, it will be useful to begin with a brief description of the nature of Hullian-type theory. While this description is sufficient for our purposes here, the interested reader should consult the works of Spence [170, 173], Bergmann and Spence [7], and Bergmann [5, 6] for a more complete and analytical account of those matters within the realm of the philosophy of science.

The nature of a Hullian-type theory. In order to characterize a Hullian-type theory, it will be helpful first to describe briefly a conceptual hierarchy of behavioral laws. Such laws, or empirical generalizations—see [170] for a description of the several kinds of psychological laws—organize the facts from behavior research into statements typically of the form "If S then R" from which predictions can be made about future instances of that S.

Even within a single field, such as psychology, laws may vary in their level of generality, i.e., in the range of phenomena to which they are relevant. For example, one might generalize from Humphreys' early experiment [75] that, "If, during the classical conditioning of the eyeblink response, the UCS follows the CS on only 50 per cent of the trials, resistance to extinction will be greater than if the stimuli are paired on every trial." If this statement is contrasted with, "If a response receives partial reinforcement during acquisition, resistance to extinction will be greater than following continuous reinforcement," one can see that the latter applies to instrumental as well as to classical conditioning, to responses other than the eyeblink, and to ratios other than 50 per cent. The second law is, therefore, at a higher level of generality because the former is deducible from it.

More general laws are desired, of course, because they subsume a wider range of phenomena under a smaller number of statements. Further generality may be gained by bringing several higher-level laws together into a system integrated by their relevance to the same behavior variables. To illustrate this fact, consider another relatively high-level behavioral law, "A response conditioned to one stimulus will tend also to occur to similar stimuli." Now the laws of stimulus generalization and partial reinforcement, together, imply more than the sum of their separate implications. One can predict, for example, that subjects trained under partial reinforcement to one stimulus will resist extinction to a generalized stimulus more than other subjects trained with continuous reinforcement. This last statement is not less general than either of the other two laws separately; the added generality has come from the combination of laws.

One might be content to seek a system of relatively high-level laws within one's own field. Such a system would serve to order the available knowledge and would permit predictions concerning a fair range of phenomena. A Hullian-type theory, however, is more than this, as can be seen if the conceptual hierarchy of behavioral laws is extended to include the several behavior sciences.

If the empirical laws of one field are, in principle, deducible from those of another, then the field whose laws are subsumable can be said to be more molar, and the subsuming field, more molecular. Level of molarity is, of course, a relative matter, psychology appearing to be molar relative to physiology but molecular relative to sociology. The laws of all behavior sciences may be conceptualized in a single hierarchy of generality, those from the more molecular fields occupying the higher levels because of their potentiality, in principle, of implying the laws of the more molar fields.

Within this conceptual schema, the postulates of a Hullian-type theory are around the level of physiological laws. The elements of the postulates, i.e., intervening variables, are around the level of physiological processes. However, the postulates are *not* asserted as genuine physiological laws. They were constructed solely to handle behavioral data in psychology, and it is important to distinguish between the mathematical statements and other possible connotations of the postulates. Thus, the postulate that habit strength grows as a function of the number of reinforced trials could imply, among other things, that there is some physiological process that could be labeled habit strength and which changes according to the specified function. Such physiological implications may be disregarded because the theory is properly evaluated only by the correctness of its psychological implications.[1]

The right of the theorist to disclaim unintended physiological interpretations is a part of his general right to delimit the range of relevant phenomena to any areas he chooses. Thus, Spence's early theory of discrimination learning was closely restricted to nonarticulate organisms in situations insuring reception of the critical cues. Also, Hull tacitly avoided the phenomena of relearning with his postulates and rejected conditions of correlated reinforcement. Ideally, all such limitations should be stated explicitly by the theorist although, in practice, he may not have recognized some of these and may not be ready to specify others because he has not yet considered them sufficiently to know whether the theory is inadequate. One who argues that the theory is proved wrong by the falseness of any such unintended implications completely misses the point of the activity. The purpose of the theory is to mediate predictions over a *specifiable* range of phenomena, and the theory is useful to the extent that it does just that.

Clearly, then, the postulates do not purport to describe the structure of the "real" organism. Instead, they describe a "model" organism whose

---

[1] For a more philosophical way of approaching these matters, consult Mac-Corquodale and Meehl [112], who attempt to distinguish between intervening variables and hypothetical constructs, and related articles by Ginsberg [48], Marx [118], and Maze [119].

construction may differ markedly from that of the real organism but whose relevant psychological input-output properties are the same. It is in this sense that one can say that the real organism behaves as if it were built like the model.

It would seem reasonable to ask why one builds such a theory rather than simply a system of empirical laws within one's own field. Actually, however, the question is fundamentally one of degree, i.e., of the level to which one attempts to generalize his knowledge. Accordingly, it is a matter of the scientist's preference, and may be influenced by a number of factors. Primarily, the ability to predict concerning a wide range of phenomena from a small number of statements is taken to be a goal of science, and theory construction is an approach to this goal. It is particularly appealing because psychological laws seem so numerous, complex, and at times mutually inconsistent that it appears more difficult to formulate a lower-level empirical system than to construct a theory. Thus, Spence [180] has collected a variety of learning curves involving different response measures, different apparatuses, and different organisms, and has shown how all of these may be seen as instances of a few hypothetical equations rather than as a miscellaneous collection of diverse empirical laws. Such a result, multiplied several times over, provides the most immediate justification of the approach.

Relation to the areas. *More molecular fields.* We have already noted that the postulates can be given physiological interpretations but that the value of the theory to psychology does not depend on whether physiologically correct interpretations can be found. Of course, the theorist need not disclaim such interpretations, or may at least be interested in the degree of correspondence between the postulates and physiological laws. Indeed, he may actively employ the available physiological knowledge when building a "model" organism.

From the point of view of an integrated behavior science, one would prefer a system of true physiological laws that would incorporate physiological as well as more molar phenomena. However, from the point of view of predicting only psychological phenomena, a model organism is just as useful as the real one. Clearly, if one can successfully predict the behavior of a model that acts like the subject being studied, then one can equally well predict the subject's behavior. Furthermore, it is not impossible that psychological phenomena could be predicted from a model that is structurally simpler than the real organism.

The writer is not competent to make a detailed comparison of the postulates with physiological facts. For that matter, the most relevant kinds of physiological work have only recently begun to appear [e.g., 182], and most physiological psychologists would probably admit that their field is not yet ready to support such an analysis. Premature attempts run the risk that apparent specific discrepancies in one part of the theory may balance unknown, but compensating, errors in other parts. In such a case, changing a postulate to make it more consistent with physiology could, at the same time, make the theory as a whole less useful for psychology. Accordingly, neither field seems ready for a concerted effort to integrate psychological and physiological phenomena within the same system.

Other areas of psychology. Although there have been a variety of attempts to apply the theory to relatively complex psychological phenomena, it is primarily concerned with classical and instrumental conditioning. We have previously noted the assumption that the basic principles derived from these simpler forms of learning will also apply to other areas of psychology, presumably with the addition of new variables. Of the new variables which will be required in order to deal satisfactorily with human behavior, language currently appears to be the most critical.

The fact that humans can talk, to themselves as well as to others, may be expected to affect essentially every variable in the system. To mention a few of the ways language can enter into a behavior situation:

1. Words, as stimuli, may modify the stimulus complex and bring in instrumental responses previously conditioned to them.

2. The human may be able to gain additional habit strength by rehearsing stimulus-response-reinforcement sequences verbally, the effect of which will depend upon the degree of correspondence between the implicitly practiced relationships and the objective situation.

3. The occurrence of words that have been conditioned as secondary drives will affect the human's motivation.

4. Similarly, the incentive motivation can be affected by verbal cues, particularly that based on delayed reward. Thus, on the one hand, words can be used as secondary reinforcers to span a long delay of reinforcement, as when one says, "I'll get paid for this tomorrow." On the other hand, a past stimulus-response sequence can be reinstated verbally immediately preceding the reinforcement, as when one says, "I'm getting paid for what I did yesterday."

Although the points listed above do not exhaust the possible effects of language, they do point to the importance of its inclusion in the theory if one wishes to deal with complex human behavior. The "pure-stimulus-act" [68] or "cue-producing-response" [37] appears to be the most promising approach, but it still remains to be formally implemented. It is one thing to predict what would happen if a sentence occurred; it is quite another thing to predict that the sentence will occur. Since words are presumably responses, learned and performed according to the principles of the theory, the solution of the problem should be possible [see, e.g., 50].

More molar areas. Psychology is to sociology, cultural anthropology, etc., much as physiology is to psychology. Accordingly, the more molar social scientist may choose to operate without reference to psychological laws, just as the learning theorist may ignore physiology. However, because a comprehensive theory of learned behavior should also apply to social phenomena, it is interesting to explore the extent to which the current theory meets this objective. At the present time, one can only do this informally because it is necessary to assume specifications of the intervening variables that have not been stated formally as yet. For example, in analyzing a problem like the resistance of a culture to change, e.g., the difficulty of introducing a new culture element, one might cast it in an approach-avoidance paradigm. Variables such as giving up money, pressures for social conformity, vicarious learning, etc., must somehow be related to existing, or possibly new, intervening variables, and the molar phenomena must be translated into familiar response terms like the probability of adopting the element. This kind of informal and incomplete analysis not only strengthens the hope for a useful comprehensive theory but may also suggest important research problems to workers in the several fields involved.

The integration of the behavior sciences seems, at mid-century, to be a natural development for the future. This does not mean, of course, that all social sciences are destined to disappear into physiology. The range of organismic behavior is so great that there probably will always be fields corresponding to circumscribed aspects of behavior. Indeed, the increasing wealth of empirical knowledge is leading to narrower specialization on subareas within each field. Integration is more likely to involve primarily a recognition of the interrelationships between the fields and the adoption of a common language system. This will permit intercommunication and cross-fertilization, and eventually a comprehensive behavior theory.

Method of postulate construction. Since the postulates are statements which, structurally, could be laws, the method of their construction is analogous to induction. There are no rigid rules for this kind of "induction" except that the result must imply the original statements deductively. Of course, a number of solutions may meet this criterion, and the postulates, therefore, cannot correctly be viewed as being unique. However, as the number of original statements is increased, the number of solutions presumably decreases, and it is then likely that various solutions will be isomorphic or differ mainly in level of generality.

Typically, in addition to the restriction that the postulates imply the statements used in their construction, the theorist will abide by other self-imposed constraints. The most common of these is parsimony, i.e., the theorist prefers the simpler of the alternatives apparent to him. Frequently, the theorist is also interested in plausibility, i.e., he will select that alternative which fits most clearly with his informal ideas of how an organism might reasonably be built. Thus, Hull was concerned that his postulates seem plausible in terms of their adaptive significance and extra confidence was attached to properties appearing to have survival value.

Disregarding these extra constraints for the moment, let us consider how the postulates are, in fact, related to the data known to the theorist. Consider a function relating some response measure to a single stimulus or antecedent condition. As a simple illustrative example, assume one had found a linear function relating performance R to the number of reinforced trials N, i.e.,

$$R = aN + b \tag{1}$$

Suppose further that one also already had the following postulates: (a) Performance is a linear function of excitatory potential ($_sE_r$), i.e.,

$$R = a'\,_sE_r + b' \tag{2}$$

(b) Excitatory potential, in turn, is the simple multiplication of drive (D) and habit ($_sH_r$), i.e.,

$$_sE_r = D(_sH_r) \tag{3}$$

(c) Reinforced trials affect only habit strength, i.e.,

$$_sH_r = f(N) \tag{4}$$

and
$$D \neq f(N) \tag{5}$$

From these, and the known empirical function, we can trace the following derivation: From (2) and (3),

$$R = a'\,D\,_sH_r + b' \tag{6}$$

From (5), D is a constant, so we may define

$$a'' = a'D$$

and therefore,

$$R = a''\,_sH_r + b' \tag{7}$$

Then, from (1) and (7),

$$aN + b = a''\,_sH_r + b' \tag{8}$$

which simplifies to

$$_sH_r = \frac{a}{a''}\,N + \frac{b - b'}{a''} \tag{9}$$

One would, therefore, know that habit must be a linear increasing function of the number of reinforced trials, which happens in this case also to be the form of the illustrative empirical function. Observe closely, however, that a conclusion could not have been made at all without the kind of assumptions contained in Eqs. (2) to (5). Furthermore, a quite different conclusion would have followed from the same procedure were these assumptions different. Thus, if N also affected drive, D would not disappear as a constant, and it would then be impossible from these data alone to separate the effects of N on $_sH_r$ from its effects on D. Were $_sE_r$ some other function of D and $_sH_r$, or were R some nonlinear function of $_sE_r$, the concluding function would be affected accordingly. Depending jointly on these matters, the theoretical function may or may not look very much like the empirical function. Despite appearance, however, each would have the same logical relation to the data, namely, that, within the constraints provided by the rest of the theory, each is the only solution which will correctly imply the empirical function.

One may question the propriety of this procedure on the grounds that the results are no better than the data used, and typical empirical data include considerable error variance. What the theorist does is freely to select and modify the data in terms of what he thinks to be the true function, the deviation from the actual data depending upon his estimate of their reliability. Fortunately, this rational procedure can be tested only by more reliable data, and these latter data can then be put back through the mill, if necessary, to generate a better postulate.

TABLE 1. TWO HYPOTHETICAL SETS OF DATA DETERMINED FROM A FACTORIAL STUDY IN WHICH BOTH HOURS OF DEPRIVATION AND MAGNITUDE OF REWARD WERE VARIED

Hours of deprivation	Amount of reward		Hours of deprivation	Amount of reward	
	High	Low		High	Low
High	4	3	High	16	8
Low	3	2	Low	8	4

The inductive process follows essentially the same logic for more complex questions requiring factorial designs of experiments. Consider, for example, a question in which Spence has been interested, the nature of the interaction between drive and incentive. In Table 1 are shown two possible sets of empirical data from which this interaction is to be determined. The matrix on the left shows no interaction in measured performance between amount of reward and hours of deprivation and, taken directly, would indicate an additive relation between the intervening variables anchored to them. The matrix on the right, however, would suggest a multiplicative interaction. Determining from these data the interaction between intervening variables, however, again requires other prior assumptions. Most critically, one must assume, as Spence has, that the performance measure is linearly related to response tendency. Thus, the matrix on the left is simply $\log_2$ of the matrix of the right, and a multiplicative performance interaction would imply an additive theoretical interaction were response tendency a logarithmic function of the response measure used, and vice versa.[2]

Since other parts of the theory are necessary to this "inductive" procedure of obtaining any one postulate, it is reasonable to ask where one first obtains these other parts. How, that is, does one begin? Unfortunately there is no simple answer to this question. Certainly the notions of parsimony and plausibility play a role, but they alone are not enough. What is needed is the spark of theoretical insight, the uttering of a sentence. The theorist scans a collection of different sets of data, methodically trying out various structures and using each failure as an additional cue to evoke more hopeful ones.[3] It would be hard to overestimate the time this trial-and-error process may consume, or properly to describe the importance a new sentence can have. Saying for the first time, "Suppose we separate the habit and performance factors," or the like, stimulates a new structure that can then be developed by the procedure just described. It is their frequency of output of just such useful sentences that has given stature to Hull, and to Spence, and to Miller, and will to others of subsequent generations.

Manner of deriving theorems. Theorems are derived from the theory by the conventional rules of logic, including mathematics. That is, the postulates serve as premises which, together with the statements describing some particular conditions, imply the theorems deductively. It is important to recognize that theorems are implied by the entire theory, not by any segment of it separately. Some parts of the theory may not be differentially involved in a particular situation, but proof of this fact is a genuine, if often ignored, part of the derivation.

Precise mathematical derivation is the ultimate goal of the theory, but until the postulates are exactly quantified, derivations must be made within the algebra of inequalities. Thus, if one wished to derive from the 1943 Hull system relative performance by two groups differing only in

[2] The theoretical interaction can be obtained without this assumption in the special case where the functions intersect at some point. Thus, learning curves diverging from the same starting point imply a multiplicative interaction with habit provided only that performance is a monotonic function of response tendency.

[3] In this context, the advantage of the simpler learning situations is that they involve fewer variables and therefore suggest a smaller number of alternative structures.

hours of food deprivation, the deprivation would be:

$$R_{hi\ D} = f(_s\dot{E}_R) = f[(_sH_R \cdot D) - _sI_R - I_R - _sO_R - _sL_R]$$
$$\lor \qquad \lor \qquad \| \quad \lor \quad \| \qquad \| \qquad \| \qquad \|$$
$$R_{lo\ D} = f(_s\dot{E}_R) = f[(_sH_R \cdot D) - _sI_R - I_R - _sO_R - _sL_R]$$

This procedure, of course, can be used equally well with more than two groups to include also second-order differences, although in such cases it is typically convenient to make the derivation graphically.

When the problem is too complex to be handled conveniently in this manner, the derivational procedure is to assume illustrative numbers for the parameters involved, and to make a mathematical derivation using these numbers. Although this procedure yields conclusions involving exact numbers, they are only illustrative and the theorems are stated in a greater-than language.

In some cases, the same greater-than result would follow regardless of the particular illustrative values used. When this is true, there can be no question about the logical correctness of the theorem. In other cases, however, one set of illustrative values gives one answer while the opposite answer can be obtained if other values are used. For example, in a choice situation, drive emphasizes any habit difference that exists. High drive, therefore, improves performance only if the correct response has the dominant habit. Therefore, whether the correct choice will be learned faster under high drive than under low drive depends upon what one assumes about the initial levels of the competing habits, and the relative rates at which habit and inhibition are built up. Under such circumstances, the most conservative approach is to reject the problem as a possible test of the theory. Frequently, however, the result changes systematically with changes in the illustrative values, and the theory can then be tested by a detailed study of the relevant variable.

One interesting illustration of this last point appears in *A Behavior System*.[4] Hull was attempting to derive that discrimination learning would be more difficult if the difference between the positive and negative stimuli was held constant and their absolute intensities increased, but he obtained the reverse relationship by the use of illustrative numbers. This result was peculiar to the illustrative dynamism and generalization functions and to his choice of the weaker stimulus as the positive one and the lower intensity pair at or near the threshold. If the same derivation is made for other pairs of stimuli, the result is more in line with the

[4] When provided with the evidence that his derivation was unique to the conditions chosen, Hull declined to use it. Partly this was because it would have required changes in other parts of the text, at a time when he was not physically up to that task. Primarily, however, Hull wanted to show by example that a theorist himself should be willing to publish the failures as well as the successes of his theory.

Weber-Fechner law. The theory actually predicts an inversion in the function, with less intense pairs being progressively less difficult to discriminate except at or near the threshold.

Quantification of the theory. Quantification is a matter of degree, varying from indications of the direction of relationships, through statements of function forms, to exact specifications of all parameters in the equations. The ultimate goal of the Hullian approach is to attain the final level of exact quantification.

Quantification is important enough in its own right to merit serious attention because only a fully quantified theory can yield exact predictions and therefore permit more rigorous tests. An even more pressing motive arises from the fact that a theory at a lower level of quantification simply cannot deal with situations in which several variables which have opposite effects upon performance are varied at the same time. That is, if one variable favors one condition and another variable favors the other condition, then no unique solution can be gained from the algebra of inequalities.

Of the difficulties which must be overcome in order to achieve full quantification, the most central concerns the unit of measurement. Data collected in psychological laboratories, even when detailed enough to permit the fitting of functions, usually seem to be unique to the particular apparatus and species of organism involved. The order of numbers varies markedly from situation to situation; achieving a general theory, stated in exact quantitative form, would, therefore, appear unlikely.

It is not yet clear how this problem will be solved, but two possible lines of attack upon it may be mentioned.

One is represented by Hull's quantification methodology. There is no need to describe this methodology here [see 74; see also 27, 28, 88] nor to repeat some of the difficulties with Hull's use of it [see 104]. The work with Hull's quantification methodology should be viewed as primarily illustrative, since Hull wished to demonstrate how it could be used, and how it would affect the postulates, if properly implemented. Adequate testing of the procedure remains to be done, but what is important in this context is to recognize that it is an attempt to scale performance in terms of a unit (based on the sigma of oscillation) which might not be peculiar to a particular situation. That is, it might be possible to transform raw data, the units of which vary from situation to situation, into a more nearly universally applicable unit.

Another possibility of surmounting the problem posed by varying units of measurement may be termed "relative" quantification. Such an approach would succeed if the parameters in the various postulates bear the same relationships to each other even though their absolute sizes vary. Thus, if inhibition always grows at (say) twice the rate of habit these postulates could be quantified relative to each other. To employ such a theory in a new situation would require a pilot study to obtain the absolute size of some parameter from which the remaining ones could then be estimated.

Implementation of either of these approaches to quantification is a project of considerable magnitude, and should reasonably be preceded by more detailed testing of the postulates at a greater-than level. The size of the task results mainly from the fact that the entire theory must be quantified at the same time.[5] Since theorems are implied by the system as a whole, numbers must be in all postulates in order to derive numerical theorems.

Other problems, hardly less serious, face the quantitatively oriented theorist. For example, the parameters may differ markedly from subject to subject so that conventional techniques of averaging the performance measures may produce serious distortions of any individual function. Spence [180] has described the techniques, based upon the selection of homogeneous groups of subjects, that he has been developing to solve this problem.

Both Hull and Spence have demonstrated their belief that the importance of quantification justifies the effort required. And despite the apparently immense difficulties, there is no way to find out to what extent a behavior theory can be quantified except by trying.

THE THEORETICAL MODELS

In this section, the independent, intervening, and dependent variables of the theory are identified and their interrelationships described. In doing this, the main focus will be on the theory as presented by Spence in his Silliman Lectures. However, he did not discuss all the kinds of simple learning data and so did not deal with all the variables that he has described in other sources and that are included in Hull's theory. In order, therefore, to provide a more comprehensive picture, ideas expressed elsewhere have been included when Spence did not state anything to the contrary.

A detailed description of Hull's theory in these regards has been made by Koch [88]. In his analysis, Koch distinguished between systematic and empirical variables, and this distinction will be maintained here. Concepts to which the intervening variables are anchored are called "systematic" variables, and specific instances of these con-

---

[5] At the early stages, some postulates may not need to be quantified at all levels, provided they are quantitatively specified at the level being used. Thus, for example, if the theorist assumes that no reactive inhibition is generated by widely distributed trials, then he may temporarily ignore that variable since it is quantitatively specified at zero.

cepts, "empirical" variables. Such variables are not different in kind but differ in their relative level of abstractness. Thus, one might tie incentive to the weight of a particular kind of food, or more abstractly, to quantity of food reward, or still more abstractly, to amount of reinforcement, etc. Whether quantity of food reward, for example, is a systematic or an empirical variable depends on the level of abstractness at which the theorist attempts to work, being a systematic variable if incentive is anchored directly to it, and an empirical variable if incentive is anchored more abstractly.

More abstract concepts provide greater generality but are difficult to formulate adequately. Frequently, therefore, the intervening variables are anchored informally at one level and more formally at another. If, at any particular time, the theorist is not able to provide a satisfactory anchoring for more than a limited portion of what he expects ultimately to achieve, he may give the more general formulation as an informal suggestion to permit trying the theoretical structure in areas outside its more formally relevant ones. For example, were amount of reinforcement adequately defined to include all sources of reward, it would be a relatively abstract concept; and although incentive is formally anchored to quantity of food reward, it may be informally employed when dealing with other sorts of situations. Similarly, the hunger drive is formally defined by hours of food deprivation, but is also conceived in terms of any operations producing hunger.

This duality exists because available empirical evidence typically permits more complete and quantitative statements about some variables than about others and also because of the difficulty of providing more abstract definitions. Formulating such definitions is an important task, but the absence of them should not be too disturbing at the present time. One may concentrate on determining the interrelations among known instances of concepts even before adequate comprehensive definitions of them have been formulated. Thus, so long as the defined concept "food to a deprived organism" is accepted as a member of the larger, partially defined class "reinforcers," one can study the effect of this known instance on behavior without being immediately concerned with the more abstract definition. Indeed, just such sorts of interrelations are used in formulating the definition, because the adequacy of a tentative definition is tested by comparing the interrelations of new instances that it suggests with those of known instances.

For this reason, theorists interested in the detailed, quantitative aspects of the system use terms defined by their studies, i.e., reinforcing events are ones previously shown to be reinforcing events, drives are operations previously shown to produce drive, etc. The circularity of this procedure, on the defining instance, is well recognized, but is avoided by generalizing the operations to new situations. One might prefer to have the defining characteristic some other than the property under concern. For example, notions such as drive reduction, stimulus-intensity reduction, etc., may be viewed as attempts to define reinforcement by some attribute other than the performance effect which it is invoked to explain. This would be advantageous should it happen to be easier to determine whether an event has the independent defining property, but is not essential to the approach.

Finally, before describing the variables of the theory, it should be noted that one of the potentially most fruitful ways to anchor input variables has not been used extensively in the formal postulates. This is the identification of some mechanism through which independent variables affect intervening variables. This can be illustrated by the fractional anticipatory goal response r_g which is the most well known of these mechanisms and which has been suggested by Spence as underlying incentive motivation. Rather than anchoring incentive directly to the number of trials and the amount and delay of reinforcement, as has been done formally, it could be tied to them indirectly through their effect upon the amplitude of r_g. This would be advantageous because, by attributing to r_g the properties of overt responses, one automatically covers a number of situations indirectly and does not have to provide separate postulates for them. Thus, how partial reinforcement affects incentive is unspecified in any of the explicit postulates, although it would follow deductively were the r_g mechanism used. Similar is a change in stimulus conditions, distribution of practice, and many others. However, not only is it difficult to formalize the r_g mechanism but it would increase the labor involved in making deductions because one then also would have to solve the theory for r_g. When this is done, other factors must be considered. For example, r_g as a classical conditioned response should, during learning, have only a probability of occurrence. This offers the possibility of removing drive, oscillation, and threshold from instrumental response tendencies directly, because the quantitative properties of those intervening variables could then enter through the response tendency for r_g. However, other characteristics, such as reactive inhibition, may have undesirable implications since r_g might fatigue during a behavior chain. It must be emphasized that r_g is an intervening variable and not a response of the real organism, and the theorist can therefore ascribe to it any properties he wishes, e.g., that it is not a fatiguable response. But since such restrictions would encroach upon the intended parsimony, it has seemed prudent to leave the mechanisms as informal suggestions until the details have been more thoroughly worked out.

Summary of Spence's theory. In describing the theory, emphasis is placed on those aspects which offer interesting contrasts and which appear to be important at the present time. The description is incomplete, therefore, and some matters are treated in greater detail than others; hence, it may be useful first to give a rather general picture of the theory as formulated by Spence.

As has already been said, the purpose of the theory is correctly to imply known and unknown S-R laws. This is done by the introduction of intervening variables which are anchored first on the stimulus, or input, side and then on the response, or output, side. The pivotal construct is excitatory potential since the independent variables feed into it and the dependent variables are determined from it. Because Spence described a two-factor theory, we must look at classical and instrumental conditioning separately.

The excitatory potential of a classical conditioned response is increased by two prior intervening variables, habit and drive, each of which is in turn related to manipulatable stimulus and antecedent conditions. Habit is the major associative variable linking the response to the stimulus and is acquired gradually as a function of reinforced trials. Normally, the pairing of the conditioned and unconditioned stimuli is sufficient. If, however, the UCS itself does not provide a reinforcing state of affairs (food, pain reduction, etc.), then habit will not increase unless some other source of reinforcement exists. Habit can also be developed by generalization from similar stimuli to which the response has been conditioned. Drive is the major motivation variable, aggregating the primary and secondary needs present at the time. The primary needs depend upon deprivation of food, water, and sex object, and upon the intensity of any noxious stimuli; the secondary needs depend upon the presence of any stimuli previously paired with noxious stimuli. Although drive is not typically referred to as an associative variable (linking the stimulus to the measured response), it may change during the course of classical defense conditioning because the cues in the situation are paired with the noxious unconditioned stimulus. In a similar vein, needs have characteristic stimuli which are a part of the total stimulus complex and so become conditioned to the response.

The excitatory potential of a classical conditioned response is reduced by several inhibitory variables. The major inhibitory factor develops as a result of nonreinforcement. Reactive inhibition, or fatigue, was not discussed by Spence but he would presumably employ such a variable when dealing with responses requiring different amounts of work. Two other notions have inhibitory properties: oscillation, which reduces excitatory potential by an amount that varies from moment to moment according to a normal probability function; and the threshold, which is the value of excitatory potential below which the response will not occur.

From the excitatory potential determined in the above way, one can predict the probability of occurrence of a conditioned response by ascertaining the likelihood that, on any trial, oscillation will not have reduced excitatory potential below threshold. Response amplitude is predicted as a simple linear function of excitatory potential. Spence did not derive the latency of a classical conditioned response from his model, although he presents data on this measure and suggests that it may be part of what gets learned (a micromolar assumption). Similarly, he does not derive resistance to extinction of a classical conditioned response both because there were no data available and because a number of factors, such as a change in drive, enter into conventional extinction procedures.

Spence's treatment of instrumental conditioning differs from that of classical conditioning in a number of ways, but all are related to the way reinforcement is handled. Instrumental habits develop simply by the contiguity of stimulus and response, but otherwise function identically. The drive variable is the same for both kinds of situations. With habit now independent of reinforcement, the properties of a reward (principally, the amount of it) affect an additional variable acting to increase excitatory potential. This is incentive, which is gradually acquired as a function of the number of times the reward has been experienced in the situation.

The fact that instrumental habits develop by contiguity suggests that the inhibitory factor in classical conditioning which is based on nonreinforcement must have a different interpretation in instrumental conditioning. This variable now represents the quantitative effects of incompatible responses which occur on nonreinforced trials. And a new inhibitory construct is introduced to reflect the effect of any incompatible responses which might occur in a delay period imposed between the completion of an instrumental response and receipt of reward. Otherwise, the inhibitory variables are the same for instrumental as for classical conditioning.

From the instrumental excitatory potential, one can again compute probability of response by the same method as for classical conditioning. Amplitude is not explicitly considered because a subject may learn particular amplitudes under conditions of correlated reinforcement. But response speed and resistance to extinction are determined as linear functions of excitatory potential.

Besides giving a brief survey of the theory, this sketch also helps point out what is meant by holding one's theorizing close to the available data. If a variable involves complications which could equally well be handled in several ways, it is simply omitted until more definitive data are collected. If the definition of a concept cannot now be made at a relatively abstract level, one goes on working with instances already identified. If

different types of situations seem to lend themselves more readily to different theoretical descriptions, separate analyses are given. Of course,
one would certainly prefer a general, abstract, and integrative theory,
but it would be unrealistic seriously to try to construct one in view of
the limited extent of present empirical knowledge. A less pretentious
theory may, indeed, better serve the role of guiding research by bringing more clearly into focus those problems which are ready for experimental attack. That is to say, a theory that is close to known data is likely
to stimulate research close to the theory.

The input intervening variables. The input intervening variables and
appropriate systematic and empirical independent variables are given in
Table 2. Since neither Spence nor Hull has provided specific definitions
for all the terms involved, the statements given reflect the present writer's
perception, and not necessarily Spence's or Hull's interpretation. They
are, therefore, only suggestive and are also partial in the sense that other
operations can later be added as more abstract definitions are formulated.

There are a number of differences in the input variables as described
by the several theories being considered. Many of these are primarily in
wording or emphasis, others refer to underlying mechanisms not explicitly postulated, and some reflect relatively important issues. It is
simply not practicable to discuss all of these in sufficient detail to expose
the bases for the differences and to describe possible tests of them. Brief
discussions of each major variable are given in order to identify the more
important contrasts, and one variable, the time of delay of reinforcement,
is treated in detail. This variable was selected because it has been dealt
with explicitly in a variety of ways and therefore offers a particularly
good illustration of the range of alternatives contained within the approach and the interaction of these with the maturing body of psychological knowledge.

Stimulus. The external stimulus complex, called the "distal stimulus"
by Hull and the "situational stimulus" by Spence, can be described in
such physical terms as frequency, amplitude, wavelength, etc. Any energy
impinging on a suitable receptor is presumed to initiate a stimulus trace
which persists with decaying effect for an interval of time. Of the total
external stimulus complex, that fraction which is perceived at any one
time is called the "proximal" or "effective" stimulus. In addition, there
are intraorganic stimuli based partly on proprioceptive feedback and
partly on cues to the state of the organism (e.g., drive stimuli). The
response is made to the stimulus complex composed of the intraorganic
and effective stimuli.

The effective and situational stimuli are not isomorphic, but the rules
by which one determines the effective stimuli from knowledge of the
situational stimuli are not yet very fully understood. One aspect of this

TABLE 2. THE INPUT VARIABLES

Empirical independent	Systematic independent	Intervening
Any physical energy impinging on a suitable receptor, as, e.g., a super-threshold tone.	Stimulus	Stimulus trace
Specification of physical energy in frequency or location, as, e.g., the pitch of a tone.	Stimulus quality	
Specification of physical energy in amplitude, as, e.g., the loudness of a tone.	Stimulus intensity	
Physical energies present at the same time, e.g., a tone and a light.	Patterning	
Hours of food deprivation on a regular feeding rhythm.	Hunger need	Drive
Hours of water deprivation on a regular drinking rhythm.	Thirst need	
Hours of deprivation of appropriate sex object.	Sex need	
Intensity of noxious stimulus, as, e.g., an electric shock.	Pain need	
Temporal coincidence of stimulus and response followed by reinforcement.	Reinforced trial	Habit (classical conditioning)
Temporal coincidence of stimulus and response.	Trial	Habit (instrumental conditioning)
Temporal coincidence of stimulus and response not followed by reinforcement.	Nonreinforced trial	Inhibition (classical conditioning)
Weight of food object given as reward.	Amount of reinforcement	Incentive (instrumental conditioning)
Time between response and receipt of reward.	Delay of reinforcement	
Experience of reward in the situation.	Trial	
Differences among stimuli in quality or intensity.	Stimulus similarity	Generalization
Cumulated work done since rest.	Fatigue	Reactive inhibition
Time since response system was active.	Rest	

problem that has been emphasized by Spence as a result of his work on discrimination learning is the importance of receptor-orienting acts. Particularly in vision, the effective stimuli depend upon the orientation of the receptor, and many behavior situations involve learning such acts as well as the behavior being recorded. For this reason, care must be taken to insure reception of the relevant cues.

Another aspect of this problem is the notion of afferent stimulus interaction. Hull assumed that each stimulus element is affected by the context in which it is embedded, so that, for example, a tone in one environment is different from the same physical tone in another environment. Spence did not discuss afferent interaction in his book, but has elsewhere stated that a stimulus element can be affected by contextual cues. When in a discrimination learning situation no single element (such as "white" vs. "black") provides a solution, the subject will learn to respond to differentially reinforced stimulus patterns or compounds (such as "white on the left" vs. "white on the right"). Spence tentatively assumed that patterning does not occur unless it is required, whereas Hull's stimulus interaction is presumably always involved. However, these might not lead to different implications because, if the effect of stimulus interaction is small, it might be observable only under conditions such as those assumed by Spence to be necessary for patterning.

One further aspect of the stimulus deserves brief mention; this is stimulus intensity dynamism. In his last postulate set, Hull assumed that stimuli not only have cue value, but also motivational properties in proportion to their intensity. This is generally recognized to be the case for very intense stimuli, but dynamism applies also to stimuli below the pain threshold. Other things equal, then, performance should be at a higher level the greater the intensity of the stimulus, and stimulus intensity discrimination should be easier if the more intense stimulus is the reinforced one. The writer [101] has elsewhere shown how such implications can be derived from Hull's theory without dynamism by attending to the fact that the subject is also learning not to respond to contextual cues. Whether there is a dynamogenic effect of stimulus intensity is an important question that can be determined from relatively straightforward empirical designs. Spence did not take an explicit stand on this question because the research has not been done and because he did not deal with problems that would be materially affected by dynamism.

Drive. Hull attempted a relatively abstract definition of drive based upon survival needs of the organism or species. It is recognized, of course, that some needs (e.g., oxygen deprivation) may not produce drive, and other conditions (e.g., curiosity) might involve drive without apparent survival need. Spence has taken the more direct approach of simply enumerating the known need-producing operations.

Spence did describe a possible mechanism underlying drive in situations involving noxious stimuli. This mechanism is an emotional response elicited by such stimuli. Not only will more intense stimuli lead to an increase in this emotional response, but different subjects may become differentially responsive when given the same intensity of stimulation. These assumptions have led to a number of studies but Spence has nevertheless formally anchored aversive drive directly to the intensity of noxious stimulation.

One important feature of the treatment of drive by both Spence and Hull is the assumption that all needs present at any one time summate into a generalized drive which then activates all habits. For example, in so far as its motivational properties are concerned, thirst will energize a response learned under hunger-food conditions as well as one learned under thirst-water conditions. Specific effects are handled by the assumption that each need produces characteristic stimuli. Thus, a subject can learn to make one response when hungry and another when thirsty because the distinctive need stimuli acquire greater habit to the appropriate responses. Similarly, a change from one need to another leads to a generalization decrement in habit because of the change in need stimuli.

Habit. Habit is the variable at which the reinforcement-contiguity issue is directly aimed. The traditional Hullian assumption is that reinforcement is a necessary condition for the development of any habit. Spence, however, has suggested a two-factor theory in which reinforcement is necessary for classical conditioning but not for instrumental conditioning.[6] Spence stated that his position resulted from the assumption that the habit strength of instrumental responses is not related to the property of a reinforcer. This assumption was highly tentative and was based on studies involving the goal gradient.

Koch [87] and Seward [155] have noted that Hull's 1949 postulates involved essentially a contiguity approach, since the growth in habit is dependent only upon some (unspecified) minimum or threshold reinforcement. One can, however, also argue that Hull's 1949 system is less similar to comparable contiguity theories than his 1943 theory, in which the increment in habit was partially a function of the amount of reward. The S-R contiguity theory of Estes [43], for example, holds that learning is independent of reinforcement, but that the amount of this learning which is retained does depend on the amount of reward. Thus, it is difficult to see any genuine difference in so far as net change in the asso-

---

[6] Actually, Spence dealt only with classical defense conditioning and instrumental reward conditioning, suggesting reinforcement as necessary for the former but not the latter. His two-factor approach may, therefore, depend as much on the nature of the need, appetitional or aversive, as on the kind of learning situation.

ciative variable is concerned as long as standard reinforcement procedures prevail. Hull's 1949 postulate set is more similar to the kind of
contiguity theory described by Spence for instrumental conditioning,
where reward affects an incentive variable and has no effect at all upon
habit. And, as Spence correctly noted, his contiguity theory is more like
the expectancy approach suggested by Tolman [187].

Inhibition. There are two general ways to handle the phenomenon
of experimental extinction. One is simply to reduce the habit built up
during acquisition; the other is to posit an inhibitory variable which
builds up during nonreinforced trials and which offsets the habit. Following the lead taken by Pavlov as a result of his studies of spontaneous
recovery and disinhibition, both Hull and Spence have chosen the latter
alternative.

Hull attempted to derive inhibition by use of a "stop-responding"
mechanism. This analysis assumes that making a response produces
fatigue, which is a kind of drive condition, and that stopping the response
is rewarded by a reduction in this fatigue. This stopping of the response
then becomes anticipatory and inhibits the overt response. There are,
however, a number of difficulties with this mechanism which Hull did
not adequately resolve [see, e.g., 49].

Spence did not deal extensively with extinction but did postulate an
inhibition variable as a direct function of the number of nonreinforced
trials in classical conditioning. This is consistent with his earlier analysis
of discrimination learning [164] in which inhibition was assumed to be
a direct function of nonreinforcement. In his Silliman Lectures, Spence
referred to the familiar contiguity assumption of counterconditioning of
incompatible responses as underlying inhibition in instrumental conditioning, but he did not describe the analysis in detail nor did he formally
introduce this mechanism.

Incentive. Incentive is affected by two major variables: the amount
and the time of delay of reinforcement. Since these have been treated
in very much the same way, only the latter is discussed here.

The time of delay of reinforcement entered into Hull's 1943 postulate
set as one of the determinants of the limit to which the habit strength of
an instrumental response can grow.[7] Such an assumption implies that the
performance of groups receiving different delays of reinforcement will

[7] Delay of reinforcement was not explicitly identified as being involved in
classical conditioning in 1943. Recently, Spence has suggested that this might
be an instance of correlated reinforcement, i.e., the delay of reinforcement will
depend upon response latency when the CS-UCS interval is constant. However, we
shall restrict ourselves here to instrumental conditioning, and to nonchaining delay
defined as the waiting time between completion of the instrumental response and
receipt of reward.

diverge with training and stabilize at different asymptotes. A considerable body of data supports this implication [e.g., 54, 135, 136, 137, 141].

However, the assumption that delay partially determines the limit of habit, coupled with the restriction that habit is relatively permanent, implies further that subjects changed from a short to a longer delay of reinforcement will not show a performance decrement, notwithstanding the fact that other subjects trained throughout with the longer delay perform at a lower level. Although some data [59] are in accord with this implication, other results [99, 155] show a drop in performance following a shift to a longer delay. Of course, the shift to an effectively infinite delay produces experimental extinction, but this could occur for other reasons, e.g., inhibition due to nonreinforcement.

In his 1949 postulates, Hull removed delay of reinforcement from habit, instead having it affect directly a new incentive variable *J*. Taking this literally, a change in delay would be expected to produce an immediate shift in performance, an implication which is not consistent with any known data. That Hull did not intend this implication,[8] however, can be surmised from his treatment of changes in amount of reward in *A Behavior System*. Since he there assumed that incentive changed gradually following a shift in amount of reward, even though the postulates literally imply an immediate change, one may reasonably assume that Hull would have treated a change in *J* in a similar fashion.

Before going further, let us identify the differences between the 1943 and 1949 positions. If all other variables are zero or unity, as appropriate, then:

$$1943 \text{ set} \qquad {}_sE_R = M(1 - 10^{-iN})$$
$$1949 \text{ set} \qquad {}_sE_R = J(1 - 10^{-iN})$$

where ${}_sE_R$ is reaction potential, M is the limit of habit strength, *J* is that part of incentive based on delay of reinforcement, and *N* is the number of reinforced trials. The most critical difference is that everything on the right side of the 1943 equation was called habit and could not decrease, while only the parenthetical portion of the 1949 equation was irreducible habit and *J* was a part of incentive and could be reduced. Had Hull kept his 1943 equation but let habit decay, the result would have been qualitatively identical to the 1949 assumption. Quantitatively, however, the 1949 equation provides a new degree of freedom, namely the rate of change of *J* following a change in delay of reinforcement. Letting habit

---

[8] Hull had simply not designed the postulates generally enough to handle changes in reward, and explicitly restricted their use to situations in which the reward conditions remained constant throughout training and testing.

decrease in the 1943 equation[9] would imply approach to the new (lower) asymptote at the same relative rate as original learning, while the 1949 equation can permit J to change at a different rate.

In 1947, Spence analyzed delayed reward in terms of immediate secondary reinforcement and, following publication of Hull's 1949 postulates, he supplemented his earlier proposal with the suggestion that the incentive variable could be related to the fractional anticipatory goal response r_g [175]. In this analysis, delay of reinforcement is translated into the stimulus asynchronism for the classical conditioning of r_g to the cues of the instrumental response, longer delays providing less favorable conditions. Then, either through the dynamism properties of the response-produced s_g, or simply directly, the amplitude of r_g is the mechanism determining incentive motivation.

The r_g-s_g analysis explicitly makes incentive a function of the number of times the reward has been experienced in the situation, i.e., the number of conditioning trials. Otherwise, the differences between it and Hull's 1949 postulates are of a detailed quantitative sort. Primarily, the r_g-s_g analysis implies a relationship between the rate of change in performance following a shift in delay of reinforcement and the rate of original learning,[10] and also a relationship to stimulus asynchronism data from classical conditioning, neither of which is necessary using Hull's approach.

In *Behavior Theory and Conditioning*, Spence retained the effect of delay of reinforcement on incentive, but noted particular doubt about it. He assumed the main effect of delayed reward to be the incompatible responses which might occur in the delay period and subsequently compete with the instrumental response. In support of this position, he reports that the gradient of delay of reinforcement has a much lower, if any, slope when trials containing incompatible responses are not included. He then provides data showing that long delays are more detrimental if the delay is suffered under conditions permitting incompatible responses to occur than if the animal is closely confined during the delay.

---

[9] There is a possible ambiguity in Hull's definitions of habit strength in 1943. The verbal statement that habit grows at a constant fraction of its yet to be attained level corresponds to the mathematical statement given above only while M is constant and trials are continuous from zero. Clearly, the mathematical statement would imply an immediate shift following a change in M and a complete shift if N were sufficiently large to make the parenthetical portion approximately 1, i.e., precisely what the 1949 equation implies. The "constant fractional increment" is the prior definition and prevails in case of conflict.

[10] This relationship is not the same as would be expected from the assumptions that delay affects the limit of habit, and that habit is reducible. In such an analysis, only one variable is changing with N; in the r_g-s_g analysis, two variables are changing during original learning but only one following a change in delay.

Finally, he argues, the change from a short to a longer delay of reward did not produce a performance decrement in the Harker study in which the subjects learned to stay at the response mechanism when initially trained with the short delay and then did not perform incompatible responses during the subsequently introduced longer delay.

Now it should be noted that an effect of incompatible responses is implicit in the Hullian system, although the analysis has not been made. Any responses occurring in a delay period will be reinforced by the subsequent reward. This provides, in effect, a fixed interval reinforcement schedule to the postresponse cues, and the responses which occur, even though causally independent of the reward,[11] are reinforced and learned. They will then tend to become anticipatory and compete with the instrumental response. However, since these anticipatory responses are analogous to anticipatory errors, there should develop a discrimination between preresponse and postresponse cues, the limit of which will depend on the difference between them. Thus, if one could insure the same amount of incompatible behavior during a delay period by two groups, for one of which the postresponse cues are more different from the instrumental cues than for the other, the effect of the delay should be different. This implication, of course, would also follow from Spence's theory.

What, then, are the differences between the Spence and Hull treatments of delayed reward? First, it must be noted that the reinforcement-contiguity issue is not critical because of the presence of a reward. The analyses could differ on the effect of a delay imposed in the goal box after the reward, because incompatible responses occurring in such a period would not be reinforced and would, therefore, not be learned according to a reinforcement interpretation. A contiguity theory implies that they would be learned, but it can be argued that the prior reward will have changed the stimulus complex in order to protect the instrumental responses from competition. Such an analysis might still imply, however, relatively greater detrimental effect of such a postreward delay the smaller the amount of reward.

Disregarding those variables that are not relevant to the present question, the equations may be written:

Hull $_sE_R = {_sH_R} \cdot D \cdot J \cdot K$

Spence $\bar{E} = H(D + K) - I_t$

In these equations, $_sE_R$ and $\bar{E}$ represent reaction potential, $_sH_R$ and H are habit strength, and D is drive. Hull separated incentive into two variables, J for delay and K for amount of reward; K in the Spence

---

[11] Skinner [161] has appropriately called these "superstitious" behaviors; see also [81].

equation is primarily dependent upon the amount of reward, [12] although delay may also affect it. The major effect of delay acts through I_t which is presumably based on incompatible responses occurring in the delay period.

Comparing these equations, if delay affects Spence's K, it is closely comparable to Hull's combined J and K. However, as we have already noted, Spence is particularly tentative on the matter, suggesting that delay might work exclusively through I_t. It should be noted that an r_g-s_g analysis of incentive would be most consonant with some effect of delay per se, but this is an issue which, while clearly formulatable, is not easily answered. From the fact that increasing the opportunity for incompatible responses increases the detrimental effect of delayed reward, one cannot confidently extrapolate that there would be no effect without any incompatible responses. Attempting to eliminate from the data trials on which incompatible responses occur is debatable not only because slightly "incompatible" responses might not be observable but also because of the danger of eliminating any inferior performance on the grounds that it must have included incompatible behavior. The Harker data, showing no drop in performance following an increase in delay of reward, are the most embarrassing to the assumption that delay affects incentive. However, the fact that subjects will learn to select that response leading to the shorter delay of reinforcement would appear to favor the incentive approach. If the only effect of delay is through incompatible responses, then some analysis would have to be provided to show how these responses mediate selection of the shorter delay response.

Actually, however, Spence has avoided such problems because, although he discussed incompatible responses as the mechanism through which delayed reward affects performance, he formally assigned the quantitative effects of delay directly to I_t. Therefore, his formulation does not depend on the incompatible response analysis, so long as the role of delay of reinforcement in determining reaction potential can be described by his equation.

Several interesting implications follow from this equation if delay affects only I_t. First, the interaction between amount and delay of reward should be additive, rather than multiplicative as assumed by Hull and as would be implied by Spence's theory if delay were also to affect his K variable. This interaction has not been studied experimentally as yet. Also implied in Spence's equation is an additive interaction with

---

[12] Spence's K is also affected by a different kind of delay than that being discussed. When the instrumental response is broken down into segments, or links of the behavior chain, early links have a delay determined by the time involved in completing the remaining links. This chaining delay affects K presumably through the r_g-s_g mechanism.

drive, which has received experimental support [142]. Finally, a more complex interaction is between delay and the instrumental habit. This interaction is postulated as additive, but since N also affects I_t (through the incompatible response habit strength), testing of this implication must be more roundabout, if at all possible.

Let us now summarize the various treatments accorded delay of reinforcement. In the several formulations, delay has been conceptualized in terms of (1) a limiting factor for habit strength, (2) a direct incentive factor, and (3) an inhibitory factor. Spence has suggested the r_g-s_g mechanism for the incentive approach, and incompatible responses as the mechanism underlying the inhibitory approach. From these several alternatives, a number of contrasting implications follow.

Thus, Hull's original assumption that delay of reinforcement affected the limit of habit strength was changed because of the effects of increasing the time of delay, although quantitative study of such shifts might support the original approach were habit permitted to decrease [38]. From the incentive and inhibitory approaches come further questions inviting detailed experimental test: the interactions of delay with amount of reward, and with trials of the instrumental habit, the effects of incompatible responses, the relative effects of delay on different responses, and the like. It is the answers to such questions which permit the theorist to select wisely from among various possible theoretical approaches. The active existence of a number of alternative interpretations can be traced largely to the deficiency of such systematic data.

The intervening variable relationships. In his last postulate set, Hull combined the intervening variables to determine reaction potential substantially as follows: [13]

$$({_sH_R} \cdot D \cdot V \cdot K \cdot J) - {_sI_R} - I_R - {_sO_R} - {_sL_R}$$

This equation is applicable to both classical and instrumental conditioning. In it, ${_sH_R}$ (habit) is determined by the number of reinforced trials, D (drive) by the conditions of drive such as food deprivation, V (dynamism) by the intensity of the stimulus, and K and J (incentive) respectively by the amount and the time of delay of reward.

[13] This equation gives the spirit of Hull's equation, but omits some of the characteristics which appear to involve problems Hull did not fully resolve. For example, Hull had two Vs in his system, one V_1 for the original training stimulus and another V_2 for the testing stimulus. Not only does this have undesirable mathematical consequences, but requires additional specification of what to do with V_2 during training, and how long to carry V_1 during testing. Also, the delay of reinforcement has been included through Hull's J, although his last equation looks somewhat different. And the inhibitory variables have been removed by arithmetic subtraction rather than by behavioral subtraction because of the effect the latter would have on extinction curves.

Opposing these excitatory variables are two inhibitory ones: $_sI_R$ (conditioned inhibition) and I_R (reactive inhibition). The latter is dependent on the work done since rest, and the former is a conditioned tendency to inhibit the response based on the reinforcement (reduction in I_R) occasioned by resting at the termination of the response.[14] The remaining two variables are calculational devices and are not tied to empirical variables. $_sO_R$ is a random variable inducing an oscillation of reaction potential from moment to moment, and $_sL_R$ is the reaction threshold below which the response cannot occur.

Spence employed two combinations for determining reaction potential:

classical conditioning	$(H \cdot D) - I_n - I_o - L$
instrumental conditioning	$[H \cdot (D + K)] - I_t - I_n - I_o - L$

As in the Hull system, H (habit) is related to the number of reinforced trials for classical conditioning,[15] but unlike Hull's system, the instrumental H is dependent simply on the number of trials. D (drive) is again dependent on conventional deprivation and noxious stimulus conditions. K (incentive) explicitly includes the number of reinforcement experiences, and is partially dependent on the amount of reinforcement. In addition, Spence has clearly related K to within-chain delay, which refers to the time between the completion of one link of a behavior chain and the completion of the remaining links. Nonchaining delay, which is the time after the entire instrumental response is completed until the reward is received, may affect K but Spence expressed doubt about this.

Nonchaining delay is the major variable determining I_t, and since incompatible responses are the possible mechanism underlying I_t, it also includes the opportunities available in the situation for incompatible behavior to occur and the number of delayed-reward trials on which such behavior might get learned. I_n is the analogue of Hull's $_sI_R$ and, for classical conditioning, is tied directly to the number of nonreinforced trials. For instrumental conditioning, however, I_n expresses the quantitative effects of incompatible responses which occur during extinction and are then learned by contiguity; but since this mechanism is not yet

---

[14] Those interested in this kind of mediated conditioned inhibition as a derived principle should note that $_sH_R$ is no longer affected by the amount of reward, hence $_sI_R$ would have to be conceived as having some kind of incentive component if the amount of I_R reduction is to affect it.

[15] The intensity of the UCS, which determines the amount of reinforcement in classical conditioning, could enter as affecting the limit of H (the assumption Hull took in 1943), or as evoking a unique amplitude of response (the micromolar assumption). Although leaning toward the latter, Spence followed his characteristic approach of reserving the decision until more definitive data have been collected.

fully developed, I_n is formally related to the number of extinction trials in instrumental conditioning.

The two calculational devices, I_o (oscillation) and L (threshold), serve the same function for Spence as for Hull. However, Spence has also assumed that both of these can be affected by the experimental conditions. Thus, oscillation is at least partially dependent upon variations in the effective stimulus and in drive which, while never identical from trial to trial, may be better controlled in some situations than in others. The threshold depends on the nature of the response so that, for example, if a rat were required to jump across a gap in order to get to the goal box, the threshold would vary with the length of the gap. Nevertheless, these variables are constant for groups of subjects in any particular situation.

We have already discussed the major contrasts between the Spence and Hull treatments of the input variables. In so far as the relationships among these variables are concerned, the most critical difference is that Spence has assumed that the motivational variables in instrumental conditioning (drive and incentive) interact additively, whereas Hull assumed that this interaction was multiplicative. In general, a multiplicative interaction implies that if any variable is zero, then the product is also zero. Thus, both drive and incentive must have some appreciable value in order for the response to occur. An additive interaction, on the other hand, implies that neither drive nor incentive is a necessary condition of performance, although at least one must be present. In the studies directed at this question, the data favor the additive relationship assumed by Spence. There have not been enough of these studies, however, and those conducted have not included near-zero values of either variable. Therefore, the answer to this question is still in doubt.

The output variables. After the input intervening variables have been determined from the appropriate independent variables and have been combined into reaction potential, the chain must be completed by relating reaction potential to the response. Technically, one calculates the expected response r of the model which is then related to the response R of the organism.[16] But since r and R are assumed to be isomorphic, it is conventional to go directly to R from reaction potential.

Behavior, as the dependent variable is psychological research, may be measured by a variety of objective operations: latency, speed, amplitude, magnitude, force, duration, rate, resistance to extinction, prob-

[16] The logic of this step is more clear when r and R are not isomorphic. Consider an electrical representation of a mathematical model. The theorist might not build the model so as to vary in speed of response, letting some other attribute r, say the number of flashing lights, indicate the speed R at which the organism is expected to respond.

ability, errors, trials to criterion, etc. These are the potential systematic dependent variables, of which four, latency (or speed), amplitude, resistance to extinction, and probability, have been explicitly related to reaction potential. Per cent correct responses in trial-and-error and discrimination situations has been related to the difference between the competing response tendencies. Presumably, other response measures can be derived from these, whereas others may require additional translations of reaction potential.

As with the independent variables, adequate definitions of the systematic dependent variables have not been made at a high level of abstractness. There are formidable problems to be resolved when one attempts to formulate such definitions. For example, latency is the time required to initiate a response. If one is running rats in an alley, one must decide how rigidly to control the subject's orientation at the time the door is opened, whether to provide any distinctive ready signal, and when to define the response as having begun. Certainly one's measures are affected by these decisions. And comparable problems of selecting criteria are involved for each response measure.

These problems are of major significance when one is attempting fully to quantify the theory. They are of less importance for greater-than kinds of studies provided the criteria used are the same for groups being compared. Thus, any condition which leads to shorter latencies defined as the time to get 2 in. out of the start box will most likely show the same relationship if latency is defined as the time to get 4 in. out of the start box. Accordingly, one can presumably interpret the definitions of the response measures quite liberally for most situations.

Latency is the time required to make the response after the stimulus is presented. Under typical conditions, time can be measured through any specified stage of the response, including time to complete it. When, however, the response is a fairly long behavior chain, it is frequently broken down into time to complete arbitrary links of the chain. It is now becoming conventional to take the reciprocals of these time scores and report data in terms of speed, since this emphasizes differences in the short time range and inverts the measure to one that has a positive relation to reaction potential.

Speed is used predominantly in instrumental conditioning, instances being the speed of running an alley, pressing a bar, etc. Hull simply postulated a function relating reaction potential to response speed, but Spence [179] has since shown how it can be derived in terms of the time required for a superthreshold reaction potential to chance to occur [see also 183]. That is, the response takes place when, as reaction potential oscillates from moment to moment, a superthreshold value occurs.

There is an advantage in deriving the response measure from properties already attributed to reaction potential over introducing a new postulate for this purpose. Clearly, one gains in parsimony; the theorist loses a degree of freedom in that he can no longer correct the theory at the terminal end by simply postulating whatever function works best. This is very much like the anchoring of the input variable through mechanisms. That is, oscillation and the threshold may be viewed as mechanisms through which reaction potential gets translated into certain measures of performance, in this case, the latency or speed of response.

These same mechanisms also apply to probability of response. This measure is most commonly used in classical conditioning, where performance is monitored over a finite interval of time to determine whether or not a response occurred. Prediction concerning probability is made by reference to the likelihood that reaction potential will chance to be superthreshold sometime during the selected interval of time.

The third measure which has been explicitly considered is amplitude. Both Hull and Spence restricted this measure to classical conditioning, where it refers to such things as the amount of change in skin resistance, the extent of eyelid closure, etc. Analogous measures in instrumental conditioning, such as the force the rat exerts on a bar, were excluded because of the possibility that particular amplitudes might be learned as different micromolar responses. No mechanism of amplitude has been proposed, its relation to reaction potential being simply postulated as a linear function of the reaction potential present at the moment of evocation.

Similarly, a separate postulate was given relating reaction potential to the number of consecutive nonreinforced trials required to extinguish the response. Actually, one mechanism for resistance to extinction is already available, namely, the amount of inhibition necessary to reduce reaction potential to threshold. However, extinction may involve a number of complications: the drive may be changed, frustration may be introduced, varying potentiality of competing responses may exist, the effective stimulus complex may be different, spontaneous recovery may be involved, etc. Extinction must be studied in greater systematic detail before a satisfactory mechanism can be proposed.

The above four measures apply to classical and instrumental conditioning, where records are taken of only one response class and discrete trials are given. In the free-responding situation, where the subject is left in the apparatus and can respond whenever he chooses, the typical measure is response rate. The interpretation of reaction potential in terms of this measure is an important undertaking but it has not yet been done. Rate would seem most clearly related to speed, since the faster one response is made, the sooner the next can occur, and so on. However, there are other complications involved in the free-responding situation, especially with a ratio schedule of reinforcement. Conditions which produce higher rates thereby lead to greater reduction in drive and more accumulated reactive inhibition as well as more reinforced trials. Clearly, a large comparative study will be required to relate response rate to measures used in the Hullian approach.

Turning now to situations in which records are kept concerning several response classes, two kinds have been considered. One is trial-and-error learning, where the subject selects from among competing responses; the other is discrimination learning, where the selection is among stimuli. A T maze can be used for both: in trial and error, the subject is required to go to the same side consistently; in discrimination, the arms of the maze are different in some way (say, white and black) and the subject is required to enter, say, the white alley regardless of its position. Differential reinforcement is given, typically reward for a correct response and no reward for an incorrect response, although other differences, such as work, punishment, etc., may be involved.

Treatment of both situations is handled through the oscillation mechanism by assuming that that reaction will occur which has the highest potential at the moment. The subject will choose the correct response every time only if its reaction potential exceeds the competing one by an amount greater than the range of oscillation. Otherwise, standard statistical procedures are used to determine the probability of the correct response, based on the difference between the reaction potentials and the variance of the oscillation distribution.

Various other measures can be derived from the ones described. For example, the number of trials to reach a performance criterion in a trial-and-error situation, say nine out of ten correct, is translated into the number of trials required to produce reaction potentials which are sufficiently different to support the criterion performance level.

In principle, a completely adequate, comprehensive behavior theory would be able to make predictions concerning any response measure an experimenter might find interesting. The Hullian approach can, indeed, already deal with a wide range of measures in the simpler learning situations. However, if one considers such a complex response as talking, there are not only probability, speed, and force, but also intonation, rhythm, volume, pitch, and all the other attributes by which one effectively communicates. It is, therefore, clear that, as with all other aspects of the theory, the anchoring on the output side is a continuing task.

Degree of formalization. Psychologists face a special hazard arising from the fact that they are themselves behaving organisms. Physical and natural scientists do not have quite the same familiarity with their subject matter and so can more easily avoid intuitive and implicit ideas based upon their own introspective experiences. In contrast, the success of most psychological theories, including the ones here under discussion, depends partly on the theorist's shrewd guesses in analyzing a situation and weighing the various factors involved.

There is only one way to insure that there are no critical implicit assumptions, and this is to insist upon a formal statement of the theory. If all terms are unequivocably defined, all postulates precisely formulated, and all steps in the derivation of theorems given in detail, then there can be no serious doubt as to what the theory implies. To the extent that these goals are not met, there is room for side-stepping embarrassing phenomena, predicting on grounds other than provided by the theory, and providing attractive postdictions.

There are other undesirable attributes of relatively informal theories. A notion can be used to advantage in one place and omitted, or at least given a quite different interpretation, in another place that is equally relevant. An example in Hull's theory is the need for short-lived stimulus traces in classical conditioning, but persisting traces for various sequential effects of repeated trials. Another result is that inconsistencies may seem more tolerable. For example, Hull derived conditioned inhibition as a habit, but whereas other habits are permanent, conditioned inhibition cannot be. And, in general, it is difficult to detect the degrees of incompleteness and redundancy.

However, even granting all these things, it is simply not practicable at the present time to write a fully formalized behavior theory of any general significance. Certainly none of the theories we have considered meets this goal, although the deficiencies are less apparent if one restricts them to the limited range of situations for which they were originally constructed.

There would be no particular virtue in attempting to identify all the difficulties in the various postulate sets without, at the same time, offering steps toward their resolution. The fact that the theories are not fully formalized, however, has the unfortunate result that it is difficult to master them solely on the basis of extant writings. Nevertheless, it does permit the theorist to fractionate the task of theory construction since tentative conventions can be used concerning problems that have not been resolved. For example, it is perfectly clear that animals can develop specific hungers based upon a deficient diet, but it is currently conventional to provide a balanced diet and consider hunger as general rather than specific. Furthermore, a less formal system provides the flexibility and modifiability necessary at the present stage of psychological knowledge, since one can hold a number of alternatives concerning the elements in which he is primarily interested while collecting the data designed to select among them.

It is impossible to hold completely in mind a theory about such complex phenomena as behavior provides; the theory must be built, written, and read in some order, with only a hazy impression of what is going to happen in the next section. Almost necessarily, new problems will develop as one goes along, and these frequently reflect back upon earlier solutions. The theorist must, therefore, come full circle and begin again, ideally bringing new data as well as new problems to the task Hull saw particularly clearly that this cycle can go on a great many times without the theorist's achieving a fully satisfactory formulation and that one must simply accept the existence of inadequacies if one is to publish at all.

All other contributions considered, the most significant heritage of the Hullian approach is that it got the enterprise vigorously under way. Probably every author has experienced the sense of accomplishment when his work is first roughly laid out. In the present larger setting, neither Hull nor Spence has claimed even to have finished this phase, much less to have gone beyond it.

THE HULLIAN APPROACH AND EMPIRICAL RESEARCH

We turn now to a consideration of the Hullian approach in action, to the role it has played in stimulating research, and to the degree of success with which it has handled the resulting data. To do this completely, however, would require considerably more time and space than presently available. Most of the articles concerning simple learning phenomena that have been published during the past decade have made explicit reference to Hull's theory or to Spence's many theoretical ideas. Accordingly, few areas in the experimental psychology of learning would not reasonably be included in an exhaustive survey of work relevant to the S-R reinforcement approach.

Therefore, all relevant research areas cannot be treated even briefly. It seems appropriate to select those which have been foci of controversy between the Hullian approach and its various alternatives. These controversies have been discussed by a number of writers, and this survey will lean heavily on citing the references where a more detailed treatment of the issues can be found. The problem of correlated reinforcement is included because of its importance and the writer's interest in it and is discussed in somewhat greater detail because it has not yet been dealt with very much in the literature. Admittedly, this selection leaves out such complex phenomena as perception, problem solving, etc., with which the theory currently is less concerned. Indeed, even presumably simpler phenomena such as exploratory behavior are omitted because they have not yet been definitely argued among learning theorists. One can object, therefore, that the most embarrassing data have been excluded.

Perhaps, in reply, the writer's attitude on such matters should be made explicit. It is an attitude which emphasizes disproving (and thence improving) one's own theory rather than someone else's. That a theory can or cannot adequately handle an apparent contradiction today may arise from so many sources that it is hardly wise to single out one with confidence. Thus the postulates may be in error, but in quite another part than apparent at first glance. The derivational procedures may be faulty or may not yet have been worked out in detail. The analysis of the situation may have incompletely specified the important boundary conditions. Indeed, the phenomena may not even be genuine, but involve various artifacts subsequently to be discovered. Our theories are not sufficiently explicit nor our laws sufficiently certain to support conclusive disproofs. For that matter, Conant [33] has correctly observed that theories are overthrown by better theories, but not by contrary evidence.

The areas described are, therefore, not presented as being crucial but rather as having occupied a prominent place in the recent history of learning theories. They are concerned with important questions, the answers to which partially characterize the theoretical approach. It is not intended, however, to discount the alternative positions, but only to suggest that, viewed across all of the issues, the S-R reinforcement approach appears to be at least holding its own.

Reinforcement (as drive reduction) vs. contiguity in classical conditioning. A one-factor S-R reinforcement theory assumes that reinforcement is a necessary condition for successful classical conditioning. An alternative approach holds that the temporal contiguity of the conditioned stimulus CS, or its trace, with the unconditioned stimulus UCS is not only necessary but itself sufficient. Since Hull adopted a specific drive-reduction hypothesis about the nature of reinforcing events, one issue that has received considerable attention concerns the hypothesized necessity for drive reduction in classical conditioning.

Among the theorists proposing the alternative position are Guthrie [e.g., 57], Tolman [187], Maier and Schneirla [114], Birch and Bitterman [11], and Mowrer [e.g., 128] in so far as autonomic conditioning is concerned. In addition to these writers, the issue has been discussed by Hilgard and Marquis [65], and by Spence [175] and Kendler and Underwood [84].

Data favoring the drive-reduction view have been provided by Loucks [106] and Loucks and Gantt [107]. If the unconditioned leg flexion in dogs was evoked by direct electrical stimulation on the motor side of the central nervous system, then there was no conditioning to a buzzer CS. Conditioning did occur under these conditions only if a reward (food) was given each trial. Furthermore, conditioning occurred without this extra reward if the electrical stimulus was applied on the afferent side, where irradiation to pain tracts could provide subsequent pain reduction.

An argument opposing the drive-reduction view stems from work by Mowrer [127], Mowrer and Aiken [129], Mowrer and Solomon [132], and Bitterman, Reed, and Krauskopf [13]. They have concluded that the form and temporal properties of the termination of a noxious UCS and presumably, therefore, the drive reduction do not affect classical defense conditioning. This argument has been challenged, however, by Miller [121, 122] and Kendler [83]. Further, using the drive-reduction principle, Zeaman and Wegner [206] have shown that whether the conditioned heart response in humans is acceleration or deceleration depends on how the heart rate was changing at the time of the shock (UCS) offset.

Spence [180] reported data favoring drive reduction in the conditioning of the human eyeblink. For example, under conditions which equate level of drive, conditioning is superior with a strong rather than with a weak UCS (airpuff). Thus, it appears that the evidence consistent with the drive-reduction hypothesis is sufficient to justify its continued consideration.

Reinforcement (as some reinforcing event) vs. contiguity in classical conditioning. The theorist need not adopt any specific hypothesis about the nature of reinforcement (identifying reinforcing events by previous demonstrations of their reinforcing property), yet still assume reinforcement to be a necessary condition for successful classical conditioning. Spence has adhered to this position, pointing to the occurrence of the UCS as the normal source of reinforcement. Accordingly, the reinforcement-contiguity issue in this sense revolves around the hypothesized necessity of the UCS, or some other identified reinforcing event, in classical conditioning.

That the UCS need not be given each trial is now a clearly established fact. Since the early experiments of Humphreys [75, 76], a number of experiments have involved partial reinforcement as summarized by Jenkins and Stanley [79]. That partial reinforcement produces only moderately slower learning, only a slightly lower asymptote, and a considerably greater resistance to extinction, appears to contradict a reinforcement interpretation. Several possible solutions to each of these, however, have been provided.

In so far as the rate of learning is concerned, the reinforcement theorist points to other identified sources of reinforcement on trials without the primary reinforcement. Mowrer [125] identified the derived primary reinforcement (reduction of the fear conditioned to the CS) in avoidance conditioning, an analysis equally applicable to defense conditioning. In so far as asymptotic performance is concerned, one can appeal to the factor of varied amount of reinforcement, or one can assume that the inhibition produced by nonreinforced trials is partially reduced on subsequent reinforced trials. Hull [69] provided an analysis of resistance to extinction following partial reinforcement based on the persisting traces of nonreinforcement being a component of the stimulus complex. Accordingly, subjects trained with partial reinforcement have learned to respond to a stimulus complex which includes traces of a preceding nonreinforcement and which is, therefore, more similar to the stimulus complex during extinction. An additional possibility was suggested by Logan, Beier, and Kincaid [105] based on the number of nonreinforced responses which may occur on any one trial. Following continuous reinforcement, the subject may respond several times to the trace of the CS during an extinction trial, and accumulate inhibition from each such nonreinforced response. Partial reinforcement provides extinction experience during training to these older ages of the CS trace, thereby reducing the number of responses per trial and increasing the number of trials necessary to inhibit the response. This can be accomplished not only by partial but by varied reinforcement, as reported by these writers, by Crum, Brown, and Bitterman [35], and by Peterson [138].

It should be noted that each of these analyses identifies the occurrence of the UCS as a necessary condition in the sense that its continued omission eventually results in extinction. That is, for example, the presumed fear reduction which reinforces the CR on non-UCS trials in partial defense conditioning depends on fear which is itself a conditioned response based on the UCS and accordingly subject to extinction.

This is illustrated in the special case of partial reinforcement in which the UCS is omitted on just those trials when an anticipatory CR occurs. This avoidance conditioning procedure was found by Brogden, Lipman, and Culler [25] to be superior to nonavoidance conditioning, a fact which appears to be a problem for reinforcement theories [see 66]. The fear analysis of avoidance conditioning, described by Mowrer [125] and Mowrer and Lamoreaux [131] and challenged by Eglash [39] and Ritchie [143], is dependent on the reinforcement provided by the UCS and implies that the CR will suffer extinction during successful avoidance trials. This implication has received support by Schlosberg [146] and Sheffield [156]. Sheffield also found that the poorer performance by the nonavoidance subjects in the Brogden, Lipman, and Culler experiment resulted from counterconditioning, an analysis consistent with the experimental findings of Logan [98] where counterconditioning was not involved and avoidance was inferior to nonavoidance.[17]

The reinforcement interpretation of classical conditioning, where re-

[17] Avoidance conditioning might also be viewed as a case of correlated reinforcement in classical conditioning, i.e., short latency responses are nonreinforced.

inforcement is viewed in general as some reinforcing event and in particular as the occurrence of the unconditioned stimulus, therefore seems consistent with the findings in these research areas to date.

Reinforcement vs. contiguity in instrumental conditioning. The theorist can take one position on the reinforcement-contiguity issue for classical conditioning and a different position for instrumental conditioning. Accordingly, a separate problem concerns the necessity of reinforcement in instrumental conditioning.

This issue has been among the most popular for discussion since the initial formulation of the law of effect. Among the theorists holding the contiguity alternative are Guthrie [57, 58], Estes [43], Tolman [187], and Birch and Bitterman [10]. Among the many analyses of the issue are Allport [1], Carr [32], Hilgard and Marquis [66], Hilgard [64, 65], Koffka [89], and Meehl [120], and also Maltzman [115, 116], Miller [122], Mowrer [126], and Spence [175]. Waters [195] and, more recently, Postman [140] have provided larger historical surveys of the issue.

The research area that has been most deeply involved in the controversy between reinforcement and contiguity interpretations of instrumental conditioning is so-called latent learning, although this phenomenon probably is more relevant to the response-learning S-R vs. stimulus-learning S-S issue. Since the early study by Blodgett [16], over fifty studies of latent learning in its several forms have appeared in the psychological literature, half or more of which have reported positive results in the sense that when subjects were for the first time appropriately motivated and/or rewarded, their performance suggested some adaptive effect of prior experience.

We shall not attempt to summarize here this large body of data, since summaries and analyses may be found in articles by Birch and Bitterman [10], MacCorquodale and Meehl [110], Seward [148], Spence [175], Thistlethwaite [184], Tolman [188], and Wolpe [204]. Despite this large amount of research and analytical activity, a systematic delineation of just what the empirical phenomena are has not yet been clearly formulated.

The S-R reinforcement theory requires some reward for learning to occur. But animals who have been given experience in a maze without the presence of a known primary reward may, when reward is later given in the goal box, very quickly learn to run the maze without error. This could be treated as extinction of the exploratory response to the culs of the maze, thereby facilitating learning by reducing the incorrect competing response tendencies. The more common interpretation is that learning (rather than unlearning) occurs during the preliminary exposure, and the reinforcement theorist must, in this case, assume that some (admittedly still unspecified) source of reinforcement is available [see 110]. The fact that performance typically improves without apparent reward is consistent with this assumption. Following this tack, a change from no apparent reward to reward is a change in amount of reward which would now be handled through an increase in the incentive variable. Consistent with this, Barry and Logan [4] found that the rat's speed of running down a straight alley increased at the same relative rate following introduction of reward as following an increase in amount of reward.

Latent learning has also been demonstrated by running rats under some identified motive-reward condition, and letting them see an irrelevant goal object somewhere in the maze. When subsequently motivated for this goal object, rats sometimes go directly to the place where it had been seen. This phenomenon has been handled by the use of the fractional anticipatory goal response, assuming that even an irrelevant goal object evokes some r_g [181]. When the drive conditions are changed, this r_g is enhanced and mediates incentive for responses leading to the now desired goal object.

There is no question but that such latent learning phenomena have forced a more detailed elaboration of the S-R reinforcement theory. It appears to this writer that what were taken as fundamental differences between learning theories are becoming markedly attenuated as such elaborations are made.

Response learning vs. stimulus learning in classical conditioning. The present approach assumes that the association formed in classical conditioning is between the trace of the CS and the response evoked by the UCS. Other responses may, of course, occur to the CS through response generalization, but the direct learning is assumed to be an S-R connection. An alternative approach argues that the association formed in classical conditioning is between the stimuli, and that the CR will, therefore, be anticipatory behavior appropriate to the UCS.

Although theorists have not been inclined to do so, there is no necessary restriction against adopting an S-S theory for classical and an S-R theory for instrumental conditioning, or vice versa. Accordingly, the issues are separated here. Spence [174, 175] has analyzed the distinction between S-S and S-R theories, and discussions of the general question may be found in Kendler [82], Campbell [31], Hilgard [63], Tolman [188, 189], Smedslund [163], and Hilgard and Marquis [66].

One sort of argument concerns the similarity between the CR and the UCR. If the association is with the response evoked by the UCS, it is argued, then the CR should be a reproduction, at least in fractional form, of the UCR. Although this is frequently the case, some experimenters [e.g., 21, 22] have noted qualitative differences between the

CR and UCR, and Wickens [198, 199] has shown the reorientation of the subject's hand may change the CR in human finger withdrawal conditioning from flexion to extension. However, until adequate definitions of the response—including mediating responses as emphasized by Dollard and Miller [37]—and of response generalization have been given, it is impossible to determine whether such results are incompatible with an S-R approach.

Another area of empirical research called forth in opposition to an S-R theory is that of sensory preconditioning. If two stimuli, A and B, neither of which evokes the response subsequently introduced, are presented contiguously a number of times, and then a response is conditioned to stimulus B, one may find that stimulus A will also evoke this response. Such sensory preconditioning has been reported by Bitterman et al. [13], Brogden [20, 23, 24], and Karn [80]. Silver and Meyer [159] reported that the asynchronism between A and B follows a function similar to that found in conventional classical conditioning, and Wickens and Briggs [200] have shown that sensory preconditioning may involve mediated or secondary stimulus generalization. More detailed discussions of the area may be found in Miller [122] and Sheffield [157]. It seems clear that further formalization of the definition of the response is necessary before the approach can adequately handle the data from these areas.

Response learning vs. stimulus learning in instrumental conditioning. The present approach assumes that the responses instrumental in obtaining reward become attached to the stimuli coincident with their occurrence. As in classical conditioning, then, the direct learning is assumed to be an S-R connection. An alternative approach assumes that the subject learns a field map of the environment and then behaves in a manner appropriate to his needs.

It should be noted that, even in an S-S theory, response learning must occur someplace, since the subject must "know" what to do. Tolman [189], for example, following the suggestion of MacCorquodale and Meehl [112], explicitly proposed as S-R-S theory, the expectation that R to one S will lead to another S, where R is a performance defined by at least two test situations.

This is illustrated by studies in spatial learning. In one variant, after a response down one alley has been learned, that alley is blocked and a number of alternative alleys are made available. Tolman et al. [191] reported that subjects chose the most direct path to food, and argued that the learning therefore involved approaching the goal place rather than the specific motor response of entering the original alley. Gentry et al. [46] have reported contrasting results. Another variant is to compare the relative ease with which subjects can learn to make different motor responses to get the same place as opposed to making the same motor response to get to different places. Tolman et al. [191] found place learning easier, although Blodgett and McCutchan [17, 18], Hill and Thune [67], and Thompson and Thompson [185] have found the opposite. Galanter and Shaw [45] have shown the importance of an environment rich in external cues for successful place learning.

Perhaps, as Seward [153] has argued, there is no real issue involved here. We have already noted that Spence's and Hull's formulations involving incentive motivation approach closely an expectancy position, and Tolman's specification of his principles of performance reduces the primarily sensory appearance of his approach. From an S-R point of view, questions such as spatial learning help to determine what response was learned, not whether a response was learned, i.e., to what extent did the subject learn to make a specific motor response and to what extent a more molar response of approaching a distinctive cue. The S-R assumption is that he learns both, which suggests quantitative analyses of their relative strengths based upon such information as the distinctiveness of the external cues.

Absolute vs. relational and configurational views of the stimulus in discrimination learning. Whenever an organism is required to respond selectively to the larger, brighter, etc., member of a pair of stimuli, the present approach assumes that each stimulus acquires a separate response tendency. These may, of course, be affected by stimulus generalization between them as well as by afferent stimulus interaction. One alternative approach assumes that the subject compares the stimuli and responds to the relationship (e.g., brightness) between them. Another alternative approach holds that the subject learns to respond appropriately to each stimulus configuration facing it.

The research area most directly concerned with the absolute vs. relational view of the stimulus has been that of transposition. If the subject is first trained to select (say) the brighter of a pair of stimuli, transposition is evidenced if he subsequently selects the brighter of a new pair of test stimuli differing in absolute brightness from the original pair. Spence [164, 166, 169] has shown that his absolute position not only implies transposition based on the generalization of excitatory and inhibitory tendencies, but also that the degree of transposition should vary in gradient fashion as the difference between the training and test stimuli is increased.

Studies of transposition, e.g., Ehrenfreund [41], Hunter [77], Kendler [83], and Thompson [186], have yielded data generally consistent with the Spence analysis. An opposing analysis can be found in James [78], and some of the studies reported by Kluver [87] are not currently subsumable under the absolute schema. These are ones in which subjects who have learned to select (say) the larger of two circles subsequently select the larger of two test triangles. Presumably, however, the single-dimension analysis by Spence could be extended to deal with qualitative as well as quantitative stimulus changes, and this form of transposition would then also follow from stimulus generalization.

Turning to the absolute vs. configurational issue, the opposing position has been stated by Gulliksen and Wolfle [56] and argued by Bitterman [12] and Weise and Bitterman [197]. This argument revolves around a comparison of the ease of learning simultaneous and successive discriminations.[18] In a simultaneous discrimination situation, two alleys (say, white vs. black) are presented together equally often in the right and left positions. The subject is required to consistently select the positive (white or black) alley regardless of its position. In the successive problem, white and black are never paired, both alleys being white on half the trials and black on the other half. The subject is here required to go left when the alleys are white and right when they are black (or vice versa).

The successive discrimination problem must be carefully distinguished from the single-presentation form of discrimination learning. The latter also does not involve joint presentation of the cues. But in that form, there is only one alley and the subject is rewarded for responding when it is one brightness and not rewarded if he responds when it is the other brightness. Therefore, in successive discrimination, each alley separately involves single-presentation discrimination, i.e., the left alley is positive when it is white and negative when it is black, while the right alley is black-positive and white-negative.

Spence's [178] analysis of the successive discrimination problem pointed out that, since no solution based on single cues is available, patterning is involved. That is, the problem cannot be solved by always going left or right, or white or black. Instead, the subject must learn the patterns, "white on the right" and "black on the left." Spence assumed that the subject can learn such a configurational discrimination if required to do so, but that such learning should be relatively difficult from an absolute point of view.

Studies of the relative ease of simultaneous and successive discrimination [15, 29, 30, 178] have yielded conflicting results, and related studies

---

[18] The discussion of this issue has emphasized the nature of the response while it is here discussed in terms of the stimulus. The absolute view holds that each stimulus element acquires an approach response tendency, and choice behavior can be predicted from these combined approach tendencies. Even when configurational learning is required, the absolute view assumes separate response tendencies to patterns or compounds of stimulus elements. In contrast, the configurational view holds that the total stimulus complex cannot meaningfully be decomposed, and that the subject learns distinctive responses to each total configuration.

[62, 97] suggest that the successive discrimination problem is a difficult one for rats. Accordingly, the question is still in doubt, and one can reasonably expect that additional work will force a further elaboration of the ways by which the absolute approach handles various kinds of patterning and relational learning.

Continuous vs. noncontinuous interpretations of discrimination learning. Whenever a response is followed by reward, this approach assumes that an increment in excitatory strength is added to each effective stimulus trace coincident with the response. Thus, if the subject responds to the brighter of two stimuli, and is rewarded, then his tendency to approach the brighter stimulus on the next trial is increased. The effective stimulus (that actually impinging on the appropriate sensorium), however, may change in the course of discrimination learning if the subject must also learn to orient his receptors in such a way as to receive maximal differential stimulation. An alternative approach assumes that the subject tests "hypotheses" in a discrimination problem, and that he learns nothing except the correctness or incorrectness of the hypothesis then being tested.

The alternative approach was initially suggested by Lashley [94] and has been adopted by Krechevsky [89, 90, 91]. According to this position, during the early trials when the subject may be testing an inappropriate hypothesis, his response tendencies to the relevant cues are unaffected. For example, if the problem is a black-white discrimination, and the subject is testing a left-going hypothesis, then he is learning nothing about the correctness of white or black. Therefore, no detrimental effect will result from reversing the discrimination (i.e., making the initially positive cue negative, and vice versa). Further analyses favoring the noncontinuous interpretation may be found in Lashley [95] and Tolman [188].

Spence's theory of discrimination learning [164, 167] clearly implies a detrimental effect of such a reversal unless the problem requires the learning of receptor-orienting acts in order to maximize differential stimulation and hence permit discrimination. His analyses of the issue [168, 175] have emphasized this point since it may account for the apparently contradictory findings of Krechevsky [93] and Lashley and Wade [96]. Indeed, Ehrenfreund [41] found a detrimental effect of reversal when differential stimulus reception was insured, but not when receptor-orienting acts were required. And the large bulk of studies [19, 52, 113, 141, 144, 165, 171, 193] have yielded results favorable to the continuous interpretation.

Correlated reinforcement. Correlated reinforcement refers to conditions in which some dimension of the reward is varied systematically with some quantitative dimension of the response. For example, a rat can be given more food the harder he presses a bar in a Skinner box. Because such conditions have not been widely studied or described, and because they provide a particularly important and interesting research area, a somewhat more detailed description is necessary here. In doing so, we shall use the force a rat exerts on a bar, and the amount of reward he gets for it, as illustrative, but it should be apparent that a similar description could be made for other response dimensions, such as speed, other responses, such as running an alley, and other reinforcement dimensions, such as the time of delay of reward.

Under conventional conditions, the amount of reward is related to the force the rat exerts on a bar in a minimal, all-or-none fashion. The rat must press the bar hard enough to be considered a response and to activate the feeding mechanism, but increasing the force above this level has no further effect on the amount of reward. This minimum force can be varied, requiring different subjects to exceed different forces in order to get reward. A maximum may also be applied, so that force must fall within set limits in order for the reward to be received. All these kinds of conditions have been studied, and generally, rats show reasonably good adjustment to the requirements which prevail.

If one permits amount of reward to vary in more than an all-or-none fashion, a large number of additional possibilities appear. The rat can be given more reward the harder he presses the bar, or the softer he presses it, or for intermediate forces. More complex conditions can be used if reward varies for the same force of response. One example would be when hard presses get a large average reward, but with a large variance in amount, whereas soft presses get less reward on the average, but with little variance.

This already enormous number of possible conditions of correlated reinforcement can be doubled by adding another dimension of the reward, say its delay. Delay can be varied with force in all of the ways that amount can: harder forces get the reward sooner, etc. And, of course, both delay and amount can be correlated simultaneously with force in any combination.

Finally, if the bar response is performed on a discrete trial basis, another response dimension can be added, response speed. Reward can then be correlated with force-speed combinations. And there are many other quantitative characteristics of the response, such as the pattern of forces over a behavior chain on a ratio schedule, with which the reward can be correlated; but since few of even the simpler conditions have been systematically studied, it would be inappropriate to speculate about the more complex ones.

The brief descriptions given, however, do emphasize the very small range of reinforcement conditions which has thus far been studied in the laboratory. This in turn is important because the more complex conditions of correlated reinforcement are common in the natural environment. This is most apparent in the case of skills where one must adjust the response so as to maximize reward: the force of a golf swing, the speed of a billiard shot, the timing of a musical performance, etc. But the rewards for many other responses depend upon quantitative characteristics of the way they are performed: the loudness with which one delivers a lecture, the vigor with which one punishes his children, the speed with which one applies the brakes of his car, etc. Indeed, most everyday behavior is geared to conditions of correlated reinforcement.

Beyond this, correlated reinforcement is particularly relevant to the question of response definition. The nature of this problem and the role of correlated reinforcement in answering it are discussed in the next section.

The macromolar-micromolar distinction. Hull's 1943 postulates were explicitly restricted to conditions in which reinforcement was not systematically correlated with any response dimension. In *A Behavior System,* however, Hull briefly described a micromolar level of analysis with which to handle correlated reinforcement. At the micromolar level, quantitatively different behaviors (e.g., different forces) are treated as different responses rather than different strengths of the same response. Hull's proposed solution was to consider different forces to be different responses whenever reinforcement is correlated with force, and to continue using the classical macromolar approach otherwise.

The writer [103] has argued exactly the reverse, that the classical macromolar approach is appropriate only for conditions of correlated reinforcement. Thus, the macromolar system can deal with response speed because how soon the subject gets the reward is correlated with how fast he responds. However, since Hull's proposal was based on an analogy with the treatment accorded qualitatively different behaviors, it will be useful to review the logic of this latter treatment.

In predicting the behavior of a rat in a Skinner box, a relatively molar response class, bar depression, is typically employed. All behaviors which involve an adequate movement of the bar are aggregated together notwithstanding any qualitative differences among them. The basis of aggregation is that all such behaviors are indiscriminately and equally reinforced. Should, however, one choose selectively to reinforce only responses by the right paw, the appropriate response class then would be "right paw bar depression." Although this latter class aggregates a narrower range of behaviors, the aggregation is on precisely the same basis, namely that all members of the class are equally reinforced. Thus, whether responses with the right paw belong in the same class with left paw responses depends upon whether they are differentially reinforced.[19]

Hull proposed to deal with quantitatively different behaviors in an analogous fashion. Thus, different forces are treated as different responses only if they are differentially reinforced. This is the micromolar level of analysis for conditions of correlated reinforcement.

The analogy, however, breaks down under further comparison. Recall that, on the qualitative side, unless right paw and left paw responses are treated as different, one does not distinguish between them either in recording data or in making predictions. Instead, because they are aggregated into the same response class, predictions and observations both concern the probability of occurrence of either paw behaviors indiscriminately. Contrariwise, on the quantitative side, when different forces are not treated as different responses, the macromolar analysis nevertheless permits observations and predictions about force, now viewed as an index of response strength. Consistent application of the analogy would require that, at the macromolar level, one does not distinguish between forces at all and is concerned only with the joint probability of occurrence of behaviors of any force.

At first thought, one might attempt to justify these divergent ways of treating quantitative and qualitative variations in behavior with the observation that force does, in point of fact, vary systematically with training. Is it not reasonable, then, to hold that this systematic variation reflects changes in response strength unless distorted by differential reinforcement of force? Further thought, however, will show that analogous changes occur on the qualitative side with training, i.e., the response becomes progressively more skillful and efficient. These latter changes, in so far as one wishes to study them, are dealt with by the theory as different responses, learned selectively on the basis of differential reinforcement. There appears to be no logical distinction, on the grounds of systematic change with practice, between qualitative and quantitative dimensions of behavior, and the preponderance of quantitative response measures can be attributed to the availability of convenient, ordered units.

There would seem to be two approaches which are consistent with this analysis. The one that is most apparent in the above comments may be summarized as follows: the response class to be used is jointly dependent upon the interests of the experimenter and the conditions of reinforcement. One may classify in a single macromolar class all behaviors, differing both quantitatively and qualitatively, which are not dif-

[19] What is meant by behaviors belonging in different response classes is that separate excitatory tendencies must be calculated. There would presumably be response generalization between classes, depending upon the degree of difference.

ferentially reinforced, and predict only about the probability of occurrence of any member of this aggregation indiscriminately. Within these upper bounds, if an experimenter wishes to observe and predict about qualitatively different behaviors within the macromolar class, then he must shift to a relatively macromolecular level, treating these behaviors as different responses. Similarly, should he wish to observe or predict about quantitatively different behaviors within the macromolar class, then he must shift to a relatively micromolar level in which these variations are treated as different responses.

The second alternative is more in keeping with the classical Hullian approach and involves treating quantitative and qualitative variations in behavior differently. Qualitative variations are handled in the same manner as above, i.e., the level of molarity is jointly dependent upon the conditions of reinforcement and the interests of the experimenter. Quantitative variations, however, are never treated as different responses, but instead are viewed as response measures which may be taken as indices of response strength.

In following the second alternative, Hull excluded conditions of correlated reinforcement, and Skinner [162] has used correlated reinforcement as one argument against the use of measures other than response rate. It is, therefore, necessary to describe in some detail the equilibrium solution to the problem of predicting behavior under conditions of correlated reinforcement within the classical Hullian approach.

The equilibrium solution. In correlated reinforcement situations, one must deal with the mutual interdependence of response and reward, i.e., not only does reinforcement affect response strength, and hence performance, but performance also affects the reinforcement received. These dependence relations, however, are temporally isolated, performance on one trial partially determining reward on that trial,[20] and this reward, in turn, affecting performance on subsequent trials. An equilibrium solution is appropriate for such situations.

A system is in stable equilibrium when the predicted variable simultaneously satisfies the several constraints acting upon it and when any deviation from such a simultaneous solution leads to forces driving the variable back toward it. Consider the force a rat exerts on a bar under conditions in which increasing forces provide decreasing amounts of reward. His performance is constrained by the two functions shown in Fig. 1. On the one hand there is the incentive function relating force to amount, determined under conditions of uncorrelated reinforcement, which shows that the force the rat exerts on the bar increases as the

---

[20] We shall ignore the more complex conditions in which response on one trial determines reward on some subsequent trial, where reward on one trial is determined by cumulative performance over a series of previous trials, etc.

amount of reinforcement increases. On the other hand, there is the function describing the terms available, i.e., the amount that will be given depending on the force exerted. Simultaneous solution of these two functions enables determination of an equilibrium.

Suppose, for example, that the rat should exert a force equal to F_1 in the figure. By referring to the terms function, we determine that he will receive M_1 amount of reinforcement. But referring an M_1 amount back to the incentive function, we observe that the rat will exert a force less than F_1 for that amount and so his performance will tend to shift

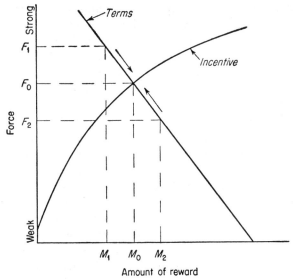

FIG. 1. Graphic presentation of the equilibrium solution for correlated reinforcement. See text for a description of this solution.

down toward a lower force more in keeping with the obtained reward. In an inversely analogous fashion, should the rat exert a force of F_2, the obtained amount M_2 will be seen to be appropriate to a response force greater than F_2. It is only force F_0 which will receive just that amount, M_0, which provides incentive for precisely that F_0 force.[21]

A variety of further complications arises if this solution is generalized to other situations. One must deal with individual differences in incentive

[21] In a situation in which the organism's behavior shifts immediately to precisely the level appropriate for the reward obtained on the preceding trial, one would have to determine whether the system is an "exploding" one. Since, however, the change in a rat's performance is relatively gradual, this problem need not be considered here.

functions, discontinuous terms functions, and other possibilities which complicate the analysis but which do not alter its basic logic. As a single, more complex example, let us briefly consider a situation in which the rat must press below a certain force in order to get reward, harder presses being nonreinforced.

Now since the rat's force will vary from trial to trial, he is viewed as being on a partial reinforcement schedule; as his average force increases, the percentage of reinforcements decreases. Clearly, then, if his average force is so high as to never involve presses below the cutoff, extinction would occur and force would decrease. If, however, his average force were so low as to never involve presses above the cutoff, he would get reward every time and thus be led to increase his force. Between these two extremes, there is an average force which gets reward just frequently enough to maintain that force.

This kind of condition is a particularly good one to point out the distinction between the macromolar and micromolar approaches. Take the instance where the reward is received on half the trials, which would occur when the median force is equal to the cutoff. By the classical macromolar approach, the response of "bar depression" is then reinforced on a 50 per cent partial reinforcement schedule. By the micromolar approach, "strong bar depressions" receive 100 per cent nonreinforcement, and "weak bar depressions" receive 100 per cent reinforcement. In the former analysis there is a single response tendency and performance must stabilize at a level insuring only enough weak responses to provide a sufficient probability of reinforcement to maintain the response. By the latter analysis, weak and strong responses have separate response tendencies and the performance level must insure only enough strong responses to maintain the response discrimination.

This description has been intended to show that the classical macromolar system can deal, in principle at least, with a wide variety of conditions of correlated reinforcement by means of an equilibrium solution. Indeed, there are other ways to view correlated reinforcement situations by means of macromolar theory. For example, in the last mentioned illustration, one could assume that the nonreinforcements which occur whenever the rat presses above the cutoff produce inhibition, and that the effective excitatory potential is in this way maintained at a low level which produces only weak responses. Accordingly, there is no a priori reason why correlated reinforcement should require alteration of the macromolar assumption. Instead, one must ask how well the analysis fits the known data.

Evaluation. To evaluate properly the equilibrium solution for correlated reinforcement, it is necessary to have a quantitative estimate of the appropriate incentive function together with obtained performance under some condition of correlated reinforcement. While there are a few studies providing the latter kind of information, the absence of the incentive function obtained on those apparatus puts the evaluation at a lower level of quantitative specificity where success is less demanding.

All the studies known to the writer have used conditions in which reward was given only if performance fell within a specified range. One type has involved varying the minimum performance that will be reinforced, as in the study by Arnold [3] where only bar responses by the rat above 5 to 30 gm were rewarded. Another type has involved setting a maximum performance above which the response is nonreinforced. Early work by Skinner [160], as recently extended by Wilson and Keller [201], required the subject to delay at least a specified interval (i.e., have a long latency) between responses in a free-responding situation. Finally, the Arnold study also included a combination of the two, where both a minimum and maximum were specified and only bar responses within a restricted range of forces were rewarded.

The equilibrium analysis would predict that the subject's adjustment to such conditions would show a shift in average performance appropriate to any shift in the minimum and/or maximum performance specified, but that variability of behavior around this average would have to insure sufficient nonreinforcements to keep response tendency at the equilibrium level. For example, in the Skinner situation, requiring say a 20-sec latency between responses, the amount and delay of reinforcement might, if received continuously, produce incentive for 5-sec latency. However, this amount and delay of reward, if received on only part of the trials, would presumably produce less incentive and hence a longer latency. Without knowledge of performance under various patterns of uncorrelated reinforcement, the most that can be said is that adjustment cannot be perfect, i.e., at least some nonreinforced responses will have to occur to reduce response tendency.

At this level of quantitative specificity, all of the results by these experimenters appear consistent with the equilibrium solution. All have obtained distributions of performance showing some but imperfect adjustment to the specified conditions.

The only research designed to permit quantitative evaluation of the equilibrium analysis is currently in progress in the writer's laboratory. Correlating amount and delay of reward with the rat's speed of running down a straight alley, we have found that some kinds of conditions seem to fit the equilibrium analysis quite well; other conditions, however, show clear deviations in that performance is affected not only by what reward is received but by how it is correlated with the response dimension. Generally, so far it appears that speed can best be predicted by attending to the differential reinforcement given different speeds. That is, the likelihood that the rat will run at a particular speed depends upon what he gets for it compared with what he can get for running at some other speed. This is, of course, the kind of result a micromolar theory would predict.

The reader should recognize that the entire discussion of correlated reinforcement has been cast at a level not unique to a Hullian theory. The functions have not been broken down into specific intervening variables with particular anchoring operations. Instead, the equilibrium solution has been left at a level appropriate to any stimulus-response approach which might choose to use it. What appears to be the singular, unique underlying assumption is one that is shared by most such systems, namely that quantitative variations in performance reflect variations in a molar response tendency. If this is true, then failure of the solution to fit empirical data would strongly favor adoption of the micromolar approach in which quantitatively different behaviors are viewed as different responses with separate response tendencies.

However, a micromolar theory is enormously complex as a derivational instrument. It would, therefore, seem sensible to resist abandoning the simpler and more conventional level of analysis until the accumulated evidence is more conclusive and until any alternative answers to the problem have been found wanting. At the same time, transition to a micromolar approach may ultimately prove fruitful.

SUMMARY AND CONCLUSION

It is hoped that bringing together under one cover even brief descriptions of a number of diverse but related matters concerning the Hullian approach will serve some value. But it must be emphasized that many of these have been dealt with by a number of others and that it has been assumed that interested readers will also avail themselves of the listed references for a more complete perspective of the Hullian approach at mid-twentieth century.

This paper has attempted to reflect a dynamic approach to theory in psychology, constantly adapting to expanding knowledge. We have briefly described what the goals of the approach are and how they are conceptualized in a larger behavior science. We have discussed the present methods for attaining these goals, emphasizing the necessity of reliable systematic data for improving the theory. We have described some of the theoretical ideas which have been suggested, particularly those by Spence and Hull, and have pointed out how these have been and are being affected by detailed, quantitative investigations.

We have seen that the Hullian approach is initially characterized by the use of intervening variables in a postulate system. It has emphasized not only the importance of formalizing the postulates, but also the possibility of quantifying them. It is more finely distinguished from other quantitative intervening variable approaches by particular assumptions about the notions of stimulus and of response, about the nature of the associative variable, and about the conditions necessary for learning.

We have discussed these latter assumptions in the context of controversies in which the approach has been involved and have seen that most of the difficulties encountered by it have arisen when one leaves the simpler situations with which it was originally concerned. The allegedly embarrassing situations are more complex either in the sense that one cannot immediately identify all the boundary conditions which must be used along with the postulates in making deductions, or in the sense that new variables which have not yet been explicitly formulated are involved. Historically, one can see that, as these situations have been analyzed for their boundary conditions and possible new variables, the present approach has not only been found to be consistent with the phenomena, but has extended our ability to predict the results of further systematic studies. It is perhaps not unreasonable to extrapolate this trend and believe that problems not now amenable to Hullian analysis will, in due time, be resolved.

REFERENCES

1. Allport, G. W. Effect: a secondary principle of learning. *Psychol. Rev.,* 1946, **53**:335–347.

2. Ammons, R. B. Acquisition of motor skills: I. Quantitative analysis and theoretical formulation. *Psychol. Rev.,* 1947, **54**:263–281.

3. Arnold, W. J. An exploratory investigation of primary response generalization. *J. comp. physiol. Psychol.,* 1947, **38**:87–102.

4. Barry, H., III, & Logan, F. A. Latent learning in a straight alley. *Psychol. Rep.,* 1957, **3**:88.

5. Bergmann, G. Outline of an empiricist philosophy of physics. I and II. *Amer. J. Physics,* 1943, **11**:248–258, 335–342.

6. Bergmann, G. Theoretical psychology. *Annu. Rev. Psychol.,* 1953, **4**:435–458.

7. Bergmann, G., & Spence, K. W. Operationism and theory in psychology. *Psychol. Rev.,* 1941, **18**:1–14.

8. Berlyne, D. E. Attention, perception, and behavior theory. *Psychol. Rev.,* 1951, **58**:137–146.

9. Berlyne, D. E. Knowledge and stimulus-response psychology. *Psychol. Rev.,* 1954, **61**:245–254.

10. Birch, H. G., & Bitterman, M. E. Reinforcement and learning: the process of sensory integration. *Psychol. Rev.,* 1949, **56**:292–308.

11. Birch, H. G., & Bitterman, M. E. Sensory integration and cognitive theory. *Psychol. Rev.,* 1951, **58**:355–361.

12. Bitterman, M. E. Spence on the problem of patterning. *Psychol. Rev.*, 1953, 60:123–126.

13. Bitterman, M. E., Reed, P. C., & Krauskopf, J. The effect of the duration of the unconditional stimulus upon conditioning and extinction. *Amer. J. Psychol.*, 1952, 65:256–262.

14. Bitterman, M. E., Reed, P. C., & Kubala, A. L. The strength of sensory preconditioning. *J. exp. Psychol.*, 1953, 46:178–182.

15. Bitterman, M. E., & Wodinsky, J. Simultaneous and successive discrimination. *Psychol. Rev.*, 1953, 60:371–376.

16. Blodgett, H. C. The effect of the introduction of reward upon the maze performance of rats. *Univer. Calif. Publ. Psychol.*, 1929, 4:113–134.

17. Blodgett, H. C., & McCutchan, K. Place versus response learning in the simple T-maze. *J. exp. Psychol.*, 1947, 37:412–422.

18. Blodgett, H. C., & McCutchan, K. Relative strength of place and response learning in the T-maze. *J. comp. physiol. Psychol.*, 1948, 41:17–24.

19. Blum, R. A., & Blum, J. S. Factual issues in the "continuity" controversy. *Psychol. Rev.*, 1949, 56:33–50.

20. Brogden, W. J. Sensory pre-conditioning. *J. exp. Psychol.*, 1939, 25:323–332.

21. Brogden, W. J. Unconditioned stimulus-substitution in the conditioning process. *Amer. J. Psychol.*, 1939, 52:46–55.

22. Brogden, W. J. Conditioned flexion response in dogs reestablished and maintained with change of locus in the application of the unconditioned stimulus. *J. exp. Psychol.*, 1940, 27:583–600.

23. Brogden, W. J. Test of sensory preconditioning with human subjects. *J. exp. Psychol.*, 1942, 31:505–517.

24. Brogden, W. J. Sensory preconditioning of human subjects. *J. exp. Psychol.*, 1947, 37:527–540.

25. Brogden, W. J., Lipman, E. A., & Culler, E. The role of incentive in conditioning and extinction. *Amer. J. Psychol.*, 1938, 51:109–117.

26. Brown, J. S. Pleasure-seeking behavior and the drive-reduction hypothesis. *Psychol. Rev.*, 1955, 62:169–180.

27. Burke, C. J. A theory relating momentary effective reaction potential to response latency. *Psychol. Rev.*, 1949, 56:208–223.

28. Burros, R. H. The application of the method of paired comparisons to the study of reaction potential. *Psychol. Rev.*, 1951, 58:60–66.

29. Calvin, A. D., & Siebel, J. L. A further investigation of response selection in simultaneous and successive discrimination. *J. exp. Psychol.*, 1954, 48:339–342.

30. Calvin, A. D., & Williams, C. M. Simultaneous and successive discrimination in a single unit hollow-square maze. *J. exp. Psychol.*, 1956, 52:47–50.

31. Campbell, D. T. Operational delineation of "what is learned" via the transposition experiment. *Psychol. Rev.*, 1954, 61:167–174.

32. Carr, H. A. The law of effect, a round table discussion. I. *Psychol. Rev.*, 1938, 45:191–199.

33. Conant, J. B. *On understanding science.* New Haven, Conn.: Yale Univer. Press, 1947.

34. Cotton, J. W. On making predictions from Hull's theory. *Psychol. Rev.,* 1955, **62**:303–314.

35. Crum, L., Brown, W. L., & Bitterman, M. E. The effect of delayed partial reinforcement on resistance to extinction. *Amer. J. Psychol.,* 1951, **64**:228–237.

36. Denny, M. R. The role of secondary reinforcement in a partial reinforcement learning situation. *J. exp. Psychol.,* 1946, **36**:373–389.

37. Dollard, J., & Miller, N. E. *Personality and psychotherapy.* New York: McGraw-Hill, 1950.

38. Dufort, R. H., & Kimble, G. A. Changes in response strength with changes in the amount of reinforcement. *J. exp. Psychol.,* 1956, **51**:185–191.

39. Eglash, A. The dilemma of fear as a motivating force. *Psychol. Rev.,* 1952, **59**:376–379.

40. Ehrenfreund, D. An experimental test of the continuity theory of discrimination with pattern vision. *J. comp. physiol. Psychol.,* 1948, **41**:408–422.

41. Ehrenfreund, D. A study of the transposition gradient. *J. exp. Psychol.,* 1952, **43**:81–87.

42. Ellis, D. S. Inhibition theory and the effect variable. *Psychol. Rev.,* 1953, **60**:383–392.

43. Estes, W. K. Toward a statistical theory of learning. *Psychol. Rev.,* 1950, **57**:94–107.

44. Freides, D. Goal box cues and pattern of reinforcement. Unpublished doctoral dissertation, Yale Univer., 1956.

45. Galanter, E., & Shaw, W. A. "Cue" versus "reactive inhibition" in place and response learning. *J. comp. physiol. Psychol.,* 1954, **47**:395–398.

46. Gentry, G., Brown, W. L., & Kaplan, J. J. An experimental analysis of the spatial location hypothesis in learning. *J. comp. physiol. Psychol.,* 1947, **40**:309–322.

47. Gibson, E. J. A systematic application of the concepts of generalization and differentiation to verbal learning. *Psychol. Rev.,* 1940, **47**:196–229.

48. Ginsberg, A. Hypothetical constructs and intervening variables. *Psychol. Rev.,* 1954, **61**:119–131.

49. Gleitman, H., Nachmias, J., & Neisser, U. The S-R reinforcement theory of extinction. *Psychol. Rev.,* 1954, **61**:23–33.

50. Goss, A. E. A stimulus-response analysis of the interaction of cue-producing and instrumental responses. *Psychol. Rev.,* 1955, **62**:20–31.

51. Goss, A. E., & Rabaioli, E. J. Response strength in a modified Thorndikian multiple-choice situation as a function of varying proportions of reinforcement. *J. exp. Psychol.,* 1952, **43**:106–114.

52. Grandene, L., & Harlow, H. F. Generalization of the characteristics of a single learned stimulus by monkeys. *J. comp. physiol. Psychol.,* 1948, **41**:327–338.

53. Grant, D. A., & Schipper, L. M. The acquisition and extinction of

conditioned eyelid responses as a function of the percentage of fixed-ratio reinforcement. *J. exp. Psychol.*, 1952, **43**:313–320.

54. Grice, G. R. The relation of secondary reinforcement to delayed reward in visual discrimination learning. *J. exp. Psychol.*, 1948, **38**:1–16.

55. Grice, G. R., & Goldman, H. M. Generalized extinction and secondary reinforcement in visual discrimination learning with delayed reward. *J. exp. Psychol.*, 1955, **50**:197–200.

56. Gulliksen, H., & Wolfle, D. A. A theory of learning and transfer. *Psychometrika*, 1938, **3**:127–149.

57. Guthrie, E. R. *The psychology of learning.* New York: Harper, 1935.

58. Guthrie, E. R. Association and the law of effect. *Psychol. Rev.*, 1940, **47**:127–148.

59. Harker, G. S. Delay of reward and performance of an instrumental response. *J. exp. Psychol.*, 1956, **51**:303–310.

60. Harlow, H. F. The formation of learning sets. *Psychol. Rev.*, 1949, **56**:51–65.

61. Harlow, H. F. Mice, monkeys, men, and motives. *Psychol. Rev.*, 1953, **60**:23–32.

62. Heyman, M. N. Transfer in discrimination learning following three conditions of initial training. Unpublished doctoral dissertation, State Univer. of Iowa, 1951.

63. Hilgard, E. R. The nature of the conditioned response. I. The case for and against stimulus substitution. *Psychol. Rev.*, 1936, **43**:366–385.

64. Hilgard, E. R. *Theories of learning.* New York: Appleton-Century-Crofts, 1948.

65. Hilgard, E. R. *Theories of learning.* (2d ed.) New York: Appleton-Century-Crofts, 1956.

66. Hilgard, E. R., & Marquis, D. G. *Conditioning and learning.* New York: Appleton-Century-Crofts, 1940.

67. Hill, C. W., & Thune, L. E. Place and response learning in the white rat under simplified and mutually isolated conditions. *J. exp. Psychol.*, 1952, **43**:289–297.

68. Hull, C. L. Knowledge and purpose as habit mechanisms. *Psychol. Rev.*, 1930, **37**:511–525.

69. Hull, C. L. Psychology seminar memoranda, 1940–41. Unpublished ms. on file in Yale Library.

70. Hull, C. L., et al. *Mathematico-deductive theory of rote learning.* New Haven, Conn.: Yale Univer. Press, 1940.

71. Hull, C. L. *Principles of behavior.* New York: Appleton-Century-Crofts, 1943.

72. Hull, C. L. Behavior postulates and corollaries—1949. *Psychol. Rev.*, 1950, **57**:173–180.

73. Hull, C. L. *Essentials of behavior.* New Haven, Conn.: Yale Univer. Press, 1951.

74. Hull, C. L., et al. A proposed quantification of habit strength. *Psychol. Rev.*, 1947, **54**:237–254.

75. Humphreys, L. G. The effect of random alternation of reinforcement

on the acquisition and extinction of conditioned eyelid reactions. *J. exp. Psychol.*, 1939, 25:141–158.

76. Humphreys, L. G. Extinction of conditioned psychogalvanic responses following two conditions of reinforcement. *J. exp. Psychol.*, 1940, 37:71–78.

77. Hunter, I. M. L. The absolute and relative theories of transposition behavior in rats. *J. comp. physiol. Psychol.*, 1953, 46:493–497.

78. James, H. An application of Helson's theory of adaptation level to the problem of transposition. *Psychol. Rev.*, 1953, 60:345–352.

79. Jenkins, W. O., & Stanley, J. C., Jr. Partial reinforcement: a review and critique. *Psychol. Bull.*, 1950, 47:193–234.

80. Karn, H. W. Sensory pre-conditioning and incidental learning in human subjects. *J. exp. Psychol.*, 1947, 37:540–545.

81. Kellogg, W. N. "Superstitious" behavior in animals. *Psychol. Rev.*, 1949, 56:172–175.

82. Kendler, H. H. Reflections and confessions of a reinforcement theorist. *Psychol. Rev.*, 1951, 58:368–374.

83. Kendler, H. H. "What is learned?" A theoretical blind alley. *Psychol. Rev.*, 1952, 59:269–277.

84. Kendler, H. H., & Underwood, B. J. The role of reward in conditioning theory. *Psychol. Rev.*, 1948, 55:209–215.

85. Kendler, T. S. An experimental investigation of transposition as a function of the difference between training and test stimuli. *J. exp. Psychol.*, 1950, 40:552–562.

86. Kimble, G. A. An experimental test of a two-factor theory of inhibition. *J. exp. Psychol.*, 1949, 39:15–23.

87. Kluver, H. *Behavior mechanisms in monkeys.* Chicago: Univer. Chicago Press, 1933.

88. Koch, S. Clark L. Hull. In Estes, W. K., et al., *Modern learning theory.* New York: Appleton-Century-Crofts, 1954.

89. Koffka, K. The law of effect in learning and its interpretation. *Int. Congr. Psychol.*, 1937.

90. Krechevsky, I. "Hypotheses" in rats. *Psychol. Rev.*, 1932, 52:516–532.

91. Krechevsky, I. "Hypothesis" vs "chance" in the presolution period in sensory discrimination learning. *Univer. Calif. Publ. Psychol.*, 1932, 6:27–44.

92. Krechevsky, I. The genesis of "hypotheses" in rats. *Univer. Calif. Publ. Psychol.*, 1932, 6:45–64.

93. Krechevsky, I. A study of the continuity of the problem-solving process. *Psychol. Rev.*, 1938, 45:107–133.

94. Lashley, K. S. *Brain mechanisms and intelligence.* Chicago: Univer. Chicago Press, 1929.

95. Lashley, K. S. An examination of the "continuity" theory as applied to discrimination learning. *J. gen. Psychol.*, 1942, 26:241–265.

96. Lashley, K. S., & Wade, M. The Pavlovian theory of generalization. *Psychol. Rev.*, 1946, 53:72–87.

97. Lawrence, D. H. Acquired distinctiveness of cues: I. Transfer between discriminations on the basis of familiarity with the stimuli. *J. exp. Psychol.*, 1949, **39**:770–784.

98. Logan, F. A. A comparison of avoidance and nonavoidance eyelid conditioning. *J. exp. Psychol.*, 1951, **42**:390–393.

99. Logan, F. A. The role of delay of reinforcement in determining reaction potential. *J. exp. Psychol.*, 1952, **43**:393–399.

100. Logan, F. A. Three estimates of differential excitatory tendency. *Psychol. Rev.*, 1952, **59**:300–307.

101. Logan, F. A. A note on stimulus intensity dynamism (V). *Psychol. Rev.*, 1954, **61**:77–80.

102. Logan, F. A., Olmstead, D. L., Rosner, B. S., Schwartz, R. D., & Stevens, C. M. *Behavior theory and social science.* New Haven, Conn.: Yale Univer. Press, 1955.

103. Logan, F. A. A micromolar approach to behavior theory. *Psychol. Rev.*, 1956, **63**:63–73.

104. Logan, F. A., Beier, E. M., & Ellis, R. A. The effect of varied reinforcement on speed of locomotion. *J. exp. Psychol.*, 1955, **49**:260–266.

105. Logan, F. A., Beier, E. M., & Kincaid, W. D. Extinction following partial and varied reinforcement. *J. exp. Psychol.*, 1956, **52**:65–70.

106. Loucks, R. B. The experimental delimitation of neural structures essential for learning: the attempt to condition striped muscle responses with faradization of the sigmoid gyri. *J. Psychol.*, 1935, **1**:5–44.

107. Loucks, R. B., & Gantt, W. H. The conditioning of striped muscle responses based upon faradic stimulation of dorsal roots and dorsal columns of the spinal cord. *J. comp. Psychol.*, 1938, **25**:415–426.

108. Luchins, A. S., & Luchins, E. H. Variables and functions. *Psychol. Rev.*, 1954, **61**:315–323.

109. Maatsch, J. L. Reinforcement and extinction phenomena. *Psychol. Rev.*, 1954, **61**:111–118.

110. MacCorquodale, K., & Meehl, P. E. On a distinction between hypothetical constructs and intervening variables. *Psychol. Rev.*, 1948, **55**:95–107.

111. MacCorquodale, K., & Meehl, P. E. On the elimination of cul entries without obvious reinforcement. *J. comp. physiol. Psychol.*, 1951, **44**:367–371.

112. MacCorquodale, K., & Meehl, P. E. Edward C. Tolman. In Estes, W. K., et al., *Modern learning theory.* New York: Appleton-Century-Crofts, 1954.

113. McCulloch, T. L., & Pratt, J. C. A study of the pre-solution period in weight discrimination by white rats. *J. comp. Psychol.*, 1934, **18**:271–290.

114. Maier, N. R. F., & Schneirla, T. C. Mechanisms in conditioning. *Psychol. Rev.*, 1942, **49**:117–134.

115. Maltzman, I. An interpretation of learning under an irrelevant need. *Psychol. Rev.*, 1950, **57**:181–187.

116. Maltzman, I. The Blodgett and Haney types of latent learning experiment. *Psychol. Bull.*, 1952, **49**:52–60.

117. Maltzman, I. Thinking: from a behavioristic point of view. *Psychol. Rev.*, 1955, **62**:275–287.

118. Marx, M. H. Intervening variable or hypothetical construct. *Psychol. Rev.*, 1951, **58**:235–247.

119. Maze, J. R. Do intervening variables intervene? *Psychol. Rev.*, 1954, **61**:226–235.

120. Meehl, P. E. On the circularity of the law of effect. *Psychol. Bull.*, 1950, **47**:52–75.

121. Miller, N. E. Learnable drives and rewards. In S. S. Stevens (Ed.), *Handbook of experimental psychology*. New York: Wiley, 1951.

122. Miller, N. E. Comments on multiple-process conceptions of learning. *Psychol. Rev.*, 1951, **58**:375–381.

123. Miller, N. E., & Dollard, J. *Social learning and imitation*. New Haven, Conn.: Yale Univer. Press, 1941.

124. Moore, O. K., & Lewis, D. J. Learning theory and culture. *Psychol. Rev.*, 1952, **59**:380–388.

125. Mowrer, O. H. A stimulus-response analysis of anxiety and its role as a reinforcing agent. *Psychol. Rev.*, 1939, **46**:553–564.

126. Mowrer, O. H. The law of effect and ego psychology. *Psychol. Rev.*, 1946, **53**:321–334.

127. Mowrer, O. H. *Learning theory and personality dynamics*. New York: Ronald, 1950.

128. Mowrer, O. H. Two-factor learning theory: summary and comment. *Psychol. Rev.*, 1951, **58**:350–354.

129. Mowrer, O. H., & Aiken, E. G. Contiguity vs. drive-reduction in conditioned fear: temporal variations in conditioned and unconditioned stimulus. *Amer. J. Psychol.*, 1954, **67**:26–38.

130. Mowrer, O. H., & Jones, H. Habit strength as a function of the pattern of reinforcement. *J. exp. Psychol.*, 1945, **35**:293–311.

131. Mowrer, O. H., & Lamoreaux, R. R. Fear as an intervening variable in avoidance conditioning. *J. comp. Psychol.*, 1946, **39**:29–50.

132. Mowrer, O. H., & Solomon, L. N. Contiguity vs. drive-reduction in conditioned fear: the proximity and abruptness of drive-reduction. *Amer. J. Psychol.*, 1954, **67**:15–25.

133. Murdock, G. P. *Social structure*. New York: Macmillan, 1949.

134. Noble, C. E. An analysis of meaning. *Psychol. Rev.*, 1952, **59**:421–431.

135. Perin, C. T. A quantitative investigation of the delay-of-reinforcement gradient. *J. exp. Psychol.*, 1943, **32**:37–51.

136. Perin, C. T. The effect of delayed reinforcement upon the differentiation of bar responses in white rats. *J. exp. Psychol.*, 1943, **32**:96–109.

137. Perkins, C. C., Jr. The relation of secondary rewards to gradients of reinforcement. *J. exp. Psychol.*, 1947, **37**:377–392.

138. Perkins, C. C., Jr. The stimulus conditions which follow learned responses. *Psychol. Rev.*, 1955, **62**:341–349.

139. Peterson, L. R. Variable delayed reinforcement. *J. comp. physiol. Psychol.*, 1956, **49**:232–234.

140. Postman, L. The history and present status of the law of effect. *Psychol. Bull.*, 1947, 6:489–563.

141. Prentice, W. C. H. Continuity in human learning. *J. exp. Psychol.*, 1949, **39**:187–194.

142. Ramond, C. K. Performance in instrumental learning as a joint function of delay of reinforcement and time of deprivation. *J. exp. Psychol.*, 1954, **47**:248–250.

143. Ritchie, B. F. Can reinforcement theory account for avoidance. *Psychol. Rev.*, 1951, 58:382–386.

144. Ritchie, B. F., Ebeling, E., & Roth, W. Evidence for continuity in the discrimination of vertical and horizontal patterns. *J. comp. physiol. Psychol.*, 1950, 43:168–180.

145. Schlosberg, H. Conditioned responses in the white rat. II. Conditioned response based upon shock to foreleg. *J. genet. Psychol.*, 1936, 49: 107–138.

146. Schlosberg, H. The relationship between success and the laws of conditioning. *Psychol. Rev.*, 1937, 44:379–394.

147. Schwartz, R. D. Social factors in the development of legal control: a case study of two Israeli settlements. *Yale Law J.*, 1954, 63:471–491.

148. Seward, J. P. A theoretical derivation of latent learning. *Psychol. Rev.*, 1947, 54:83–98.

149. Seward, J. P. Secondary reinforcement as tertiary motivation: a revision of Hull's revision. *Psychol. Rev.*, 1950, 57:362–374.

150. Seward, J. P. Delayed reward learning. *Psychol. Rev.*, 1952, 59: 200–201.

151. Seward, J. P. Hull's system of behavior: an evaluation. *Psychol. Rev.*, 1954, 61:145–159.

152. Seward, J. P. The constancy of I–V: a critique of intervening variables. *Psychol. Rev.*, 1955, 62:155–169.

153. Seward, J. P. Reinforcement and expectancy: two theories in search of a controversy. *Psychol. Rev.*, 1956, 63:105–113.

154. Seward, J. P. Drive, incentive, and reinforcement. *Psychol. Rev.*, 1956, 63:195–205.

155. Seward, J. P., Weldon, R. J. Response latency as a function of change in delay of reward. *J. comp. physiol. Psychol.*, 1953, 46:184–189.

156. Sheffield, F. D. Avoidance training and the contiguity principle. *J. comp. physiol. Psychol.*, 1948, 41:165–177.

157. Sheffield, F. D. The contiguity principle in learning theory. *Psychol. Rev.*, 1951, 58:362–367.

158. Sheffield, V. F. Extinction as a function of partial reinforcement and distribution of practice. *J. exp. Psychol.*, 1949, 39:511–526.

159. Silver, C. A., & Meyer, D. R. Temporal factors in sensory preconditioning. *J. comp. physiol. Psychol.*, 1954, 47:57–59.

160. Skinner, B. F. *The behavior of organisms.* New York: Appleton-Century-Crofts, 1938.

161. Skinner, B. F. "Superstition" in the pigeon. *J. exp. Psychol.*, 1948, 38:168–172.

162. Skinner, B. F. Are theories of learning necessary? *Psychol. Rev.,* 1950, 57:193–216.

163. Smedslund, J. The problem of "what is learned?" *Psychol. Rev.,* 1953, 60:157–158.

164. Spence, K. W. The nature of discrimination learning in animals. *Psychol. Rev.,* 1936, 43:427–449.

165. Spence, K. W. Analysis of the formation of visual discrimination habits in chimpanzees. *J. comp. Psychol.,* 1937, 23:77–100.

166. Spence, K. W. The differential response in animals to stimuli varying within a single dimension. *Psychol. Rev.,* 1937, 44:430–444.

167. Spence, K. W. Gradual versus sudden solution of discrimination problems by chimpanzees. *J. comp. Psychol.,* 1938, 25:213–224.

168. Spence, K. W. Continuous versus non-continuous interpretations of discrimination learning. *Psychol. Rev.,* 1940, 47:271–288.

169. Spence, K. W. The basis of solution by chimpanzees of the intermediate size problem. *J. exp. Psychol.,* 1942, 31:247–271.

170. Spence, K. W. The nature of theory construction in contemporary psychology. *Psychol. Rev.,* 1944, 51:47–68.

171. Spence, K. W. An experimental test of the continuity and noncontinuity theories of discrimination learning. *J. exp. Psychol.,* 1945, 35: 253–266.

172. Spence, K. W. The role of secondary reinforcement in delayed reward learning. *Psychol. Rev.,* 1947, 54:1–8.

173. Spence, K. W. The postulates and methods of behaviorism. *Psychol. Rev.,* 1948, 55:67–78.

174. Spence, K. W. Cognitive versus stimulus-response theories of learning. *Psychol. Rev.,* 1950, 57:159–172.

175. Spence, K. W. Theoretical interpretations of learning. In S. S. Stevens (Ed.), *Handbook of experimental psychology.* New York: Wiley, 1951.

176. Spence, K. W. Theoretical interpretations of learning. In C. P. Stone (Ed.), *Comparative psychology.* (3d ed.) Englewood Cliffs, N.J.: Prentice-Hall, 1951.

177. Spence, K. W. Mathematical formulations of learning phenomena. *Psychol. Rev.,* 1952, 59:152–160.

178. Spence, K. W. The nature of response in discrimination learning. *Psychol. Rev.,* 1952, 59:89–93.

179. Spence, K. W. The relation of response latency and speed to the intervening variables and N in S-R theory. *Psychol. Rev.,* 1954, 61:209–216.

180. Spence, K. W. *Behavior theory and conditioning.* New Haven, Conn.: Yale Univer. Press, 1956.

181. Spence, K. W., Bergmann, G., & Lippitt, R. A study of simple learning under irrelevant motivational-reward conditions. *J. exp. Psychol.,* 1950, 40:539–551.

182. Stellar, E. The physiology of motivation. *Psychol. Rev.,* 1954, 61: 5–22.

183. Taylor, J. S. Reaction latency as a function of reaction potential and behavior oscillation. *Psychol. Rev.*, 1950, 57:375–389.

184. Thistlethwaite, D. A critical review of latent learning and related experiments. *Psychol. Bull.*, 1951, 48:97–129.

185. Thompson, M. E., & Thompson, J. P. Reactive inhibition as a factor in maze learning: II. The role of reactive inhibition in studies of place learning versus response learning. *J. exp. Psychol.*, 1949, 39:883–891.

186. Thompson, R. Transposition in the white rat as a function of stimulus comparison. *J. exp. Psychol.*, 1955, 50:185–190.

187. Tolman, E. C. *Purposive behavior in animals and men.* New York: Century, 1932.

188. Tolman, E. C. Cognitive maps in rats and men. *Psychol. Rev.*, 1948, 55:189–208.

189. Tolman, E. C. Principles of performance. *Psychol. Rev.*, 1955, 62: 315–326.

190. Tolman, E. C., Hall, C. S., & Bretnall, E. P. A disproof of the law of effect and a substitution of the laws of emphasis, motivation, and disruption. *J. exp. Psychol.*, 1932, 15:601–614.

191. Tolman, E. C., Ritchie, B. F., & Kalish, D. Studies in spatial learning. I. Orientation and the short cut. *J. exp. Psychol.*, 1946, 36:13–24.

192. Tolman, E. C., Ritchie, B. F., & Kalish, D. Studies in spatial learning. II. Place learning versus response learning. *J. exp. Psychol.*, 1946, 36: 221–229.

193. Walk, R. D. Effect of discrimination reversal on human discrimination learning. *J. exp. Psychol.*, 1952, 44:410–419.

194. Wasserman, H. N. A unifying theoretical approach to motor learning. *Psychol. Rev.*, 1952, 59:278–284.

195. Waters, R. H. The law of effect as a principle of learning. *Psychol. Bull.*, 1934, 31:408–425.

196. Weinstock, S. Resistance to extinction of a running response following partial reinforcement under widely spaced trials. *J. comp. physiol. Psychol.*, 1954, 47:318–322.

197. Weise, P., & Bitterman, M. E. Response selection in discrimination learning. *Psychol. Rev.*, 1951, 58:185–195.

198. Wickens, D. D. Studies of response generalization in conditioning. I. Stimulus generalization during response generalization. *J. exp. Psychol.*, 1943, 33:221–227.

199. Wickens, D. D. Stimulus identity as related to response specificity and response generalization. *J. exp. Psychol.*, 1948, 38:389–394.

200. Wickens, D. D., & Briggs, G. E. Mediated stimulus generalization as a factor in sensory preconditioning. *J. exp. Psychol.*, 1951, 42:197–200.

201. Wilson, M. P., & Keller, F. S. On the selective reinforcement of spaced responses. *J. comp. physiol. Psychol.*, 1953, 46:190–193.

202. Wilson, W., Weiss, E. J., & Amsel, A. Two tests of the Sheffield hypothesis concerning resistance to extinction, partial reinforcement, and distribution of practice. *J. exp. Psychol.*, 1955, 50:51–60.

203. Wolpe, J. The neurophysiology of learning and delayed reward learning. *Psychol. Rev.*, 1952, **59**:192–199.

204. Wolpe, J. Theory construction for Blodgett's latent learning. *Psychol. Rev.*, 1953, **60**:340–344.

205. Wyckoff, L. B., Jr. The role of observing responses in discrimination learning. Part I. *Psychol. Rev.*, 1952, **59**:431–442.

206. Zeaman, D., & Wegner, N. The role of drive reduction in the classical conditioning of an autonomically mediated response. *J. exp. Psychol.*, 1954, **48**:349–354.

A CASE HISTORY IN SCIENTIFIC METHOD[1]

B. F. SKINNER
Harvard University

INTRODUCTION

A scientist is an extremely complex organism, and his behavior still resists a successful empirical analysis. Nevertheless, if anything useful is to be said about him, either in trying to understand his behavior or in inculcating similar behavior in others, it will be by way of an empirical, rather than a formal, analysis. As an antiformalist it would be inconsistent of me to describe my own scientific activity in the formal framework of Project A. I have therefore reacted to the proposal of the director by illustrating my own philosophy of science with a personal history.

It has been said that college teaching is the only profession for which there is no professional training, and it is commonly argued that this is because our graduate schools train scholars and scientists rather than teachers. We are more concerned with the discovery of knowledge than with its dissemination. But can we justify ourselves quite so easily? It is a bold thing to say that we know how to train a man to be a scientist. Scientific thinking is the most complex and probably the most subtle of all human activities. Do we actually know how to shape up such behavior, or do we simply mean that some of the people who attend our graduate schools eventually become scientists?

Except for a laboratory course which acquaints the student with standard apparatus and standard procedures, the only explicit training in scientific method generally received by a young psychologist is a course

[1] This paper, originally conceived in response to the invitation to contribute to the present study, was presented in substantially similar form as the presidential address to the Eastern Psychological Association, April, 1955, and published in *The American Psychologist,* May, 1956.

in statistics—not the introductory course, which is often required of so many kinds of students that it is scarcely scientific at all, but an advanced course which includes "model building," "theory construction," and "experimental design." But it is a mistake to identify scientific practice with the formalized constructions of statistics and scientific method. These disciplines have their place, but it does not coincide with the place of scientific research. They offer *a* method of science but not, as is so often implied, *the* method. As formal disciplines they arose very late in the history of science, and most of the facts of science have been discovered without their aid. It takes a great deal of skill to fit Faraday with his wires and magnets into the picture which statistics gives us of scientific thinking. And most current scientific practice would be equally refractory, especially in the important initial stages. It is no wonder that the laboratory scientist is puzzled and often dismayed when he discovers how his behavior has been reconstructed in the formal analyses of scientific method. He is likely to protest that this is not at all a fair representation of what he does.

But his protest is not likely to be heard. For the prestige of statistics and scientific methodology is enormous. Much of it is borrowed from the high repute of mathematics and logic, but much of it derives from the flourishing state of the art itself. Some statisticians are professional people employed by scientific and commercial enterprises. Some are teachers and pure researchers who give their colleagues the same kind of service for nothing—or at most a note of acknowledgment. Many are zealous people who, with the best of intentions, are anxious to show the nonstatistical scientist how he can do his job more efficiently and assess his results more accurately. There are strong professional societies devoted to the advancement of statistics, and hundreds of technical books and journals are published annually.

Against this, the practicing scientist has very little to offer. He cannot refer the young psychologist to a book which will tell him how to find out all there is to know about a subject matter, how to have the good hunch which will lead him to devise a suitable piece of apparatus, how to develop an efficient experimental routine, how to abandon an unprofitable line of attack, how to move on most rapidly to later stages of his research. The work habits which have become second nature to him have not been formalized by anyone, and he may feel that they possibly never will be. As Richter [5] has pointed out, "Some of the most important discoveries have been made without any plan of research," and "there are researchers who do not work on a verbal plane, who cannot put into words what they are doing."

If we are interested in perpetuating the practices responsible for the present corpus of scientific knowledge, we must keep in mind that some very important parts of the scientific process do not now lend themselves to mathematical, logical, or any other formal treatment. We do not know enough about human behavior to know how the scientist does what he does. Although statisticians and methodologists may seem to tell us, or at least imply, how the mind works—how problems arise, how hypotheses are formed, deductions made, and crucial experiments designed —we as psychologists are in a position to remind them that they do not have methods appropriate to the empirical observation or the functional analysis of such data. These are aspects of human behavior, and no one knows better than we how little can at the moment be said about them.

Some day we shall be better able to express the distinction between empirical analysis and formal reconstruction, for we shall have an alternative account of the behavior of Man Thinking. Such an account will not only plausibly reconstruct what a particular scientist did in any given case, it will permit us to evaluate practices and, I believe, to teach scientific thinking. But that day is some little distance in the future. Meanwhile we can only fall back on examples.

Some time ago the director of Project A of the American Psychological Association asked me to describe my activities as a research psychologist. I went through a trunkful of old notes and records and, for my pains, reread some of my earlier publications. This has made me all the more aware of the contrast between the reconstructions of formalized scientific method and at least one case of actual practice. Instead of amplifying the points I have just made by resorting to a generalized account which is not available, I should like to discuss a case history. It is not one of the case histories we should most like to have, but what it lacks in importance is perhaps somewhat offset by accessibility. I therefore ask you to imagine that you are all clinical psychologists—a task which becomes easier and easier as the years go by—while I sit across the desk from you or stretch out upon this comfortable leather couch.

A CASE HISTORY

The first thing I can remember happened when I was only twenty-two years old. Shortly after I had graduated from college, Bertrand Russell published a series of articles in the old *Dial* magazine on the epistemology of John B. Watson's behaviorism. I had had no psychology as an undergraduate but I had had a lot of biology, and two of the books which my biology professor had put into my hands were Loeb's *Physiology of the Brain* and the newly published Oxford edition of Pavlov's *Conditioned Reflexes*. And now here was Russell extrapolating the principles of an objective formulation of behavior to the problem of knowledge. Many years later when I told Lord Russell that his articles were responsible for my interest in behavior, he could only exclaim, "Good Heavens! I had always supposed that those articles had demolished Behaviorism!" But at any rate he had taken Watson seriously, and so did I.

When I arrived at Harvard for graduate study, the air was not exactly full of behavior, but Walter Hunter was coming in once a week from Clark University to give a seminar, and Fred Keller, also a graduate student, was an expert in both the technical details and the sophistry of behaviorism. Many a time he saved me as I sank into the quicksands of an amateurish discussion of "What is an image?" or "Where is red?" I soon came into contact with W. J. Crozier, who had studied under Loeb. It had been said of Loeb, and might have been said of Crozier, that

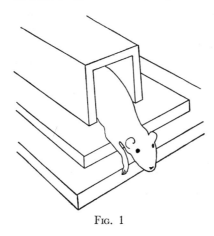

FIG. 1

he "resented the nervous system." Whether this was true or not, the fact was that both these men talked about animal behavior without mentioning the nervous system and with surprising success. So far as I was concerned, they canceled out the physiological theorizing of Pavlov and Sherrington and thus clarified what remained of the work of these men as the beginnings of an independent science of behavior. My doctoral thesis was in part an operational analysis of Sherrington's synapse, in which behavioral laws were substituted for supposed states of the central nervous system.

But the part of my thesis at issue here was experimental. So far as I can see, I began simply by looking for lawful processes in the behavior of the intact organism. Pavlov had shown the way; but I could not then, as I cannot now, move without a jolt from salivary reflexes to the important business of the organism in everyday life. Sherrington and Magnus had found order in surgical segments of the organism. Could not something of the same sort be found, to use Loeb's phrase, in "the organism as a whole"? I had the clue from Pavlov: control your conditions and you will see order.

It is not surprising that my first gadget was a silent release box, operated by compressed air and designed to eliminate disturbances when introducing a rat into an apparatus. I used this first in studying the way a rat adapted to a novel stimulus. I built a soundproofed box containing a specially structured space. A rat was released, pneumatically, at the far end of a darkened tunnel from which it emerged in exploratory fashion into a well-lighted area. To accentuate its progress and to facilitate recording, the tunnel was placed at the top of a flight of steps, something like a functional Parthenon (Fig. 1). The rat would peek out from the tunnel, perhaps glancing suspiciously at the one-way window through which I was watching it, then stretch itself cautiously down the steps. A soft click (carefully calibrated, of course) would cause it to pull back into the tunnel and remain there for some time. But repeated clicks had less and less of an effect. I recorded the rat's advances and retreats by moving a pen back and forth across a moving paper tape.

The major result of this experiment was that some of my rats had babies. I began to watch young rats. I saw them right themselves and crawl about very much like the decerebrate or thalamic cats and rabbits of Magnus. So I set about studying the postural reflexes of young rats.

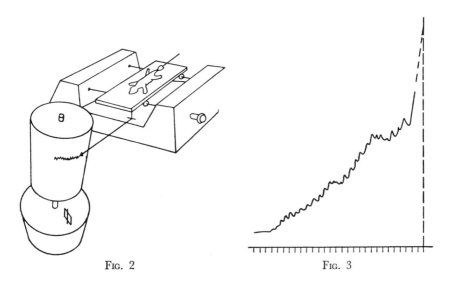

Fig. 2   Fig. 3

Here was a first principle not formally recognized by scientific method-ologists: when you run onto something interesting, drop everything else and study it. I tore up the Parthenon and started over.

If you hold a young rat on one hand and pull it gently by the tail, it will resist you by pulling forward and then, with a sudden sharp spring which usually disengages its tail, it will leap out into space. I decided to study this behavior quantitatively. I built a light platform covered with cloth and mounted it on tightly stretched piano wires (Fig. 2). Here was a version of Sherrington's torsion-wire myograph, originally designed to record the isometric contraction of the tibialis anticus of a cat, but here adapted to the response of a whole organism. When the tail of the young rat was gently pulled, the rat clung to the cloth floor and tugged forward. By amplifying the fine movement of the platform, it was possible to get a good kymograph record of the tremor in this motion and then, as the pull against the tail was increased, of the desperate spring into the air (Fig. 3).

Now, baby rats have very little future, except as adult rats. Their behavior is literally infantile and cannot be usefully extrapolated to everyday life. But if this technique would work with a baby, why not try it on a mature rat? To avoid attaching anything to the rat, it should be possible to record, not a pull against the substrate, but the ballistic thrust exerted as the rat runs forward or suddenly stops in response to my calibrated click. So, invoking the first principle of scientific practice

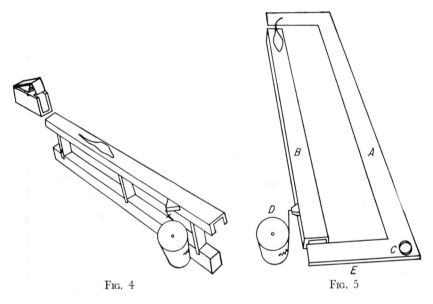

Fig. 4   Fig. 5

again, I threw away the piano-wire platform and built a runway, 8 ft long. This was constructed of light wood, in the form of a U girder, mounted rigidly on vertical glass plates, the elasticity of which permitted a very slight longitudinal movement (Fig. 4). The runway became the floor of a long tunnel, not shown, at one end of which I placed my soundless release box and at the other end myself, prepared to reinforce the rat for coming down the runway by giving it a bit of wet mash, to sound a click from time to time when it had reached the middle of the runway, and to harvest kymograph records of the vibrations of the substrate.

Now for a second unformalized principle of scientific practice: some ways of doing research are easier than others. I got tired of carrying the rat back to the other end of the runway. A back alley was therefore added (Fig. 5). Now the rat could eat a bit of mash at point C, go down the back alley A, around the end as shown, and back home by runway B. The experimenter at E could collect records from the kymograph at D in comfort. In this way a great many records were made of the forces exerted against the substratum as rats ran down the alley and occasionally stopped dead in their tracks as a click sounded (Fig. 6).

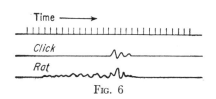

Fig. 6

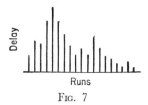

Fig. 7

There was one annoying detail, however. The rat would often wait an inordinately long time at C before starting down the back alley on the next run. There seemed to be no explanation for this. When I timed these delays with a stop watch, however, and plotted them, they seemed to show orderly changes (Fig. 7). This was, of course, the kind of thing I was looking for. I forgot all about the movements of the substratum and began to run rats for the sake of the delay measurements alone. But there was now no reason why the runway had to be 8 ft long and, as the second principle came into play again, I saw no reason why the rat could not deliver its own reinforcement.

A new apparatus was built. In Fig. 8 we see the rat eating a piece of food just after completing a run. It produced the food by its own action. As it ran down the back alley A to the far

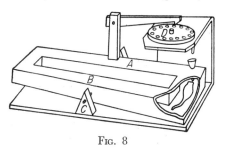

Fig. 8

end of the rectangular runway, its weight caused the whole runway to tilt slightly on the axis C and this movement turned the wooden disc D, permitting a piece of food in one of the holes around its perimeter to drop through a funnel into a food dish. The food was pearl barley, the only kind I could find in the grocery stores in reasonably uniform pieces. The rat had only to complete its journey by coming down the home stretch B to enjoy its reward. The experimenter was able to enjoy *his* reward at the same time, for he had only to load the magazine, put in a rat, and relax. Each tilt was recorded in a slowly moving kymograph.

A third unformalized principle of scientific practice: some people are lucky. The disc of wood from which I had fashioned the food magazine was taken from a storeroom of discarded apparatus. It happened to have a central spindle, which fortunately I had not bothered to cut off. One day it occurred to me that if I wound a string around the spindle and allowed it to unwind as the magazine was emptied (Fig. 9), I would get a different kind of record. Instead of a mere report of the up-and-down movement of the runway, as a series of pips as in a polygraph, I would get a *curve*. And I knew that science made great use of curves, although, so far as I could discover, very little of pips on a polygram. The difference between the old type of record at A (Fig. 10) and the new at B may not seem great, but as it turned out the curve revealed things in the rate of responding, and in changes in that rate, which would certainly otherwise have been missed. By allowing the string to unwind rather than to wind, I had got my curve in an awkward cartesian quadrant, but that was easily remedied. Psychologists have adopted cumulative curves

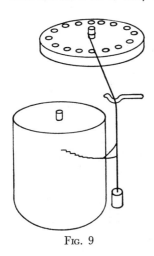

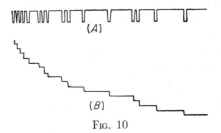

(A)

(B)

Fig. 9   Fig. 10

only very slowly, but I think it is fair to say that they have become an indispensable tool for certain purposes of analysis.

Eventually, of course, the runway was seen to be unnecessary. The rat could simply reach into a covered tray for pieces of food, and each movement of the cover could operate a solenoid to move a pen one step in a cumulative curve. The first major change in rate observed in this way was due to ingestion. Curves showing how the rate of eating declined with the time of eating comprised the other part of my thesis. But a refinement was needed. The behavior of the rat in pushing open the door was not a normal part of the ingestive behavior of *Rattus rattus*. The act was obviously learned but its status as part of the final performance was not clear. It seemed wise to add an initial conditioned response connected with ingestion in a quite arbitrary way. I chose the first device which came to hand—a horizontal bar or lever placed where it could be conveniently depressed by the rat to close a switch which operated a magnetic magazine. Ingestion curves obtained with this initial response in the chain were found to have the same properties as those without it.

Now, as soon as you begin to complicate an apparatus, you necessarily invoke a fourth principle of scientific practice: apparatus sometimes breaks down. I had only to wait for the food magazine to jam to get an extinction curve. At first I treated this as a defect and hastened to remedy the difficulty. But eventually, of course, I deliberately disconnected the magazine. I can easily recall the excitement of that first complete extinction curve (Fig. 11). I had made contact with Pavlov at last! Here was a curve uncorrupted by the physiological process of ingestion. It was an orderly change due to nothing more than a special contingency of reinforcement. It was pure behavior! I am not saying that I would not have got around to extinction curves without a breakdown in the apparatus; Pavlov had given too strong a lead in that direction. But it is still no exaggeration to say that some of the most

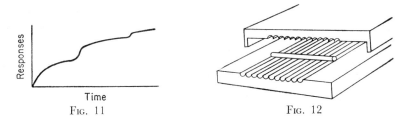

Fig. 11   Fig. 12

interesting and surprising results have turned up first because of similar accidents. Foolproof apparatus is no doubt highly desirable, but Charles Ferster and I in recently reviewing the data from a five-year program of research found many occasions to congratulate ourselves on the fallibility of relays and vacuum tubes.

I then built four soundproofed ventilated boxes, each containing a lever and a food magazine and supplied with a cumulative recorder, and was on my way to an intensive study of conditioned reflexes in skeletal behavior. I would reinforce every response for several days and then extinguish for a day or two, varying the number of reinforcements, the amount of previous magazine training, and so on.

At this point I made my first use of the deductive method. I had long since given up pearl barley as too unbalanced a diet for steady use. A neighborhood druggist had shown me his pill machine, and I had had one made along the same lines (Fig. 12). It consisted of a fluted brass bed across which one laid a long cylinder of stiff paste (in my case a MacCollum formula for an adequate rat diet). A similarly fluted cutter was then lowered onto the cylinder and rolled slowly back and forth, converting the paste into about a dozen spherical pellets.

These were dried for a day or so before use. The procedure was painstaking and laborious. Eight rats eating a hundred pellets each per day could easily keep up with production. One pleasant Saturday afternoon I surveyed my supply of dry pellets and, appealing to certain elemental theorems in arithmetic, deduced that unless I spent the rest of that afternoon and evening at the pill machine, the supply would be exhausted by 10:30 Monday morning.

Since I do not wish to deprecate the hypothetico-deductive method, I am glad to testify here to its usefulness. It led me to apply our second principle of unformalized scientific method and to ask myself why *every* press of the lever had to be reinforced. I was not then aware of what had happened at the Brown laboratories, as Harold Schlosberg later told the story. A graduate student had been given the task of running a cat through a difficult discrimination experiment. One Sunday the student found the supply of cat food exhausted. The stores were closed and so, with a beautiful faith in the frequency theory of learning, he ran the cat as usual and took it back to its living cage unrewarded. Schlosberg reports that the cat howled its protest continuously for nearly forty-eight hours. Unaware of this I decided to reinforce a response only once every minute and to allow all other responses to go unreinforced. There were two results: (1) my supply of pellets lasted almost indefinitely and (2) each rat stabilized at a fairly constant rate of responding.

Now, a steady state was something I was familiar with from physical chemistry, and I therefore embarked upon the study of periodic reinforcement. I soon found that the constant rate at which the rat stabilized depended upon how hungry it was. Hungry rat, high rate; less hungry rat, lower rate. At that time I was bothered by the practical problem of controlling food deprivation. I was working half time at the Medical School (on chronaxie of subordination!) and could not maintain a good schedule in working with the rats. The rate of responding under periodic reinforcement suggested a scheme for keeping a rat at a constant level of deprivation. The argument went like this: suppose you reinforce the rat, not at the end of a given period, but when it has completed the number of responses ordinarily emitted in that period. And suppose you use substantial pellets of food and give the rat continuous access to the lever. Then, except for periods when the rat sleeps, it should operate the lever at a constant rate around the clock. For, whenever it grows slightly hungrier, it will work faster, get food faster, and become less hungry, while whenever it grows slightly less hungry, it will respond at a lower rate, gets less food, and grow hungrier. By setting the reinforcement at a given number of responses it should even be possible to hold the rat at any given level of deprivation. I visualized a machine with a dial which one could set to make available, at any time of day or night, a rat in a given state of deprivation. Of course, nothing of the sort happens. This is "fixed-ratio" rather than "fixed-interval" reinforcement, and as I soon found out, it produces a very different type of performance. This is an example of a fifth unformalized principle of scientific practice, but one which has at least been named. Walter Cannon described it with a word invented by Horace Walpole: *serendipity*—the art of finding one thing while looking for something else.

This account of my scientific behavior up to the point at which I published my results in a book called *The Behavior of Organisms* is as exact in letter and spirit as I can now make it. The notes, data, and publications which I have examined do not show that I ever behaved in the manner of Man Thinking as described by John Stuart Mill or John Dewey or as in reconstructions of scientific behavior by other philosophers of science. I never faced a Problem which was more than the eternal problem of finding order. I never attacked a problem by constructing a Hypothesis. I never deduced Theorems or submitted them to Experimental Check. So far as I can see, I had no preconceived Model of behavior—certainly not a physiological or mentalistic one, and I believe, not a conceptual one. The "reflex reserve" was an abortive, though operational, concept which was retracted a year or so after publication in a paper at the Philadelphia meeting of the APA. It lived up to my opinion of theories in general by proving utterly worthless in suggesting further experiments. Of course, I was working on a basic Assumption—that there was order in behavior if I could only discover it—but such an assumption is not to be confused with the hypotheses of deductive theory. It is also true that I exercised a certain Selection of Facts, not because of relevance to theory but because one fact was more orderly than another. If I engaged in Experimental Design at all, it was simply to complete or extend some evidence of order already observed.

Most of the experiments described in *The Behavior of Organisms* were done with groups of four rats. A fairly common reaction to the book was that such groups were too small. How did I know that other groups of four rats would do the same thing? Keller, in defending the book, countered with the charge that groups of four were too *big*. Unfortunately, however, I allowed myself to be persuaded of the contrary. This was due in part to my association at the University of Minnesota with W. T. Heron. Through him I came into close contact for the first time with traditional animal psychology. Heron was interested in inherited maze behavior, inherited activity, and certain drugs—the effects of which could then be detected only through the use of fairly large groups. We did an experiment together on the effect of starvation on the rate of pressing a lever and started the new era with a group of 16 rats. But we had only 4 boxes, and this was so inconvenient that Heron applied for a grant and built a battery of 24 lever-boxes and cumulative recorders. I supplied an attachment which would record not only the mean performance of all 24 rats in a single averaged curve, but mean curves for 4 subgroups of 12 rats each and 4 subgroups of six rats each [3]. We thus provided for the design of experiments according to the principles of R. A. Fisher, which were then coming into vogue. We had, so to speak, mechanized the latin square.

With this apparatus Heron and I published a study of extinction in maze-bright and maze-dull rats using 95 subjects. Later I published mean extinction curves for groups of 24, and W. K. Estes and I did our work on anxiety with groups of the same size. But although Heron and I could properly voice the hope that "the possibility of using large groups of animals greatly improves upon the method as previously reported, since tests of significance are provided for and properties of behavior not apparent in single cases may be more easily detected," in actual practice that is not what happened. The experiments I have just mentioned are almost all we have to show for this elaborate battery of boxes. Undoubtedly more work could be done with it and would have its place, but something had happened to the natural growth of the method. You cannot easily make a change in the conditions of an experiment when 24 apparatus have to be altered. Any gain in rigor is more than matched by a loss in flexibility. We were forced to confine ourselves to processes which could be studied with the base lines already developed in earlier work. We could not move on to the discovery of other processes or even to a more refined analysis of those we were working with. No matter how significant might be the relations we actually demonstrated, our statistical Leviathan had swum aground. The art of the method had stuck at a particular stage of its development.

Another accident rescued me from mechanized statistics and brought me back to an even more intensive concentration on the single case. In essence, I suddenly found myself face to face with the engineering problem of the animal trainer. When you have the responsibility of making absolutely sure that a given organism will engage in a given sort of behavior at a given time, you quickly grow impatient with theories of learning. Principles, hypotheses, theorems, satisfactory proof at the .05 level of significance that behavior at a choice point shows the effect of secondary reinforcement—nothing could be more irrelevant. No one goes to the circus to see the average dog jump through a hoop significantly oftener than untrained dogs raised under the same circumstances, or to see an elephant demonstrate a principle of behavior.

Perhaps I can illustrate this without giving aid and comfort to the enemy by describing a Russian device which the Germans found quite formidable. The Russians used dogs to blow up tanks. A dog was trained to hide behind a tree or wall in low brush or other cover. As a tank approached and passed, the dog ran swiftly alongside it, and a small magnetic mine attached to the dog's back was sufficient to cripple the tank or set it afire. The dog, of course, had to be replaced.

Now I ask you to consider some of the technical problems which the psychologist faces in preparing a dog for such an act of unintentional heroism. The dog must wait behind the tree for an indefinite length of time. Very well, it must, therefore, be intermittently reinforced for waiting. But what schedule will achieve the highest probability of waiting? If the reinforcement is to be food, what is the absolutely optimal schedule of deprivation consistent with the health of the dog? The dog must run to the tank—that can be arranged by reinforcing it with a practice tank—but it must start instantly if it is to overtake a swift tank, and how do you differentially reinforce short reaction times, especially in counteracting the reinforcement for sitting and waiting? The dog must react only to tanks, not to a refugee driving his oxcart along the road, but what are the defining properties of a tank so far as a dog is concerned?

I think it can be said that a functional analysis proved adequate in its technological application. Manipulation of environmental conditions alone made possible a wholly unexpected practical control. Behavior could be shaped up according to specifications and maintained indefinitely almost at will. One behavioral technologist who worked with me at the time (Keller Breland) is now specializing in the production of behavior as a salable commodity and has described this new profession in the *American Psychologist* [2].

There are many useful applications within psychology itself. Ratliff and Blough have recently conditioned pigeons to serve as psychophysical observers. In their experiment a pigeon may adjust one of two spots of light until the two are equally bright or it may hold a spot of light at the absolute threshold during dark adaptation. The techniques which they have developed to induce pigeons to do this are only indirectly related to the point of their experiments and hence exemplify the application of a behavioral science [4]. The field in which a better technology of behavior is perhaps most urgently needed is education. I cannot describe here the applications which are now possible, but perhaps I can indicate my enthusiasm by hazarding the guess that educational techniques at all age levels are on the threshold of revolutionary changes.

The effect of a behavioral technology on scientific practice is the issue here. Faced with practical problems in behavior, you necessarily emphasize the refinement of *experimental* variables. As a result, some of the standard procedures of statistics appear to be circumvented. Let me illustrate. Suppose that measurements have been made on two groups of subjects differing in some detail of experimental treatment. Means and standard deviations for the two groups are determined, and any difference due to the treatment is evaluated. If the difference is in the expected direction but is not statistically significant, the almost universal recommendation would be to study larger groups. But our experience with practical control suggests that we may reduce the troublesome variability by changing the conditions of the experiment. By discovering, elaborating, and fully exploiting every relevant variable, we may eliminate *in advance of measurement* the individual differences which obscure the difference under analysis. This will achieve the same result as increasing the size of groups, and it will almost certainly yield a bonus in the discovery of new variables which would not have been identified in the statistical treatment.

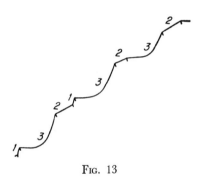

Fig. 13

The same may be said of smooth curves. In our study of anxiety, Estes and I published several curves, the reasonable smoothness of which was obtained by averaging the performance of 12 rats for each curve. The individual curves published at that time show that the mean curves do not faithfully represent the behavior of any one rat. They show a certain tendency toward a change in slope which supported the point we were making, and they may have appeared to justify averaging for that reason.

But an alternative method would have been to explore the individual case until an equally smooth curve could be obtained. This would have meant, not only rejecting the temptation to produce smoothness by averaging cases, but manipulating all relevant conditions as we later learned to manipulate them for practical purposes. The individual curves which we published at that time do not point to the need for larger groups but for improvement in experimental technique. Here, for example, is a curve the smoothness of which is characteristic of current practice. Such curves were shown in the making in a demonstration which Ferster and I arranged at the Cleveland meeting of the American Psychological Association (Fig. 13). Here, in a single organism, three different schedules of reinforcement are yielding corresponding performances with great uniformity under appropriate stimuli alternating at random. One does not reach this kind of order through the application of statistical methods.

In *The Behavior of Organisms* I was content to deal with the overall slopes and curvature of cumulative curves and could make only a rough classification of the properties of behavior shown by the finer grain,

The grain has now been improved. The resolving power of the microscope has been increased manyfold, and we can see fundamental processes of behavior in sharper and sharper detail. In choosing rate of responding as a basic datum and in recording this conveniently in a cumulative curve, we make important temporal aspects of behavior *visible*. Once this has happened, our scientific practice is reduced to simple looking. A new world is opened to inspection. We use such curves as we use a microscope, X-ray camera, or telescope. This is well exemplified by recent extensions of the method. These are no longer part of my case history, but perhaps you will permit me to consult you about what some critics have described as a *folie à deux* or group neurosis.

An early application of the method to the behavior of avoidance and escape was made by Keller in studying the light aversion of the rat. This was brilliantly extended by Murray Sidman in his shock-avoidance experiments. It is no longer necessary to describe avoidance and escape by appeal to "principles," for we may *watch* the behavior develop when we have arranged the proper contingencies of reinforcement, as we later watch it change as these contingencies are changed.

Hunt and Brady have extended the use of a stable rate in the study of anxiety-producing stimuli and have shown that the depression in rate is eliminated by electroconvulsive shock and by other measures which are effective in reducing anxiety in human patients. O. R. Lindsley has found the same thing for dogs, using insulin-shock therapy and sedatives. Brady has refined the method by exploring the relevance of various schedules of reinforcement in tracing the return of the conditioned depression after treatment. In these experiments you *see* the effect of a treatment as directly as you see the constriction of a capillary under the microscope.

Early work with rats on caffeine and Benzedrine has been extended by Lindsley with dogs. A special technique for evaluating several effects of a drug in a single short experimental period yields a record of behavior which can be read as a specialist reads an electrocardiogram. Dr. Peter Dews of the Department of Pharmacology at the Harvard Medical School is investigating dose-response curves and the types and effects of various drugs, using pigeons as subjects. In the Psychological Laboratories at Harvard additional work on drugs is being carried out by Morse, Herrnstein, and Marshall, and the technique is being adopted by drug manufacturers. There could scarcely be a better demonstration of the experimental treatment of variability. In a *single* experimental session with a *single* organism one observes the onset, duration, and decline of the effects of a drug.

The direct observation of *defective* behavior is particularly important. Clinical or experimental damage to an organism is characteristically

374   B. F. SKINNER

unique. Hence the value of a method which permits the direct observation of the behavior of the individual. Lindsley has studied the effects of near-lethal irradiation, and the effects of prolonged anesthesia and anoxia are currently being examined by Thomas Lohr in cooperation with Dr. Henry Beecher of the Massachusetts General Hospital. The technique is being applied to neurological variables in the monkey by Dr. Karl Pribram at the Hartford Institute. The pattern of such research is simple: establish the behavior in which you are interested, submit the organism to a particular treatment, and then look again at the behavior. An excellent example of the use of experimental control in the study of *motivation* is some work on obesity by J. E. Anliker in collaboration with Dr. Jean Mayer of the Harvard School of Public Health, where abnormalities of ingestive behavior in several types of obese mice can be compared by direct inspection.

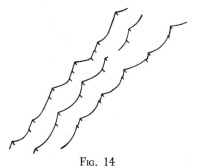

Fig. 14

There is perhaps no field in which behavior is customarily described more indirectly than psychiatry. In an experiment at the Massachusetts State Hospital, under the sponsorship of Dr. Harry Solomon and myself, O. R. Lindsley is carrying out an extensive program which might be characterized as a quantitative study of the temporal properties of psychotic behavior. Here again it is a question of making certain characteristics of the behavior visible.

The extent to which we can eliminate sources of variability before measurement is shown by a result which has an unexpected significance for comparative psychology and the study of individual differences. Figure 14 shows tracings of three curves which report behavior in response to a multiple fixed-interval fixed-ratio schedule. The hatches mark reinforcements. Separating them in some cases are short, steep lines showing a high constant rate on a fixed-ratio schedule and, in others, somewhat longer "scallops" showing a smooth acceleration as the organism shifts from a very low rate just after reinforcement to a higher rate at the end of the fixed interval. The values of the intervals and ratios, the states of deprivation, and the exposures to the schedules were different in the three cases, but except for these details the curves are quite similar. Now, one of them was made by a *pigeon* in some experiments by Ferster and me, one was made by a *rat* in an experiment on anoxia by Lohr, and the third was made by a *monkey* in Karl Pribram's laboratory at the Hartford Institute. Pigeon, rat, monkey, which is which? It doesn't matter. Of course, these three species have behavioral repertoires which are as different as their anatomies. But once you have allowed for differences in the ways in which they make contact with the environment, and in the ways in which they act upon the environment, what remains of their behavior shows astonishingly similar properties. Mice, cats, dogs, and human children could have added other curves to this figure. And when organisms which differ as widely as this nevertheless show similar properties of behavior, differences between members of the same species may be viewed more hopefully. Difficult problems of idiosyncrasy or individuality will always arise as products of biological and cultural processes, but it is the very business of the experimental analysis of behavior to devise techniques which reduce their effects except when they are explicitly under investigation.

We are within reach of a science of the individual. This will be achieved, not by resorting to some special theory of knowledge in which intuition or understanding takes the place of observation and analysis, but through an increasing grasp of relevant conditions to produce order in the individual case.

A second consequence of an improved technology is the effect upon behavior theory. As I have pointed out elsewhere, it is the function of learning theory to create an imaginary world of law and order and thus to console us for the disorder we observe in behavior itself. Scores on a T maze or jumping stand hop about from trial to trial almost capriciously. Therefore we argue that if learning is, as we hope, a continuous and orderly process, it must be occurring in some other system of dimensions —perhaps in the nervous system, or in the mind, or in a conceptual model of behavior. Both the statistical treatment of group means and the averaging of curves encourage the belief that we are somehow going behind the individual case to an otherwise inaccessible, but more fundamental, process. The whole tenor of our paper on anxiety, for example, was to imply that the change we observed was not necessarily a property of behavior, but of some theoretical state of the organism ("anxiety") which was merely *reflected* in a slight modification of performance.

When we have achieved a practical control over the organism, theories of behavior lose their point. In representing and managing relevant variables, a conceptual model is useless; we come to grips with behavior itself. When behavior shows order and consistency, we are much less likely to be concerned with physiological or mentalistic causes. A datum emerges which takes the place of theoretical phantasy. In the experimental analysis of behavior we address ourselves to a subject matter which is not only manifestly the behavior of an individual and hence accessible without the usual statistical aids but also "objective" and "actual" without recourse to deductive theorizing.

Statistical techniques serve a useful function, but they have acquired a purely honorific status which may be troublesome. Their presence or absence has become a shibboleth to be used in distinguishing between good and bad work. Because measures of behavior have been highly variable, we have come to trust only results obtained from large numbers of subjects. Because some workers have intentionally or unconsciously reported only selected favorable instances, we have come to put a high value on research which is planned in advance and reported in its entirety. Because measures have behaved capriciously, we have come to value skillful deductive theories which restore order. But although large groups, planned experiments, and valid theorizing are associated with significant scientific results, it does not follow that nothing can be achieved in their absence. Here are two brief examples of the choice before us.

How can we determine the course of dark adaptation in a pigeon?

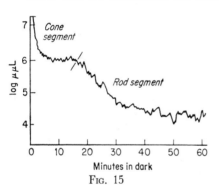

FIG. 15

We move a pigeon from a bright light to a dark room. What happens? Presumably the bird is able to see fainter and fainter patches of light as the process of adaptation takes place, but how can we follow this process? One way would be to set up a discrimination apparatus in which choices would be made at specific intervals after the beginning of dark adaptation. The test patches of light could be varied over a wide range, and the percentages of correct choices at each value would enable us eventually to locate the threshold accurately. But hundreds of observations would be needed to establish only a few points on the curve and to prove that these show an actual change in sensitivity. In the experiment by Blough already mentioned, the pigeon holds a spot of light close to the threshold throughout the experimental period. A single curve, such as the one sketched in Fig. 15, yields as much information as hundreds of readings, together with the means and standard deviations derived from them. The information is more accurate because it applies to a single organism in a single experimental session. Yet many psychologists who would accept the first as a finished experiment because of the tables of means and standard deviations would boggle at the second or call it a preliminary study. The direct evidence of one's senses in observing a process of behavior is not trusted.

As another example, consider the behavior of several types of obese mice. Do they all suffer from a single abnormality in their eating behavior or are there differences? One might attempt to answer this with some such measure of hunger as an obstruction apparatus. The numbers of crossings of a grid to get to food, counted after different periods of free access to food, would be the data. Large numbers of readings would be needed, and the resulting mean values would possibly not describe the behavior of any one mouse in any experimental period. A much better picture may be obtained with one mouse of each kind in single experimental sessions, as Anliker has shown [1]. In an experiment reported roughly in Fig. 16, each mouse was reinforced with a small piece of food after completing a short "ratio" of responses. The hypothalamic-obese mouse shows an exaggerated but otherwise normal ingestion curve. The hereditary-obese mouse eats slowly but for an indefinite length of time and with little change in rate. The gold-poisoned obese mouse shows

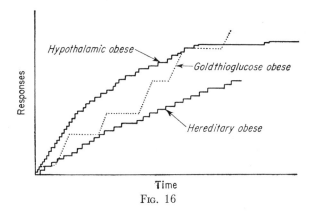

Fig. 16

a sharp oscillation between periods of very rapid responding and no responding at all. These three individual curves contain more information than could probably ever be generated with measures requiring statistical treatment, yet they will be viewed with suspicion by many psychologists because they are single cases.

It is perhaps natural that psychologists should awaken only slowly to the possibility that behavioral processes may be directly observed, or that they should only gradually put the older statistical and theoretical techniques in their proper perspective. But it is time to insist that science does not progress by carefully designed steps called "experiments" each of which has a well-defined beginning and end. Science is a continuous and often a disorderly and accidental process. We shall not do the young psychologist any favor if we agree to reconstruct our practices to fit the pattern demanded by current scientific methodology. What the statistician means by the design of experiments is design which yields the kind of data to which *his* techniques are applicable. He does not mean the behavior of the scientist in his laboratory devising research for his own immediate and possibly inscrutable purposes.

The organism whose behavior is most extensively modified and most completely controlled in research of the sort I have described is the experimenter himself. The point was well made by a cartoonist in the Columbia *Jester* (Fig. 17). The caption read: "Boy, have I got this guy conditioned! Every time I press the bar down he drops in a piece of food." The subjects we study reinforce us much more effectively than we reinforce them. I have been telling you simply how I have been conditioned to behave. And of course it is a mistake to argue too much from one case history. My behavior would not have been shaped as it was were it not for personal characteristics which all psychologists fortunately do not share. Freud has had something to say about the motivation of scientists and has given us some insight into the type of person who achieves the fullest satisfaction from precise experimental design and the intricacies of deductive systems. Such a person tends to be more concerned with his success as a scientist than with his subject matter, as is shown by the fact that he often assumes the role of roving ambassador. If this seems unfair, let me hasten to characterize my own motivation in equally unflattering terms. Several years ago I spent a pleasant summer writing a novel called *Walden Two*. One of the characters, Frazier, said many things which I was not yet ready to say myself. Among them was this:

Fig. 17

I have only one important characteristic, Burris: I'm stubborn. I've had only one idea in my life—a true *idée fixe* . . . to put it as bluntly as possible, the idea of having my own way. "Control" expresses it, I think. The control of human behavior, Burris. In my early experimental days it was a frenzied, selfish desire to dominate. I remember the rage I used to feel when a prediction went awry. I could have shouted at the subjects of my experiments, "Behave, damn you, behave as you ought!" Eventually I realized that the subjects were always right. They always behave as they ought. It was I who was wrong. I had made a bad prediction.

(In fairness to Frazier and the rest of myself, I want to add his next remark: "And what a strange discovery for a would-be tyrant, that the only effective technique of control is unselfish." Frazier means, of course, positive reinforcement.)

We have no more reason to say that all psychologists should behave as I have behaved than that they should all behave like R. A. Fisher. The scientist, like any organism, is the product of a unique history. The practices which he finds most appropriate will depend in part upon this history. Fortunately, personal idiosyncrasies usually leave a negligible mark on science as public property. They are important only when we are concerned with the encouragement of scientists and the prosecution of research. When we have at last an adequate empirical account of the behavior of Man Thinking, we shall understand all this. Until then, it may be best not to try to fit all scientists into any single mold.

REFERENCES

1. Anliker, J. E. Personal communication.

2. Breland, K., & Breland, Marion. A field of applied animal psychology. *Amer. Psychologist*, 1951, **6**, 202–204.

3. Heron, W. T., & Skinner, B. F. An apparatus for the study of behavior. *Psychol. Rec.*, 1939, **3**, 166–176.

4. Ratliff, F., & Blough, D. S. "Behavioral studies of visual processes in the pigeon," Report of Contract N5ori-07663, Psychological Laboratories, Harvard Univer., Sept., 1954.

5. Richter, C. P. Free research versus design research. *Science*, 1953, **118**, 91–93.

THE STATISTICAL APPROACH TO
LEARNING THEORY[1]

W. K. ESTES

Indiana University

[1] Although responsibility for the present report must rest with the writer, the theory under discussion is to an important extent a cooperative enterprise. Specific citations in the text cannot do full justice to the contributions of present and former associates at Indiana University who have collaborated in many researches, both experimental and theoretical; Cletus J. Burke and Donald W. Lauer must especially be mentioned. Also, I have profited by opportunities to discuss technical problems and exchange ideas and results with a number of individuals who have been conducting related research at other institutions, particularly Robert R. Bush, Frederick Mosteller, and Patrick Suppes. Preparation of this manuscript was facilitated by a fellowship period at the Center for Advanced Study in the Behavioral Sciences. Finally, I am indebted to Douglas G. Ellson and to the editor of this volume for detailed critical comments on the manuscript.

Part I. Orienting Attitudes and Systematic Viewpoint

Just as in any form of psychological investigation, the conclusions that will emerge from a study of theorists and theories are bound to be influenced by the choice of methods. As usual, we have available both the behavioral and the introspective approaches. We can look at what a theorist has done and try to infer his rules of operation, or we can simply ask him what he is trying to do and why. The difficulty with the behavioral approach in this instance is that we can rarely get adequate protocols; a theorist is usually happy enough to communicate his successes, but he can hardly be expected to rush into print with his failures, not, at least, if he recognizes them in time. The weakness of the introspective approach is that we cannot be sure of the causal relations between a man's scientific activities and his systematic views. It is my suspicion that methodologies and philosophies of science rarely guide either research or theory construction and in fact usually take form only when we try in retrospect to give a plausible rationale for what we have been doing. We ask, in effect, from what principles it can be deduced that our methods have been sound and our results good.

Does it follow that an exposition of one's systematic views on theory and method can serve no purpose but to cover up the trail of trial and error and make the process of theory construction appear unrealistically logical and systematic? This would be too hasty a conclusion. If the explorer of a new territory has been thoughtful enough to prepare us a map, we may find it useful even though we would not assume for a minute that the map played any guiding role in the original exploration.

What is the import of these remarks for our present assignment, which is to give an account of the development and present status, the characteristic assumptions, methods, and results of the statistical approach to behavior theory? Firstly, since I believe that this theoretical enterprise represents a response to particular circumstances rather than the unfolding of a philosophical position, I shall be inclined to emphasize the behavioral rather than the introspective approach. The major part of the job will be to fill in the fragmentary and unsystematic protocol available in the published record. This I hope to accomplish by chronicling as objectively as possible the circumstances that led to the first concrete attempts at formulating a statistical theory of learning and the events that have been responsible for its subsequent growth and modification. By way of over-all orientation, I shall preface this account with a summary sketch of the systematic viewpoint that I associate with the statistical approach— but with the warning that the systematic viewpoint may be more a result than a cause of this line of theoretical development. And to further the comparative aims of the Project A committee, I shall conclude the account with an analytical summary of the morphological features of statistical learning theory as it appears frozen in cross section at the time of writing.

To locate my systematic viewpoint in a familiar reference frame, we might characterize it as physicalistic, operational, and empirical. Individuals vary in their interpretation of these categorizing adjectives, however, so we had better pause for a bit of elucidation.

By physicalism, I refer to a frank preference for carrying over the methods and goals of physical science into psychology and maintaining a common language in so far as it is possible to do so. Like all psychologists I have been duly exhorted to beware of modeling psychology on physics and regaled with example after example of once promising psychological theorists who succumbed to the fatal disease. But who has never detected a hollow ring to these exhortations or noticed possible reinterpretations of the horrible examples? Perhaps in looking to physics we have taken the wrong models for psychological theory construction; perhaps, on the other hand, we have taken excellent models but have been distracted by some of the glittering superficialities from carrying over their more essential features. As a matter of fact I am inclined to suspect that our habits of thinking about natural phenomena are so deeply grounded in the history of physics, and to some extent biology, that we cannot even communicate what we mean by scientific progress, law, or theory except by reference to these disciplines. If this is true, then we really have little choice in the initial stages of behavioral theory construction but to start with the concepts and techniques of the more mature sciences and modify or replace these as need arises. The alternative, to strike off across a new area armed only with faith and intuition, would make a fine show of independence, but it might also minimize our chances of profiting by experience.

"Operationism" is not, so far as I can tell, a very well-defined concept, but in common usage it generally indicates a persisting desire to make one's ideas clear and a preference for concepts with direct experimental reference. Although subscribing cheerfully to these connotations, I intend further to emphasize the utility of distinguishing between the basic descriptive terms, or "data language," and the theoretical terms associated with a scientific system or theory. It does not seem likely that anyone will question the importance of this distinction in principle. Unless we are to set a theory above both competition and empirical test, we must have some means of describing comparative judgments and tests without prejudicing the results; i.e., the theorist, the critic, and the experimenter must have a common language which is theoretically neutral in the sense that it does not involve tacit assumptions favoring either the given theory or its competitors.

Implementing the distinction is no trivial matter, however, for our everyday language is saturated with informal psychological theory. Everyman's theory is not necessarily always bad, but its terms and concepts—perception, motivation, purpose, expectation, goal, sentiment, emotion, cognition, and all the rest—are so bound up with long-established linguistic habits that our every application of them inevitably and inextricably confounds description and interpretation. If we are to know when we are describing and when interpreting behavior, we need to begin our systematizing with a clear view of experimental facts, a view free of distortion by unrecognized theoretical assumptions. The descriptive system developed by Skinner and his followers [61, 85] and the deductive system of Hull's later period [55, 56], despite differences on other points of methodology, attest to the possibility of basing fruitful psychological theories directly upon descriptions of observed behavior, without the intervention of intuitively familiar "psychological" categories.

It is instructive to note that both Hull and Skinner began their theoretical programs by attempting to remodel inherited vocabularies. For Hull it was purpose, goal, and idea; for Skinner, reflex terminology, which gradually faded out of the theoretical picture as emphasis shifted from refurbishing jaded concepts to formulating new ones better attuned to the demands of experimental data. In this aspect of their development, these systems have recapitulated a sequence of events which is to be found in the history of every branch of natural science. Each new theoretical enterprise necessarily begins with terms and concepts carried over either from the vernacular or from other disciplines. Initially, the connotations these terms bring with them are often fruitful in suggesting new lines of investigation; but like other servants they are apt to outlive their usefulness without loosening their hold on our affections. Permitted to linger on because of habit or sentimental attachments, they become restrictive and misleading, and at the same time more firmly entrenched, so that eventually we can dislodge them only at the cost of diverting much energy from constructive research.

These comments are not intended to set the stage for an announcement that the statistical approach to learning theory has a magic formula for avoiding all the travails of its predecessors. They may, however, serve to explain why many familiar psychological terms will be conspicuously missing from the following pages. The omission of terms having to do with motivation, perception, and cognition from the system developed by myself and my coworkers will undoubtedly qualify our theories automatically as narrowly behavioristic, rigidly mechanical, and blindly associationistic. Still, it is not unheard of for a theory to prove fruitful despite these sinister attributes. Progress in many disciplines has rewarded those who were fortunate enough to be narrow and rigid in the right place at the right time. In most matters of form and method, the statistical approach can, I think, claim to have been guided more by facts than by preconceptions. In one respect, real inflexibility must be conceded. The inductive bases of statistical learning theories are strictly limited to theoretically neutral descriptions of behavior. It will be interesting to see whether phenomena associated with motivation, perception, and cognition can be reached "from below" by an approach which builds upon objective descriptions of behavior or whether, as many psychologists appear to believe, these phenomena will be reserved exclusively for more intuitive or holistic approaches.

In characterizing my systematic position as empirical I mean to signify more than an intention to keep one foot in the laboratory. I shall take no stand on a number of the most debated issues of systematic psychology simply because I regard them as matters to be settled by experiment, not by argument. These include questions as to the proper level of analysis for psychological constructs, the reducibility of psychological to physiological theory, limitations on the level of psychological measurement, and the degree of quantitative specificity psychological theories should aim for. On such points I prefer to think in terms of testing hypotheses rather than defending opinions. Indeed, in a sense, the theoretical enterprise to be described may be regarded as an experiment intended to test the hypothesis that learning data are amenable to interpretation by abstract quantitative theories comparable in predictive power to those of the physical sciences. The progress report to be given here will try primarily to make clear the "apparatus and procedure" of this experiment. Some preliminary results are available, but not enough, I am afraid, to warrant the customary section on "conclusions."

Part II. The Development of Statistical Learning Theory

ORIGINS AND INITIAL FORMULATION

Emergence of the Statistical Viewpoint

At times in the history of a science, the empirical situation seems uncompromisingly to demand a particular kind of theory. The demand becomes evident, of course, only after the fact when one observes that several very similar theories have blossomed simultaneously and independently. From evidence of this sort, a reader of the contemporary literature on learning must conclude that the state of the field in the late 1940s was ripe for a probabilistic or statistical type of learning theory.

In retrospect, one can discern several lines of influence pointing toward quantitative learning theory, and specifically toward theory of a probabilistic rather than deterministic character. Pressures came from both theoretical and empirical developments of the immediate prewar and postwar periods. Attempts to decide experimentally among the qualitatively stated postulates or principles of reinforcement, contiguity, and expectancy theories had reached a virtual impasse. It became gradually clear that effective differential testing of assumptions concerning the necessary and sufficient conditions of elementary learning had to wait upon more precise formulations of hypotheses and more effective machinery for deriving their testable consequences. At the same time, experimental programs associated with the systems of Hull and Skinner were beginning to accumulate sets of orderly and reproducible data concerning functional relationships in elementary learning that appeared suitable for quantitative analysis.

The first major attempt to formulate a general quantitative theory of learning, that of Hull [55], followed the classical tradition in proposing essentially a deterministic growth model. Learning was to be represented by the growth and decay of two hypothetical entities, habit strength and inhibition. Specifically, it was assumed that for any fixed set of conditions, each reinforcement produces a definite, predictable increment in habit strength, the increments summating to an exponential growth curve over a series of trials, and that each response evocation produces a definite, predictable increment in inhibition, the total amount of inhibition decaying as an exponential function of time following the response. A simple growth and decay model was clearly inadequate, however, to cope with the observed variability of behavior, and Hull supplemented it by postulating an autonomous oscillatory process which permitted the effective excitatory strength of a response to vary from moment to moment around the mean value determined by such independent variables as preceding reinforcements. The resulting hybrid model has been applied to instrumental conditioning data with some success, [57, 68, 86, 87], but in situations of only slightly greater complexity, e.g., multiple choice problems with partial reinforcement, it becomes all but unmanageable for calculational purposes. Inevitably an alternative strategy to Hull's had to be tried. The obvious alternative was to assume that learning is basically a probabilistic rather than a deterministic process and to formulate theoretical assumptions in terms of changing behavioral probabilities rather than in terms of an underlying growth process.

During the period from about 1948 to 1951, there appeared at least four distinct and independent attempts to recast learning theory in a probabilistic form. These were Mueller's application of a Poisson model to measures of conditioning [75], Miller and Frick's application of information theory to operant behavior [73], Bush and Mosteller's stochastic model [12], and my own first approximation to a statistical model for associative learning [19]. All four of these approaches are alike in taking probabilities of observed responses as primary theoretical dependent variables and deriving relationships among experimental measures (e.g., response times, rates, relative frequencies) by straightforward applications of probability theory. The last approach attempts also to represent the independent variables of learning experiments in terms of statistical distributions of events and may appropriately be termed *statistical* learning theory to distinguish it within the more general class of *probabilistic* or *stochastic* theories.

The interrelationships of statistical learning theory and its contemporaries will have to be studied in some detail if we are to attain a reasonable perspective with respect to the current theoretical scene; this we shall try to accomplish. For convenience in exposition, I shall first review the development and present status of the particular theory with which I have had firsthand experience, and then undertake a comparative analysis in a final section.

In one sense, statistical learning theory is by no means new. Many of the basic ideas can be traced back at least through a generation or two of behavioral theorists, and some of them have been developed along different lines by other contemporary theorists. The question of genealogy I shall not try to push very far. The more remote origins of the present theory would be hard to track down, and the task of separating the influences of heredity and environment is well known to be always difficult and frequently unrewarding, even when one is not working under the handicap of personal involvement.

The mathematical model which provided the formal basis for my 1950 paper on statistical learning theory [19] was initially formulated in the summer of 1948. During the preceding year, I and another Skinner-trained experimentalist, Norman Guttman, had finished

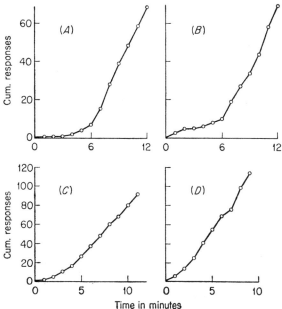

Fig. 1. Cumulative bar-pressing curves exhibiting the orderly acquisition characteristic of most animals.

constructing a fairly elaborate apparatus for studying operant behavior in the rat [47], and by way of breaking in the apparatus we had replicated several of Skinner's basic experiments on acquisition and extinction of the bar-pressing habit. The acquisition curves obtained during this "warm-up" period furnished the immediate instigation to formulate a statistical model for learning. Some of the properties of these curves which seemed to cry out for quantitative treatment will be apparent from the examples shown in Fig. 1. Let us now attempt to reconstruct the reasoning which led from data to theory.

Perhaps the most striking features of the acquisition curves are their orderliness and reproducibility. The course of acquisition is typically a smooth acceleration to a stable asymptotic response rate;

the form of the curve is very similar from one animal to another, and (note, e.g., curves A and B or C and D in Fig. 1) from one occasion to the next for a given animal. But where does one go from here? The cause of science will not be properly served if we do no more than mount our fine graphs on the laboratory wall where they are readily available for rapturous contemplation. If the important features of the course of acquisition are to be summarized, communicated, and integrated with other findings, we must have a mathematical description of these curves. And since the curves are smooth and reproducible, obtaining such a description should not be difficult. In fact, upon trying our hand at a bit of curve fitting we find that on the contrary, it is

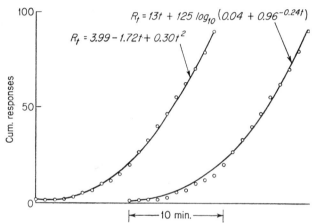

FIG. 2. A single cumulative response curve fitted by two different equations: a quadratic polynomial and a function derived from statistical learning theory [19].

too easy. Any number of simple mathematical functions can be fitted to the observed acquisition curves. In Fig. 2 we see the result of fitting a single empirical curve with two different mathematical functions. If we require only descriptive adequacy, then our choice of functions is clearly going to be quite arbitrary. If we are not willing to settle for an arbitrary choice, then some further reflection is in order.

Why are we so reluctant to make an arbitrary choice of functions? Obviously because we are hoping eventually to achieve more than an accurate description of acquisition in one particular situation. We would like to arrive at a description which will hold for a variety of situations. And we would like to find that the parameters in our functions have theoretical significance, i.e., that their values reflect manipulations of variables in some reasonable way. These aspirations bring us up against a conservation law which has been recognized more or less explicitly since the time of John Locke to hold for all theoretical undertakings. Theories transform information; they do not create it. If we hope to get more out of our mathematical model than a description of a particular set of facts, then we will have to take a broader range of facts into account when formulating the model.

One additional source of relevant information concerning the acquisition of bar pressing is immediately at hand. Although we were initially most impressed by the smoothly accelerated acquisition curves generated by the majority of animals, we have not overlooked the fact

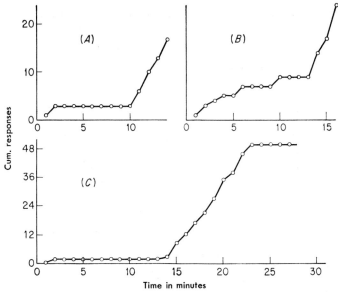

Fig. 3. Deviations from the characteristic curve form for acquisition of bar pressing.

that exceptions occur. The exceptions are of two main types, as illustrated in Fig. 3. Some animals, e.g., those represented by curves A and C in Fig. 3, exhibit an almost instantaneous shift from near-zero to near-maximum rate of responding. On the other hand, some animals, e.g., those represented by curves B and C in Fig. 3, make a few responses and appear to be following the normal course of acquisition, then inexplicably cease responding, sometimes for considerable periods. Clearly all these cases cannot readily be handled by a model which assumes that acquisition is described by the same simple function in all animals. We might get around the difficulty by assuming that there are several types of learners, each with its own learning function. But this way out would yield little satisfaction. We have no independent criteria for classifying types of learners; and once started on such a course we could look forward to nothing but an endless series of *ad hoc* classifications as the same problem recurred in new situations.

Before giving serious consideration to any classificatory scheme, we might well examine our working assumptions. Conceivably our initial efforts at model building have been guided by some tacit assumptions which reflect traditional views about the nature of learning rather than the properties of the data we are trying to account for. This line of inquiry brings an immediate flood of light. In looking for a simple function to describe acquisition in all animals, we have followed the lead of

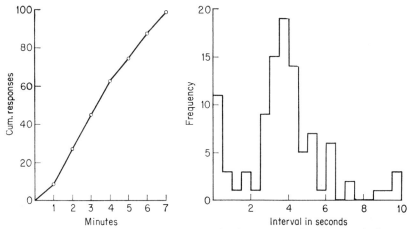

FIG. 4. Bar-pressing data for a single animal represented as a cumulative response curve, on the left, and as a frequency distribution of inter-response times, on the right.

numerous predecessors [e.g., 41, 45, 55] to the extent of tacitly assuming that learning may be treated as some sort of deterministic growth process. Once this assumption is made explicit, we see that it is by no means a necessary one. Possibly the learning process is basically statistical. The changing correlations between empirical response and stimulus variables which provide the observable symptoms of learning might result either from the formation of many associative relations, bonds, or connections at a more "molecular" level, or from the formation of unitary "molar" connections on a probabilistic basis. If there were trial to trial sampling variations at either the "molecular" or the "molar" level, the typical smooth acquisition curve might be a resultant of averaging. At the same time the atypical results shown in Fig. 3 might also be accounted for, since in any statistical process exceptional sequences are bound to occur occasionally.

Closer examination of the "typical" acquisition curves brings further evidence in support of a statistical hypothesis. Initially we considered only cumulative curves of the sort shown in the first three figures. If we amplify these records, or better yet take noncumulative records on a faster tape, and measure the times between successive responses, we find that even the smooth curves of Fig. 1 are the result of an averaging process. In Fig. 4 we can see what very different impressions concerning the nature of the learning process are generated by a cumulative response curve as compared to a frequency distribution of interresponse times for the same data.

If we yield to the demands of the data and adopt provisionally the view that acquisition is a basically statistical process, then we must also change our whole approach to the problem of model construction. We shall no longer expect to find any one single equation that will describe learning in all animals. Rather than continue what is apparently destined to be a fruitless search for "the learning function" we must ask what particular set of concepts and assumptions will enable us both to deduce an average curve descriptive of the over-all course of acquisition and at the same time to account for deviations from group trends.

Formulation of a Probabilistic Response Model

Since we wish first of all to arrive at precise descriptions of elementary forms of learning, we have little latitude in our initial choice of dependent variables. In the kind of experimental situation we have taken as our empirical starting point, the response variable to be used in tracing the course of learning is chosen at will by the experimenter. The behaviors available to the organism at any given time are classified in accordance with objective criteria. In this context, then, the term *response* refers not to a physiologically or anatomically defined unit, but to a class of activities, e.g., all behaviors which result in depression of a bar, all behaviors which result in cutting a photocell beam or entering an end box of a maze, all behaviors which eventuate in the appearance of the syllable VEC in a particular blank space of an answer sheet. Testable predictions of behavior in the Skinner box, T maze, or paired-associate learning situation must refer to frequencies or times of these operationally defined "responses." Yet we can only afford to follow the lead of the experimenter up to a point. It would be extremely inconvenient for theoretical purposes to have one set of acquisition laws relating to response frequencies, another set relating to latencies, and so on. Some unifying construct is necessary.

We could at this point simply introduce a new construct, similar to Hull's $_sE_R$ and relate it to the various experimentally defined response measures by special postulates. Such a course would have the obvious attraction of allowing us to get on quickly to the more central problems of learning; but it would have the equally obvious drawback of leaving us with a number of arbitrary functions intervening between our learning theory and the testable predictions derivable from the theory. We would have to look forward to continual difficulties in deciding whether discrepancies between theoretical predictions and experimental results reflect inadequacies in our assumptions about learning or merely unfortunate choices of the intervening functions.

Our unwillingness to face an unending sequence of *ad hoc* assumptions about response measures in each new situation, together with the fact that we have found strong reasons to regard behavior as essentially probabilistic, suggests a possible way out. Suppose that we take as our basic theoretical dependent variable the probability of occurrence associated with any given operationally defined response class. The desired unification can then be achieved by formulating laws of learning in terms of response probability as a dependent variable. At the same time the need for a multiplicity of postulates relating to response measures is minimized. By taking time out for some paper and pencil investigations, we find that by applying the mathematical theory of probability we can derive once and for all the relations between response probability and such empirically definable measures as frequency, rate, and latency or reaction time. Further, it becomes clear that once we have laws of learning stated in terms of changes in response probability, continued application of the same mathematical theory will enable us to generate predictions of empirical relationships involving such measures as trials to a criterion of learning, errors to a criterion, responses to extinction, and so on.

Let us digress for a moment in order to illustrate the last point. Suppose that the minimum time required to execute a given response is h min. Then in a free responding situation the maximum rate of occurrence of the response is certainly $1/h$ responses per minute; and it is fairly obvious that if the probability of the response during any one interval h is p, then the average rate of responding will be

$$r = \frac{p}{h} \qquad (1)$$

For example, if $h = 0.05$ min and $p = .75$, then the maximum rate of responding is 20 responses per minute and the average predicted rate is 15 responses per minute. Further it can be shown [19] that if p is constant within a trial, the mean predicted latency of the response will be given by

$$L = \frac{h}{p} \qquad (2)$$

Now suppose that a learning theory yields the following acquisition law for a given situation,

$$p_n = 1 - (1 - \Theta)^{n-1} \tag{3}$$

where p_n is response probability after $n - 1$ reinforced trials and Θ is a parameter $0 < \Theta \leq 1$. We cannot test the law directly, since probabilities are purely theoretical entities, but we can readily obtain predicted relationships among observables. Thus for the situation in question we must predict that the rate of responding will be related to number of reinforcements by the equation

$$r_n = \frac{1}{h} - \frac{1}{h}(1 - \Theta)^{n-1}$$

where r_n is to be read as "average rate after $n - 1$ reinforcements," and that mean latency will be related to number of reinforcements by

$$L_n = \frac{h}{1 - (1 - \Theta)^{n-1}}$$

These expressions result simply from substituting Eq. (3) into Eqs. (1) and (2), respectively. A little algebra yields still other relationships. If p_n represents probability of a correct turn in a T maze, then $1 - p_n$ must represent probability of an error. Therefore $e(K)$, the predicted number of errors in K trials, can be obtained by adding the values of $1 - p_n$ for $n = 1, 2, \ldots, K$.

$$\begin{aligned} e(K) &= \sum_{n=1}^{K}(1 - p_n) \\ &= \sum_{n=1}^{K}(1 - \Theta)^{n-1} \\ &= \frac{1 - (1 - \Theta)^{K}}{\Theta} \end{aligned}$$

The technique for performing the summation is given in [82], and in almost any text on college algebra. As K becomes large, $(1 - \Theta)^{K}$ approaches zero, so the expected total number of errors during learning is equal to $1/\Theta$. Thus given the form of the acquisition function and the value of the parameter Θ for a given subject, we can make predictions about rate, latencies, total errors, and many other measures. How we can ascertain the value of Θ is a pertinent question, but to deal with it now would be getting ahead of the story. We shall come back to this question later. For the present, I wish only to emphasize the fact that once response probability has been chosen as our basic dependent variable, it can be related to a variety of observables by derivations which depend only on the assumptions common to all applications of probability theory.

One may also note that our response model is in all essentials the same as the one assumed tacitly or explicitly in many other branches of psychology, e.g., psychophysics, test theory, communication theory. In one salient respect our strategy is almost exactly the reverse of that which has typified many preceding learning theories. The more common procedure has been to start by formulating assumptions or postulates about learning and only at a later stage to begin worrying about making contact between the theory and observables. One of the distinctive features of the present approach is that in the early stages of theory building we have concentrated our efforts primarily on establishing a secure foundation. We have no guarantee that our approach will lead to anything passable as a learning theory, but we can have some confidence that if we do arrive at a theory, it will not be found floating idly in mid-air while the constructors try belatedly to drop a few *ad hoc* mooring lines down to the plane of observables.

Stimulus-Response Relationships and Learning

Construction of what appears to be a serviceable response model represents tangible progress, but it does not quite complete our theoretical foundation. Before we can proceed with the superstructure, we will have to deal with one additional preliminary matter, namely, the question of precisely what we are going to mean by "learning." So long as we thought only in terms of a particular set of data this question did not arise. Everyone will agree that acquisition of the bar-pressing habit, as represented by the curves of Fig. 1, is an instance of learning. Starting from this example, we might surmise that learning can be provisionally defined as a systematic change in response probability. Not all systematic changes in response probability will qualify, however. If the experimental sessions had been sufficiently prolonged, the curves shown in Fig. 1 would have begun to decelerate and rate of bar pressing would have fallen nearly to zero even though all responses were being rewarded. We would want to attribute the decline in response probability to satiation, however, not to unlearning. Similarly, if we changed the situation radically, e.g., by turning off the lights in the boxes, by adding buzzers or vibrators, or by changing the inertia of the bar, we would certainly produce a change in probability of bar pressing; but again we would want to distinguish this from the change in probability that occurred during acquisition and from the change that would occur if we disconnected the magazine and permitted extinction to occur.

These distinctions are apparently based on the extent to which the changes in response probability can be reversed without additional exposure to the given experimental situation. If response probability declines as a result of feeding, the original level can be restored by a period of fasting; if probability is changed as a result of a shift in stimulus conditions, the original probability will again obtain if we restore the original stimulus conditions. But the changes produced by a series of reinforced learning trials evidently cannot be entirely undone except by extinction trials, and the changes produced by unreinforced trials cannot be entirely undone except by reacquisition.

Further, it seems clear that we want to include under "learning" only changes in response probability relative to given stimulus variables. In the elementary operant conditioning situation, response probability is defined relative to the entire stimulating situation. But we can foresee that later we will want to deal with experiments in which learning is represented by changes in response probability relative to some independently manipulable component or property of a situation. In the Skinner box, the rat may learn to press the bar only when a tone is sounding; in a paired-associate experiment the subject learns to make a given response only in the presence of one particular stimulus word, and so on. We can allow for all these possibilities if we agree to conceptualize learning in terms of probability relations (referred to in the sequel as conditional relationships, or, for brevity, connections) between operationally defined response classes and operationally defined classes of stimulating situations.

These preliminaries disposed of, we move into an area of considerably greater uncertainty. The decisions we have made up to this point have been dictated closely by empirical considerations. Barring major changes in our over-all objective or our underlying philosophy, the probabilistic framework we have developed should remain relatively fixed while we proceed to fill in the outline with detailed assumptions concerning the nature of stimulus response relations and the manner of their formation and abolishment. We shall try to continue following the facts, but we may not always be sure where they are trying to lead us. Probably the most we should hope for is that by trying out reasonable appearing assumptions, testing their consequences, and modifying them as necessary, we may converge through a series of approximations toward an adequate theory.

In order to make further progress toward a quantitative learning theory, we now must make some specific and detailed assumptions about the form of the probability relations between stimulus and response variables. One of the first questions to be settled is whether we shall conceive the relation between a response class and a stimulating situation to be unitary or to be composed of more elementary component relations. Two considerations nudge us toward the latter alternative. First, a considerable body of data from elementary learning experiments (e.g., experiments on "continuity" in discrimination learning, stimulus compounding, transfer of training, retroactive inhibition, stimulus generalization) seems to demand a property which we might call "transposability." By this I refer to the fact that when a period of learning has increased the probability that a complex stimulus will evoke a given response, then, other things equal, various components or aspects of that stimulus will exhibit an increased probability of evoking the response if tested in a new situation. This property of transposability will characterize our theoretical model if we assume that the conditional relations between a response class and the various components or aspects of a stimulating situation are mutually independent. In order to be noncommittal, for the moment, about the nature of the components or aspects, let us refer to them simply as elements. It will be a task for future research to determine just what features of a stimulating situation may correspond to the stimulus elements defined in the model.

The second consideration favoring a "molecular" hypothesis is the necessity of accounting both for the typical gradual course of learning illustrated in Fig. 1 and the abrupt changes seen in Fig. 3. The appearance of both types of curves under apparently identical circumstances suggests that some kind of sampling process might be involved. And the term sampling at once brings to mind two ideas which prove extremely helpful in the touchy business of converting our somewhat vague and qualitative notions into an explicit quantitative model— one is a chemical analogy and the other is Guthrie's treatment of learning by repetition.

The chemical analogy will become apparent if we pause a moment to summarize the properties which appear to be demanded of an acquisition model:

1. The average course of acquisition is given by a curve which is negatively accelerated in its terminal phase and which approaches a stable asymptote.

2. The smooth mean curve is the result of averaging over a Poisson-like distribution of latencies or interresponse times, and the asymptote of the observed learning curve represents merely a point of statistical equilibrium.

3. A relation between observed stimulus and response variables is decomposable into numerous component relations which are formed via some kind of sampling process.

We see that the quantitative properties which characterize simple acquisition are the same as those which characterize mass-action chemical processes. Therefore it is reasonable to hope that the mathematical model which is known to describe the latter will provide at least a good starting point for a description of the former.

With our preliminary analyses completed and the chemical analogy to guide us through the next stage, we are finally ready to set down our assumptions in quantitative form. We recall that the simplest mass-action chemical process is described by a relation of the form:

$$\Delta x = q(S - x) \tag{4}$$

where x is the momentary concentration of a given reaction product, S is the maximum concentration, q is a proportionality constant, and Δx is the change in x during a unit time interval. The formula can be reinterpreted in terms of the learning situation. If we represent a stimulating situation by a set, or population, of stimulus elements, then S will be the number of elements in the set and q will be the proportion of these elements representing the effective stimulation on any one trial.

We have already decided that the organism's possible behaviors in the situation are to be categorized into operationally defined classes. For simplicity we shall limit ourselves at the start to experiments in which only two response classes, call them A_1 and A_2, are recognized. (In the operant conditioning experiment, for example, A_1 will be any behavior which results in depression of the bar during a given time interval and A_2 will be any behavior which does not result in depression of the bar during this interval.) Continuing the interpretation, we assume that at any time each element in the stimulus set S bears a conditional relation to (is connected to) one or the other of these response classes. This relation is such that if all elements are equally likely to be sampled on any trial, the probability of A_1 is equal to the proportion of elements connected to A_1. If A_1 is the response that is being recorded during learning, then the quantity x in Eq. 4 represents the number of stimulus elements in S that are connected to A_1 at a given time, and Δx represents the average change in the number of elements connected to A_1 on any one learning trial. (In the bar-pressing experiment a "trial" will correspond to the occurrence and reinforcement of a bar-pressing response.) Since by our assumptions the ratio x/S is equal to p, the probability of response A_1, we can divide both sides of Eq. 4 by S and obtain the relation

$$\Delta p = q(1 - p) = \Theta(1 - p)$$

or equivalently $\quad\quad p_{n+1} = p_n + \Theta(1 - p_n) \tag{5}$

where n represents ordinal number of the trial and the constant of proportionality q has been relabeled Θ in accord with the notation used in later work.

Before discussing the empirical implications of Eq. (5), it may be helpful to summarize the concepts and assumptions underlying it.

Response variables. The organism's possible behaviors in the given experimental situation are categorized into mutually exclusive and exhaustive response classes on the basis of objective criteria. With each response class, we associate a probability. In the operant conditioning situation, the momentary probability of the bar pressing response is the theoretical dependent variable. Relations between response probabilities and experimentally defined response measures are derivable by application of probability theory.

Stimulus variables. The stimulating situation is represented by a set of S stimulus elements and the effective stimulation on any trial is represented by a randomly drawn subset of elements. At any time each element in S is connected to exactly one response class. As a first approximation it is assumed that all stimulus elements are equally likely to be sampled and that the probability of a response at any time is equal to the proportion of elements in S that are connected to it.

Learning. On any acquisition trial all stimulus elements sampled by the organism become connected to the response reinforced on that trial.

It will be noted that our rudimentary theory shares several important properties with Guthrie's [46] treatment of associative learning. On any one trial, learning occurs on an all-or-none basis relative to the components or aspects of the stimulating situation which actually affect the organism, but not all components are available on any one trial. Over a series of trials, response probability changes by a series of discrete jumps, the size of the jump being a random variable; but if we average over a number of replications of an experiment (i.e., over the set of empirical learning functions generated by a group of organisms or by a series of learnings and relearnings by the same organism), the random variation will be smoothed by the averaging. The mean curve may turn out to be as simple in form as that arising from a continuous-growth postulate such as Hull's.

It might seem at a first glance that our model is incomplete, even as a limited theory, in that we have not introduced any assumptions about extinction, or unlearning. Further analysis reveals, however, that the assumptions already made provide a mechanism for unlearning. At any time the response which is reinforced receives an increment in probability according to Eq. (5). Since the response classes defined for a given situation are mutually exclusive and exhaustive, their probabilities must add up to unity at all times; therefore, any increase in the probability of one response must be accompanied by a compensating decrease in the probability of other responses. If, for example, response classes A_i, A_j, and A_k are defined for a given situation, and if the probability p_i of response A_i increases by the amount

$$\Delta p_i = \Theta(1 - p_i)$$

on a given trial, then the combined probability of A_j and A_k must decrease by the amount

$$\Delta(p_j + p_k) = -\Theta(1 - p_i) = -\Theta(p_j + p_k)$$

If the two changes are added together, we get

$$\Delta p_i + \Delta(p_j + p_k) = \Theta(1 - p_i - p_j - p_k) = \Theta(1 - 1) = 0$$

as required.

This result may be stated another way in terms of the model. Suppose a particular element of the stimulus set S is connected to response A_j; if now this element becomes connected to a different response A_k on some learning trial, it is at the same time disconnected from A_j. In more familiar psychological terms we could say that given an association, or conditioning, principle and a probability model for response variables, a principle of unlearning by interference follows as a theorem.

With a provisional model in hand, we are naturally eager to try some applications. One technicality must be taken care of first however. Our assumptions concerning the "hows" of acquisition are completely summarized in Eq. (5), but the latter cannot be used directly to describe empirical acquisition curves. Equation (5) is a difference equation, a mathematical form which may be destined to play much the same role in behavioral theories that differential equations have in physics. Using this mode of expression, we can state basic laws and assumptions in general terms, without reference to the particular conditions peculiar to individual experiments. Then starting with the general law in the form of a difference equation, and taking due account of the experimental conditions characterizing a given situation, we can derive expressions which relate observables (e.g., response rate and time, latency and number of reinforcements) by explicit formulas suitable for comparison with empirical curves. If the rate of change in response probability were given by the differential equation

$$\frac{dp}{dn} = \Theta(1 - p)$$

we could integrate the latter and obtain a formula expressing p as a growth function of n. Happily, it turns out that we can carry out an analogous mathematical operation on difference equations such as our Eq. (5). The operation is called finite integration, or more generally, "solving" the difference equation. The derivation is not difficult [for details, cf. 13, 37, 60, 82] and yields the formula

$$p_n = 1 - (1 - p_1)(1 - \Theta)^{n-1} \qquad (6)$$

where p_n represents probability of response A_1 on the nth acquisition trial.[2] Just as we did before in the case of Eq. 3, we can substitute from Eq. (1) or (2) into Eq. (6) and obtain learning functions in terms of response rate or mean latency.[3] The fact that these functions are in-

[2] For our present purposes it really does not matter how we arrive at Eq. (6), provided we can prove that it is correct. We had better run through the proof briefly in order to leave no gaps in the route of anyone who is trying to follow the argument closely. We start by considering the hypothesis that Eq. (6) is correct. If so, response probability after the next trial should be given by

$$p_{n+1} = 1 - (1 - p_1)(1 - \Theta)^n$$

and by subtraction we should get the change in probability resulting from a single acquisition trial

$$\begin{aligned}
\Delta p_n &= p_{n+1} - p_n \\
&= 1 - (1 - p_1)(1 - \Theta)^n - 1 + (1 - p_1)(1 - \Theta)^{n-1} \\
&= (1 - p_1)[(1 - \Theta)^{n-1} - (1 - \Theta)^n] \\
&= (1 - p_1)(1 - \Theta)^{n-1}(1 - 1 + \Theta) \\
&= \Theta(1 - p_1)(1 - \Theta)^{n-1}
\end{aligned}$$

Referring back to Eq. (6) we see that

$$(1 - p_1)(1 - \Theta)^{n-1} = (1 - p_n)$$

and, therefore (by substitution into the last line above)

$$\Delta p_n = \Theta(1 - p_n)$$

which is precisely what we should have if Eq. (6) is the solution of Eq. (5).

[3] By further mathematical operations we can if desired change the independent variable from trials to time. To obtain a new difference equation representing the expected change in response probability during a unit time interval, we multiply the right side of Eq. (5) by the momentary response probability p, yielding

$$\Delta p = \Theta p(1 - p) \qquad (7)$$

This mathematical manipulation amounts to assuming that p is changed at each reinforcement in accordance with Eq. (5) but remains constant during intervals between successive responses. Equation (7) is not so easily solved as Eq. (5), but it can be shown [cf. 12, 19 for details] that when Θ is small an approximate solution is given by

$$p_t = \frac{1}{1 + [(1 - p_1)/p_1]e^{-Bt}} \qquad (8)$$

where p_t is response probability at time t, e is the base of natural logarithms, and $B = \Theta/h$ (as before, h represents the minimum time required for execution of the response whose probability is p). Substituting r for p by means of Eq. (1), we now can rewrite Eq. (8) in terms of rate of responding, and the cumulative form of this rate curve, illustrated in Fig. 2, should describe cumulative acquisition curves in operant conditioning situations.

deed appropriate in form to describe empirically obtained curves is illustrated in Fig. 5; curves derived from Eq. (6) are fitted to curves of median running time against number of reinforcements from a runway experiment, mean bar-press duration and mean response rate against number of reinforcements from bar-pressing experiments, and number of errors against reinforced trials from a T-maze experiment.[4]

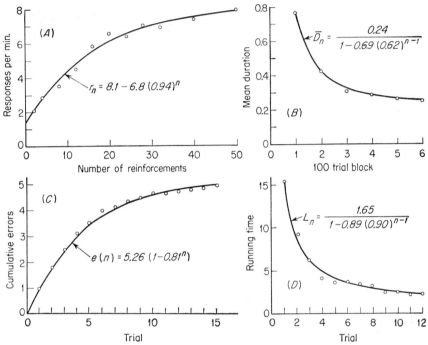

FIG. 5. Four kinds of simple acquisition data described by functions derived from statistical learning theory: curves A, B, C, and D, respectively, represent rate of bar pressing vs. number of reinforcements, mean bar-press duration per 100-trial block, mean cumulative errors vs. trials in T-maze learning, and median running time vs. trials in a runway experiment.

Let us review our progress briefly. We started out to formulate a model which would provide quantitative descriptions of operant conditioning curves and at the same time account for deviations from the typical curve forms. In some respects we now stand fairly well. From our provisional model it has been possible to derive acquisition functions, not only for the bar-pressing experiment, but for a variety

[4] I am indebted to Dr. Solomon Weinstock for the running-time data. The bar-pressing data come from unpublished studies by the writer, and the T-maze data from a study by Estes and Lauer [36].

of elementary learning situations. Further, by virtue of the assumption that learning occurs on an all-or-none basis relative to the sample of stimuli effective on any trial, the model is able to provide both for sudden and for gradual learning, both for variability among individual protocols and for orderly group trends. When we take a mean curve from a group of animals in a maze experiment or cumulative responses over time in a bar-pressing experiment, the trial variation averages out, and we obtain the typical smooth acquisition curve. We have shown how the forms of the average curves can be deduced from the model; by further mathematical development, we can also derive functions for the standard deviations around these curves and even, in some cases, descriptions of the complete distribution of response measures on any trial [for details see 13, chap. 14; 32].

Appropriately enough, we conclude our reconstruction of the formative period of statistical learning theory just as we started—immersed in the idiosyncrasies of acquisition data. We may have done a little more than come a full circle, however, for we return with a small but functional theoretical model under our arm, and we find with some pleasure that the model can handle a larger collection of facts than the very limited set we started with. Also, it will soon become clear that en route we have turned up some new and perplexing problems which cannot be handled by the 1950 model and which start us off on another cycle.

Reinforcement and Contiguity

Before proceeding with further adventures, we should try to clear up some questions the reader may have as to how the 1950 model stands relative to the explanatory concepts which appear in other contemporary learning theories. Do we have a contiguity theory or a reinforcement theory?

In my 1950 paper [19] I attempted to formulate my assumptions about the conditions of elementary learning in terms of Guthrie's contiguity theory as I understood it. A response was assumed to become conditioned to all stimuli affecting the organism at the time of its evocation. The term *reinforcement* was regarded simply as a convenient label for procedures which serve to evoke responses in the presence of new stimuli and to protect newly formed associations by removing the stimuli before interfering responses can occur. Presumably one could derive from the contiguity assumptions an account of the fact that some events or procedures are effective reinforcers and others are not. I still find these ideas attractive in a programmatic sense, and in Part III of this article I shall try to summarize the progress to date in working out the program.

To anticipate a bit, I might remark that early in the development of statistical learning theory, it became clear that research could not wait upon an adequate definition of reinforcement in terms of more primitive concepts. In order to make empirical applications of the developing theory, it was expedient to take advantage of the fact that there are a number of commonly studied learning situations for which all experimenters can agree that certain operations are reinforcing, i.e., lead to acquisition when appropriately correlated with response occurrences. Thus it is natural enough that our quantitative theory yields statements, not about what reinforcement is, but about how it operates. All theorems (laws) about learning derivable from the theory take the form of "if . . . then" statements; e.g., "if a given operation yields an increment in response probability satisfying Eq. (5), then repeated reinforcement of a response via this operation will generate a mean learning curve of the form described by Eq. (6)." Later on we shall see that deductions of this type sometimes yield predictions of genuinely new empirical phenomena. To the extent that such predictions are both intrinsically interesting and empirically confirmed, the theory is accomplishing precisely what we ask of a theory and no one should complain if we continue to operate on the same descriptive level indefinitely. As the theory is applied to a variety of experimental situations primarily to refine and extend our account of how learning proceeds under various schedules, conditions, and contingencies of reinforcement, we incidentally accumulate considerable information as to the kinds of operations which serve as reinforcers.

I am convinced that given a sufficiently austere temperament one could develop a fruitful descriptive theory without ever straying into speculative bypaths. The proposition is largely academic though, for where are we to find the theorist who *never* finds himself wishing, albeit guiltily, for a deeper understanding of some empirical phenomenon that can be provided by the most detailed quantitative description? The student of learning is especially beset by temptations. The fact that a wide variety of superficially diverse operations turn out to have quantitatively equivalent effects on learning demands some kind of explanation, and almost every learning theorist has tried his hand at answering this call. In the case of me and my associates, the drive for explanation has taken the form of continuing attempts to derive the independently established quantitative laws of reinforcement from more primitive assumptions concerning contiguity, interference, and stimulus sampling.

For certain areas of application, especially classical conditioning and the simpler types of verbal learning (e.g., paired-associate learning), the contiguity principle seems to prescribe the conditions of reinforcement more directly than does any alternative theory. In more complex situations involving rewards, punishments, and the like, contiguity interpretations become more speculative and really cannot be defended against alternative theories on grounds of parsimony. Whether the interpretations are worth while comes down to a question of whether they have fruitful consequences in the theoretical and experimental analysis of new empirical situations. As we follow the more recent development of statistical learning theory in these pages, we shall see a number of instances in which the contiguity principle has been useful in mediating extensions and applications of the theory to new problems and situations. I believe it is the function of contiguity theory as a tool of analysis that is responsible for its continued viability.

In brief, our answer to the question "reinforcement or contiguity?" is simply, "both." Whether we can have our cake and eat it and still not grow fat is a much more difficult question. Some materials which may be of use in formulating an answer to it will be provided in the following sections.

GROWTH OF STATISTICAL LEARNING THEORY SINCE 1950

The year 1950 marks a turning point in our narrative. In the preceding section we could speak of "the theory" or "the model" with no real ambiguity. We had only to deal with a single clearly defined mathematical model and its range of application was limited to an almost as clearly defined class of elementary acquisition experiments. In 1957, the problem of communication is much more formidable. During the intervening years, many people have had a hand in the enterprise. Many generalizations and extensions of the original theory have been attempted—some proving obviously fruitful, some as obviously negative, some indeterminate. Giving a neatly organized account of these developments is made difficult by the fact that they have not been directed by any master plan. Rather, we have been led along by a series of problems. Some of these are primarily empirical problems, some primarily theoretical; the principal feature that they have in common is that none is ever solved without first giving rise to at least two more. For expository purposes it will be convenient to organize the following account around two main groups of problems: (1) those arising from attempts to provide direct experimental tests of theoretical assumptions and (2) attempts to generalize the original theory by removing various simplifying assumptions and to extend it to new empirical areas.

Tests of theoretical assumptions. *Invariance of parameters.* As we have illustrated in preceding sections, the experimental application of a quantitative theory involves a number of steps, starting with the abstract and formal assumptions of the theory and terminating with derivations of predicted functional relationships among observables. The last phrase must be qualified, however: the dependent and independent variables in the derived functions are operationally definable in terms of observables, but the same is not always true of the parameters. Consider, for example, Eq. (6) above. As written, the dependent variable p_n is purely theoretical; but since we have assumed a probability model for response variables, we know that if Eq. (6) is to be applied, say, to a T-maze experiment, the theoretical variable p_n can be replaced by an observable $\bar{p}_n$, the expected proportion of occurrences of a given response by a group of similar organisms on the nth acquisition trial. With this identification agreed upon, we are in a position to provide numerical values for all of the terms in Eq. (6) except the parameter Θ.

Now we must face up to the question, postponed earlier, of precisely how we are to evaluate Θ in any particular experiment. We know that in terms of our conceptual model, Θ represents rate of learning in terms of the average proportion of stimulus elements sampled per trial from the stimulus set, or population, representing a given stimulating situation. The conceptual definition is not of much help, however, for we have no means of identifying individual stimulus elements and determining when they are sampled. From the definition we should expect that, other things equal, the value of Θ should depend on the observable variability in the stimulating situation, but it must also depend in part on characteristics peculiar to the individual organism. One could hardly avoid assuming, for example, that a visual defect would influence the organism's sampling of its visual environment, or that gradations in auditory acuity would be reflected in rate of sampling of auditory cues.

These considerations lead to a methodological restriction which I believe will hold for all behavioral theories. Any theory which predicts individual behavior in quantitative detail will contain parameters whose values depend at least in part on characteristics peculiar to the individual organism, and in general, the values of these parameters can be determined only from behavioral data. In principle, one must concede that ultimately the values of some behavioral parameters may turn out to be predictable from physiological or biophysical theories, but there appears to be no danger of arriving at this stage in the foreseeable future. To return to our illustrative situation, it becomes clear that the value of Θ for any particular organism or group of organisms must be obtained by statistical estimation, i.e., curve fitting or some equivalent procedure.

All estimation procedures amount roughly to this: given a set of empirical data, e.g., any of the empirical curves plotted in Fig. 5, which should be describable by a given theoretical function, one selects some criterion of goodness of fit, e.g., least squares or maximum likelihood, then by appropriate statistical procedures selects the parameter values which yield the best agreement between the theoretical function and the data. (In Fig. 5, the value $\theta = .19$ yields the best fit of Eq. (6) to the empirical curve C according to a least squares criterion.)

The necessity for evaluating parameters from the data to be described raises a question of circularity in the theory. In what sense, a critic may ask, are we making theoretical predictions about learning if application of the theory always includes this step of parameter estimation? The point is well taken, and deserves detailed consideration. In order to answer the question fully, it is necessary to distinguish three levels of prediction, the first involving only extrapolation; the second, overdetermination; and the third, situational invariance.

The first form of prediction is the most that can be accomplished when we fit a function such as Eq. (6) to a single set of empirical data. If all the data are used in evaluating the parameter θ, then we really cannot be said to be predicting the behavior in any sense. All that can be claimed is that the application provides a test of the theory to the extent that it gives the theory a chance to be wrong; it might turn out to be impossible to describe the data with the given function by any choice of parameter values. (Try fitting the acquisition curves of Fig. 5 with $y = e^{-an^2}$ or $y = a + bn$.) Therefore, if a reasonable description of the data is achieved, one must concede that the result provides some mild support for the theory ("mild" because the result will be of little help in choosing between this theory and alternative theories that may come under consideration). If only part of the data is used in estimating the parameter, then a genuine prediction is possible. If, for example, in an experimental application of Eq. (6), the value of θ were determined by using only data from the first few trials of a learning series, then the curve for the remainder of the series could be considered as testing a theoretical prediction. This is a rather low-level and unglamorous form of prediction, but for all that it should not be taken too lightly; we shall see some examples later on in which predictions of this sort are so markedly superior to what could be accomplished without a theory that they represent no small achievement.

When a quantitative theory is in the process of development, the first tests of any newly derived functions are usually of the simple curve-fitting type. Once this first hurdle has been passed, however, we are always eager to move on to higher-level forms of prediction which involve an element of overdetermination. We speak of a parameter as "overdetermined" if its value can be empirically determined in two or more independent ways. We have already found (cf. Formulation of a probabilistic response model) that the parameter h of our response model and the parameter Θ of our acquisition model are overdetermined. Indeed the structure of our theory is such that not only these but any additional parameters which may be introduced in the course of further developments and extensions will similarly be overdetermined in the sense of entering into numerous predicted functional relationships among operationally defined variables.

The determination of a parameter by two or more independent procedures has always been regarded as one of the critical tests of physical theories, and there seems to be no reason why the same will not be true of behavioral theories. Tests of this sort have been among the primary objectives of several research studies involving applications of the statistical model for acquisition. In some cases [11, 27], the results have been clearly confirmatory; more often [1, 8, 37, 89], the results have included a mixture of successes and failures, thus leading either to reconsideration of the theoretical assumptions or to further analysis of the experimental situation, or both. For illustrative purposes we might consider briefly an instance of the latter sort which has arisen in connection with certain human learning experiments.

When acquisition functions for the simple two-alternative verbal conditioning experiment are derived from the present theory—see [37] for details—the parameter Θ turns up both in the equation for the mean acquisition curve, Eq. (9) below, and in the formulas for the conditional probabilities of a given response on trials following the two types of reinforcing events. In several experiments [1, 37] estimates of Θ obtained from mean acquisition curves and estimates obtained from conditional relative frequencies have failed to agree. These disparities gave rise first of all to mild chagrin on the part of the theorist, then to more constructive reactions of two kinds. Noting that all of the experiments in question had been conducted with temporally massed trials, Estes and Straughan [37] hypothesized that some extraneous factor associated with massed trials might be responsible for sequential effects in the data. Such effects have, for example, been found in psychophysical studies [15, 90]. If so, then more adequate trial spacing might tend to minimize the extraneous factors and thus eliminate the disparity. The hypothesis has not been decisively tested, but the evidence so far available [27, 89] favors the conclusion that the disparity is reduced by more adequate trial spacing.

The question also arises whether the theory might not be extended to take account of the sequential effects observed with massed trials. An attempt to handle one possible source of sequential effects has been reported by Straughan [88]. Straughan considered the possibility that there might be a certain amount of lag, or inertia, in the stimulus sampling process, so that a stimulus element which has been sampled on a given trial would be more likely to be sampled on the following trial than an element which has not. Introducing this "lag" assumption into the acquisition model, Straughan showed that predictions concerning forms and asymptotes of acquisition curves are unaffected but that sequential effects of the kind observed in massed-trial experiments are predictable from the revised model.

By exploiting the notion of overdetermination, it is possible to conduct exceedingly stringent tests of a model while working entirely within a single experimental situation. Yet even if these tests are successfully passed, our theoretical ambitions are not satisfied. Next we begin to hope that predictions may be possible on a still higher level of generality, that involving situational invariance. That is, we would like to evaluate the parameters of the model in one situation and then use the obtained values to generate completely a priori predictions of behavior in new situations. This is always a difficult step; in order to achieve it, one needs not only an adequate model but also a sufficiently detailed understanding of the variables involved in a number of different experimental situations. Failing the latter, the best model will have little chance of succeeding at cross-situational prediction.

The first attempt to achieve the third level of prediction with the present model was carried out on a very modest scale. In preliminary investigations it had been found that functions derived from the model provided satisfactory descriptions of bar-pressing acquisition curves, both for individual animals and for groups. The acquisition function contained the two free parameters which have been previously mentioned, the sampling parameter Θ and the minimum response time h, and it was a clear implication of the theory that other things equal, the values of these parameters should be independent of the particular response classification. Therefore, once these parameters were evaluated for a group of animals during acquisition of one bar-pressing habit, it should be possible to predict in advance the detailed course of acquisition of a second bar-pressing habit. Using an apparatus which contained two bars in different locations, the indicated experiment was carried out with clearly confirmatory results [20]. This instance of successful prediction, even on a very limited scale, was the first concrete evidence that we might be on the path toward a theory of some generality.

A second type of experiment which had been sufficiently studied to provide a promising test situation was T-maze learning in the rat. If the model gives an adequate representation of T-maze learning, then not only should an appropriate function derived from the model, namely, Eq. (6), describe acquisition of a particular maze response, e.g., turning left, but once the parameter Θ has been evaluated, the model should provide a priori predictions of the course of learning during a series of reversals. However, judging from the extant literature on simple reversal learning [e.g., 50, 71, 77, 85] prospects of successful prediction were anything but bright. All previously reported studies agree that rate of learning improves during successive reversals; if so, then the value of Θ, which determines the slope of the learning curve, could not remain constant over a series of reversals, and the theoretical predictions would be bound to fail.

Critical study of the literature revealed one possible loophole; all the preceding studies had been conducted with temporally massed trials, and we already had some evidence from verbal conditioning experiments that some of the simplifying assumptions of the model were not well satisfied under these conditions. Consequently, D. W. Lauer and the writer planned and carried out a study of successive reversals in the T-maze situation with a design which permitted a comparison of learning rates under widely spaced trials with learning rates under closely massed trials [36]. Since our spaced condition involved single daily trials, it took over four months to run through five series. The results, however, were enlightening. The usual progressive improvement in learning rate was observed in our massed-trial groups, but not in our spaced-trial group. For the latter, the value of the slope parameter remained so clearly constant over successive reversals that values could be estimated from the data of earlier series and used to predict the learning curves of later series.

Attempts at series-to-series prediction in simple two-choice experiments with human subjects have run into similar problems. When trials are temporally massed, rate of learning characteristically increases over successive series [37], but as spacing is increased, this effect is reduced and the slope parameter Θ becomes more nearly recoverable from one series to the next [27, 33, 89].

Effects of reinforcement. The achievement of our acquisition theory that has aroused the widest interest, extending to statisticians, game theorists, and economists, as well as psychologists, is the successful prediction of asymptotic response probabilities under a variety of random reinforcement schedules and in both animal and human cases. These predictions are generated by the acquisition model sketched above, with occasional guidance from contiguity principles. The type of reasoning involved can be illustrated nicely in terms of the well-known T-maze experiment of Brunswik [9], with which is associated the origin of the now popular term *probability learning*. In Brunswik's experiment, rats were run under random reinforcement with a correction procedure. Under 75 per cent reinforcement, for example, food was available on one side of the T with probability .75 and on the other side with probability .25. Since in this procedure the animal is permitted to correct errors, each trial terminates with a reinforced run to one side of the maze; and according to contiguity-interference principles, the response which occurs last on a trial should become connected to all cues sampled on the trial. Therefore, our acquisition function, Eq. (5), should describe the change in probability of the terminal response on each trial. Knowing the position of the food on each trial, we are in a position to make repeated application of Eq. (5) and thus predict the course of learning over a series of trials. This trial by trial computation would be laborious, however, and we prefer to take a shortcut. Given that on any trial one of the two alternative responses is reinforced with probability π and the other with probability $1 - \pi$, it can be proved by mathematical induction that p_n, the expected probability of the first response after n trials, is given by the simple formula

$$p_n = \pi - (\pi - p_1)(1 - \Theta)^{n-1} \tag{9}$$

Since the value of Θ is between 0 and 1, the term $(1 - \Theta)^{n-1}$ must approach zero for large n, and we see at a glance that asymptotically the expected probability of a given response should be equal to the probability of reinforcement.

The results of Brunswik's experiment were not obviously incompatible with our prediction, but his series of trials was so abbreviated that one could not be confident his animals had reached asymptotes. In order to provide a more decisive test, D. W. Lauer and the writer have more recently conducted an experiment which essentially replicated Brunswik's $\pi = .75$ condition except that our animals were run one trial per day over a much longer series. This study [65] yielded mean asymptotic response probabilities (estimated from relative frequency of a given response over the last 16 days of a 56-day series) in close agreement with the theoretical predictions from Eq. (9).

In a very similar manner the model can be applied to the type of verbal conditioning experiment originated by Humphreys [58]. In this situation the experimenter assigns fixed probabilities, π and $1 - \pi$, to a pair of alternative events; these events might, for example, be occurrences of one or the other of a pair of "reinforcing" lights, saying of "right" or "wrong" by the experimenter, appearance of heads or tails on the toss of a biased coin. On each trial the subject predicts which event will occur and then observes the actual outcome. On the assumption that occurrence of a given event reinforces the response of predicting that event, one again arrives at Eq. (9) as the predicted learning function—for derivation see [37].

The interesting prediction, implied by Eq. (9), that mean probability of predicting an event should be asymptotically equal to the actual probability of the event did not have to wait long for experimental test. During the same year in which Eq. (9) was first derived, two independent studies by Grant, Hake, and Hornseth [43] and by Jarvik [59] appeared, both confirming the predicted asymptotic relationship. To check further on the generality of the result, J. H. Straughan and the writer proceeded during the following year to study both original acquisition of a guessing response and reacquisition following a shift in probability of reinforcement; we obtained the predicted asymptotic relationship in both cases, and also demonstrated that Eq. (9) describes not only group curves but learning curves of individual subjects [37]. Equation (9) has been generalized and applied to guessing experiments involving more than two alternatives by Neimark [76] and Detambel [18] with uniformly confirmatory results.[5]

The last two studies represent a step forward, for the most convincing tests of a theory are always those which involve new experimental arrangements. Going from two to three alternatives in the guessing situation may seem too minor a generalization to qualify as an instance of "predicting new facts," but further study of the model suggests the possibility of dealing with some rather more radical innovations. Initially we thought only in terms of constant probabilities of reinforcement simply because experiments on partial reinforcement had traditionally been limited to this case. There is nothing in our theoretical assumptions, however, to restrict us to situations where probability of reinforcement is constant over trials. The assumptions specify how response probability changes on any given trial; therefore if π in Eq. (9) were replaced by some function π_n giving probability of reinforcement as a function of trials, it should be a purely mathematical problem to deduce the predicted course of learning. The mathematical problem has indeed been solved for a wide variety of cases [30]. The gist of the theoretical result is that response probability "tracks" probability of reinforcement much as one tracks a moving target; if π_n is any reasonably orderly function, then asymptotically the curve of p_n is described by a function of similar form. It can be predicted, for example, that if probability of reinforcement varies linearly with trials (i.e., π_n is a straight line) then the curve of response

---

[5] Results of a study, "Probability learning with two and three choices," reported by R. A. Gardner at the 1957 meetings of the Midwestern Psychological Association suggest that under some, as yet incompletely specifiable, conditions, asymptotic response probabilities for the three-choice case tend to overshoot the predicted values.

probability will approach a straight line with the same slope. M. Johns and the writer have recently tested this prediction in a modified verbal conditioning situation, with results typified by the empirical curve shown in Fig. 6.

Another natural application of the random reinforcement model arises if we permit the probability of reinforcement to depend on the response made by the subject. In conditioning terminology, this amounts to going over from the classical to the instrumental paradigm. Suppose, for example, that in a verbal conditioning situation the subject's task is to predict which of a pair of alternative events E_1 and E_2

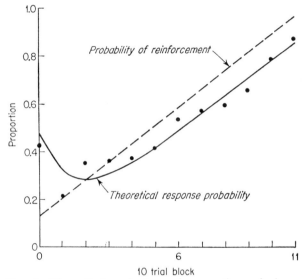

FIG. 6. Theoretical and observed proportions of A_1 responses for a verbal conditioning study in which probability of reinforcement varies linearly with trials.

will occur on each trial. In the type of experiment previously discussed, which we will call the noncontingent case, the actual probability of E_1 is π and the probability of E_2 is $1 - \pi$ regardless of the subject's response. In the type of experiment now to be considered, the contingent case, the events E_1 and E_2 have one set of probabilities, say π_{11} and $1 - \pi_{11}$ if the subject's response on the trial is a prediction of E_1, but a different set of probabilities, π_{21} and $1 - \pi_{21}$, if the subject predicts E_2. When the model is applied to this case [23, 30], the predicted learning curve has the same form as that of Eq. (9) but has the asymptote

$$p_\infty = \frac{\pi_{21}}{1 - \pi_{11} + \pi_{21}} \tag{10}$$

where p_∞ represents the probability, after a large number of trials, of the response corresponding to reinforcing event E_1. As in the noncontingent case, the model for the contingent case can be generalized to any number of alternatives [30]. In all instances, noncontingent and contingent, two or more than two alternatives, it turns out that expected asymptotic response probability depends only on the probabilities of reinforcement, and thus can be predicted in advance of an experiment. Predictions of this sort for contingent cases with two and three alternatives have been confirmed experimentally by A. Brody and the writer in a camouflaged[6] guessing experiment. Experiments by Detambel [16, 18] and Neimark [76] could also be taken as yielding confirmatory evidence, but they involve a procedural complication which will be discussed below.

Still another variation on classical random reinforcement procedures was suggested by the analogy between some of the guessing experiments successfully treated by our theory and simple game situations. To illustrate the analogy, suppose two individuals, whom we will label as E and S, play at matching pennies. If E resolves always to turn up heads with probability π and tails with probability $1 - \pi$, then he can apply Eq. (9) to predict changes in S's probability of guessing "heads." But following this strategy, E will not make any money; if he chooses $\pi = .5$ he can expect to break even; otherwise S will be able to match him more than half the time. In order to improve his chances, E may complicate his strategy, perhaps by making his selection of heads or tails on any trial depend on S's guess on one or more preceding trials; for example, E might decide to choose heads with probability $\pi_1 = .25$ if S has guessed heads on the preceding trial and with probability $\pi_2 = .75$ if S has guessed tails on the preceding trial. A very direct extension of our acquisition model, requiring no new assumptions, will enable us to predict S's learning curve under these modified circumstances. In fact, an interesting theorem can be derived [30] which applies to all similar types of reinforcement contingency. If in a two-alternative learning situation the probability of reinforcing event E_1 on trial n is equal to π_{11} or π_{21} according as response A_1 or A_2, respectively, has occurred on trial $n - v$, then the rate of learning depends upon the "lag" v, but the asymptote is independent of v—and in fact is always given by Eq. (10). A preliminary experimental test of this theorem by M. Johns and the writer has yielded results in support of both predictions. With $\pi_{11} = .66$ and

---

[6] The situation was presented to the subject as one involving psychophysical judgments; the reinforcing events were signals purportedly indicating correct and incorrect choices but actually occurring randomly with probabilities π_{ij} and $1 - \pi_{ij}$. A report of the results is in preparation.

$\pi_{21} = 1.0$, in a guessing situation, progressively slower rates of learning were obtained as we went from $v = 0$ to $v = 1$ and then to $v = 2$, but the terminal relative frequency of A_1 responses was close to the predicted value

$$p_{1,\infty} = \frac{1}{1 - .66 + 1} = .75$$

in all three cases (.75, .80, and .74, respectively, for three independent groups of subjects).

Applications of the theory to predict simultaneously the behavior of both players in simple two-person games have been worked out and tested by the writer [31] and by Atkinson and Suppes [4]. Judging from the results of these exploratory studies, it seems quite a promising possibility that continued cultivation of the model for acquisition under determinate reinforcement will yield accounts of learning in a variety of situations which arise in the study of games and economic behavior.

Effects of nonreinforcement. The studies of Detambel and Neimark raise an issue which we have delicately skirted so far—namely, what to do about nonreinforcement. The T-maze experiment with a correction procedure and all the human learning experiments we have treated up to this point have an important characteristic in common: we can specify without ambiguity precisely what response is reinforced on each trial. There are many common learning situations which lack this characteristic, e.g., operant conditioning in the Skinner box, maze learning with a noncorrection procedure, human learning experiments which involve nonreward or incomplete information on some trials. For convenience in reference, let us refer to these two types of experimental arrangement as *determinate reinforcement* and *indeterminate reinforcement*, respectively.

From the standpoint of contiguity theory, this classification should be expected to be of critical importance. In determinate situations, each trial terminates with the occurrence of one or another of a set of mutually exclusive reinforcing events ($E_1, E_2, \ldots, E_r$), and each of these events, whenever it occurs, evokes a response belonging to the corresponding experimentally defined response class in the set ($A_1, A_2, \ldots, A_r$). In a guessing experiment, for example, the occurrence of event E_j is assumed to evoke from the subject a reaction compatible with (belonging to the same class as) A_j, the response of predicting E_j. Similarly, if the left goal box of a T maze is open and contains food whereas the door of the right goal box is locked, we can be confident that the last locomotor response on the trial will be going left and approaching the food. Whether or not one is intuitively comfortable with our assumptions about the conditions of reinforcement in determinate situations, the fact remains that they lead to correct predictions.

By contrast, consider, say, the T maze with a noncorrective procedure. Now, on "incorrect" runs, the animal is confined for a given interval in the empty goal box. What effect will an unreinforced run have on probability of going to the given side? A natural first thought is that nonreinforcement of a right turn should reduce its probability $(\Delta p_R = -\Theta p_R)$ and therefore increase the probability of a left turn $\Delta p_L = \Theta(1 - p_L)$ just as in the correction procedure. If so, then Eq. (9) should describe T-maze learning under a noncorrection procedure in which food is placed on one side with probability π and on the other with probability $1 - \pi$. The prediction, however, turns out to be contrary to fact. Several studies[7] have shown that with a noncorrective procedure almost all animals learn to go 100 per cent of the time to the more frequently reinforced side. These results have instigated an active line of theoretical and experimental investigation devoted to ascertaining the precise effects of an unreinforced maze trial. A rather oversimplified interpretation of contiguity theory might lead one to expect that an unreinforced T-maze trial should yield reinforcement of the incorrect turn, since that was the last response made at the choice point on the given trial; this assumption would, however, lead to even worse predictions than the preceding one. What is obviously left out of account is the fact that after entering an empty goal box the animal may attempt to retrace while still under the influence of some of the stimuli that were effective during the maze run. If we assume that such attempts at retracing do occur, and more specifically that the probability of the retracing response is equal to the momentary probability of the "correct" response, then one can derive the interesting prediction [19] that, on the average, response probabilities will remain unchanged on such trials. Introducing the assumption into our model for partial reinforcement[8] we find that the observed results are now predicted quite accurately.

Still our treatment of the noncorrection case is not entirely satis-

---

[7] These include studies, all unpublished, by J. C. Stanley [cited in 13, chap. 13], D. R. Meyer (reported at the Midwestern Psychological Association meetings in 1954), R. Hickson and T. Carterette (reported at the Midwestern Psychological Association meetings in 1955), and S. Weinstock and A. J. North (personal communication).

[8] Now the equation

$$p_{n+1} = (1 - \Theta)p_n + \Theta$$

is to be applied on trials when a response is reinforced and the equation

$$p_{n+1} = p_n$$

on trials when it is not,

fying. To handle acquisition under a partial reinforcement schedule we must assume that an unreinforced trial yields no mean change in response probability. But this assumption has the embarrassing consequence of leading to the prediction that extinction will never occur even if reinforcement is permanently discontinued. I cannot claim, at the time of writing, to have escaped entirely from this predicament, but a series of as yet unpublished experiments has suggested a way out. Studying the effects of blocks of forced reinforced and forced unreinforced maze runs, I have found that in the naïve animal an unreinforced trial produces no apparent change in response probabilities, but that after a series of reinforced runs to a given side of a T maze, the introduction of nonreinforcement yields a decrement in probablity of response to that side describable by the difference equation $p_{n+1} = (1 - \Theta)p_n$. Apparently under partial reinforcement schedules, the effect of nonreinforcement varies between these extremes; the quantitative description of this variation remains a problem for further research.

In human learning experiments, the introduction of unreinforced trials raises problems analogous in many respects to those brought out by the T-maze example. Nonreinforcement arises in the Thorndikian situation if reward or knowledge of results is withheld, in the guessing experiment if on some trials none of the events E_j occurs. As in the animal case, contiguity principles are of no help in predicting the effect of an unreinforced trial unless we can specify just what nonreinforcement leads the subject to do. Certainly this will depend on the nature of the task and the instructions, so no one specification is likely to hold in general. By considering particular experimental procedures, we may, however, be able to define classes of procedures which yield similar outcomes. One class for which we might expect to find considerable homogeneity comprises situations in which either the nature of the instructions or the nature of the task leads the subject to interpret a blank trial (i.e., one on which none of the experimentally defined reinforcing events occurs) as indicating neither correctness nor incorrectness of his response. In such situations, contiguity assumptions lead to the prediction that the effect of a blank trial on response probability will be described, on the average, by

$$p_{n+1} = p_n$$

Incorporating this hypothesis into our acquisition model, we can derive learning curves for a modified guessing experiment in which the subject's task is to guess which of a set of reinforcing events (E_1, E_2, . . . , E_r) will occur but in which the probabilities of these events do

not add up to unity. The predicted curve has the same form as that of
Eq. (9), but the new asymptote is

$$p_{j,\infty} = \frac{\pi_j}{\pi_1 + \pi_2 + \cdots + \pi_r}$$

where $p_{j,\infty}$ is the mean asymptotic probability of predicting event E_j;
and $1 - (\pi_1 + \pi_2 + \cdots + \pi_r)$ is, of course, the probability of a
blank trial. Derivations of the learning function for this case have
been reported by Neimark [76], Estes [24], and Bush and Mosteller
[13, chap. 13], and experimental results which appear generally confirmatory have been reported by Neimark [76], and by Anderson [1].
Very recently, a more stringent test of the "neutral" hypothesis has
been provided by Atkinson [2], who showed that under a specially
contrived reinforcement schedule differential outcomes are predictable
from three different hypotheses about the effect of a blank trial. The
hypotheses are

(A) *The "neutral" hypothesis: on the average a blank trial leaves all response
probabilities unchanged.*
(B) *The response which occurs on a blank trial is conditioned to all cues
sampled on the trial.*
(C) *All the alternative responses are equally likely to be conditioned to the
cues sampled on the blank trial.*

Atkinson's experimental results appeared incompatible with B or C,
but compatible with A.

　　In a second important class of experiments, the instructions to the
subject state or imply that omission of reinforcement indicates a wrong
response. An experiment of this type reported by Detambel [16]
utilized two response keys and a single "reinforcing" light; the subject's task was to attempt on each trial "to choose the key that will
turn on the light." In one of Detambel's groups, the light appeared
following responses to key A_1 with probability .5 and following responses to key A_2 with probability zero. Assuming that under these
conditions nonreinforcement of A_2 will have the same effect on the
response probabilities as reinforcement of A_1, and vice versa, we can
enter the values $\pi_{11} = .5$ and $\pi_{21} = 1$ in Eq. (10) and obtain for the
predicted asymptotic probability of response A_1,

$$p_{1,\infty} = \frac{1}{1 - .5 + 1} = .67$$

which proves to be in good agreement with Detambel's data.[9]

　　[9] Data for a variety of reinforcement schedules in this experimental situation have
been reported by Brand, Woods, and Sakoda [7].

When this last type of experiment involves more than two alternative response classes, a new theoretical problem arises which has instigated considerable investigation but has not been adequately solved. Imagine an experiment identical to that of Detambel described above, except that three response keys are available to the subject. Now, as before, a response will be expected to receive an increment in probability $p_{j,n+1} = (1 - 0)p_{j,n} + 0$ when it is followed by the reinforcing light and a decrement $p_{j,n+1} = (1 - \Theta)p_{j,n}$ when it is not. In either case the change in $p_{j,n}$ must be compensated by a change in one or both of the other response probabilities. If, e.g., A_1 occurs and the reinforcing light does not appear, we must have

$$p_{1,n+1} = (1 - \Theta)p_{1,n}$$

and $\quad p_{2,n+1} + p_{3,n+1} = (1 - \Theta)(p_{2,n} + p_{3,n}) + \Theta$

in order to keep the probabilities adding up to unity. But how is the increment to be distributed between classes A_2 and A_3? The mathematical theory will be satisfied by any mode of distribution which conserves total probability. One might expect that the increment would be divided equally among the remaining response classes, but Neimark has shown that predictions based on this assumption deviate systematically from observed terminal mean response probabilities [76]. Several investigators have suggested that some sort of weighting scheme should be employed, so that the increment will be most likely to go to the response which has been most frequently reinforced. A purely *ad hoc* weighting system is not particularly satisfying, however, and no one has yet succeeded in deriving an adequate weighting system from more general theoretical assumptions.

How can we summarize the present status of the theory relative to interpretations of nonreinforcement? For situations involving only two response classes, satisfactory interpretations can be provided for two extreme cases. If instructions or preliminary training ensure that nonreinforcement of a given response either produces no change in response probability or else produces a decrement equivalent to that resulting from reinforcement of a competing response, then accurate predictions of curve forms and asymptotes are generated by the theory. Experimental conditions can be specified which appear to satisfy the assumptions associated with these two cases. For experiments in which the effect of nonreinforcement is not well determined by instructions or preliminary training, obtained learning curves appear always to fall between those corresponding to the "neutral" and "decremental" cases [see, e.g., 13, chap. 13; 42, 76]. The model for the "neutral" case has been successfully extended to include situations involving more than two response classes, but a comparable extension has not been achieved for the "decremental" case.

The series of problems generated by our attempts to handle non-reinforcement has been instructive in a number of respects. In it we have found numerous reminders that the role of a theory, at any level of analysis, is to process information, not to substitute for empirical investigations. When, for a given situation, we are able to specify the response which is reinforced by each distinguishable outcome of an experimental trial, our mathematical theory generates accurate quantitative predictions as to the course and asymptote of learning, but when our specification is incomplete, the theory remains silent. Similarly, when we are able to specify the response that will be evoked by an experimental event, the contiguity principle is helpful in indicating what reinforcing effect the event will have; but when we lack this specification, the contiguity principle cannot be applied. Always a theory first asks us what we know, then tells us what we can predict.

We also have seen illustrations of how theoretically significant classifications evolve from the interaction of theory and experiment. Even the most familiar empirical landscape may be quite altered in appearance when viewed through the medium of a new theory. New distinctions are forced upon us; old lines of demarcation sometimes disappear, sometimes take on new significance. Time after time we find that with a modification of some assumption, or merely on recombination of assumptions, the theory delivers a new set of theorems (experimental laws). In applying the theory we are led, then, to classify together sets of situations which are described by the same sets of laws. Thus we find that experiments of the maze type run with correction procedures and human learning experiments involving complete knowledge of results (full information as to which response is correct on each trial) are described by the same quantitative laws; therefore we group these together under the label *determinate reinforcement*. Experiments which involve nonreinforcement or incomplete knowledge of results are not all describable by a single set of laws, however, and must be further analyzed.

Independence of learning rates and asymptotes. The unsettled question of what to do about nonreinforcement has not been the only roadblock on our way to an adequate account of acquisition under partial reinforcement. Another cluster of vexing problems has been associated with two parameters, π and Θ in Eq. (9), which should behave independently but which persistently refuse to do so. According to our assumptions, the sampling parameter Θ depends only on stimulus variables (plus characteristics of the organism) and, therefore, should be unaffected by variation in the probability of reinforcement. In both animal and human cases, however, it is found that the rate of learning, and therefore the value of Θ, varies directly with the difference between initial response probability and probability of reinforcement in any series [37, 65, 76, 89]. The hypothesis has been suggested [37] that this relation may be, in a sense, an artifact of massed trial procedures. In the derivation of Eq. (9) it was assumed that a single population of stimulus elements is sampled independently on each trial. If, however, trials occur in close temporal succession, then the stimulus complex affecting the subject on any one trial may include traces of the stimulation associated with the responses and reinforcing events of one or more preceding trials. Then Θ might well depend on π, for the pattern of trace stimulation would be more variable for π near .5 than for π near 1 or 0. However, the relationship should break down if the intertrial interval is increased or if other measures are utilized to reduce the carry-over of trace stimulation from one trial to the next. Experimental tests of this hypothesis have yielded curiously mixed outcomes. In experiments with human subjects, increasing the effective trial spacing has usually resulted in decreasing the dependence of Θ on π and improving the fit of the model [27, 33, 89]. In the T-maze experiments, however, the same does not appear to be true; acquisition is faster (Θ is greater) with uniform reinforcement than with partial reinforcement even when maze trials are spaced at 24-hr intervals [36, 65].

It would be convenient if we could settle each problem before moving on to the next. However, nature is not always so obliging as to permit this, and we cannot allow our general theoretical advance to be held up indefinitely by a few isolated pillboxes. While some of our forces remain pinned down by refractory problems associated with nonreinforcement and parameter invariance, we continue to make progress on other fronts.

Stimulus variability. We have seen that the statistical model assumes learning to be basically a sampling process. On each trial the organism samples the population of stimulus elements defined by the experimental situation and only the elements sampled on the trial influence response probability or undergo changes of state as a consequence of reinforcement. These assumptions are reflected in such acquisition functions as Eqs. (6), (7), and (9) where Θ, defined in the model as the mean sampling probability of stimulus elements, appears as a slope parameter. The fact that various derived functions containing Θ as a parameter have turned out to provide good descriptions of empirical acquisition curves may be taken as supporting the theory in a general way, but it is not critical with respect to any particular aspect of the theory. In any one acquisition series, the stimulating situation is fixed; therefore, no matter how well we succeed in fitting a theoretical function to an empirical curve, we obtain no information as to how the value of Θ depends on stimulus properties. To obtain such information, we must ascertain whether Θ behaves appropriately when stimulus conditions are systematically varied.

There are no standard methods for controlling the variability of a stimulating situation,[10] so it has been necessary to improvise methods for the desired test experiments. Burke, Estes, and Hellyer [11] introduced gradations in stimulus variability by assigning varying sampling probabilities to the components of a complex stimulus. Subjects in a two-alternative verbal conditioning situation were presented with a pattern of lights on a display panel as the ready signal at the beginning of each trial. In the first experiment, the probabilities of reinforcement were independent of the signal pattern, but the individual panel lights were assigned sampling probabilities of $1/3$, $2/3$, and 1 for three groups of subjects. Therefore, stimulus elements associated with any one light should have Θ values in the ratio $1/3:2/3:1$ for the three groups. Results of the experiment confirmed the quantitative predictions that the rate of learning should be directly related to stimulus sampling probability while the asymptote of learning should be independent of it, and also agreed well with quantitative predictions derived from the theory.

A follow-up experiment [33] used a discriminative situation; the procedure differed from that just described only in that the subject's task was to discriminate between two sets of signal lights, and the sampling probabilities for individual lights were $1/2$ and 1 for "variable" and "constant" stimulus groups. Again the principle trends in the data were in agreement with theoretical predictions. As usual, however, the correspondence between theory and data, although promising, was not perfect. The principal disparity in this case was that for the discrimination group, the predicted effects of stimulus variability on learning rate were smaller than expected, and in fact not statistically reliable, during original acquisition; only during a reversal series were the effects significant and of the expected order of magnitude. The same disparity has appeared in further, unpublished, studies, and therefore probably cannot be written off to sampling error. It has been suggested [33] that the effects of experimentally controlled stimuli, e.g., the panel lights, may be attenuated on early

[10] Several investigators, e.g., Voeks [91], Wolfle [94], have reported effects of stimulus variability on learning rate which appear to be in qualitative agreement with theoretical expectation; the techniques used for manipulating stimulus variability in those studies do not, however, lend themselves to quantitative tests of the present theory.

trials by the presence of uncontrolled stimulation, primarily verbal, associated with the giving of instructions and initial adjustment to the experimental situation on the part of the subject; this hypothesis should not be difficult to check on experimentally.

Transfer and stimulus compounding. All successful applications of statistical learning theory provide indirect support for the assumption that probability of a response is equal to the proportion of stimulus elements in the trial sample that are connected to the response. So long as the stimulating situation remains fixed, however, no evidence is obtainable that could be considered critical with respect to this assumption. As we shall see in a later section, other investigators, starting with quite different assumptions, sometimes arrive at learning functions identical in form to functions derived from our assumptions. To obtain more direct tests, we must determine response probability in the presence of two or more stimulus situations, then predict the probability in a new situation which comprises portions of the other situations in a new combination. An experiment of this type by Fink and Patton [39] has yielded qualitatively confirmatory findings, but for a more rigorous test we must turn to Schoeffler's carefully controlled quantitative study [83].

As the first stage in his study, Schoeffler trained human subjects to discriminate between two randomly selected, nonoverlapping sets of signal lights, S_1 and S_2, on a display panel. After the subjects had attained a criterion of 100 per cent correct responding (i.e., one response A_1 reached a probability of approximately unity in the presence of S_1 and a second response A_2, a probability of approximately unity in the presence of S_2) they were tested on various new combinations, e.g., all of S_1 plus all of S_2, half of S_1 plus one fourth of S_2, all of S_1 plus a new set S_3 which had not been presented during discrimination training. Determinations of response probability on a sample of 180 subjects yielded close agreement between predicted and obtained values. In the cases just cited, for example, the predicted probabilities of the A_1 response were .5, .67, and .75, respectively; the observed probabilities were .54, .63, and .73. Comparable accuracy of prediction has been obtained in tests of compounding following the "probabilistic discrimination" training described in a later section, and, by Peterson [78], in tests of compounding following verbal association training.

Generalizations of the original statistical model. Behavioral theories have always to deal with extremely complex empirical situations. Consequently, in order to get started on the formulation of a new theory, it is always necessary to resort to ruthless simplification and idealization of the empirical system. All but a very few variables are ignored completely, and those that remain are permitted only the simplest properties. Once the enterprise has gained some momentum and the initial maximally simplified model has survived some preliminary empirical tests, it is time to begin asking how the theory would be modified if some of the simplifying assumptions were relaxed. At a minimum, the ensuing analyses yield improved perspective as to the direction and magnitude of errors of approximation involved in working with the original model. In some cases the results are much more far reaching and lead to important generalizations of the theory.

Variation in stimulus sampling probabilities. During the initial formulation of the stimulus sampling model it was expedient to assume that all stimulus elements in a given population have equal probabilities of being sampled on any learning trial. Utilizing this simplifying assumption, we arrived at a set of simple laws, e.g., those represented by Eqs. (4) and (5) above, which have been the basis for a variety of empirical applications. The first occasion for seriously questioning this assumption arose in the fall of 1951 when C. J. Burke and I were invited to contribute a paper on set-theoretical models to a symposium on learning theory at the meetings of the Institute of Mathematical Statistics. In order to give a systematic account of the class of models represented by the original statistical model, we undertook to investigate the consequences of removing the assumption of equal sampling probabilities. The result of this investigation [cf. 32] was a more general model which included the original one as a special case (the "equal θ case").

The general model ("unequal θ case") is not very convenient to work with for practical purposes, but study of its properties has led to some interesting conclusions. One of these is the finding that under all conditions of reinforcement so far investigated, predicted asymptotes of learning are independent of variation in stimulus-sampling probabilities. If we compare the acquisition curve derived for any particular situation from the general model with the corresponding equal θ case, we find that in each instance the curves not only go to the same asymptotes but have similar forms. Further, even when there is considerable dispersion of θ values, the curves derived on the equal θ assumption provide adequate approximations to the exact curves for most purposes of experimental application. A finding of somewhat different character is that when there is dispersion of θ values in a stimulus population, the predicted slope of a curve of relearning following extinction will be steeper than that of the original learning curve.

Stimulus fluctuation model for time-dependent processes. From what we know of the structure and function of organisms it seems clear that the process of stimulation must involve at least two sources of variability, one with a locus primarily in the environment and one with a locus primarily in the organism. Effective stimulation occurs when energy changes in the environment give rise to activity in a receptor system. Any variation in the energy input from the environment must be expected to produce variation in effective stimulation. For some purposes it is convenient to assume that stimulating conditions can be held perfectly constant throughout an experimental period and can be exactly reproduced from one period to the next. Even if this assumption were satisfied, variability in stimulation would still be produced both by variations in the gross orientation of the subject relative to sources of stimulation and by variation in physiological properties of receptor systems. The subject-determined variability was taken into account in the original statistical model by the assumption that the subject draws random trial samples of stimulus elements from a fixed population. It was immediately apparent, however, that the theoretical restriction to a fixed stimulus population was paralleled by a restriction on empirical applicability of the model to situations in which such time-dependent processes as forgetting and spontaneous recovery could be assumed negligible.

These considerations led me to investigate the consequences of permitting a stimulus population to vary in composition during the course of learning; this variation would, of course, be the conceptual counterpart of variation in environmental conditions. The results of the ensuing mathematical analyses have been incorporated into a more general model which includes population constancy as a special case and which also permits treatment of a variety of distributional phenomena which were beyond the scope of the original formulation.

The extended theory assumes that the stimulus events which correspond to stimulus elements in the set model depend upon numerous independently variable aspects or components of the environmental situation. The dependency is such that a given stimulus element is available for sampling during a given experimental period only if a particular set of conditions is present in the environmental situation. Presumably systematic variation in environmental conditions can be ruled out by appropriate experimental controls, but there must always be some residual random variability in physical properties of the situation. Intuitively, one would expect random fluctuation in environmental conditions to be readily observable in most learning experiments but perhaps detectable only by instrumental measurement in the best controlled situations. In any event, no sweeping commitment as to magnitude of these effects is necessary. We simply assume that the sources of stimulation in any experimental situation undergo constant random fluctuation and proceed to derive the testable consequences of this assumption.

The mathematical properties of the fluctuation process—cf. [25]

for details—are such that each stimulus element has some fixed probability of being available for sampling during any given period. The important consequence of stimulus fluctuation for learning theory is that stimulus elements which are available for sampling during a learning period may be replaced by other, previously unavailable, elements prior to a subsequent test period; thus response probabilities

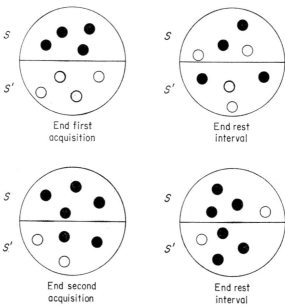

End first
acquisition

End rest
interval

End second
acquisition

End rest
interval

Fig. 7. Representation of retention losses during acquisition in terms of stimulus element model. During the rest interval following each acquisition period, conditioned and unconditioned elements (closed and open dots, respectively) are randomly interchanged between the available and unavailable portions of the stimulus population (S and S', respectively) until mean densities in the two portions are equalized. Proportion of closed dots in the upper half of each circle represents momentary response probability.

may change over a period of time during which there has been no opportunity for learning.

Consider, for example, the hypothetical conditioning situation schematized in Fig. 7. The total set of stimulus elements potentially available in the situation is partitioned into the subset S of elements available for sampling by the subject during any one period and the subset S' of elements unavailable for sampling during the period. Open and closed circles represent elements that are or are not, respectively, connected to the conditioned response. Initially, let us assume, all elements are unconditioned. At the end of the acquisition period, all elements in S have become conditioned and probability of the conditioned response has reached unity. During a rest period, however, the random fluctuation process leads to an interchange of elements between S and S'. As this interchange continues, the proportion of conditioned elements in S decreases until the proportions in S and S' reach equality. Consequently, if subjects are returned to the experimental situation and tested after various rest intervals, we will find that probability of the conditioned response decreases from 1.0 to .5 along a negatively accelerated curve as a function of the rest interval. If a second period of conditioning is given after a rest interval, the total number of conditioned elements will be increased over the previous

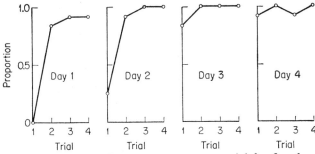

Fig. 8. Proportion of correct responses per trial for first four trials of four successive days in a T-maze study with continuous reinforcement.

total (from 4 to 6 in the example) and therefore response probability will exhibit a smaller decline (from 1.0 to .75 in the example) during a rest period following the second acquisition period. Over a series of acquisition periods, the amount of retention loss ("forgetting") between periods will continue to decline until eventually all elements are conditioned and the interchange of elements between periods leads to no further change in response probability. In other words, amount of retention increases with the number of acquisition periods. In Fig. 8 are shown empirical curves for successive periods of acquisition of a maze response [for experimental details cf. 36]. The intraperiod and interperiod changes in response proportions demonstrate nicely the effects anticipated from the schema of Fig. 7.

From the assumption of constant fluctuation, taken together with the original statistical model, it has been possible to derive a set of quantitative laws describing curves of spontaneous recovery and forgetting, and to account for numerous phenomena relating to distribution of practice [25, 26]. Also, the extended theory provides for a distinction between the two aspects of learning represented by reaction potential and habit strength in Hull's system [55] or reflex strength and reflex reserve in Skinner's [85]. In the statistical theory, momentary response strength is defined in terms of the set of elements that is available for sampling during a given period, habit strength in terms of the total population of elements that may become available at any time during an experiment. Resistance to extinction may continue to increase even after momentary response probability has reached an asymptote if the additional learning trials are spaced out sufficiently so that there is opportunity for interchange of previously available and previously unavailable elements.

Quantitative predictions generated by the fluctuation model have been tested in several experimental studies. A number of predicted characteristics of spontaneous recovery and regression (retention loss) in simple instrumental learning situations have been demonstrated by Lauer and Estes [36, 65]. The most elaborate quantitative application of the model is Homme's study of spontaneous recovery in a bar-pressing situation [54]. Homme obtained evidence confirming predicted relations between the number and distribution of reinforcements of a response and properties of curves for subsequent extinction and recovery. He also showed that in order to provide a detailed quantitative description of the bar-pressing data it is necessary to modify my simplifying assumption of equal fluctuation probabilities for all stimuli in a situation; Homme's modification consists in assuming that some of the stimulus elements in a population are constantly available while the remainder undergo random fluctuation. Another elaboration of the original model has been proposed by McConnell [69] who derived regression and recovery curves applicable to situations in which appreciable stimulus fluctuation occurs within as well as between experimental periods.

The fluctuation model yields also a variety of detailed predictions concerning phenomena of retroactive and proactive interference. This type of application is illustrated for a hypothetical retroaction experiment in Fig. 9. The experiment is assumed to be one in which the stimulus situation remains the same and only reinforcement contingencies change from original to interpolated learning. Solid circles in the diagram represent stimulus elements connected to the response reinforced during original learning; open circles, elements connected to the response reinforced during interpolated learning. The sets S and S' are defined as in Fig. 7. From the same assumptions discussed in relation to the example of Fig. 7, it clearly follows that probability of the originally reinforced response on the test period will be inversely related to amount of interpolated learning and directly related to duration of the rest interval between interpolated learning and the test period. A preliminary test of these predictions has been provided by Frankmann's recent study of retroactive inhibition in a T-maze situation [40]. The study was exploratory in nature, utilizing only two values of each independent variable, and the results, although generally in accord with expectation, are hardly conclusive. It does seem clear, however, that quantitative predictions concerning

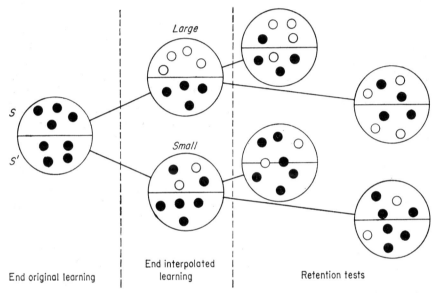

Fig. 9. Representation of retroactive inhibition in terms of stimulus sampling model. Closed and open dots, respectively, represent stimulus elements connected to the response reinforced during original learning and the response reinforced during interpolated learning. "Large" and "small" denote relative amounts of interpolated learning. Each "amount" condition is further subdivided according to the duration of rest interval before the retention test.

the principal variables involved in studies of retroactive and proactive interference can be derived and tested, provided that the experimental situations conventionally used in this area are simplified enough to permit unambiguous identification of stimulus and response variables.

Learning models as stochastic processes. As in the case of nearly all quantitative theories that have their roots in data, the development of statistical learning theory has been, at the mathematical level, a story of progressively increasing abstraction. The initial formulations were strongly molded by the characteristics of particular empirical relationships, and formal assumptions were inextricably intermingled with substantive hypotheses. In order to clarify the structure of the theory and pave the way for extension and generalization, it was necessary to disentangle assumptions as to how learning proceeds from assumptions concerning necessary and sufficient conditions of learning. This had been largely accomplished by the time Burke and I reported our generalization of the set-theoretical model for stimulus variables [32].

Once the mathematical structure of a theory has been clarified, a natural next step is to study the class of mathematical models or systems which it represents. Such analysis often brings out close interrelationships among models that have initially taken diverse forms owing to peculiarities of empirical origins or predilections of particular investigators. In the case of statistical learning theory, it has been found that a number of superficially very different models can best be understood as instances of the class of stochastic (probabilistic) models known as Markov processes. This finding has had a number of useful outcomes. It has facilitated formal comparison among different particular models, e.g., those developed by Bush and Mosteller and those developed by Estes and Burke [29]. It has brought new mathematical methods to bear on problems which arise in working with the models. And researches which are in progress at the time of writing suggest that this line of investigation may yield a modification of present statistical models which will improve and extend the treatment of discrimination learning.

Extension to new empirical areas. Complementing the internal forces that lead to generalizations of a model are external ones arising from attempts to handle new empirical problems. Space will not permit us to discuss all of the researches in progress which are attempting to extend the empirical scope of statistical learning theory. It will suffice, perhaps, for the purpose of sketching the present front line of theoretical advance, if we merely indicate briefly the nature of some of these lines of combined experimental and theoretical investigation.

Elementary discrimination learning. It should be possible to handle the simplest forms of discrimination learning by a rather obvious extension of our acquisition model. The only complication is that we must define a set of stimulus elements to correspond to each of the stimulus situations to be discriminated. Communality, or similarity, between the situations will be represented by common elements. At one extreme, a discrimination problem involving two totally different situations will be represented by two non-overlapping stimulus sets, say S_1 and S_2. If one response A_1 were always reinforced in the presence of S_1 and a second response A_2 were always reinforced in the presence of S_2, then we would simply have two simultaneous acquisition processes; if we considered only trials on which S_1 was presented, we would predict an acquisition curve of the form of Eq. (6), and if we considered only trials on which S_2 was presented, we would predict a similar acquisition curve for the other response. Therefore, a curve for probability of correct responding against trials would have the same form as both of these and would go to unity as an asymptote. If, however, the two sets had some elements in common, then at any given time some of these common elements would be connected to A_1 and some to A_2 (50 per cent to each under the conditions we are considering if S_1 and S_2 are presented equally often), and asymptotic probability of correct responding would be less than unity.

Unfortunately, most conventional discrimination experiments are too complicated to provide suitable test situations for the model. In experimental situations of the Lashley type, for example, the duration of exposure to the discriminative stimulus is uncontrolled, and may vary systematically during the course of learning. Data on discrimination in classical conditioning situations [53, chap. 8] and simple operant situations [44] appear qualitatively in accord with theoretical expectations, but there have been no parametric studies suitable for testing quantitative predictions.

In the Indiana laboratory, we have carried out some quantitative tests using the same apparatus described above in connection with studies of stimulus variability. The light-guessing situation is modified by defining for each subject two sets of panel lights, S_1 and S_2, which are to be discriminated. The two sets may be disjoint or they may have some lights in common, and individual lights can be assigned any desired probabilities of appearing in a trial sample. On the positive side, studies with this situation have found the predicted form for the curve of discrimination learning [33, 83] and have confirmed predictions as to the effect of introducing partial reinforcement [33]. Also, the model has suggested a new type of discrimination experiment in which the two stimulus situations to be discriminated are identical except for the sampling probabilities of the components. In the situation described above, a "probabilistic discrimination" learning experiment will arise if the two sets of lights, S_1 and S_2, are identical, but for trials on which response A_1 is reinforced the lights have one set of sampling probabilities and for trials on which A_2 is reinforced they have a different set of sampling probabilities. For example, suppose each set included the same two lights, L_1 and L_2; we could establish a probabilistic discrimination by assigning L_1 and L_2 the probabilities .9 and .4, respectively, of appearing on trials when A_1 is reinforced, and .4 and .9, respectively, on trials when A_2 is reinforced. The gist of the theoretical prediction for this type of situation is that the probability of response A_1 in the presence of a given stimulus component, say L_1, should change exponentially over a series of trials and should tend to an asymptote equal to the conditional probability that A_1 will be reinforced when L_1 is present. Confirmatory findings have been obtained in a recent experiment [34].

On the negative side, the prediction that in conventional discrimination experiments the asymptotic probability of incorrect responding should be directly related to the proportion of common elements appears to fail in many situations. Even under relatively simple and well-controlled conditions, we find both human and animal subjects attaining virtually perfect discriminations between stimulus complexes or patterns which under any reasonable interpretation must be assumed to have many components or properties in common [see, e.g., 17, 63, 78, 80]. What strategy to adopt in the face of these disparities is not easy to decide. The stimulus element model has proved so useful in accounting for acquisition phenomena and in dealing with stimulus-compounding and time-dependent processes, that we can hardly think of giving it up entirely. One course of action that has been explored by several recent investigators is to supplement the statistical acquisition model with some higher-order process. Burke, in an unpublished study, and Wyckoff [95] have proposed models incorporating the assumption that, in a discrimination situation, the organism learns "observing responses" which permit it to attend to the relevant cues in a situation (those on which differential reinforcement is based) and ignore the common cues; then discrimination learning relative to the relevant cues proceeds as in the simpler acquisition model. Restle [80, 81] has proposed a similar two-process theory which assumes that the organism simultaneously "adapts to" the irrelevant cues (common elements) in a situation and undergoes conditioning to the relevant cues. A somewhat different possibility, now under investigation by the writer, is to develop a more general sampling model which allows for learning with respect both to stimulus patterns and to stimulus components as special cases.

Classical conditioning and habituatory decrement. It may seem odd that these situations, traditionally considered the simplest in the area of learning, have not been treated in detail by statistical learning theory. The reason for this apparent oversight is related to the fact that the simplicity of experiments on conditioning and habituation is paralleled by a refinement in level of measurement. Duration of stimuli and time intervals between conditioned and reinforcing stimuli are accurately measured in conditioning experiments and are known to be important independent variables. Present statistical models can handle classical conditioning experiments at the same relatively gross level of analysis which characterizes treatments of maze learning or learning of verbal associations, but as yet they do not handle relationships involving durations and magnitudes of stimuli or interstimulus intervals. Much effort has been expended on attempts to remedy this deficiency, but no adequate solution is yet at hand or even clearly foreseeable. The basic difficulty is that available data are inadequate to guide the theorist at a number of critical choice points. An adequate statistical model will have to include assumptions concerning the detailed course of growth and decay of stimulus samples. Unfortunately, there are several different sets of assumptions for which reasonable cases can be made, and available quantitative data on temporal relationships in conditioning are insufficient to decide among the alternatives. Thus theoretical progress in this area will have to go hand in hand with parametric experimentation. A start toward handling the variable of conditioned stimulus intensity in conditioning has been reported by Barnes [5], and an extensive research program concerned with temporal and intensive variables in conditioning has been initiated by D. W. Lauer and his associates in the Indiana laboratory.

Parameters of reinforcement. It seems reasonable to expect that such parameters as magnitude and delay of reinforcing stimuli should prove amenable to treatment by statistical models. Again, however, progress is slowed by a paucity of quantitative data suitable to guide extension of present theories. Investigations of amount of reinforcement in animal learning have accomplished more toward testing explanatory hypotheses and turning up new empirical phenomena than toward determining quantitative relationships.

According to a contiguity interpretation, magnitude of a reinforcing stimulus should be related to characteristics of learning only in so far as it influences the relative frequencies of responses compatible or incompatible with the reinforced response. Consider, for example, a runway situation with food as the reinforcing agent. Other things equal, increasing the quantity of food per reinforcement will normally have at least the following two consequences for behavior in the goal box. Firstly, a larger quantity of food can be seen or smelled at a greater distance and thus will be more likely to evoke an approach response while the animal is still exposed to cues from the portion of the runway path anterior to the goal box. Conditioning of approach responses to cues associated with progressively earlier portions of the runway will in turn lead to the reductions in running time and latency which are taken as indices of learning. Secondly, a larger quantity of food will require longer to consume and thus will delay the occurrence of interfering responses, e.g., exploratory responses or attempts to escape from the goal box, which might otherwise become conditioned to runway cues and lead to increases in running time.

There have been several attempts to test this interpretation. A study by the writer [21] demonstrated that the usual differential effects of large as compared to small magnitudes of reinforcement upon a runway response are eliminated if similar reactions to the goal box are established by appropriate pretraining for the groups of animals which are to receive large vs. small amounts of reinforcing agent on runway trials. Following up this investigation, Hellyer [51] reasoned that if when distance cues are controlled, increasing the amount of reinforcing agent is effective primarily because it serves to delay the occurrence of competing responses in the goal box, then similar effects should be obtained by alternative procedures which operate in the same way. In an ingeniously designed runway experiment, Hellyer manipulated rate of delivery of water independently of amount. His intuitively surprising finding was that the effects of slowing the rate of delivery of a given amount of water were qualitatively similar to those of increasing the amount given; he also found that a statistical control for duration of ingestive behavior reduced the effect of both variables to insignificance.

The contiguity interpretation of reinforcement does not, so far at least, stand on its own feet as a determinate and testable theory. The principal difficulty is that the intuitive notion of varying degrees of compatibility between different pairs of response classes has not been spelled out in sufficient detail. One cannot, in general, state in advance of an experiment for any particular pair of stimuli whether the second will evoke a response which interferes with the response to the first or one which facilitates it.

The contiguity interpretation does, however, suggest the form of a testable descriptive theory. If the magnitude of a reinforcing stimulus determines the probability that the stimulus will evoke a response compatible with the reinforced response, then we can associate with any reinforcing stimulus a parameter c which, for any given set of experimental conditions, takes on the same mathematical role as the parameter π in Eq. (9) above.[11] Thus we can predict that the asymptote of response probability will be directly related to magnitude of reinforcement whereas relative rate of learning will be independent of this parameter.[12] For purposes of more detailed quantitative prediction, the value of c characterizing a given reinforcing procedure for a

[11] On any single trial, c and $1 - c$ represent the probabilities that the reinforced response will become connected to all stimulus elements in the trial sample [then $\Delta p = \Theta(1 - p)$] or will lose all its connections to elements in the trial sample (then $\Delta p = -\Theta p$), respectively.

[12] Data which appear to confirm these predictions have been reported by L. H. Hughes, Jr., in a paper, Saccharine reinforcement in a T maze, *J. comp. physiol. Psychol.*, 1957, **50**, 431–435.

given population of organisms must be evaluated from experimental data. As in the case of the rate parameter Θ circularity is avoided by virtue of the fact that the parameter c appears in numerous independent predictive relationships all derivable from the same model.

When relationships among variables in a problem area are not thoroughly understood, useful parametric data cannot always be had for the asking. A number of years ago I initiated a study with the modest purpose of determining the functional relationship between rate of bar pressing and concentration of sucrose solution used as reinforcing agent for the range of concentrations below those covered in Guttman's [48] experiment. Substantial quantities of data were collected, but the relationship at issue has yet to be determined. The first unexpected finding was that most animals could not be conditioned with a reinforcement of 4 per cent sucrose solution, yet after training with a more concentrated solution, the same animals would maintain maximal rates of responding, apparently indefinitely, on the 4 per cent solution. The second, and for my original purpose still more inconvenient complication, was that even for well-trained animals, no orderly rate function could be obtained at low concentrations. For any given animal, near maximal response rates could be maintained by concentrations down to a critical region, near 4 per cent sucrose in most cases, but at lower concentrations, extinction occurred; the originally anticipated result of low but stable response rates at low concentrations simply did not materialize. Prospects of accounting for this complex set of findings in terms of statistical learning theory appear promising [22], but a comprehensive and detailed treatment of magnitude of reward in the free-responding situation is certainly not at hand.

In many human learning experiments, magnitude of reinforcement can be interpreted in terms of the amount of information given concerning the correctness or incorrectness of the subject's responses. From the standpoint of contiguity theory, the basic difficulty in handling this type of experiment is that we ordinarily have no way of specifying in advance how a subject will respond to an ambiguous or uninformative outcome. A recent approach to this problem has employed a combination of methods, drawing upon learning theory, information theory, and psychophysics. The first step was to arrange an experimental situation in which stimuli of varying degrees of ambiguity could be presented, and in which the ambiguity could be scaled by a psychophysical procedure and related to the scale of response probabilities. In this situation the subject is presented on each trial with a pair of geometrical figures which differ in form; the subject's task is, first, to guess at the beginning of each trial whether the larger figure will appear on the left or on the right, and second, when the stimuli are presented, to judge which is the larger. Now if by appropriate preliminary experimentation we obtain a set of stimulus pairs which evokes, on the average, a proportion π of right judgments (i.e., judgments that the right-hand figure is larger in area), we can enter this value of π in Eq. (9) and predict the curve of learning in terms of probability of right responses (guesses). As in the simple Humphreys-type guessing situation, the parameter π should determine the asymptotic probability of the guessing response.

Some evidence concerning the adequacy of this approach is presented in Table 1. The data were obtained from four groups[13] of

TABLE 1

Group	N	Asymptotic response probability	
		Theoretical	Observed
1	10	.85	.87
2	10	.73	.66
3	10	.36	.39
4	10	.14	.11

subjects run for 216 trials in the situation described above (unpublished study by M. Johns and the writer). The observed values of asymptotic response probability are mean proportions of "right" guesses over the last 72 trials of the series; the theoretical values (estimates of π) are mean proportions of "right" judgments. These results are encouraging enough to suggest that other human learning situations in which reinforcement is identified with knowledge of results may yield to similar analyses. For such situations, it appears that reinforcing value of a stimulus is inversely related to the ambiguity, or uncertainty, associated with the stimulus, and that by virtue of this relationship, the reinforcing value can be quantitatively scaled by an independent set of operations.

Partial reinforcement and resistance to extinction. The almost ubiquitous finding that resistance to extinction is greater after partial than after continuous reinforcement has been a challenge to all varieties of reinforcement theory, and the present theory is no exception. Some research indirectly related to this problem has been discussed above in connection with our attempts to account for the vagaries of non-

---

[13] For groups 1 and 4, the two figures of every pair differed slightly in area. For groups 2 and 3, the two figures of each pair were actually equal in area, but one figure of each pair was judged larger with significantly greater than 50 per cent frequency by our population of subjects.

reinforcement in T-maze learning. In an extensive series of studies, Weinstock[14] [92, 93], Lauer [64, 66], and the writer have found that the decremental effect of nonreinforcement varies systematically as a function of number and distribution of reinforcements and nonreinforcements, and Weinstock [92] has investigated possible modifications in present statistical models which might account for the observed relationships.

At a qualitative level, all these researches provide indirect evidence at least mildly favorable to a contiguity-interference interpretation. According to the present theory, the mechanism for extinction of an instrumental response is conceived as follows. The function of nonreinforcement is to establish a stimulating situation in which competing responses have high probabilities. When the competing responses are evoked in the presence of stimulus elements which are connected to the formerly reinforced response, conditioning occurs in accordance with the contiguity principle, and the competing responses gain connections at the expense of the formerly reinforced one. During a series of reinforced trials, some one response, e.g., approaching a food tray, becomes well conditioned to the reinforcing situation, e.g., the goal box of a maze. Then when reinforcement is first omitted, cues from the changed situation and cues arising from the disrupted response sequence evoke competing responses with high probability.[15] Consequently, extinction tends to be rapid following a series of continuously reinforced trials. Under a partial reinforcement schedule, the situation is somewhat different. Competing responses which become conditioned following a nonreinforcement early in the series will tend to occur on later reinforced trials; therefore, response-produced stimuli associated with them will become conditioned cues for the reinforced response and will tend to maintain the latter during a subsequent extinction series.

An advantageous feature of the interference interpretation is that, unlike other hypotheses that have been proposed, it accounts for the relationship between partial reinforcement and resistance to extinction

---

[14] A valuable byproduct of Weinstock's experiments is a quantity of data on distribution of running times; Bush and Mosteller [13, chap. 14] have reported some analyses of these data in terms of a response model substantially the same as the one discussed in an earlier section of this paper.

[15] As in the interpretation of reinforcement discussed above, the initial application of contiguity-interference principles to any experiment involving extinction suffers ambiguity because there are no general rules for prescribing just what responses will "compete" with a given response. However, once definite assumptions have been made concerning the conditions of response competition in a given situation in order to predict or explain some particular experimental result, the theory becomes determinate for that situation and can be expected to yield additional testable predictions.

under conditions of widely spaced trials. When trials are temporally massed, the "trace hypothesis" proposed by Hull [57] enters the picture. According to my interpretation of Hull's hypothesis, some of the stimulus elements associated with nonreinforcement on a given trial of a partial series may, if the intertrial interval is not too great, appear in the sample of elements available at the beginning of a subsequent reinforced trial. Consequently, cues associated with nonreinforcement may become conditioned cues for the reinforced response and tend to maintain it during a following extinction series. In a recent paper on discrimination learning [10], C. J. Burke and I have shown that a quantitative account of this type of trace-conditioning can be derived from the assumptions of statistical learning theory.

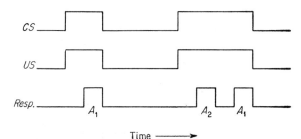

Time ⟶

Fig. 10. Schematic representation of temporal relations among stimulus and response events in an escape learning experiment.

Escape and avoidance learning. In Fig. 10 we have schematized the two kinds of trials that may occur in a simple escape learning experiment. Response class A_1 represents all actions that result in termination of the unconditioned (to-be-escaped) stimulus and class A_2 all actions that do not. Each trial begins with presentation of the conditioned stimulus and, either simultaneously or after a short interval, the unconditioned stimulus. In the first trial shown in Fig. 10, response A_1 occurs immediately and terminates both stimuli. In the second trial, one or more responses belonging to class A_2 occur first, then A_1 occurs and terminates both stimuli. According to the statistical model, the populations of stimulus elements associated with the conditioned and unconditioned stimulus sources are available for sampling whenever the sources are operative. On trials of the first type, only the A_1 response is evoked contiguously with the conditioned stimulus sample and therefore should become conditioned to it. On trials of the second type, the A_1 response is the last to occur in the presence of the conditioned stimulus sample and therefore should remain connected to all elements in the sample at the end of the trial.[16] Thus on trials of both types, the terminal response should receive the increment in probability specified by Eq. (5).

Data suitable to test a number of predictions from this theory of escape learning have been obtained by Straughan [88]. In Straughan's study, human subjects learned to terminate a loud tone by selecting the correct one of two motor responses. For some of Straughan's subjects, reinforcement was partial rather than continuous, the A_1 and A_2 responses being reinforced by termination of the tone with probabilities .7 and .3, respectively. Utilizing Eq. (9), we can predict that terminal probability of the A_1 response should be 1.0 and .7 in the continuously and partially reinforced groups, respectively. Also, by means of a derivation that is straightforward but too lengthy to review here, we can predict that terminal latencies of the A_1 and A_2 responses will be equal for each group (although not necessarily the same for different reinforcement schedules). Observed A_1 proportions over the last 20 trials of an 80-trial series for Straughan's continuously and partially reinforced groups ($N = 64$ for each group) were .999 and .714, respectively. Mean latencies of the A_1 and A_2 responses over the same trial block for the partially reinforced group were 1.40 and 1.45 sec; no comparison of terminal latencies could be made for the continuously reinforced group, of course, since the A_2 response had virtually ceased to occur.

The effective scope of statistical learning theory in this general class of human learning experiments has been further extended by Brody [8] who introduced additional complications by including both avoidance and escape contingencies. Brody's subjects were permitted to choose between two mutually exclusive responses on any trial. A given response served to prevent the occurrence of a to-be-avoided stimulus with a predetermined probability, say π_a. On trials when this stimulus occurred, the same response served to terminate it with a second predetermined probability, say π_e. Utilizing for nonavoidance trials the same analysis discussed above in relation to escape learning trials, and assuming that on avoidance trials the successful avoidance response becomes connected to all stimulus elements in the trial sample, Brody derived functions which provided good fits to his empirical acquisition curves. As can be seen in Table 2, Brody also succeeded in

---

[16] It is possible that on extended trials of the second type, more than one sample would be drawn from the conditioned stimulus population. Since only the last sample would become conditioned to the A_1 response, the increment in response probability would be less than on a trial of the first type. The consequences of this modified assumption will not be pursued here, but it should be mentioned that the predictions concerning asymptotic probabilities, discussed below, would not be changed.

predicting the asymptotic probabilities of partially reinforced avoidance responses with accuracy comparable to that achieved by previous investigators for simple verbal conditioning experiments. The theoretical probabilities in Table 2 are computed from the formula

$$p_{\infty} = \frac{\pi_e \pi_a}{1 - \pi_a + \pi_e(2\pi_a - 1)}$$

A subsidiary aspect of Brody's study had to do with temporal relations between termination of the conditioned stimulus and occurrence of the avoidance or escape response. Each trial began with presentation of the conditioned stimulus, or "signal," and the unconditioned stimulus followed only if the predesignated avoidance response failed to occur within a critical interval of approximately 2 sec. For half the subjects, the signal terminated at the end of the critical

TABLE 2

Group	N	Reinforcement probabilities		Asymptotic response probabilities	
		π_a	π_e	Theoretical	Observed
I	32	.66	1.0	1.0	.92
II	32	.66	.66	.79	.72
III	32	.66	.34	.50	.53
IV	32	.90	.30	.79	.77

interval regardless of the subject's response (noncontingent condition). For the remaining subjects, conditions were arranged so that the signal terminated with the avoidance response, if the response occurred within the critical interval, and otherwise terminated with the unconditioned stimulus when the escape response occurred (contingent condition). In terms of contiguity theory, optimal conditions for acquisition prevailed for the contingent group, since the successful avoidance or escape response was always the last response to occur in the presence of a trial sample from the conditioned stimulus population. For the noncontingent group, however, the last response to occur in the presence of a conditioned stimulus sample, particularly on early trials, would sometimes be an incorrect response, and for these trials no increment in probability of the correct response could be predicted. Brody's data demonstrated that, as anticipated, the contingent procedure significantly facilitated acquisition of the avoidance response.

Drive and conditioning. Throughout the preceding sections of this report, no explicit attention has been given the variables and relationships subsumed under the concept of "drive" in the theories of Hull [55, 56] and Spence [87]. The omission is attributable largely to the fact that most of the experimental situations to which statistical learning theory has been applied do not involve changes in motivating conditions as independent variables. One should not conclude, however, that these conditions have been ignored, or even regarded as unimportant.

In my first paper on statistical learning theory [19], I assumed that "drive-inducing" operations, e.g., food deprivation, electric shock, affect either the makeup of the stimulus population characterizing a given situation or the rate at which the population is sampled by the organism. This assumption has been routinely taken into account in the designing of experiments to test other features of the theory. Especially in animal experiments, deprivational conditions, if they are not undergoing systematic variation as part of an experimental design, must be held constant from trial to trial during learning. In order to satisfy this requirement, I and my associates have come to rely increasingly upon 24-hr trial spacing in maze and runway experiments.

When occasion arises to represent deprivational variables formally in the present theory, it is assumed that an operation such as food deprivation controls the availability of a specific population of stimuli, presumably largely visceral in origin. Degree of deprivation influences the probability that any cue ("stimulus element") in this population will be sampled on any single trial. Shifts in drive level (as operationally defined) produce changes in the relative contribution of the drive population to the stimulus sample affecting the organism on any trial. If, owing to previous training, the drive stimuli are preponderantly connected to the response that is being recorded, a sudden increase in drive level will yield a sudden increase in probability of that response; if the drive stimuli are preponderantly connected to competing responses, a sudden increase in drive level will yield a decrease in probability of the recorded response. Populations of stimuli associated with two different operationally defined drives, say hunger and thirst, may have elements in common. The degree of communality will determine the extent to which effects of reinforcement or extinction under one of the drives will generalize to the other and will also determine the limiting accuracy of discrimination attainable between the two drive conditions. The parameters representing sizes of drive-stimulus populations, associated Θ values, and degrees of communality between populations associated with different operationally defined drives must be evaluated from behavioral data for any given situation, but then can be used, just as any parameters of the model, to generate predictions about behavior under new combinations of conditions.

Detailed assumptions concerning the populations of drive stimuli involved in problems of generalization between hunger and thirst drives in an operant conditioning situation have been formulated and tested at a qualitative level by Bishop [6]. Parametric studies are needed to determine functional relationships between properties of drive-stimulus populations and such observable independent variables as deprivation time in standard experimental situations.

Verbal learning. From the standpoint of the present theory, paired-associate learning is regarded as an instance of multiple discrimination learning. Therefore we should expect experimental laws for paired-associate learning to be derivable from the statistical model developed in connection with simple acquisition and discrimination experiments. In a typical paired-associate study, the subject is given repeated presentations of a list of stimuli, usually printed words or nonsense syllables, and is required to associate a particular response word with each item of the list. The stimulus items are presented singly, in varying orders from one showing of the list to the next, and reinforcement consists in exhibiting the correct response word after the subject's response on each trial. To represent such an experiment theoretically, we define a collection of stimulus sets, $S_1, S_2, \ldots, S_K$, one for each item in the stimulus list, and corresponding response classes, $A_1, A_2, \ldots, A_K$. Response A_h is reinforced on a given trial if and only if stimulus S_h is presented. Probability of a correct response to stimulus S_h on the nth showing of the list should, then, be given by the same function as Eq. (6) above, namely,

$$p_{h,n} = 1 - (1 - \theta)^{n-1}$$

From this relation, one can readily compute theoretical curves for mean proportion of correct responses against trials, families of curves for the probability of any designated number of correct responses per trial, and numerous other testable functional relationships. For purely illustrative purposes, I have plotted two of the theoretical curves derivable for learning of a 10-item list in Fig. 11, together with empirical data representing 108 protocols from a group of relatively slow-learning subjects.[17] Systematic tests of the analysis sketched here are in progress in the Indiana laboratory, but none of this research has yet been published.

Serial verbal learning involves more difficult theoretical problems, partly because there are so many quantitative relationships to be accounted for. Atkinson [3] has constructed a statistical model which describes a number of serial position effects. Probably the most valuable immediate outcome of Atkinson's theoretical investigation is its

[17] I am indebted to Dr. Benton J. Underwood for these paired-associate data.

empirical byproducts. In order to facilitate applications of his theoretical functions, Atkinson conducted a series of carefully designed experiments which have clarified a number of relationships between the serial position curve and independent variables. The model itself, still in a preliminary form, involves several new assumptions which require independent tests before it can be properly evaluated.

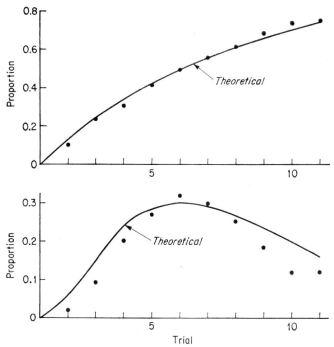

FIG. 11. Theoretical and empirical curves of paired-associate learning. Upper panel: proportion of correct responses per trial for the set of 108 protocols. Lower panel: proportion of protocols exhibiting exactly two correct responses on each trial. The θ value of .13 determined from the upper curve was used to compute a priori predictions for the lower curve.

Critically needed research. The items mentioned in this section will represent a very small sample from a very large population. Our best experimental efforts seem only to whet the insatiable demand of a growing quantitative theory for more and better data. The simplest problems turn into complex ones when we try to progress from qualitative to quantitative description and from description to prediction. We should like to place a standing order for more good parametric experiments in all areas of learning; but who will fill the order? Research designed to refine our measurements and descriptions of functional relationships ordinarily seems too much like drudgery to attract many investigators. It begins to take on glamour, however, when there are quantitative theories to be tested. Under the instigation of contemporary theoretical developments, the output of needed types of parametric research is increasing, but I can see no immediate danger of a surplus.

Some of the most critical areas for the immediate needs of statistical learning theory have become apparent in the course of our review. In many instances, curiously enough, these involve, not new research problems, but classical ones in areas that the nonspecialist looks upon as "all worked out." To review just one example, time relations in classical conditioning and habituatory decrement require clarification before much progress toward an adequate quantitative theory can be anticipated. There have been numerous studies of the CS-US interval in eyelid conditioning, but none that suffices to determine whether the asymptotes or the slope constants of conditioning curves, or both, are affected by variation of the interval; an empirical decision on this point is needed to guide formulation of a stimulus trace model within statistical learning theory. There have been a few studies of US duration, but none that have partialed out the interval from completion of the UR to termination of the US; the role of this independent variable must be understood before we can even tentatively appraise the adequacy of an interference account of response decrement in conditioning situations.

In general, research on learning in classical situations has been all but dominated by "critical ratio," and more recently "analysis of variance" research. Much is known about methods of producing significant group differences in standard learning situations, but little about the limits within which learning can be modified by manipulation of standard independent variables. For all the studies of distribution of practice in conditioning or in simple verbal learning, we do not know even roughly within what extremes learning rate can be varied by manipulation of intertrial intervals. Only after decades of research on eyelid conditioning have there begun to appear studies [e.g., 91] showing how rapidly conditioning can be achieved when radical measures are taken to reduce stimulus variability from trial to trial. Countless similar examples could be adduced. Quantitative learning theories would pay their way if they did nothing but lead to increased emphasis on exploring the full range of effects of independent variables and on determining forms of functional relationships between variables.

Another critically needed shift in conventional research strategies has been urged most eloquently by Harlow [50], although for somewhat different reasons from those I shall emphasize. In the vast majority of studies of learning, the yield is a single set of data for the groups of organisms investigated. This one limitation in itself makes the data of most experiments almost useless for purposes of testing a new quantitative theory. As we have demonstrated in the case of numerous specific problems in the preceding pages, the testing of a quantitative theory normally involves at least two distinct steps: evaluating the parameters of the model from one set of data generated by a given subject or group of subjects, and then making predictions concerning new sets of data obtainable from the same subjects. So simple an experiment as repeated acquisition and extinction of a classical conditioned response with well-spaced trials would be of more value to statistical learning theory at the present time than any number of significant statistics demonstrating effects of ingeniously contrived new variations on conventional conditioning procedures.

Finally, it should be mentioned that the learning theorist shares with his fellows in numerous related disciplines a need for truly comparative studies of learning. By this I mean, not explorations of behavioral oddities in little-known bypaths of the animal world, but rather systematic investigations in which experiments of standard types are conducted "in parallel" at a number of phylogenetic levels. All the published research pertaining to statistical learning theory has been conducted with vertebrates, and indeed almost all with either rats or men. I have tacitly assumed that all general assumptions and laws of the theory can be applied at least throughout the range of the vertebrates with only numerical values of parameters changing as we go from one particular animal form to the next. At present, however, this assumption amounts to little more than an article of faith. Available comparative data concerning the quantitative effects of the major independent variables treated in this report are insufficient even to spell out in detail what we mean when we speak of "the same law" applying to different animal forms.

Part III. Systematic and Comparative Analysis

FORMAL STRUCTURE OF STATISTICAL LEARNING THEORY

It will be apparent from the preceding account of the development of statistical learning theory that we shall have trouble in assembling an exhaustive yet logically arranged and neatly rounded summarization of "the theory" or "the system." The crux of the difficulty is that we cannot give any sharply defined referent for "the theory" or "the system." If, like many of the earlier psychological systematists, we had started with a comprehensive program for theory construction, we could simply present the master plan and indicate how far it had been filled in. But we have no program. What we now call the statistical, or probabilistic, approach to learning theory began, not with a blueprint, but merely with a handful of promising (or more accurately, tantalizing) experimental findings and an interest in seeing what progress could be made toward a rigorous quantitative theory. If we had started out to account for a definite set of facts, we might hope to be approaching a definite and clearly delimited theoretical model representing those facts. But many of the facts that are now being described and predicted by statistical learning theory have been discovered during the period of its development, frequently as a direct result of applications and tests of the developing theory. Consequently, the outlines of "the system" are as uneven, and often hazy, as the lines of experimental advance in the study of learning.

In the preceding sections of this report, *statistical learning theory* has designated an evolving collection of concepts, formal methods, and empirical laws organized by these concepts and methods. Now that our attention turns to structural considerations, our usage of the term *theory* shifts to the more static, conventional sense, i.e., a cross-sectional description at a given point in time, emphasizing the formal concepts and deductive machinery, and ignoring the messy complications that characterize any interaction of formal and empirical systems. This type of description, taken alone, is misleading, for it involves the same kinds of simplification, idealization, and abstraction that inevitably occur when we go from empirical phenomena to conceptual representations of them. It is only in the perspective provided by the more naturalistic account given in Part II that we can even attempt the summary and systematic analysis needed for purposes of a comparative survey of contemporary systems and theories. With the reservations indicated above, I shall now attempt to outline the formal model emerging from some ten years of interaction between the statistical approach to learning theory and associated experimental research.

By the term "model" I shall denote specifically the formal system associated with a scientific theory, i.e., the mathematical symbols and the assumed interrelationships among them. When a model has been interpreted in terms of a system of empirical events, it becomes a theory. Thus a theory may be conceived as a mapping of an empirical system onto a formal system, as illustrated for statistical learning theory by the following schema. Within the empirical system, two principal types of entities must be distinguished: events and properties or aspects of events. The rules of correspondence similarly fall into two categories: coordinating definitions, which set elements of the formal system in correspondence with classes of events[18] in the empirical system; and interpretive rules, which specify how mathematical functions, variables, and parameters defined within the formal system may be evaluated from data representing observable, and usually measurable, properties or aspects of empirical events.

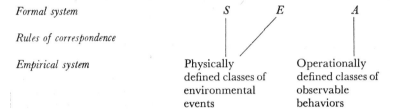

Formal system	S	E	A
Rules of correspondence			
Empirical system	Physically defined classes of environmental events	Operationally defined classes of observable behaviors	

In this section of Part III, I shall first summarize the formal terms (referred to in the Project A outline as "systematic concepts") of statistical learning theory and the assumed relations among these terms, then proceed to consider empirical interpretations and derivations of theorems which, upon interpretation and experimental confirmation, become the empirical laws of the theory.

Itemization of Systematic Concepts

It will be convenient to divide our itemization of theoretical ingredients into two main parts. The first part, summarized in Table 3, will comprise the primitive set-theoretical constructs which are basic to all of our formal theorizing. The second part will comprise the theoretical variables which appear either as systematic dependent or independent variables or as parameters in the assumptions (axioms) of the theory and, therefore, in all descriptive statements derived from them. This second list, presented in Table 4, is by no means complete, but it includes all the theoretical variables that have appeared prominently in published presentations or applications of the theory up to the time of writing. These constructs and variables have all been introduced in Part II, so we can proceed directly to questions of their definition and formal status.

Mode of Definition of Systematic Concepts

The constructs listed in Tables 3 and 4 have the status of primitive notions within statistical learning theories and are strictly definable

---

[18] More accurately, coordinating definitions establish correspondences between terms of the formal system and terms of the data-language [cf. 35, pp. 320–322].

only in mathematical terms. Our technique of formalization is to represent stimuli, responses, and reinforcing events[19] by finite mathematical sets and then to generate the systematic dependent and independent variables and parameters of models for learning experiments by defining functions on these sets.

The sets and their elements serve as abstract conceptual devices which are useful in deriving quantitative laws but which never appear in the final product. It will make no sense to ask where a stimulus element is located, or even whether it "intervenes" between observed

TABLE 3. SET-THEORETICAL CONSTRUCTS OF STATISTICAL LEARNING THEORIES

Construct	Characterization
A_j $(j = 1, 2, \ldots, r)$	Set of r mutually exclusive and exhaustive response classes.
S^*	Set of "stimulus elements" representing all stimulus events (all stimulation) that can affect the organism† in any situation at any time.
S_*	Subset of S^* representing all stimulus events that can occur in a particular experimental situation at any time.
S	Subset of S_* representing all stimulus events that can occur in a particular experimental situation during a particular experimental period.
$S' = S_* - S$	Subset of S_* representing stimulus events which sometimes occur in a given experimental situation but are unavailable during a particular experimental period.
S_h $(h = 1, \ldots, k)$	Subsets of S_* (or of S, depending on the assumption made in a particular application), one corresponding to each experimenter-defined stimulating situation (pattern of stimulation) that may occur in a given experiment.
$S_j^*, S_{*j}, S_j, S_{hj}$	Subsets of elements in S^*, S_*, S, or S_h, respectively, that are connected to response A_j.
E_k $(k = 1, 2, \ldots, r)$	Set of reinforcing events, one corresponding to each response class.

† It is to be understood that all the stimulus sets are associated with some individual organism in any psychological application.

stimuli and responses, for stimulus sets and their elements belong to the formal, not the empirical, system. Properties or aspects of these mathematical entities are, however, assumed to represent properties or aspects of observable behavioral events. Thus Θ, the sampling probability of a stimulus element, or N, the number of elements in a stimulus set, does appear in the descriptive statements derivable within the

[19] Presumably "reinforcing events" can ultimately be reduced to stimulus-response terms, and one of the chief purposes of contiguity-interference theory is to effectuate this reduction. However, applications of our mathematical theory require only that one be able to locate experimenter-defined events whose effects on response probabilities conform to the assumptions of the theory.

theory, and rules must be given specifying how values of these variables can be determined from empirical data.

For purposes of comparing the present theory with others, it might be helpful to indicate how the theoretical variables of Table 4 fit into the conventional intervening-variable paradigm. For simplicity, only a few of the most important variables are included in the schema shown on page 450. In this schema it is assumed that the "empiri-

TABLE 4. THEORETICAL VARIABLES

Construct	Characterization
n	Number of trials.
r	Number of response classes.
K	Number of experimenter-defined stimulus situations.
h_j	Time required to execute response A_j.
$p_{hj,n}$	Probability of A_j on trial n in presence of stimulus situation corresponding to S_h. If there is only one stimulus situation, the subscript h is dropped; if there are only two response classes, the subscript j is dropped and p_n is taken to refer to A_1; if reference to trial number is unnecessary, the n is omitted (yielding such variants as $p_{j,n}, p_n, p$). The argument n may be replaced by t when appropriate.
$F_{hij,n}$	Probability that the ith stimulus element in set S_h is connected to A_j on trial n. As above, unnecessary subscripts and arguments are dropped, yielding $F_{ij,n}, F_{i,n}, F_i$, etc.
Θ_{hi}	Sampling probability of the ith element in S_h. The subscript h is dropped if only one set is defined for a given experiment, yielding Θ_i.
j	Probability that any given element in S becomes unavailable (enters S') during an interval Δt.
j'	Probability that any given element in S' becomes available (enters S) during an interval Δt.
$\pi_{hjk,n}$	Probability of E_k given that A_j occurs in the presence of S_h on trial n. The most common variants are π_{jk} (constant probability of E_k following A_j in a single stimulus situation), and π (constant probability of E_1 in a single-stimulus, two-alternative experiment).
$N^*, N_*, N, N', N_h, N_{hj}$	Number of elements in S^*, S_*, S, S', S_h, or S_{hj}, respectively.

cal" variables are strictly definable in terms of the data-language without reference to the theory. The lines between different pairs of variables signify either interpretive rules or assumed functional relationships, as appropriate.

The conceptual status of such theoretical variables as N and p in the present theory is formally analogous to that of such terms as D (drive strength) and $_sE_R$ (reaction potential) in Hull's system [55]. In each case, simplicity of theoretical structure is gained by stating assumptions about learning in terms of theoretical variables rather than directly in terms of empirical dependent and independent variables.

It should be pointed out that although constructs of the kind listed in Table 4 will fill the roles of mathematical dependent and independent variables in all functions derived within the theory, no one construct can be rigidly classified in either category. In an acquisition function, for example, p might be the dependent variable, n the independent variable, and Θ a parameter. But in a function predicting responses to extinction as a function of stimulus variability, n might appear as the dependent variable, Θ as the independent variable, and p as a parameter.

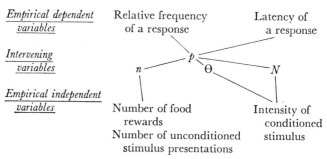

Major Interrelations among Constructs

In this section we shall bring together the assumptions, or more formally, axioms, specifying interrelations among the constructs itemized in Tables 3 and 4, and some theorems which are of wide applicability in empirical interpretations of the model. Derivations of the theorems are available in published sources and will not be repeated here. For convenience of reference, the assumptions will be grouped under headings which indicate the major areas of application.

Response model. The set $[A_1, A_2, \ldots, A_j \ldots, A_r]$ may be interpreted as a sample space representing the possible behavioral outcomes of a trial. The element A_j then represents the event "response A_j occurs." The probability of A_j is defined as p_j, i.e.,

$$Pr(A_j) = p_j \qquad (j = 1, 2, \ldots, r)$$

The mutually exclusive and exhaustive character of the response classes is expressed by the following assumptions:

1. $$\sum_{j=1}^{r} p_j = 1$$

2. $$Pr(A_j \cup A_k) = p_j + p_k$$

and similarly for any combination of response classes. Or, verbally expressed, the probabilities of the response classes sum to unity, and the probability that the response which occurs on a trial will belong to a specified subset of response classes is equal to the sum of the probabilities associated with those response classes. Using only these assumptions together with the classical calculus of probabilities [see Feller, 38, for details], many important theorems are derivable, e.g.:

  a. The expected number of occurrences of A_j in n trials is equal to

$$p_{j,1} + p_{j,2} + \cdots + p_{j,n}$$

  where $p_{j,v}$ represents probability of A_j on trial v. If p_j is constant over the series, this sum reduces to np_j.

  b. The probability that A_j occurs for the first time on the nth trial of a series is equal to

$$(1 - p_{j,1})(1 - p_{j,2}) \cdots (1 - p_{j,n-1})p_{j,n}$$

If p_j is constant over the series, this product reduces to $(1 - p_j)^{n-1}p_j$. These theorems are of frequent application in deducing relations between response probabilities and empirical dependent variables.

Stimulus sampling model. For simplicity of exposition we shall consider only assumptions referring to a single stimulus set S (and where appropriate, its complement S') in the remainder of this section. The following two assumptions are basic to derivations involving stimulus sets:

  1. The probability that the ith element in S is sampled on any trial equals Θ_i. Except when specified otherwise, Θ_i is assumed to be a parameter which has a fixed value associated with any given combination of stimulus and response sets.

  2. The probability that the ith and jth elements of S are both sampled on any given trial equals $\Theta_i\Theta_j$, and similarly for any combination of elements.

Two important relations derivable from these assumptions are:

  a. The mean stimulus sample size on any trial, designated s, equals the sum of the Θ values over all elements of S, i.e.,

$$s = \sum_{i=1}^{N} \Theta_i$$

  If all of the Θ_i are equal, this expression reduces to

$$s = N\Theta$$

  b. The probability that the ith element of S is sampled at least once during the first n trials of a series equals $1 - (1 - \Theta_i)^n$.

These theorems are frequently useful in the derivation of learning functions [see, e.g., 11, 32].

Stimulus fluctuation model. There are two principal assumptions:

1. The set S_*, representing all potential stimulation associated with a given experimental situation, is partitioned at any time into two subsets, S and S', representing stimulus elements that are and are not, respectively, available for sampling.

2. There is constant, random interchange of elements between S and S'. During any unit time interval Δt there is probability j that any given element in S goes into S' and probability j' that any given element in S' goes into S. From these assumptions one can derive [25, 26] theorems basic to the statistical theory of spontaneous recovery, forgetting, and other distributional phenomena. If we let $f(t)$ represent the probability that any given element of S_* is in S at time t following an experimental trial (or period), then

   a.
   $$f(t) = J - [J - f(0)]a^t$$
   where $J = \dfrac{j'}{j + j'}$ and $a = 1 - j - j'$

   b. When t becomes sufficiently large, the mean numbers of elements in S and S' stabilize at values which satisfy the relation
   $$J = \frac{N}{N + N'}$$

As a corollary, we note that if trials are given at widely spaced intervals, the sampling probability, on any trial, of the ith element of S is equal to $J\Theta_i$. Strictly speaking, fluctuation should be taken into account in all applications of the model, but in deriving learning functions for experiments which take place in a single relatively short experimental period, it is usually expedient to assume that the amount of fluctuation during the period is small and to treat S as fixed.

Stimulus-response relations. Stimulus and response sets are connected by the assumptions:

1. For any combination of stimulus and response sets, each element of the stimulus set bears a conditional relation to (is connected to) exactly one element of the response set. More formally, we may say that at any time the response set generates a partition of S into subsets S_1, S_2, . . . , S_r, one subset corresponding to each of the response classes A_1, A_2, . . . , A_r. It is implied by the concept of a partition that each element of S is in one and only one of these subsets.

Finally, the stimulus and response sets are related to response probability by the following assumption:

2. The value of p_j on any trial is equal to the proportion of elements in the trial sample that are connected to A_j (i.e., that are in S_j).

Now, defining F_{ij} as the probability that the ith element of S is connected to A_j (i.e., is in S_j), we can state a number of important relations:

a. If the Θ values are equal for all elements of a given set S, then, on the average,

$$p_j = \frac{\sum_i F_{ij}}{N} = F_j$$

where F_j is the proportion of the elements of S that are in S_j.

b. For any set S

$$p_j \cong \frac{\sum_i \Theta_i F_{ij}}{\sum_i \Theta_i} = \frac{1}{N\overline{\Theta}} \sum_i \Theta_i F_{ij}$$

where $\overline{\Theta}$ represents the mean value of Θ and $\cong$ means "tends to equality for large N."

c. If the Θ values are equal for all elements of two nonoverlapping stimulus sets S_g and S_h containing N_g and N_h elements, respectively, and the expected probabilities of response A_j in the presence of the two sets separately are p_{gj} and p_{hj}, respectively, then the expected probability of A_j in the presence of the combined set $S_{gh} = S_g \cup S_h$ is given by

$$p_{(gh)j} = \frac{N_g p_{gj} + N_h p_{hj}}{N_g + N_h}$$

Theorems *a* and *b* are of frequent application in the derivation of learning functions, theorem *c* in predicting results of experiments on transfer or stimulus compounding.

Learning. In general, learning is represented by changes in the connections between response classes and stimulus elements. We assume that learning, so defined, can occur only with respect to elements sampled on a trial.

In the theoretical representation of any learning experiment, the term *trial* refers to an experimental trial as defined for the given type of experiment. A trial always begins with the drawing of a sample of elements from a stimulus set S (corresponding to the experimental presentation of a CS, discriminative cue, or ready signal to the subject) followed by the occurrence of one of the responses $A_1, A_2, \ldots , A_r$ (corresponding to the subject's response to the CS, cue, or ready signal). The response may in turn be followed by occurrence of one of the reinforcing events $E_1, E_2, \ldots , E_r$ (corresponding to such experimental operations as presenting a US, reward, or knowledge of results). It is assumed that when no reinforcing event occurs on a trial, no learning occurs, but when some reinforcing event occurs, all elements sampled become connected to the reinforced response. In more formal terms:

1. If element i is not sampled on trial $n - 1$, or if element i is sampled on trial $n - 1$ and no reinforcement occurs, then

$$F_{ij,n} = F_{ij,n-1}$$

2. If reinforcing event E_j occurs on trial $n - 1$, then

$$F_{ij,n} = (1 - \Theta_i)F_{ij,n-1} + \Theta_i$$

and $\quad F_{ik,n} = (1 - \Theta_1)F_{ik,n-1} \quad$ for all $k \neq j$

i.e., the probability that the element is connected to A_j increases and the probability that it is connected to any other response class decreases.

The following theorems are basic to most of the learning functions that have been utilized in applications of the theory.

If Θ values are equal for all elements of a stimulus set S, then:

a. if no reinforcing event occurs on trial $n - 1$,

$$p_{j,n} = p_{j,n-1}$$

i.e., expected response probability does not change; and

b. if reinforcing event E_j occurs,

$$p_{j,n} = (1 - \Theta)p_{j,n-1} + \Theta$$

and $\quad p_{k,n} = (1 - \Theta)p_{k,n-1} \quad$ for all $k \neq j$

i.e., the probability of A_j increases and the probabilities of all other responses decrease.

Itemization of Empirical Dependent and Independent Variables

Dependent variables. In all cases, dependent variables are measures relating to experimentally defined response classes. For any particular experiment, the response classification is defined by the recording procedures. In a runway experiment, for example, the possible behaviors during any time interval Δt may be categorized into classes A_1 and A_2, i.e., behaviors which result in breaking of a photocell beam and behaviors which do not. In a verbal conditioning experiment, the subject's behavior on any trial may be categorized into classes A_1, A_2, . . . , A_r where A_j includes all behaviors associated with prediction of the jth reinforcing event. The dependent variables most frequently utilized in interpretations of the theory are:

1. Number of occurrences of a given response A_j (for brevity we shall use "response A_j" or simply A_j for "an instance of response class A_j") on a given trial for a group of subjects.

2. Number of occurrences of A_j in a block of trials for a given subject.

3. Number of (unreinforced) occurrences of A_j to a criterion of extinction.[20]

4. Number of trials to a criterion of acquisition or extinction.

5. Rate of occurrence of A_j in a free responding situation.

6. Time before first occurrence of A_j on a given trial.

Independent variables. I assume that all empirical independent variables (causal variables, antecedent conditions, or determinants of behavior) which enter into behavioral laws influence behavior by way of stimulation. This does not mean that hormones, genetic determiners, surgical interventions, and the like are considered unimportant, but simply that they are considered in a formal behavioral theory only as determiners of parameter values. Since the term *stimulus* and its variants have many common meanings [cf. 35, pp. 284–287 for a discussion], I had best indicate my own usage before continuing this section. By way of orientation, it should be emphasized at the outset that by *stimulus* and all variants of the term I refer to environmental conditions describable in physical terms without reference to the behavior of the organism. By *stimulating situation* or simply *situation* I mean to indicate all sources of stimulation that are mentioned in the experimenter's description of the experimental situation,[21] and by *stimulus* or *cue* any independently manipulable part of a

---

[20] Such theoretical terms as *response*, *learning*, and *extinction* do not properly belong in this section and should be taken merely as shorthand for corresponding data-language specifications which would be unduly tedious to spell out in detail.

[21] This appeal to the experimenter's description may seem to make us unduly vulnerable to errors or omissions in conventional categorizations. I believe, however, that we are merely recognizing the existing state of affairs, not adding any new complications. As in any research program, we hope to refine our descriptions by successive approximations. Initially we accept the distinctions and classifications of contemporary experimental practice; but we expect later to use the developing theory to sharpen them.

situation. No situation is precisely reproducible, so just as in the case of response variables, the itemization of stimulus variables involves classification. In a conditioning experiment, for example, we designate by "the CS" the class of situations an instance of which occurs at the beginning of each trial; in the usual discrimination experiment we recognize two classes of situation, one correlated with reinforcement and one with nonreinforcement of a given response class. With these understandings, we can proceed to summarize the three principal types of empirical independent variables involved in studies of learning, transfer, and retention:

1. Number of reinforced or unreinforced trials in a given situation. In this context, reinforcement and nonreinforcement refer, of course, to experimentally defined classes of events.

2. Variations in components or properties of a stimulating situation.

3. Time between learning trials in a given situation or time interval during which the organism is not exposed to a given stimulating situation.

Interpretation of Formal Theory in Terms of Empirical Variables

Rules of correspondence between set-theoretical constructs and empirical variables. Strictly speaking, the correspondences between set-theoretical constructs and experimentally defined variables always have the status of hypotheses; in many common experimental situations, however, the correspondences are either so intuitively obvious or so well established by successful applications of the theory that we tend to lose sight of their hypothetical character. The problems and issues involved are somewhat different for constructs associated with stimuli, responses, and reinforcing events, so we shall discuss them separately.

Stimuli. In formulating a set-theoretical representation of a stimulating situation, we must, initially at least, assume that the experimenter's description of the situation is sufficiently accurate to indicate which sources of variation may be considered negligible and which must be taken into account. If we represent the CS or ready signal in a simple acquisition experiment by a single set S, we are assuming the situation to be sufficiently reproducible from trial to trial so that fluctuations in the available stimulation can be considered negligible. Usually it is fairly obvious a priori whether the assumption is reasonable. An advantage of using a standard experimental situation for theoretical tests is that once particular coordinating assumptions have been found satisfactory they become conventions for the given situations and need not be reconsidered for each new experiment.

With the proviso that we keep track of our simplifying assumptions and correct them when necessary in the light of experience, the procedures for defining stimulus sets are straightforward. If an experiment is assumed to involve only repeated occurrences of a single stimulating situation (more precisely, instances of a single class of situations), its formal representation requires only a single set S. If an experiment involves discrimination between two stimulating situations, these are represented by two sets S_1 and S_2, which may have elements in common.

There have been few parametric studies of stimulus compounding, so formal representations of such experiments are more definitely provisional. Each independently manipulable stimulus in an experiment is represented by a set of elements, but a combination of two stimuli cannot always be represented by the union (sum) of the corresponding sets. If two stimuli belong to different modalities, then there is usually good reason to assume that a combination of the two can be represented by the union of the sets, but if two stimuli belong to the same modality, special problems (e.g., masking) may arise. The experiments so far conducted as tests of theoretical predictions on compounding [34, 78, 83] have used visual stimuli (signal lights or printed words) and the assumption of additivity has worked out satisfactorily. In the case of two auditory stimuli, however, we would not ordinarily expect combinations to be additive.

Responses. So long as we are dealing only with behavior in a single stimulating situation, the representation of response variables is straightforward. For any unambiguous response classification provided by the experimenter, we can define a corresponding set of response classes. In a classical conditioning experiment, for example, we may represent by A_1 the class of behaviors which meet the criterion of a CR during a prescribed interval after onset of a CS and by A_2 the class of behaviors which do not. If two dependent variables are defined for a given situation, we may require two independent response classifications. Suppose that running time and frequency of correct choices are to be recorded in a T-maze experiment. We first define, for all trials, two mutually exclusive and exhaustive classes, A_1 and A_2, corresponding to running and not-running, respectively;[22] then for all trials on which the animal runs the maze, we define a second, orthogonal

---

[22] In order to derive quantitative predictions about running time, we conceive the maze path as a series of segments and define A_1 as the response of running from one segment into the next. If there are k such segments along the correct path, minimum running time will be the time required for k successive A_1 responses. Longer running times will occur if the A_1 responses are interspersed with one or more A_2 responses.

classification of the runs into, say A_L and A_R, those which terminate in the left and right goal boxes, respectively. Whether or not the two dependent variables, running time and frequency of correct choices, are correlated is not a matter of definition; it is a matter to be predicted by the theory and tested by experiment.

Even transfer can be represented, up to a point, without any special difficulty. Transfer involves two or more situations, corresponding to which are stimulus sets S_1, S_2, etc. Suppose there are two situations and that we have defined the response classes A_1, A_2, . . . , A_r in the first and A'_1, A'_2, . . . , A'_r in the second. Now we can speak of transfer from the first situation to the second if any systematic change in the probabilities of A_1, A_2, . . . , A_r which results from a period of learning in the first situation is accompanied by some systematic change in the probabilities of A'_1, A'_2, . . . , A'_r. Only if we wish to go further and treat not only transfer but positive transfer and negative transfer do we run into complications. When we speak of positive transfer, or generalization, we mean to imply that the same response which has its probability increased in S_1 during learning will exhibit increased probability in S_2 upon a subsequent test. Thus we have not only to define response classifications in the two situations, but also to assume that the classification is the same in the two cases; if we have, say, reinforced response A_1 in S_1 and propose to test for generalization by evaluating the probability of A_1 in S_2, we are assuming that the criteria used to identify the class of behaviors corresponding to A_1 in the first situation are appropriate for identifying "the same response" (i.e., the response to which positive transfer will occur) in a second situation. In a few relatively well-standardized learning experiments—e.g., eyelid conditioning, simple verbal learning—appropriate criteria for response classification are established beyond much doubt. In other cases, e.g., discrimination learning [cf. 28, pp. 6–7; 35, pp. 218–231], response criteria are highly controversial.

A statistical model can offer no special sources of insight into the ambiguous cases; what it should provide is more effective means for testing hypotheses pertaining to response classification. Assumptions that prove fruitful can be incorporated into a broader theory which will prescribe the conditions of application of particular mathematical models. Up to the present time, little progress in this direction can be reported, however. In the early stages of development of statistical and probabilistic learning theories (as in the case of all previous quantitative theories), it has seemed necessary to restrict attention to experimental situations in which ambiguities of response classification are minimal.

Reinforcing events. In order to complete the formal representation of a learning experiment, the possible experimentally distinguishable outcomes of a trial must be classified according to their effects on response probabilities. A class of outcomes which produce increments in probability of response A_j is represented by an element E_j in the set of "reinforcing events." As in the case of stimuli and responses, our model has nothing to tell us about the nature of reinforcing events. It does, however, facilitate the formulation and testing of explanatory hypotheses which relate reinforcing events to other classes of events or operations. In any test situation, the role of an explanatory principle, e.g., the contiguity principle, is to generate a hypothesis specifying the empirical events which will reinforce a given response; the role of the statistical model is to generate testable predictions as to how learning will proceed if the latter hypothesis is correct. Obviously no one test can be definitive. Repeated failures of prediction or repeated failures of an explanatory principle to generate testable hypotheses lead in time to rejection. The more common outcome, a mixture of successes and failures, indicates clearly enough that something is wrong, but not so clearly what should be done to improve matters. The rapid progress of reinforcement theory in recent years has been made possible by the fortunate circumstance that, as experimenters, we can identify a considerable number of experimental operations which serve regularly and reliably as reinforcing events even though, as theorists, we may not agree concerning the independently definable properties these reinforcers have in common.

In the research program associated with statistical learning theory, persistent attempts have been made to effect an independent definition of reinforcing events in terms of contiguity-interference principles. The principle of conditioning by contiguity, taken alone, appears simple and straightforward enough: a response becomes conditioned to all stimuli temporally contiguous[23] with the stimulus that evokes it. One might think, then, that a reinforcing event could be defined as any stimulus which originally evokes the to-be-reinforced response. But this definition specifies neither sufficient nor necessary conditions for an increment in probability of the response. It is not sufficient, for even though the response is evoked in the presence of the appropriate

---

[23] The precise definition of "contiguous" poses difficult problems. Originally, following the lead of Guthrie [46], I interpreted contiguity to mean strict temporal simultaneity. However, prolonged and strenuous attempts to develop a theory of reinforcement based on this interpretation have convinced me that no such theory can be constructed without the addition of further assumptions. At present, my inclination is to modify the interpretation of temporal contiguity in the direction of Hull's stimulus trace hypothesis [55, 56]. With this modified interpretation, we assume, in effect, that the response which occurs at any time becomes connected to any stimulus elements sampled during a short preceding interval (of the order of 0.5 sec). More rigorous quantification of the "trace" interpretation is desirable but has not yet been worked out in detail.

stimulus, if a cue for some competing response occurs before the first stimulus is terminated, the newly formed association will suffer interference. And the condition specified by the definition is not necessary, for a reinforcing event may consist in the termination rather than the onset of stimulation (as, for example, in the case of an escape learning experiment).

Upon reviewing the many attempts to formulate simple, closed explanatory principles of reinforcement and the still more numerous attempts to test the formulations, I have been led strongly to suspect that no hypothesis as simple or unitary as those envisaged by contemporary contiguity or drive-reduction theorists is going to prove adequate. It appears, rather, that associative learning depends upon a complex of causal factors or conditions. The experimental operation we refer to as a reinforcement for a given response in a given situation is one which supplies the factor or factors missing from the complex needed for acquisition in that situation.

The two reasonably well-established principles of reinforcement derivable from contiguity theory may be summarized as follows. Other things equal, the likelihood that an experimental operation will reinforce a given response is directly related to (a) the probability that stimuli associated with the operation will evoke behaviors that do not interfere with the given response and (b) the extent to which stimulation effective at the time of evocation of the response is terminated immediately after occurrence of the response on each trial. These principles will enable us to make a priori predictions about the reinforcing effects of events or procedures when, and only when, we are in a position to state precisely how the events or procedures will change the stimulus situation prevailing when the to-be-reinforced response occurs and precisely what behaviors will be evoked by stimuli occurring simultaneously with or following that response. When we do not have the necessary information, we cannot make definite predictions, but we may still be able to formulate testable hypotheses. Finally, I should like to emphasize that I do not expect these two principles alone to prescribe adequately the necessary and sufficient conditions for reinforcement, except perhaps in a few of the simplest conditioning situations, even when we have enough information to apply the principles without ambiguity.

Experimenter-determined variables. Once we have specified the set-theoretical representation of a learning experiment, we are in a position to prescribe the values of at least two and usually three of the theoretical variables listed in Table 4. The variable r will be the number of response classes and also the number of possible reinforcing events; K will be the number of stimulus sets. The variable π_k, probability of reinforcing event E_k, is usually, but not always, experimenter-determined. In a given experiment, E_k might, for example, represent a signal, unequivocably discriminable by the subject, indicating that response A_k is correct. Then the value of π_k, probability that the signal is given on any trial, is prescribed by the experimenter. In the same type of experiment one might, however, present the signal indicating correctness of A_k on every trial but make it so faint, or the "noise" level so high, that there is only probability π_k that the subject will detect the signal. Then π_k would be a subject-controlled variable, and its value would have to be determined either from a psychophysical experiment or from the data of the learning experiment itself.

The remaining items in Table 4 are all subject-controlled variables in the sense that their values must be ascertained from behavioral data. In order to complete the linkage between the theory and any particular experiment, one must derive experimental laws which contain subject-controlled variables as dependent variables or parameters. Formally, these laws may be theorems especially derived for a particular application of the theory or they may be general theorems with values of the experimenter-controlled variables appropriate to the particular application. In the next section, we shall illustrate the derivation of experimental laws for a number of important applications and discuss the final step of estimating parameter values and comparing theoretical with observed relationships.

Derivation of experimental laws. Deriving theorems from a mathematical theory may seem at first thought to be an almost mechanical process. So far as the actual derivations are concerned, this impression is quite correct. It is intended that all theorems, or laws, of the theory should be strict logical consequences of the assumptions. Still, in practice the derivation of laws is far from mechanical, and in fact, may involve a high degree of art. From any mathematical theory an infinite number of theorems can be derived, but only a few of these are of any scientific interest. One of the artistic, or intuitive, functions of the scientist is to diagnose empirical situations and sense occasions on which a theory can fruitfully be applied. A second intuitive function is to foresee clearly enough what a theory will have to say about a given empirical problem so that the appropriate mathematical derivations can be initiated. A third is to make simplifying assumptions that are necessary for any particular application of a theory without distorting the problem under investigation.

In the remainder of this section, I shall sketch at a rather nontechnical level some of the techniques of derivation used to generate important classes of experimental laws, and at the same time I shall try to illustrate at least the third of the intuitive functions mentioned above. The presentation will necessarily involve more mathematical notation than the preceding portions of this article, and the reader with a low tolerance for symbols and equations may be well advised to skip ahead to the following section, which is concerned with more general matters of methodology.

Relations among response measures. Theorems *a* and *b* under the heading Response model, above, are already in form for direct application to any situation in which probability of a given response is assumed constant (as might, e.g., be the case at the asymptote of learning). Taken together, they overdetermine the variable p_j, and therefore, provide a consistency check on the theory. The first of these theorems states that the expected number of occurrences of a response A_j in n trials is equal to np_j. Since n is known for any experiment, once we have computed the observed mean number of occurrences of A_j we can set this empirically determined quantity equal to np_j and solve for p_j. If, e.g., the mean number of occurrences of response A_j in a block of 50 trials were 35, our estimate of p_j would be .70. Having estimated p_j, we would be in a position to make a genuine prediction. According to the second theorem, the probability that A_j occurs for the first time on the nth trial is equal to $(1 - p_j)^{n-1}p_j$. Using our estimate of p_j obtained by application of the first theorem, we could predict the exact frequency distribution for "first occurrences." If the estimate $p_j = .70$ in the numerical illustration were based on 100 blocks of 50 trials (using either the same subject or a group of subjects with like values of p_j) we could predict that in .70 × 100 = 70 instances A_j would occur as the first response in a block; in .30 × .70 × 100 = 21 instances A_j would occur for the first time on the second trial of the block; and so on.

The same two theorems provide a basis for deriving laws relating to latencies or response time. Consider, for example, a situation in which the subject makes successive choices between two responses, A_1 and A_2, that require h_1 and h_2 sec, respectively, to execute; latency is defined as time from onset of the stimulus to completion of the first A_1 response. The probability of a latency of exactly $L = (n - 1)h_2 + h_1$ sec is equal to $(1 - p_1)^{n-1}p_1$ and it can easily be shown [19; 13, pp. 311–313] that the predicted mean latency is

$$\bar{L} = h_2 \frac{(1 - p_1)}{p_1} + h_1$$

If $h_1 = h_2$, this relation simplifies to

$$\bar{L} = \frac{h}{p_1}$$

Time-dependent phenomena. Numerous functions describing changes in response probability during retention intervals follow directly from theorem *a* under Stimulus fluctuation model, above. According to this theorem, if the component of a stimulating situation corresponding to any given stimulus element has probability $f(0)$ of being present in the situation (available for sampling) during a given learning trial, then it has probability $f(t)$ of being present in the situation on a test trial after a rest interval t, where

$$f(t) = J - [J - f(0)]a^t$$

and J and a are parameters with values between zero and unity.

Now consider a learning experiment involving a single stimulating situation; the latter is represented formally by a set S_* with subsets S and S' corresponding to the elements of S_* which are and are not, respectively, available for sampling by the subject during any single learning period. Suppose that at the end of the first acquisition period all elements of S and no elements of S' are connected to response A_j. Then $f(0)$ equals unity and if all elements have equal sampling probabilities, $f(t)$ will be equal to the mean proportion of elements in S connected to A_j after time t and therefore to $p_j(t)$, the probability of A_j in the situation after time t. Making the appropriate substitutions in the formula of theorem *a* under Stimulus fluctuation model, we have the function

$$p_j(t) = f(t) = J + (1 - J)a^t$$

describing the predicted course of spontaneous regression, or short-term forgetting.

Now the dependent variable $p_j(t)$ can be evaluated in any appropriate manner. We might, for example, test either the same subjects or different groups of subjects after different intervals t and take the observed proportion of A_j responses at each interval as an estimate of $p_j(t)$. Then by curve-fitting procedures we could determine, in turn, the values of the parameters J and a which produce best agreement, according to an appropriate criterion, between the empirical and theoretical curves of $p_j(t)$.

Spontaneous recovery from extinction can be handled similarly. Suppose that conditioning has been continued over several periods until all elements in S_* are connected to A_j, and then extinction is carried out during a single period until p_j goes to zero. At the termination of extinction, all elements in S' but none in S are connected to A_j. Reasoning as in the preceding paragraph, we can set $f(0)$ equal to zero in the formula of theorem *a* under Stimulus fluctuation model, and, substituting $p_j(t)$ for $f(t)$, obtain for the predicted curve of spontaneous recovery

$$p_j(t) = J(1 - a^t)$$

Since the same parameters, J and a (both derived from j and j' of Table 4), appear in the functions for both regression and recovery, it is possible to make quantitative predictions for one situation after the parameters have been evaluated in the other [25, 54]. Functions applicable to various other distributional phenomena have been derived from the statistical theory [25, 26, 40, 54] by the same general methods illustrated here.

Stimulus manipulation. The simplest type of experiment on stimulus compounding provides the most direct means for evaluating sizes of stimulus sets. Suppose that we wish to compare the numbers of elements, N_1 and N_2, in the sets S_1 and S_2 corresponding to two stimuli which are assumed on empirical grounds to have no common elements. In the interest of simplicity it will be convenient also to suppose we are dealing with a situation for which it is reasonable to assume equal Θ values over both sets. Our first step is to give appropriate training to experimental subjects until probability of some response A_j is brought approximately to unity in S_1 and zero in S_2. (Successful achievement of this step will corroborate our assumption that the sets are nonoverlapping.) Then we will present the two stimuli together and evaluate the probability of A_j in the presence of the combination. By theorem c under Stimulus-response relations, above, p_j should be related to N_1 and N_2 by the relations

$$p_j = \frac{N_1}{N_1 + N_2}$$

and

$$1 - p_j = \frac{N_2}{N_1 + N_2}$$

from which it obviously follows that

$$\frac{p_j}{1 - p_j} = \frac{N_1}{N_2}$$

Substituting observed values for p_j and $1 - p_j$, we have a numerical estimate of the relative size of sets S_1 and S_2.

This technique can be used to prepare a rigorous quantitative test of our stimulus model. By repeated application of the technique, we select a set of nonoverlapping stimuli for which the corresponding sets, $S_1, S_2, \ldots, S_K$, are all of the same size, i.e.,

$$N_1 = N_2 = \cdots = N_K = N$$

Then by appropriate training [see 83 for an account of an actual experiment of this type] we bring probability of a response A_j to approximately unity in the presence of some of the stimuli, say the odd-numbered ones, and to zero in the presence of the remainder. Now by applying theorem c under Stimulus-response relations we can make exact a priori predictions of response probabilities in the presence of any desired combination; e.g., given a combination of S_1, S_2, and S_3,

$$p_j = \frac{N_1 + N_3}{N_1 + N_2 + N_3} = \frac{2N}{3N} = \frac{2}{3}$$

or given the combination S_1, S_2, S_4, S_6, S_8,

$$p_j = \frac{N_1}{N_1 + N_2 + N_4 + N_6 + N_8} = \frac{N}{5N} = \frac{1}{5}$$

and so on.

For a second example of predicting consequences of stimulus manipulations, let us consider an experiment on stimulus generalization. Suppose that we condition a response A_j to a stimulus, say a light of wavelength 500 mμ. Assume that the probability of A_j in the presence of the CS is zero before conditioning and unity at the end of conditioning. Now suppose that we test with lights of 520 and 540 mμ and obtain .90 and .60 as empirical estimates of p_j in the presence of the two test stimuli. Assuming that the stimulus set S_{500}, corresponding to the CS, comprises N elements all of which were connected to A_j at the end of conditioning, we conclude that the sets S_{520} and S_{540}, corresponding to the test stimuli, have 90 and 60 per cent, respectively, of their elements in common with S_{500}. Having established these correspondences between empirical and theoretical variables, we are ready to test the model by making some predictions. We might, for example, replicate the experiment with new subjects but this time carry conditioning only far enough so that $p_j = .5$ in the presence of the CS. We could predict by application of theorem c under Stimulus-response relations that the probabilities of A_j in the presence of the test lights should be for S_{520},

$$p_j = .5 \times .90 = .45$$

and for S_{540},

$$p_j = .5 \times .60 = .30$$

Although this example is purely hypothetical, the predictions do not seem implausible in the light of data reported by Guttman and Kalish [49].

Simple learning. For purposes of theoretical treatment the simplest learning experiments are those involving two alternative response classes and determinate reinforcement. By the latter we mean that a reinforcing event corresponding to one or the other of the defined response classes occurs on every trial, and that we can specify in advance of a trial the probability that any given response will be followed by any given reinforcing event.

From our previous discussions of reinforcement and contiguity theory it follows that acquisition of a runway response with 100 per cent reinforcement should represent one of the simplest determinate cases. The animal's behavior during any time interval is categorized into two classes, running and not-running, and the former is reinforced at the termination of each experimental trial. If we make the simplifying assumption that all stimulus elements in the set corresponding to the situation which begins each trial have equal sampling probabilities ("equal Θ case"), then by theorem b under Learning, above, the probability of running changes from one trial to the next in accordance with the relation

$$p_n = (1 - \Theta)p_{n-1} + \Theta$$

As it stands, this difference equation is not convenient for experimental application; however, we can prove by mathematical induction that if the difference equation holds for any pair of successive trials, then over a series of trials response probability must change according to the formula

$$p_n = 1 - (1 - p_1)(1 - \Theta)^{n-1}$$

Now by substituting for p_n in this function its equivalent in terms of mean latency from the relation $\bar{L} = h/p$ given in Part II above under Formulation of a Probabilistic Response Model, we finally obtain a function

$$\bar{L}_n = \frac{h}{p_n} = \frac{h}{1 - (1 - h/L_1)(1 - \Theta)^{n-1}}$$

suitable for experimental application. The values of h and Θ can be determined by curve-fitting procedures from an empirical curve of mean latency against trials. With estimates of h and Θ in hand, we can then generate independent tests of the theory by deriving other functions containing these parameters to predict changes in variances or other statistics of the latency distribution during the acquisition series.

A second example of determinate reinforcement is provided by the verbal conditioning experiment. In the two-choice version, the subject responds to the ready signal on each trial by predicting which of two reinforcing events, E_1 or E_2, will occur. Again making the equal Θ assumption, we can apply theorem b under Learning, above, to obtain the expected probability of A_1 (the response of predicting E_1) on trials following occurrences of E_1 or E_2: if E_1 occurs on trial $n - 1$,

$$p_{1,n} = (1 - \Theta)p_{1,n-1} + \Theta$$

if E_2 occurs on trial $n - 1$,

$$p_{1,n} = (1 - \Theta)p_{1,n-1}$$

where, as usual, $p_{1,n}$ represents probability of A_1 on trial n. From these difference equations, or "trial operators," we can predict that the probability of A_1 will increase following reinforcement of A_1 and decrease following reinforcement of A_2, but we are not yet in a position to make any predictions about the over-all course or limit of learning under any particular reinforcement schedule.

Starting with the trial operators, we can, however, make a start in the desired direction by deriving a difference equation for the average change in response probability per trial under any given conditions. Suppose the design of an experiment prescribes noncontingent, random reinforcement with E_1 and E_2 having probabilities π and $1 - \pi$, respectively, on any trial. Then to obtain the average change in probability of A_1 on a trial, we need only weight each of the trial operators by its probability of application and add them, viz., on the average,

$$p_{1,n} = \pi[(1 - \Theta)p_{1,n-1} + \Theta] + (1 - \pi)(1 - \Theta)p_{1,n-1}$$
$$= (1 - \Theta)p_{1,n-1} + \Theta\pi$$

It can be shown by mathematical induction that if this equation is applied repeatedly the resulting curve of probability against trials is given by

$$p_{1,n} = \pi - (\pi - p_{1,1})(1 - \Theta)^{n-1}$$

a negatively accelerated function which has π as an asymptote regardless of the initial probability $p_{1,1}$ or of the value of Θ. As we have indicated in Part II, considerable research has been directed toward determining experimental conditions for which curves of learning under new reinforcement schedules are predictable once Θ has been evaluated from data obtained under some one schedule.

In more complicated cases, e.g., those in which probability of a given reinforcing event on any trial is contingent upon the response made on the same or a preceding trial, or those in which probabilities of reinforcement vary in some systematic manner from trial to trial, the procedure for deriving experimental laws is essentially the same as that illustrated here for the simple noncontingent case [see 30 for details].

Discrimination learning. For the simplest discrimination experiments, i.e., those characterized by determinate reinforcement and by controlled stimulus exposures which are independent of the organism's behavior, we should be able to derive predictive laws from the theory already presented. Suppose a discrimination is to be formed between two stimulus situations, S_I and S_{II}, which are presented in a random sequence with equal relative frequencies. Response A_1 is to be reinforced whenever S_I is present on a trial and A_2 whenever S_{II} is present. To conceptualize this experiment we require three stimulus sets: S_1 representing stimulation available only in S_I; S_2 representing stimulation available only in S_{II}; and S_c representing stimulation available on all trials. In the terminology used by a number of recent investigators [see, e.g., 67, 80] S_1 and S_2 represent relevant cues and S_c irrelevant cues. For simplicity, we shall assume equal Θ values for all elements in all three sets; therefore, the probability that an element in S_c will be sampled on any trial is equal to Θ, and the probability that an element in S_1 or S_2 will be sampled on any trial is equal to $\Theta/2$. Now beginning with theorem *b* under Learning, above, we can proceed as in the preceding section and obtain expressions for the proportions of elements in S_1, S_c, and S_2, respectively, that are connected to A_1 after $n-1$ discrimination trials:

$$p_{11,n} = 1 - (1 - p_{11,1})\left(1 - \frac{\Theta}{2}\right)^{n-1}$$

$$p_{c1,n} = \tfrac{1}{2} - (\tfrac{1}{2} - p_{c1,1})(1 - \Theta)^{n-1}$$

and
$$p_{21,n} = (p_{21,1})\left(1 - \frac{\Theta}{2}\right)^{n-1}$$

where $p_{hj,n}$ is to be read "proportion of elements in set S_h connected to A_j on trial n." In order to predict response probability in either S_I or S_{II}, we must take into account the sizes of the three stimulus sets, N_1, N_c, and N_2. It will be convenient to introduce the abbreviations

$$w_1 = \frac{N_1}{N_1 + N_c}$$

and
$$w_2 = \frac{N_2}{N_2 + N_c}$$

for the proportions of "relevant cues" in the two situations. Now application of theorem *c* under Stimulus-response relations yields the desired expressions for probability of A_1 in situations S_I and S_{II} as a function of number of trials:

$$p_{I1,n} = w_1 p_{11,n} + (1 - w_1)p_{c1,n}$$

and
$$p_{II1,n} = w_2 p_{21,n} + (1 - w_2)p_{c1,n}$$

If the initial values $p_{11,1}$, $p_{21,1}$, and $p_{c1,1}$ are all assumed equal to $\frac{1}{2}$, these expressions reduce to the simple, negatively accelerated "growth" and "decay" functions

$$p_{\mathrm{I}1,n} = \frac{1}{2} + \frac{w_1}{2}\left[1 - \left(1 - \frac{\theta}{2}\right)^{n-1}\right]$$

$$p_{\mathrm{II}1,n} = \frac{1}{2} - \frac{w_2}{2}\left[1 - \left(1 - \frac{\theta}{2}\right)^{n-1}\right]$$

Thus it turns out that the predicted asymptotes, but not the slopes, of discrimination learning curves depend on the proportions of common elements in the stimulus sets. As the proportion of common elements tends to zero, w_1 and w_2 tend to unity, and the curves of $p_{\mathrm{I}1,n}$ and $p_{\mathrm{II}1,n}$ tend to asymptotes of unity and zero, respectively. Empirical estimates of the parameters w_1 and w_2 are obtainable directly from the observed asymptotic relative frequencies of A_1 responses in S_{I} and S_{II}, respectively. Once the parameters have been evaluated for a given situation, we can derive a priori predictions for learning under modified conditions (e.g., with unequal relative frequencies of presentation of S_{I} and S_{II} or with partial reinforcement in one or both situations).

METHODOLOGY

Stages in theory construction. Having just emerged from the rough-and-ready business of everyday theory construction long enough for the analytical interlude of the preceding pages, I find the tidy and formal appearance of the system outlined in Part III under Formal Structure of Statistical Learning Theory as unfamiliar as that of a small boy in a Sunday suit. The formal structure was not blueprinted in advance; hence it must have evolved via a series of approximations. Reviewing the semihistorical account given in Part II, and imposing a certain measure of abstraction and idealization on the disorderly flow of events, we can distinguish the following phases in the cycle of operations that has generated the present theory.

Exploration. As the statistical approach attempts invasion of each new empirical area, we have to explore alternative modes of description and measurement until we succeed in isolating simple empirical relations which exhibit symptoms of reproducibility and generality. The rapid growth of statistical learning theories from about 1948 has been possible only because these exploratory analyses were essentially completed for a number of empirical situations by reinforcement theorists, especially Skinner and Hull, during the preceding decade.

Conceptualization. Once promising empirical variables have been identified, we require a conceptual representation which will enable us to use mathematical reasoning in working out the consequences of assumptions about relations among the variables. The general method of conceptualization we have found fruitful is to represent collections of empirical events by mathematical sets and empirical relations by relations and functions on the sets.

Axiomatization. The best constructs do not make a theory until they are interrelated by definite assumptions. Not all the assumptions on the roster are on an equal footing at any given time, however. Always some have merely the character of tentative hypotheses that will be dropped at a moment's notice if they fail to produce. Others have survived enough trials and tests to acquire tenure and will be the last to be relinquished when the theory runs into factual difficulties. The assumptions with most seniority are regarded as axioms when we turn to structural analysis of the theory, but we do not ordinarily attempt to achieve quite the degree of formalism that the logician associates with axiomatization.

Although there can be no limitations in principle on the sources of a theorist's hypotheses, strategic considerations may lead to some restrictions in practice. The investigators who have had a part in the development of statistical learning theories share a strong distrust of speculative theorizing. Like many of our fellows, we find it difficult enough to test theories that arise in close conjunction with experimental analyses, and usually beyond our capacities to test those that do not. A distaste for untestable theories does not, however, by any means consign us to a permanent role as passive followers of paths set by the experimentalist. When formulating theoretical assumptions we prefer to begin with severely limited hypotheses, often representing no more than simple smoothing and extrapolation of observed relations among empirical variables. After a theory has begun to take shape, we expect to derive predictions of new empirical phenomena and then have our turn at setting the pace for the experimenter.

Mathematical analysis. Once assumptions have been stated in mathematical form, it is necessary to analyze the formal system with respect to internal consistency and fruitfulness in generating a multiplicity of relationships among the theoretical variables. The end result of this phase, often attained only after many revisions of the formal system, is a body of theorems which, once appropriately interpreted, may prove to be experimental laws. Now we have a model, i.e., a theory that describes a class of idealized situations in which only the variables of the theory play a role. The question remains how well the model will approximate actual experimental situations.

Empirical test. The empirical facts or problems that give rise to a particular line of theorizing usually mark also the point to which we return for preliminary assay of the theoretical product. We do not, however, consider that we have really tested a theory until we have established some reasonably firm rules of correspondence between theoretical and empirical variables and then have gone on to predict new empirical phenomena.

Exploitation. Once the theory has begun to acquire some empirical standing, it can begin to serve us as a theory should. We always see facts in the light of theories and always hope to see them more clearly with better theories. A useful theory not only guides experimental designs and interpretations of data, but also provides machinery for formulating and testing new hypotheses.

Generalization and extension. One of the distinctive characteristics of quantitative theories is a constant pressure in the direction of increasing generality. Each restriction and simplifying assumption imposed at a given stage of development serves as a challenge to further investigation. Whenever a restriction is removed, the outcome is a broader theory which includes its predecessor as a special case. A second medium of extension and generalization is the incorporation into the theory of hypotheses which have been formulated in terms of the theoretical model and confirmed by subsequent experimental tests.

Of necessity, statistical learning theories have had their empirical origin in the simpler and better-analyzed experimental situations. It is only in these situations that one can hope to make apt initial choices of empirical variables and relationships. Further, it is likely that the statistical approach to learning theory will continue indefinitely to devote considerable attention to the most elementary forms of learning. One of the reasons for this prognosis is the recognition that empirical simplicity is relative to the current degree of refinement of experimental and theoretical methods. What appear at the moment to be extremely simple learning situations become continually less so as they are more delicately probed with the aid of quantitative theories.

Naturally we are eager to extend our theories to more complex situations whenever tactical circumstances permit. When a complex situation can be considered to be compounded of simpler ones, the extension of the theory can often be accomplished with little modification. Thus, we have treated discrimination learning as a resultant of two or more concurrent acquisition processes and paired-associate learning in terms of concurrent discriminations. When complex forms of learning resist analysis into simpler components, we may find it possible to account qualitatively for certain aspects of the learning by means of general laws which have been established in simpler situations. We may, for example, hope to clarify distributional phenomena even in complex learning experiments by application of our stimulus fluctuation principles. Retention from trial to trial or period to period should be affected in qualitatively predictable ways by stimulus fluctuation regardless of particular experimental arrangements. Finally, there is the possibility, as yet relatively unexplored, that the same methods used in developing present statistical theories of elementary learning may be applied directly to the construction of theories for more complex variables and relationships.

Formal organization. Our cross-sectional analysis of statistical learning theory in its present form reveals numerous points at which ambiguity or indeterminacy might enter into the system: in the data-language descriptions of empirical variables, in the definitions of set-theoretical concepts and theoretical variables, in the correspondence between theoretical concepts and empirical variables, in the estimation of parameter values. We should like to eliminate all traces of indeterminacy from the system, but that is too much to hope for. Our descriptions and analyses of empirical situations are never complete or final; therefore, at any stage of a scientific investigation there is a residue of uncertainty which must be reflected in our theoretical system.

The strategy adopted for dealing with uncertainty and ambiguity is one of the distinctive aspects of the present approach to learning theory. One frequently hears the argument that so long as an empirical science is in a primarily exploratory stage, theories must be informal and qualitative. I do not question that informal and qualitative theorizing is sometimes necessary and even rewarding, but I do have doubts as to both the necessity and the wisdom of being long satisfied with it. The disadvantage of permitting a haze of ambiguity to cover an entire theory is that the theorist, like anyone trying to navigate in a fog, can never really tell how far he has come or whither he is heading. Although we cannot get rid of ambiguity entirely, we can localize it by making our theoretical concepts and assumptions precise and permitting indeterminacy only in the correspondences between theoretical and empirical variables. In the early stages of theory construction, it may still be impossible to localize the sources of an erroneous prediction, but as rapidly as we accumulate instances of successful prediction and description in any empirical area, we become committed to particular rules of correspondence, or coordinating definitions, and the entire theory becomes determinate.

It will be clear from our analysis of the present theory that all linkages among constructs are explicit and determinate and all derivations of theorems are accomplished by exact mathematical reasoning.[24] Interpretive rules, on the other hand, are somewhat open ended. We can not, for example, say once and for all what kinds of events or operations will serve as reinforcing events. But in all the experimental situations that have been used for empirical tests of the theory we have had to make specific assumptions as to which operations correspond to reinforcing events, and if we wish to retain the ground we have gained, we must remain committed to these correspondences.

I would like to emphasize that my brief for rigor in theorizing does not imply any great love of formality for its own sake. In the developmental stages of a science it is not healthy for theories to stand still long enough for exhaustive logical analysis. The kind of formalization I consider necessary to sound theory construction consists in progressively sharpening the definitions of concepts and exposing concealed assumptions at the same time that the theory continues to undergo correction and refinement in the light of experimental applications.

Mensurational and quantificational procedures. Presentations of even the most formal and quantitative learning theories do not include discussions of the logic of measurement. To one with a background in mental testing or traditional psychophysics it may seem that the learning theorist must either be shirking his scientific responsibilities or else be possessed of some unfair advantages over workers in those fields. I believe that neither is the case. The advantageous position of the learning theorist arises from the fact that he has not been lured into searching for elaborate scales of measurement before the development of quantitative theories.

There may, of course, be differences in usage of the term *measurement*. By it I mean the coordination of an empirical system to a particular type of mathematical system[25] within the framework of a theory. In the case of fundamental physical measurement, the theories involved are so firmly accepted and so inextricably imbedded in our habits of thinking about nature that reference to theories is usually suppressed. In the case of derived physical measurements, e.g., those having to do with heat, electrical conduction, the theoretical reference remains explicit; and the generally healthy condition of the theories is reflected in the associated scales of measurement. The severe growing pains of psychological measurement are largely attributable, I would suggest, to unfortunate early experiences in the house of dualism. Once it has

[24] A strict axiomatization of a portion of the present theory was completed by Professor Patrick Suppes and the writer during our period in residence at the Center for Advanced Study in the Behavioral Sciences. This study is in preparation for publication.

[25] An elucidation of the properties of this mathematical system has been given by Campbell [14].

been assumed that there must be psychological scales, or dimensions of measurement, paralleling physical scales, what is more natural than to carry out in a psychological testing situation some operations that yield numbers and assume that the numbers represent measurements on a "psychological scale." This accomplished, the way is open for endless discussion of subtle mathematical questions whose answers have no empirically testable consequences and which are related in no direct way to the development of substantive theories.

Investigations of learning begin with measurements of empirical variables but without an a priori assumption that the numbers obtained really represent measures on psychological scales. The investigator who measures the latency of a runway response in a learning experiment is not operating under the assumption that there must be scales of "psychological time" and "psychological distance" corresponding to ordinary physical time and distance; therefore, he is not immediately confronted with such questions as whether he is justified in using a ratio scale or whether his units are additive. The investigator may still become embroiled in logical difficulties by making the assumption that he is really measuring "learning," but modern learning theorists usually avoid this trap also. In the reinforcement theories of Hull and Skinner and in the statistical theories of the writer and others, one bypasses the hopeless problem of defining some unitary measurable variable to serve as a referent for the term "learning" and proceeds directly to relate such physically measurable behavioral variables as latency to physically measurable independent variables by means of laws or theories.

Once a theory has begun to take shape, measurement is a matter of assigning numerical values to the variables and parameters of the theory. The problems of measurement may still be difficult enough, but they are technical, not philosophical. In the case of statistical learning theories, the one special problem of measurement is the problem of statistical estimation. Having cast our methodological lot with the statistical theories of other disciplines, we share not only their problems, but also their methods and results. Also, new problems of statistical estimation arise in learning theory that have not been solved elsewhere, and the solution of these is becoming an important area of theoretical research [see 13, 72].

RANGE OF APPLICATION

Numerous questions can be asked about the empirical scope and fertility of statistical learning theories. Probably the reader will have been able to derive his own answers to most of them from the material given in Part II of this report. Here I shall limit myself to brief summary comments on some of the specific questions raised in the Project A outline.

I would prefer to define the present scope of the system, not in terms of the problems for which it is always right, but in terms of the area in which it is presently undergoing development in association with experimental researches. So defined, the area of application is roughly coextensive with that in which the experimental analysis of learning has reached the stage of yielding data suitable for quantitative treatment. I say "roughly" because, on the one hand, some problems in this area have not so far been touched by the statistical approach and, on the other, predictions derived from statistical theories often run ahead of available experimental data. Generally speaking, applications of statistical learning theory in its present form are limited to situations in which measures are taken on well-defined response classes and in which reinforcing events can be identified. Among the standard experimental situations dealt with so far are classical and instrumental conditioning, runway and T-maze learning, simple discriminative learning, simple verbal learning in Thorndikian, paired-associate, and guessing experiments, simple escape and avoidance learning. Within these situations, only restricted sets of variables have been treated. For example, considerable progress has been made in dealing with random reinforcement schedules, but only a bare start in dealing with magnitudes of reinforcing stimuli; relationships involving stimulus variability have been formalized but those involving stimulus traces have not. In nearly all cases, tests of theoretical predictions have been most successful under conditions of temporally spaced trials. Under conditions of extremely massed trials or continuous work, complications enter that have not been analyzed in terms of statistical models.

Rigorous empirical tests have been carried out only in a very restricted set of experimental situations. Statistical learning theorists are not the first to find that the assumptions underlying quantitative tests of a theory are rarely satisfied except in experiments carried out especially for the purpose. This state of affairs is bound to continue. What we hope for, and in some instances have reason to expect, is that once particular concepts and principles of the theory become established by rigorous tests in special experiments, they will prove useful aids to the interpretation of empirical phenomena in a wider range of situations, perhaps in some cases extending even beyond the laboratory walls.

EVALUATION OF THE SYSTEM

One function always expected of a theory is to replace the detailed descriptions of fact provided by the experimenter's protocol with descriptions which, though less complete, are more compact and more useful. How well this function is served depends in part upon how well the laws derived from the theory fit the facts. In the case of a quantitative theory, it is usually easy to decide whether predictions are in agreement with data (or at least whether there is significant disagreement) but often not so easy to decide whether an experimental application has resulted in confirmation or refutation of the theory.

Quantitative theories are occasionally completely wrong but they are rarely completely right. Among the researches cited in Part II, we have seen numerous instances in which statistical learning theory is superior to any competitor in handling a particular kind of data, but still falls short of what we would like to achieve with it. Each step forward in our coverage of empirical data brings us at the same time to new problems and a new view of what remains to be accomplished. Thus the first applications of the theory to simple selective learning under random reinforcement were intended to test predictions concerning curve forms and asymptotes. The results in these respects left little to be desired, but they immediately suggested the possibility of evaluating the parameters of the system under one set of experimental conditions and then making entirely a priori predictions of behavior under other conditions.

Some of these more exacting tests of the theory have led to accurate predictions of quantitative relationships and some have not. Should the entire set of findings be taken as evidence for the theory or against it? A simple balance sheet would not be particularly illuminating. We can say that in each of the empirical situations to which it has been applied, the theory has generated accurate descriptions of some, at least, of the principal trends in the data. Perhaps more important, the disparities between theory and observation have led to more detailed experimental analyses and, in some cases, to new empirical distinctions and classifications which appear to further the interpretation and organization of learning phenomena.

For the experimentalist, evaluation of the theory comes down to evaluation of the research instigated, and organized by it. Lacking any generally accepted standards for this kind of assessment, I have tried to report in Part II, as objectively as my personal involvement would permit, the history of the theory in mediating research. This account may permit one who has also the benefit of hindsight and detachment to provide the value judgments. By way of summary, I shall simply list here by topics the chief lines of empirical research instigated by the theory up to the present time:

1. Effects of competing responses [20], magnitude of reinforcement [22], and deprivational conditions [6] upon curves of operant conditioning (bar pressing in a free responding situation)

2. Effects of stimulus variables upon curves of classical conditioning [5] and verbal conditioning [11]

3. Conditions of constancy and modifiability of acquisition and extinction rates [27, 36, 64, 66]

4. Resistance to extinction in relation to partial reinforcement under conditions of widely spaced trials [92, 93]

5. Forms and asymptotes of acquisition curves in relation to conditions of random reinforcement and nonreinforcement [1, 2, 37, 65, 76]

6. Effects of new random reinforcement procedures: probability of reinforcement variable over trials [31], probability of reinforcement contingent on outcomes of preceding trials, probability of reinforcement controlled by ambiguity of the reinforcing stimulus[26]

7. Extensions of the treatment of random reinforcement in simple human learning to escape learning [88, 89] and avoidance [8] situations

8. Simple human discrimination learning in relation to stimulus variables and partial reinforcement [17, 31, 33, 34, 44, 63, 79]

9. Quantitative prediction of stimulus compounding [34, 39, 78, 83]

10. Spontaneous recovery, regression, and related distributional phenomena in relation to number and spacing of acquisition and extinction trials [36, 40, 54, 66, 69]

11. Quantitative analyses of paired-associate and serial learning of verbal responses [3]

12. Learning in elementary forms of social interaction, e.g., two-person games [4, 31]

This list has been organized in terms of research cited in Part II of this report and associated with the Indiana branch of statistical learning theory. Among the studies associated with related statistical or probabilistic models are those of Bush and Mosteller and their associates on parameters of learning functions under partial reinforcement and learning in simple social situations [13, chaps. 12, 13]; those of Restle on the role of relevant and irrelevant cues in discrimination learning

---

[26] Estes, W. K., & Johns, M. Probability-learning with ambiguity in the reinforcing stimulus. *Amer. J. Psychol.*, 1958, **71**, 219–228.

[80]; and those of Wyckoff on "observing responses" in discrimination learning [95].

What specific aspects of statistical learning theories have been responsible for the research instigated by them? One of the most critical features is probably a matter of timing. Unlike some of their predecessors, these theories have taken root in areas where the way has been prepared by considerable experimental analysis and the isolation of quantifiable empirical variables. The experimental spadework has provided both a tissue of empirical relationships from which promising theoretical assumptions could be extracted and also possibilities of prompt empirical testing for the embryo theories. The quantitative character of the theories tends in itself to facilitate research. The exact and specific predictions generated by them call irresistibly for observational tests. When experimental outcomes confirm the predictions, the investigator has reason to feel rewarded; he has won a point in his running game against nature. Disparities between quantitative predictions and data are momentarily less satisfying than successful correspondences, but in a way more important for the long-term fruitfulness of the system. If one restricted applications of a theory to problems for which successful outcomes were highly probable, a period of unadulterated pleasure might ensue, but in time the system would grind to a halt. Although maintenance of the investigator's morale requires a sprinkling of happy outcomes, the theory is nurtured more by its errors of prediction.

Associated with any fruitful theory are constant attempts to refine and extend the network of predictive relationships. A successful application consists in collecting and processing information as prescribed by the theory, i.e., evaluating theoretical variables, and then correctly predicting a relationship among empirical variables. When in any instance this much has been accomplished by application of the statistical model, the next step has been to ask whether, using the same information, i.e., the same parameter values, further predictions could be generated relating the given variables to others or specifying relationships among the variables in new situations.

Sooner or later, these attempted extensions of the predictive network lead to disparities between theory and data. And at this point again, strategic considerations are important. One must yield to the facts, but not too readily. Our increasing confidence in the basic soundness of the statistical approach is not only a result but also a cause of its fruitfulness in leading to new lines of research. Our initial response to an erroneous prediction is not immediate modification of the theory, but continued experimentation, with the expectation that in each new situation suitable analyses will enable us to distinguish conditions under which the theory does and does not hold. Isolation of such conditions may provide the starting point for revision or extension of the theory. As we have seen in a preceding section, the history of the present system has been structured largely by a series of these critical situations in which a mixture of successes and failures of prediction has led both to new experimental analyses and to modifications of the formal model.

At the time of writing, we can distinguish a number of key problems which represent foci of current research efforts and whose resolution will probably determine the next lines of theoretical development. One of these problems arises from the ubiquitous tendency for parameters representing rates of learning to vary systematically with probability of reinforcement and with previous learning history. A second is associated with stimulus overlap in discrimination experiments, a third with the complex pattern of dependencies between effects of nonreinforcement and other experimental conditions. More could be enumerated, but I believe that if even these three problems could be added to those already handled effectively, we would have something bearing more than casual resemblance to a workable descriptive theory of elementary learning.

The various components and aspects of statistical learning theories that we have reviewed differ widely with respect to probable longevity. Particular mathematical forms and formulas are likely to be revised many times, subject, however, to the restriction that the well-confirmed experimental laws derivable from the theory in its present form should appear as approximations or special cases in successor theories. Some of the more general features of the present system, e.g., the probabilistic response model, the view of learning as a sampling process, the method of defining and representing reinforcing events, the exploitation of contiguity principles as a source of hypotheses relative to conditions of reinforcement and nonreinforcement, the assumptions of additivity and transposability of stimulus-response relations, may be expected to weather many seasons.

In some instances, concepts and methods developed within the present system may prove useful in other areas of application. Especially likely candidates for this interdisciplinary function are the techniques of representing classes of empirical variables by mathematical sets, the probabilistic methods of deriving relations among response measures, the general procedure for formulating basic assumptions in terms of difference equations which represent the momentary effects of causal variables and then from these deriving descriptive laws for particular combinations of experimental conditions.

INTERRELATIONS WITH OTHER SYSTEMS

Classical learning theories. It does not seem possible to make any direct comparison between the statistical approach to learning theory and that of such "field" or "cognitive" theorists as Tolman, Lewin, or Köhler. The two approaches are characterized by different descriptive frames of reference and different immediate objectives; and there is almost no overlap in problems investigated, methods, or results. It is possible that some of the methods of statistical learning theories may prove applicable to empirical problems that have interested cognitive theorists, but there is at present no real basis for prognosticating the forms or probable outcomes of such applications.

The present theory embodies many features of Skinner's "descriptive behaviorism," especially the emphasis on descriptions of learning in terms of functional relationships between experimentally defined classes of behavioral and environmental events and the operational treatment of reinforcement. I would consider the most important difference between the two approaches to be one of emphasis. Although he speaks of response probability as a systematic dependent variable, Skinner has preferred to concentrate his research almost entirely on the formulation of laws that can be shown to hold uniformly for individual organisms in highly reproducible situations. Investigators associated with the present system are interested also in statistical regularities which can be demonstrated only by averaging data over groups of subjects or over repeated experiments with individual subjects. When there is a choice, all would agree, I think, that laws which provide unerring predictions for individual cases are the most satisfying. However, there is no guarantee that the choice is always open to us. In psychology, as in other fields of science, there may be important predictive relationships that can be studied only at a statistical level of analysis. And I have been able to find no tangible empirical basis for anticipating that with progressive refinements of experimental control, probabilistic laws of behavior will always converge to deterministic ones.

A number of ideas which have played important roles in the development of statistical learning theory bear obvious signs of Guthrie's influence. These include especially the stimulus-response contiguity principle and the conception of gradual learning as an outcome of all-or-none laws operating on many components of a situation. To what extent the utilization and modification of these concepts within the present system are in harmony with Guthrie's thinking I shall not try to decide. The quantitative methodology of statistical learning theory has so little in common with the informality and intuitive emphasis of

Guthrie's approach that comparative analyses for any but historical purposes are apt to be unrewarding.

Whether statistical learning theory should be regarded as either a competitor or a successor to Hull's system is hard to say. The statistical approach grew out of attempts to refine and quantify certain aspects of contemporary reinforcement theory, and the contributions of Hull and his followers to the latter are too well known to require comment. At present, the empirical scope of statistical learning theory is much more restricted than that envisaged by Hull's quantification program. On the other hand, I believe it can fairly be said that in the common areas of application, the statistical theory is more determinate and testable. In any case, it should be possible within a reasonable time to determine which approach is the more advantageous as a research instrument and as a basis for further theory construction in the common areas. As I have indicated elsewhere [28], my own forecast for the immediate future is that Hull's system, together with the other broadly programmatic theories of recent decades, will be superseded by a loosely related federation of more restricted theories, statistical or otherwise, with the basic frame of reference and descriptive vocabulary of stimulus-response reinforcement theory serving a unifying function by providing a common connective link between model builders and experimenters.

Stochastic models. The stochastic model developed by Bush and Mosteller [12, 13] is similar in many respects to the statistical model for acquisition phenomena described in this paper. The communalities are not entirely accidental, for those investigators and I have kept in relatively close communication, with numerous exchanges of methods and results over a period of years. It will be instructive to compare the two programs, bringing out points of similarity and difference with respect to methodology, empirical scope, and types of mathematical models employed.

Comparisons among contemporary quantitative learning theories are facilitated by the fact that nearly all of them treat learning as a stochastic process. By this I mean that response probabilities serve as systematic dependent variables and laws derived from the theories take the form of mathematical operators or equations describing changes in response probabilities during learning. The theories developed by Bush and Mosteller, Detambel [18], Miller and McGill [74], Restle [80, 81], Wyckoff [96], and me and my colleagues at Indiana all follow this pattern, and there are indications that even Hull's quantitative theory, as revised by Spence [86], is coming into the fold. In fact, all these theories except that of Hull employ substantially the same response model. Differences in approach among the theorists are associated in large part with different starting points. Miller and Mc-Gill, Restle, Wyckoff, and Detambel all began with specific empirical problems. I and my colleagues have begun theory construction in some cases with specific empirical problems and in some cases with attempts to formalize and test explanatory hypotheses; the latter include, for example, hypotheses having to do with stimulus fluctuation and with contiguity-interference principles. Bush and Mosteller began with a particular limited mathematical system which seemed likely to have applications to learning and other psychological phenomena; they have proceeded to develop this mathematical system in great detail and have applied it to a number of experimental problems, e.g., symmetric choice problems, avoidance learning, and imitation, thus generating limited descriptive theories for these situations.

The empirical scope of Bush and Mosteller's work has been confined largely to certain aspects of acquisition and extinction, especially in situations involving partial reinforcement. Some correspondences between their approach and mine in this area may be illustrated in terms of one of the experimental situations that both have dealt with, the verbal conditioning experiment. In our approach to this situation, Straughan and I [37] showed that starting with assumptions of stimulus sampling and association by contiguity, one can derive the quantitative laws (discussed in a preceding section)

$$p_{n+1} = (1 - \Theta)p_n + \Theta$$

expressing the increment in response probability resulting from a reinforcement of the given response, and

$$p_{n+1} = (1 - \Theta)p_n$$

expressing the decrement resulting from reinforcement of an opposed response. Bush and Mosteller [13, chap. 13] arrive at the same laws by a different route. Their general model is assumed to be applicable to any learning situation in which events, e.g., reinforcements or non-reinforcements, produce changes in response probabilities describable by the linear transformation

$$Qp_n = \alpha p_n + (1 - \alpha)\lambda$$

where p represents response probability before the given event has occurred, and Qp the new value of response probability after the event. In Estes and Straughan's equations, Θ represents the stimulus sampling ratio; in Bush and Mosteller's, α and λ are free parameters which must be evaluated in terms of the conditions of a particular application.

To deal with the two-choice guessing situation, Bush and Mosteller define two operators, say

$$Q_1 p_n = \alpha_1 p_n + (1 - \alpha_1)\lambda_1$$

and
$$Q_2 p_n = \alpha_2 p_n + (1 - \alpha_2)\lambda_2$$

to represent the effects of reinforcement and nonreinforcement, respectively. By considering known experimental facts, they place restrictions on the parameters. It is known, for example, that in this type of experiment, 100 per cent reinforcement and 100 per cent nonreinforcement of a response lead to asymptotic probabilities of unity and zero, respectively. In order to represent this fact in the model, Bush and Mosteller impose the restriction $\lambda_1 = 1$ and $\lambda_2 = 0$. Other experimental facts concerning asymptotic probabilities under partial reinforcement appear to require the further restriction $\alpha_1 = \alpha_2 = \alpha$. Now their equations take the form

$$Q_1 p_n = \alpha p_n + 1 - \alpha$$

and
$$Q_2 p_n = \alpha p_n$$

for this situation. Since the name given a parameter is of no consequence, their parameter α could be relabeled $1 - \theta$, and their equations would become

$$Q_1 p_n = (1 - \theta)p_n + \theta$$

and
$$Q_2 p_n = (1 - \theta)p_n$$

It is clear that, except for unessential differences in notation, the equations resulting from specialization of Bush and Mosteller's general model have the same form as those derived by Estes and Straughan from the assumptions of statistical learning theory. Bush and Mosteller use the same general methods of derivation as do I and my colleagues, so the mean curves of learning derived for given experiments with various schedules of random reinforcement turn out to be identical in form no matter with which of these approaches one has started.

The fact that two models have been found to deliver the same learning functions when applied to one or more common situations does not imply that they will always do so, for the models may differ with respect to properties which do not reveal themselves in those particular applications. From a mathematical viewpoint there are a number of important differences between the linear operator model developed by Bush and Mosteller and the corresponding model associated with statistical theory. The former may be characterized as an infinite, Markovian, stochastic model. By stochastic we refer simply to the fact that changes in behavior during learning are represented in terms of changing response probabilities. By Markovian we mean that the entire course of learning is, in principle, predictable given the set of response probabilities characterizing a subject's state at any one time. The model is infinite in the sense that response probability is permitted to vary over an infinite set of possible values.

By contrast the set-theoretical model developed by Estes and Burke [32], which is basic to the learning functions discussed in earlier sections of this review, may be characterized as a finite, non-Markovian, stochastic model: finite because response probability is restricted to a finite set of values; non-Markovian because in the general case, prediction of the course of learning requires not only information concerning response probabilities at some particular time but also a complete specification of the distribution of Θ values over the subsets of stimulus elements connected to the various response classes. In the "equal Θ" case, however, the set model is Markovian, and, because it is also finite, has even simpler mathematical properties than Bush and Mosteller's infinite model.

What is the import of these mathematical differences for problems of learning theory? One obvious conclusion is that where both are applicable, a choice between the linear operator model and the equal Θ case of the set model comes down pretty much to a matter of personal preference on the part of the investigator. Theoretically it is possible to derive differential predictions from the two models (in the application to verbal conditioning experiments, for example, this could be done for variances around mean learning curves), but I doubt that the differences would be empirically detectable with present levels of experimental control and mensurational precision. Bush and Mosteller have investigated the mathematical properties of the infinite model extensively, and many of their results, e.g., those having to do with bounds on mean curves, the combining of classes theorem, and statistical estimation procedures, are applicable to the finite model as well. In the case of problems for which stimulus variables are important, the set model will be the natural choice since it provides a natural means for representing stimulus properties. Even here there is a parallelism between finite and infinite models, for, as Bush and Mosteller have pointed out [13, chap. 2], one can construct an infinite set model from which the operators of an infinite stochastic model are derivable.

It is interesting to note that other investigators have arrived by very different routes at stochastic models similar in formal properties to those discussed above. Consider, for example, the work of Miller and McGill on free-recall verbal learning [74]. They started with no apparent attachment to any particular variety of learning theory, and set themselves the task of constructing a model that would account in detail for a specific set of data. Their work is remarkable for the extent to which the form of their model was dictated by the quantitative properties of the data. Only after their model, an infinite, Markovian, stochastic model in the classification used above, had taken definite form did its close interrelations with those of Bush and Mosteller and Estes and Burke become apparent. The difference equations, or operators, expressing the effects of successful recalls and failures of recall, respectively, in Miller and McGill's model turn out to be identical in form with those expressing effects of reinforcement and nonreinforcement in the others.

In the area of discrimination learning, Restle [80, 81] has developed a model which, from a mathematical viewpoint, may be regarded as a modification of Estes and Burke's "equal Θ" case. Restle assumes that two processes go on concurrently in discrimination learning; the subject simultaneously associates relevant cues with appropriate responses and "adapts" (learns to ignore) irrelevant cues. The equations describing the combined process are relatively complex, but for a situation in which all cues are relevant, they reduce to those of the "equal Θ" model.

Extrapolating somewhat the trends disclosed by the present review, I would guess that the outcome of the various contemporary research programs in quantitative learning theory will be, not a number of competing schools or systems, but a stock of common methods and a descriptive frame of reference upon which reasonably general agreement can be reached. The mathematical fruits of these researches —e.g., set models, linear operator models, Markov models, techniques for dealing with response sequences—quickly become common property and frequently find application in problem areas quite different from those in which they have originated. The general conception of learning as a probabilistic or statistical process has been taken up by so many contemporary investigators of diverse backgrounds and research interests that it seems likely to dominate forthcoming lines of theoretical development.

Within the collection of limited theories generated by the various statistical and probabilistic approaches, we may distinguish three main types which pose somewhat different problems relative to integration and generalization.

1. At one extreme are miniature theories in the strict sense, i.e., those associated with models that have been constructed to order for a particular set of data. Only under favorable conditions of diligent cultivation and cross-fertilization do such theories show any great tendency to grow and expand. As one may see vividly in Hilgard's

review [52], it is all too common for miniature theories to bloom and wither away in a single season, leaving almost no trace on the broader field of learning theory. Some of the measures which can be taken to avoid isolation and sterility of a miniature theory are illustrated in the work of Miller and McGill [74]. After constructing a model to represent a particular type of verbal learning data, they proceeded to study the general class of models to which theirs belonged and thereby to make contact with related approaches.

2. A family of formally related miniature theories may be generated by a series of particular interpretations of a general mathematical model or system. This technique is exemplified in Part 2 (applications) of Bush and Mosteller's book [13]. The common mathematical system does not guarantee the emergence of a general theory but it may facilitate attempts to generalize and integrate the local models.

3. A theory may be both limited and general: limited in that it is restricted to relationships among a small set of variables, but general in that these variables and relationships are assumed to play similar roles in a variety of empirical situations. Illustrative of this category are the theories of reinforcement, stimulus sampling, and stimulus fluctuation discussed in earlier sections of the present report. This approach stands or falls on the consequences of testing the general assumptions in a series of particular situations. When successful, it generates a family of both formally and substantively related miniature theories. Such an outcome probably represents the closest approximation to general learning theory that we can hope to achieve in the foreseeable future.

REFERENCES

1. Anderson, N. H., & Grant, D. A. A test of a statistical learning theory model for two-choice behavior with double stimulus events. *J. exp. Psychol.*, 1957, **54**, 305–317.

2. Atkinson, R. C. An analysis of the effect of nonreinforced trials in terms of statistical learning theory. *J. exp. Psychol.*, 1956, **52**, 28–32.

3. Atkinson, R. C. A stochastic model for rote serial learning. *Psychometrika*, 1957, **22**, 87–96.

4. Atkinson, R. C., & Suppes, P. "An analysis of two-person game situations in terms of statistical learning theory." Tech. Report No. 8, Contract Nr 171–034, Stanford Univer., Stanford, Calif., 1957 (Mimeographed).

5. Barnes, G. Conditioned stimulus intensity and temporal factors in spaced-trial classical conditioning. Unpublished doctoral dissertation, Indiana Univer., 1954.

6. Bishop, C. K. Summation and generalization of response strength in

relation to hunger and thirst drives. Unpublished doctoral dissertation, Indiana Univer., 1953.

7. Brand, H., Woods, P. J., & Sakoda, J. M. Anticipation of reward as a function of partial reinforcement. *J. exp. Psychol.*, 1956, **52**, 18–22.

8. Brody, A. L. Statistical learning theory applied to an instrumental avoidance situation. *J. exp. Psychol.*, 1957, **54**, 240–245.

9. Brunswik, E. Probability as a determiner of rat behavior. *J. exp. Psychol.*, 1939, **25**, 175–197.

10. Burke, C. J., & Estes, W. K. A component model for stimulus variables in discrimination learning. *Psychometrika*, 1957, **22**, 133–145.

11. Burke, C. J., Estes, W. K., & Hellyer, S. Rate of verbal conditioning in relation to stimulus variability. *J. exp. Psychol.*, 1954, **48**, 153–161.

12. Bush, R. R., & Mosteller, F. A mathematical model for simple learning. *Psychol. Rev.*, 1951, **58**, 313–323.

13. Bush, R. R., & Mosteller, F. *Stochastic models for learning.* New York: Wiley, 1955.

14. Campbell, N. R. *Physics: the elements.* London: Cambridge Univer. Press, 1920.

15. Collier, G. H. Probability of response and intertrial association as functions of monocular and binocular stimulation. *J. exp. Psychol.*, 1954, **47**, 75–83.

16. Detambel, M. H. A re-analysis of Humphreys' "Acquisition and extinction of verbal expectations." Unpublished master's thesis, Indiana Univer., 1950.

17. Detambel, M. H. The role of "stimulus overlap" and "stimulus sample size" in discrimination learning. Unpublished doctoral dissertation, Indiana Univer., 1952.

18. Detambel, M. H. A test of a model for multiple-choice behavior. *J. exp. Psychol.*, 1955, **49**, 97–104.

19. Estes, W. K. Toward a statistical theory of learning. *Psychol. Rev.*, 1950, **57**, 94–107.

20. Estes, W. K. Effects of competing reactions on the conditioning curve for bar pressing. *J. exp. Psychol.*, 1950, **40**, 200–205.

21. Estes, W. K. Need reduction vs. stimulus characteristics as determiners of response latency. Paper given at Midwest Psychol. Ass. meetings, 1951. ADI abstract file, Library of Congress, Document 3277. (Abstract)

22. Estes, W. K. Analysis of the relation between amount of reinforcement and rate of conditioning in a bar pressing situation. *Amer. Psychologist,* 1954, **9**, 361. (Abstract)

23. Estes, W. K. Individual behavior in uncertain situations. In R. M. Thrall, C. H. Coombs, & R. L. Davis (Eds.), *Decision processes.* New York: Wiley, 1954. Pp. 127–138.

24. Estes, W. K. Models for learning theory. In Committee on Human Resources, Research and Development Board, Department of Defense, *Symposium on psychology of learning basic to military training problems.* Washington, D.C., HR-HTD 201/1, 1954. Pp. 21–38.

25. Estes, W. K. Statistical theory of spontaneous recovery and regression. *Psychol. Rev.*, 1955, 62, 145–154.

26. Estes, W. K. Statistical theory of distributional phenomena in learning. *Psychol. Rev.*, 1955, 62, 369–377.

27. Estes, W. K. Theory of elementary predictive behavior. In Dunlap and Associates, Inc. (Sponsors), *Mathematical models of human behavior—proceedings of a symposium.* Stamford, Conn.: Sponsors, 1955. Pp. 63–67

28. Estes, W. K. Learning. *Annu. Rev. Psychol.*, 1956, 7, 1–38.

29. Estes, W. K. Review of Bush and Mosteller's *Stochastic models for learning. Contemp. Psychol.*, 1956, 1, 99–101.

30. Estes, W. K. Theory of learning with constant, variable, or contingent probabilities of reinforcement. *Psychometrika*, 1957, 22, 113–132.

31. Estes, W. K. Of models and men. *Amer. Psychologist*, 1957, 12, 609–617.

32. Estes, W. K., & Burke, C. J. A theory of stimulus variability in learning. *Psychol. Rev.*, 1953, 60, 276–286.

33. Estes, W. K., & Burke, C. J. Application of a statistical model to simple discrimination learning in human subjects. *J. exp. Psychol.*, 1955, 50, 81–88.

34. Estes, W. K., Burke, C. J., Atkinson, R. C., & Frankmann, Judith P. Probabilistic discrimination learning. *J. exp. Psychol.*, 1957, 54, 233–239.

35. Estes, W. K., et. al. *Modern learning theory.* New York: Appleton-Century-Crofts, 1954.

36. Estes, W. K., & Lauer, D. W. Conditions of invariance and modifiability in simple reversal learning. *J. comp. physiol. Psychol.*, 1957, 50, 199–206.

37. Estes, W. K., & Straughan, J. H. Analysis of a verbal conditioning situation in terms of statistical learning theory. *J. exp. Psychol.*, 1954, 47, 225–234.

38. Feller, W. *Probability theory and its applications.* New York: Wiley, 1950.

39. Fink, J. B., & Patton, R. M. Decrement of a learned drinking response accompanying changes in several stimulus characteristics. *J. comp. physiol. Psychol.*, 1953, 46, 23–27.

40. Frankmann, Judith P. Effect of amount of interpolated learning and time interval before test on retention in rats. *J. exp. Psychol.*, 1957, 54, 462–466.

41. Graham, C. H., & Gagne, R. M. The acquisition, extinction, and spontaneous recovery of a conditioned operant response. *J. exp. Psychol.*, 1940, 26, 251–281.

42. Goodnow, Jacqueline J. Determinants of choice-distribution in two-choice situations. *Amer. J. Psychol.*, 1955, 68, 106–116.

43. Grant, D. A., Hake, H. W., & Hornseth, J. P. Acquisition and extinction of a verbal conditioned response with differing percentages of reinforcement. *J. exp. Psychol.*, 1951, 42, 1–5.

44. Green, E. J. Stimulus-variability and operant discrimination in human subjects. *Amer. J. Psychol.*, 1956, 69, 269–273.

45. Gulliksen, H. A rational equation of the learning curve based on Thorndike's law of effect. *J. gen. Psychol.*, 1934, 11, 395–434.

46. Guthrie, E. L. *The psychology of learning.* (2d ed.) New York: Harper, 1952.

47. Guttman, N., & Estes, W. K. A modified apparatus for the study of operant behavior in the rat. *J. gen. Psychol.*, 1949, 41, 297–301.

48. Guttman, N. Operant conditioning, extinction, and periodic rein forcement in relation to concentration of sucrose used as reinforcing agent. *J. exp. Psychol.*, 1953, 46, 213–224.

49. Guttman, N., & Kalish, H. I. Discriminability and stimulus generalization. *J. exp. Psychol.*, 1956, 51, 79–88.

50. Harlow, H. F. The formation of learning sets. *Psychol. Rev.*, 1949, 56, 51–65.

51. Hellyer, S. The duration of the consummatory response as a variable in amount of reinforcement studies. Unpublished doctoral dissertation, Indiana Univer., 1953.

52. Hilgard, E. R. *Theories of learning.* (2d ed.) New York: Appleton-Century-Crofts, 1956.

53. Hilgard, E. R., & Marquis, D. G. *Conditioning and learning.* New York: Appleton-Century-Crofts, 1940.

54. Homme, L. E. Spontaneous recovery and statistical learning theory. *J. exp. Psychol.*, 1956, 51, 205–212.

55. Hull, C. L. *Principles of behavior.* New York: Appleton-Century-Crofts, 1943.

56. Hull, C. L. *Essentials of behavior.* New Haven, Conn.: Yale Univer. Press, 1951.

57. Hull, C. L. *A behavior system.* New Haven, Conn.: Yale Univer. Press, 1952.

58. Humphreys, L. G. Acquisition and extinction of verbal expectations in a situation analogous to conditioning. *J. exp. Psychol.*, 1939, 25, 294–301.

59. Jarvik, M. E. Probability learning and a negative recency effect in the serial anticipation of alternative symbols. *J. exp. Psychol.*, 1951, 41, 291–297.

60. Jordan, C. *Calculus of finite differences.* New York: Chelsea, 1950.

61. Keller, F. S., & Schoenfeld, W. N. *Principles of psychology.* New York: Appleton-Century-Crofts, 1950.

62. Kemeny, J. G., Snell, J. L., & Thompson, G. L. *Introduction to finite mathematics.* Englewood Cliffs, N.J.: Prentice-Hall, 1957.

63. LaBerge, D. L., & Smith, A. Selective sampling in discrimination learning. *J. exp. Psychol.*, 1957, 54, 423–430.

64. Lauer, D. W. Progressive changes in response measures over repeated acquisitions and extinctions of a running habit. ADI Publication Project, Library of Congress, Document 4576. (Abstract)

65. Lauer, D. W., & Estes, W. K. Observed and predicted terminal distributions of response probability under two conditions of random reinforcement. *Amer. Psychologist*, 1954, 9, 413. (Abstract)

66. Lauer, D. W., & Estes, W. K. Successive acquisitions and extinctions of a jumping habit in relation to schedule of reinforcement. *J. comp. physiol. Psychol.*, 1955, **48**, 8–13.

67. Lawrence, D. H. Acquired distinctiveness of cues: II. Selective association in a constant stimulus situation. *J. exp. Psychol.*, 1950, **40**, 175–188.

68. Logan, F. A. Three estimates of differential excitatory tendency. *Psychol. Rev.*, 1952, **59**, 300–307.

69. McConnell, D. G. Spontaneous regression and recovery of a bar-pressing response during a sequence of acquisition and extinction periods. Unpublished doctoral dissertation, Indiana Univer., 1957.

70. McGeoch, J. A., & Irion, A. L. *Psychology of human learning.* (2d ed.) New York: Longmans, 1952.

71. Meyer, D. R. Food deprivation and discrimination reversal learning by monkeys. *J. exp. Psychol.*, 1951, **41**, 10–16.

72. Miller, G. A. Finite Markov processes in psychology. *Psychometrika*, 1952, **17**, 149–168.

73. Miller, G. A., & Frick, F. C. Statistical behavioristics and sequences of responses. *Psychol. Rev.*, 1949, **56**, 311–324.

74. Miller, G. A., & McGill, W. J. A statistical description of verbal learning. *Psychometrika*, 1952, **17**, 369–396.

75. Mueller, C. G. Theoretical relationships among some measures of conditioning. *Proc. nat. Acad. Sci.*, 1950, **36**, 123–130.

76. Neimark, Edith D. Effects of type of non-reinforcement and number of alternative responses in two verbal conditioning situations. *J. exp. Psychol.*, 1956, **52**, 209–220.

77. North, A. J. Improvement in successive discrimination reversals. *J. comp. physiol. Psychol.*, 1950, **43**, 442–460.

78. Peterson, L. R. Prediction of response in verbal habit hierarchies. *J. exp. Psychol.*, 1956, **52**, 249–252.

79. Peterson, L. R., & Peterson, M. J. The role of context stimuli in verbal learning. *J. exp. Psychol.*, 1957, **53**, 102–105.

80. Restle, F. A theory of discrimination learning. *Psychol. Rev.*, 1955, **62**, 11–19.

81. Restle, F. Axioms of a theory of discrimination learning. *Psychometrika*, 1955, **20**, 201–208.

82. Richardson, C. H. *Introduction to the calculus of finite differences.* New York: Van Nostrand, 1954.

83. Schoeffler, M. S. Probability of response to compounds of discriminated stimuli. *J. exp. Psychol.*, 1954, **48**, 323–329.

84. Simon, H. A. A comparison of game theory and learning theory. *Psychometrika*, 1956, **21**, 267–272.

85. Skinner, B. F. *The behavior of organisms.* New York: Appleton-Century-Crofts, 1938.

86. Spence, K. W. The relation of response latency and speed to the intervening variables and *N* in *S-R* theory. *Psychol. Rev.*, 1954, **61**, 209–216.

87. Spence, K. W. *Behavior theory and conditioning.* New Haven, Conn.: Yale Univer. Press, 1956.

88. Straughan, J. H. An application of statistical learning theory to an escape learning situation using human subjects. Unpublished doctoral dissertation, Indiana Univer., 1953.

89. Straughan, J. H. Human escape learning in relation to reinforcement variables and intertrial conditions. *J. exp. Psychol.,* 1956, **52**, 1–8.

90. Verplanck, W. S., Collier, G. H., & Cotton, J. W. Nonindependence of successive responses in measurements of the visual threshold. *J. exp. Psychol.,* 1952, **44**, 273–282.

91. Voeks, Virginia W. Gradual strengthening of S-R connections or increasing number of S-R connections. *J. Psychol.,* 1955, **39**, 289–299.

92. Weinstock, S. Acquisition and extinction of a partially reinforced running response at a 24-hour intertrial interval. Unpublished doctoral dissertation, Indiana Univer., 1953.

93. Weinstock, S. Resistance to extinction of a running response following partial reinforcement under widely spaced trials. *J. comp. physiol. Psychol.,* 1954, **47**, 318–322.

94. Wolfle, D. L. The relative efficiency of constant and varied stimulation during learning. III. The objective extent of stimulus variation. *J. comp. Psychol.,* 1936, **22**, 375–381.

95. Wyckoff, L. B., Jr. The role of observing responses in discrimination learning. *Psychol. Rev.,* 1952, **59**, 431–442.

96. Wyckoff, L. B., Jr. A mathematical model and an electronic model for learning. *Psychol. Rev.,* 1954, **61**, 89–97.

LEARNING SET AND ERROR FACTOR THEORY

University of Wisconsin

INTRODUCTION

The experimental data emanating from the Wisconsin Primate Laboratory during the last quarter-century created in the author vast skepticism concerning the learning systems which were developing and attaining popularity. There appeared, however, to be no point in opposing or attacking such systems, since their fundamental limitations lay not in the underlying logic, but in the fact that they were based on circumscribed and inadequate information. It became apparent that a major contribution to theoretical psychology could be made only by developing an alternative system which could incorporate these data that failed to fit into the current theoretical schemata.

Both simple observation and experimentation made it obvious that the role of the internal drives had been overemphasized in the dominant contemporary theories. This overemphasis appeared not only in the untenable position of drive-reduction learning, but was also indicated by the undue percentage of studies, stemming from many laboratories, in which some deprivation condition was the primary variable under consideration. Our own investigations made it quite clear that internal states are variables of small importance in most learning situations and that in many situations, their importance lies more in the suppression than in the augmentation of behaviors essential to successful environmental adaptations by organisms.

Similarly, it was evident that overemphasis upon internal motivational agents had led to underestimation of the role of external motivational agents—the stimuli producing forced movements or tropisms in primitive organisms, releaser functions in higher fish, birds, and reptiles, and exploratory-curiosity motivation in our common laboratory animals, including man. In an effort to assign proper emphasis to external stimuli as motivating agents, we conducted a series of studies on exploration and curiosity motives, and these data, supplemented by data on the subprimates, now provide a wealth of information on the importance of incentives. It may be noted that these data of ours are far more in keeping with Tolman's general position than with that of any other learning theorist.

We became convinced that many of the shortcomings of contemporary theoretical systems stemmed from the fact that there exist practically no data on the ontogenetic development of learning, perception, and motivation in any animal other than man, and unfortunately, it is difficult to assess with accuracy the relative roles of maturational and learning factors in the human organism's development. In an effort to determine how and when various perceptual, learning, and motivational processes develop, we initiated a major program in which macaque monkeys were separated from their mothers at birth. After three years of effort we have obtained a large body of facts which may be exchanged for the deductive psycho-ontogeny of the past. We are quite certain now that form discrimination is almost entirely a function of maturation rather than the learned formation of cell assembly systems or any other postulated learning mechanism. We know that exploratory motives are not derived from internal drives, which in many cases they antedate ontogenetically; we have presumptive evidence that many or most social motives also are not derived from internal drive states. We know, too, that single-problem learning is a much simpler process than the formation of learning sets. These are all data which may be used in a formulation of a system, if adequate frameworks and integrations can be developed.

Learning theory, after Tolman, repressed the higher mental processes—complex learning and problem solution. Tolman had, of course, attempted to deal with these processes in terms of inferential expectation, insight, or creative ideation, but Tolman failed here because at the time nothing was known of the mechanisms that would enable us to trace the development and organization of these complex behaviors. We are uninterested in any system that cannot in an orderly way attack the problems of complex behaviors because our paramount concern transcends the study of the comparative psychology of the subprimate forms. Furthermore, we are firmly convinced that the analysis of simple behavior gives relatively little information about the nature of complex behavior, whereas the successful analysis of complex behavior may give vast insight into the nature of simple behavior.

We believe that learning set formation and error factor analysis are fundamental and effective techniques for analyzing complex learned behaviors and for understanding the simpler learned behaviors. Furthermore, we believe that the detailed understanding of learning sets and error factors will lead to the integration of a very considerable body of psychological information. Firm in this belief, we agreed in 1954 to cover the topic of "Systematic Implications of 'Learning Sets' and Related Matters."

When we accepted the task of contributing to Project A, we were in no position to attempt the development of a psychological system in the sense that this term is presently understood. Whether this would be true if we could start now may be open to question, but unfortunately we cannot live life backward. Actually, the materials here presented will be basic to any system we may present in the future.

In 1949 the author [20] demonstrated that rhesus monkeys learn successive nonspatial discrimination problems with progressively greater facility and referred to this phenomenon as the result of the formation of a "learning set," a term abbreviated as "LS." Just as learning is generally regarded as a hypothetical construct—an intervening variable—so, also, is learning set treated. Learning set formation has also been called "interproblem learning" to contrast it with "intraproblem learning," which is limited to the learning that occurs during the solution of a single problem.

Study of the effect of the learning of a single problem on the learning of subsequent problems has a long psychological history—the problem area of transfer of training. Learning set formation represents a particular type of transfer of training, the transfer between many problems of a single class instead of the more commonly studied transfer between problems of disparate classes or transfer between a few problems of a single class. Transfer of learning between problems within a single class was studied before Pavlov, by Pavlov [53], and after Pavlov, but early investigators failed to develop techniques for effective analysis or to recognize the significance of the phenomenon.

Previous workers studied interproblem learning over a narrow range of problems and usually trained their subjects to mastery, or near mastery, of all problems. After some equivocation, the author [21] departed radically from these procedures; he ran each individual problem for a small number of trials and analyzed learning in relatively large blocks of problems.

INTRAPROBLEM AND INTERPROBLEM LEARNING CURVES

The apparatus and test situation which we have commonly used in learning set studies is shown in Fig. 1. In the discrimination problem being tested two stimulus objects differing in multiple characteristics

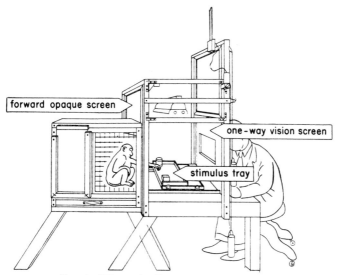

Fig. 1. Wisconsin General Test Apparatus.

cover the two foodwells of the test tray. In this instance the barrel-shaped stimulus object is correct and rewarded, the cube incorrect and not rewarded. The positions of the objects on the tray shift from left to right in a balanced, predetermined order in the series of six trials. A noncorrection method is used. Regardless of the animal's performance level, a new problem employing new objects follows directly after the completion of trial 6. Ten different sequences of position rewards are randomly presented in each block of 10 six-trial problems. Animals are given a number of problems in a single session, each problem presenting new stimulus objects. In some experiments, monkeys have completed as many as 14 problems a day (84 trials) every day for several months.

Interproblem learning experiments are not, of course, limited to the apparatus, method, or kind of learning task described. They may utilize any apparatus or task the experimenter chooses, and procedures must be devised to fit the experimenter's needs. The only invariable requirement is that there be multiple problems of comparable difficulty level.

With rhesus monkeys as subjects, learning sets evolve even though each problem is run for only a limited number of trials [21]. If six-trial nonspatial discrimination (hereafter called "discrimination") problems are used, the development of the interproblem learning curves and the change in the form of the intraproblem learning curves are very clearly

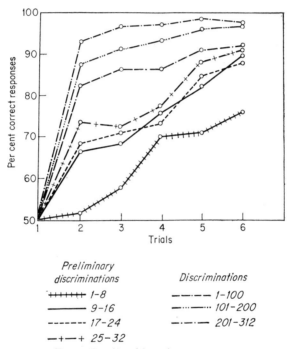

Preliminary
discriminations

++++++ 1-8
———— 9-16
------- 17-24
—+—+ 25-32

Discriminations

—·—·— 1-100
—···—··· 101-200
—·—·— 201-312

Fig. 2. Family of learning set curves.

illustrated. As is shown in Fig. 2, the learning of the early problems takes place slowly, and the learning curve is typical of what has been called trial-and-error learning. Little, if any, demonstrable gain occurs during the early trials of any particular problem, and the form of the intra-problem learning curve, or the obtained segment of a particular intra-problem learning curve, is positively accelerated. As successive problems are presented, progressively greater performance gain occurs during the early intraproblem trials, and the form of the learning curve becomes sigmoidal and then changes to a curve of negative acceleration. By the time a hundred problems have been presented, there is indication of the formation of a sharp break in the learning curve; now, the trial 1–trial

2 segment of the curve is best described by a different mathematical function from that which best describes the segment from trials 2 to 6. From approximately one hundred problems onward, the intraproblem learning curve partakes of the properties of the classical insight learning curve. Performance changes from chance to perfection or near perfection in a single trial, and subsequent errors are insignificant. From 90 to 97 per cent correct responses are made on the second trial, and individual animals may run dozens of successive problems with no trial 2 errors, or no errors throughout trials 2 to 6. If the monkey by chance makes a correct response on trial 1, it solves the problem without error, and if it by chance makes an error on trial 1, it immediately shifts to the correct object and makes no subsequent errors.

Thus, the formation of an LS results in a complete transformation in the form of the intraproblem learning curves. The early problems are learned slowly, the learning curves are positively accelerated, and each learning curve is continuous. The late problems are learned rapidly or immediately, and the resulting learning curve is discontinuous, having two distinct components, a rapid component from trial 1 to trial 2 and a slow component from trials 2 to 6 [20].

FORM OF LEARNING SET CURVE

The nature of the development of interproblem learning curves is well illustrated by plotting the percentage of correct responses made on a particular trial, such as trial 2, or a sequence of trials, such as trials 2 to 6, during training on successive blocks of problems. In other words, just as the individual-problem learning curve is plotted with trials on the abscissa and performance efficiency on the ordinate, so is the LS curve commonly plotted with problems on the abscissa and performance efficiency on the ordinate. Interlocking information may be given by plotting successive problems or problem-blocks as the parameter on the individual-problem graph, or by plotting successive individual trials or selected trials or groups of trials as the parameter on the LS graph. These facts are illustrated in Fig. 3a and 3b. From these data it is self-evident that intraproblem learning becomes discontinuous after the LS has been formed, but that the interproblem learning curve, or LS curve, is continuous.

The classical discrimination LS curve for rhesus monkeys that have been carefully tamed and preadapted to the Wisconsin General Test Apparatus (WGTA) is negatively accelerated with no indication or suggestion of discontinuity. Fortunately, we now have LS data on rhesus monkeys on a variety of learning problems and discrimination LS data on a considerable number of primate species and some nonprimates,

Most rhesus LS curves, including discrimination, discrimination-reversal, and oddity, are negatively accelerated, but the LS curve for moderately difficult discrimination problems, such as the planometric (flat) problems studied by Harlow and Warren [28], have an initial flat portion during which little or no improvement is to be found. Similar results have been reported for individual rhesus monkeys on oddity problems [45] and may be demonstrated in occasional individual cases on almost

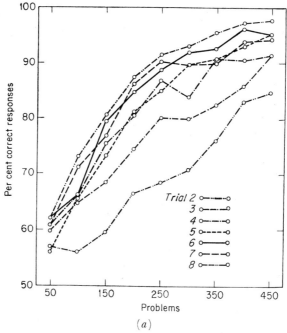

Per cent correct responses

Trial 2 o——··——o
3 o——·—o
4 o——·—·o
5 o————o
6 o————o
7 o— — —o
8 o——·——o

Problems

(a)

Fig. 3. Intraproblem and interproblem learning curves based on the same data. (a) Discrimination learning curves with problem blocks as the parameter.

any kind of learning problem. Furthermore, inadequate taming or abbreviated adaptation to the test situation will characteristically produce an initial flat portion in the learning curve for any animal on any test. In some of the more primitive primates, including the marmoset and the squirrel monkey, a prolonged initial flat portion is found in which there is little or no learning over a long series of discrimination problems. The data on the nonprimate forms are not of such technical elegance as to make direct comparison possible, but such data as exist are concordant with the trends described. In general, it may be stated that LS curves

which have an initial flat function subsequently assume a negatively accelerated function, i.e., the curves become S-shaped with a shorter or
longer foot to the S.

These data also make it quite obvious that there is no single or ideal
form of LS curve, but, rather, the form is a function of the problem, the

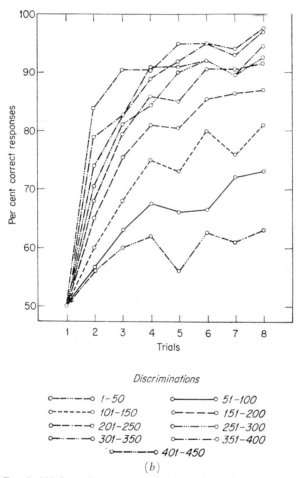

Discriminations

o———o 1-50   o———o 51-100
o———o 101-150   o———o 151-200
o———o 201-250   o———o 251-300
o———o 301-350   o———o 351-400
o———o 401-450

(b)

Fig. 3. (b) Learning set curves with trials as the parameter.

subject, and the experimenter's whimsies, recognized or unrecognized.
All the LS data, however, yield continuous learning curves, and this continuity of the LS curves is in striking contrast with the discontinuity of
the intraproblem learning curves typically found late in LS formation.

Regardless of any differences in the form of intraproblem and interproblem learning curves it would seem almost self-evident that some close relationship exists between single-problem learning and multiple-problem learning. Furthermore, as we shall subsequently see, this presumption is strongly supported by detailed analyses of the error factors (EF's) whose elimination underlies learning. Other presently existing techniques for demonstrating or analyzing the relationship between intraproblem learning curves on successive blocks of problems are worthy of note. Meyer [43] plotted the learning curve derived from the day 1 error data—the first four problems in a series of discrimination reversals—and showed this curve to be the decay function commonly found when percentage of

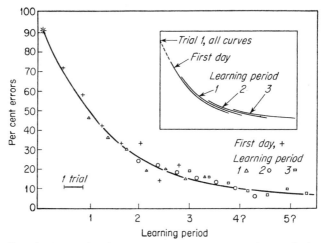

FIG. 4. A graph of the general reversal equation and the overlapping intraproblem functions from which it was derived. *Redrawn from J. exp. Psychol.* [43].

errors is plotted against trials in a single problem. He then grouped the rest of the problems into three successive blocks and obtained the averaged intraproblem learning curve for each block. Plotting these three curves on the same axis as the day 1 curve in such a way that the trial 2 value of each averaged curve coincided with the point of equivalent value on the day 1 curve, he found two results making for startling orderliness, as shown in Fig. 4. First, the scores for the rest of the trials fit extremely closely to the function described by the day 1 trials data. Meyer, in fact, concluded that one function fitted all the data when they were plotted this way. Secondly, the interval between the points at which trial 2 values matched the day 1 values was constant from block to block. Unfortunately, no retest has been made of this ingenious and surprising finding, nor has any measure of its generality been attempted.

LEARNING SET AND EFFICIENCY OF LEARNING

Comparison of LS curves obtained in a few studies suggests that the number of trials presented per problem is an important determiner of the over-all slope of the LS curve and the efficiency with which a predetermined criterion is reached. Although major systematic studies manipulating this variable have not been done, comparisons among existing experiments indicate that the smaller the number of trials per problem, the greater the number of problems required to reach a given criterion of learning, but the fewer the total number of trials to reach this criterion. There appear to be two major aspects to the trials per problem variable: the number of trials per problem and the amount learned on any given problem. Because the relationship between these two aspects of the variable depends upon the stage of LS development, we would expect somewhat different predictions about interproblem transfer at different developmental periods.

Early in LS acquisition the intraproblem learning curve is positively accelerated. Little learning takes place on the first few trials of any problem. One would expect, then, that if transfer were dependent upon amount learned, a small number of trials during the early stages of LS development would produce little or no improvement from problem to problem, whereas a number of trials large enough to allow effective intraproblem learning would produce considerable transfer. During advanced stages of LS development, however, the intraproblem learning curve becomes negatively accelerated and eventually discontinuous. Maximal intraproblem performance gain occurs by the second trial, with very small gain in the later trials. At this stage of LS development one would expect, if amount of intraproblem learning rather than sheer number of trials per problem were critical, that a few, in fact, two, trials per problem would be most efficient.

As we will subsequently show, this hypothetical analysis very closely fits the facts. The available data support the hypothesis that the amount learned on a given problem is an important variable determining the amount transferred to the succeeding problem. Transfer from problem $n - 1$ to problem n, according to this hypothesis, is a monotonic increasing function of the amount learned on problem $n - 1$, rather than a function of the sheer number of trials presented on that problem. A few interesting predictions follow from this hypothesis. For one thing, from knowledge of the changes in the intraproblem learning curve during LS formation, one can estimate what would constitute the most efficient way to plan LS experiments. Maximal efficiency would be the attainment of a given criterion of LS performance in the fewest over-all number of trials. In general, the technique is to run the animal, on any given problem, through the trials on which the gains are greatest. To run the animal on further trials, where there is diminishing gain, would be wasteful of trials. Thus, on the early problems, when the intraproblem curves are S-shaped, it would be most efficient to run the animal a few trials beyond the point of inflection because it is around this point that the increase in learning is greatest. Several trials after the point of inflection we begin to enter the realm of diminishing returns, and the problem should be discontinued and the next problem begun. Late in LS formation, when the intraproblem curve is a negatively accelerated growth curve, it would be most efficient to run the animal for two trials per problem and no more, since it is from trial 1 to trial 2 that the greatest increment in learning is made. Between the very early and very late problems the number of trials per problem would be gradually reduced.

Although the currently available data do not warrant greater specificity of speculation than we are engaging in at present, nevertheless the trial at which the animal should be switched to the next problem may be precisely determined if we assume some exactly specifiable relationship between learning and transfer, e.g., amount transferred is directly proportional to the amount learned $(T = KL)$. Marvin Levine at our laboratory has demonstrated as an exercise that when the relationship is stated in such a mathematically precise manner, exact predictions may be made.

Other predictions which follow from our assumption that transfer is a direct function of amount of learning deal with variables producing differences in intraproblem learning. Thus, within a group of animals receiving identical LS training procedures we would predict a significant positive correlation between average intraproblem performance and the speed with which a given LS criterion is reached. Also, if number of trials is held constant, the more difficult the intraproblem learning conditions (e.g., greater similarity of the stimuli), the slower the LS acquisition. As we shall see later, the dependence of interproblem transfer upon intraproblem learning is subject to an important limitation. The capacity to acquire LS may not always be present in an organism even though it can learn single discriminations. The hypothesis of transfer, therefore, must be modified to hold only when animals of equal capacity are considered. Within this limit, however, the hypothesis promises to be fruitful.

The available data appear to substantiate the hypothesis that it is the amount of intraproblem learning which determines the interproblem transfer. Hayes, Thompson, and Hayes [29] found that a chimpanzee which began training at a fixed rate of two trials per problem remained at about chance level for 300 problems but improved rapidly when shifted to 10 trials per problem. Unpublished Wisconsin data on two rhesus monkeys trained under similar schedules yielded comparable results. Miller, Murphy, and Finocchio [48] demonstrated the development of LS using three trials per problem from the beginning. Early learning was slow. After 192 problems, correct performance on trial 2 approximated 60 per cent. Similar results were obtained by Davis, McDowell, and Thorson [9] on four-trial discrimination problems. After 128 problems, the animals had not yet attained 60 per cent correct responses on trial 2.

With respect to performance late in LS development, several studies indicate that a small number of trials produces efficient learning. In one study, Harlow [20] switched the animals after 32, 50-trial problems to 6-trial problems without significant disruption in the rate of improvement in LS development. Braun, Patton, and Barnes [6] showed efficient acquisition late in learning when the number of trials per problem had been reduced to three. Finally, Hayes, Thompson, and Hays [29] report that two trials per problem are effective for the chimpanzee in advanced stages of discrimination LS formation, and these data are in keeping with unpublished results obtained on monkeys at Wisconsin.

A MATHEMATICAL FORMULATION OF LEARNING SET

Currently, an attempt is being made to give mathematical formulation to LS phenomena. Restle is expanding a mathematical model developed to handle simple discrimination learning.[1] He conceives of the stimulus situation in simple discrimination learning as containing two types of cues: cues which are relevant or correlated with the reward and cues which are irrelevant or uncorrelated with the reward. During learning, relevant cues become conditioned and irrelevant cues become adapted. Both processes are exponential, and the rates are determined by the numbers of both types of cues.

By adding a few postulates, he has extended the model to handle LS data. His basic postulate is that in the LS situation there exist certain cues which are *relevant* and *common to all problems.* In oddity LS, "oddness" provides such a cue. In discrimination LS, the cue is the object reinforced on the preceding trial. In LS formation there are, then, three types of cues: *type a cues,* which are relevant throughout and permit transfer from problem to problem; *type b cues,* which are relevant within any one problem but which vary from problem to problem; and *type c cues,* which are irrelevant within any one problem. Type c cues become adapted in a manner analogous to their adaptation in simple discrimination. Type b cues, though relevant within any one problem, are irrelevant in the long run, and therefore eventually become adapted. The type a cues, of course, become conditioned.

[1] Dr. Frank Restle, Michigan State University, has given us permission to present this outline form of his mathematical formulation of learning set theory.

Stating in mathematical terms the assumption that the processes of conditioning and adaptation proceed exponentially, Restle is able to derive equations expressing the probability of a correct response at any point on an LS curve. Also, he has derived theoretical descriptions of findings which already exist in the LS literature. He has produced curves which closely fit data obtained by Riopelle [57] in a reversal learning situation, and a curve describing the within-problems learning curve found by Meyer [43]. Using data obtained by Warren [68], he has predicted performance in a discrimination learning situation in which combinations of cues are relevant (color + form, form + size, size + color, and color + size + form), on the basis of performance in situations where only one of the three types of cues is relevant.

Although Restle notes several limitations which currently exist in his formulation, it is nevertheless clear that his model provides the most rigorous attempt to date to give theoretical organization to LS data.

ONTOGENETIC AND PHYLOGENETIC DEVELOPMENT AND LEARNING SET FORMATION

The importance of LS has sometimes been questioned on the grounds that it is merely an instance of transfer of training. The assumption has also been made that intraproblem learning and interproblem learning are the same process. Interproblem learning, according to this view, is no new phenomenon of particular psychological importance. There is evolving, however, a considerable body of evidence showing that, in spite of the similarities between intraproblem and interproblem learning, the LS learning is dependent upon some capacity factor or factors transcending those needed for intraproblem learning of equivalent problems.

Probably the most definitive measure of learning difficulty is the absolute or relative age at which various problems can be solved by representative members of a species, particularly if past experience is equated or controlled. This technique has been used with human beings in the construction of mental maturity scales and intelligence tests and has given us such constructs as maturation and mental age. The age at which most of our standard laboratory learning problems can be solved by infant and young monkeys, separated from their mothers at birth and raised in a standardized laboratory environment, is now being determined by the Wisconsin workers [27]. One of the most striking facts already disclosed is the large temporal separation between the development of effective individual-problem learning and the development of LS's for the same kind of problem.

Rhesus monkeys can solve individual discrimination problems in the

WGTA situation by 60 days of age. The learning is reasonably rapid and efficient on the first problem, requiring from 50 to 100 trials. In spite of the fact that these young animals are capable of effective intra-problem learning, they appear to be completely incapable of forming a discrimination LS. They can learn a discrimination problem or a series of discrimination problems, but there is no indication, or practically no indication, of interproblem transfer. The capacity to form a discrimination LS certainly does not develop before 150 days of age in the rhesus monkey; at 200 days of age these animals show only limited interproblem learning capability, and full LS capacity probably does not develop until well into the second or third year of life.

The operation of some capacity factor or factors in the formation of LS's is illustrated as clearly by the phylogenetic as by the ontogenetic data, although these data are limited both in terms of species and problems which have been studied. All available evidence indicates that subprimate animals possess only the most rudimentary capabilities for solving discrimination LS's. Koronakos and Arnold [38] have recently presented evidence that rats may show limited interproblem discrimination learning. Twenty rats were trained on each of seven discrimination problems to a criterion of 80 per cent correct responses in 20 consecutive trials or on a total of 80 trials if this criterion was not attained. Five subjects met the criterion for all problems, and their composite performance curve shows improvement, attaining a maximum of approximately 70 per cent correct responses on trials 1 to 20 of problem 6. It must be recognized that the number of problems was small and the basis for the improvement is not specifically defined.

Somewhat more precise evidence for discrimination LS formation has been demonstrated by Warren and Baron [69] for the cat. Four subjects were trained on 340 discrimination problems. The first 4 problems were learned to a criterion of 20 correct out of 25 consecutive responses, and the others were presented for fixed periods of trials, 50 trials for problems 5 to 80, 25 trials for problems 81 to 140, and 10 trials for problems 141 to 300. The asymptote for performance on trials 2 to 10 is approximately 70 per cent. The trial 2 performance data are not given. The authors state that: "Although the data presented here show that the capacity for acquiring learning sets is not restricted to the order *Primates*, it is clear that the learning set curves for cats quickly reach an asymptotic level of performance which is much lower than for monkeys" [69, p. 230].

Actually the LS formation of nonprimates and primates is not only differentiated by the asymptotic level of performance but also by the level of performance throughout most of the learning. For the primates the intraproblem learning curve after LS formation shows clear evidence of discontinuity, a phenomenon not reported for any subprimate form to date.

An extremely interesting picture relating LS capacity to evolutionary development is obtained by comparing discrimination LS formation by representative families and genera within the primate order. The relatively primitive marmoset and squirrel monkey have been shown by Miles and Meyer [47] and by Miles [46] to develop discrimination LS's much more slowly than the rhesus monkey. Performance by the three tested subjects of each species is hardly above chance after 200 six-trial problems, and at the end of 1,000 problems the trial 2 performance is far from perfect, as is evident in Fig. 5. It should be pointed out, how-

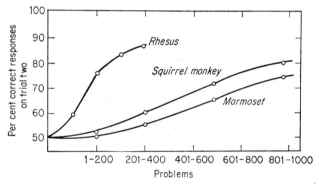

Fig. 5. Learning set performance of squirrel monkeys and marmosets compared with rhesus monkeys. *Reproduced from J. comp. physiol. Psychol.* [47].

ever, that the trial 2 performance is far better than any that has been demonstrated for any subprimate form, and the intraproblem learning curve late in LS formation is similar to that found for the rhesus monkey. As would be predicted in terms of cortical structure, the performance of the squirrel monkey is superior to that of the marmoset, and there is very little overlapping on LS performance.

Additional data on LS formation among various genera within the primate order have been supplied by Riopelle [58], who tested squirrel monkeys, cebus monkeys, and spider monkeys on series of six-trial discrimination problems. Figure 6 shows that performance of the cebus monkeys lay between that of the squirrel monkeys and the spider monkeys, and the performance of the spider monkeys closely approximated that of rhesus macaques. It is interesting in passing to note that the cebus monkey, the most able of the subanthropoids in instrumental, tool-using tasks, proves to be inept on the "academic-type" discrimination problems, and that the spider monkey performs very efficiently on discrimination problems despite its missing or vestigial thumbs.

Comparable discrimination LS performance has been obtained on rhesus and Java macaques, and similar performance was obtained on a single well-motivated langur at the Wisconsin laboratory. There is every reason to believe that the mangabey and baboon would perform equally effectively. The small variance in LS performance in the catarrhine monkeys contrasts with the great interspecies differences found in the platyrrhine forms. All existent discrimination LS data on all measured species are in keeping with the anatomical data bearing on cortical complexity, and it is obvious that LS techniques are powerful measures for the intellectual ordering of primate and possibly even nonprimate forms.

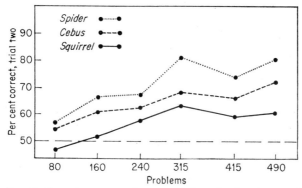

Fig. 6. Learning set performance of squirrel, cebus, and spider monkeys. *Courtesy of Dr. A. J. Riopelle.*

The chimpanzee and human data are not directly comparable with the monkey data because of experiential factors with human subjects and motivational differences in the testing situations with chimpanzees and human subjects, but such data as exist are in accord with phyletic predictions. Although Hayes, Thompson, and Hayes state that "the data available suggest that when pre-experimental experience is equated, man, chimpanzee, and rhesus monkeys differ very little in their ability to acquire sets for object-discrimination learning" [29, p. 103], their position must be challenged on a number of bases, including data of other experiments. The human subjects used by Hayes were quite immature, ranging from two to four years of age; our data suggest that infant rhesus monkeys of roughly comparable maturational age are also inept in LS formation. The comparison of the behavior of young children and adult monkeys departs from a strict interspecies comparison. Furthermore, human children and presumably young chimpanzees are harder to motivate than well-tamed monkeys, which typically respond with the machinelike characteristics of institutionalized subnormal children. Hayes, Thompson, and Hayes are obviously aware of these problems relating to species differences, differences in living conditions, and differences in adaptation to the test situation. The remarkable behavior of the occasional mature chimpanzee [52] that remains emotionally tractable and test-motivated makes it appear unlikely that this species would negate the generalization that position in the primate order and LS capability are highly related. The data obtained by Harlow [20] and Roberts [60] on nursery school children indicate that these subjects possess LS ability well beyond that of mature monkeys. The relative status of the mature rhesus monkey and man is self-evident.

By and large the phylogenetic data demonstrate that LS formation is closely related to evolutionary position, as conventionally described, and to cortical complexity in so far as this characteristic has been effectively measured. These data contrast with the little that is known about single-problem discrimination learning, for at present there is no evidence to indicate that single problems are learned more rapidly by members of one genus, family, or order than another within the class of mammals if conditions of maturation and past experience are, or can be, equated and if equally effective test conditions, adapted to the subjects, are used. Hebb has even gone so far as to conclude: "In the infant, the evidence is conclusive that the rate of the first learning is slowest in the highest species, quite apart from maturation" [30, p. 115]. We would question this conclusion because initial discrimination learning in the infant monkey is at least as rapid as initial discrimination learning in the infant rat, but we would concede that single-problem learning is relatively uncorrelated with phyletic position among mammals, whereas LS learning is highly related to phyletic position. These data, therefore, support the position that some capacity factor or factors operate to differentiate single-problem and multiple-problem acquisition.

One may conclude, then, that there is a capacity factor or factors which influence speed of LS formation, asymptote of maximally efficient LS performance, and even the ability to form effective LS's. The factor or factors may also determine the minimal number of trials per problem essential to establish the LS, and probably determine the maximal complexity of problems amenable to LS formation, such as conditioned response, spatial discrimination, nonspatial discrimination, oddity problem, or problems of greater complexity.

LEARNING SET FORMATION AND CORTICAL LOCALIZATION

Above and beyond the ontogenetic and phylogenetic data which assign a higher level of capacity to LS than to single-problem learning, there exist data from psychophysiology offering support to the separability of these two learning functions. In recent years, the effect of various temporal lobe lesions on visually guided behavior has attracted wide interest. Much of the temporal lobe lies within the classically described posterior associative cortex, and although the temporal lobe is rostral to the classical visual associative cortex, studies involving simulation [54] or extirpation [44] give unequivocal proof that the temporal lobe, or portions of the temporal lobe, serves visual associative functions.

It was first suggested by Riopelle, Alper, Strong, and Ades [59] that large temporal lesions which involve both the hippocampus and hippocampal gyrus abolish object-discrimination LS's without producing equivalent deficit in single-problem discrimination learning. Such a finding might be taken as providing additional evidence which differentiates single-problem and multiple-problem learning. Supporting data were provided by Chow [7], who showed that bilateral extirpation of the neocortex abolishes the LS for pattern discriminations during the brief period of postoperative testing, but at the same time, it does not affect to a measurable degree performance on individual pattern-discrimination problems. Meyer's [44] study lends general support to the position that LS's are more vulnerable to temporal resection than are single problems, but the issue is clearly complicated by the monkey's past experience, the size of lesion, and individual differences. The greater susceptibility of multiple- as contrasted with single-problem learning to temporal lesions may result from either quantitative or qualitative differences in difficulty. Both Warren and Harlow [70] and Chow [7] have shown that pattern-discrimination LS's are more susceptible to temporal lesions than are object-discrimination LS's. Here again the differences could be attributable to qualitative or quantitative differences in difficulty inherent in the two kinds of LS's. The problem is, however, unresolvable at our present state of knowledge. Regardless of the mechanisms involved, the operative studies suggest some separability of single-problem learning from LS learning and give supporting evidence to that already provided by the ontogenetic and phylogenetic data.

THE SIGNIFICANCE OF LEARNING SET THEORY

Up to this point we have concerned ourselves primarily with the technical aspects of LS formation. We conceive of LS, however, as more than a technique; we believe it to be a model with broad explanatory capabilities for a wide range of psychological phenomena.

One of the most striking phenomena associated with LS formation is the change in problem difficulty following multiple-problem practice. The initial problems of a class are learned slowly in a trial-and-error fashion. After LS formation the same kind of problem is solved immediately in an insightful fashion. Furthermore, we believe that this phenomenon has great generality and that all insightful learning of all problems by all animals is the resultant of LS formation. In other words, no animal can solve problems insightfully, or with maximal efficiency, without a history of earlier solutions of similar problems.

The evidence for learning-setless insight was summarized by the author in an earlier publication [23, pp. 457–466]. Köhler's [37] observations of insightful learning by chimpanzees has not stood the test of time or experimentation as indicated by the researchers of Schiller [61], Birch [5], and Bingham [4]. Maier's [41] discovery of reasoning in rats represented an intellectual tour de force independent of the data. It is, of course, impossible to control experience with human adult subjects. The Tolman [67] insight or inferential expectation studies were not adequately controlled, and the interpretations have been questioned by subsequent investigators [11, 34]. The two classical studies on insight learning by young children in problem situations [2, 42] demonstrated a surprising absence of insight even though at least some of the situations were of a kind that must have appeared frequently in the children's past experience, and so the children must have had opportunities for LS formation. As of the present time there is no satisfactory evidence for the existence of unlearned insight.

Using monkey subjects whose experience was controlled, we have obtained evidence that insightful learning through LS formation is a widely generalized principle. The phenomenon appears in discrimination learning, discrimination-reversal, oddity learning, and nonoddity learning, and doubtless would appear in many other problems.

It is the author's hypothesis that all concepts such as triangularity, middle-sizedness, redness, number, and smoothness evolve only from LS formation. Unfortunately, most of the major concept-formation studies on naïve subjects antedated LS theory, and as a result, the data provide no definitive test. The study by Andrew and Harlow [3], involving the training and testing of monkeys on a concept of triangularity, approaches an LS model for testing concept formation. These investigators trained 16 monkeys to discriminate a triangle and circle and then tested for generalization on 100 new pairs of stimuli. Performance was only 6 per cent better than chance. The monkeys were then trained to select the more triangular member in 50 of the original 100 pairs, after which they were given generalization tests on the other 50 pairs. Performance was now beyond 70 per cent correct responses, indicating a significant improvement in the formation of a generalized concept of triangularity. It is probable that unlimited training on a single problem would never produce significant concept formation; indeed, the inverse should occur:

with increased practice on a single problem, generalization tendencies should decrease, thus narrowing the possibilities for the formation of a concept.

It is not surprising that none of the classical concept-formation studies obtained efficient generalization to a wide range of stimuli by training on a single problem. Broad stimulus generalization, which is what we call concept formation, was obtained only after extensive training on a wide range of problems of a class, even though the informal nature of the experimental designs makes impossible real quantification of the mechanism involved. The studies by Fields [12, 13], Gellermann [14, 15], Karn and Munn [33], Smith [63], Neet [51], Andrew and Harlow [3], Weinstein [71], and Hicks [31] make it quite clear that concept formation is dependent on an LS mechanism, and this generalization holds for all mammalian species that have been tested.

In view of the extensive literature on transposition, both human [1, 40] and subhuman [35, 65, 66], it is surprising that no attempt has been made to extend these reasearches beyond the model of single-problem training and subsequent transposition testing. Actually, Spence in his original study on the intermediate-size problem tested his chimpanzees on a short series of single problems followed by individual tests and reported: "The data of two subjects, Lia and Cuba, suggest that response might have been on the basis of configurational or relational properties of the stimulus complexes" [66, p. 270]. Such findings suggest that a thorough attack on the family of transposition problems by means of LS methods might provide data making possible the integration of divergent theories.

Consideration of the changing intraproblem learning curves leads to predictions relating motivation to learning. Early intraproblem learning is slow and attended with multiple errors. Late intraproblem learning is rapid and essentially errorless. Errors lead to response refusals and relatively random intertrial behavior, characteristic of responses to frustration. One would, therefore, predict a progressive reduction in responses indicative of emotional disturbance as an LS develops. General observation supports this position even if experiments controlling learning experience as contrasted with LS learning experience are lacking. One would also predict that frustration would be minimized if the problems presented early in LS formation were run until a considerable degree of mastery had been obtained, and that late in LS formation frustration would be uncorrelated with problem length. Generalizing broadly to human behavior, we hold that original learning within an area is difficult and frustrating, but after mastery, learning within the same area becomes simple and effortless. Both the intellectual and emotional problems associated with learning to read disappear so completely that reading becomes an automatic process for most students. Similar phenomena are associated with such learnings as those involved in arithmetic and foreign languages. It remains as a possibility that the resistance of elderly people to new learning may relate more to associated problems of frustration than to learning limitations.

THE NATURE OF ERROR FACTOR THEORY

The conventional graphical way of presenting learning data is in terms of a curve demonstrating improved performance, defined as a reduction in the number or percentage of errors or response time or an increase in the number or percentage of correct responses, over a series of trials. The effect of other variables such as drives, incentives, temporal ordering of trials, and attributes of the stimuli on efficiency of problem solution are indicated by plotting families of learning curves on a single graph. This treatment of problem solution carries the suggestion that the learning involved is some unfractionable unit, such as habit strength, with which other variables interact.

It is the author's contention, however, that in most learning problems multiple factors are operating differentially on every trial to determine the course of the plotted learning curve. Such a concept is implicit in Spence's [64] analysis of discrimination learning, in which changes in two factors, a positional and a nonpositional factor, are described. The long struggle to attain precise nonspatial delayed responses presented a wealth of factual and theoretical information on antagonistic operation of positional and nonpositional factors during nonspatial delayed response learning [22, pp. 223–231].

As long as one studies only single problems it is difficult or impossible to conduct more than limited analyses of the multiple factors which operate to affect learning on the various trials. Single-problem learning at the level of difficulty of nonspatial discrimination is usually slow, and the patterns of rewards and nonrewards over the long succession of trials are too complex for differential analysis. The considerable variability among animals, particularly on problems which are learned slowly, adds to the difficulty of analysis. Still another complication is that imposed by the stimulus preferences animals bring to the experimental situation, and with single problems these preferences may distort the learning data.

Effective analyses of the factors underlying learning are possible only if one utilizes data from relatively large numbers of problems given to each of a number of subjects. The time factor in the collection of such extensive data is considerably reduced if the problems are presented for only a small number of trials, as has been done in the LS studies. Two techniques have proven useful in this kind of analysis: one is the utilization of a number of different balanced sequences controlling the positions of the correct and incorrect stimulus objects within each problem and over blocks of problems. The author's original analysis [21, p. 27] employed ten such sequences, which included four sequences in which the position of the correct stimulus object shifted on the second trial, and six sequences in which the first-trial position of the stimuli remained constant on the second trial. On two of these last six sequences, the position of the positive stimulus remained constant through the first three trials.

A second technique involves presentation of a single stimulus for a predetermined number of trials, followed by the conventional two-stimulus discrimination presentation. This method offers many possibilities for controlling experimental conditions relating to position, stimulus-object properties, and incentives. Actually, the general method was devised to test generalization [16, 65] and incentive conditions [18] before its potentialities for error factor (EF) analysis were explored [26].

Analysis of the data from a discrimination LS experiment employing multiple positional sequences enabled the author [21] to demonstrate in 1950 that it was possible to identify and trace the course of several distinct classes of errors made by monkeys on successive trials and over the series of problems. These classes of errors were described as being produced by EF's, which may be conceived of as reaction tendencies, or interactions between or among reaction tendencies, in the monkeys, leading to ordered, but inappropriate, responses to the problems presented. As these orderly but inappropriate responses are reduced, the percentage of errors diminishes progressively, and learning is said to be taking place.

In his first analytical study, the author identified four EF's operating in the discrimination situation and named them stimulus-perseveration, differential-cue, response-shift, and position-habit EF.

The operation of the *stimulus-perseveration EF* is deduced from errors involving repetitive choice of the incorrect stimulus object. An exact determination of the number and percentage of errors attributable to stimulus perseveration is difficult or perhaps impossible because these errors are confounded with those produced by other EF's. One can, however, by various computational devices [21] approximate the number and percentage of stimulus-perseveration errors, and a very good estimate can be made of the relative importance of this EF during the course of both intraproblem and interproblem learning.

It is presumed that this EF results from the subjects' stimulus preferences, absolute or relative, innate or learned. If an animal's responses were completely dominated by stimulus preference, and if this were not influenced by learning, no errors would be made on half the problems and 100 per cent errors would be made on the others. Observation of the monkey's behavior indicates that certain classes of stimuli, including large stimuli, tall, unstable stimuli, and many-pointed, bright, metallic stimuli characteristically elicit avoidant or hesitant behavior. Other stimulus objects elicit positive or approach responses although at the present time we cannot define their characteristics precisely. In a series of problems generalization from the physical properties of previously encountered stimuli, correct or incorrect, must also operate to produce preferential responses, either adient or avoidant.

Even after considerable pretraining and adaptation, stimulus-preference errors are important. Early in discrimination learning, a monkey may choose the unrewarded stimulus on every trial of a six-trial problem, and frequently it makes four or five consecutive errors. To date, several variables have been found to affect the course of stimulus perseveration

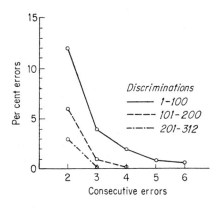

Fig. 7. Reduction in stimulus-perseveration errors during learning set formation.

during LS formation. The actual number and percentage of stimulus-perseveration errors will be a function of the criterional trial or trials chosen, amount and nature of adaptation, discrimination learning experience, and the stimuli chosen for presentation. The age of the animal appears to be important in that stimulus perseveration is stronger and more persistent for young monkeys than for mature monkeys with comparable laboratory experience. The importance of stimulus perseveration, of course, varies with successive blocks of problems during LS formation. Figure 7 shows the reduction of perseverative errors during the course of testing on 312 discrimination problems [21]. It will be noted that both the numbers of consecutive errors and the maximal length of consecutive-error sequences are progressively reduced during learning. Usually, the response tendencies producing stimulus perseveration are among the first to be suppressed or inhibited.

Bearing on the learned generalization aspect of stimulus perseveration and its suppression is an experiment by Riopelle [57], who studied the role of specific stimulus objects in a succession of problems with rhesus monkeys by presenting each day five discrimination problems on a six-trial basis and then presenting, again, the stimulus objects from either the first or the fourth problem of the day. The reappearance of the objects, however, was with reversed reward values, i.e., a discrimination-reversal problem. Five new problems and one reversed problem were tested each day for 63 days. Learning data on the new problems over the course of the experiment closely paralleled other discrimination LS data. Reversal-problem learning developed more slowly. Until midway in training, the monkeys chose the previously correct object on trial 1 of the reversal problems significantly more often than chance, but late in training they approached chance on trial 1 performance. Through the first 21 days, the subjects showed marked stimulus perseveration on trial 2 of the reversals, but during the last 42 days, performance closely paralleled that on the new problems. For trials 3 to 6, stimulus perseveration was marked on reversals only during the first week of training. Comparison of performance on reversals utilizing problem 1 and problem 4 revealed that negative transfer was greater for problem 4 reversals through the first two-thirds of training, but during the last third there was no difference. Riopelle termed these phenomena of progressive reduction in transfer "transfer suppression," and his findings provide evidence that monkeys are able to transfer learned stimulus values and, more important, they can learn to suppress this transfer effect.

A more persisting EF than stimulus perseveration is that of *differential cue*. The operation of the interacting response tendencies which produce these errors was described in detail and given theoretical importance by Spence [64] in 1936. Spence pointed out that on any particular trial of a nonspatial discrimination there is ambiguity between the object rewarded and the position rewarded. When a subject displaces a stimulus and obtains a reward, both the stimulus object hiding the food and the position of the object and food are simultaneously rewarded. To solve the nonspatial problem, however, the animal must learn to choose the object previously rewarded whether or not on a particular trial it occupies the position previously rewarded.

The importance of differential-cue errors may be determined by comparing the difference in the number of errors made, e.g., on trial 2 of problems in which the position of the correct stimulus does not change from trial 1 with problems in which the position of the correct stimulus does change. If the number of problems under each of the two conditions is equal, and if the number of errors made on the problems with changed position is divided by the number of errors made on the problems with unchanged position, one obtains a ratio, the comparable-trial error ratio (CTE ratio), which approaches unity as the response tendencies toward position are inhibited or suppressed. By holding position and object constant for more than two trials and meeting the conditions of changing the position of the correct stimulus on half the problems, it becomes possible to measure differential-cue errors on trials subsequent to trial 2.

The combined existing data on the differential-cue EF indicate that it is considerably more persisting than that of stimulus perseveration. Harlow's [21] data (see Fig. 8) showed that this EF persisted on both trials 2 and 3 throughout the first 200 problems but was not important during the next 112 problems. Braun, Patton, and Barnes [6] reported the differential-cue factor to be operating during problems 289 to 384, and it apparently was operating during a portion of the next 96 problems. The results reported by Davis, McDowell, and Thorson [9] are

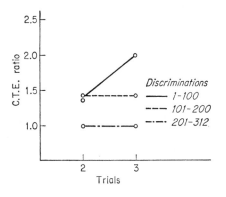

Fig. 8. Reduction in differential-cue errors during learning set formation as indicated by decrease in CTE ratio.

similar to those obtained by Braun et al. The differences probably result from the varying number of trials given per problem—six by Harlow, three by Braun et al., and four by Davis et al.

It would be predicted that as the number of trials of ambiguous reward increases before the shift of the rewarded object to a new position, the greater would be the error frequency on the shift trial and, consequently, the higher the comparable-trial error ratio. This prediction is generally borne out by the data [6, 9, 21].

Perhaps the most persistent EF is *response shift*, which may be described as a strong tendency of the monkey to respond to both stimuli in the object-discrimination learning situation. Response shift was initially discovered in the six-trial discrimination problem when the data revealed that more errors were made on trial 4 following three successive correct responses than following an initial error and two subsequent correct responses. The fact that fewer errors were made on trial 4 after the sequence with the initial error trial is particularly surprising because the initial incorrect choice implies that the trial 1 negative object was preferred or, at least, that it had no strong negative value for the animal.

In Harlow's [21] original analysis, response-shift errors were demonstrated only on trials 4 to 6, being obscured on the earlier trials by other confounding error sources. Davis, McDowell, and Thorson [9], on the other hand, were able to demonstrate response-shift errors from trials 2 through 4 during problems 257 to 448. By this time the confounding EF's of stimulus perseveration and differential cue had been suppressed or inhibited to a degree that permitted the more persistent response-shift EF to be identified in the earlier trials of the individual problems.

The existence of the response-shift EF had doubtless been demonstrated in 1947 by Moss and Harlow [50], who used the technique of training to a single stimulus and then testing in the conventional two-stimulus situation on the following trial. The monkey was presented on trial 1 with a single stimulus object covering one foodwell; the other foodwell was uncovered. On half the problems, the trial 1 stimulus was rewarded, and on the remaining problems it was not rewarded. Trial 2 presented the previously encountered stimulus over one foodwell and a new object over the other foodwell. The trial 1 reward condition also prevailed on trial 2; i.e., if the single stimulus was rewarded on trial 1, it was rewarded on trial 2, and the new stimulus was unrewarded. If the trial 1 stimulus was unrewarded, it was also unrewarded on the second trial, and the new stimulus was rewarded.

This method gives unequivocal evidence of a response-shift factor since performance following an unrewarded stimulus is clearly superior to performance following a rewarded stimulus, and this difference remains constant throughout training on hundreds of problems [21, 26]. If the single stimulus used on trial 1 is placed over a centered foodwell rather than over one of the two peripheral foodwells, the typical 10 per cent error difference quintuples (unpublished experiment by Schrier and Harlow). This almost unbelievable demonstration of the power of the response-shift EF is in keeping with its importance and persistence and indicates why no investigator has found response shift to be completely suppressed or inhibited even though hundreds of problems involving thousands of trials may have been completed by every subject.

We conceive of the response-shift EF as resulting from an exploratory tendency [24] in the subjects. Furthermore, it would appear that this is primarily a tendency to explore the test situation in terms of its incentive possibilities. This is particularly striking in that it occurs in animals with a history of extensive experience with food incentives. Additional data bearing on this point will be presented subsequently.

Response shift could well be a function of a number of interacting variables, one of which might conceivably be work inhibition. We regard this explanation as extremely remote, however, since Davis [8] found little evidence that work inhibition is either an important or consistent variable influencing performance of rhesus monkeys. Response shift in monkeys may well be related to the spontaneous alternation originally reported in rat maze-behavior by Dennis [10].

Position habit errors, which are consistent responses to either the right or left foodwell regardless of the position of the correct object, appear to represent an essentially unimportant error source for primates. Although many monkeys show clear-cut preference for either the right or left side of the cage, these preferences operate as a negligible error source in discrimination learning. The data [6, 9, 21, 57] show that positional error tendencies either do not exist or are suppressed during the first hundred problems. A most significant finding of Riopelle [57] is that the monkey's trial 1 choices reflect positional preferences through hundreds of problems although these preferences are apparently completely suppressed during the subsequent trials of the individual problems.

The four error-producing factors which we have described as operating in the discrimination learning situation are not regarded as comprising a complete system of EF's for either the discrimination learning problem or any other problem. Any condition which leads to indiscriminate responses to either or both of the stimuli will produce errors, and included in such conditions are external disturbances, internal emotional disturbances, and inadequate attention. All the described states would tend to produce random or unsystematic errors, i.e., errors without regard to objects, position, or arrangement of trial sequences.

It is obvious that the number of EF's varies in terms of the complexity of problems. A spatial discrimination with identical objects would eliminate any possibility of the operation of the stimulus-preference and differential-cue EF's. The oddity problem involves all the EF's described as operating in object discrimination learning and other EF's too [49]. Particularly important here is the rewarded-object perseveration error, the tendency to respond to the object last correct without regard to the configurational cue of oddity. Similarly, the oddity-nonoddity problem must introduce at least one additional EF, a tendency to respond in terms of the preceding configurational cue.

Recently Levine and Schrier have suggested a reformulation of the definition of EF's. They define EF's as unique patterns of responses made to irrelevant aspects of the stimulus situation, i.e., responses to those stimuli which are not correlated with the reward to the same degree as the correct object or cue. The irrelevant stimulus acts as an "error-factor producer" (EFP) when the responses of the subject are correlated with the stimulus for a given number of trials. Thus, in object discrimination, position preference means that the subject is responding consistently to one side. Stimulus preference means that the subject is responding consistently to the incorrect stimulus.

They distinguish four classes of stimuli which may serve as EFP's. The first class contains those cues which are spatially differentiated, though constant from trial to trial. This includes the cues associated with each position in object discrimination and is the basis of position preference. The remaining three classes contain the cues which change from trial to trial. The second stimulus class consists of changing cues in what is traditionally described as the external environment. All environmental stimuli which appear and disappear from trial to trial, or which shift position or change in some way, are potential EFP's. The animal may respond systematically to these. Whether it does or not will depend on its capacity to perceive these changes and on the laws governing the manner in which stimuli gain control over behavior. One may note here that irrelevant stimuli which vary in this manner will, if responded to by the animal but not perceived by the experimenter, produce behavior which appears random, i.e., uncorrelated with any aspect of the situation. A tester, e.g., who periodically unconsciously tapped his foot, would be the source of such a stimulus. The third class of stimuli contains those which result from the behavior of the subject. A response to the right side yields different stimulation from a response to the left side. An organism, then, can respond to its own preceding responses and yield such behavior sequences as response alternation, double alternation, and so forth. How long a sequence of behavior the animal responds to again depends upon its capacity and can probably be decided only empirically. Included in this class of stimuli are those deriving from emotional reactions and preresponse movements. Since these stimuli are normally not recorded by the experimenter, they probably constitute the major source of random response sequences. The fourth class of stimuli to which the animal can respond comprises rewards and nonrewards on preceding trials. Response shift is considered to be a factor in this class. If the animal goes to object A consistently on the first few trials and then switches to the B object, the interpretation would be that the response-reward sequence on the first few trials has determined the switch on the critical trial. Another type of factor falling into this category is that of "rewarded-object perseveration," in which the subject's response is determined by whether or not it was rewarded on the preceding trial.

The authors point out that certain implications follow from this systematic cataloguing of the stimuli:

1. Random behavior may be defined as response sequences which do not correlate with any of the recorded changes in the stimulus situa-

tion. Since the major source of stimuli producing random sequences is probably the behavior of the subject, they predict that animals that are very active between trials should yield a more random-appearing sequence of responses than placid animals.

2. In delayed response, anything which eliminates the ability to retain the cue information, such as a prefrontal operation, would alter the pattern of EF's. Whereas a normal animal just learning delayed response can respond to its preceding behavior and preceding rewards, the animal no longer able to retain information over the delay period should no longer be able to retain the information about its preceding response or the preceding reward condition, since these took place even before the critical cue. With such an animal, one would expect either an increase in random sequences or in the frequency of position preferences.

3. The oddity task has the feature that learning can be manifested on the first trial of a given problem. If the task is arranged so that a series of one-trial problems is presented, then, from the standpoint of EF's, the situation becomes simpler than it is on a single, multiple-trial oddity problem or a series of multiple-trial problems. In the latter the subject can alternate objects, can manifest object shift, and can show rewarded-object perseveration. The last is a particularly powerful EF. These EF's cannot occur in the one-trial learning situation. They predict, therefore, that the animal would learn oddity faster with one-trial problems than it would with the equivalent number of trials presented in a single problem or series of multiple-trial problems.

Levine and Schrier have also considered the relation of problem difficulty to EFP's. They acknowledge that tasks can be conceived of as falling along a continuum of number of EFP's, and they offer some evidence that the greater the number of EFP's, the more difficult the task. They argue, however, that the converse is not true. One cannot say that the more difficult a problem, the more EFP's present. Thus, increasing the similarity of the stimuli to be discriminated increases the number of errors but does not alter the number or nature of the EFP's. The patterns and frequency of the EF's themselves would be different in the two situations, but the stimuli which control the behavior in one situation would also exist in the other. It is as though increasing the similarity of the stimuli increases the potentiality of the irrelevant stimuli for eliciting the EF's. Other variables which affect errors without altering EFP's are spatial discontiguity of the objects from the foodwells, the size of the patterns to be discriminated, and in general, the detectability of the stimuli to be discriminated. Thus, to increase problem difficulty, one can increase the number of EFP's or one can increase the eliciting potential of the irrelevant cues which already exist by making the relevant stimulus harder to discriminate or detect.

APPLICATION OF ERROR FACTOR THEORY

Although a wide range of learning tasks can be ordered in terms of the complexity of EF's which operate, EF theory offers little new in so far as classification of problem difficulty per se is concerned. The progressive increase in number of ambiguous factors as we pass from spatial discrimination, to object discrimination, to increasingly complex multiple-sign problems has already been described [22]. Error factor analyses, however, permit us to predict and subsequently to validate the nature of the underlying conditions producing positive and negative transfer

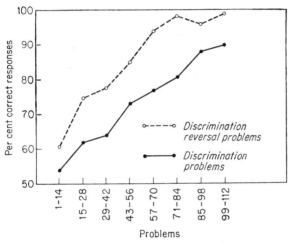

Fig. 9. Comparison of discrimination learning set curve with discrimination-reversal learning set curve based on data from the same subjects.

among many problems and provide parsimonious explanations for some previously inadequately explained phenomena.

There is an impressive literature which discusses in theory the relative difficulty of a discrimination and a discrimination-reversal, the common-sense assumption being that it is much harder to change a well-learned response than to learn it. Having been reared in this tradition, the author was unprepared to find that rhesus monkeys that had formed a discrimination LS formed a discrimination-reversal LS with considerable facility, as Fig. 9 indicates [20].

Only after we had developed EF theory did the answer become obvious. The learned inhibition of all the error-producing factors which operate in discrimination learning transfers positively to the discrimination-reversal learning situation with a single exception, that of stimulus perseveration. Successful discrimination and discrimination-reversal learning necessitate suppression of positional, differential-cue, and response-shift EF's. The only negative effect of the previous discrimination learning on reversal is the exaggeration of the stimulus-perseveration EF. The original learning produces a high object-preference which must be overcome in the reversal phase of the problem. But this analysis makes it obvious that there are more factors exhibiting positive transfer than negative transfer, and furthermore, that positive transfer operates on two of the more persistent EF's.

Reid's [56] apparently puzzling finding that overlearning facilitates rather than hinders black-white discrimination-reversal learning has been confirmed [55], and a number of explanations have been offered. Perhaps the simplest explanation is the one we have presented above: discrimination learning and reversal are not antithetical processes. So far as EF elimination is concerned, the two learning problems have more in common than at variance. From this point of view, there is no reason to predict anything but increased reversal efficiency with discrimination overlearning. Certainly there is no reason at the present time to assume, as do Reid [56] and Pubols [55], that a different kind of learning, a "response of discriminating," takes place, particularly during the overlearning period.

Any radical change in a problem situation, such as shifting from discrimination to oddity, oddity to nonoddity, or discrimination to discrimination-reversal, results in a very striking phenomenon: the first problem or block of problems following the change may result in a cascade of errors, accompanied by other behavioral signs such that the subject may be described as "emotional," "disorganized," or "frustrated." This finding has been frequently reported in series of black-white discrimination-reversals for mature rats [see 55, 56] and infant monkeys [27]. The first reversal may entail a very large number of errors, perhaps more errors than were made in the original learning. The subsequent reversals and rereversals are usually made more efficiently, with error scores falling below those in the original learning. Similar results have been reported for problem changes and reversals in a wide variety of learning situations. Changing a solvable problem into one that is insolvable produces extreme examples of disruption, which in this instance cannot be overcome. The resulting behaviors have been described in the frustration literature, which is outside the scope of this paper.

It is our belief that EF analysis offers possibilities of determining the effects of reversal or change in a problem more efficiently and objectively than these changes have previously been analyzed. We believe that change in a problem will result in the reappearance of previously suppressed EF's, and that the nature of this EF reappearance can be predicted with considerable success in terms of the nature of the problem and the subject's past history. Furthermore, we would predict that the degree of problem change or shift and the resulting increase in problem difficulty will be related in a quantitative manner to the type and number of EF's which reappear.

The actual test of this hypothesis is difficult since one must show not only that problem change or reversal is disruptive but that the nature and the order of appearance of the suppressed EF's which this change releases are highly systematic. An approach to the problem has been made by Moon and Harlow, who studied oddity learning in monkeys that had previously learned object discrimination [49] and uncovered two categories of errors that appeared only when the subject was attempting solution of the problem in terms of the reactions appropriate to object-discrimination learning. Subsequently, Moon and Harlow analyzed the oddity-nonoddity learning of the same monkeys and found that during the first hundred oddity-nonoddity problems the monkeys rapidly came to respond to the nonoddity trials as if they were object-discrimination trials. In other words, their responses were not appropriate to the previously learned oddity problem, but to a more primitive problem, object discrimination.

We would predict that had the nonoddity problem been unsolvable and had testing been continued, the typical form of the errors would have become progressively more primitive, regressing to position habits, stimulus perseveration, and eventual randomness—inattentive or emotional responses. The experimental testing of this hypothesis poses a few difficulties, but it unquestionably can be done. In favor of such a hypothesis there already exists a considerable body of quantitative and semiquantitative data of a nondefinitive type.

This concept of regression to more primitive error patterns is reminiscent of Krechevsky's classical studies of "hypotheses" in rats [39]. Subjects tested on insolvable problems for hundreds of trials showed frequent periods of consistent behavior such as response to the right position, left position, light selection, or light avoidance. Furthermore, these islands of consistent, patterned behavior were commonly surrounded by long series of random or inconsistent responses. Even though different rats and strains of rats showed preferences for different response patterns, the general picture is quite clear: Krechevsky was probably measuring unlearned patterns, not patterns arising from change or shift in a previously learned response.

Progressive reappearance of previously suppressed EF's following protracted failure in a problem-solving situation would appear to be a mechanism of high adaptive value. If an animal possesses a repertoire of LS's permitting facile solution of a half-dozen problems, it should utilize all these patterns or "hypotheses" when a new problem appears. Reaction of the animal with initial randomness upon the appearance of any new problem would represent a waste of its previous learning. The initial use of existing LS's and the consequent appearance of complicated EF patterns is probably efficient, and regardless of efficiency, it appears as a rather generalized approach by all higher primates. Indeed, one of the difficulties from which human subjects often suffer when faced with a simple problem is a stubborn insistence on trying to solve it by some hypothesis or LS of a level of complexity inappropriate to the presented task.

If it is assumed that learning is the elimination of all EF's operating within a particular problem, it should be possible for animals to learn problems partially by eliminating individual EF's before formal training in the test situation begins. Actually, psychologists have been doing this for decades, e.g., "adapting" rats on a straightaway before training them on a multiple-unit maze, thereby doubtless reducing error-producing factors in advance of the "learning" situation.

At Wisconsin we systematically engage in "adaptation" procedures in order to prepare the animal emotionally for experimentation, but this preliminary training must also reduce EF's, though we have conducted few formal experiments to test this assumption. We consistently start experimental work with naïve monkeys by giving them experience on 20 objects presented individually over a single, centered foodwell. We probably reduce stimulus preference by this technique, but we have not as yet conducted a formal experiment to determine the extent to which this is accomplished by our single-stimulus preliminary training.

An intriguing experiment by Jarvik [32] demonstrates that essentially perfect discrimination performance can be accomplished without any paired-stimulus training. Jarvik [32] soaked small square pieces of bread in either a saccharin solution or a solution containing capsicum, dehydrocholic acid, and quinine and dyed one kind red and the other, green. Half the subjects had the saccharin bread red, half green. The animals were given preliminary experience with one piece of each color of bread, the positive or saccharin-soaked bread being presented first. The subjects, 10 chimpanzees and 8 monkeys, were then tested for 25 trials with both stimuli present. No errors were made by 12 of the subjects, and a maximum of 2 errors was made by 2 chimpanzees. These data clearly show that immediate discrimination learning may be effected by establishing strong stimulus preferences before instituting formal training.

The importance of stimulus preferences is demonstrated by data that we are presently obtaining on groups of 60-, 90-, and 120-day–old monkeys and on 16 young adults. Approximately 25 per cent of the animals, on their initial discrimination problem, which in this experiment is 500 trials in length, solved the problem with few or relatively few errors. Strong preferences apparently exist in some monkeys for certain stimuli in spite of our best efforts to prevent such an occurrence.

In 1944 the author developed the technique of adapting monkeys to the WGTA by presenting a series of stimuli, one at a time, on the test tray. Each stimulus was presented an equal number of times over the right and the left foodwell, and each trial was rewarded. The extremely efficient performance by the subjects on their initial and subsequent discrimination problems [19] suggested that the adaptation procedures actually constituted training procedures.

The truth of this presumption has now been established by an unpublished study by Harlow and Meyer, who demonstrated that the above procedures, which never involve paired-stimulus presentation, reduce the differential-cue EF significantly. The monkey learns to suppress the effect of reward of position and respond consistently to object rewards. Lest it be suggested that this is accomplished by eliminating position preferences, it should be stated that direct tests indicate that these procedures have not affected position preferences. Position preferences existed before these single-stimulus training procedures and equally strong preferences existed afterward. Since obtaining these results, we have abandoned the two-hole board for our standard adaptation technique and resorted to the one-hole board, for we prefer to minimize learning prior to the formal experimentation.

Still another error factor has been demonstrated to be amenable to experimental manipulation: response shift. In this instance the EF was exaggerated, not reduced, through a modification of reward conditions. Schrier and Harlow [62] tested eight Java monkeys on 432, 10-trial discrimination problems, three problems per day, rewarding the subject with one, two, or four food pellets for correct responses within a problem. The three reward conditions were balanced over each three-day test period. Over-all learning curves, i.e., curves based on trials 1 through 10, were progressive for all incentive conditions combined and for each incentive condition plotted independently. Frequency of response-shift errors was inversely related to the amount of incentive, but neither differential-cue errors nor position-preference errors related in any systematic way to incentive amount. Analysis of trial 2 responses following correct trial 1 responses showed an interesting relation to incentive amount. Such responses under intermediate- and high-reward conditions showed a fairly constant percentage of errors over the course of the experiment, but under the low-reward condition the percentage of errors increased significantly from 40 per cent in the first third of the experiment to 50 per cent in the next third and 65 per cent in the final third. The monkeys actually had "learned" to perform below chance on trial 2, although they received no food reward for these response-shift errors,

In summary it may be stated that in spite of the limited research conducted thus far on EF analysis, a number of interesting phenomena are evolving. It is a reasonable hypothesis that the suppression of all EF's defines perfect learning, and that learning is nothing but suppression or inhibition of EF's. Several EF's have been shown to be subject to suppression or augmentation by training outside the test situation. Finally, in at least one case, we find completely different interaction between an incentive condition and the EF's operating within a problem. These data suggest that EF's are functional units whose suppression underlies learning.

LEARNING SET, ERROR FACTORS, AND UNIPROCESS LEARNING THEORY

The development of the thesis that learning involves nothing other than the elimination of responses and response tendencies inappropriate

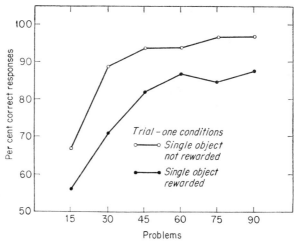

Fig. 10. Discrimination learning set curves based on trial 2 responses following rewarded and unrewarded trial 1 responses. *Reproduced from Psychol. Rev.* [26].

to a particular learning situation leads us to question the commonly held concept that learning is the resultant of two processes, excitation, which follows reward, and inhibition, generated when no reward is received. It seems more consistent with EF theory to assume that instead of two processes only a single process underlies learning, and the reasoning favoring this assumption is presented at length in a recent paper [26]. Also reported in that paper is an experiment testing duoprocess as opposed to uniprocess theories by means of LS methods. We found under carefully controlled conditions that trial 1 reward and trial 1 nonreward give rise to LS curves which are alike in form and parallel each other throughout their course. Furthermore, the constant difference between the curves, as shown in Figs. 10 and 11, can be explained by the operation of the independently measured response-shift EF. Constant differences are, however, immaterial inasmuch as it is differential curve form rather than a constant rate difference which would result if reward and nonreward showed differential strengthening and weakening effects during the course of learning.

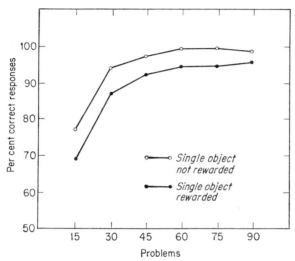

FIG. 11. Discrimination learning set curves based on trial 2–6 responses following rewarded and unrewarded trial 1 responses. *Reproduced from Psychol. Rev.* [26].

Since the publication of the study just discussed, we have completed two additional experiments testing the contrasting duoprocess-uniprocess learning theories. A group of 10 monkeys was tested on a total of 720 two-trial discrimination problems. A single stimulus object was presented on trial 1, and it was rewarded on half the problems and not rewarded on the others. After a delay of 5, 10, or 20 sec, trial 2 began, introducing a pair of stimuli, which included the singly presented stimulus of trial 1. The LS curves for these two-trial problems with intertrial delay lack the regularity of the LS curve for six-trial problems without intertrial delay, but the form of the six trial 2 curves following rewarded and nonrewarded trial 1's, plotted independently for reward condition and delay condition, is similar for each delay interval. The

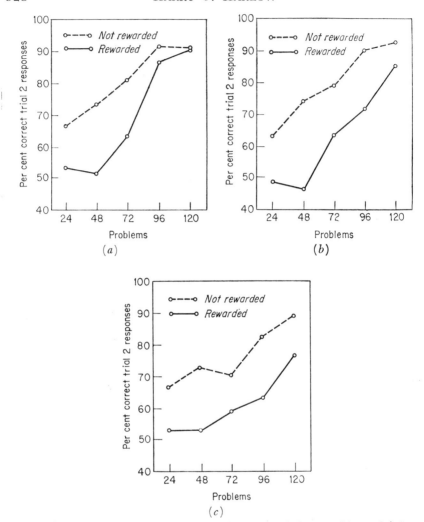

FIG. 12. Discrimination learning set curves for intertrial delay problems. (a) 5-sec. delay. (b) 10-sec delay. (c) 20-sec. delay. In each instance, the solid-line curve is for the trial 1 reward condition and the broken-line curve is for trial 1 not rewarded.

differences in performance following the various delay intervals are not great, but the relative superiority of the nonrewarded over the rewarded trial remains quite constant at all delay intervals (see Fig. 12). Certainly, these data give no indication of the operation of two different mechanisms, one associated with reward and the other with nonreward.

The next experiment involved testing the same 10 monkeys on a total of 960 delayed response trials, 120 trials on each of four delay-conditions, 0, 5, 10, and 20 sec, and for each of two prechoice or incentive conditions. Each trial was initiated with one of the two identical stimulus objects covering one foodwell on a tray and the second stimulus 2 in. behind the remaining foodwell. For one incentive condition, food was visible in the uncovered foodwell. The experimenter tapped three times behind the well, then covered it with the block and started the timer. At the end of the appropriate delay period, the tray was pushed forward to within the animal's reach. For the second incentive condition, food was in the covered foodwell. The experimenter tapped behind the uncovered foodwell, which was visibly empty, then covered it with the second block. The remainder of the trial procedure was the same as for the first condition.

Superior performance was obtained for those trials in which the subjects saw food in the well during the predelay period. Long experience with delayed response testing suggests that the critical factor is attention; it is easier to attract and hold the animal's attention if it sees the food in the well than if it sees only an empty well.

The effects of the delays were thus much greater than in the discrimination learning experiment. The curves for the two incentive conditions (Fig. 13), which are based on the percentage of correct responses as a function of delay, are not significantly different in form, and the advantage of the visible reward

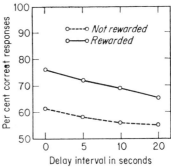

FIG. 13. Delayed response performance as a function of incentive condition and delay interval. The solid-line curve is for the visible-food condition; the broken-line curve is for the empty foodwell condition.

over the nonvisible reward presentation condition is consistent. When the data are plotted separately for each of the eight conditions, essentially parallel learning curves are found for the 0- and 5-sec delay intervals, and the 10-sec curves parallel the shorter-delay curves except for the last point. At the 20-sec delay interval the visible reward presentation produces a smooth, negatively accelerated curve, but the nonvisible reward condition yields a flat, chance curve which fails to rise above 56 per cent at any point.

In general, we believe that the data of these two experiments give strong additional support to the uniprocess learning thesis. Temporal delay in both experiments produced comparable deficits under conditions of trial 1 reward and nonreward in one instance, and visible reward and nonvisible reward in the other. Generally, these two incentive conditions produced parallel learning when delay interval was held constant. The sole exception was a failure to obtain any learning under one test condition.

The concept of uniprocess learning is by no means original. Guthrie [17] has long espoused such a position, and Hebb [30] can be similarly categorized. Both these authorities imply that the fundamental process is one of growth or excitation. Analysis of EF elimination led us, however, to examine the possibilities of a uniprocess position based on inhibition. Later, speculation on the nature of learning per se seemed to be consistent with an inhibition learning theory, for we could find no evidence that learning evolves from the formation of new associations. To this iconoclastic statement we now give fuller explanation.

Let us first consider what learning really is. To obtain learning in any situation we must have a subject motivated to achieve an incentive, and the situation is so arranged that there are various impedimenta of varying orders of complexity in the way of the subject's response to the incentive. The subject must circumvent these impedimenta if it is to learn. In the Skinner box the various patterns of temporal ordering are these impedimenta, and on the Klüver tray in the WGTA they are the patterns of objects placed over the foodwells. In a very real sense the subject in either of these situations, and in all other learning situations, is not responding to the impedimenta; it is responding to the incentive, and it is responding in spite of the impedimenta. Observation of responses of monkeys in the WGTA situation makes it obvious that the monkey is responding to the food, and the animal makes or attempts the food-getting response in spite of the road-blocking stimuli. So long as an animal actually responds to the stimuli and not the incentive, learning is inefficient or impossible. During the adaptation process, we attempt to prevent our monkeys from responding to the stimulus objects by chewing them, tearing them, or playing with them in the cage. Those deviant monkeys that persist in responding to the stimuli per se never learn, and they make their scientific contribution in subsequent neurophysiological experiments. The difficulty encountered in training infant monkeys, most chimpanzees, and all human children is their persistent tendency to disregard both appetite and hunger and to respond to the stronger motives afforded them by the impedimenta.

Successful monkey learners, regardless of the situation, gradually inhibit responses and response tendencies interfering with the minimal essential responses of prehending and/or ingesting the incentive, and as this is achieved, the latency of the correct response, the response remaining after all the incorrect responses have been inhibited, gradually approaches, but never attains, the latency of the direct response to the incentive. The responses inhibited include any response to incorrect stimuli and any unnecessary response to the correct stimuli. For learning viewed in this way, we see no need to postulate formations of new associations.

Recently the author has reviewed the experimental materials relating to the evolution of learning and attempted to fit them into a theoretical framework [25]. The learning of primitive organisms appears to be nothing more than the gradual suppression or inhibition of extraneous response tendencies. In view of modern genetic theory, which holds that evolution takes place by the selection of multiple small mutations, it is not unreasonable to hypothesize that the fundamental process of learning has probably remained essentially unchanged for near-countless millions of years. Furthermore, there is nothing relating to the slow, but progressive, evolution of the nervous system to suggest any great master mutation giving rise to a new learning mechanism. For countless generations, development has gone along the line of slowly increasing the number and complexity of neural structures without evidence for development of essentially new anatomical units which might give basis for a sudden change in the nature of learning. Unless the assumption is made that there have been one or more large mutations which could have resulted in new learning processes, inhibition learning theory is not inconsistent with evolutionary theory. Data such as these, of course, can never be definitive but must always be judged on a "best-guess" basis.

CONCLUDING COMMENTS

The materials on learning set and error factor theory have now been presented. We have described how our data led us to take sides on an issue which we believe to be a firm basis for the establishment of a system, the issue of uniprocess vs. duoprocess learning. We have made a rather arbitrary decision to investigate how far it is profitable to exploit the concept that the single learning process is inhibitory, and that learning consists only in the elimination of incorrect response tendencies elicited in the learning situation. We are satisfied with this arbitrary position because we believe it has a high probability of being fundamentally meaningful.

Experimental and observational data, in large part obtained from our "baby monkey" research since this paper was written, have strengthened our opinion that the most important mammalian motives are the incentives provided by the physical stimuli of the external world—exteroceptive, chemoreceptive, and nociceptive. No stimuli of any of these classes have developmental priority over the others, and the actual order of appearance in many cases is at variance with textbook descriptions. Thus, solid foods develop as effective incentives from responses to exteroceptively motivated curiosity-manipulatory responses. If we were to follow the common psychological paradigm of "derived motives," responsiveness to solid food would be a derived motive conditioned to curiosity responses.

It is these external incentives that form the motivating conditions constantly eliciting behavior in the waking organism. The animal is no more able to avoid responding to these incentives than it is able to ignore hunger, thirst, or elimination. Attainment of these incentives in sufficient amount produces satiation, and the primary function of drive states is to delay this satiation effect. We grant the fact that primary drive states may have other functions, such as alteration of threshold states.

The direct response to these incentives is blocked, made difficult, or made variable in learning situations. The suppression of the extraneous, or nonadaptive, responses or response tendencies elicited by the blocking (problem) agents constitutes learning, but their suppression is not a function of the response to the incentive, e.g., the eating of food. The response to the incentive gives the animal information about the characteristics of the incentive, such as its quality and quantity. This learning about particular incentive characteristics may influence the likelihood that subsequently the incentive will consistently elicit responses over less prepotent external stimuli simultaneously acting upon the organism.

We have already presented our basic theoretical position in regard to learning, but we will summarize it again. When a psychologist decides to study learning in an animal, he initially trains the animal to form an expectancy that some response or sequence of responses in a particular situation will be followed by an incentive. This is done by "shaping" the behavior of the rat or pigeon in the Skinner box, by training the rat on a straightaway before subsequently running it on a maze, and by adapting the monkey to the test tray in the WGTA. In all these learning situations the animals are trained to make some response or responses that lead to an incentive. The subjects learn that responsiveness in a particular situation will provide an incentive or that there is a certain probability that it will provide an incentive.

Let us now take any discrimination problem and note what "learning" is from this point forward. Having mastered the straightaway, the rat may be put in a maze. As Snygg has so clearly shown, it is possible to design multiple-unit mazes in such a way that the natural response tendencies of the rat will lead it usually to make errorless performances. It is also possible to devise mazes which will invariably produce errors. If the maze patterns are such that they elicit errors, the rat must inhibit responsiveness to those segments which lead to errors before the experimenter will state in print that the rat learned the maze.

The pigeon has been trained to press a lever in a Skinner box according to some predetermined schedule. It is presented with a green light, and the previously introduced schedule of reward is continued. The bird is now presented with a red light and not rewarded. At first the pigeon responds as it did to the green light in the total test situation, but gradually it learns to inhibit this response. When the inhibition is complete, the pigeon is described as having learned the discrimination.

When infant monkeys 60, 90, 120, or 150 days of age face their first discrimination problem, choice between two multidimensional objects on a test tray, their performances fall into two classes. In this learning situation, learning to push the object which covers the baited food-well, some infants make no errors or as few as five errors before reaching the criterional level of learning. The other monkeys make many errors, indeed, they may make 90 per cent or more errors on the first 25 trials, and as many as 70 errors totally before mastering the problem. The meaning of these data is perfectly clear: if the preferred stimulus is the one rewarded, "learning" may take place in zero trials; if the nonpreferred stimulus is the one rewarded, the monkey must come to inhibit these response tendencies before learning is complete.

Our theoretical position differs from that of Hull in that his is a duoprocess reinforcement theory and ours a uniprocess nonreinforcement position. Similarly, our position differs from Spence's, whose 1936 treatment of discrimination learning, like Hull's, favors reinforcement and two learning processes, excitation and inhibition. To Spence, however, we are indebted for the concept of differential-cue errors. Guthrie's position resembles ours in that he favors nonreinforcement, but differs from ours in that he proposes the formation of new associations whereas we propose the elimination of preestablished nonadaptive responses or response tendencies. Our position has much in common with that of Tolman in the treatment of incentives. Because of the incompleteness of our theory at the present time, more detailed comparison with current theories is best left to the future.

Our purpose in this paper has been to present a point of view, or pretheory, based on a quarter-century of experimental work at the Wisconsin Primate Laboratory. Since certain of the present systematic considerations are novel, and have not before been brought together in this way, the primary initial task was necessarily one of exposition. Though at many points questions germane to the Project A discussion outline are touched upon, more detailed analysis of the present formulation would be pretentious at this phase.

REFERENCES

1. Alberts, E., & Ehrenfreund, D. Transposition in children as a function of age. *J. exp. Psychol.*, 1951, **41**, 30–38.

2. Alpert, A. The solving of problem-situations by preschool children. *Teach. Coll. Contr. Educ.*, 1928, No. 323.

3. Andrew, G., & Harlow, H. F. Performance of macaque monkeys on a test of the concept of generalized triangularity. *Comp. Psychol. Monogr.*, 1948, 19, No. 3 (Serial No. 100).

4. Bingham, H. C. Chimpanzee translocation by means of boxes. *Comp. Psychol. Monogr.*, 1929, 5, No. 3 (Serial No. 25).

5. Birch, H. G. The relation of previous experience to insightful problem-solving. *J. comp. Psychol.*, 1945, 38, 367–383.

6. Braun, H. W., Patton, R. A., & Barnes, H. W. Effects of electroshock convulsions upon the learning performance of monkeys: I. Object-quality discrimination learning. *J. comp. physiol. Psychol.*, 1952, 45, 231–238.

7. Chow, K. L. Effects of temporal neocortical ablation on visual discrimination learning sets in monkeys. *J. comp. physiol. Psychol.*, 1954, 47, 194–198.

8. Davis, R. T. Problem-solving behavior of monkeys as a function of work variables. *J. comp. physiol. Psychol.*, 1956, 49, 499–506.

9. Davis, R. T., McDowell, A. A., & Thorson, N. Four-trial object-quality discrimination learning by monkeys. *Proc. So. Dak. Acad. Sci.*, 1953, 32, 132–142.

10. Dennis, W. Spontaneous alternation in rats as an indicator of the persistence of stimulus effects. *J. comp. Psychol.*, 1939, 28, 305–312.

11. Evans, S. Flexibility of established habit. *J. gen. Psychol.*, 1936, 14, 177–200.

12. Fields, P. E. Studies in concept formation. *Comp. Psychol. Monogr.*, 1932, 9, No. 2 (Serial No. 42).

13. Fields, P. E. Studies in concept formation: IV. A comparison of white rats and raccoons with respect to their visual discrimination of certain geometrical figures. *J. comp. Psychol.*, 1936, 21, 341–355.

14. Gellermann, L. W. Form discrimination in chimpanzees and two-year-old children: I. Form (triangularity) *per se*. *J. genet. Psychol.*, 1933, 42, 3–27.

15. Gellermann, L. W. Form discrimination in chimpanzees and two-year-old children: II. Form versus background. *J. genet. Psychol.*, 1933, 42, 28–49.

16. Grandine, L., & Harlow, H. F. Generalization of the characteristics of a single learned stimulus by monkeys. *J. comp. physiol. Psychol.*, 1948, 41, 327–337.

17. Guthrie, E. R. *The psychology of learning.* New York: Harper, 1935.

18. Harlow, H. F. Studies in discrimination by monkeys: II. Discrimination learning without primary reinforcement. *J. gen. Psychol.*, 1944, 30, 13–21.

19. Harlow, H. F. Studies in discrimination learning in monkeys: V. Initial performance by experimentally naive monkeys on stimulus-object and pattern discrimination. *J. gen. Psychol.*, 1945, 33, 3–10.

20. Harlow, H. F. The formation of learning sets. *Psychol. Rev.*, 1949, **56**, 51–65.

21. Harlow, H. F. Analysis of discrimination learning by monkeys. *J. exp. Psychol.*, 1950, **40**, 26–39.

22. Harlow, H. F. Primate learning. In C. P. Stone (Ed.), *Comparative psychology.* (3d ed.) Englewood Cliffs, N.J.: Prentice-Hall, 1951.

23. Harlow, H. F. Thinking In H. Helson (Ed.), *Theoretical foundations of psychology.* New York: Van Nostrand, 1951.

24. Harlow, H. F. Mice, monkeys, men, and motives. *Psychol. Rev.*, 1953, **60**, 23–32.

25. Harlow, H. F. The evolution of learning. In G. G. Simpson & A. Roe (Eds.), *Behavior and evolution.* In press.

26. Harlow, H. F., & Hicks, L. H. Discrimination learning theory: uniprocess vs. dualprocess. *Psychol. Rev.*, 1957, **64**, 104–109.

27. Harlow, H. F., & Mason, W. A. Behavior of the infant monkey. In W. F. Windle (Ed.), *Neurological and psychological deficits of asphyxia neonatorum.* Springfield, Ill.: Charles C Thomas, 1958.

28. Harlow, H. F., & Warren, J. M. Formation and transfer of discrimination learning sets. *J. comp. physiol. Psychol.*, 1952, **45**, 482–489.

29. Hayes, K. J., Thompson, R., & Hayes, C. Discrimination learning sets in chimpanzees. *J. comp. physiol. Psychol.*, 1953, **46**, 99–104.

30. Hebb, D. O. *The organization of behavior.* New York: Wiley, 1949.

31. Hicks, L. H. An analysis of number-concept formation in the rhesus monkey. *J. comp. physiol. Psychol.*, 1956, **49**, 212–218.

32. Jarvik, M. E. Discrimination of colored food and food signs by primates. *J. comp. physiol. Psychol.*, 1953, **46**, 390–392.

33. Karn, H. W., & Munn, N. L. Visual pattern discrimination in the dog. *J. genet. Psychol.*, 1932, **40**, 363–374.

34. Keller, F. S., & Hill, L. M. Another "insight" experiment. *J. genet. Psychol.*, 1936, **48**, 484–489.

35. Kendler, T. S. An experimental investigation of transposition as a function of the difference between training and test stimuli. *J. exp. Psychol.*, 1950, **40**, 552–562.

36. Klüver, H. *Behavior mechanisms in monkeys.* Chicago: Univer. Chicago Press, 1933.

37. Köhler, W. *The mentality of apes.* New York: Harcourt, Brace, 1925.

38. Koronakos, C., & Arnold, W. J. The formation of learning sets in rats. *J. comp. physiol. Psychol.*, 1957, **50**, 11–14.

39. Krechevsky, I. "Hypothesis" versus "chance" in the pre-solution period in sensory discrimination learning. *Univer. Calif. Publ. Psychol.*, 1932, **6**, 27–44.

40. Kuenne, M. R. Experimental investigation of the relation of language to transposition behavior in young children. *J. exp. Psychol.*, 1946, **36**, 471–490.

41. Maier, N. R. F. Reasoning in rats and human beings. *Psychol. Rev.*, 1937, **44**, 365–378.

42. Matheson, E. A study of problem solving behavior in preschool children. *Child Develpm.*, 1931, **2**, 242–262.

43. Meyer, D. R. Food deprivation and discrimination reversal learning by monkeys. *J. exp. Psychol.*, 1951, **41**, 10–16.

44. Meyer, D. R. Some psychological determinants of sparing and loss following damage to the brain. In H. F. Harlow & C. N. Woolsey (Eds.), *Biological bases of behavior*. Madison, Wis.: Univer. Wis. Press, 1958.

45. Meyer, D. R., & Harlow, H. F. The development of transfer of response to patterning by monkeys. *J. comp. physiol. Psychol.*, 1949, **42**, 454–462.

46. Miles, R. C. Learning set formation in the squirrel monkey. *J. comp. physiol. Psychol.*, 1957, **50**, 356–357.

47. Miles, R. C., & Meyer, D. R. Learning sets in marmosets. *J. comp. physiol. Psychol.*, 1956, **49**, 219–222.

48. Miller, R. E., Murphy, J. V., & Finocchio, D. V. A consideration of the object-quality discrimination task as a dependent variable. *J. comp. physiol. Psychol.*, 1955, **48**, 29–31.

49. Moon, L. E., & Harlow, H. F. Analysis of oddity learning by rhesus monkeys. *J. comp. physiol Psychol.*, 1955, **48**, 188–195.

50. Moss, E., & Harlow, H. F. The role of reward in discrimination learning in monkeys. *J. comp. physiol. Psychol.*, 1947, **40**, 333–342.

51. Neet, C. C. Visual pattern discrimination in the Macacus rhesus monkey. *J. genet. Psychol.*, 1933, **43**, 163–196.

52. Nissen, H. W. Analysis of conditional reaction in chimpanzees. *J. comp. physiol. Psychol.*, 1951, **44**, 9–16.

53. Pavlov, I. P. *Conditioned reflexes: an investigation of the physiological activity of the cerebral cortex.* London: Oxford Univer. Press, 1927.

54. Penfield, W., & Erickson, T. C. *Epilepsy and cerebral localization: a study of the mechanism, treatment and prevention of epileptic seizures.* Springfield, Ill.: Charles C Thomas, 1941.

55. Pubols, B. H. The facilitation of visual and spatial discrimination reversal by overlearning. *J. comp. physiol. Psychol.*, 1956, **49**, 243–248.

56. Reid, L. S. The development of noncontinuity behavior through continuity learning. *J. exp. Psychol.*, 1953, **46**, 107–112.

57. Riopelle, A. J. Transfer suppression and learning sets. *J. comp. physiol. Psychol.*, 1953, **46**, 108–114.

58. Riopelle, A. J. Progressive discrimination learning in platyrrhine monkeys. *J. comp. physiol Psychol.*, 1958, **51**, 467–470.

59. Riopelle, A. J., Alper, R. G., Strong, P. N., & Ades, H. W. Multiple discrimination and patterned string performance of normal and temporal-lobectomized monkeys. *J. comp. physiol. Psychol.*, 1953, **46**, 145–149.

60. Roberts, K. E. Learning in preschool and orphanage children: an experimental study of ability to solve different situations according to the same plan. *Univ. Iowa Stud. Child Welf.*, 1933, **7**, No. 3 (Whole No. 251).

61. Schiller, P. H. Innate constituents of complex responses in primates. *Psychol. Rev.*, 1952, **59**, 177–191.

62. Schrier, A. M., & Harlow, H. F. Effect of amount of incentive on

discrimination learning by monkeys. *J. comp. physiol. Psychol.*, 1956, **49**, 117–122.

63. Smith, K. U. Visual discrimination in the cat: I. The capacity of the cat for visual figure discrimination. *J. genet. Psychol.*, 1934, **44**, 301–320.

64. Spence, K. W. The nature of discrimination learning in animals. *Psychol. Rev.*, 1936, **43**, 427–449.

65. Spence, K. W. Failure of transposition in size discrimination of chimpanzees. *Amer. J. Psychol.*, 1941, **54**, 223–229.

66. Spence, K. W. The basis of solution by chimpanzees of the intermediate size problem. *J. exp. Psychol.*, 1942, **31**, 257–271.

67. Tolman, E. C. *Purposive behavior in animals and men.* New York: Appleton-Century-Crofts, 1932.

68. Warren, J. M. Additivity of cues in visual pattern discriminations by monkeys. *J. comp. physiol. Psychol.*, 1953, **46**, 484–486.

69. Warren, J. M., & Baron, A. The formation of learning sets by cats. *J. comp. physiol. Psychol.*, 1956, **49**, 227–231.

70. Warren, J. M., & Harlow, H. F. Learned discrimination performance by monkeys after prolonged postoperative recovery from large cortical lesions. *J. comp. physiol. Psychol.*, 1952, **45**, 119–126.

71. Weinstein, B. The evolution of intelligent behavior in rhesus monkeys. *Genet. Psychol. Monogr.*, 1945, **31**, 3–48.

ROTE LEARNING

ARTHUR L. IRION
Tulane University

INTRODUCTION

In a sense, the reader of this chapter is confronted with an insoluble problem. He is being asked to follow an analysis of a system that does not exist, for, despite the fact that the earliest experiments in learning were concerned with rote learning, and despite the existence of the enormous amount of data that has been gathered in this rather limited learning situation, no comprehensive, systematic treatment of these data exists. Partly for this reason, and partly because the field of rote learning is idiosyncratic in other respects, the outline that is being used as a guide in many of the other papers in this series cannot be followed in detail.

The fact that systematic treatment of rote-learning data exists only in rudimentary form is rendered even more remarkable by the circumstance that the overwhelming majority of rote-learning experiments have followed, more or less closely, the tradition established by Ebbinghaus. Thus, the would-be systematizer has not been plagued with data gathered by experimenters holding to different systematic and presystematic viewpoints. What the systematic biases of those who did gather these data may have been, we shall have occasion to examine presently, and certainly no implication is intended that psychologists in general were in agreement with these points of view. It is sufficient to note here that, in general, the psychologists who held widely different systematic views from those of workers in the area of rote learning tended to reject the rote-learning situation altogether either as being artificial or as being less fruitful than other areas of learning experimentation. Their opinion that rote-learning data are relatively worthless has led them to investigate and to speculate about learning with reference to other learning situations, thereby leaving the bulk of rote-learning data to be gathered by those whose systematic leanings were more or less homogenous.

The field of rote learning, of course, is not entirely devoid of theory. The *Mathematico-deductive Theory of Rote Learning* of Hull and others [7] represents an attempt to bind together a considerable number of the independent and dependent variables of rote learning within a single systematic framework. Unfortunately, and perhaps because of the formidable nature of the theory, this work does not seem to have had a great deal of influence upon subsequent experimentation, and only a minute fraction of rote-learning experiments since 1940 have been squarely coordinated with the theory. On the other hand, if there has been a dearth of comprehensive systematizing in the field of rote learning, there has certainly been no shortage of special theories and limited hypotheses. This plethora of special hypotheses suggests that those who have worked in the field of rote learning have been concerned with the explanation of the results of particular experiments or small groups of experiments rather than with the incorporation of large amounts of data into a single framework.

There may be a reason for this. It is well known, of course, that there is a logic of science. It is, perhaps, less well understood that there is also a psychology of science and that psychologists, no less than other scientists, are subject to its laws. Such a psychology of science concerns itself with the ways in which scientists behave in their scientific endeavors, and we should not be surprised to find that their behavior does not always conform to the rules of the scientific game, that is, to the logic of science. For example, according to the logic of science, no theory can be maintained in the face of one single, well-established, contradictory fact. Conant [1] and others, however, have pointed out that scientists do not often reject a theory, particularly one that is well established, on this basis. Instead, theories tend to persist until more adequate ones are presented and, indeed, even under these circumstances, scientists have often seemed loath to discard some of their theoretical beliefs.

It is also true that a theory that appears to be removed from the historical context of the time of its emergence may die by neglect rather than by disproof. Hull's theory of rote learning [7] is an example of this phenomenon. It is entirely possible that, had this theory been advanced at the present time, it would have aroused a considerable amount of scientific activity among workers in the field of rote learning. Arriving on the scene too early, the theory has had virtually no impact upon the research in this area. This fact is one of the reasons why this theory will not be discussed in detail in this chapter.

Now in considering the psychology of science, it is apparent that one of the functions of a systematic formulation is to facilitate communication among research workers. Although this function of systems has been largely neglected, it is possible that this may be one of the chief reasons why systems are formulated and gain adherents. This factor may be particularly important in a young science in which the preconditions for realizing other goals of systematization (of the sort customarily emphasized in the logic of science) may not have been achieved. Thus, two students of Lewin can discuss their experimental work with relatively complete understanding by making reference to the concepts employed by Lewin, even though their words might need a considerable amount of translation if they were to be clearly comprehended by a student of Hull or Guthrie. It is significant to note, therefore, that those who have worked in the field of rote learning have typically "spoken the same language." In this way, they have fulfilled one of the functions of a system, and a very important one. It is possible that, once the communication function of a system is established by other means, the need for systematization becomes considerably less pressing. If true, this would account, at least in part, for the relative lack of systematic theory in the field of rote learning. There is another reason, and probably a more important one, for the lack of systematization, but we shall discuss this cause in a later section.

BACKGROUND FACTORS AND ORIENTING ATTITUDES

It is not always true that the person who first works in a particular research area continues to dominate the development of that kind of research for any great length of time. Concerning the influence of Ebbinghaus on the field of rote learning, however, there can be no doubt that his influence has been, and continues to be, profound. Twenty-five years after the publication of *Uber das Gedächtnis* [2], Titchener, a man who did not bestow indiscriminate praise upon the works of his colleagues, could make the following statement [15]:

Here, then, were pure perceptions, sights and sounds that had no meaning and no associates; here was material so varied and yet so simple, so rich and yet so uniform, that experiments could be made under laboratory conditions, and the results of one experiment could be compared, directly with the results of another.

It is not too much to say that the recourse to nonsense syllables, as a means to the study of association, marks the most considerable advance, in this chapter of psychology, since the time of Aristotle.

Thirty-two years later, or nearly sixty years after the appearance of Ebbinghaus's work, McGeoch began his *Psychology of Human Learning* [9] as follows:

Systematic experimental study of human learning dates from 1885, when Ebbinghaus stated some of its fundamental problems, devised methods for studying them, and in many ways set the pattern for later research. His monograph, *Memory: a contribution to experimental psychology* . . . , is a landmark in the history of psychology and is still a model which will repay careful study.

Today, seventy years after Ebbinghaus's initial work, the situation has not changed materially. Many of the fundamental problems that Ebbinghaus stated are still being investigated and Ebbinghaus's invention, the nonsense syllable, is still in widespread use, as are several of his methods of investigation. Of course, the apparently great influence of Ebbinghaus is enhanced by an artifact. We tend to count as rote-learning experiments only those that follow more or less closely the tradition Ebbinghaus created. Thus, the work of Thorndike might not be considered by some to be "pure" rote-learning experimentation. In the same way, many of the recent studies that employ rote-learning techniques to investigate problems that do not fall in the classical rote-learning tradition (the use of such techniques to study personality variables, for example) may be ignored by some individuals when they are considering the rote-learning literature. Nevertheless, it would be as foolish as it would be inaccurate to discount the influence of Ebbinghaus entirely. A brief inquiry into the systematic preferences of Ebbinghaus, therefore, would seem to be in order.

Ebbinghaus, whose work belongs to the latter part of the nineteenth century, could hardly have failed to have been strongly influenced by the British school of associationism and especially by the formulations of John Stuart Mill. In being influenced in this way, Ebbinghaus was certainly not alone among early German psychologists; in fact, one could make a fairly strong defense of the proposition that modern psychology was created by the synthesis of British associationism and German natural science. In a sense, the work of Ebbinghaus represents a fairly exact application of the doctrine of associationism to laboratory experimentation. The "ideas" of the associationists, into which mind was supposedly analyzable, became the nonsense syllables which formed the units of analysis for Ebbinghaus, and quite obviously, most of the "laws" of association propounded by the associationists became subject to experimental attack by means of the techniques that Ebbinghaus devised. Beyond this, it is possible that the temperament of Ebbinghaus himself may have been responsible for the way in which the field of rote learning developed. More so than many another of his contemporaries (or ours, for that matter), Ebbinghaus was committed to the empirical approach. Thus, in his free translation of Ebbinghaus's *Abriss der Psychologie* [3], Meyer [10] notes in the preface that he "became interested in this book because of the fact that the author has succeeded in keeping entirely free of all fads, and has presented only that which is generally accepted by psychological science. . . ." I shall not strain this point, but it is worth noting that the bulk of the work in rote learning has maintained this tradition, and indeed, this work has more than once been attacked because of its crass empiricism.

One other chain of circumstances that has determined the present status of research and theory in rote learning should also be mentioned. Learning research, in general, has exhibited a marked change of orientation in the comparatively recent past. The earlier experiments were largely exploratory in character, and although they frequently involved the systematic variation of variables, their usual purpose was to determine what the important conditions of learning might be. The later experiments tended to be crucial experiments that tested opposed theoretical predictions. Still more recently, experiments that systematically vary variables that are *theoretically* important have appeared. By the latter statement, I am referring to experiments that seek to determine the properties of intervening variables. Experiments, for example, that attempt to determine the functions of development of such intervening concepts as $_sH_R$, D, $_sO_R$, etc., fall within this classification. In such investigations, the intervening variables become, through a process of induction on the part of the experimenter, the dependent variables. This general shift of orientation appears to have taken place during the middle 1930's. Of course, a definite date cannot be set. There were certainly experiments before 1930 that were theoretically oriented, and in a sense, the shift in orientation is still going on. Nevertheless, the fact remains that there *has* been a change of orientation. The important thing, from the standpoint of this discussion, is that the shift of orientation in the field of rote learning has been much more gradual than has been the shift in other areas of learning research.

If we wish to understand why this should be so, we must keep in mind several facts. An examination of the experimental literature of rote learning reveals the fact that the overwhelming majority of authors have contributed but a single experiment to the literature. That these are frequently converted Ph.D. dissertations is something that we shall have to consider in a moment. If we plot number of authors against number of papers per author, a typical *J* function is obtained, so that the number of individuals who have contributed 10 or more papers to the literature of rote learning is exceedingly small. This means, of course, that at any one time the field of rote-learning research tends to be dominated by a handful of individuals. The same general phenomenon may be observed with respect to laboratories. In any given ten-year period, most active laboratories will produce one or two papers in the field of rote learning while a very few laboratories will be tremendously productive. If we examine the literature of rote-learning experimentation for the fifteen-year period immediately preceding the time when learning experiments began to shift toward a systematic, theoretical orientation (1920 to 1935), we can observe that a small number of persons and schools dominated the scene.

The University of Chicago, for instance, clearly led the field with respect to number of papers produced, and although most of these were of the one-paper-to-an-author variety, footnote credits as well as the nature of the experiments make it clear that the influence of such men as Carr and Robinson must have been considerable. It would be more difficult to select the individuals who exerted the greatest influence on the development of rote learning during this period, but Carr, McGeoch, and Robinson would unquestionably be among the first five or six individuals to be named in this respect. Thus, the general empirical biases of Chicago Functionalism were well represented. Those who knew John McGeoch, who was undoubtedly the most important single contributor to the rote-learning literature of his period, may have objected to certain aspects of his work, but I have never heard him criticized for spending a disproportionate amount of time and effort attempting to systematize large amounts of rote-learning data in a single, precise, theoretical framework.

It is also, perhaps, significant that there appears to have been a considerable amount of academic inbreeding among those who worked in the area of rote learning. McGeoch was a student at Chicago in the days of Carr and Robinson. Melton was a student of McGeoch's at Washington, then was with Robinson at Yale, and later returned to succeed McGeoch as head of the department at the University of Missouri, which was, in the days of McGeoch and Melton, one of the important centers of rote-learning research. Bunch, of course, was a student at Chicago in the days of Carr. Hovland was at Yale in the days of Robinson, although in this case the influence of Hull is clearly discernible. Underwood studied under Melton at Missouri and McGeoch at Iowa and has since become one of the major contributors to this area of research. Unquestionably, the preceding few sentences present an oversimplification of the setting in which rote-learning research has been accomplished. Nevertheless, it is instructive to note that approximately 40 per cent of the rote-learning studies published in the *Journal of Experimental Psychology* during the five years from 1949 through 1954 were written by students of Carr, McGeoch, or Melton.

SOME CHARACTERISTIC PROBLEMS AND THEORIES

In the field of rote learning, a relatively small number of phenomena has received the bulk of research attention, and in each case, one or more relatively cogent hypotheses have been advanced. Before turning our attention to these subjects, however, a word should be said about three problems that underlie most of the research in rote learning.

The problem of the unit of material to be learned. One assumption has been made, more or less implicitly, from the time of the earliest research down to the present day. This assumption is that, for purposes of experimental design and (sometimes) analysis of the data, the proper unit of the material to be learned is the individual item (or, in the case of paired-associate learning, the pair of items) in the list to be learned. Stated in another way, the assumption is that the characteristics of a list are determined in a relatively simple way by the characteristics of the individual items making up the list. It was on the basis of this assumption that much of the work on the calibration of materials by Glaze [4] and others [5, 20] was undertaken. The assumption is a natural one to have made considering the heritage of classical associationistic thought and the nature of the materials themselves—the materials being lists composed of discrete items or pairs of items.

The matter is not so simple, however, for there is a considerable amount of evidence to indicate that, at least under certain circumstances, the organization of the list as a whole determines the characteristics of the individual item. This is another example of a familiar problem, the neglect of possible interaction effects. There are numerous suggestions in the published literature that such interaction effects exist. Perhaps the most striking demonstration of these effects was obtained by Hall [6]. In a preliminary experiment, Hall scaled nonsense syllables with respect to difficulty by the method of having subjects learn them. She then constructed two lists of six items each, one list being homogeneous with respect to difficulty but composed of easy items; the other list also being homogeneous with respect to difficulty but composed of difficult items. She then ran four groups of subjects. The first group learned the entire easy list. The second group learned the entire difficult list. The third group, however, learned the easy list from which the last item had been deleted and the corresponding item from the difficult list substituted for it. Finally the fourth group learned the difficult list from which the last item had been deleted and the corresponding item from the easy list substituted for it. Difficulty of the terminal item in each condition was determined by computing the mean number of trials required for *that item* to be given correctly. What was found was that the difficulty of the terminal item was determined very largely by the over-all difficulty of the list in which it was embedded. The easy terminal item in the difficult list was much more difficult to learn than was the same syllable in the easy list. Similarly, the difficult item when presented in the easy list became almost as easy to learn as the original easy item had been.

The problem of the well-practiced subject. This problem also concerns itself with the neglect of possible interaction effects. The typical rote-learning experiment is designed somewhat as follows: let us assume that the experimenter wishes to determine the relative effects of four interpolated activities in determining amount of retroactive inhibition. He assembles a group of subjects, gives each subject one or more practice sessions to familiarize him with general rote-learning procedures, and then administers each condition of the experiment to each subject. Usually, the order in which each subject is given the various experimental treatments is determined by a counter-balanced practice order. In its simplest form, the counterbalanced practice order merely ensures that each condition occurs equally often in each order. More elaborate counterbalancing procedures demand, in addition, that each condition precede and follow each other condition an equal number of times. The inadequacy of such a procedure should have been recognized as soon as Ward's [17] data, showing that the curve of learning to learn is not linear, became available.

In addition, there is the further difficulty that there may be an interaction effect between the effects of a particular independent variable and the order in which it occurs. Moreover, it is frequently impossible to determine whether or not such an interaction effect exists. For example, some years ago Lee Thune and I had an opportunity to go over the data of an experiment in which it was possible to analyze the interaction of state of practice with the dependent variable which was, in this case, retroactive inhibition. The conclusion of the experiment for the pooled results was quite valid. One of the several conditions *did* produce more retroactive inhibition than any of the others. However, this effect was concentrated in the earlier stages of the counterbalanced practice order. When that condition was analyzed for the *last* day of the experiment, retroactive facilitation rather than retroactive inhibition was discovered. Fortunately, there is some indication that rote-learning experimenters are beginning to abandon this type of procedure, although it would not be difficult to find numerous examples of the use of counterbalancing procedures in the contemporary literature. The use of subjects in several conditions does have advantages, of course. Within subjects, variability is probably reduced, particularly if several practice sessions are given. That is to say, the subjects in each condition are automatically "matched" with respect to ability. Finally, and perhaps most importantly, a large total number of subjects is not needed. Nevertheless, in the opinion of this writer, the use of counterbalancing procedures is basically unsound unless it is known that order and the effects of the independent variables do not interact. In any event, experimenters should design their experiments so that this interaction effect, if it exists, can be determined. This goal can be accomplished, of course, by designing the experiment so that a sufficient number of replications of each order of counterbalancing exists to make such an analysis possible.

The problem of standardizing conditions. Earlier, in our discussion of the reasons why workers in the field of rote learning have produced so little in the way of comprehensive and systematic theory, we said that there was an additional reason for this lack of systematic theory. This reason is that the workers in this field have not had very many systematic data with which to work.

Of the thousands of studies that have been conducted on rote learning, it would be difficult to find more than a handful that have been conducted under comparable conditions. The same experimenter will often vary his technique of experimentation between successive experiments, and if the variability of technique within experimenters is considerable, the variability of technique among experimenters is enormous. True, most of the experiments of, let us say, McGeoch tend to resemble the other experiments of McGeoch with respect to methodology more than they resemble the experiments of Underwood or Hovland. It is also true that there are isolated bodies of experiments in which the data have been gathered under conditions that are as comparable as conditions can be made to be. But these are exceptions. Generally, each experimenter determines the conditions under which practice in his experiment is to be conducted, with little attention being paid to the techniques employed by other investigators working in the same area.

Some of these variations of technique are inevitable and some may be of little consequence. Since we have no aptitude tests for the abilities involved in rote learning, this must remain an uncontrolled factor, and these abilities probably vary from one laboratory to another. Frequently, because of practical considerations, an experimenter must use a particular piece of equipment rather than one he would prefer to use. It would be difficult for an experimenter working in Florida to reproduce the temperature and humidity conditions of an experimenter working in Colorado. Between investigators there are bound to be differences in amount of experience and degree of technical skill. Such differences are unavoidable, and it is possible that many such variables have little effect upon the results of experimentation, although there can be no doubt that, in combination, they contribute to the variability of results between experiments. But most procedural variations between experiments are not of this unavoidable type. They result from the whimsy of individual investigators and most of them are as unnecessary as they are inexcusable. Furthermore, many of these variations in procedures concern variables known to be important in determining performance. The most casual review of the literature will reveal an astonishing number of methodological variations, a few of which are listed below.

1. Different experimenters give different instructions to their subjects, even when dealing with almost identical learning situations.

2. Some experimenters give their subjects practice in rote learning before the beginning of the experiment; others do not. In the case of the former group, there is variation in the amount of pretraining that is given.

3. Some experimenters use a counterbalancing technique; others use the "one shot" approach. There are also variations in the techniques used for counterbalancing.

4. Usually, the specific materials learned by the subjects are not published. More frequently, the reader is told that the words or syllables were taken from somebody's collection of materials and that they have a certain mean association value. There has been relatively little work done in the calibration of rote-learning materials. However, as might be expected, there has been a considerable amount of variation in the methods of calibration employed by those who have worked in this important field. The result of this state of affairs is that only rarely do we find two experimenters who have used exactly the same set of materials. More usually different experimenters, working on the same general problem, use lists that differ in length and difficulty as well as in the specific items making up the list.

5. Although the 2-sec rate of presentation has been fairly well established as a standard rate, variations in rate of presentation can be found.

6. Different experimenters use different intertrial intervals.

7. Different investigators fill short retention intervals in different ways.

8. In the learning of nonsense syllables, some experimenters require their subjects to spell the syllables whereas others require them to pronounce them.

These are but examples. However, if one takes any two papers on the same subject but prepared by different investigators, one is likely to find that the experimental procedures have differed in several (if not in all) of these ways. Under such circumstances, construction of a precise quantitative theory is almost impossible. Even the *generality* of any lawful relationship obtained under such circumstances must be indeterminate and unspecifiable.

The point is not that a list of nonsense syllables used by Thune is better than a list used by Archer, or that one person's set of instructions is necessarily better than the set of instructions used by someone else. The point is that gratuitous variation of practically every circumstance under which learning occurs, and this without plan or design, has made it impossible to compare results from different experiments that should be, at least roughly, comparable.

This situation exists in most other areas of psychology, of course, although this fact does not particularly help the situation in the field of rote learning. There is no standard T maze, no standard Skinner box, no standard jumping stand. Amounts, kinds, and frequencies of reinforcement differ from one animal experiment to another. It is often argued that standardization of conditions would restrict the experimenter; that it would let him do only particular kinds of things. The truth is that standardization would increase the scope of his activities, for it would permit him to rely upon previously obtained experimental results with much more confidence than he is able to rely upon such results at the present time. The argument is not that an experimenter should be prevented from using any variable that he thinks is relevant as an independent variable. The argument is that he should do this within a standard frame of reference and that he should depart from that frame of reference by intention rather than by whimsy.

I feel that perhaps it is time for those who are primarily interested in rote learning, and there are not too many of them, to get together and decide, arbitrarily if necessary, upon a set of standard conditions. In the case of most of the variables I have listed, it should not be difficult for them to reach agreement. The calibration of lists presents the thorniest problem. In order to do the job properly, a great amount of very tedious and unglamorous work would be required. Still, on the basis of calibrations of materials that now exist, it would not be difficult to prepare a group of lists, each list being designated by a code number. There would have to be several lists, each of several lengths and levels of difficulty. Moreover, there would have to be pairs of lists varying in length, difficulty, and similarity. There would have to be paired-associate lists as well as serial lists; and in all cases, lists of nonsense syllables, consonant syllables, nouns, and adjectives should be constructed. Fortunately, a great deal of this work has already been done. What is needed is the arbitrary designation of the lists that already exist. Furthermore, experimenters should not be given absolute freedom to use any list they choose from among the collection of lists. For example, agreement might be reached that experimenters wishing to work on the serial anticipation learning of nonsense syllables would work with a 10-item list taken from the 50 per cent association value group of lists. If such agreement could be reached, and if a report could be published, it would be a considerable aid to scientific communication. Furthermore, editors of journals could be enjoined, and, I feel, with considerable success, to reject papers that did not conform to the standard conditions of experimentation.

This is not to say, of course, that experimenters should not vary length of list, intertrial interval, the instructions to the subjects, and all the other variables that might be listed. To require this would be to reduce rote-learning research to the endless repetition of a single experiment, the experiment of the standard condition. What *is* implied is that if an experimenter wishes to determine the effects of intertrial interval upon learning or retention or reminiscence, he should not also use original instructions, a nonstandard rate of presentation, and a list of dubious ancestry. It would also be perfectly legitimate to vary two or more variables using a more complicated experimental design. Indeed, it would be very desirable to do so, for in this way possible interaction effects might be discovered. But, always, research should be conducted within the frame of reference established by the set of standard experimental procedures. In a perfect world, it would be very desirable if the specific standard conditions could be established empirically. However, the arbitrary designation of a set of standard conditions would represent a tremendous scientific advance. There can be no doubt that this is one of the most pressing problems of contemporary research in the area of rote learning.

A TYPICAL PROBLEM AND SOME OF THE THEORIES RELATING TO IT

It is clearly impossible to discuss all the problems with which workers in the field of rote learning have dealt. Such problems as serial position effects, transfer phenomena, remote associations, and retroactive and proactive inhibition come immediately to mind. To discuss them all would require the writing of a book rather than a paper. In view of this fact, I have selected one phenomenon, the effects of distributing practice. This includes, of course, the special case of reminiscence. It is not that distribution of practice is more important than many of the other problems that might be considered. Rather, in a discussion of distribution of practice and the theories that have been advanced to explain the data that have been gathered in this area, we are considering an area of study that may be considered to be a typical example. What may be said of distribution of practice might also be said about most other areas of rote-learning research.

The phenomena relating to distribution of practice are well known and there is no need to review them here. It should be sufficient to note the general fact that the introduction of rest periods into a series of practice sessions tends to increase the efficiency of acquisition and that, in general, the longer the rests, the more the improvement in performance. Naturally, there must be an optimal length of rest for any given type of task. Similarly, it is a fairly general finding that the amount of practice between rests is important, shorter practice periods between rests being more effective than longer ones. Again, we should expect that there is an optimal length of practice period for a given task and for a given length of the interpolated rest periods. Thus, in learning a list of 12 nonsense syllables, if one trial is given every two years, this pattern of distribution would probably not be as effective as massed practice, trial for trial. It certainly would not be as effective as massed practice in terms of the total time required to learn the list. Our primary concern here, however, is not to review the literature on distribution of practice, but, rather, to consider the theoretical approaches that have been made in an attempt to explain the phenomena of distribution.

Concerning the classification of theories. A considerable amount has been said in recent years about the classification of theories. We have classified theories as being either S-R or R-R theories, as being behavioral or physiological, molar or molecular, or reinforcement rather than non-reinforcement in orientation. Everyone is familiar with these distinctions and there is no need to go into a detailed description of them. We shall, however, examine rote-learning theories in the light of these classifications. Before doing this, there is one more classificatory distinction that should be made because it is applicable to most of the theories that have been advanced in the field of rote learning. This is the distinction between theories that are vague and those that are precise in terms of prediction. Vague theories never die, nor do they usually fade away. This is because they are very nearly incapable of being disproved. Consider, for example, the classical perseveration theory as it applies to reminiscence and distribution phenomena. The only predictions that can be made on the basis of this theory are that performance will be better shortly after the end of practice than it was at the end of practice and that distributed practice will be more effective, trial for trial, than will be massed practice. No other specific predictions are made. Of course, there is a body of data concerning a host of the variables upon which distribution effects and reminiscence depend. These, however, can be incorporated into the theory by verbal fiat, since it is merely necessary to explain any specific datum by saying that this is the way in which perseveration operates. Precise theories are much more vulnerable. If specific predictions are made concerning, let us say, the exact time that reminiscence reaches its maximum following a specified amount and kind of practice on a particular task, then the theory must be very nearly correct. With even a slight inaccuracy of prediction, it is only necessary for an experimenter to run a sufficient number of subjects to demonstrate that the divergence between prediction and data is too large to be accounted for by errors of measurement for the theory to be discredited. Thus, however much we may yearn for precise, quantitative theories, such theories tend to die young. Vague theories march on through the years and are eventually abandoned (usually to be resurrected once again) only because people are bored with them or because some more attractive hypotheses have been advanced.

Of course, it goes without saying that a theory need not be quantitative in order to be precise. Most precise theories are quantitative, but a qualitative theory that makes definitive predictions cannot be classed as vague. For instance, a theory that predicts that one individual would suffer from schizophrenia during his lifetime whereas another would not could scarcely be called a quantitative theory, yet it would not be vague in its predictions. The accuracy of the theoretical prediction is, of course, beside the point. The prediction is made, and in terms of the prediction, the theory can be tested.

One further word should be said about rote-learning theory. Practically no attempt has been made to set forth physiologically oriented theory in this area. To be sure, the perseveration theory that we mentioned a moment ago has the sound of physiological explanation. Similarly, Hull et al. [7] have used such concepts as the stimulus trace. It is also true that individuals working within the framework of information theory have appealed to a physiological model, but it would probably be more correct to say that some physiologists have appealed to an information theory model. For example, the work of von Förster [16] on memory uses the formal model of quantum theory and relates this, somewhat vaguely, to physiological theory. Actually, however, these theories could exist as behavioral theories without carrying an additional cargo of physiological speculation. The reason for this lack of physiologizing is, of course, that so little is known of the neurophysiology of learning that theories are behavioral out of necessity even though some of them use a terminology that smacks of physiology.

As to the status of rote-learning theories with respect to the classifications of theories mentioned earlier, it must be noted that almost all rote-learning theorizing has been done in the framework of S-R concepts. This undoubtedly arises from the fact that the materials used in rote-learning research lend themselves so well to this type of analysis. The question as to whether rote-learning theories have tended to be molar or molecular is more difficult to answer. In order to answer the question, some definition must be given to the terms molar and molecular. It is true that most rote-learning theories, in so far as they use any unit of analysis at all, tend to use the individual item in the list as the unit. To this extent they tend to be molecular. Indeed, such theories have frequently been criticized as being too atomistic. Some of this criticism may be justified. It is true that any given list of nonsense syllables or other verbal material is likely to have some sort of organization within itself. It is also true that the individual learner organizes the material that is presented to him. Both of these factors may be important in determining the individual's response to a particular item. On the other hand, it would be unfair to accuse the workers in this field of being blind to these problems. The literature concerning serial position effects, for example, (and it is a large literature) represents an attempt to study intraserial organization. The same thing may be said for much of the work on remote associations or transfer of training. But does analysis at the level of the individual nonsense syllable constitute atomism? No theories have been advanced that considered rote learning in terms of the movements made when the individual syllables were pronounced or concerning the nerve impulses that give rise to these movements. On the whole, however, it must be conceded that rote-learning theory is approximately as molecular as our knowledge and experimental techniques will permit it to be.

As far as the reinforcement issue is concerned, the issue is confused. There have been nonreinforcement theorists who have worked in the area of rote learning. However, it is probably safe to say that the majority of workers in this area, at least in recent times, have subscribed to some kind of reinforcement principle. The difficulty is that almost no work has been done in which amount, kind, and delay of reinforcement have been the independent variables. Those who subscribe to the reinforcement position tend to feel that rewards are "built in" to the rote-learning situation. This is usually rationalized by an appeal to the somewhat vague notion of knowledge of results. Not nearly enough is known about knowledge of results and its effects upon learning, and unfortunately, the classical rote-learning situation is one in which the systematic manipulation of this variable is extremely awkward. As a result of this situation, a considerable amount of lip service has been paid to reinforcement principles, but little theoretical or experimental work has been done on this problem.

From what has already been said, it should be apparent that the great majority of rote-learning theories have been delightfully vague and that, as a result of this fact, many of them are hoary with age.

With respect to specific theories of reminiscence and the distribution of practice, these theories tend to fall into three main groups. Within each group except one there are several more or less independent hypotheses.

Work theories. The first group of theories may be termed work theories. The general notion is that practice, although serving to strengthen habits, also produces some negative state that interferes with performance. With rest, this negative condition, always postulated to be more transitory than habit, tends to dissipate and performance is improved. In simple language, this is the fatigue theory. Some years ago, however, psychologists decided that *fatigue* was not a nice word to use, and as a result of this decision, a number of more or less synonymous terms have been coined. Thus, unfashionable though it may be to talk about fatigue, it is perfectly proper to talk about reactive inhibition. Of course, the definition of reactive inhibition as given by Hull [8] comes about as close as one could wish to being an excellent working definition of fatigue considered as an intervening variable. The concept of reactive inhibition does have one advantage over the older concept of fatigue. It opens the door to quantification. Perhaps it would be more precise to say that it unlocks the door in view of the fact that no one has attempted to apply the concept to rote-learning data in any strict sense. Even in the areas for which the concept of I_R was designed, the concept has proved to be cumbersome and somewhat confused. In the field of rote learning, the difficulties are even greater. The principal difficulty lies in the extreme difficulty of obtaining a measure of the amount of work done in making rote-learning responses.

Work theories break down into several hypotheses concerning the way in which work accomplishes its negative effect. These hypotheses vary according to the theoretical predilections of their formulators. In few instances do the several hypotheses yield different predictions. This is partly because most of the work theories make very vague predictions and partly because different hypotheses employ the same independent variables to predict the same dependent variables, but use a different name for the mediating cause or intervening variable. For example, both the fatigue theory and the motivation theory can predict the same events. In one case, it is maintained that the individual, having performed a certain amount of work during practice, becomes fatigued and that, as a consequence, his efficiency is impaired. The motivation theory would hold that the individual, having performed a certain amount of work during practice, loses motivation to continue and that this loss of motivation, in turn, depresses the efficiency of his performance. In each case, presumably, the individual will accumulate fatigue or suffer from decreased motivation in proportion to the amount of work done, and he will recover from these negative states in proportion to amount of rest given. Much the same thing can be said for a stimulus saturation type of hypothesis. The classical example of such a hypothesis is contained in Pavlov's [13] concept of internal inhibition. Internal inhibition supposedly builds up through the presentation of stimuli rather than through the making of responses. However, since the presentation of the conditioned stimulus is often followed by the making of a response, the work factor is confounded with the stimulation factor, at least in part. A possible crucial experiment would consist of having the subjects participate in rote learning under conditions of massed and distributed trials and also under circumstances in which it would be impossible to respond (as under the influence of curare). Following a standard number of trials of practice, a delayed retention test could be given.

It will be noted that all the work theories employ two theoretical variables in order to explain the phenomena of distribution of practice and of reminiscence. One of these variables is positive with respect to performance and is usually termed habit strength or excitatory potential or something that resembles these terms closely. This variable is considered to be relatively permanent in the sense that it does not dissipate rapidly in time. The other variable is negative with respect to performance. As we have seen, the negative variable may have a number of different names. The negative variable is held to be relatively transitory. Usually, it is held that the positive and negative variables interact by simple subtraction.

The weakness of a theory that employs two opposed theoretical variables is obvious. Unless the operations that define the independent variables are tied to the theoretical variables specifically and in detail and unless the theoretical variables are related specifically to the measurement of the dependent variables, the theoretician can "explain" almost any experimental finding by manipulating the supposed values of the intervening variables. Under these circumstances, however, he is unable to predict his results in advance.

An analogy might prove helpful in connection with this point. If a railroad car is shunted onto a straight level siding, it should be possible to predict with some precision how far the car will roll before it comes to rest. In order to make this prediction, we would have to know the mass of the car, its initial velocity, and certain factors that would enable us to compute the amount of rolling friction. Again, we have two theoretical variables, momentum and friction. Again, the latter variable detracts from the former. Now, if we were in the position of the rote-learning theorist, we would not know how to compute momentum nor would we be able to estimate the amount of friction in the system. As a result of this state of affairs we could explain any result. If the car did not roll as far as anticipated, we could explain this by saying that there was high friction or low momentum or both. It is apparent that an infinite number of combinations of numbers representing the two variables could be devised, any one of which would "explain" perfectly why the car rolled a certain distance and no farther. It is also apparent that, under such circumstances, prediction would be haphazard.

The argument that is being advanced does not apply only to work theories of the distribution phenomena or to rote-learning theory in general. It has been a favorite device of a great many psychological theorists in many areas to set up a pair of opposed theoretical variables (without defining their characteristics specifically, of course). Once this is done any result can be "explained" after it has been obtained, but preexperimental prediction is nearly impossible. Many examples of this type of theorizing come immediately to mind. Positive and negative valences (combined with barriers), unless they are defined in precise detail, can explain almost anything—after it has happened. Many of the Freudian explanations suffer from the same flaw. These other inadequacies of psychological theory, of course, do not excuse the existence of the same flaws in rote-learning theory.

The differential forgetting theory. In some ways the differential forgetting theory resembles the work theories we have already discussed, at least in a formal sense. Because different theoretical concepts are used, however, this similarity may escape notice. Nevertheless, again we are dealing with a theory that postulates two factors, one positive and one negative. It is true that, in the case of the differential forgetting theory, the two theoretical variables are of the same nature. Briefly, the differential forgetting theory holds that, during practice, two sets of habits are acquired. One set represents the correct responses. The other set represents incorrect responses that presumably interfere with the execution of the correct responses. It is further held that the incorrect habitual responses are, on the average, weaker than the correct habitual responses. If one then assumes that weak habits are forgotten at a faster *rate* than strong habits, one could deduce that after a short rest interval, a net benefit should accrue to the strong habits. It should be noted that this is precisely the same mechanism of prediction employed by the work theories. One theoretical variable (the strong correct responses) tends to resist the ravages of time. The other variable (the weak incorrect responses) tends to dissipate in time.

It should be emphasized that there are no "pure" measures of the strengths of either the correct or the incorrect habits. It has been suggested that overt errors might prove to be a reliable index of the strength of the incorrect habits, but the use of this measure rests upon the assumption that the number of overt errors (a known quantity) is related to the total incorrect habits' strength in a fixed ratio, regardless of the stage of practice. Quite apart from the fact that we have no way of arriving at a reasonable value for the fixed ratio, it is extremely doubtful that such an invariant relationship exists. For example, if an individual is able to recite a 12-unit list of nonsense syllables perfectly on a single trial there are, of course, no overt errors on that trial. It would be foolish, however, to conclude that intraserial interference had been reduced to zero. About the best that can be done is to demonstrate that, in the learning of whole lists, those lists that are given more practice or are learned to a higher performance criterion tend to be forgotten less rapidly than those lists that are less well learned. This would, to some extent, demonstrate the reasonableness of the theory. On the other hand, it should not be forgotten that, in following this procedure, the measurements are very gross and the results of such experiments contain the effects of forgetting of the incorrect, interfering responses as well as the forgetting of the correct responses.

We have talked about the dissipation of strong and weak habits in time, and in a sense this was proper since, in distribution experiments, time is one of the independent variables. However, if one holds to an interference theory of forgetting, an interesting prediction can be made. If one combines an interference theory of forgetting with the differential forgetting theory of distribution effects, one has to conclude that, during the rest periods, the subjects learn (informally) material that interferes with both the strong, correct habits and the weak, incorrect habits. Furthermore, one would have to conclude that the interference affects these two sets of habits differentially. If this is the case, it should be possible to enhance distribution effects by introducing minute amounts of interpolated material designed to cause interference during the rest periods. By increasing the amount and similarity of the interpolated material, of course, this trend should be reversed and distribution (with interpolated learning in the rests) should be less effective than continuous practice.

The perseveration theories. In contrast to the "two-factor" theories we have discussed above, perseveration theories use but a single theoretical variable. In all these theories the general notion is that practice (or stimulation) sets in motion learning processes that continue after formal practice has ended. As is true of work theories, the perseveration theories do not differ sharply among themselves with respect to their formal characteristics although there may be considerable differences in terminology. Here is the fundamental question: are we to consider distribution effects to be a result of the interaction of two theoretical variables, or will one theoretical variable suffice to illuminate the data?

The clearest example of a perseveration theory is the rehearsal theory.

At a naïve level, what is implied is that the subject employs the rest intervals in a distribution experiment to rehearse the material to which he has been exposed. Again, at a naïve level the rehearsal theory is usually differentiated from the classical perseveration theory of Müller and Pilzecker [11] on the basis of whether or not the subject *intended* to rehearse or whether or not the rehearsal was *conscious*. These distinctions imply an involvement with the mind-body problem which we cannot and, indeed, should not, discuss here. Needless to say, the distinctions are not mutually exclusive. A person may be aware, i.e., be able to verbalize, that the learning materials have been subvocally rehearsed during the rest intervals, but he may be completely unaware of a verbalized intention to rehearse them. Some of the most frequently heard, and hence the most banal, singing commercials may be whistled or subvocally sung by an individual for hours at a time even though he earnestly desires to put those particular sequences of tones from his existence forever. Similarly, it is possible that inarticulate rehearsal occurs, the individual being able to verbalize neither his intentions nor the fact of his rehearsal. In other words, the distinctions between classical perseveration theory and rehearsal theory are probably misleading.

At the same time it should be pointed out that psychologists have spent a great deal of time and have exercised a considerable amount of ingenuity in order to prevent rehearsal (and, hence, perseveration) from taking place during the rest intervals of distribution experiments. These efforts to control the effects of rehearsal and perseveration, incidentally, may very possibly have introduced more variability into the data than would have been the case if no such control had been attempted. It is interesting to note, however, that little has been done to determine what the effects of rehearsal (considered as an independent variable) might be. The almost universal assumption has been that rehearsal during the rest periods would enhance postrest performance. The results obtained by Rohrer [14], who instructed his subjects to rehearse during the rest period, certainly do not support this assumption.[1] If rehearsal, as a form of perseveration, has any effect upon post-rehearsal performance, it should be possible to treat rehearsal as an independent variable and to determine how rehearsal relates to other variables in the

---

[1] Some years ago G. R. Grice, J. Kling, and I performed an experiment that was intended to expand Rohrer's findings. The data have never been published owing to the fact that the randomly selected groups did not seem to be reasonably well matched with respect to rote-learning ability. However, the data suggest quite strongly that, if subjects are instructed to rehearse during a rest interval introduced early in practice, rehearsal is beneficial to subsequent performance. If rehearsal is introduced after a moderate degree of practice, rehearsal appears to have little effect. Late in practice, the data suggest that rehearsal may cause a decrement in subsequent performance.

determination of learning performance. Far too little work has been done on this important topic.

In addition to the classical perseveration theory and the rehearsal theory, the stimulus-maturation hypothesis should also be mentioned. This theory, proposed by Wheeler [18] and Wheeler and Perkins [19], clearly belongs with perseveration theories. According to the stimulus-maturation hypothesis, learning is a form of maturation or growth, dependent upon stimulation, but relatively independent of the rate of stimulation. If enough initial practice is given to initiate this growth, presumably the growth will continue without additional stimulation. This implies that performance will be closely related to the amount of time that has elapsed since the beginning of practice but that performance will not be closely related to the number of trials. There are obvious limits to this concept of perseverating growth, although these limits have not been spelled out in the theory. It is apparent that practice can be so widely spaced that little or no learning takes place. On the other hand, we have ample evidence to support the view that moderate distribution enhances performance. These facts make it necessary to add to the theory (if it is to be stated in specific form) a statement as to the amount of time the growth process will continue to operate following stimulation. If the stimulus-maturation hypothesis is considered in this way, it is at once placed on the same basis as other perseveration theories. That is, something continues after practice has ended to produce increments in performance. This continuing process operates for a certain period of time and then stops, unless additional practice is given. Wheeler prefers to refer to this continuing process as growth or maturation. Others have preferred to speak in terms of the perseveration of the neurophysiological processes that underlie learning. Still others have preferred to speak of rehearsal. In terms of a behavioral formulation, all are saying the same thing while using different words.

A FINAL WORD

Except for the *Mathematico-deductive Theory of Rote Learning,* little has been produced in the way of comprehensive systematic theory in the field of rote learning. A tremendous quantity of data exists however. Most of these data are subsumed under various hypotheses that were designed to cover only a limited range of phenomena. Within each area of rote-learning research (such as transfer, serial phenomena, reminiscence, etc.), we usually find several different special hypotheses. More frequently than not, these differ with respect to their terminology to a greater extent than they do to their formal characteristics. Quantitative theory is virtually nonexistent.

One reason for the lack of quantitative theory is that the independent variables have never been properly scaled and dimensionalized. Perhaps there is no way in which this can be accomplished. Perhaps we shall never have units comparable to the meter, gram, and second against which our independent variables can be plotted. However, an attempt at scaling the important variables could be made. Little has been accomplished in this area. Another reason we have already mentioned: the fact that no set of standardized conditions has ever been devised for the research that is being done in this area.

What does the future hold? I feel that it is safe to say that experiments in the field of rote learning will continue to appear in our journals. The frequency of such experiments will probably decrease relative to the frequency of experiments in other areas of learning experimentation. In addition, I feel that the time is propitious for some people who are interested in this area to attempt to review the enormous amount of information that has been gathered and to attempt to incorporate large amounts of these data within a single theoretical framework. Some of this work has already been undertaken. Osgood's [12] attempt to cast data on transfer of training into a single system is an example of this type of activity. Unfortunately, in this instance, Osgood was hampered by the fact that neither of the two independent variables he employed could be quantified in any very meaningful way. This, of course, leaves the shape of the transfer surface which he drew somewhat indeterminate. Nevertheless, further attempts of this sort should be made. Finally, and above all, there is a desperate need for standardization of conditions. With standardization, quantification of our data and our theories becomes a potentiality. Without standardization, the present state of relative chaos is likely to continue for an indefinite period.

REFERENCES

1. Conant, J. B. *On understanding science.* New Haven, Conn.: Yale Univer. Press, 1947.
2. Ebbinghaus, H. *Uber das Gedächtnis: Untersuchungen zur experimentellen Psychologie.* Leipzig: Duncker and Humblot, 1885.
3. Ebbinghaus, H. *Abriss der Psychologie.* Leipzig: Veit & Co., 1908.
4. Glaze, J. A. The association values of non-sense syllables. *J. genet. Psychol.,* 1928, **35**, 255–267.
5. Haagen, C. H. Synonymity, vividness, familiarity, and association value ratings of 400 pairs of common adjectives. *J. Psychol.,* 1949, **27**, 453–463.
6. Hall, V. P. Interaction of list and item difficulty in rote-serial learning. Unpublished master's thesis, Univ. of Illinois, 1950.
7. Hull, C. L., et al. *Mathematico-deductive theory of rote learning:*

a study in scientific methodology. New Haven, Conn.: Yale Univer. Press, 1940.

8. Hull, C. L. *Principles of behavior.* New York: Appleton-Century-Crofts, 1943.

9. McGeoch, J. A. *The psychology of human learning: an introduction.* New York: Longmans, Green, 1942.

10. Meyer, M. *Ebbinghaus' psychology.* Boston: Heath, 1910.

11. Müller, G. E., & Pilzecker, A. Experimentelle Beiträge zur Lehre vom Gedächtniss. *Z. Psychol.,* 1900, Ergbd. 1.

12. Osgood, C. E. The similarity paradox in human learning: a resolution. *Psychol. Rev.,* 1949, 56, 132–143.

13. Pavlov, I. P. *Conditioned reflexes.* G. V. Anrep. (Trans.) London: Oxford Univer. Press, 1927.

14. Rohrer, J. H. Factors influencing the occurrence of reminiscence: attempted formal rehearsal during the interpolated period. *J. exp. Psychol.,* 1949, 39, 484–491.

15. Titchener, E. B. *A text-book of psychology.* New York: Macmillan, 1910.

16. Von Förster, H. *Das Gedächtnis: eine quantenphysikalische Untersuchung.* Vienna: Franz Deuticke, 1948.

17. Ward, L. B. Reminiscence and rote learning. *Psychol. Monogr.,* 1937, 49, No. 220.

18. Wheeler, R. H. *The science of psychology: an introductory study.* New York: Crowell, 1929.

19. Wheeler, R. H., & Perkins, F. T. *Principles of mental development: a text-book in educational psychology.* New York: Crowell, 1932.

20. Witmer, L. R. The association value of three-place consonant syllables. *J. genet. Psychol.,* 1935, 47, 337–359.

SOME RECENT TRENDS IN ETHOLOGY

R. A. HINDE

Field Station for the Study of Animal Behaviour, Madingley; Department of Zoology, Cambridge University

BACKGROUND FACTORS AND ORIENTING ATTITUDES

Background Factors

The term ethology, formerly used in a broad sense for the study of animal behavior and ecology, is now taken to refer primarily to the former. Used in this way it should refer to a field of study, and not to any particular theories or methods used within that field. In recent years it has come to be employed particularly by a group of workers who, though differing widely themselves in the problems they tackle and in the theoretical interpretations (if any) which they adopt, share certain basic orienting attitudes which are perhaps more important as unifying factors than any particular theoretical scheme [129, 207, 222]. Partly because of the difficulties of international communication during the period when the early work was done, these workers happen at the moment to be mostly Europeans. They have, of course, no exclusive right to the term "ethologist"—indeed, similar approaches have been used independently with great effect by other workers in America and elsewhere. But it is convenient, for the purposes of this volume, to restrict discussion mainly to the work of this group, even though this necessitates the use of "ethology" in a restricted, and perhaps already outmoded, sense.

Although this work can be said to have sprung primarily from the publication of Lorenz's *Der Kumpan in der Umwelt des Vögels* in 1935 [121], a shortened English version of which was published in 1937 [122], the seeds had been sown a generation earlier by such workers as O. Heinroth in Germany, C. O. Whitman and W. Craig in the United States, and J. Huxley and E. Eliot Howard in England. During the pre-war and war years the literature was little known in the English-speaking world, but in the last decade it has had an increasing influence among zoologists and psychologists. At the present time, papers appear principally in *Zeitschrift für Tierpsychologie, Behaviour, British Journal of Animal Behaviour* (now called *Animal Behaviour*), and a number of other biological and psychological journals. Tinbergen [216] has provided a recent summary of much of the work discussed here in his book *The Study of Instinct.* Thorpe [209] has provided a link with studies in other fields in *Learning and Instinct in Animals.*

Since ethologists are now numerous and hold divergent views on many topics, it is no easy task to present a summary or analysis of their views. Indeed, now that their attitudes and ideas have spread to related fields also concerned with animal behavior, it was difficult to decide which work should be included in the present discussion. Therefore, although the author is deeply indebted to those (Professor G. P. Baerends, Dr. D. S. Lehrman, Dr. P. Marler, Dr. W. H. Thorpe, Dr. N. Tinbergen, Dr. W. S. Verplanck) who have read this chapter in draft and made innumerable helpful criticisms and suggestions, he cannot claim that, in its final form, it represents any opinion but his own.

Orienting Attitudes

The three whys. The men whom Lorenz [128] describes as the "pioneers" of this approach—Whitman, Heinroth, Huxley, Verwey, and others—were for the most part zoologists. This zoological bias has greatly influenced the development of the school and has been especially important in determining the kind of questions asked. For the zoologist, the answer to the question "What causes it to be here?" gives only a partial understanding of the structure concerned. Other problems also are raised—"How does it work and what is its function?" "What is its evolutionary origin and history?" and so on. Similarly, when the ethologist asks "Why does the animal behave in this way?" he requires at least three answers— causal,[1] functional,[2] and historical.

It is, apparently, still necessary to emphasize that the study of function and evolution, as well as causation, does not imply a confusion between them—the three questions are distinct. Nor does it imply that all behavior is functional in that it contributes to survival or reproduction: of course it is not. (However, even apparently nonfunctional behavior may be the product of mechanisms or potentialities of biological significance in other contexts.)

Although these three aspects of behavior study are quite separate, advances in one may assist progress in another. For example, knowledge of the role of "releasers" (p. 584) in the causation of behavior is essential for an understanding of the evolution and function of bird courtship display (p. 590). This sort of liaison between the different approaches has been particularly fertile because it was an interest in evolution which first focused attention on the relatively stereotyped motor coordinations known as "Fixed Action Patterns" (p. 573) and promoted research into their causation [cf. Lorenz, 128, 129].

Nevertheless, the greatest part of the work discussed here was directed at problems of causation, and in conformity with the other chapters in this book, it is with this that we shall be principally concerned.

Scope. The work of these ethologists cannot be characterized by the kind of phenomena studied—although attention has been concentrated mainly on the behavior of insects and lower vertebrates, work has also been done on animals ranging from Protozoa to man, and has been concerned with both relatively simple reflexes and complicated learned behavior. In fact the approach is essentially a broad one, and many of these "ethological" studies could equally be classified as psychological, zoological, taxonomic, ecological, physiological, neurophysiological, endocrinological, pharmacological, genetic, or even botanic. The specific characteristics of the work thus lie not in its scope but in matters of attitude and emphasis. It is the purpose of the following pages to make these explicit.

Levels and aims. The material with which ethologists are concerned is usually at the behavior level. If prediction of behavior, given the antecedent conditions, were the sole aim, there might be no need to analyze further than this: reference to underlying mechanisms could be un-

[1] Ethologists have not been over-sophisticated about the word "cause," and so far no confusion has resulted. For those who prefer it, read "variable, of which behavior is a mathematical function."

[2] In asking questions about the function of a type of behavior, it can usually be understood that the ethologist wants to know about the nature of the selection pressure to which the animal species has been subjected for individuals to behave in this way (see p. 577).

necessary. But even if the complete prediction of behavior were possible, we should still have advanced only one stage towards its full understanding: a further stage would be reached when the organization of behavior could be understood in terms of the physiological organization which it reflects. Thus the hypotheses of ethologists must be judged not only at the behavior level, but also in terms of their compatibility with work at lower ones.

Indeed, a theoretical system which by its nature cannot be related to physiological data is unlikely to have a wide validity even at the behavior level. To take a parallel from physics, Toulmin [228] has pointed out that it is "a great virtue of a good model that it does suggest further questions, taking us beyond the phenomena from which we began, and tempts us to formulate hypotheses which turn out to be experimentally fertile." Thus the Greek antenna-model of sight, and the models of thermal and gravitational phenomena as the effects of caloric and gravitational fluids, prompted unprofitable questions; on the other hand "the model of light as a substance in motion is a good model, not only because it provides us with an easily intelligible interpretation of the diagrams of geometrical optics, but also because it . . . leads us to speculate about light-particles or light-waves as the things which travel, or are propagated: these speculations have borne fruit" [228]. Of course, just as an explanation of shadow-casting in terms of the wave theory of light tends to be laborious, prediction of behavior via all the physiological intermediaries would be hopelessly cumbersome. But the behavior model should be at least compatible with, and—if possible— translatable into, the physiological one. For the ethologist, therefore, analysis down to a physiological level is a desirable, but not at present usually attainable, aim.

"Physiologizing" is, however, more than a long-term aim. Physiology is a valuable source of information for the behavior student. A fertile psychology cannot afford to ignore physiological data which may suggest useful concepts. Further, psychologists who deny themselves such data may be neglecting an important source of evidence on which to base their predictions of behavior. Ethologists aim, therefore, at an analysis of behavior into units which the physiologist will be able to handle— and believe that they can be guided in that analysis by a consideration of present physiological knowledge [cf. 69].

Description and classification. Psychologists who try to model their approach on that of classical physics fail to recognize that it dealt largely with everday events—falling apples, stick in water, or melting ice. It could, therefore, often afford to pass quickly over the descriptive phase which is so important in the development of other sciences. In biology, by contrast, the work of generations of taxonomists and systematists was necessary before much progress could be made, and in the study of behavior description and classification are equally essential.

Psychologists whose theoretical systems have been based on limited experimental techniques have ignored this, concentrating their attention on a few responses and neglecting the rest of the behavior of the animal. Indeed the laboratory experimenter, in an attempt to reduce variability, often not only purposely restricts the behavior of the animal in which he is interested, but also limits sharply the aspects which he is willing to record.[3] The initial data of ethology, on the other hand, often refer to animals living free in nature, whose behavior is not controlled by the limitations of experimental surroundings: the behavior must thus first be described and classified. Much of the preliminary work in ethology consists of this: it forms an essential first stage before analysis can be undertaken.

Experimental techniques. The experiments which follow this description and classification must be flexible, and the techniques used suited to the problem in hand and the stage of analysis reached. Sometimes apparently crude experiments in the field yield more useful results than superficially sophisticated ones in the laboratory, where the meaning of the results is obscure. The investigator who overemphasizes the role of precise laboratory experiments may limit his own view, for it becomes less likely that the animal will do anything which the experimenter does not expect. Of course, controlled experiments are essential in the study of behavior, but should come after qualitative study.

Comparative approach. Generalizations about behavior which are to be valid for many species must be based on comparative work: generalizations which precede comparison can never be more than guesses. However, the comparative method must be used cautiously, for apparently close similarities may be merely parallel evolutionary adaptations to a similar environment, and rest on quite different causal bases. It is thus necessary to choose for comparison first species believed on other grounds to be closely related phyogenetically, and only then more distantly related ones.

Pursued in this way, a comparative approach does more than permit generalization. Even in the initial stage of selective description, knowledge of the behavior of one species may be helpful in the study of a related one. The present writer would certainly never have noticed the occasional pivoting movements made by Greenfinches (*Chloris chloris*) if he had not already been familiar with the highly ritualized (p. 595) and thus conspicuous pivoting display of the related Goldfinch (*Carduelis carduelis*) [79]. At many other levels complex behavioral

---

[3] Just because of this, the "displacement activities" shown by rats in mazes and puzzle boxes often went unnoticed.

phenomena which have been elaborated after a long evolutionary history may be more easily understood if first studied in a relatively primitive and uncomplicated form. Further, comparison is the only method available for investigating the evolution of behavior—the origin of many display postures would be quite obscure if it were not possible to observe them in a less ritualized form in related species [128, 129].

Finally it must be emphasized that the differences revealed by comparative study may be as interesting and important as the similarities: both will provide new theoretical insight into problems of causation, function, and evolution. Such differences must, however, be considered in relation to the biology of the species: for example, measures of "intelligence" obtained by applying the same test to widely differing species are meaningless unless this is done [9, 216].

Quantitative specificity. Analysis of behavior must start from a qualitative basis and by stages become more quantitative: the early qualitative work is an essential preliminary to a more precise analysis.

When generalizations are made, the broader the generalization the less quantitative specificity can it have. There is, therefore, a limit to the precision which is necessary before principles of broad application can be stated. On the other hand, of course, for detailed prediction a high degree of specificity is essential. The degree of quantitative precision which is desirable in any particular case thus depends on the immediate aim.

Organization. Informal exposition is at present best suited to the varied nature of the work discussed here and the tentative status of the concepts employed. In some branches of the subject a more formal approach may become desirable in the near future.

Use of models. Three models which have played a part in the development of ethology (as here defined, p. 562) must be mentioned. Lorenz [e.g., 124, 128] used a hydraulic reservoir model in discussing problems of motivation: this was an "as if" model manifestly remote from the mechanisms it was supposed to represent. Lorenz himself referred to it as a "crude model" which was used merely "to symbolize a surprising wealth of facts really encountered in the reactions of animals" (see p. 582). Tinbergen [e.g., 215, 216] used a basically similar model in his "hierarchical system" of "nervous centres" which are "loaded" with "motivational impulses." Though he recognized the "provisional and hypothetical nature" of his scheme, Tinbergen described it as "a graphic picture of the nervous mechanisms involved." These models have been very useful in synthesizing the products of analysis and in orienting ideas, but they are unlikely to continue to be fertile in the future. Tinbergen's scheme contains a number of properties which result from its hydraulic nature and are misleading when applied to the original: the passage from the remote "as if" Lorenzian model to the "close" Tinbergen one has resulted in a confusion between the properties of the model and those of the original [78, 80].

Von Holst [e.g., 86, 87, 150], considering the relations between the central nervous system and peripheral sense organs, has developed a theory of "Reafferenz" which bears similarities to the feedback loops of control systems. He claims that his "functional schemata, constructed in order to illustrate definite causal relationships, are quite abstract, although the consequences they predict are concrete and experimentally verifiable." This scheme is being applied in a number of contexts on the boundary between physiology and behavior study.

Synthesis and analysis. Analysis alone cannot provide an understanding of biological organization—wholes as well as parts must be studied [165]. The importance of resynthesizing the products of analysis must therefore be stressed. It enables emphasis to be laid on the inter-relations between factors, and thus permits the adequacy of the initial analysis to be assessed. Further, it provides a means of envisaging the behavior of the animal as an organized whole, and thus not only complements the initial analysis of causation, but also shows up the functional relations between the parts.

THE DESCRIPTION AND CLASSIFICATION OF BEHAVIOR— SOME BASIC CONCEPTS

General

Just as the systematist of organisms has "to break up the almost unlimited and confusing diversity of individuals in nature into easily recognizable groups, to work out the significant characters of these units, and to find constant differences between similar ones" [147], so the ethologist must break up the complex stream of behavior into units suitable for study, and classify these into groups for ease of reference. A constant awareness of the problems involved in description and classification is essential, for the future course of research may depend on the choice of units, and the criteria by which they are recognized become the bricks from which hypotheses are built.

Description and Classification into Behavior Types

The terms "response," "reaction," and so on can refer either to a single unique event occurring over a limited space of time, or to a group of such events, classed together as having certain characteristics in common. There is a reciprocal relation between the criteria of the behavior classes, and the way the unique events are described in the first instance. Either the description will be influenced by the way the behavior is to be grouped or, since the criteria of the behavior classes must be drawn from the data available, the nature of the classes will be influenced by the description given. In practice, descriptions of behavior fall into two main types:

Physical description. For some purposes, an adequate description can be given in terms which refer ultimately to the strength, degree, and pattern of muscular contractions (or glandular activity, change in some other physiological property, etc.). In practice such "physical descriptions" are often limited to patterns of limb or body movement, for a complete description would be not only impracticable but also unnecessarily refined and cumbersome. Terms such as "knee jerk," "positive supporting reaction," "sleeping posture" are of this type.

In classifying on the basis of such descriptions, we are grouping together similar spatio-temporal patterns of muscular contraction— though the classification will depend only on selected characteristics, others being ignored. The choice of the characteristics employed should, of course, have an objective justification, but they may vary greatly in complexity. Thus "crouching" by a bird may be characterized merely by a certain degree of bending in the tarsal joint, but in other cases a complex spatio-temporal pattern of muscular contractions (e.g., as in tail flicks), or simultaneous or sequential occurrence of a number of different component patterns (e.g., as in the courtship postures of birds), may be used. In this latter case the selection of criteria is further complicated by the disappearance of some components when the response is given at low intensity. The usual practice here is to describe low and high intensity forms and indicate the intermediate variations—a method roughly comparable to that used by taxonomists for clines [94], but often leading to the description only of rare extreme cases.

Description by consequence. A second method for the description of behavior may be called "description by consequence." "Picking up nest material," "pressing down the lever," or "approaching" do not refer to particular patterns of muscular contraction but cover all patterns which lead (or could lead, and there is room for ambiguity here) to the specified result. Descriptions of this type are normally used when the behavior involves orientation to objects in the environment, and when the motor patterns, though leading to a constant result, are themselves diverse. They thus tend to be used especially for "appetitive" [33, see p. 572] behavior.

There are two advantages in descriptions of this type. First, a brief description may cover a multitude of motor patterns each of which is variable—thus "approaching" covers hopping, walking, flying, sidling, etc.: they therefore provide an essential shorthand. Naturally each behavior-class characterized by consequence could be subdivided into smaller groups characterized by physical description. The number of these may be very limited. Thus the Herring Gull (*Larus argentatus*) uses only one method for retrieving eggs which have rolled out of its nest—it puts its beak beyond them and tries to maneuver them back under its breast. In spite of the inefficiency of this technique, the bird never attempts to use its apparently more suitable webbed feet or wings [220]. In other cases the number of smaller groups characterized by physical description, into which a behavior class characterized by consequence could be divided, may be large. Even within one method of locomotion it would be theoretically possible to specify an unlimited number of time units in each of which the pattern of muscular contraction was different from that in every other, and to group these in an unlimited number of classes. However, few of these classes would have objective justification and few would be of any help in analyzing the behavior. This is a reflection of the fact that extensive variability of motor patterns does not necessarily mean extensive variability of mechanisms—just as, although touching a point with the finger could involve an infinite variety of motor patterns, it involves localization in only three dimensions.

A second advantage of descriptions by consequence is that they often call attention to essential features of the behavior which may not appear in physical descriptions—such as orientation with respect to the environment, or responsiveness to external stimuli. Thus an animal's behavior may change radically (e.g., from one type of appetitive behavior to another) with little change in the motor pattern; or, alternatively, a radical change in the patterns of muscular contraction (e.g., from flying to walking) may be, for some purposes, of little significance. Description by consequence is thus often essential for a full understanding of the behavior.

There are, however, also dangers in descriptions of this type. First, the manner in which categories of behavior are described may have important consequences on subsequent hypotheses—whether, for instance, we say "entering the goal box" or "escaping from the alley."

Second, as stressed by Meehl and MacCorquodale [148], such descriptions are susceptible to overinterpretation. The statement "the rat learned to press the lever" can be interpreted as pure description, but can also be overinterpreted to imply reciprocal relations between the various behavior classes by which the lever could be depressed, such that a decrease in frequency of one is followed by a compensatory increase in another. This *may* be so, but does not necessarily follow from the initial descriptive statement. As we have seen in the case of the egg-rolling response, the number of alternative response classes which can be used in bringing about a given consequence may be surprisingly limited.

Whichever type of description is used, it inevitably involves the rejection of some of the data and a selection (arbitrary, intuitive, or rational) of the features to be studied—as soon as we move away from the initial cinematographic record of the behavior we are rejecting information. Just because description and classification involve rejection of data and the selection of criteria, there are always the dangers that the essential data are rejected, that the units used are irrelevant, too small or too large for the task in hand.

For instance, descriptions of reproductive behavior in terms of "maternal behavior," "sexual behavior," etc., are inadequate for a proper analysis of the stimuli controlling them [216]. Similarly, the understanding of the apparently "insightful" tool-using behavior of primates is greatly facilitated by examination of its components [185].

On the other hand, insufficient rejection of data may lead to a hopelessly confusing mass of detail, and divert attention from the essentials of the problem. Thus any attempt to describe precisely the patterns of muscular contraction involved when a fighting bird strikes its adversary with its beak would be hopelessly difficult because of the variations in the initial posture and relative positions of the combatants—the only possible criteria by which the behavior can be categorized are of the consequence type. Similarly, Nissen [162], as a result of his work with chimpanzees, has argued that there is a logical necessity for descriptions of this type in much complex behavior.

The two types of description are thus not always alternative. Description in terms of muscular contraction is unsuitable in some cases because of the complexity of the data which it provides, and in others because the data cannot be subdivided into classes with an objective validity. In other cases, description by consequence is equally unsuitable. Sometimes —as in the threat and courtship postures of birds, which involve both a relatively stereotyped motor pattern and an orientation with respect to the environment—both must be used.

We must now consider the ways in which these behavior classes can be grouped together.

Classification of Behavior Types

The classificatory systems used by the systematist of organisms are based on common characters—the characters being chosen in such a way that they indicate phylogenetic relationships between groups. In classifying behavior types it is necessary to use systems which lay emphasis on causal and functional relations as well as on phylogenetic ones. Characters derived solely from physical descriptions are sometimes of little use for the first two purposes, and other types of criteria must be employed. A brief survey of these will serve to introduce some basic concepts.

Four principal systems of classification are used: first, a broad division into appetitive and consummatory behavior, and then further independent classifications according to causation, function, and evolutionary and ontogenetical history. Although any particular pattern of behavior can be examined by any of these methods, the classificatory systems themselves must, of course, remain independent. Examples of behavior grouped by one set of criteria need not share characteristics relevant to one of the others.

Like its structure, the behavior of each species has undergone a greater or lesser degree of evolutionary differentiation. There is thus no a priori reason why the categories useful for one species should necessarily also be useful for another; once again, comparison is necessary before generalization is possible. In practice, a degree of compromise is often necessary—the most useful categories may be those which are applicable over a moderately wide field with a moderate degree of precision. Further, categories useful at a given stage of research may later become superfluous: many of those discussed below have proven value as working tools but may not be fundamental.

Appetitive Behavior and Consummatory Acts

The value of moderately precise categories can immediately be seen in the division of behavior into "appetitive" and "consummatory"—the former refers to the variable initial "searching" phase of a behavior sequence, the latter to the final, more or less stereotyped and relatively simple activity [Lorenz, e.g., 128; Tinbergen, 216]. This distinction, first made by Sherrington [194] and Craig [33], is not absolute but one of degree, and many responses do not fit easily into either category [76]. Indeed, since the behavior of animals has developed by innumerable routes in adaptation to innumerable environments, we must expect any dichotomous classification of this sort to mark the extremes of a continuum—absolute dichotomies will be exceptional. It must also be noted that a form of behavior is labeled as appetitive or consummatory by its properties as a piece of behavior: there is no necessary implication that all examples of appetitive behavior have similar causal mechanisms [cf. Lehrman, 115]. Nevertheless, the distinction between appetitive and consummatory behavior is a useful one.

Each type of appetitive behavior shown by an animal has three characteristics which may be a help in labeling it—the motor pattern(s), the orientation component, and the stimuli to which the animal is particularly responsive while showing the behavior. Thus a feeding Great Tit (*Parus major*) may hop (motor pattern) over the ground (orientation component) "looking for" (to use a convenient shorthand without teleological implications) beechmast (stimuli to which it is particularly responsive) [76]. In different kinds of appetitive behavior each of these characteristics may vary independently of the others—e.g., a nest-building Great Tit may hop over the ground "looking for" a piece of moss. There are, therefore, grounds for believing that they depend on more or less independent mechanisms.

The nature of these three characteristics has not yet been discussed in detail. The "motor pattern" can usually be described fairly easily, but if it consists primarily of locomotion it may give no indications of the nature of the behavior unless other patterns (e.g., snarling and other facial expressions, crest-raising) are superimposed. "Orientation component" usually involves a spatial relation to environmental objects, and may be an important characteristic of the behavior. Of the three, "stimuli to which it is particularly responsive" is the most difficult to investigate but perhaps the most fundamental, for it is by this that most forms of appetitive behavior are ultimately categorized.[4] Thus if a Great Tit, which had previously been pecking at nest-material, begins to peck at food and ignores the nest-material, this is an indication that it is now showing a new type of appetitive behavior. Of course, the use of this type of characteristic involves observation of the behavior over a considerable time span, and "natural experiments" of the type indicated above often have to serve instead of precise tests of responsiveness. Further, the criterion is relative—the animal is "particularly responsive." Whatever a Great Tit is looking for, it will nearly always respond to a flying hawk, but it is not necessarily useful to say that Great Tits are nearly always showing "predator appetitive behavior." This example shows that a classification of this type, though often valuable, cannot be absolute.

The same three characteristics can also be identified in many consummatory acts. Thus Lorenz and Tinbergen [130], in an early paper, identified distinct motor and orientation components in a response—the "egg-rolling" of the Grey Lag Goose (*Anser anser*)—which is near the consummatory-act end of the appetitive behavior–consummatory act continuum. The two are distinguishable in that the former (the Fixed Action Pattern, FAP, or *Erbkoordination*)[5] is elicited but not guided by external stimuli—and, once started, always goes through to completion—whereas the orientation or "taxis" component depends continuously on environmental stimuli. Further, with much consummatory behavior it is possible to identify "consummatory stimuli" [e.g., "food in stomach," "eggs against brood patches"—see 16, 78, 207, 209] which are responsible for

---

[4] It is for this reason that it is often convenient to label appetitive behavior by the behavior which usually follows it. This is not teleology.

[5] The terms *Instinkthandlung* and *Instinktbewegung* were formerly both used in this context. The former (= instinctive activity) is now often used to refer to the combination of FAP and taxis component.

the subsequent fall in motivation and may be compared with the "stimuli to which the animal is particularly responsive" when showing appetitive behavior. It must be emphasized, however, that the identification of these characters in some types of consummatory behavior does not mean that they can be distinguished in all. There has been a tendency to regard the egg-rolling response as a type of all consummatory behavior, but this is not justifiable. Often, for instance, the stimuli eliciting the Fixed Action Pattern are the same as those producing the orientation; and many consummatory acts, such as swallowing and ejaculation, lack an orientation component. Similarly, all cases of a fall in response strength are not due to the perception of new consummatory stimuli—they may be due to the disappearance of the eliciting stimuli, habituation, and so on.

Although the distinction between Fixed Action Pattern and orientation component is not absolute, the isolation of FAPs led to important advances in ethology, for here is a unit which can be easily recognized and studied. Although relatively complicated, consisting usually of a temporal pattern of muscular contraction, an FAP cannot be split up into successive responses depending on qualitatively different external stimuli: in other words, it is not a chain reaction [213]. Since FAPs are relatively stereotyped and characteristic of the species, they have provided excellent material for phylogenetic studies. Lorenz [e.g., 128] has also emphasized their apparent spontaneity (see p. 583) and the way in which their performance may act as a reinforcing agent in learning.

In a number of cases FAPs have been shown to be "inborn." Since the way in which ethologists have used the term "inborn" has caused some confusion recently, elaboration is necessary.

The appearance of any character of behavior depends on a number of factors including (a) the genetic constitution of the individual and (b) his past environment. The terms "inborn" or "innate," as Spurway [200] has pointed out, should strictly speaking be reserved for differences between characters, not for the characters themselves. Thus, in the ideal case, differences in behavior between two birds reared in identical environments can be said to depend ultimately on inborn differences.

In practice, ethologists have often used "inborn" to mean not learned—i.e., not influenced by conditioning, imitation, or those other processes commonly grouped together as learning. This of course is etymologically inaccurate, and "not learned" would be a better term. Although the behavior differences between two animals brought up in identical environments must depend ultimately on inborn differences, the behavior itself may be "learned." A valuable critical discussion of these terms is given by Lehrman [115] and Schneirla [188; see also, 70, 136].

The terms "inborn" and "not learned" have been applied both to motor patterns and to the relations between motor patterns and stimuli.

In the former case "practice" sometimes occurs before the movement appears in its final form, but the direction of the "improvement" does not depend on external reward: ethologists have sometimes grouped such cases together with those in which there is no practice. When "not learned" and "inborn" refer to the connection between motor pattern and stimulus they do not preclude the possible importance of learning processes which do not involve the specific behavior in question. Thus canaries with no experience of nest-building or nest material, if provided with material at ten months, will pick it up within a few seconds and carry it to a possible nest site [Hinde, unpublished observation]. This does not mean that learning plays no part in the development of (e.g.) the sensorimotor skills involved: what is significant is that the canary picks up the material and does not (e.g.) court it; and that it carries it to the nest site, not to the center of the floor.

There are obvious disadvantages in defining "not learned" behavior by exclusion, especially when there are no clear limits to the excluded group, and there are no a priori reasons for thinking that the group thus defined is homogeneous [cf. 19]. Further, since the ontogeny of behavior is invariably complex, such a dichotomous classification inevitably leads to difficulties. Nevertheless, the importance of behavior which has not been influenced by specific learning processes is immediately apparent to anyone familiar with animals: the extent to which examples of such behavior share common properties is being elucidated by research.

Finally it must be emphasized that the real distinction comes not between learned and unlearned *behavior,* but between learning and the other factors that influence behavior. In fact the development of behavior always involves a complex interaction of genetic and environmental factors, into which learning may or may not enter [see also 83, 222].

One point, relating properly to an earlier stage in the discussion, can conveniently be made here. Before a classification of behavior can be made, the size of the units must be determined. How far is the analysis to proceed before the resulting portions are classified? In the case of consummatory behavior, the isolation of the Fixed Action Pattern provides a convenient practical answer to this, for the movement is relatively stereotyped and cannot be analyzed into parts which are elicited by stimulus situations different from those which elicit the whole.

Subsequently more detailed analyses may, of course, subdivide the FAP of consummatory behavior into smaller units, such as "acts" [180] or "components" [75, 79, 143]. Russell et al. [180] define an "act" as "a set of observable activities in different effectors (e.g., muscle tensions), regularly observed in combination (and thus not analyzable into separately occurring components . . .), hence recognizably different from other such acts observed in the same species": different acts may be elicited by the same external stimulus situation, and may in fact constitute stages in intensity of the same response[6] (super act, in their terminology[7]).

With appetitive behavior the problem is more difficult, for alternative motor patterns and orientations may be used. Indeed, few types of appetitive behavior have so far been studied in detail by ethologists and none is known so well as that shown by a rat in a maze. [But see 140, 233.] However, a sequence of appetitive behavior can often be divided into a series of links, each with a single set of consummatory stimuli (i.e., in each "link" the animal is responsive to a particular set of stimuli). Each such link can legitimately be treated as a unit, in spite of the (limited) variability of the motor behavior (which is, of course, itself a major problem), because, like the fixed action pattern of consummatory behavior, it has a set of eliciting causal factors specific to it. In other words, the sequence of appetitive behavior as a whole is a chain response, each link having its own eliciting (and often consummatory) stimuli [76]. Often the consummatory stimuli of one link seem to be the eliciting stimuli of the next.

"Reflexes." The difference between "instinctive" behavior and "reflexes" has often been emphasized in order to underline the importance of changes in threshold of some instinctive acts in contrast with reflexes. This distinction has, however, caused some confusion because there is no agreement between those ethologists [e.g., 216, 207] who restrict the term reflex to simple S-R sequences in which changes in threshold are insignificant, holding that it becomes valueless if used in a wider sense, and other workers who include all S-R sequences as reflexes, to be investigated by the methods of "reflexology" [e.g., 99].

Further confusion has arisen because some ethologists have contrasted "reflex" (in their sense) with "response" (signifying S-R sequences of greater complexity in which changes of threshold are important); whereas for other workers the "response" forms part of the reflex, and cannot be contrasted with it.

[6] The terms "response" and "reaction" are used by some ethologists in an extremely broad sense—in fact almost any change in behavior or responsiveness (i.e., motor pattern, orientation, or readiness to respond) may be so described. Thus Tinbergen [214] states that a reaction "may be a special motor response in one case, a change in readiness to react with a special motor response in another case, or even a change in readiness to respond with a whole pattern of functionally related movements in many other cases."

[7] Although the "act," in the same sense indicated by these authors, may turn out to be a useful unit of behavior, the employment of this particular term may lead to confusion. The term "consummatory act," which has been widely used by ethologists, usually refers to a "super act" in the terminology of these authors, and may contain a number of "acts."

The difference between instinctive and reflex behavior is, as Tinbergen [216] and Thorpe [207] imply, of course only one of degree.

Causal Classification

The various types of behavior shown by an animal can be classified according to the causal factors on which they depend, activities which share causal factors being classified together. Thus all activities whose frequency or intensity is significantly increased by male sex hormone can be grouped together as male sexual behavior. All activities similarly influenced by the stimulus situation "rival male" can be described as "agonistic behavior" [cf. 189]. This type of classification is essential for an understanding of the behavior of the whole animal, and it works well in practice. There are, however, some difficulties. Two methods are used to assess whether patterns of behavior share causal factors. One is to administer the factor in question and see whether the patterns in question both increase in frequency. The other is to investigate the temporal correlations between the appearances of various activities [11, 95]. In either case, a positive result does not necessarily mean a *direct* effect of any factor on both patterns [e.g., 3]. Further, the nonoccurrence of a pattern after administration of the factor does not mean that the factor is without influence on the behavior in question—additional factors may be necessary before the behavior appears.

The term "intention movement," used for movements which are incomplete by comparison with other examples of the "same" (see p. 569) response, may be included here, since it may be inferred that the incompleteness is due to a deficiency in the "internal" (central or peripheral) or external causal factors, or to the presence of factors for incompatible behavior. This term, however, though extremely valuable in particular cases, has never been given a satisfactory general definition [38; see also p. 595].

Functional Classification

Activities may be classified according to the functions which they serve—e.g., "threat," "courtship," "hunting," and so on.[8] Two rather different types of criteria are, however, used here. If interest is centered on the evolution of behavior, the statement that a type of behavior has a given function implies that the behavior is maintained in the repertoire of the species by selection acting through a consequence related to the

---

[8] Such terms correspond to words such as "legs," "eyes," etc., in morphology. A structure is classed as a leg because of its function, and there is no implication that the legs of, e.g., arthropods and vertebrates are related either embryologically, i.e., causally, or phylogenetically. A similar structure which has a different function is given a different name, e.g., maxilliped.

function in question (e.g., copulation has a function related to reproduction). On the other hand, if we are interested primarily in the function itself, we may argue that a pattern of behavior has a given function
merely because it contributes to a certain biological end. For instance, if
we were interested in the behavior patterns of passerine birds which function in reducing disease, we might include territorial behavior which, by
spacing the birds out, probably helps to prevent the spread of epidemics.
But the territories of many species are so large that it seems improbable
that a small change in territory size would make any significant difference
to disease, and so selection cannot be acting through disease to maintain
territorial behavior in its present form [81].

In practice, when any one species is being considered, a functional
classification of behavior very often corresponds to a causal one: considered from the point of view of evolution, this is not hard to understand—the mechanisms which underlie adaptive behavior need be far less
complex if functionally related activities share causal factors than if the
various causal factors are distributed at random among the functional
groups. It is for this reason that ethologists often use functional-sounding
words, e.g., reproductive behavior, parental behavior, when they are
referring to a category which they believe to be related in terms of *causal*
factors. *Often* the functional classification is a good guide to the causal.
This is not always the case, however, and in many animals it may be
quite unjustifiable to talk about a "reproductive instinct" if instinct is
used in the causal sense, for sexual and parental behavior may depend
on quite different causal factors [76]. Causal analysis must precede
causal classification if functional and causal categories are not to be
confused. Further, as Tinbergen [218, 220, 221] has shown, the same
functional category, courtship, may rest on quite different causal bases
in different animals; and great care is necessary in generalizing from
species to species.

Functional categories are often used to include behavior patterns
from unrelated species. This is quite justifiable just so long as the categories are used only in discussions of function. Care is necessary, however, for almost identical behavior elements may have dissimilar functions in different species.

Historical Classification

Two quite distinct systems must be recognized:

1. Classification according to source. Here patterns of behavior believed to have a common historical origin are grouped together. This is
much used in the study of the evolution of behavior—especially the
evolution of Fixed Action Patterns. The basic criterion for grouping together is then similarity in the pattern of muscular contraction, but as

in the systematics of organisms, due allowance must be made for possibilities of convergence, divergence, etc. [83].

2. Classification according to method of acquisition. Here behavior classes are grouped not according to their historical source but according to the nature of intervening changes which have occurred—for instance, "learned," "ritualized."

Finally, mention must be made of categories of behavior based on descriptive criteria other than descriptions of movement patterns. Such groupings have no implications about causation, function, or evolution. The division of behavior into appetitive and consummatory (see p. 572) is a classification of this type. Kühn's classification of orienting mechanisms is another—applicable to a wide variety of organisms, it is based mainly on descriptive characters, and must not be interpreted as having any deeper significance. Many other terms applying to a wide variety of species are also of this nature—"territorial behavior," "migratory behavior," and so on. "Intention movement" when used to refer to a movement which is incomplete by comparison with another, otherwise similar, movement is also of this type (see p. 577).

The Independence of the Classificatory Systems

Although the classificatory systems discussed in the previous section are basically independent of each other, possibilities of confusion constantly arise. Perhaps the best known examples have arisen through misuse of the term "instinct," which is used sometimes for a functional and sometimes for a causal category of behavior, sometimes for a mechanism and sometimes for factors controlling that mechanism. As Kortlandt [106] has recently pointed out, Lloyd Morgan's classification of instincts involves such a confusion, the top-level instincts being functional categories, the rest carrying implications of a causal nature.

Indeed because, for reasons we have already seen, functional and causal categories often overlap, the temptation to confuse them is often severe. This is particularly dangerous when the functional categories are nothing more than descriptive generalizations. Reference to "self-preservative" as opposed to "reproductive" instincts, for instance, both confuses functional and causal categories and implies something causally in common between, for example, feeding and preening.

Another cause of confusion is the assumption that members of a descriptive class also share common characteristics of other types. Descriptive categories are often useful tools for research even when they carry no references to other characteristics. Kühn's classification of taxes, for instance, is primarily (though not exclusively) descriptive, and to argue that such "a preliminary classification has heuristic value only if the members of a given class are thought to be representative of similar dynamic processes which can be investigated" [115] merely reveals a misunderstanding of the classification employed.

NATURE OF THE SYSTEM

General

Ethologists have not all concentrated on a precise analysis of the behavior of only one species in one particular situation, but have tackled a variety of problems posed by animals as they found them in nature. This has required flexibility in the concepts used. The optimum balance between rigidity and plasticity of concepts changes with the diversity of phenomena studied and with the stage of the analysis reached. Frequently, some plasticity is still desirable, for an attempt at overrigid formalization would both narrow and stultify research. As the subject develops, some lines require more precisely defined concepts; in their new form these may then become valueless in other contexts where analysis has not proceeded so far, but they may nevertheless remain related to their forerunners of broader application.

So far, ethologists have attempted precise quantification at only a few points—though the number is now rapidly increasing. For the most part only tentative suggestions about "what affects what," qualified by indications of the direction of the effect, have been made.

The terms "independent," "intervening," and "dependent" variables have seldom been used in the work discussed in this chapter, but the variables which have been used can conveniently be discussed under these headings.

Dependent Variables

Although the behavior studied by ethologists varies greatly in complexity, it is generally at the level of responses of the whole animal. For instance, in analyzing the stimuli which elicit the pecking response of young Herring Gulls (*Larus argentatus*) Tinbergen and Perdeck [227] used as dependent variable number of pecks per unit of time.

Studies such as this, where the behavior observed consists of a relatively stereotyped pattern, differ from experiments involving lever pressing and similar tasks. Although each peck is, of course, different from every other peck in at least some respects, these differences lie mainly in the orientation components; other features are nearly constant from one response to the next. When the response is distinguished in terms of achievement, e.g., lever pressed down, it need have no such constant features [cf. 131].

Of course, this does not imply that all ethologists aiming at some degree of quantitative precision have used a relatively stereotyped response—what is measured must depend on the nature of the case. In experiments on the orientation of homing birds, for instance, the mean deviation of the bird's course from the homing direction may be used [e.g., 146]. Because of the diversity of the behavior studied, it is not possible to generalize further about the dependent variables used by ethologists: some further examples are given below.

Independent Variables

The following are the principal types of independent variables which have been manipulated in ethological studies:

1. Stimuli

Verplanck [231] has pointed out that the term "stimulus" has been used in at least four senses by psychologists:

Sense I. For a part, or a change in a part, of the environment.
Sense II. "Any form of energy which elicits a response"—the kind of response, organism and prevailing conditions being unspecified.
Sense III. A class of environmental events which control a specified activity of the organism according to specified laws.
Sense IV. As II, but including hypothetical or inferential classes of physical events (usually intra-organismic).

Ethologists have used stimulus in all these ways. For instance:

Sense I. "We want to know what stimuli the sense organs of a given animal can receive" [216].
Sense II. "Motion may be a powerful stimulus."
Sense III. The term "sign stimulus" is always used in this way. Thus Tinbergen, after discussing a number of examples showing that "As a rule, an instinctive reaction responds to only very few stimuli, and the greater part of the environment has little or no influence . . . " [216, p. 27] says "Russell . . . has called these essential stimuli 'sign stimuli' " [216, pp. 36, 172]. Thorpe [205] defines "releaser" [which in his usage is synonymous with sign stimulus, but see p. 58] as "Any specific feature or complex of features in a situation eliciting an instinctive activity or mood."
Sense IV. "That external stimuli sent out by some object can evoke definite instincts or activities in an animal, nobody will call in question; that internal stimuli are also playing a role in arousing these behaviour elements appears from the often observed fact that an animal which has not performed a certain activity for a long time, because it did not encounter an object adequate for pro-

ducing a reaction to react to, at the end may show this activity towards a completely inadequate object" [10].

That a single term may be used for a number of different categories in this way may be unfortunate, but it has not in practice led to any difficulties.

Direct quantitative treatment of stimulus variables is difficult, and has been possible in only a few cases where size, distance, or some similar property was concerned [e.g., 13, 95, 226]. The very nature of the stimuli to which animals respond is often incompatible with precise measurement, and qualitative descriptions such as "red belly underneath" are necessary. Stimulus situations of this type can at present be evaluated only in terms of the behavior they evoke.

2. Among other independent variables which have been manipulated in ethological studies are: (a) previous experience, (b) hormone dosage, (c) individual or specific characteristics, (d) age and/or phase of life cycle.

Intervening Variables

A number of terms used in ethological literature refer to intervening variables. In only a few cases have formal definitions of these terms been attempted, and their meaning is indicated either by informal exposition or by usage. They can be subdivided into two groups:

1. Terms employed in the hydraulic models previously used by Lorenz and Tinbergen.
2. Hypothetical constructs" [in the sense of MacCorquodale and Meehl, 131] describing hypothesized functional parts or aspects of the nervous system. The extent of the neurophysiological implications carried by such concepts varies; in some cases, they are almost absent.

Terms used in hydraulic models: the problem of spontaneity. The "hydraulic" models used by Lorenz and Tinbergen in discussing problems of motivation were mentioned on p. 567. Lorenz's model consisted of a *"reservoir"* of *"reaction specific energy"* which flowed away in action and was subsequently replenished from an unspecified source. Tinbergen [e.g., 216] has used a basically similar model in speaking of *"motivational impulses"* which flow from one *"nervous centre"* to another, and are eventually expended in action. (The concept of reaction specific energy is similar in some respects to Skinner's "reflex reserve.")

Though these models have never, as Kennedy [99] suggests, formed the "central idea" of ethology, they have often been useful in providing a "working hypothesis of a type that helps put one's thoughts in order"

[216]. Their present status has been discussed elsewhere [78, 80; see also p. 567]; they belong to an early phase of research, and as analysis proceeds, they have become less useful.

One concept which must be mentioned here is "spontaneity." This term has been used in at least two different ways by ethologists, and some confusion has resulted. Lorenz, struck by the extent to which many inborn behavior patterns are independent of external stimulation, postulated "the endogenous generation of motor stimuli" (roughly corresponding to the accumulation of reaction specific energy in his model). It is to this supposed "endogenous generation" that the term "spontaneity" sometimes refers.

Tinbergen, however, uses "spontaneity" in a rather different way—namely, to mean "without apparent external stimulus." He lists three types of internal factors which may play a part in the causation of behavior: (a) hormones, (b) internal sensory stimuli, and (c) intrinsic central nervous factors. It is to (c) only that Lorenz refers when discussing spontaneity. In a 1952 paper [217] Tinbergen distinguishes clearly between these two uses of the term. " 'Spontaneity' of the animal as a whole, meaning behaviour independent of factors external to the animal, is an established fact; 'spontaneity' of the central nervous system, a part of the animal, has not been proved, though it seems probable." Tinbergen also emphasizes the important distinction between the initiation and the coordination or patterning of movements: of course one may depend on external stimuli while the other does not.

By "intrinsic nervous factors" Tinbergen presumably means changes in the central nervous state which occur independently of a change in the extraneural states and stimuli, and which lead to a change in responsiveness. The existence or importance of such factors cannot be discussed here [see 11, 172 for recent reviews].

Other hypothetical constructs. Since ethologists are interested not only in the prediction and control of behavior, but also in the physiological mechanisms involved, a number of ethological terms carry neurophysiological implications.

Ethologists differ in the degree of neurophysiological specificity which they impute to such constructs. As far as the immediate study of behavior is concerned, they often need have none. But some neurophysiological implications are necessary if the concepts are to be useful as a convenient shorthand for discussing, for instance, the common features of the mechanisms mediating similar Fixed Action Patterns in related species, or for providing a point of reference for coordination with actual or projected physiological studies. In practice such "existence postulates" —to borrow a phrase from MacCorquodale and Meehl [131]—have sometimes been introduced unnecessarily and surreptitiously, with a consequent reduction in the utility of the concepts [80]. In any case, all these concepts are highly provisional, and no claim is made except that they are useful at the present stage in research.

Motor coordination mechanism. Any recurring pattern of behavior must depend on certain constant features of anatomy or physiology. Such features need not be anatomically localized, or even have a constant diffuse location—they could involve specific patterns of activity. Thus for each "Fixed Action Pattern," a "motor coordination mechanism" can be postulated. This concept has proved useful, especially in comparative studies, e.g., in discussions of the nature of ritualization. In causal contexts it represents an entity which has so far proved rather elusive.

Innate Releasing Mechanism. IRM corresponds to "das Schema" [von Uexkull, 229], "angeborener auslösender Mechanismus" [Lorenz, e.g., 121]. This construct was first introduced to account for the observations that (a) animals will often respond to a particular stimulus situation with a specific group of responses, even though they have never been confronted with the situation before; and (b) in such cases, the animal responds to only a very limited part of the total stimulus situation. Thus Tinbergen and Perdeck [227] describe the IRM as a mechanism which is "selectively responsive to a special stimulus situation."

To some extent, of course, this is true of all behavior. Hick [quoted by Broadbent, 25] has shown that even the human nervous system is simply incapable of dealing with all the information reaching it through its sense organs, so that selection must be continuous. The matter is, however, raised in a particularly acute form by many animal experiments. Thus Lack [112, 113] has shown that a territory-holding Robin (*Erithacus rubecula*) will attack or threaten a bunch of red breast feathers more readily than a whole stuffed juvenile Robin, which resembles the adult in all features except that it lacks the red breast. The red breast is more important than all other morphological characters together. Many similar cases are cited by Tinbergen [214, 216], and lead to the important concept of "sign stimuli" [178], or essential features of an object or situation which elicit a particular pattern of inborn behavior. It seems that "unlearned" [see p. 57] behavior is *characteristically* elicited by only a few sign stimuli—though later conditioning may, of course, complicate the releasing situation.[9]

The concept of the IRM, however, involves a number of difficulties:

[9] The term "releaser" is used primarily for organs which have undergone evolutionary adaptation to a signal function. Lorenz uses it for structures used in intraspecific communication, but Baerends [10] extended its use to any organ or structure "especially serving to send out sign stimuli," regardless of whether actor and reactor belong to the same species. Strictly speaking, therefore, all objects which are instrumental in releasing responses are not "releasers." The use of the term releaser has implications about both function and evolutionary history.

1. The term itself is an unfortunate one because (a) releasing mechanisms are not necessarily innate [e.g., 209], (b) stimuli responded to selectively may not merely "release" (see p. 592), and (c) the mechanism of selective response to stimuli is unlikely to be a unitary one, but complex and diffuse.[10]

2. The usual method of studying the sign stimuli eliciting a response is to vary characteristics of the situation which normally elicits the response and record the response strength in each case. If change in a particular characteristic produces a change in response strength, then that characteristic is relevant to the response. It has, however, often also been assumed that there must be a mechanism, peculiar to the response, selectively responsive to that feature. This, of course, is not necessarily the case: responsiveness to objects which contrast with their backgrounds is likely to be greater than that to objects which do not for all responses mediated by vision—responsiveness to contrast is not a property of an IRM specific to any particular response but of the perceptory mechanisms used in all responses. Properties of sense organs and perceptory mechanisms will influence the effectiveness of all stimulus situations independently of the response being studied. This criticism of the IRM concept, raised by Lehrman [117], is an important one. In reply, Tinbergen suggested that "we apply the term (I)R.M. to those cases where a stimulus situation has been shown to be typical of one response and not of others." This, however, has rarely been done in the past.

3. The concept of the IRM has been closely associated with the Lorenz-Tinbergen hydraulic models (p. 582), as a result of which it has acquired a number of properties which are incompatible with observational data. This has been discussed elsewhere [80, 170].

Finally, it must be emphasized that the concept of the IRM is basically a descriptive one. Reference to IRMs in unrelated species merely implies the presence of descriptive similarities in their behavior and not in the underlying mechanisms.

Drive. This has been used in at least three ways by ethologists:

Drive I. Refers to a central nervous state caused by stimuli, hormones, etc., and itself causing the animal to behave in a particular way [e.g., 216, 218].

Drive II. Refers to the internal causal factors leading to a given behavior—that is, to all causal factors other than those received through exteroceptors [157].

Drive III. Refers to all the causal factors influencing behavior, whether internal or external. Thus Thorpe [205] defines drive as "the

---

[10] Baerends [11] emphasizes that the releasing mechanism may include everything between sense organ and motor coordinating mechanism and that the use of the term IRM does not imply that the mechanism is either localized or unitary.

complex of internal and external states and stimuli leading to a given behaviour."[11] [Tinbergen, 222, uses "motivation" in this way.] One term has thus come to be used in three different senses because of the different interests of the authors concerned and the different stages which their analyses have reached. Very little confusion has resulted so far.

It will be noted that, in all three usages, the concept of drive as used hitherto involves no distinction between exciting and directing factors. All drives are regarded as specific to a more or less limited group of responses. Thus Tinbergen [218] writes that the "drive can be of different kinds, each giving rise to a different behaviour pattern." Similarly, in Tinbergen's hierarchical scheme of nervous centers (p. 582) each causal factor (stimulus, hormone, etc.) can influence only a limited group of responses. It is possible that ethologists will require a concept closer to the learning theorists' "general drive" to deal with phenomena such as displacement activities (see p. 593) and irrelevant drive phenomena [78]. Neurophysiological data also seem in favor of a move towards a "general drive" concept, e.g., the work on the reticular activating system of mammals [2] as well as experiments on lower vertebrates [23, 170].

There are, however, other difficulties associated with all three usages of "drive," and in practice the concept has often carried hidden and misleading "existence postulates" originating from the Lorenz-Tinbergen hydraulic models [80]. At present there is no agreement amongst ethologists as to how "drive" should be used. Other terms have been suggested for particular contexts, where they have rendered the use of "drive" unnecessary. Thus "Specific Action Potential" (SAP) has been suggested as a direct measure of responsiveness to a given stimulus [78]. Since the intensity of a response may be influenced in a number of ways, e.g., "motivational" factors, learning processes, presence of compatible or incompatible response tendencies, etc., SAP depends on many variables. Specific Action Potential was originally suggested to replace Lorenz's "Reaction Specific Energy" [205]. Since the concept of RSE is obsolete, SAP is unlikely to be of much use in that context and, as used here, has no connection with RSE or any similar construct.

"Tendency" has been used in the preliminary analyses of agonistic and courtship behavior (see p. 590) where causal factors for two or more incompatible types of behavior are simultaneously present. An animal can be said to have a strong tendency to behave in a particular way,

[11] Baerends [9] uses "Trieb" to mean potential "Drang" (= "Stimmung" or mood). "Drang ist aktivierte Trieb, Trieb ist potentielle Drang." This use of *Trieb* does not correspond to the present use of the English word "Drive" by ethologists, though in some contexts it approaches the first of the three uses given above. It is often synonymous with Tinbergen's use of "Instinct."

although the SAP for that type of behavior may be low because of another incompatible response tendency [79].

Mood. Another descriptive term which, in some senses, comes close to drive.

Tinbergen [213] describes "mood" ("Stimmung") as a word "which does not pretend to be more than a convenient descriptive term to denote the 'psychological condition' of the animal"; and later [214] as "a readiness to respond with one group of functionally related motor patterns." Lorenz [128] defines it as the animal's "present internal state of specific readiness for certain activities." Thorpe's [205] definition refers to a "state" of "readiness for action." Baerends [9] emphasizes that "Stimmung" refers to the state of activity of a group of mechanisms.

Recently this term has been avoided by ethologists because its subjective associations in everyday speech have given rise to frequent misunderstandings. As it has often been used in practice to refer particularly to the animal's responsiveness to stimuli (e.g., "in nest building mood" meant the animal was particularly likely to respond to nest-material if it encountered any), it may come to be useful when the relationship between susceptibility to stimuli and strength of response once released has been worked out in more detail.

Construction of function forms. It has already been pointed out that ethologists, engaged in studying the diverse patterns of behavior shown by widely differing species, have not yet attempted to specify precise relations between variables in even one case, let alone to make generalizations applicable to many species.

Mensurational and quantificational procedures. No mensurational or quantificational procedures are presupposed.

In the case of independent variables, it is accepted that the great majority of the stimuli which are important in nature cannot (at present) be measured against a physical scale; stimuli differing in physically measurable dimensions have been used in only a few studies (see p. 582).

On the dependent variable side, the method of measurement must be adapted to suit the particular problem in hand. Three types of procedure can be recognized:

1. Qualitative judgments of the "more intense, less intense" type. These are often sufficient for the initial analysis of complex types of behavior into simpler types (see p. 590).

2. Quantal intensity [e.g., 125, 128, 180]. Many responses involve more and more "acts" (see p. 576) as the internal or external causal factors are increased. For instance, with increasing intensity, the mobbing response given by Chaffinches to owls involves slight movements of the head, followed by lateral movements of the body and vertical movements of the tail; then these become more intense, the bird begins

to call "chink, chink," and finally the rate of calling increases [77]. It is often possible to produce an arbitrary scale of increasing intensity of the response according to the components which are present. Although it is, of course, not possible to ensure that the various steps on the scale are of equal value, such a method is often sufficiently precise and reliable for many purposes.

3. Sometimes some features of the response can be measured against a physical scale. At least five varieties of measure may be used—quantitative intensity, frequency (i.e., ratio of occurrence to number of trials), latency, number of occurrences in a fixed period, and duration in a fixed period.

Russell et al. [180] point out that measures of intensity differ from the others in that there are as many separate measures as there are occurrences of the act. The remaining measures ("tendency" measures) can all be reduced in principle to frequencies, and are related to the threshold of occurrence. They therefore suggest that only two behaviorally measurable (dependent) variables are related to each act—Intensity and Tendency. Measures of frequency, duration, etc., are all to be functionally related to "Tendency." These functional relations are varied, "so that it would be reckless at present to pay too much attention to, for instance, the types of curves we can fit to the relation between any of these measures and a given controlled variable, but quite reasonable to use any of them in the attempt to determine whether change in a given controlled variable has any influence on the Tendency of a particular Act." Unfortunately these authors offer no experimental evidence in support of their hypotheses.

As yet few attempts to investigate the nature of the relations between different measures of the same response have been made outside the field of learning [21, 77]. More such studies are needed (a) in order that adequate measures of response strength can be gained, (b) because it is necessary to know if the various measures are affected differently or differentially by the independent variables, and (c) because such information will give some indication of the complexity of the underlying mechanisms.

ORGANIZATION OF ETHOLOGY

General

So far, for reasons we have already seen, no ethologist has attempted to build up a formal system. Research has rather been directed towards the elucidation of principles, usually stated informally, with clusters of research projects indicating the extent of their validity. Such principles are embodied in informal statements, thus:

"Dependence on only one or a few sign stimuli seems to be characteristic of innate responses" [216].

"The various sign stimuli required for the release of an instinctive activity co-operate according to the rule of heterogenous summation" [216; see p. 592].

"In the breeding season most birds defend territories from other individuals of the same species and sex."

All such statements require a qualification defining their scope—thus the statement about bird territories is true for most male passerine birds but not, e.g., for the Emperor Penguin (*Aptenodytes forsteri*) [202]. The degree of generality of any such statement is, of course, a function of the quantitative specificity with which it is stated—if principles are to have any general application, only a limited degree of precision is desirable.

The framework of ethological ideas can thus include both purely qualitative analyses of broad categories of behavior (e.g., the analysis of courtship behavior, see p. 590), where the results are likely to have a fairly general validity, and more detailed analyses of particular problems, where the precise quantitative results are relevant only to the problem in hand (though of course they may point the way to less precise but broader generalizations). Both types of approach are necessary for an understanding of animal behavior.

History of ethology in mediating research. The scope and trends of ethological research can be seen only by considering the principal general topics with which it has been concerned. This has been attempted in the following paragraphs, but it must be noted that the selection of topics is necessarily an individual one—to some extent it reflects the personal interests of the present writer, and other ethologists might not agree that the studies chosen represent the growing points of current research. Further, those topics lying near (or within) the borders of physiology have not been considered. This involves the omission of many studies which have influenced ethologists (e.g., the work of von Holst, Gray, Lissmann, Weiss, and many others) as well as those in which ethological ideas have played an incidental role. Selection has also been in favor of European rather than American work, in order to include especially references with which the readers of this volume may not be familiar: this has involved omission of many writers (e.g., Aronson, Beach, Carpenter, Evans, Nice, Noble, Schneirla, and others), whose work is extremely pertinent to the subjects discussed. Further, except for a few classical studies, recent work has been included in preference to prewar work: in some cases, recent reviews have enabled previous detailed studies to be omitted from the bibliography. The literature cited is thus intended to be representative but by no means comprehensive.

Finally, references to some of the principles which are emerging are intended to show the direction research is taking, and not as formal statements.

Studies of the whole or a large part of the behavior of a species. General studies of the behavior of a species under natural or near-natural conditions are essential both for the more detailed study of limited portions of its behavior repertoire and, of course, for understanding the significance and relation of these parts with respect to the whole. Many such studies have been made by zoologists and naturalists who would not call themselves ethologists. The following is a selection of studies in which an ethological approach (see p. 562) has been especially evident:[12] arthropods [9, 34, 35, 52, 61, 96, 97], fish [12, 13, 57, 95, 151, 153, 164, 190, 191, 236], amphibia and reptiles [42, 45, 46, 107], birds, passerines [4, 8, 38, 63, 66, 74, 90, 112, 120, 126, 143, 161, 211], other groups [30, 71, 72, 73, 91, 101, 102, 105, 114, 127, 137, 138, 158, 197, 220, 230, 234, 235], and mammals [36, 41, 43, 44, 47, 118, 163, 166, 184, 192].

Qualitative analyses of relatively complex types of behavior (e.g., aggression, courtship) into simpler components. This includes a number of studies in many of which it has been shown that:

1. When behaving agonistically, the animal is under conflicting tendencies (see p. 586) to attack and flee from its rival. Sometimes one or another of these tendencies overrides the other and the animal actually attacks or flees. When the two tendencies are approximately equal, the animal may either alternate rapidly between the one and the other, show an ambivalent ("threat") posture, or a displacement activity (see below). Where a species has a number of different threat postures, each is probably correlated with different strengths or relative strengths of the two tendencies. The following references deal with analyses of this type in fish [12, 95, 153, 155, 190, 191, 223] and birds [4, 74, 75, 79, 143, 144, 152, 158, 159, 218, 220, 221].

2. Courtship. Similarly, courtship occurs when the animal is under the influence of conflicting tendencies, though here three are primarily involved—to attack, flee from, and behave sexually towards the mate. The nature of courtship "displays" depends on the strengths and relative strengths of the associated tendencies.

In both threat and courtship displays, particular components of the displays (e.g., crest-raising, wing-drooping in birds) are often correlated with the strength of one or other of the component tendencies. The

---

[12] Latin names of species and groups have been omitted from this section in the interests of brevity, but may be found in the list of references.

following studies deal with fish [12, 13, 151, 153, 154, 155, 164, 190, 191, 223] and birds [74, 75, 79, 93, 126, 143, 152, 158, 159, 161, 218, 220].

3. Various complex displays to predators similarly depend on conflicting tendencies [5, 7, 77, 143, 195].

This type of investigation thus results in an analysis of the behavior into "displays," "postures," etc., and of these into "components," and a subsequent separation of the components into groups, each associated with a particular tendency (e.g., attacking, fleeing, etc.) and thus presumably depending on more or less distinct sets of causal factors [79, 221]. The more detailed investigation of these causal factors represents a further step in the analysis. The evidence at present available indicates that the conclusions which are emerging in this field are widely applicable among fishes, birds, and probably, mammals. The courtship of other groups may, of course, rest on quite different bases [14, 171, 237].

Nature of the stimulus situation evoking each response. Of the total stimulus situation present at the time, only a very small proportion is relevant in the elicitation of a particular "unlearned" response. Such stimuli are termed "sign stimuli." For example, Tinbergen found that male Sticklebacks (*Gasterosteus aculeatus*) would attack very crude models which had the character "red belly underneath" but usually ignored models which, although closely similar to real sticklebacks, lacked this color. "The fish reacted essentially to the red and neglected the other characteristics" [164, 216]. Such sign stimuli are usually configurational, and the response to them not learned (p. 574). One consequence of this is that different responses normally given to the same object (e.g., courtship responses to the female) may be elicited by different characters of that object. (As defined in this way, the statement that a character is a sign stimulus for a particular response has not necessarily meant that it is specific to that response. Thus a color character which involves contrast with the normal background is likely to be effective in many different contexts—see p. 584.) The following references contain analyses of the stimulus situations eliciting particular responses: parental behavior in *Ammophila* (a hunting wasp) [9], courtship of Lepidoptera and Odonata [26, 133, 134, 135, 199, 226], hunting and courtship of spiders [40, 169], feeding in Honey-bees [59], fright responses of Minnows [60], schooling of fish [98], aggression and courtship of Sticklebacks [164, 216], parental behavior of Sticklebacks [95, 193], various responses of Cichlids [12, 190, 191], fighting of Fighting Fish [119], courtship of various Syngnathid fish [57], egg-rolling of Grey Lag Goose and other species [130, 168], response of young birds to flying predators [216], begging of young passerine birds [225], fighting of the European Robin [112], pecking of young Herring Gulls [227], hunting in owls [174], response of passerines to owls [68, 77], fighting of Chaffinches [142], auditory social signals of domestic hen [29], mating of rat [17].

Mode of action of the stimulus in evoking a response.

1. Changes in threshold. Changes in internal factors (*e.g.*, hormones) may affect the responsiveness to a particular external stimulus: such changes in responsiveness may occur even though the strength of the response once elicited is unaffected [21, 170]. Baerends [13] has shown that in *Lebistes reticulatus* the color pattern of the male can be used as an index of the internal state; and he has used this to demonstrate the effect of changes in the internal state on responsiveness to a constant stimulus [see also van Iersel, 95]. In exceptional cases practically no external stimulus may be necessary to elicit the response [*Leerlaufreaktionen,* Vacuum Activities, Overflow Activities, 6, 128, 216]. On the other hand, extra-strong stimuli (supernormal stimuli) may be effective when the animal is unresponsive to a normally adequate one [135, 216, 227].

2. Diverse nature of stimulus effects. In earlier ethological studies emphasis was laid on the function of the stimulus in releasing a response which was already "ready." Later work has also underlined the following factors:

a. The stimulating or motivating effect of the stimulus. The validity of the distinction between releasing and motivating effects is, however, still uncertain [77, 95].

b. Some stimuli (consummatory stimuli) serve to "switch off" the behavior in progress at the moment [16, 78, 207: see p. 573].

c. Some stimuli function mainly in the orientation of the response: homing of hunting wasps [22, 210, 224], hunting in *Ammophila* [9], orientation of ants [27, 232, 233], hunting in mantids [149], foraging of bees [61], orientation of fishes (demonstrating influence of internal factors) [85], various responses of fishes [12, 13, 95, 216], egg-rolling of goose [130], begging of young passerine birds [225], homing of birds [65, 84, 108, 109, 110, 111, 146, 183].

3. Principle of Heterogenous Summation (*Reizsummenregel*). If some of the sign stimuli which normally evoke a response are absent, the response may be reduced quantitatively but not qualitatively. The intensity of the response depends on how many of the sign stimuli are present but not on which (except in so far as the sign stimuli are of differing effectiveness). It is sometimes possible to construct models which combine sign stimuli in such a way that they are even more effective than the normal object [13, 55, 119, 135, 190, 191, 214, 216, 220, 227].

Analysis of the response. Many (but not all) forms of appetitive and consummatory behavior can be analyzed into a Fixed Action Pattern and an orientation component (see p. 573). The following references illustrate this: cichlid fishes [12, 190, 191], egg-rolling of goose [130], begging of young passerines [225].

Analysis of internal factors. So far only a few ethological studies in which internal factors were manipulated directly have been made by European ethologists, who have relied on the results of work by others (e.g., Beach and his pupils) in this field. The following, however, may be noted: gonadotrophins in sexual behavior of *Xenopus laevis* [179], parental behavior of doves [116], factors influencing the change from one phase of the reproductive cycle to another in the Three-Spined Stickleback [95].

Investigation of the factors affecting one particular response. In a number of other studies attempts to analyze the factors affecting one particular response have been made. In some of these the effects of re- peated stimulation, in others the effects of varying "internal" factors, and in others the effects of varied external stimuli as well were studied. Par- ticular attention has been paid to the processes underlying the changes in responsiveness when a stimulus is presented continuously or repeti- tively: these processes can be characterized by (1) the degree of per- manence of the waning, and (2) the degree of specificity of the waning to the particular stimulus used. Among the responses investigated from this point of view have been the following: hunting of *Ammophila* [9], various patterns in *Gryllus* [92], hunting and sexual behavior of spiders [40, 169], fanning of the Three-spined Stickleback [95, 193], courtship of Guppy [13], wiping, equilibrating, hunting, etc., responses of Amphibians [23, 51, 58], breathing in newts [201], egg-laying of dove [32], parental behavior of dove [116], mobbing response of Chaffinches to predators [77], gobbling of Turkey [186], begging of young passerines [170]. [See also reviews in 129, 172.]

Displacement activities. Sometimes when an animal is behaving in one way (e.g., aggressively) it suddenly shows behavior normally char- acteristic of a quite different context (e.g., feeding). Thus fighting Great Tits may suddenly start to peck at a bud or to pick up leaves and throw them over their shoulders—activities normally used in feeding. Such cases are grouped under the term "displacement activities" [104, 212, 216, 218]. The concept of displacement activities thus has reference primarily to apparent irrelevance, and thus often to the known historical origin of the behavior pattern in question—a pattern developed (phylo- genetically or ontogenetically) in one context appears in another. Such activities sometimes occur when the animal has tendencies to behave in two incompatible ways, or is in the presence of difficult or insoluble problems, etc. It is, therefore, sometimes said that they are activities "activated by a strange drive" or some similar phrase [6, 157, 218]. Tinbergen [218], however, makes it quite plain that this is only a *theory* about causation, not a matter of fact. "Displacement activities" are only one of a number of types of behavior which appear in "conflict" situations [e.g., ambivalent behavior, 216; redirection activities, 16; threat the courtship postures, see references on p. 591; etc.]. Further, although the category of displacement activities has been a useful one at the state of research reached, it certainly contains very heterogeneous phenomena. It is now clear that the causal basis of many displacement activities is less different from that of the same motor patterns when appearing in their "normal" context than was formerly supposed [3, 156]. In other cases displacement activities may necessitate a radical revision of the ethologists' concept of drive (p. 585). Indeed, the implied dichotomy between "displacement" and "nondisplacement" behavior—or, as they are sometimes called, autochthonous and allochthonous behavior—can be a source of confusion: the distinction is not a clear one.

Ontogeny of behavior—learning.

1. The various patterns of behavior shown by an animal are not all equally easily modified by learning. Thus the homing behavior of the wasp *Philanthus* is easily modifiable, but the hunting behavior is not [216]. The extent to which the different parts of the behavior are modifiable is characteristic of the species and, presumably, an adaptive feature [216 and references cited, 220].

Further, when any particular response becomes modified by conditioning, the features of the environment which are selected are often characteristic of the species. Thus various species of *Hymenoptera* use visual landmarks in orientation, but the sort of landmarks which are selected varies from species to species [216].

2. The tendency for particular behavior patterns to be modified rather than others, and the tendency to learn some aspects of the situation rather than others, are particularly revealed in the phenomena of "imprinting." The classic example is the Grey Lag gosling which, on hatching from the egg, will follow the first moving object (within wide limits of shape, size, etc.) that it sees, and will thenceforward direct towards that object all the activities which are normally directed to the parent. Lorenz [121] claimed that imprinting is absolutely different from other types of learning—on the grounds that it (a) is irreversible, (b) is limited to a brief period of the life cycle, (c) sometimes occurs before the specific behavior patterns in which it will play a role have developed, (d) involves a learning of species rather than individual characteristics— but this absolute distinction cannot be maintained. It is however, particularly interesting in that learning occurs without any conventional

reward, and involves a modification to "consummatory stimuli" [28, 29, 54, 71, 82, 121, 122, 123, 129, 160, 161, 173, 175, 198].

The acquisition of song by some passerine birds seems to have some features in common with imprinting [167, 208, 209].

3. Other types of learning in animals have been reviewed by Thorpe [204, 206, 209]. The detailed comparisons which he makes between animals of different phyletic levels give a perspective to the study of learning which cannot be achieved by studies, however detailed, of a single species.

4. Complex types of learning such as "counting" by birds and mammals [102, 103, 209].

5. Changes in responsiveness to a constant stimulus (see p. 593).

6. The development of behavior and the relation between maturation and learning has been studied by a number of writers [e.g., 20, 28, 41, 43, 44, 47, 89, 105, 106, 118, 161, 181, 182, 192, 208].

Evolution of behavior.

1. Evolution of social releasers. The integration of social behavior depends on the elicitation of specific responses in one individual (the "reactor") by sensory patterns provided by the structure or behavior of another (the "actor"). Communication of this sort has been facilitated by evolutionary changes in both the structure and behavior of the actor, making them more improbable and striking, and in the responsiveness (i.e., in the "IRM") of the reactor to these signals of the actor [122, 129, 145, 156, 214, 216, etc.].

So far, three sources of "displays" serving social communication have been recognized—"intention movements" (p. 577), "displacement activities" (p. 593) (including autonomic responses), and redirection activities [158]: all have become modified in evolution for a signal function [39, 145, 156, 218, 221]. In addition, courtship displays have sometimes been evolved by the further modification of threat postures. The evolutionary changes involved include the development of conspicuous structures, changes in the threshold, intensity, and form of the movements, and also changes in the relations between the components of the movements ("ritualization"). In some cases "emancipation" from the causal factors which primitively controlled the movement may also have occurred. (Similar changes may, of course, occur in movements not serving social communication.) The changes are such as to make the movement more conspicuous, more species-specific, or (in the case of certain "submissive," etc., displays) more different from displays of opposite significance [10, 39, 79, 83, 121, 122, 123, 125, 127, 128, 143, 152, 164, 214, 216, 220, 221].

Nonvisual communication has also been studied by ethologists [28, 29, 53, 67, 141, 144, 145, 181, 182, 208, 216].

2. The evolution of behavior as revealed by species differences. The comparative study of closely related forms enables deductions to be drawn about both the evolution of behavior and the phylogenetic relationship between species. Although complex behavior systems (e.g., "social nesting") have sometimes been used in such studies, they are often less certainly homologous between species, and their taxonomic utility is less easily assessed than that of simpler patterns. Fixed Action Patterns, especially those which are used in social communication between species, have been most valuable [83, 121, 127, 129, 221]: Arthropods [1, 14, 26, 34, 35, 52, 53, 96, 97, 187, 199], fish [12, 57, 155, 190, 191], birds [4, 8, 30, 64, 71, 72, 73, 74, 79, 120, 127, 128, 158, 168, 196, 235], mammals [166].

Functional aspects of behavior. These are discussed in many ethological papers but see particularly [7, 37, 81, 139, 144, 176, 177, 219].

Synthesis and links with neurophysiology. Complete understanding of behavior cannot be obtained merely by analysis into component variables. It is necessary (a) to resynthesize the products of the analysis in order to check its thoroughness, and to provide a picture of the behavior of the whole animal, and (b) to push the analysis still further to physiological levels.

Tinbergen [213, 215, 216] and Baerends [9, 12] have indicated one way in which such a resynthesis can be performed. The various causal factors (independent variables) affecting the behavior of an animal can be arranged in a series of interlinked hierarchical schemes. Thus some factors (e.g., male sex hormone) influence many different activities, whereas others (e.g., the situation "female laying eggs in nest" for the male stickleback) influence only one. Such a scheme can be described as a "hierarchy of causal factors."[13]

This concept of a hierarchy of causal factors, besides providing a means of synthesis and a way of looking at the whole behavior of the animal, is important in a number of other ways. For instance, as Tinbergen has pointed out [213], much useless discussion and argument as to the validity of generalizations can be avoided if the *level* in such a hierarchical scheme which is being discussed is specified.

It also provides an opportunity for a further link-up with physiological work. In a bold hypothetical scheme, Tinbergen has gone further than this to give a graphic representation of a hierarchical system of *causally related* nervous centers, each with its own IRM and each governing a particular type of behavior. This model can be of great value in "helping

---

[13] A rather different type of scheme is given by Kortlandt [106]. This makes use of the concept of "goal" but unfortunately fails to define it adequately. See *Brit. J. Anim. Behav.*, 1957, 5, 116–118.

us to put our thoughts in order." The general hierarchical arrangement is supported in some respects by both ethological and neurophysiological data [76, 216] though evidence is now accruing that the scheme as propounded requires rather fundamental modification [78, 80] (see p. 582).

SCOPE AND RANGE OF APPLICATION OF ETHOLOGY

The work discussed in the preceding sections is not part of a self-contained system. Much of it consists of attempts to establish bridgeheads for liaison both with workers in peripheral fields and also with investigators of the same phenomena at a different level, such as physiologists and biochemists. Its success must be judged by the extent to which these bridgeheads are secured—by the usefulness of ethological principles to both the psychologist running a rat in a maze and the physiologist pushing electrodes into its brain. It has already been emphasized that the aims and methods used by European ethologists are similar to those used by many American workers; and in some cases very similar conclusions have been reached independently. Links with S-R theory, expectancy theory [e.g., 209], information theory, and many other branches of psychology as well as with physiology and zoology are becoming increasingly apparent.

ETHOLOGICAL METHODS BELIEVED TO BE VALUABLE IN CONTEXTS OUTSIDE THE SCOPE OF ETHOLOGY

These have been mentioned in the preceding discussion and can be summarized here:

1. The necessity for observation, description, and classification before analysis
2. The validity of the functional and evolutionary as well as the causal study of behavior, and the cross-fertility of these separate approaches
3. The importance of qualitative studies as a necessary preliminary to quantitative work
4. The importance of designing experiments with a view to their biological relevance for the species concerned
5. The role of a comparative approach

    a. In facilitating observation
    b. In elucidating the evolution of behavior
    c. In taxonomy

    d. In providing a basis for generalization
    e. In leading to an understanding of function

  6. The importance of synthesis as well as analysis

NOTE ON TERMINOLOGY

    Although no definitions of the terms used by ethologists are given in this paper, page references to discussions of a few of the more important concepts are given below. Some of them have been defined by Thorpe [205] and, more recently, Verplanck (in press) has provided a glossary of terms for behavior students on both sides of the Atlantic.

Act, p. 576
Allochthonous behavior, p. 594
Appetitive behavior, p. 572
Autochthonous behavior, p. 594
Center, p. 582
Component, p. 590
Consummatory act, p. 572
Consummatory stimuli, p. 573
Displacement activity, p. 593
Display, p. 590
Drive, p. 585
Emancipation, p. 595
Fixed Action Pattern (*Erbkoordination*), p. 573
Heterogeneous Summation (*Reizsummenregel*), p. 592
Imprinting, p. 594
Inborn, p. 574–5
Innate, p. 574–5
Innate Releasing Mechanism (*Schema, angeborenen auslösender Mechanismus*), p. 584

Intention movement, p. 577
Mood (*Stimmung*), p. 587
Motivational impulses, p. 582
Motor coordination mechanism, p. 584
Orientation component, p. 573
Overflow activity, p. 592
Reaction, p. 568, 576
Reaction specific energy, p. 582
Reafferenz, p. 568
Redirection activity, p. 595
Reflex, p. 576
Releaser, p. 584
Response, p. 576
Ritualization, p. 595
Sign stimulus, p. 584, 591
Specific Action Potential, p. 586
Supernormal stimulus, p. 592
Tendency, p. 586
Vacuum activity (*Leerlaufreaktion*), p. 592

REFERENCES

  1. Adriaanse, M. S. C. A. *Ammophila campestris* Latr. and *Ammophila adriaanse* Wilke. *Behaviour*, 1947, **1**, 1–35.
  2. Adrian, E. D., Bremer, F., & Jasper, H. H. Brain mechanisms and consciousness. *Sym. Council int. Organisation med. Sci.* Oxford: Blackwell, 1954.
  3. Andrew, R. J. Some remarks on conflict situations, with special reference to *Emberiza* species. *Brit. J. Anim. Behav.*, 1956, **4**, 41–45.
  4. Andrew, R. J. A comparative study of certain behaviour patterns in

the Yellowhammer, Corn Bunting and related species. Unpublished doctoral dissertation, Cambridge Univ., 1955.

5. Armstrong, E. A. Diversionary display. 1. Connotation and terminology. 2. The nature and origin of distraction display. *Ibis*, 1949, **91**, 88–97, 179–188.

6. Armstrong, E. A. The nature and function of displacement activities. *Sym. Soc. exp. Biol.*, 1950, **4**, 361–384.

7 Armstrong, E. A. The ecology of distraction display. *Brit. J. Anim. Behav.*, 1954, **2**, 121–135.

8. Armstrong, E. A. *The wren*. London: Collins, 1955.

9. Baerends, G. P. Fortpflanzungsverhalten und Orientierung der Grabwespe *Ammophila campestris*. *Tidschr. Entomol.*, 1941, **84**, 68–275.

10. Baerends, G. P. Specializations in organs and movements with a releasing function. *Sym. Soc. exp. Biol.*, 1950, **4**, 337–360.

11. Baerends, G. P. The ethological analysis of fish behaviour. In M. E. Brown (Ed.), *The physiology of fishes*. Vol. 2. New York: Academic Press, 1957.

12. Baerends, G. P., & Baerends, J. M. An introduction to the ethology of Cichlid fishes. *Behaviour*, 1950, Supplement No. 1, 1–242.

13. Baerends, G. P., Bronwer, R., & Waterbolk, H. Tj. On the ethology of *Lebistes reticulatus* Peters. 1. Analysis of the male courtship pattern. *Behaviour*, 1955, **8**, 249–335.

14. Bastock, M. A gene mutation which changes a behavior pattern. *Evoln.*, 1957, **10**, 421–439.

15. Bastock, M., & Manning, A. The courtship of *Drosophila melanogaster*. *Behaviour*, 1955, **8**, 85–111.

16. Bastock, M., Morris, D., & Moynihan, M. Some comments on conflict and thwarting in animals. *Behaviour*, 1954, **6**, 66–84.

17. Beach, F. A. Analysis of the stimuli adequate to elicit mating behaviour in the sexually inexperienced male rat. *J. comp. Psychol.*, 1942, **33**, 163–207.

18. Beach, F. A. Effects of testosterone propionate upon the copulatory behaviour of sexually inexperienced male rats. *J. comp. Psychol.*, 1942, **33**, 227–247.

19. Beach, F. A. The de-scent of instinct. Presidential address, Eastern Psychol. Ass., 1952.

20. Beach, F. A. In B. Schaffner (Ed.), *Transactions of the First Conference on Group Processes*. New York: Macy Foundation, 1955.

21. Beach, F. A., & Holz-Tucker, A. M. Effects of different concentrations of androgen upon sexual behaviour in castrated male rats. *J. comp. physiol. Psychol.*, 1949, **42**, 433–453.

22. Beusekom, G. van. Some experiments on the optical orientation in *Philanthus triangulum* Fabr. *Behaviour*, 1948, **1**, 195–225.

23. Birukow, G. Ermüdung und Umstimmung bei Gleichgewichtsreaktionen der Amphibien. *Verh. dtsch. Zool. Ges.* Wilhelmshaven: 1951. Pp. 144–150.

24. Birukow, G. Studien über statisch-optisch ausgelöste Kompensations-bewegungen und Körperhaltung bei Amphibien. *Z. vergl. Physiol.,* 1952, **34,** 448–472.

25. Broadbent, D. Pavlovian conditioning and vigilance tasks. Medical Research Council, 1952, A.P.U. 175/52.

26. Buchholtz, C. Eine vergleichende Ethologie der orientalischen Calopterygiden (*Odonata*) als Beitrag zu ihre systematischen Deutung. *Z. Tierpsychol.,* 1955, **12,** 364–386.

27. Carthy, J. D. The orientation of two allied species of British ant. I and II. *Behaviour,* 1951, **3,** 275–303; 304–318.

28. Collias, N. E. The development of social behaviour in birds. *Auk,* 1952, **69,** 127–159.

29. Collias, N., & Joos, M. The spectrographic analysis of sound signals of the domestic fowl. *Behaviour,* 1953, **5,** 175–189.

30. Craig, W. The expressions of emotion in the pigeon. I. The blond ring-dove (*Turtur risorius*). *J. comp. Neurol. Psychol.,* 1909, **19,** 29–80.

31. Craig, W. The expressions of emotion in the pigeon. II. The mourning dove (*Zenaidwa macrowahinn*). *Auk,* 1911, **28,** 398–407.

32. Craig, W. Oviposition induced by the male in pigeons. *J. Morphol.,* 1911, **22,** 299–305.

33. Craig, W. Appetites and aversions as constituents of instincts. *Biol. Bull.,* 1918, **34,** 91–107.

34. Crane, J. Comparative biology of Salticid spiders at Rancho Grande, Venezuela. *Zoologica,* 1948–50, **33–35.**

35. Crane, J. A comparative study of innate defensive behaviour in Trinidad Mantids. *Zoologica,* 1952, **37,** 259–293.

36. Crowcroft, P. Notes on the behaviour of shrews. *Behaviour,* 1955, **8,** 63–80.

37. Cullen, E. Adaptations in the Kittiwake to cliff-nesting. *Ibis,* 1957, **99,** 275–302.

38. Daanje, A. Über das Verhalten des Haussperlings. *Ardea,* 1941, **30,** 1–42.

39. Daanje, A. On the locomotory movements of birds and the intention movements derived from them. *Behaviour,* 1950, **3,** 48–98.

40. Drees, O. Untersuchungen über die angeborenen Verhaltensweisen bei Springspinnen. *Z. Tierpsychol.,* 1952, **9,** 169–207.

41. Eibl-Eibesfeldt, I. Uber die Jugendentwicklung des Verhaltens eines männlichen Dachses (*Meles meles* L.). *Z. Tierpsychol.,* 1950, **7,** 327–355.

42. Eibl-Eibesfeldt, I. Ein Beitrag zur Paarungsbiologie der Erdkröte. *Behaviour,* 1950, **2,** 217–237.

43. Eibl-Eibesfeldt, I. Beobachtungen zur Fortpflanzungsbiologie und Jugendentwicklung des Eichhörnchens (*Sciurus vulgaris* L.). *Z. Tierpsychol.,* 1951, **8,** 370–400.

44. Eibl-Eibesfeldt, I. Gefangenschaftsbeobachtungen an der persischen Wüstenmaus (*Meriones persicus persicus* Blanford). *Z. Tierpsychol.,* 1951, **8,** 400–423.

45. Eibl-Eibesfeldt, I. Nahrungserwerb und Beuteschema der Erdkröte (*Bufo bufo* L.). *Behaviour*, 1952, **4**, 1–36.

46. Eibl-Eibesfeldt, I. Vergleichende Verhaltensstudien an Anuren. I. Zur Paarungsbiologie des Haubfrosches *Hyla arborea* L. *Z. Tierpsychol.*, 1952, **9**, 383–395.

47. Eibl-Eibesfeldt, I. Zur Ethologie des Hamsters (*Cricetus cricetus*). *Z. Tierpsychol.*, 1953, **10**, 204–254.

48. Eibl-Eibesfeldt, I. Der Kommentkampf der Meerechse. *Z. Tierpsychol.*, 1955, **12**, 49–62.

49. Eibl-Eibesfeldt, I. Ethologische Studien am Galápagos Seelöwen. *Z. Tierpsychol.*, 1955, **12**, 286–303.

50. Eibl-Eibesfeldt, I. Zur Biologie des Iltis (*Putorius putorius*). *Verh. dtsch. Zool. Ges.* Erlangen: 1955. Pp. 304–323.

51. Eikmanns, K-H. Verhaltensphysiologische Untersuchungen über den Beutefang und das Bewegungssehen der Erdkröte. *Z. Tierpsychol.*, 1955, **12**, 229–253.

52. Evans, H. E. An ethological study of the Digger Wasp *Bembecinus neglectus*, with a review of the ethology of the genus. *Behaviour*, 1955, **7**, 287–304.

53. Faber, A. *Laut- und Gebärdensprache bei Insekten*. Vol. 1. *Orthoptera*. Stuttgart: 1953.

54. Fabricius, E. Zur Ethologie junger Anatiden. *Acta. Zool. Fenn.*, 1951, **68**, 1–178.

55. Fabricius, E. Aquarium observations on the spawning behaviour of the Char, *Salmo alpinus. Inst. Freshwater Research*, Report 34. Drottningholm, 1953.

56. Fabricius, E. Aquarium observations on the spawning behaviour of the Burbot, *Lota vulgaris* L. *Inst. Freshwater Research*, Report No. 35. Drottningholm, 1954.

57. Fiedler, K. Vergleichende Verhaltensstudien an Seenadeln, Schlangennadeln und Seepferdchen (*Syngnathidae*). *Z. Tierpsychol.*, 1954, **11**, 358–416.

58. Franzisket, L. Untersuchungen zur Spezifität und Kumulierung der Erregungsfähigkeit und zur Wirkung einer Ermüdung in der Afferenz bei Wischbewegungen des Rückenmarkfrosches. *Z. vergl. Physiol.*, 1953, **34**, 525–538.

59. Free, J. B. A study of the stimuli which release the food-begging and offering responses of worker honey-bees. *Brit. J. Anim. Behav.*, 1956, **4**, 94–101.

60. Frisch, K. von. Über einer Schreckstoff der Fischhaut und seine biologische Bedeutung. *Z. vergl. Physiol.*, 1941, **29**, 46–145.

61. Frisch, K. von. *An account of the life and senses of the honey bee.* London: Methuen, 1954.

62. Goethe, F. Beobachtungen bei der Aufzucht junger Silbermöwen. *Z. Tierpsychol.*, 1955, **12**, 402–434.

63. Goodwin, D. Some aspects of the behaviour of the Jay (*Garrulus glandarius*). *Ibis*, 1951, **93**, 414–442; 602–625.

64. Goodwin, D. A comparative study of the voice and some aspects of behaviour in two old-world Jays. *Behaviour*, 1952, 4, 293–316.

65. Griffin, D. R. Bird navigation. *Biol. Rev.*, 1952, 359–400.

66. Haartman, L. von. Der Trauerfliegenschnäpper. I. Ortstreue und Rassenbildung. II. Populationsprobleme. III. Die Nahrungsbiologie. *Acta Zool. Fenn.*, 1949, 56, 1–104; 1951, 67, 1–60; 1954, 83, 1–92.

67. Haartman, L. von., & Löhrl, H. Die Lautäusserungen des Trauer- und Halsbandfliegenschnäppers. *Orn. Fenn.*, 1950, 4, 86–97.

68. Hartley, P. H. T. An experimental analysis of interspecific recognition. *Sym. Soc. exp. Biol.*, 1950, 4, 313–336.

69. Hebb, D. O. Drives and the C.N.S. (Conceptual Nervous System). *Psych. Rev.*, 1955, 62, 243–254.

70. Hebb, D. O. Heredity and environment in mammalian behaviour. *Brit. J. Anim. Behav.*, 1953, 1, 43–47.

71. Heinroth, O. Beiträge zur Biologie, namentlich Ethologie und Psychologie der Anatiden. *Verh. V. Int. Ornithol. Kongr.* Berlin: 1911. Pp. 589–702.

72. Heinroth, O., & Heinroth K. Verhaltensweisen der Felsentaube (Haustaube) *Columba livia livia* L. *Z. Tierpsychol.*, 1949, 6, 153–201.

73. Heinroth, O., & Heinroth, M. *Die Vögel Mitteleuropas.* Berlin: Bermuhler, 1928.

74. Hinde, R. A. The behaviour of the Great Tit (*Parus major*) and some other related species. *Behaviour*, 1952. Supplement No. 2. Pp. 1–201.

75. Hinde, R. A. The conflict between drives in the courtship and copulation of the Chaffinch (*Fringilla coelebs*). *Behaviour*, 1953, 5, 1–31.

76. Hinde, R. A. Appetitive behaviour, consummatory act, and the hierarchical organisation of behaviour—with special reference to the Great Tit. *Behaviour*, 1953, 5, 191–224.

77. Hinde, R. A. Factors governing the changes in strength of a partially inborn response, as shown by the mobbing behaviour of the Chaffinch (*Fringilla coelebs*). I. The nature of the response, and an examination of its course. II. The waning of the response. *Proc. roy. Soc. B.*, 1954, 142B, 306–331, 331–358, and in preparation.

78. Hinde, R. A. Changes in responsiveness to a constant stimulus. *Brit. J. Anim. Behav.*, 1954, 2, 41–55.

79. Hinde, R. A. A comparative study of the behaviour of certain finches. *Ibis*, 1955, 97, 706–745; 98, 1–23.

80. Hinde, R. A. Ethological models and the concept of drive. *Brit. J. Philos. Sci.*, 1956, 6, 321–331.

81. Hinde, R. A. The biological significance of the territories of birds. *Ibis*, 1956, 98, 340–369, and other papers in this number.

82. Hinde, R. A., Thorpe, W. H., & Vince, M. A. The following response of young moorhens and coots. *Behaviour*, 1956, 9, 214–242.

83. Hinde, R. A., & Tinbergen, N. The comparative study of species-characteristic behaviour. In *Evolution and Behavior.* New Haven, Conn.: Yale Univer. Press, in press.

84. Hoffmann, K. Versuche zu der im Richtungsfinden der Vögel enthaltenen Zeitschätzung. *Z. Tierpsychol.*, 1954, **11**, 453–475.

85. Holst, E. von. Quantitative Messung von Stimmungen im Verhalten der Fische. *Sym. Soc. exp. Biol.*, 1950, **4**, 143–172.

86. Holst, E. von. Relations between central nervous system and peripheral sense organs. *Brit. J. Anim. Behav.*, 1954, **2**, 89–94.

87. Holst, E. von, & Mittelstaedt, H. Das Reafferenzprincip. *Naturwissenschaften*, 1950, **37**, 464.

88. Holzapfel, M. Über Bewegungsstereotypen bei gehaltenen Säugérn. I–IV. *Z. Tierpsychol*, 1938, **2**, 46–60, 60–72; *Zoologische Garten*, 1939, **10**, 184–193; *Z. Tierpsychol.*, 1939, **3**, 151–160.

89. Holzapfel, M. Die Beziehung zwischen den Trieben junger und erwachsener Tiere. *Schweizerische Z. Psychol.*, 1949, **8**, 32–60.

90. Howard, H. E. *The nature of a bird's world.* Cambridge: Cambridge Univer. Press, 1935.

91. Howard, H. E. *A waterhen's worlds.* Cambridge: Cambridge Univer. Press, 1940.

92. Hubert, F. Sitz und Bedeutung nervöser Zentren für Instinkthandlungen beim Männchen von *Gryllus campestris* L. *Z. Tierpsychol.*, 1955, **12**, 12–48.

93. Huxley, J. S. The courtship habits of the great crested grebe (*Podiceps cristatus*). *Proc. Zool. Soc. Lond.*, 1914, **2**, 491–562.

94. Huxley, J. S. *Evolution: the modern synthesis.* London: Allen and Unwin, 1942.

95. Iersel, J. A. A. van. An analysis of the parental behaviour of the male Three-spined Stickleback. *Behaviour*, 1953. Supplement No. 3.

96. Jacobs, W. Vergleichende Verhaltensttudien an Feldheuschrecken. *Z. Tierpsychol.*, 1950, **7**, 169–216.

97. Jacobs, W. Verhaltensbiologische Studien an Feldheuschrecken. *Z. Tierpsychol.* Supplement, 1953.

98. Keenleyside, M. H. A. Some aspects of the schooling behaviour of fish. *Behaviour*, 1955, **8**, 183–249.

99. Kennedy, J. S. Is modern ethology objective? *Brit. J. Anim. Behav.*, 1954, **2**, 12–29.

100. Koenig, L. Beiträge zur einem Aktionssystem des Bienenfressers (*Merops apiaster* L.). *Z. Tierpsychol.*, 1951, **8**, 169–210.

101. Koenig, L. Beobachtungen am afrikanischen Blauwengenspint (*Merops superciliosus chrysocercus*) im freier Wildbahn und Gefangenschaft. *Z. Tierpsychol.*, 1953, **10**, 180–204.

102. Köhler, O. "Zahl"-versuche an einem Kohlraben und Vergleichsversuche an Menschen. *Z. Tierpsychol.*, 1943, **5**, 575–712.

103. Köhler, O. The ability of birds to count. *Bull. Anim. Behav.*, 1951, **9**, 41–45.

104. Kortlandt, A. Wechselwirkung zwischen Instinkten. *Arch. Néerl. Zoöl.*, 1940, **4**, 443–520.

105. Kortlandt, A. Eine Übersicht der angeborenen Verhaltensweisen des

Mitteleuropäischen Kormorans (*Phalacrocorax carbo sinensis*). *Arch. Neérl. Zoöl.*, 1940, **4**, 401–442.

106. Kortlandt, A. Aspects and prospects of the concept of instinct (vicissitudes of the hierarchy theory). *Arch. Neérl. Zoöl.*, 1955, **11**, 155–284.

107. Kramer, G. Beobachtungen über Paarungsbiologie und soziales Verhalten von Mauereidechsen. *Z. Morph. Ökol. Tiere*, 1937, **32**, 752–783.

108. Kramer, G. Experiments on bird orientation. *Ibis*, 1952, **94**, 265–285.

109. Kramer, G. Wird die Sonnenhöhe bei Heimfindorientierung verwertet? *J. Ornithol.*, 1953, **94**, 201–219.

110. Kramer, G. Die Sonnenorientierung der Vögel. *Verh. dtsch. Zool. Ges.* Freiburg: 1952. Pp. 72–84.

111. Kramer, G. Ein weiterer Versuch, die Orientierung von Brieftauben durch jahreszeitliche Änderung der Sonnenhöhe zu beeinflussen. *J. Ornithol.*, 1955, **96**, 173–185.

112. Lack, D. The behaviour of the robin. I & II. *Proc. Zool. Soc. Lond.*, 1939, A, **109**, 169–178.

113. Lack, D. *The life of the robin.* London: H. F. & G. Witherby, 1943.

114. Laven, H. Beiträge zur Biologie des Sandregenpfeifers (*Charadrius hiaticula*). *J. Ornithol.*, 1940, **88**, 183–288.

115. Lehrman, D. S. A critique of Konrad Lorenz's theory of instinctive behaviour. *Quart. Rev. Biol.*, 1953, **28**, 337–363.

116. Lehrman, D. S. The physiological basis of parental feeding behaviour in the Ring Dove (*Streptopelia risoria*). *Behaviour*, 1955, **7**, 241–286.

117. Lehrman, D. S. In B. Schaffner (Ed.), *Transactions of the First Conference on Group Processes.* New York: Macy Foundation, 1955.

118. Lindemann, W. Uber die Jugendentwicklung beim Luchs (*Lynx l. lynx* Kerr) und bei der Wildkatze (*Felis s. silvestris* Schreb). *Behaviour*, 1955, **8**, 1–45.

119. Lissmann H. W. Die Umwelt des Kampffisches (*Betta splendens* Regen). *Z. vergl. Physiol.*, 1932, **18**, 65–111.

120. Lorenz, K. Beiträge zur Ethologie sozialer Corviden. *J. Ornithol.*, 1931, **79**, 67–127.

121. Lorenz, K. Der Kumpan in der Umwelt des Vögels. *J. Ornithol.*, 1935, **83**, 137–213; 289–413.

122. Lorenz, K. The companion on the bird's world. *Auk*, 1937, **54**, 245–273.

123. Lorenz, K. Über den Begriff der Instinkthandlung. *Folia Biotheor.*, 1937, **2**, 18–50.

124. Lorenz, K. Über die Bildung des Instinktbegriffs. *Naturwissenschaften*, 1937, **25**, 289–300; 307–318; 324–331.

125. Lorenz, K. Vergleichende Verhaltensforschung. *Zool. Anz. Suppl.*, 1939. Bd. 12, 69–102.

126. Lorenz, K. Die Paarbildung beim Kohlrabe. *Z. Tierpsychol.*, 1939, **3**, 278–292.

127. Lorenz, K. Vergleichende Bewegungsstudien an Anatiden. *J. Ornithol.*, 1941, **89**. Sonderheft 194–294.

128. Lorenz, K. The comparative method in studying innate behaviour patterns. *Sym. Soc. exp. Biol.*, 1950, **4**, 221–268.

129. Lorenz, K. In B. Schaffner (Ed.), *Transactions of the First Conference on Group Processes.* New York: Macy Foundation, 1955.

130. Lorenz, K., & Tinbergen, N. Taxis und Instinkthandlung in der Eirollbewegung der Graugans. I. *Z. Tierpsychol.*, 1938, **2**, 1–29.

131. MacCorquodale, K., & Meehl, P. E. On a distinction between hypothetical constructs and intervening variables. *Psych. Rev.*, 1948, **55**, 95–107.

132. MacCorquodale, K., & Meehl, P. E. Edward C. Tolman. In Estes, W. K., et al., *Modern learning theory.* New York: Appleton-Century-Crofts, 1954.

133. Magnus, D. Beobachtungen zur Balz und Eiablage des Kaisermantels *Argynnis paphia* L. *Z. Tierpsychol.*, 1950, **7**, 435–449.

134. Magnus, D. Experimentelle Untersuchungen am Kaisermantel zu Analyse optischer Auslösungsreize. *Deutscher Entomologentag in Hamburg*, 1953, 58–75.

135. Magnus, D. Zur Problem der "überoptimalen" Schlüsselreize. *Verh. dtsch. Zool. Ges.* Tubingen: 1954.

136. Maier, N. R. F., & Schnierla, T. C. *Principles of animal psychology.* New York and London: McGraw-Hill, 1935.

137. Makkink, G. F. An attempt at an ethogram of the European avocet (*Recurvirostra avosetta* L.) with ethological and psychological remarks. *Ardea*, 1936, **25**, 1–60.

138. Makkink, G. F. Contribution to the knowledge of the behaviour of the Oystercatcher (*Haematopus ostralegus*). *Ardea*, 1942, **31**, 23–74.

139. Manning, A. The effect of honeyguides. *Behaviour*, 1956, **9**, 114–139.

140. Manning, A. Some aspects of the foraging behaviour of bumblebees. *Behaviour*, 1956, **9**, 164–201.

141. Marler, P. Characteristics of some animal calls. *Nature*, 1955, **176**, 6.

142. Marler, P. Studies of fighting in Chaffinches. I, II, III. *Brit. J. Anim. Behav.*, 1955, **3**, 111–117; 137–146; 1956, **4**, 23–30; 1957, **5**, 29–37.

143. Marler, P. The behaviour of the Chaffinch. *Behaviour*, 1956. Supplement No. 5.

144. Marler, P. The voice of the Chaffinch and its function as a language. *Ibis*, 1956, **98**, 231–261.

145. Marler, P. Specific distinctiveness in the communication signals of birds. *Behaviour*, **11**, 13–39.

146. Matthews, G. V. T. *Bird navigation.* Cambridge: Cambridge Univer. Press, 1955.

147. Mayr, E. *Systematics and the origin of species.* New York: Columbia Univer. Press, 1942.

148. Meehl, P. E., & MacCorquodale, K. Some methodological comments concerning expectancy theory. *Psych. Rev.,* 1951, **58**, 230–233.

149. Mittelstaedt, H. Uber die Beutefangmechanismus der Mantiden. *Verh. dtsch. Zool. Ges.* Freiburg: 1950. Pp. 102–106.

150. Mittelstaedt, H., & Holst, E. von. Reafferenzprincip und Optomotorik. *Zool. Anzeiger,* 1953, **151**, 253–257.

151. Morris, D. Homosexuality in the Ten-spined Stickleback (*Pygosteus pungitius* L.). *Behaviour,* 1952, 4, 233–262.

152. Morris, D. The reproductive behaviour of the Zebra Finch (*Poephila guttata*) with special reference to pseudofemale behaviour and displacement activities. *Behaviour,* 1954, **6**, 271–322.

153. Morris, D. The reproductive behaviour of the River Bullhead (*Cottus gobio* L.) with special reference to the fanning activity. *Behaviour,* 1954, **7**, 1–32.

154. Morris, D. The causation of pseudofemale and pseudomale behaviour: a further comment. *Behaviour,* 1955, **8**, 46–56.

155. Morris, D. The reproductive behaviour of the Ten-spined Stickleback (*Pygosteus pungitius* L.). *Behaviour,* 1958. Supplement No. 6.

156. Morris, D. The feather postures of birds and the problem of the origin of social signals. *Behaviour,* 1956, **9**, 75–113.

157. Moynihan, M. Some displacement activities of the Black-headed Gull. *Behaviour,* 1953, **5**, 58–80.

158. Moynihan, M. Some aspects of reproductive behaviour in the Black-headed Gull (*Larus ridibundus* L.) and related species. *Behaviour,* 1955. Supplement No. 4, 1–201.

159. Moynihan, M., & Hall, M. F. Hostile, sexual and other social behaviour patterns of the Spice Finch (*Lonchura punctulata*) in captivity. *Behaviour,* 1954, **7**, 23–76.

160. Nice, M. M. Some experiences in imprinting ducklings. *Condor,* 1953, **55**, 33–37.

161. Nicolai, J. Zur Biologie und Ethologie des Gimpels. *Z. Tierpsychol.,* 1956, **13**, 93–133.

162. Nissen, H. W. Description of the learned response in discrimination behaviour. *Psych. Rev.,* 1950, **57**, 132. (See also *Psych. Rev.,* 1952, **59**, 161–167.)

163. Nolte, A. Freilandbeobachtungen über das Verhalten von *Macaca radiata* in Südindien. *Z. Tierpsychol.,* 1955, **12**, 77–87.

164. Pelkwijk, J. J. ter, & Tinbergen, N. Eine reizbiologische Analyse einiger Verhaltensweisen von *Gasterosteus aculeatus* L. *Z. Tierpsychol.,* 1937, **1**, 193–204.

165. Picken, L. E. R. The study of minute biological structures and their significance in the organisation of cells. *School Sci. Rev.,* 1955, **129**, 262–268; **130**, 332–338; **131**, 30–37.

166. Pilters, H. Untersuchungen über angeborene Verhaltensweisen bei

Tylopoden unter besonderer Berucksichtigung der neuweltlichen Formen. *Z. Tierpsychol.*, 1954, **11**, 213–303.

167. Poulsen, H. Inheritance and learning in the song of the Chaffinch. *Behaviour*, 1951, **3**, 216–228.

168. Poulsen, H. A study of incubation responses and some other behaviour patterns in birds. *Vidensk. Medd. fra Dansk naturh. Foren.*, 1953, **115**, 1–131.

169. Precht, H. Über das angeborene Verhalten vom Tieren: Versuche an Springspinnen. *Z. Tierpsychol.*, 1952, **9**, 207–230.

170. Prechtl, H. F. R. Zur Physiologie der angeborenen auslösenden Mechanismen. *Behaviour*, 1953, **5**, 32–50.

171. Prechtl, H. F. R. Zur Paarungsbiologie einiger Molcharten. *Z. Tierpsychol.*, 1951, **8**, 337–348.

172. Prechtl, H. F. R. Neurophysiologische Mechanismen des formstarren Verhaltens. *Behaviour*, 1956, **9**, 243–319.

173. Räber, H. Analyse des Balzverhaltens eines domestizierten Truthahns. *Behaviour*, 1948, **1**, 237–266.

174. Räber, H. Das verhalten gefangener Waldohreulen (*Asio otus otus*) und Waldkäuze (*Strix aluco aluco*). *Behaviour*, 1949, **2**, 1–95.

175. Ramsay, A. O. Familial recognition in domestic birds. *Auk*, 1951, **68**, 1–16.

176. Ruiter, L. de. Some experiments on the camouflage of stick caterpillars. *Behaviour*, 1952, **4**, 222–233.

177. Ruiter, L. de. Countershading in caterpillars. *Arch. Néerl. Zool.*, 1955, **11**, 285–341.

178. Russell, E. S. Perceptual and sensory signs in instinctive behaviour. *Proc. Linn. Soc. Lond.*, 1943, **154**, 195–216.

179. Russell, W. M. S. Experimental studies on the reproductive behaviour of *Xenopus laevis* L. I. The control mechanisms for clasping and unclasping and the specificity of hormone action. *Behaviour*, 1954, **7**, 113–188.

180. Russell, W. M. S., Mead, A. P., & Hayes, J. S. A basis for the quantitative study of the structure of behaviour. *Behaviour*, 1954, **6**, 153–206.

181. Sauer, F. Die Entwicklung der Lautäusserungen vom Ei abschalldichtgehaltener Dorngrasmücken (*Sylvia c. communis* Latham) im vergleich mit später isolierten und mit wildleben Artgenossen. *Z. Tierpsychol.*, 1954, **11**, 10–93.

182. Sauer, F. Uber das Verhalten junger Gartengrasmücken *Sylvia borin*. *J. Ornithol.*, 1956, **97**, 156–187.

183. Sauer, F., & Sauer, E. Zur Frage der nächtlichen Zugorientierung von Grasmücken. *Rev. Suisse Zool.*, 1955, **62**, 250–259.

184. Schenkel, R. Ausdruck—Studien an Wölfen. *Behaviour*, 1947, **1**, 81–130.

185. Schiller, P. H. Innate constituents of complex responses in primates. *Psych. Rev.*, 1952, **59**, 177–191.

186. Schleidt, M. Untersuchungen über die Auslösung des Kollerns beim Truthahn (*Meleagris gallapagos*). *Z. Tierpsychol.*, 1952, **11**, 417–435.

187. Schmidt, R. S. Termite nests—important ethological material. *Behaviour*, 1955, **8**, 344–357.

188. Schneirla, T. C. A consideration of some conceptual trends in comparative psychology. *Psych. Bull.*, 1952, **49**, 559–597.

189. Scott, J. P., & Fredericson, E. The cause of fighting in mice and rats. *Physiol. Zool.*, 1951, **24**, 273–309.

190. Seitz, A. Die Paarbildung bei einigen Cichliden. *Z. Tierpsychol.*, 1940, **4**, 40–84; 1941, **5**, 74–101.

191. Seitz, A. Vergleichende Verhaltensstudien an Buntbarschen. *Z. Tierpsychol.*, 1949, **6**, 202–235.

192. Seitz, A. Untersuchungen über angeborene Verhaltensweisen bei Caniden. *Z. Tierpsychol.*, 1955, **12**, 463–489.

193. Sevenster, P. A quantitative study of "displacement" fanning in the Three-spined Stickleback as compared with parental fanning, in preparation.

194. Sherrington, C. S. *The integrative action of the nervous system.* New York: Charles Scribners' Sons, 1906.

195. Simmons, K. E. L. The nature of the predator-reactions of breeding birds. *Behaviour*, 1952, **4**, 161–172.

196. Simmons, K. E. L. Some aspects of the aggressive behaviour of three closely related plovers (*Charadrius*). *Ibis,* 1953, **95**, 115–127.

197. Simmons, K. E. L. Studies on Great Crested Grebes. *Avic. Mag.,* 1951, **61**.

198. Spalding, D. A. Instinct, with original observations on young animals. *MacMillan's Magazine,* 1873, **27**, 282–293 (reprinted *Brit. J. Anim. Behav.,* 1952, **2**, 2–11).

199. Spieth, H. T. Mating behaviour and sexual isolation in the *Drosophila virilis* species group. *Behaviour*, 1950, **3**, 105–145.

200. Spurway, H. Territory and evolution in Sticklebacks. *Penguin new biology,* 1953, **4**, 33–43.

201. Spurway, H., & Haldane, J. B. S. The comparative ethology of vertebrate breathing. I. Breathing in newts, with a general survey. *Behaviour,* 1954, **6**, 8–34.

202. Stonehouse, B. The Emperor Penguin (*Aptenodytes forsteri*). Falkland Islands Dependencies Survey, *Scientific Reports,* No. 6, 1953.

203. Stride, G. O. On the courtship behaviour of *Hypolimnas misippus* L. (Lepidoptera, Nymphalidae). *Brit. J. Anim Behav.,* 1956, **4**, 52–68.

204. Thorpe, W. H. Types of learning in insects and other arthropods. *Brit. J. Psychol.,* 1943–44, **33**, 220–234; **34**, 20–31; 66–76.

205. Thorpe, W. H. The definition of some terms used in animal behaviour studies. *Bull. Anim. Behav.,* 1951, **9**, 34–40.

206. Thorpe, W. H. The learning abilities of birds. *Ibis,* 1951, **93**, 1–52; 252–296.

207. Thorpe, W. H. Some concepts of modern ethology *Nature,* 1954, **174**, 101–105,

208. Thorpe, W. H. The process of song-learning in the Chaffinch as studied by means of the sound-spectrograph. *Nature,* 1954, **173**, 465–469.

209. Thorpe, W. H. *Learning and instinct in animals.* London: Methuen, 1956.

210. Tinbergen, N. Über die Orientierung des Bienenwolfes (*Philanthus triangulum* Fabr.). *Z. vergl. Physiol.,* 1932, **18**, 305–335; 1935, **21**, 699–716.

211. Tinbergen, N. The behaviour of the Snow Bunting in spring. *Trans Linn. Soc. N.Y.,* 1939, **5**, 1–94.

212. Tinbergen, N. Die Übersprungbewegung. *Z. Tierpsychol.,* 1940, **4**, 1–10.

213. Tinbergen, N. An objectivistic study of the innate behaviour of animals. *Biblioth. Biotheor.,* 1942, **1**, 39–98.

214. Tinbergen, N. Social releasers and the experimental method required for their study. *Wilson Bull.,* 1948, **60**, 6–52.

215. Tinbergen, N. The hierarchial organization of the nervous mechanisms underlying instinctive behaviour. *Sym. Soc. exp. Biol.,* 1950. Pp. 305–312.

216. Tinbergen, N. *The study of instinct.* London: Oxford Univer. Press, 1951.

217. Tinbergen, N. Recent advances in the study of bird behaviour. *Proc. Xth int. Ornithol. Congr. Uppsala,* 1950, 360–374.

218. Tinbergen, N. Derived activites: their causation, biological significance, origin and emancipation during evolution. *Quart. Rev. Biol.,* 1952, **27**, 1–32.

219. Tinbergen, N. *Social behaviour in animals.* London: Methuen, 1953.

220. Tinbergen, N. *The herring gull's world.* London: Collins, 1953.

221. Tinbergen, N. The origin and evolution of courtship and threat display. In A. C. Hardy, J. S. Huxley, & E. B. Ford, (Eds.), *Evolution as a process.* London: Allen & Unwin, 1954.

222. Tinbergen, N. In B. Schaffner (Ed.), *Transactions of the First Conference on Group Processes.* New York: Macy Foundation, 1955.

223. Tinbergen, N., & van Iersel, J. A. A. "Displacement reactions" in the Three-spined Stickleback. *Behaviour,* 1947, **1**, 56–63.

224. Tinbergen, N., & Kruyt, W. Über die Orientierung des Bienenwolfes. III. *Zeits. vergl. Physiol.,* 1938, **25**, 292–334.

225. Tinbergen, N., & Kuenen, D. J. Über die auslösenden und die richtunggebenden Reizsituation der Sperrbewegung von jungen Drosseln. *Z. Tierpsychol.,* 1939, **3**, 37–60.

226. Tinbergen, N., Meeuse, B. B. D., Boerema, L. K., & Varossieau, W. W. Die Balz des Samtfalters *Eumenis* (= *Satyrus*) *semele* (L.) *Z. Tierpsychol.,* 1942, **5**, 182–226.

227. Tinbergen, N., & Perdeck, A. C. On the stimulus situation releasing the begging response in the newly-hatched Herring Gull chick (*Larus a. argentatus* Pont.). *Behaviour,* 1950, **3**, 1–38.

228. Toulmin, S. E. *The philosophy of science.* London: Hutchinson, 1953.

229. Uexküll, J. von. *Umwelt und Innenwelt der Tiere.* Berlin: Springer, 1909.

230. Verwey, J. Die Paarungsbiologie des Fischreihers (*Ardea cinerea* L.). *Verh. VI int. Ornithol. Kong., Kopenhagen,* 1926, 390–413.

231. Verplanck, W. S. Burrhus F. Skinner. In Estes, W. K., et al., *Modern learning theory.* New York: Appleton-Century-Crofts, 1954.

232. Vowles, D. M. The orientation of ants. I and II. *J. exp. Biol.,* 1955, **31,** 341–355; 356–375.

233. Vowles, D. M. The foraging of ants. *Brit. J. Anim. Behav.,* 1955, **3,** 1–13.

234. Weidmann, U. Some reproductive activities of the Common Gull, *Larus canus* L. *Ardea,* 1955, **43,** 85–131.

235. Whitman, C. O. The behavior of pigeons. *Publications, Carnegie Inst. Wash.,* 1919, **257,** 1–161.

236. Wickler, W. Das Fortpflanzungsverhalten des Keilflickbarbe *Rasbara heteromorpha. Z. Tierpsychol.,* 1955, **12,** 220–228.

237. Zippelius, H. M. Die Paarungsbiologie einiger Orthopteren-arten. *Z. Tierpsychol.,* 1949, **6,** 372–390.

INFORMATION THEORY[1]

F. C. FRICK

Lincoln Laboratory, Massachusetts Institute of Technology

INTRODUCTION

Information theory is a formal—as opposed to substantive—theory. It could be regarded as simply an extension of correlation theory. It is not a model of behavior, not even communicative behavior, but rather a tool that may be used in the construction of such models.

In barest outline, the theory consists of a measure, defined for any "message," where messages are considered to be the outputs of a Markoff process. The theory justifies the particular measure chosen in that it permits us to establish equivalences among messages (the "coding theorem") and in that it permits us to establish a limit to the degree of association, or correlation, that may be achieved between messages (the "channel theorem"). It states nothing about the meaning or value of a message, nor how or why messages are correlated or transmitted.

Strictly speaking, the structure of the theory is laid out in the mathematical proofs of the central theorems, and because of its formal nature, it cannot readily be warped into an analytic rubric of the sort that might be used in the exposition of substantive theories. The "independent-intervening-dependent variable" schema is not only inappropriate to the analysis of formal theory but may be misleading. Such a treatment inevitably focuses attention on the observational basis for the theory and is, in fact, specifically designed to expose the translations between experimental data and the theoretical model. Although a formal theory often develops out of experimental research or the examination of some

[1] The research reported in this document was supported jointly by the Department of the Army, the Department of the Navy, and the Department of the Air Force under Air Force Contract No. AF 19(122)-458.

class of physical phenomena, such a theory is no more validated by experiment than cartesian coordinates are validated by the data which are plotted on them. In short, formal theories do not have empirical predictive value, nor do they suggest hypotheses other than the original hypothesis that this particular organization of the data may be interesting, i.e., may lead to substantive theory.

Why then should information theory be included in a volume devoted to the analytic exposition of psychological theory? One reason, of course, is that the distinction between formal and substantive theory is not always obvious. Information theory, in particular, has suffered from those (not only psychologists) who have interpreted it as a substantive model and have, for instance, been able to confound thermodynamics and the statistical structure of language [1]. Of more importance, however, is the fact that formal theories very often have an effect outside their immediate province. To borrow an expression from Bush and Mosteller [2], they serve as models for experiments rather than models of the organism, and in this way they have a profound, though indirect, influence on the behavioral model which may be developed from the experimental data.

This is to say more than simply that the use of the information measure entails certain assumptions about the data, or that it places certain constraints on experimental design. Clearly it does this, even as the use of coordinate theory requires ratio scales of measurement for the variables considered. And the assumptions that are involved in the use of information measure are pointed out as clearly as possible in the exposition of the theory which follows. In addition, however, the information-theoretic approach reflects an attitude, or opinion, about the subject matter to which it is directed. This viewpoint is, perhaps, not immediately apparent from an exposition of the formal model and is worth summarizing here.

Information theory is one item in an entire context of related theories devoted to the description and analysis of time series, or stochastic processes. An informational analysis is appropriate, therefore, only where it is believed that the process under investigation is intrinsically statistical. Historically, it was the prior recognition of communication as a statistical process in this sense that led to the development of information theory. As a belief, with respect to psychological experimentation, it is important because it necessitates a consideration of the temporal sequence of events and the sampling space, or context, in which behavior occurs. It leads us away from the immediate stimulus and observed response and demands that we consider the set of alternative possible stimuli and responses. The usual S-R functional $R = f(S)$ is interpreted as a statistical distribution function and the algorithm of differential equations is no longer appropriate to the description of the data.

It is possible, of course, to regard the variables of behavior as random, in the statistical sense, without adopting the particular formalism of information theory. This, for instance, is the point of view adopted by Estes, Bush and Mosteller, Cronbach, and others who are in no sense information theorists. However, the existence of information theory as a ready-made formal model of considerable generality has stimulated this sort of approach to a number of physical and psychological phenomena. It has, in fact, been argued [see 11] that this indirect contribution may be the most important consequence of the theoretical development.

Aside from the assumption of a statistical process, the viewpoint of information theory reflects a somewhat more subtle bias. Formal theories are often motivated by the study of some class of physical events, and information theory, in particular, grew directly out of the investigation of electronic communication systems. As is essential to the formulation of any theory, the development proceeded by the abstraction of some property of the process under consideration. In the present case, what was considered to be the significant feature of the process was the *difficulty* of communicating. Thus, the coding theorem establishes an equivalence between messages in terms of the length of a standard message. The channel theorem sets limits on the degree of correlation that can be achieved between messages (the input and output of the channel) as a function of the channel characteristics. In short, the formalism of the theory is directed at a determination of the efficiency of communication, and the application of information theory to psychological data implies an interest in the efficiency, rather than the structure, of the process under study. The theory is, in this sense, normative.

A normative approach to behavioral processes tends to discount the usual schema for categorizing behavior. For example, the distinctions that are often made among various types of learning—motor, verbal, concept formation, conditioning, etc.—do not seem particularly relevant in a context that examines how closely the subject approaches the maximum possible correlation between one random variable, the stimulus process, and another random variable, the response process. The interest is in how the subject selects and codes the available stimuli, how effectively he processes his inputs, rather than the particular form in which the input is presented. Here, too, however, it should be emphasized that such a viewpoint does not necessarily imply adoption of the formalism of information theory. Most of the normative studies of behavior, investigations of decision making, the strategies of concept attainment, and the efficiency of various training procedures have not, in fact, employed information theory.

The point to be made is that the use of information theory entails a systematic position: the viewpoint that behavior is stochastic and that the efficiency of the behavioral process is a significant aspect for study. The converse is not true, and we may adopt the viewpoint without the verbal or mathematical trappings of information theory.

Unfortunately it is still too early to evaluate the effects on psychology of information theory itself, or the conceptual position which it represents. The present author's biases in this respect should, however, be stated. Essentially they are: (1) the viewpoint represented by the theory is fruitful and important, and (2) the mathematical formalism does not lend itself to uncritical, mechanical application. Even if the data are believed to meet the mathematical requirements, the computation of information transmission, say, does not in itself insure any deeper understanding of the process under study. This is, of course, characteristic of formal theory in the sense that we have been using the term; it is, however, a point that may be disguised by the computational complexities involved.

THE BASIC THEORY

The insight that led to the development of information theory was the realization that all the processes which might be said to convey information are basically selection processes. Speech, for example, can be regarded as a sequence of selections from a number of possible choices—the phonemes, letters, or words of the language. Alternatively, we need information only when we are faced with a choice of some sort. If I know the road to Boston, I do not need a route sign at the intersection. In the same sense, a completely determinate process would not be regarded as an information source. For as it moves through its appointed course, I can predict its motions in advance, and I receive no new information when it actually carries out its function.

Thus, information and ignorance, choice, prediction, and uncertainty are all intimately related. On the other hand, complete ignorance or indeterminance also precludes information transmission. A lecture in German is not informative to a listener who does not understand German. There must be some degree of agreement, some sort of common language established between the information source and the receiver. Put somewhat more precisely: information processes are selection processes, but these selections must be made from a *specific* set of alternatives, and if the sequence of selections is to convey information, the possible choices must be known to the receiver. To say "yes" or "no" to someone who has not asked a question is not informative in any usual sense of the word. It is this restriction on the set of alternatives that makes it possible to speak precisely and quantitatively about information.

Within these bounds of complete knowledge and complete ignorance, it seems intuitively reasonable to speak of degrees of uncertainty. The wider the choice, the larger the set of alternatives open to use, the more uncertain we are as to how to proceed—the more information we require in order to make our decision. Thus, color alone will distinguish an apple from an orange, but we will have to know more than just color if we are to distinguish among apples, oranges, grapefruit, and lemons.

In much the same way, the informational value of a choice seems also to depend upon the likelihood of that choice. If we feel certain of what a man is going to say, it is not very informative when he says it. If a process is highly predictable, we need only a few observations to establish its present state quite accurately. Our uncertainties are intimately tied up with probability estimates and if we are to fit our intuitive notions regarding information, we must consider not only the range of choices available but the probabilities associated with each. This reflects the second basic insight behind the development of information theory. We may summarize the position by stating two premises: (1) information is associated with a selection process. (2) Such a process is basically statistical in the sense that it involves probability considerations.

From these premises, it has been possible to develop a measure of amount of information and a set of limit theorems which justifies the particular measure chosen. The ultimate justification of the theory will lie in the extent to which it gives precision to our intuitive notions regarding information and information transmission and opens the way to a clearer understanding of the basic processes involved.

Accordingly, we will start our discussion of information theory by defining a unit of information which we will state to be the amount of information associated with a selection between two equally likely alternatives. A binary choice is clearly the minimum condition for any information transmission at all, and the maximum uncertainty, and hence the maximum information associated with such a situation, would seem to exist when the alternatives are equally likely. This amount of information we will term one "bit," and if we use the symbols $H(N)$ to stand for the amount of information associated with a choice among N equally likely alternatives we can write:

$$H(2) = 1 \text{ bit}$$

Consistent with our intuitions, we shall also postulate that n independent selections of this type shall constitute n bits of information.

Our first problem will then be to extend this definition to choices among any finite number of alternatives. There are several ways in which we could proceed with such an extension but we shall, in general, follow Fano's development [8, 9]. This is mathematically less elegant than

Shannon's [32], but it exhibits the important concept of "coding" in a clearer fashion.

We shall begin by considering a set of N elements, where N is some power of 2. It is very easy to demonstrate that any element of this set can be encoded into a sequence of independent selections from a set of two equally likely choices. That is, we can set up a one-to-one correspondence between each element of our original set and a set of binary numbers. Each binary digit will carry one bit of information according to our definition. The number of such selections required will equal the informational value in bits associated with each element in our original set. This coding procedure, by which we establish a correspondence between a given set of elements and a set of known informational value, is, as we shall see, basic to the development and understanding of information theory.

To illustrate the procedure, let $N = 8$, and arrange these eight alternatives in a row, the order of arrangement being arbitrary. We can now

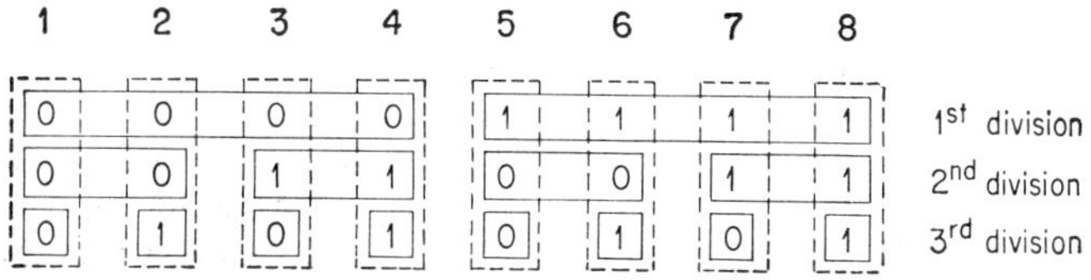

Fig. 1. Simple binary coding procedure.

divide this set into two equal subsets, assigning the number O to one and the number 1 to the other. We now further divide each subset into two equal subsets, again assigning binary digits as before. If we now halve these subsets and assign binary digits we will have associated with each alternative in our original set, a unique three-digit binary number as shown in Fig. 1. Thus, we see that a selection from N alternatives can be indicated by a sequence of selections from a smaller number of alternatives. In general, where $N = 2^n$, the number n of binary digits required so as to uniquely represent each element of N will be $\log_2 N$. Accordingly, we may write:

$$H(N) = \log_2 N$$

which is the amount of information, in bits, associated with the selection of one out of a set of N equally probable alternatives.

Strictly speaking, however, this result will hold only if N is a power of 2, in which case H is an integer. What Shannon has been able to do is to develop another information function with no such restriction on N. In order to accomplish this, however, we must restrict our definition of information as applying only to the average of a large number of selections, and in so doing the basically statistical nature of information becomes apparent. As we are seldom, if ever, interested in any single, or unique, selection from a set of choices this restriction will not bother. It does, however, put us in the realm of probability theory, and any application of information theory must be made with an awareness of the basic assumptions underlying such a probability model.

Consider, for example, the case where $N = 3$. We encode into binary selections as before:

N	Binary code
1	11
2	10
3	01

It is clear that alternative 3 requires only the first digit to specify it uniquely. Intuitively, the number of bits associated with N lies somewhere between 1 and 2. At this stage, however, it is not clear what meaning can be given to a fraction of a selection.

Accordingly, let us consider long sequences made up of n successive selections from some set of N alternatives. A sample of written English, where the alternatives consist of the letters of the alphabet, would be an example. To simplify our description at this point, we will, however, assume that unlike English sequences the selections are independent and equally likely, such sequences as might be generated by successive rolls of a die.

The set of sequences thus formed we will call an *ensemble of messages*, and the number of different messages in the ensemble will be:

$$M = N^n$$

We can encode this number into binary digits, but unless N is a power of 2, the length of the binary sequence required will, as before, depend on the particular message selected. However, it now becomes meaningful to · ask how much information is associated with each symbol in the message, *on the average*. This can be shown to equal $\log_2 N$ as follows:

Let $B(M)$ equal the number of binary, equally likely selections required to represent each message. Then

$$B(M) = \log_2 M + d$$

where d is a number, smaller than unity, required to make $B(M)$ an integer. If N is a power of 2, $d = 0$. In general, however, d will depend on the particular message or sequence selected. The average amount of information per selection, $H(N)$, will equal the amount of information in the message, divided by the number of selections in the message:

$$H(N) = \lim_{n \to \infty} \frac{1}{n} \log_2 (N^n + d)$$

Since N is a constant and d is smaller than unity, this equation yields:

$$H(N) = \log_2 N$$

In words, the amount of information associated with each selection of a sequence of selections from N equally likely alternatives will, on the average, equal $\log_2 N$. Alternatively, independent selections from N equally likely alternatives can be represented by sequences of binary digits, the average length of which will, for sufficiently long messages, equal $\log_2 N$.

It remains for us now to remove the remaining restrictions on the measure we have defined. We shall first consider the case where the selections, though independent, are not equally likely. In order to deal with this case, it will clearly be necessary to introduce probability distributions over the set of alternatives.

We begin by defining a source S which makes selections (with replacement) from a finite set of alternatives. For the time being, we shall assume that these selections are independent; i.e., the present selection is in no way influenced by previous selections. Such a source will generate a sequence of symbols representing the selections made, and it will be necessary to assume that the series of symbols thus generated is ergodic. This is to say that the statistical parameters characterizing the selective process do not vary with time. If we let $p(i)$ be the average frequency with which the symbol i turns up, this average will be approached to any small error in samples taken anywhere in the series—if the samples are sufficiently long or sufficiently numerous. Alternatively, we can say that the source is statistically stationary.

Assuming such a source S we will now introduce some necessary notation. Let k be the number of mutually exclusive alternatives from which the source makes its selections. Then $p(i)$, where $i = 1, 2, \ldots,$ $i, \ldots, k,$ is the probability that the symbol i will be selected and $p(ij)$ the probability that the symbols i and j are selected in that order. Such a source will generate an ordered sequence of symbols $i_1 i_2 i_3 \cdots i_k$, with a probability of occurrence $p(i_1 i_2 \cdots i_k)$. Our assumption of independence in selection means that for every k and every possible sequence $i_1 i_2 \cdots i_k$

$$p(i_1 i_2 \cdots i_k) = p(i_1) p(i_2) \cdots p(i_k)$$

The source is thus completely specified by the set of probabilities $p(i_1) p(i_2) \cdots p(i_k)$ over the k selections available to S. What is required is a function that will assign a number to such a probability distribution in a fashion analogous to the way in which we have previously assigned an information measure.

A plausible way of accomplishing this task is simply to extend our preceding definition in the following manner. Consider any event of probability $p = 1/n$; we may treat this event as one among n equally likely alternatives, and the amount of information associated with its selection is

$$\log_2 n = \log_2 \frac{1}{p} = -\log_2 p$$

If we assume that probability is a continuous function over the set of alternatives, we may extend this definition to irrational p values, by using an approximation by rationals. Thus we will assign to the selection of symbol i, which occurs with probability $p(i)$, an information value of $-\log_2 p(i)$ bits. Clearly, alternatives of differing probability will have different information values with less information attributed to higher probability alternatives, thus fitting our intuitive notion that the unexpected event is somehow more informative than the relatively certain occurrence.

Each selection generated by the source S will, in general, have a different informational value. As before, we consider long sequences of selections (messages) and under these conditions the average, or expected, value of the function $-\log_2 p$ becomes meaningful. This value we can obtain by summing over the amount of information associated with each selection, weighted by the probability that the selection will occur. Accordingly, we define the average amount of information associated with any selection to be

$$H = -\sum_{i=1}^{k} p(i) \log_2 p(i)$$

which is the expected value of the function $-\log_2 p$.

It remains for us to extend this definition to the most general case, where no assumption is made regarding the independence of the source selections. Here, we consider the selection of one symbol, i, from the set $S = 1, 2, \ldots, k$ followed by a second selection j. Where before we assumed that $p(ij) = p(i)p(j)$, we will now assume that in general, $p(ij) \neq p(i)p(j)$.

Strictly speaking this case is subsumed under our assumption of an ergodic source. The statistical properties of such a source are completely defined by the set of $p(i)$, and as the selections can be selections of single symbols, or groups of symbols (for example, single letters, or words, or texts of any length), the set of $p(i)$, in this general sense, already takes into account such correlations as may exist between the more elementary symbols composing the selection i. Furthermore, any correlations that do exist must fade out over sufficiently long messages, as they cannot have any influence on the averages of shorter messages, picked at random. In short, the ergodic assumption permits us, with only a notational difference in the $p(i)$, to extend our definition of H to those cases where the source selections are not independent.

Such highhanded treatment, however, serves only to indicate the breadth of the assumption of statistical homogeneity. Because most sources of interest are not independent, it is worth examining this case in somewhat more detail.

As noted above, we are concerned with sequences exhibiting internal dependencies. This is to say that the current choice will be affected by the immediately preceding choice, or choices. Such a situation is most easily described in terms of conditional probabilities—the probability of a particular choice j, given the immediately preceding choice i. This joint probability, $p(ij)$, can be written:

$$p(ij) = p(i)p_i(j)$$

in words, the probability of a sequence ij is equal to the probability of the occurrence of i times the conditional probability of j, given i. If selections are independent

$$p_i(j) = p(j)$$

and
$$p(ij) = p(i)p(j)$$

Following any given selection i, the situation will differ from the independent case only in that the information value will depend on the conditional probabilities $p_i(j)$ rather than the unconditional $p(j)$. Accordingly, we can write:

$$H_i(y) = - \sum_{j=1}^{k} p_i(j) \log_2 p_i(j)$$

where $H_i(y)$ is the amount of information associated with the selection made whenever the system is in the state of having just selected i. We can expect to be in state i with a probability $p(i)$, so in a long sequence of choices we will have $p(i)H_i(y)$ bits of information associated with the state i. If, as before, we take the expected value over all the states of the system we get:

$$H = \sum_{i=1}^{k} p(i)H_i(y) = - \sum_{i,j} p(i)p_i(j) \log_2 p_i(j)$$

which is the average amount of information per symbol of the sequence.

It should be noted that this definition continues to hold where dependencies extend over more than one symbol. In this case, the summation must simply be extended to cover all possible sequences of length n preceding the choice j, hence, the earlier reference to i as the "state" of the system, rather than the immediately preceding choice.

At this point, it is probably worth looking back over what we have accomplished. We have defined, on an intuitive basis, a unit of information, the "bit," and we have indicated how any set of alternatives can be mapped into sequences of one-bit selections. In addition, we have defined a measure H for any set of events whose probabilities p_1, p_2, . . . , p_k are known. This measure is, in fact, simply the mean logarithmic probability of the events or symbols considered. The justification for terming this measure an "amount of information" is given in what has been called Shannon's Fundamental Coding Theorem, in which it is stated that messages of an ensemble having an average information value H can be encoded into not less than H binary, equally likely symbols. Furthermore, this number can be approached as closely as desired by encoding together increasingly long sequences of messages.

We shall not give the proof of this theorem. However, its plausibility is evident from the following coding procedure, developed independently by Shannon [32] and Fano [8]. The procedure parallels the scheme used before. In this case, however, we cannot partition the ensemble of messages into equal sets, as the messages are of unequal probability, and our selections of sets and subsets would no longer be selections between equally likely alternatives; i.e., the selections would no longer meet our definition of a bit. The trick now is to make the probability of each subset as nearly equal as possible, rather than to equate the number of messages in each.

To accomplish this, we consider all messages of length n and arrange them in order of decreasing probability. We divide this collection into two sets of as nearly equal probability as possible and assign binary digits as before. In a similar fashion we divide the two sets into equally probable subsets and continue the process until each subset contains only one message. This is, of course, an approximation procedure, the success of which will depend on how closely we can equalize the probabilities between subsets. It should be intuitively clear, however, that as we consider longer messages our accuracy can be improved as the probability of each message approaches zero.

It is perhaps surprising—and of considerable importance in practical applications of information theory—how good an approximation we can obtain with very short messages. The following example illustrates this point, as well as the coding procedure.

Consider a source which generates messages by independent selections among three alternatives, A, B, C, with probabilities: $p(A) = .5$, $p(B) = .3$, $p(C) = .2$. By our definition of H, the average information associated with each selection will equal:

$$-(.5 \log_2 \cdot 5 + 3 \log_2 \cdot 3 + 2 \log_2 \cdot 2) = 1.486 \text{ bits}$$

If we consider messages of length two, we can arrange them, in order of decreasing probability, $p(i)$, and encode as follows:

Message	$p(i)$	Recoded message				$p(i)$ ("Bits" per recoded message)
AA	.25	0	0			.50
AB	.15	0	1	0		.45
BA	.15	0	1	1		.45
AC	.10	1	0	0		.30
CA	.10	1	0	1		.30
BB	.09	1	1	1	0	.30
BC	.06	1	1	0	1	.24
CB	.06	1	1	1	0	.24
CC	.04	1	1	1	1	.16
						3.00 (Av. bits per message)

In the recorded version, the average information per selection $= 1.5$ bits, contrasted with the 1.486 bits computed by the equation for H. If we recode into messages of length three, the average information per selection works out to be 1.496 bits.[2]

The coding theorem essentially states that all message ensembles having the same information measure are equivalent for coding purposes. The importance of this result will be apparent when we consider the problem of information transmission and the applications of information theory.

In the preceding discussion, we have gone to some length to present the concept of selective information as defined by information theory. We have done this primarily to emphasize the difference between the technical usage of the term and our ordinary conversational usage. "Information" as used in information theory is a measure of the size of a message set. It establishes equivalences among message sets with respect to coding, but it says nothing about the value, importance, or consequences of the message.

The central result of the theory has been a set of limiting theorems regarding the transmission of information, and the concept of information transmission has been applied extensively to psychological problems. Before taking this up, however, we will state two theorems concerning H. These establish intuitively reasonable properties of the measure, and their proofs may be found elsewhere [32] by those interested in proofs.

1. $H \geqq 0$ always and $H = 0$ only if all $p(i)$ except one are zero.

---

[2] This coding is not always so well behaved and may approach the limiting value $-\Sigma p(i) \log_2 p(i)$ in an oscillatory fashion.

This simply says that the measure is nonnegative and that no information is involved when the selection is certain.

2. The maximum value of H is $\log_2 N$ and this is achieved only when all the $p(i)$ are equal.

According to this theorem, the amount of information associated with a sequence of independent binary selections is a maximum when the selections are equally likely. Conversely, it will always be possible to represent a sequence of binary, not equally likely selections with a sequence which will on the average be shorter. It follows that no binary representation of a message can be made with a number of selections smaller than the amount of information associated with that message. Consequently, the average amount of information associated with a message equals the *minimum* number of independent, binary, equally likely selections (bits) required to specify that message. By much the same reasoning it is possible to show that a larger number of selections will be required, if the selections are not independent.

We turn now to a consideration of information transmission. This could be treated as simply an extension of the concept of coding which we have already developed; however, there is considerable heuristic value in considering information transmission within the framework of a physical communication system. Such an approach also ties in with the historical development of the theory and permits us to introduce in a natural way such terms as "equivocation," "noise," and "channel capacity" which have become so closely associated with information theory.

Basically, a communication system consists of three parts: a message *source* of the type that we have already defined, a *channel*, which is a fixed transmission system that establishes a connection between the source and the *destination*. The physical realization of such a system will ordinarily be somewhat more complicated. In general, the decisions made by the source will have to be encoded into a form that is suitable to the channel. A communication system will thus often include a *transmitter* which "matches" the channel to the source, for example, changing sound pressure into electrical current. A *receiver* may be necessary to perform a similar matching between the channel and the destination. In many cases, these will be inverse operations where we can think of the transmitter as encoding a message and the receiver as decoding it.

In any physical system, we must also consider the possibility of "noise." The message received at the destination will seldom, if ever, be a perfect representation of the message generated by the source. The received message will thus be a function of the source message plus something else. It is as if there were a second source operating through the same channel, and we have so represented it in Fig. 2. The characteristic of this second source is that it introduces messages into the channel which neither the original source nor the destination can predict in detail.

It should be noted that this is a restrictive definition of noise. For instance, the hum in a radio set is not noise in this sense. It is a fixed distortion that we can, in principle, build a network to filter out. The case in which we are interested here is that in which the message does not always undergo the same change in transmission. Under these conditions noise can be thought of as a statistical process analogous to the statistical process which generates messages.

Using this abstract model of a communication system as a basis, we can begin to clarify the concept of information transmission. We are essentially concerned with the relations between a number of information sources. Viewed from the destination we have a sequence of selections or symbols, generated by the channel,[3] which is regarded as a fixed transmission system with a fixed set of transmission symbols among which the selections are made. These selections are related through the channel to

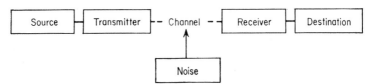

Fig. 2. Generalized representation of a communication system.

the selections made by the message source, and the amount of information transmitted clearly depends on the correspondence between the selections made by the message source and the sequence of symbols received at the destination.

The possible correspondences that might exist are schematized in Fig. 3. In I, we have represented the simple coding operation. There is a one-to-one correspondence between the input symbols (x) and the output (y). In communication terms this would correspond to transmission through a noiseless channel and the conditional probabilities, $p_{x_1}(y_1), p_{x_2}(y_2), \ldots ,$ are all equal to 1.

II and III represent, respectively, one-many and many-one relations. In II it is not possible to predict the output, given the input. If we assume that the input selections are equally likely we can compute $H(x) = 1$ and $H(y) = 2$ from the conditional probability matrix shown

[3] Strictly, we should speak of the input to the transmitter and the output from the receiver. This, however, tends to complicate description and it should be obvious that the formal model is not affected by what we choose as input or output. Abstractly, we are simply dealing with the relations between two random variables —whatever their source.

and we see that, in effect, information has been added by the channel. This corresponds to "noise" as we defined it above and justifies our representation of noise as a separate information source.

III is the transpose of II. Here it is possible to predict the output,

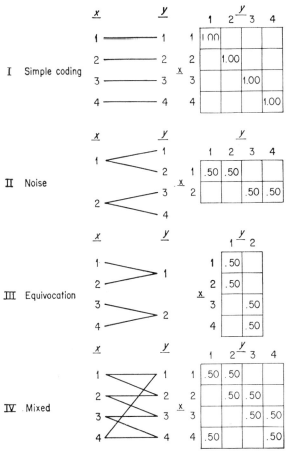

Fig. 3. Schema of the possible correspondences between the inputs (x) to a channel and the outputs (y). The right-hand figure in each case represents the conditional probability matrix; cell entries are the probability of y, given $x = p_x(y)$. The conditional probabilities indicated for Cases II, III, and IV are arbitrary.

given the input. The output, however, is equivocal in that knowing the output alone does not permit us to specify the input. In communication theory terms a many-one coding of this sort corresponds to "equivocation,"

In most physical systems, both noise and equivocation are present as represented by IV. Here again the channel is completely defined by a set of conditional probabilities specifying the relation between the message generated by the source and the sequence of transmission symbols.

Perhaps the strongest result of information theory has been the development of a limit theorem for information transmission in the general case of a noisy channel as represented in Fig. 3, IV. Before stating this fundamental theorem it will, however, be necessary to state several theorems regarding the information associated with joint distributions.

We now consider two sources, as defined before. These sources will generate sequences of symbols, x and y respectively. We let $p(i)$ be the probability of $x = i$ and $p(j)$ be the probability of $y = j$. For each source we have an information measure $H(x)$ and $H(y)$. In an analogous fashion we can define an information measure for the joint distribution,

$$H(xy) = - \sum_{i,j} p(ij) \log_2 p(ij)$$

noting that the distribution $p(ij)$ differs only in notation from any of the sources that we have considered before.

Furthermore, it can be shown that:

$$H(xy) \leq H(x) + H(y)$$

with $H(xy) = H(x) + H(y)$ only if the sequences x and y are independent.

Just as before we can define informational measures for the conditional probability distributions

$$H_x(y) = - \sum_{i,j} p(ij) \log_2 p_i(j)$$

and

$$H_y(x) = - \sum_{i,j} p(ij) \log_2 p_j(i)$$

$H_x(y)$ is the amount of information added in transmission—the amount of information associated with the noise source. Alternatively, it can be interpreted as a measure of the average uncertainty we have regarding the output, when we know the input. Similarly, $H_y(x)$ is a measure of equivocation and can be regarded as the average uncertainty of the input, knowing the output.

Using the definition of a conditional probability $P_i(j) = p(ij)/p(i)$ and a little algebra, it is easy to show the following relations between these measures:

$$H(x) + H(y) \geq H(xy) = H(x) + H_x(y) = H(y) + H_y(x)$$

They are schematized in Fig. 4, using the Euler circle diagram suggested by Miller [23].

From this diagram it is also apparent that we may compute another quantity T which is the amount of information that is common to x and y. If we think of x as the input and y as the output from the channel, T will measure the amount of information associated with the input that appears in the output, i.e., the amount of information transmitted. This quantity can be defined:

$$T = H(x) + H(y) - H(xy) = H(x) - H_y(x) = H(y) - H_x(y)$$

a set of equalities, that is easily checked by reference to the diagram. Also, it can be seen that if x and y are independent, $H(xy) = H(x) + H(y)$ and $T = O$. There is, as we should expect, no information transmission.

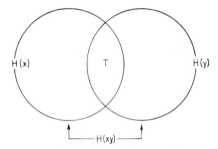

Fɪɢ. 4. Schematic representation of the relations between the information measures of two associated sources.

This definition gives us a measure of the average amount of information per selection that we can transmit over a given channel. However, we have no assurance that the receiver will be able to sort out the information associated with the source from the information which has been "added" by the noise. If, for example, I know that some percentage of the symbols received is incorrect, I have not been helped much until I know which symbols are in error. In short, the output of the channel may still be equivocal. If our measure of information transmitted is to have any practical significance, we must somehow insure that this amount of information is received *correctly*.

This problem has been solved by Shannon, who has been able to show that by appropriate coding it is possible to reduce the per symbol equivocation to any desired tolerance and still transmit T bits of information per selection, on the average. This result justifies the use of T as a measure of information transmission, for it states that we can (in theory) "make the probability of incorrect reception of a message as small as desired; and the number of binary selections used in the transmission does not need to be larger, on the average, than the information content of the message divided by T" [10]. An indication of the way in which such a result can be achieved is given below, adapted from Fano.

Noise in the channel entails that we are never completely certain that the signal received corresponds to the signal sent. However, it is clear that if we utilize only particular signals, or particular sequences of signals, we can reduce the probability of error. For instance, the two binary sequences 00000 and 11111 will never be confused so long as not more than two digits are changed by the noise. If we use long enough sequences of symbols, we can select particular sequences such that the probability of confusion among them is as small as we like. We then encode the messages generated by the source into this set of channel outputs. The first operation is generally referred to as "matching" the channel because the procedure used in any given case will depend on the channel characteristics, i.e., the particular set of conditional probabilities associated with the particular channel under consideration. It is a one-many coding, and the, perhaps, surprising result of Shannon's theorem is the fact that the average amount of information per symbol does not approach zero but converges on T.

With this result we have essentially concluded our outline of the formal aspects of information theory. Two addenda are needed before taking a summary look at the basic assumptions and psychological interpretations of the model.

In the first place, we have developed the theory without reference to the *rate* of information transmission. For the communication engineer the rate of transmission is of prime importance. In psychological applications time does not often enter in as natural a way. There are, however, no difficulties involved in using a rate measure which will, of course, equal the bits per symbol times the number of symbols generated per second. Thus we can define the channel capacity as the maximum possible information transmission in either bits per symbol or bits per second, where the maximum is with respect to all possible information sources used as inputs to the channel.

In the second place, we have not included in our discussion the extension of the theory to information sources whose outputs are continuous functions of time. Here again the concern of the communication engineer and the psychologist appears to differ, and to date, the theory of continuous transmission has not been of great interest in psychological applications. Suffice it to say that Shannon has shown that continuous transmission in the presence of noise does not differ essentially from transmission of information by discrete selections of the sort that we have considered. The information measure of a continuous source which is defined:

$$H(x) = - \int_{-\infty}^{\infty} p(x) \log_2 p(x)$$

is not an exact analogue of the measure of a discrete source in that it is a measure relative to a coordinate system. If the coordinate system is changed, the measure changes. Information transmission, on the other hand, involves a difference between two sources, so that it is invariant under coordinate transformation, and the results of the theory can be obtained essentially by substituting integration for the summation that we have used in the preceding discussion. For those interested in the continuous theory a brief summary is available in Luce [19].

THE APPLICATION OF INFORMATION THEORY IN BEHAVIORAL STUDIES

Information theory is a *probability* model and suffers from all the conceptual difficulties associated with probability theory. In particular, the definitions and theorems of the theory assume that it is meaningful to speak of infinite samples of past symbol occurrences and the expected value for infinite samples of future messages. The theory assumes that we know the parameter values of a statistical process and is thus subject to the same cricticisms in application that have been leveled at Bayes' theorem. In fact the expression for T can be derived from Bayes' result [3].

This is not a new problem to psychologists, but it is worth pointing out that the passage from probability theory to statistics has not yet been achieved for information measure. In applications of the theory, the experimenter must be prepared to assume that the frequencies with which events occur are reasonable estimates of the true probabilities with which the model deals. In fact, the maximum likelihood estimates, $\hat{H}$ and $\hat{T}$, have been shown to be biased [24] and general corrections for these biases are not available. Nor do we know the sampling distribution of H.

Despite these clear difficulties with the application of information measures to finite sequences and limited data, the large number of experimental studies that have appeared in recent years using information measures is an indication that many researchers are willing to make statements about the probability distributions characterizing their data. Actually, the use of information theory to describe empirical data is not as unreasonable as it might at first appear.

In the first place, as a formal and normative theory, in the sense discussed in the introduction, information theory does not lead to deductions amenable to critical test, where precision of measurement might be vital. Rather, it establishes boundary conditions for maximally efficient coding. In general, it is the observed large deviations from the model and the search for their sources that have proven of most interest to psychologists and engineers who have applied information theory in their work.

In the second place, as Fano has demonstrated [8], the statistical characteristics assumed a priori can be quite different from the frequencies actually observed without the efficiency of transmission or coding being lowered very much. This arises from the fact that H varies rather slowly with any one of the $p(i)$ unless that $p(i)$ is close to zero or unity. In a similar fashion, the fundamental coding theorem assumes an unlimited delay, or message length, to achieve the optimum representation given by H. Yet we were able, in our illustration of coding procedure, to achieve a better than 99 per cent efficient code by considering messages only out to length three.

On the assumption, then, that applications to empirical data are to some extent tenable, information theory has played a number of roles in psychology. Not the least of these has been that of a general reorientation in thinking about various behavioral problems. It is very easy to substitute psychological terms into the verbal structure of the model, or to extend the technical terms of the formal theory to describe the classic concerns of the psychologist. Thus, the inputs and outputs of a channel are easily and naturally translated into the stimuli and responses of the organism. Proceeding in the other direction, as Crossman [5] suggests, we can say: "Instead of a *stimulus* causing a *reaction* when the *threshold* is exceeded, we now think rather in terms of a *signal* which may be obscured by *noise,* providing the *information* needed to *select* a response."

Verbal recodings of this sort are not simply playful. As suggested in the introduction, they influence the choice of variables and the design of experiments. Crossman, for example, continues his discussion by pointing out that, unlike a stimulus, a signal (which should be regarded as the output of a transmitter as we have defined it) implies a set of alternatives and thus emphasizes the effect on behavior of what might have been as well as what is immediately present. Furthermore, a signal in this sense functions purely as the basis for response selection. It can, according to the theory, be coded into a variety of physical forms and embedded in a variety of signal sets, without effect on its selective function.

The respective dependence and invariance suggested by this reformulation of the basic psychophysical problem have stimulated a great deal of research in recent years [4, 5, 6, 7, 15, 16, 18, 19, 22, 23, 28, 29, 30, 31]. This work has been directed to the study of human information processing and considers, in Miller's [23] terminology, the "transmission situation." The observer is regarded as a "channel" and the interest has been in estimating his channel capacity under various conditions and for various input stimuli.

The apparent contradiction in terms—channel capacity is defined in the theory as the maximum transmission for all possible input sources—is avoided by the intuitively reasonable assumption that man is a multichannel system. Because the information measure is invariant under operations of coding, it becomes possible to compare information transmission among these various channels and to determine the efficiency of various coding schemes. For example, the same amount of information can be presented to an observer by exchanges between the number of symbols per second and the amount of information per symbol. Similar exchanges can be made by distribution of the input simultaneously over different channels, or by permitting different aspects of the stimuli to vary and hence "carry" information.

Studies like these which are directed at optimizing the display of information in the sense of maximizing the amount of information transmitted have been of considerable value to the growing field of engineering psychology. Perhaps, of most importance, the results of these studies indicate the existence of a minimal discriminative difference, proportional to the range of variation and invariant for different discriminable aspects of the stimulus. This is the stuff of which substantive theory is made, and indeed, it has suggested hypotheses regarding the manner in which people process, or organize, the sensory inputs from their environment [22]. It must, however, be emphasized that such developments are not an extension of information theory. The theory simply provides a conceptual framework and set of measures by means of which we can analyze a number of diverse situations. Any "model building," in the usual sense, must develop from the empirical results obtained.

As we have attempted to show in our development, the theory deals primarily with the coding problem and in particular with the question of optimal coding. Such a theory requires some measure of variation and of contingency, and Shannon has demonstrated that H and T are peculiarly appropriate for the analysis of a communication system, which is his main interest. The abstract structure of such a system is, however, much more general than the terminology associated with the theory might suggest, and mean logarithmic probability measures are applicable to many situations where terms like "information transmission" are awkward or quite inappropriate.

Consider, for instance, the conditional probability matrices of Fig. 3. These present the possible relations between an input and an output, or, as we have suggested, between stimuli and responses. More generally, we might say that these tables represent the various ways in which any set of events can be mapped into another set of events. Phrased this way, it is apparent that we could also consider mapping the set that we are concerned with into itself. Here x and y represent the same set of responses and the contingency could be sequential or temporal dependence. In this case, we would read for the conditional probabilities $p_x(y)$, "the probability that the response x is followed by the response y." As x and y are representative of the same set, we can adopt our earlier notation and represent the alternative responses and their probabilities by $p(i)$, where $i = 1, 2, \ldots, i, \ldots, k$, the set of alternative responses recorded. As before, $p(ij)$ is the probability of the responses i and j occurring in that order and equals $p(i)p_i(j)$. It should then be apparent that, by a somewhat devious route, we have arrived back at the point in our earlier development where we considered the definition of H for nonindependent source selections. In short, H may be used as a measure of the internal dependencies, or degree of patterning, within a sequence of responses.

This result is obtained, much more elegantly, by Shannon in a theorem which shows that a series of approximations to H can be obtained by considering sequences extending over $1, 2, \ldots, n$ symbols. The estimates of H thus obtained are a monotonic decreasing function of n. The function will equal H in the limit, or when the length of sequence considered has exhausted the statistical dependencies within the sequence.

It is thus apparent that information theory offers a ready-made tool for the description of behavior patterns and the analysis of sequential behavior [13, 19, 23, 25]. In this connection, it appears to be most convenient to consider the relative uncertainty of the sequence, which is the ratio of the obtained value of H to the maximum value that would obtain for the same set of alternatives if they were equally likely and occurred independently. One minus this quantity is the percentage of *redundancy* in the sequence, and in application to response sequences, redundancy may be used as a measure of the degree of stereotypy, or organization, of the observed behavior.

In fact, informational measures have been little used in the description of behavioral strategies and organization except in the study of language [26, 27, 33]. As suggested in the introduction, the effect of the theory may well be indirect. Psychologists have long recognized that successive responses are seldom independent. Information theory, or more properly the probability model on which it is based, explicitly recognizes sequential dependencies and demonstrates that they can be taken into account in a reasonable fashion. Again, the particular formulation of the theory may not be optimal, and indeed, in a particularly simple demonstration of the effects of an anxiety-producing stimulus on the pattern of responding [12] an alternative time series analysis was employed. However, it is exactly these peripheral effects that give power to the formal theory, emphasizing its generality as well as the distinction between information measures and the mathematical theory of communication for which they were originally derived.

As we have indicated, information measures are applicable wherever the data in which we are interested can be arranged into a contingency table. So are a number of other measures, and the common logical structure underlying them has been pointed out in papers by McGill [21] and Garner and McGill [17].

The similarities between information analysis and the analysis of variance first became apparent as a result of McGill's work on multivariate information transmission [20]. He points out that the basic equation for information transmission essentially decomposes a measure of response uncertainty $H(y)$ into a part determined by the stimulus $T(x,y)$ and a part, $H_x(y)$, which consists of unexplained variation. There are cases, however, in which some portion of this residue $H_x(y)$ might be accounted for by the action of another variable in the stimulus situation, and it would be useful to extend the definition of transmitted information to include two sources u and v. This can be accomplished by replacing x in the equation,

$$T(x,y) = H(x) + H(y) - H(x,y)$$

with the symbol (uv). If we eliminate the extra parentheses, we can then write:

$$T(u,v;y) = H(u,v) + H(y) - H(u,v,y)$$

where $T(u,v;y)$ can be regarded as a measure of the association between the variables u, v, and y.

McGill then shows that it is possible to separate the dependence of y on u and on v in a fashion completely analogous to the way in which the variance of a criterion variable can be partitioned and associated with the predictor variables, certain interactions, and a residue, or "error variance." As with analysis of variance, informational analysis can be extended to any number of sources or predictor variables. Because informational measures require no assumptions about the metric properties of the variables involved, informational analysis can be regarded as a nonparametric analysis of variance. However, just because variance is metric it is obvious that information and variance cannot, in general, be related by an equation. The relation rather derives from a formal similarity which is explored by McGill and Garner in the papers cited above.

Furthermore, this isomorphism extends to correlational analysis. In all three methods, the attempt is made to account for the variation of some variable by the variation of one or more predictor variables. Following McGill's notation we can write

$$M(y;w,x) = \frac{M(y,x) + M_x(y,w)}{M(y,w) + M_w(y,x)}$$

where $M(y;w,x)$ is a generalized measure of the amount of variation in the dependent variable y that can be predicted from w and x. As indicated, this variation can be analyzed in two different ways. The important point is that the effects of any particular variable are analyzed only after removing, or fixing, the influences of variables studied previously.

The general structure of the analysis is illustrated by the formulas

$$T(y;w,x) = T(y,x) + T_x(y,w)$$
$$V(y;w,x) = V(y,x) + V_x(y,w)$$
$$V^1(y;w,x) = V^1(y,x) + V_x^1(y,w)$$

The T measure is transmitted information. The V measure is the variance of the subclass means $\bar{y}_w$ and $\bar{y}_x$ around the grand mean $\bar{y}$. The V^1 measure is the variance of points on the regression plane or regression line.

McGill has thus been able to generalize the concepts developed by Shannon, and in so doing gives us a proper perspective on the mathematical formalism of information theory.

REFERENCES

1. Bell, D. A., & Ross, A. S. C. Negative entropy of Welsh words. In C. Cherry (Ed.), *Information theory*. New York: Academic Press, 1956. Pp. 149–153.

2. Bush, R. B., & Mosteller, F. *Stochastic models for learning*. New York: Wiley, 1955.

3. Cherry, E. C. A history of the theory of information. *Proc. Inst. electr. Engrs.*, 1951, **98**, 383–393.

4. Cronbach, L. J. On the non-rational application of information measures in psychology. In H. Quastler (Ed.), *Information theory in psychology*. Glencoe, Ill.: Free Press, 1955. Pp. 14–25.

5. Crossman, E. R. F. W. The measurement of discriminability. *Quart. J. exp. Psychol.*, 1955, **7**, 176–195.

6. Eriksen, C. W., & Hake, H. W. Absolute judgments as a function of the stimulus range and the number of stimulus and response categories. *J. exp. Psychol.*, 1955, **49**, 323–332.

7. Eriksen, C. W., & Hake, H. W. Multidimensional stimulus differences and accuracy of discrimination. *J. exp. Psychol.*, 1955, **50**, 153–160.

8. Fano, R. M. "The transmission of information," Tech. Report No.

65, Massachusetts Institute of Technology, Research Laboratory of Electronics, 1949.

9. Fano, R. M. "The transmission of information," Part II, Tech. Report No. 149, Massachusetts Institute of Technology, Research Laboratory of Electronics, 1950.

10. Fano, R. M. Information theory point of view in speech communication. *J. acoust. Soc. Amer.*, 1950, **22**, 691–696.

11. Fano, R. M. Information theory, past, present and future. *Convention Record*, I.R.E., 1954, **2**, Part 4, 2–5.

12. Frick, F. C. The effect of anxiety—a problem in measurement. *J. comp. physiol. Psychol.*, 1953, **46**, 120–123.

13. Frick, F. C., & Miller, G. A. A statistical description of operant conditioning. *Amer. J. Psychol.*, 1951, **64**, 20–36.

14. Gabor, D. A summary of communication theory. In W. Jackson (Ed.), *Communication theory.* New York: Academic Press, 1953. Pp. 1–23.

15. Garner, W. R. An informational analysis of absolute judgments of loudness. *J. exp. Psychol.*, 1953, **46**, 373–380.

16. Garner, W. R., & Hake, H. W. The amount of information in absolute judgments. *Psychol. Rev.*, 1951, **58**, 446–459.

17. Garner, W. R., & McGill, W. J. Relation between uncertainty, variance and correlation analyses. *Psychometrika*, 1956, **21**, 219–228.

18. Klemmer, E. T., & Frick, F. C. Assimilation of information from dot and matrix patterns. *J. exp. Psychol.*, 1953, **45**, 15–19.

19. Luce, E. D. "A survey of the theory of selective information and some of its behavioral applications," Tech. Report No. 8, Bureau of Applied Social Research, Columbia Univer., 1954.

20. McGill, W. J. Multivariate information transmission. *Psychometrika,* 1954, **19**, 97–116.

21. McGill, W. J. Isomorphism in statistical analysis. In H. Quastler (Ed.), *Information theory in psychology.* Glencoe, Ill.: Free Press, 1955. Pp. 56–62.

22. Miller, G. A. The magical number seven, plus-or-minus two, or, some limits on our capacity for processing information. *Psychol. Rev.*, 1956, **63**, 81–96.

23. Miller, G. A. What is information measurement? *Amer. Psychologist*, 1953, **8**, 3–11.

24. Miller, G. A. Note on the bias of information estimates. In H. Quastler (Ed.), *Information theory in psychology.* Glencoe, Ill.: Free Press, 1955. Pp. 95–100.

25. Miller, G. A., & Frick, F. C. Statistical behavioristics and sequences of responses. *Psychol. Rev.*, 1949, **56**, 311–324.

26. Newman, E. B. The pattern of vowels and consonants in various languages. *Amer. J. Psychol.*, 1951, **64**, 369–379.

27. Newman, E. B., & Gerstman, L. S. A new method for analyzing printed English. *J. exp. Psychol.*, 1952, **44**, 114–125.

28. Pollack, I. The information of elementary auditory displays. *J. acoust. Soc. Amer.*, 1952, **24**, 745–749.

29. Pollack, I. The information of elementary auditory displays. II. *J. acoust. Soc. Amer.,* 1953, **25,** 765–769.

30. Pollack, I., & Ficks, L. Information of elementary multidimensional auditory displays. *J. acoust. Soc. Amer.,* 1954, **26,** 155–158.

31. Pollack, I. Assimilation of sequentially encoded information. *Amer. J. Psychol.,* 1953, **66,** 421–435.

32. Shannon, C. E. A mathematical theory of communication. *Bell Syst. Tech J,* 1948, **27,** 623–656

33. Shannon, C. E. Prediction and entropy of printed English. *Bell Syst. Tech. J.,* 1951, **30,** 50–64.

LINEAR FREQUENCY THEORY AS BEHAVIOR THEORY

DOUGLAS G. ELLSON

Indiana University

INTRODUCTION

The discussion outline for this set of theoretical papers asks each author to do some serious soul-searching concerning "background factors and orienting attitudes" which influenced the objectives, methods, and content of the system that he describes. This presumably takes for granted that the author of the paper is the author of the theory, which in my case is not true. The theory that is presented in this paper, or at least the model upon which it is based, is very old as age is counted in psychological theories, and I do not propose to probe the souls of the engineers and mathematicians who were originally responsible for it.

Linear frequency theory was presented ready-made to psychologists [16]. It had been tested and found useful as a description of certain behavior of machines, and engineers who had used this description in the design of machine components of man-machine systems suggested to me and to other psychologists that it might be equally useful as a description of certain behavior of man. The task of these engineers would be greatly simplified if the behavior of both man and machine components of such systems could be described in terms of the same variables. This suggests one reason for my own interest in linear frequency theory. It is always gratifying to a psychologist to know that the results of his investigations may be useful to someone who is not a psychologist.

Perhaps more important, linear frequency theory meets two methodological requirements that must be satisfied by any theory if it is to be successful. First, the theory is formulated in unambiguous language, in this case the language of mathematics, in which the rules of transformation are so sufficiently explicit and unambiguous that it is possible to determine whether one statement is or is not a consequence of another. Second, there is at least one important class of unambiguously observable behavioral events to which the theory is clearly applicable. Linear frequency theory is applicable to simple movements, a kind of behavior that can be observed with maximum precision. A theory that satisfies the methodological requirements of a purist and at the same time has immediate practical implications is all too rare in psychology.

Analysis of human motor behavior in terms of linear frequency theory provides an example of a rigorous theoretical approach to a very practical problem, namely, the design and analysis of the performance of complex man-machine systems. Some aspects of frequency analysis in this context are not new to psychologists. Some of the most fruitful procedures in the study of language from the point of view of both scientific and social significance are those associated with the application of linear frequency theory to speech and hearing. From all the complex response configurations which we call spoken language, this analysis abstracts a single characteristic, the physical frequencies represented in speech sounds. The analysis of speech behavior in terms of this abstract variable has made possible a very precise description of speech which has been utilized in the design of a wide variety of mechanical and electronic systems for communication by means of the spoken word. Scientifically the frequency analysis of speech represents one of the most successful theoretical treatments of behavior that has ever been developed. The social significance of this peculiarly abstract analysis becomes obvious if we ask what would happen to our society if all mechanical and electronic devices whose design incorporates knowledge of the frequency characteristics of human speech were to disappear. Telephone and radio communication, hearing aids, auditorium acoustics, and many similar devices which, together with a human speaker and hearer, constitute man-machine communication systems would disappear with them.

In the absence of the machine components of speech communication systems the frequency analysis of human speech would have only academic interest: it would probably be of concern only to the purest of scientists. Similarly, the frequency analysis of human motor behavior has scientific value as a contribution to basic knowledge, but like the frequency analysis of speech, it has immediate interest because of the prac-

tical applications which await this knowledge. In a context of systems engineering, it provides an excellent example of a basic scientific analysis that, potentially, can contribute very significantly to the solution of practical problems.

DESCRIPTIONS OF MAN-MACHINE SYSTEM PERFORMANCE

A wide variety of formal procedures has been developed by systems engineers and others for the analysis and description of complex organizations or systems, ranging from the relatively simple and empirical representations of static aspects of systems such as wiring diagrams and organization charts, to highly theoretical analyses of dynamic or time-varying characteristics. Two of the latter, information theory, associated with digital computers and discrete-variable communication systems, and servo theory, associated with analogue computers and continuous-variable amplifying systems, are of special interest to psychologists since they provide mathematical models which show promise of adaptation to aspects of human behavior. Applied to the analysis and design of systems, these two approaches have much in common, although their similarities are obscured by differences in the vocabularies associated with each and by the fact that certain characteristics of the systems to which they are likely to be applied are quite different.

In both approaches, the emphasis is upon the precision of relationship between input and output variables rather than upon the efficiency of energy and materials utilization which has been the major consideration in traditional engineering design. Both are concerned primarily with the tracing of signals through complex devices or organizations within which the signal may take many different physical forms: the signal may be manifested as the opening and closing of switches or of relay connections or hydraulic valves, as human speech, as changes in temperature, voltage, or pressure, as linear or rotational movements, etc. The practical effectiveness of both theories for the analysis of the functioning of complex systems results primarily from their reduction of a great variety of superficially quite different concrete events to a single abstract variable—a signal characteristic which may be followed through many physical transformations. For information analysis, this "system variable" is information, expressed in terms of the unit *bit* and as a time function as *bits per second*. For servo theory, the comparable variable is change in any of many empirical variables expressed as a time function whose component units are single-frequency sine waves.

Differences between the two approaches are associated with this difference in basic variable. The *bit* of information theory is empirically represented as the occurrence of one of two possible events. It is best adapted to systems within which the obviously important events can conveniently be recognized and described as discrete states, and in which details of intermediate or transitional states can be ignored. Information theory has been applied, for example, to the design of digital computers and to those parts of telephone circuitry concerned with making connections. In such systems, the basic component is a device similar to a switch or relay and the data represent the occurrence of discrete events or operations. The performance of the system is evaluated in terms of accuracy and speed with which discrete operations are performed. Ambiguous data, classified according to the principle of the excluded middle and transitional states, e.g., the detailed path taken by a relay armature as it moves from open to closed position, are ignored except as the total time required for the transition affects the speed with which the system can perform its function accurately. Applied to human behavior, information theory is best adapted to the theoretical simplification of decision processes manifested in responses such as button-pushing, switch operations, telegraph, typewriter, and piano key pressing, neuron action, and in molar and qualitative units of language such as letters, numerals, and words. Servo theory, on the other hand, is applied to systems or parts of systems in which data are conveniently treated as continuous variables. In such systems, the signals are wavelike and the details of continuous changes in state are of importance. Examples of continuous-variable systems are a-c circuits, including human speech and the speech-transmission components of telephone circuits, and steering and aiming devices which often include human operators as components performing the function called tracking.

In systems whose operations involve discrete events, accuracy of transmission is attained by procedures similar to those which contribute to the precision (and the limitations) of two-valued logic: alternatives are chosen so as to be maximally distinguishable and intermediate values are arbitrarily excluded. Input signals such as words or other language units introduced into the systems are engineered or coded in such a way as to minimize the occurrence of intermediate signals or responses to such signals which produce error. Operational error is reduced by this technique and by the use of components which respond to or transmit alternative signals with maximum reliability. Since wires, switches, and relays with the necessary high reliability are available, the digital systems that incorporate them as components have what is called "intrinsic" precision. A similar intrinsic precision is not a necessary characteristic of continuous-variable systems—in fact these may almost be said to be characterized by an intrinsic inaccuracy. A system which transmits or performs other operations upon continuous variables might be expected to increase in accuracy as its sensitivity to small variations increases. But as its sensitivity to signals increases, so does its sensitivity to irrelevant characteristics of the signal introduced by imperfect transmission within the systems or by imperfect shielding of the signal from external influences. Scientists who have worked with maximally sensitive recording equipment are well aware that maximum sensitivity does not guarantee maximum accuracy of transmission of the signal they may wish to record. In the design of servo systems sensitive to continuously varying signals, this paradox of sensitivity is associated with the fact that a servo system is an amplifier which (a) may multiply error in a signal just as effectively as it multiplies relevant characteristics of a signal and (b) may itself introduce the error which it multiplies. Examples of such error are the vacuum tube noise of electronic amplifiers and the lag and overshoot resulting from the inertia of massive parts of a system such as motors and gears.

THE FEEDBACK CIRCUIT

Servo theory makes use of two basic techniques for the elimination of error, the feedback circuit and selective frequency amplification. The

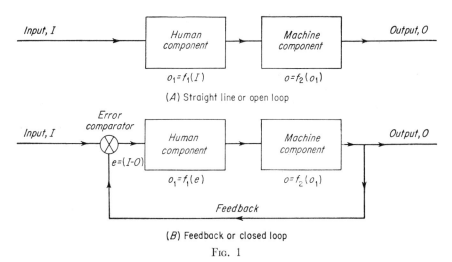

(A) Straight line or open loop

(B) Feedback or closed loop

Fig. 1

feedback circuit is a structural characteristic of certain systems in which a signal follows a path which when diagrammed appears as a loop. There are many forms and uses of the loop circuit, perhaps the simplest of which is the negative feedback loop. Having passed through all or part of the system, the output signal or a suitable function of it is returned by a different path to a device which compares it with the input. The difference, which is the error of the system, is reversed in sign, and added to the input. (This reversal is indicated by the term *"negative* feedback.") In effect the output of an ideal feedback system of this sort is a negative function of its error: it responds so as to reduce error and it stops responding when error is zero.

In its simplest form the negative feedback loop may easily be demonstrated as in the following example:

Example 1. Let you, the reader, function as a signal amplifier, with a vertical line across the room providing a signal to be amplified in energy by the arm movement involved in pointing at it with a pencil. Holding the arm to one side, look at the line, close your eyes, point at the line, then open your eyes and correct the pointing error. A few repetitions will illustrate the increase in accuracy which can be obtained by adding a reasonably well-designed feedback loop to a straight line (open loop) amplifier circuit. In this example, looking while pointing completes a feedback loop from output to input comparator. The open and closed loop systems are represented schematically in Fig. 1.

FREQUENCY ANALYSIS

Although the notion of the feedback loop is extremely useful in the design and analysis of dynamic systems, it actually represents only a small part of the theory of such systems—chiefly the nonquantitative part which can be represented in a schematic diagram. Its primitive character as theory is indicated by the fact that the use of negative feedback does not at all guarantee the improvement in performance suggested by our example. If components are improperly chosen or matched, the addition of the feedback loop to a functioning system may produce a wild oscillation in response to certain signals, increasing rather than decreasing the performance error. The real power of servo theory in the design of systems which amplify with a minimum error is based upon a far more detailed mathematical model of system operation provided by a combination of frequency analysis of the signal with a description of the system and its components in terms of equations such as those accompanying Fig. 1. A system is described theoretically as a set of mathematical operations performed (in an order specified by the nature of the circuit network connecting the components which perform each operation) upon an input signal described as the sum of a set of sine functions of various frequencies, amplitudes, and phase relations. The "system equation" of the form $O = f(I)$ relating output and input is obtained by appropriate combination of the equations representing each component. It is important to note that the equation for each component has the same basic form as the equation for the system as a whole—its output is some function of its input. Any component in a system may itself be a complex system whose internal operations can be ignored if the summarizing input-output function is known. In this case the engineer calls it a "black box," an exact synonym of the psychologist's "empty organism."

The value of describing the signal in terms of its frequency characteristics may be illustrated by an extension of Example 1, making use of some dynamic relationships intuitively familiar to everyone, namely, the input-output function for the simple pendulum.

Example 2. In the previous example, the machine component is the relatively rigid pencil which transmits arm movements essentially without change or delay, and the feedback loop is completed through even more rigid light rays. In consequence the performance of the system is essentially equivalent to the transmission characteristics of its human component. In Example 2, we shall hypothetically modify this system to emphasize the characteristics of a machine component. Let us hang a long and heavy free-swinging pendulum from the pencil and consider the movements of the pendulum bob to be the output of the system. The pencil but not the pendulum will be visible to the human operator. We shall make the simplifying (and for some situations involving only low frequency inputs, correct) assumption that the pencil follows the movement of the line with negligible error. For the portion of the system between the vertical line and the pencil supporting the pendulum, we shall assume that the operation represented by f in the equation $O = f(I)$ is simply multiplication by a constant, 1.0. In this case the critical performance characteristics of the system are essentially those of the pendulum. The pendulum is, of course, a very simple machine, but it is one which exhibits most of the basic characteristics of all machine components in man-machine systems. It has an input, movement of its supporting pivot, and an output, movement of its bob; it has inertia; its movements are subject to damping, etc.; and all these characteristics may be known and subject to manipulation by the design engineer.

If the pendulum bob weighs, say, 10 pounds, the wire it is suspended on is 10 feet long, and its pivot is relatively friction-free, the resulting man-machine system will follow irregular movements of the vertical line with negligible error only if the movements of the line are very slow and smooth. If the line jerks to a new position and stops, two kinds of error will develop, both associated with the inertia and elasticity of the pendulum: first a lag as the pendulum bob falls behind, and second an overshoot as the bob catches up and swings past. The bob will then continue to oscillate around the line, slowing down and reducing error to an acceptable minimum only after some lapse of time as a result of friction and the viscous damping of the air. If the line oscillates regularly at certain frequencies, the pendulum will begin to oscillate at the same frequency with increasing amplitude (resonating) to produce very large error by exaggerating the amplitude of the input. If the line oscillates at higher frequencies, the pendulum may stand stationary, producing errors of a different kind. There is, of course, an infinite variety of possible movements the line might make, and to each of these the pendulum would respond differently. Should we wish to describe the performance of this machine in great detail we could go on indefinitely at the empirical level describing the possible movements of the line and the response which the pendulum bob makes to each of them. We could also determine a comparable set of these input-output relationships for each of all possible values of bob weight, wire length, air density, and pivot friction and for every combination of these and of any other variable which

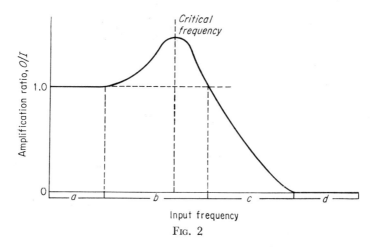

Fig. 2

influences the performance of this and similar machines. But to put the resulting empirical knowledge in tabular form for reference would only emphasize by its cumbersome magnitude the necessity for theory to simplify and summarize, to provide a condensed description of a few relationships among a few critical variables which in proper combination produce or at least approximate the infinite variety of empirical input-output configurations which can be observed. Frequency analysis, together with the component and system equations, provides a basis for such a simplifying theory.

If we examine only the performance of the pendulum or machine component in Example 2 (which in this case is essentially equivalent to the performance of the system as a whole), we find that tremendous simplification of its input-output relationships can be accomplished by describing the input, movements of the pendulum support, and the output, the movements of the bob, as the sum of a set of sine functions of varying frequency, phase relations (relative displacement in time), and relative amplitude. When inputs are classified according to these variables and the corresponding outputs described similarly are examined, a number of regularities become apparent. For any simple pendulum, for example, inputs composed of single sine wave form oscillations whose frequencies are *below* a certain critical frequency are reproduced in the output almost exactly, i.e., with the same frequency and amplitude and only slightly and predictably delayed in time. Input frequencies *at or near* the critical frequency appear in the output with increased amplitude, and input frequencies *above* the critical frequency are reproduced with decreased amplitude, approaching zero amplitude as frequency increases. These relationships may be summarized in a "frequency response curve" such as that in Fig. 2, which might be obtained for an undamped pendulum if amplification ratio were plotted as a function of input frequency. The general form of this curve is characteristic of the response of a large class of machines.

LINEARITY

Although the summary of the performance of a machine provided by a function relating amplification ratio to the frequency of simple sine form inputs would probably be useful, it has very limited applicability, since inputs in the form of simple sine waves are relatively rare—they represent only a small sample of the possible inputs to a system. However, tremendous generality for this description of the behavior of a machine is developed when it can be shown that, for any input which is the sum of two or more sine waves, the output is the sum of the responses made by the machine to waves of each of these frequencies separately, i.e., when each sine wave *component* of the input is reproduced as a component of the output with its amplitude multiplied by the factor (O/I ratio) associated with its frequency. A system which has this additive characteristic is called a *linear system*. This meaning of the term "linear" is not to be confused with the more familiar trade usage which describes an amplifier as linear between certain frequency limits when it is linear in the additive sense and satisfies the added restriction that its amplification ratio is a constant within the specified limits.

Since a motion of any form can in principle be reduced to a set of sine form components of appropriate frequencies, amplitudes, and phase relations, the frequency analysis of the performance of linear systems has great generality, limited in application only by the requirement of linearity for the system in question and by the availability of practical techniques for the frequency analysis of input and output into their component sine waves. Formal methods of analysis applicable to certain nonlinear systems are available but have not been developed to the extent that they are widely used in systems engineering.

APPLICATIONS OF LINEAR FREQUENCY THEORY

Before examining the application of linear frequency theory to human motor behavior, let us look briefly at some of its practical uses in the design of systems, since these contribute to an understanding of the questions concerning human behavior which are relevant in terms of this theory. First, notice that the curve in Fig. 2 indicates that the machine it describes will act as a low-pass filter. Any input frequency in the range c will be transmitted with decreased amplitude and any frequency in the range d will be eliminated entirely as the signal passes through the system or component represented. This characteristic of a machine may be utilized to correct certain "errors," e.g., to eliminate unwanted high-frequency oscillation. This correction is made at the expense of sensitivity to corresponding frequencies in the input, which may or may not be desirable. It is desirable to exclude high-frequency "static" produced by atmospheric electricity in a radio transmission system but to do so by the means we have just described undesirably reduces the fidelity of reproduction of the input introduced at the microphone by the musician or speaker. A low critical frequency is desirable in the steering mechanisms of an automobile in order to reduce or eliminate the high-frequency tremor of the driver's hand or bumps in the road, but the critical frequency cannot be decreased indefinitely without reducing sensitivity to the input frequencies represented by curves in the road, i.e., without reducing maneuverability.

Resonance in the neighborhood of the critical frequency occurs when signals with frequencies in the range b occur. This characteristic is utilized in a-c amplifiers such as radio-frequency tuning circuits, which selectively amplify the rf carrier wave and provide selective tuning by varying the critical frequency. An undesirable consequence of resonance at the critical frequency is illustrated by the shimmy of the front end of early automobiles which occurred when the driver or irregularities in the road introduced the critical frequency into the system. Resonance of this sort may be eliminated by proper design of the system to change or filter or damp the critical frequency.

The constant amplification ratio represented in the frequency response curve in Fig. 2 by a horizontal line at low frequencies (range a) is a desirable characteristic of the audio-frequency amplifier component of a radio, one which is necessary for high fidelity reproduction, but a similar constant ratio throughout the radio-frequency band would be highly undesirable since it would preclude selective tuning.

FREQUENCY THEORY AND HUMAN BEHAVIOR

These examples suggest some of the uses for frequency analysis in the design of systems. Aside from the manipulation of the connecting network which determines the flow of signals and the interaction of components, e.g., in feedback loops, a system is constructed to perform its required function by selection of components with the desired frequency response characteristics. If the response characteristics of available components are known, the response of the system as a whole to any input can be calculated and the performance of alternative systems may be compared before their construction. This fact, which has very great economic consequences, has led to the questions concerning the frequency characteristics of human behavior which the systems engineer has asked the psychologist to answer. The design engineer's decision to use a human component rather than a machine component in particular systems can be made with confidence only if the response characteristics of the human component as well as machine components are known. In order to permit a meaningful comparison of potential human and machine components, however, the response characteristics of both types of component must be expressed *in terms of the same variable* which in this case is the time function specified by frequency analysis. This fact, it may be mentioned parenthetically, suggests the reason that engineers responsible for the basic design of dynamic man-machine systems have largely ignored most of the psychologists' carefully collected data on human motor behavior. Most of the research performed by psychologists in this field utilizes time-on-target or integrated error score as a dependent variable. Information provided by such research is completely useless to the design engineer. In the case of either score the response is integrated over time and frequency analysis is applicable only to the unintegrated data, i.e., to the response as a detailed function of time. Psychologists, including the author, have often gone to a great deal of trouble to construct integrating scoring devices for use in motor behavior studies. From the point of the design engineer, these devices destroy the aspect of the signal which is of greatest value to him, namely, its time-varying characteristics, including the possibility of determining its component frequencies. Once a time-varying signal has passed through a device which integrates over time, the crucial time function is irretrievably lost.

In requesting information concerning the frequency characteristics of human behavior, the systems engineer has in effect handed the psychologist a mathematical model and suggested coordinating definitions which are sufficient to convert the model into an S-R theory. These definitions specify input and output as a tracking task (stimulus) variable and a tracking response variable, time functions of each of these, a relationship between them, and a set of limiting conditions. If counterparts of the relationships between input and output variables specified by this model can be observed consistently between stimulus and response of man under any single set of limiting conditions, then the model becomes an empirical law of human behavior. If relationships described by the model are found for many different situations, e.g., for many tracking responses, task inputs, and limiting conditions, and these relationships are adequately systematized, then the model becomes a theory of human behavior. (Since the model in question systematically describes relationships among a variety of input and output variables of a variety of machines it is already properly described as a theory of machine system behavior.) The limiting conditions mentioned above are variables that are known to affect the relationships described by the theory but are not necessarily included in it as variables. In a given application of the model, they must be held constant or to a range within which their effect is negligible.

A simple and most concise statement of the general form of the frequency analysis model was prepared several years ago at my request by Dr. David Gilbarg of the Graduate Institute for Mathematics and Mechanics at Indiana University and published together with a commentary in which I attempted to present some applications to tracking behavior in nonmathematical language [6]. Since Dr. Gilbarg's presentation is brief and I could not improve upon it, I shall reproduce it verbatim:

The method of operational and frequency analysis described in the body of this report is based on certain mathematical facts which are roughly summarized as follows: If the response of a linear system to certain "elementary" stimuli or inputs is known, the response to any input, however complex, can be predicted. The purpose of this Appendix is to formulate these mathematical facts in a form in which they can be used for actual calculation.

Let a system, such as the human operator, transform an input function, $f(t)$, into the output, $g(t)$. For the purpose of brevity we shall state this symbolically in operational notation, $T[f(t)] = g(t)$, where T is the "operator" which transforms $f(t)$ into $g(t)$. The system is called *linear* if, for arbitrary inputs $f_1(t)$ and $f_2(t)$, and constants a, b,

$$T(af_1 + bf_2) = aT(f_1) + bT(f_2) = ag_1 + bg_2 \qquad (1)$$

where $g_1(t)$, $g_2(t)$ are the outputs corresponding to $f_1(t)$, $f_2(t)$. We shall demand, in addition, of the linear system, that if $f(t, w)$ is a family of inputs, depending on the parameter w, (e.g., a family of sine waves, sin wt, of different frequencies), then,

$$T\left[\int_{w_1}^{w_2} a(w)f(t,w)dw\right] = \int_{w_1}^{w_2} a(w)T[f(t,w)]dw = \int_{w_1}^{w_2} a(w)g(t,w)dw \qquad (2)$$

where $T[f(t,m)] = g(t,w)$.

The two classes of "elementary" inputs most frequently used in analyzing linear systems are (1) the sine waves, and (2) the step functions. The analysis based on these two classes is discussed here.

Let $F(t)$ be an arbitrary input function. If $F(t)$ satisfies certain general mathematical conditions, it is possible to express it as an integral sum of sines and cosines by means of the Fourier integral theorem,* as follows:

Let
$$a[w] = \frac{1}{\pi} \int_{-\infty}^{+\infty} F(x) \sin wx \, dx$$

$$b(w) = \frac{1}{\pi} \int_{-\infty}^{+\infty} F(x) \cos wx \, dx$$

then
$$F(t) = \int_{0}^{-\infty} (a(w) T(\sin wt) + b(w) T(\cos wt)) dw \tag{3}$$

It follows from the linearity of the operator, as expressed in Eq. (2), that

$$T[F(t)] + \int_{0}^{\infty} [a(W) T(\sin wt) + b(w) T(\cos wt)] dw \tag{4}$$

Thus, if the responses $T(\sin wt)$, $T(\cos wt)$ are known for every value of w, the output $T[F(t)]$ can be calculated by means of this equation.

If $F(t)$ happens to be a periodic function of period τ, the above method of the Fourier integral simplifies to analysis in terms of harmonic components. We have in this case,†

$$F(t) = a_o + \sum_{n=1}^{\infty} \left(a_n \sin \frac{2\pi nt}{\tau} + b_n \cos \frac{2\pi nt}{\tau} \right) \tag{5}$$

where
$$a_n = \frac{2}{\tau} \int_{-\tau}^{+\tau} F(x) \sin \frac{2\pi nx}{\tau} \, dx$$

$$b_n = \frac{2}{\tau} \int_{-\tau}^{+\tau} F(x) \cos \frac{2\pi nx}{\tau} \, dx; \qquad n = 1, 2, \ldots$$

$$a_o = \frac{1}{\tau} \int_{-\tau}^{+\tau} F(x) dx$$

and the response to $F(t)$ is

$$T[F(t)] = T(a_o) + \sum_{n=1}^{\infty} \left[a_n T \left(\sin \frac{2\pi nt}{\tau} \right) + b_n T \left(\cos \frac{2\pi nt}{\tau} \right) \right] \tag{6}$$

Hence, if the outputs to all harmonics are known, the response to $F(t)$ can be calculated by means of this sum.

If the basis of the analysis is to be the response to step functions, the

* See, for example, Courant, *Differential and Integral Calculus*. Vol. 2, pp. 318ff.

† See, for example, Courant, *Differential and Integral Calculus*. Vol. 1, pp. 437ff.

procedure is as follows: Let $u(t)$ represent the unit step function,

$$u(t) = 0, t < 0$$
$$= 1, t \geq 0$$

Let $A(t) = T[u(t)]$ be the response to the unit step input. It will be assumed that, if the step input is applied at $t = \tau$, the response is simply displaced by the amount τ, i.e., $T[u(t - \tau)] = A(t - \tau)$. Now consider any input function $F(t)$, then the response of the linear system is given by*

$$T[F(t)] = F(0)A(t) + \int_0^t \frac{dF(\tau)}{d\tau} A(t - \tau)d\tau \qquad (7)$$

Thus, if the response to the unit step function is known, the right hand side can be calculated for any input $f(t)$, and the output determined.

The formulas (3), (6), and (7) are the means of predicting the response of a linear system to any input, (3) and (6) using the response to sine waves as basis, and (7) the response to a step function. The two methods are equivalent when they are both valid [6].

Dr. Gilbarg's references to the analysis of complex input and output functions into step function components may be ignored for our purposes here except to say that the general treatment is the same as in the linear frequency model and that the two forms of the model are mathematically translatable, since a step function can be reduced to a set of sine wave components and vice versa.

Considering only the frequency form of the general linear model it is apparent that it is applicable to relationships between stimuli and responses which vary continuously in a single dimension. To make this application the input function $f(t)$ is defined in terms of a particular stimulus variable and the output function $g(t)$ in terms of a tracking response, both being stated as functions of time. Empirical tests of the resulting theory require a determination of the transform T, which is most easily done experimentally by presenting a single sine wave input of constant amplitude at each frequency over the range of interest, e.g., from zero frequency to the frequency above which the amplitude ratio is zero, and determining the amplitude of the resulting sine form tracking responses associated with each input frequency presented. The transform T may be represented by expressing amplitude ratio and phase shift (delay in transmission through the system) as functions of input frequency. Once having determined the transform, a variety of complex input functions $f(t)$ are presented and the corresponding output functions $t[f(t)]$ are computed and compared with observed outputs $g(t)$. To the extent that there is agreement between computed and observed

* See, for example, Karman and Biot, *Mathematical Methods in Engineering*. p. 403.

outputs the condition of linearity is satisfied, and the theory is verified for the set of limiting conditions represented in the empirical test.

EXPERIMENTAL TESTS OF FREQUENCY THEORY FOR HUMAN BEHAVIOR

The experimental conditions under which this theory has been tested so far are relatively uniform and, from the point of view of the subject, rather simple. The typical experimental apparatus displays two indicators, such as a pointer and a vertical line, one or both of which move horizontally. The subject manipulates a control, usually a stick or lever, sometimes a wheel, movement of which affects the position of one of the indicators. His task is to keep the two indicators continually in alignment. There are two basic types of tasks, pursuit and compensatory tracking. In pursuit tracking, an input indicator moves independently of any action of the subject. Using his manual control, the subject moves the second or output indicator so as to follow the input, attempting to minimize the error or discrepancy between the positions of the two indicators. Movements of the output indicator or of the subject's manual control may be treated as output for purposes of analysis. Aiming a hand-held gun at a moving target is a nonlaboratory example of pursuit tracking, the target and sight corresponding to input and output indicators respectively and the gun itself to the control.

In compensatory tracking, one indicator is fixed with respect to the tracker, usually in the center of his visual field. The movements of the second indicator are in effect the algebraic sum of an imposed input and some function of the output, the control movement of the subject. Beginning with the two indicators superimposed, if the subject holds his control stationary any input produces error in the form of a discrepancy between the fixed and moving indicators. The subject's task is to move his control and the indicator controlled by it in such a way as to minimize or compensate for the error. Aiming a rotating turret with the human operator inside is an example of compensatory tracking. A sight mounted on the turret provides the fixed indicator; the target functions as a moving indicator, its movements providing an input. The subject's manipulations of the manual control device rotate the turret so as to reduce discrepancies between the positions of target and sight.

From the point of view of frequency theory, the two types of tracking are mathematically equivalent and are therefore theoretically interchangeable at the convenience of the engineer or the experimenter. Psychologically, the two might appear to be very different tasks, but although both have been used in experimental work (usually in different laboratories), no significant difference in the frequency characteristics of tracking behavior because of this factor has so far been demonstrated. However, the apparent absence of behavioral significance of this variable may well be due to the crudity of methods used so far.

Since the basic theoretical problem concerns the relationship between input and output as time functions, precise knowledge of the input characteristics is required. Inputs used experimentally have chiefly taken three forms:

1. White noise, in which the distributions of frequencies, amplitudes, and phase relationships of components are defined only statistically.

2. Complex waves composed of a few sine-form components of known frequency, amplitude, and phase relationships.

3. Simple sine waves of constant frequency and amplitude.

A number of technical problems which will not be discussed here are associated with the decision to use inputs that are known statistically rather than inputs that are fully defined. The frequency analysis research performed at the Indiana laboratory has been restricted to inputs of known composition.

In practice, empirical application of the linear frequency model to human tracking behavior has not been at all simple. A major difficulty is the magnitude of the data reduction problem, which exceeds that to which psychologists are accustomed. Adequate treatment of a two-minute sample of tracking may require several hundred hours of hand computation. As one consequence, large-scale studies are not common: a single study sponsored by the United States Air Force and carried out under the direction of Dr. O. J. Benepe [2] probably includes half the available data on tracking behavior of the human operator which has been analyzed according to the requirements of frequency analysis. This study is based on 221 power spectra obtained for 99 subjects, together with a number of summarizing analyses based on autocorrelation techniques. Most other studies have been limited to data obtained from one or a few subjects or to less detailed analyses.

LINEARITY OF HUMAN RESPONSE

The results of empirical studies have so far been largely negative. It may be stated categorically that linearity of response over the entire range of interest for tracking input frequencies (from zero to approximately 10 cycles per second) has not been demonstrated for any set of limiting conditions. In addition there is ample evidence of nonlinear relationships between tracking stimuli and tracking responses. However, it does not follow, as some have concluded, that man is a nonlinear system. We would not conclude that a pendulum was a nonlinear system if we tested it outdoors in a thunderstorm and found that the relationship between horizontal movements of its pivot and its bob did not satisfy the conditions of linearity. We should properly conclude that this particular input-output relationship was not linear under the limiting conditions of the environment provided by a thunderstorm, but we should leave open the question whether (a) the pivot-bob movements were linearly related under other limiting conditions, and (b) the movements of the bob were linearly related to a more inclusive input, including, for example, the movement of the pivot and forces applied by the wind. This analogy suggests the status of research on the linearity of the human operator today. Under the conditions that have been examined there is positive evidence of nonlinearity in the relationship between certain inputs and outputs. But only a few conditions have been investigated and there are tantalizing hints in the available data that a very high degree of linearity may be demonstrated (a) under other limiting conditions that have not yet been examined in the laboratory, and (b) under the same limiting conditions when more inputs than movements of a visual tracking stimulus are controlled or taken into account.

First, let us examine the evidence of nonlinearity. Some of this evidence is obvious without resort to laboratory demonstration. We know, for example, that we can instruct a subject (a) to track or (b) not to track and that he will do as instructed. This is a most obvious change of the transform T from whatever it may be when tracking to an amplitude ratio of zero for all frequencies when not tracking, indicating that instructions are one of the critical limiting conditions. We know also that a man can steer a bicycle down a curved path with his hands on the grips (a) at the ends of the handle bars or (b) near the steering column, which implies different input-output amplitude ratios in each case, i.e., that T varies if we define output as hand movement. He can also ride a bicycle with his arms crossed, i.e., with his right hand on the left grip and left hand on the right one, in which case if output is measured as right-hand movement the *sign* of the transform is changed. It is clear therefore that task conditions markedly affect the transform T, indicating that man is not a simple system giving a uniform response to the particular portion of his environment we call the tracking input. These facts are taken for granted in all laboratory research, and the attempt is made to hold instruction and other task-variables constant during any test of linearity. However, given apparent constancy of these limiting environmental conditions there is further evidence of nonlinearity. Linearity requires that the same transform be recoverable when inputs differ in composition, and it goes almost without saying that this is possible only if the responses to inputs of the same composition presented at different times are the same. The transform must be a process which is stationary in time, a requirement which can be tested by presenting any input of fixed composition repeatedly or continuously under constant conditions and comparing two or more samples of the responses obtained. Differences in response to an input of constant composition, which provides clear evidence of a nonstationary T in a highly uniform limiting environment, have been demonstrated over a long period of time during which learning occurred and also during a relatively short period of tracking after the learning asymptote (as indicated by integrated error scores) had been reached [2, exp. II and III]. Even more obvious evidence of nonlinearity is provided in a study [7] in which inputs consisting of single frequencies ranging from 0.5 cycles per second to 4 cycles per second were presented at two amplitude levels. It was found that input-output amplitude ratios decreased by approximately 10 per cent input amplitudes were tripled. Further, at the higher frequencies most subjects responded at frequencies higher than the input frequency, an effect indicating a rather startling instability of T above the critical frequency. At these frequencies the subjects acted as though they responded to the amplitude of the input signal but not to its frequency: they duplicated the amplitude characteristic only.

Another indication of nonlinearity, related to the last example, is the occurrence of "noise," i.e., frequencies in the output which are not present in the input. This noise or error may be random in terms of frequency, resembling thermal noise or "static" or it may be especially prominent at certain frequencies. An example of the latter type of error is the 60-cycle hum in a radio amplifier. Irregular tracking error, familiar to all investigators of tracking responses, is evidence of "random" noise. A number of investigators have also pointed to a prominent error component at approximately 1 cycle per second which appears in the output of the human tracker when it is completely absent from the input. The characteristic tremor frequency of approximately 10 cycles per second might be expected to appear in human outputs, but this frequency is considerably above the critical frequency of most apparatus used in tracking studies and in consequence has seldom been reported as tracking error. The noise or error which is identified by spectral analysis in the Benepe report, corroborating reports of other analyses, includes "random" error, error with a frequency near 1 cycle per second, and error with frequencies corresponding to those of input components. In addition a 5-cycles per second error component appeared under some conditions, e.g., when other error was suppressed.

All of this might appear to be overwhelming evidence that the human being performing a tracking task is best described as nonlinear. However, it may be pointed out that most of the evidence of nonlinearity just presented is associated with variables not mentioned in the theory. A theory which states a relationship between input and output is not invalidated by evidence that output is related to other variables. The fact that changes in instructions and changes in posture (e.g., in operating a bicycle) affect output characteristics is irrelevant to the question of linearity. The knowledge that these variables do affect output simply means that these are system variables included in S which must be held constant in testing for a linear relationship between input and output variables. The evidence for changes in T, the input-output relationship, under fixed task conditions is restricted to very few of the possible configurations of limiting conditions—the actual amount of research investigating linearity in the human operator while tracking is almost infinitesimal in comparison with the amount of research which has been conducted to determine the response characteristics of machines. And finally, the reported tracking error and other nonlinearity of the human operator under many circumstances are no greater than those of many machines considered to be linear in terms of practical standards.

The human tracking error is likely to become important in practical situations only when it occurs in high-amplification systems requiring the man to respond to maximally high frequencies, and especially when the human or scientific or economic or military penalties for even small error are great. In such cases we build research equipment which amplifies the error so that we can examine it in detail. But we should not lose perspective merely because we look at the error through a research microscope and its consequences through a social or a physical amplifier. The error which appears as nonlinearity in spectral analysis may be, and in published research often is, less than 1 or 2 per cent of the total signal, decreasing relatively as input amplitude increases. Consider the expected performance of a man driving a car at a uniform 20 mph, 8 hours a day from Denver to San Francisco with all traffic cleared from the road. With proper instruction and motivation, how often would we expect his front wheels to leave the road? Assuming that he could perform this task at least once without ever leaving the road, we have described a set of limiting conditions under which the deviations from linearity are extremely slight. The ratio of the width of the road to the wandering of the road, which represents the maximum proportion of nonlinearity under these conditions, is obviously very small, whether or not we consider it negligible for scientific or social purposes. Over the range of input frequencies defined by the curves in the road taken at the rate of 20 mph, a man driving a car is a highly linear system with a uniform amplification ratio of 1. Since at 20 mph the path of the car is relatively rigidly related to the movements of the steering wheel we may conclude that this measure of linearity of the transform for the system as a whole is equally characteristic of the transform for its human component.

There are many similar situations in which a human output very closely approximates a linear transform of a stimulus input. These are apparently limited to inputs containing no frequencies higher than approximately 0.5 cycle per second. Above this frequency, linearity is more subject to question.

There is one extremely interesting suggestion [2, exp. IV] of limiting conditions which result in marked reduction of the error occurring at low input frequencies. In a pursuit tracking task, a single sine wave input of $\frac{1}{3}$ cycle per second was presented as a visible pointer movement (a) together with auditory stimulation consisting of the uncontrolled ambient noise of the laboratory, (b) together with a tone varying in (auditory) frequency at 0.25 cycle per second, i.e., auditory stimulation not in synchrony with the visual input, and (c) together with a tone varying regularly in aduitory frequency at $\frac{1}{3}$ cycle per second, the variation in auditory frequency being synchronized with the movements of the pointer providing the visual input. Under condition (c) error was markedly reduced, not only that near the input frequency and 1 cycle per second, but throughout the entire frequency spectrum examined, from 0.2 to 6.0 cycles per second. This is an isolated result, but the reduction in error is great and is consistent for 16 subjects. It strongly suggests that better control of stimulation through other modalities than that receiving the arbitrarily defined "input" may contribute to successful application of the linear model to human behavior.

In any case, it is quite obvious that if we consider the relationship of a single input to a single response output in the human operator without regard for other variables, he is a nonlinear system. But any system which has alternative transforms, such as a linear amplifier with an on-off switch, is nonlinear if we ignore conditions which select the transform, e.g., the state of the switch. The human operator is obviously a complex system in which many possible transforms are available, these being selected by means of variables other than the immediate single-dimension characteristic of a stimulus arbitrarily called "the" input for purposes of a given system or experiment. The first question to be answered in applying the linear frequency analysis model to human behavior is not "Is man a linear system?" but "Are there any conditions under which linearity of input-output relationship can be shown for man?" The answer to the latter question is certainly positive in spite of the fact that most laboratory research has emphasized nonlinearity by magnifying error for purposes of analysis. Conditions are known now under which a man's response to a continuously varying stimulus is at least as linear as many of the machines which are considered to be linear. Under these conditions of linear operation, the transform T is a constant multiplier. The associated error is sufficiently small to be negligible for many technological purposes, and there are suggestions that the stricter requirements of scientific theory verification may be satisfied by more carefully controlled empirical research.

METHODOLOGICAL COMMENTARY

Since neither the theoretical treatments of systems-engineering concepts and their application to human behavior nor the reports of supporting empirical research, even that conducted by psychologists, are generally available in psychological journals, I have tried in the preceding section to summarize the engineering context, the basic theoretical notions, and some of the relevant empirical data, mentioning methodological matters only incidentally. In the present section linear frequency theory will be examined as an example of a limited theory of the behavior of systems. From the methodological point of view, whether the systems are called human beings or machines is irrelevant.

Linear frequency theory is based on a mathematical model, i.e., a set of statements which are completely expressed in conventional mathematical notation. As a result, generally accepted rules are available which permit the derivation of certain statements of relationship among variable terms and do not permit the derivation of certain others. Questions as to whether a given statement is or is not a consequence, i.e., whether it can or cannot be derived from the statements comprising the mathematical model, can be answered. The formal model is converted to a theory by the addition of a few empirical definitions which assert equivalence between (a) empirical operations and (b) terms and logical operations in the model or in statements derived from it. The variables defined by these operations may be directly observed or obtained from sets of directly observed values of such variables by "empirical," i.e., observable, data reduction operations. To the extent that these operations are unambiguously described, these definitions make it possible to specify that certain empirical consequences are derivable or are not derivable from the model.

There are six basic coordinating definitions utilized to convert formal statements of the linear frequency model to an empirically testable form, i.e., to a theory. These define I, an input variable, O, an output variable, $f(t)$ and $g(t)$ time functions of each of these, T, the transform stating the relationship of $f(t)$ and $g(t)$, and S, the system and the conditions under which it operates.

The input variable I is an empirical independent variable, defined by operations which provide instantaneous values of a variable such as position, distance, pressure, temperature, brightness, auditory frequency, etc., which is in the environment of the system. The output variable O is the corresponding empirical dependent variable, some response or activity of the system whose instantaneous values are measured. Although definition of these empirical variables is implied in every application of the theory to a particular system, the actual theoretical analysis is based on a characteristic abstracted from sequential sets of measurements of I and O, namely, their changes as a function of time. The temporal changes in I and O are presumably observable if I and O are observable, but since direct observations (estimates) of time functions are likely to be highly ambiguous, the precise time functions are redefined as data reduction operations performed upon sequential sets of I and O measurements. The reduction of ambiguity which results is, of course, the primary function of such operational definitions. The particular operations chosen to define $f(t)$ and $g(t)$ are selected in terms of the second criterion applied to definitions in science, namely, their usefulness. Particular data reduction operations which have defined $f(t)$ and $g(t)$ usefully—in this case by permitting demonstrations of their relation to each other—are those which describe a sequential set of instantaneous values of I and O as the sum of a set of sine functions of appropriate frequency, amplitude, and in some cases phase relations. Two common operations are represented (a) by Fourier analysis, which reduces the input and output sequences to power spectra, and (b) by autocorrelation. The data reduction may be performed by the instrument used in observation, e.g., a wave analyzer, in which case $f(t)$ and $g(t)$ are directly observed empirical variables rather than constructs, and I and O, which may not be observed at all, become somewhat vestigial constructs.

In the context of the present theory little more need be said concerning the variables just discussed. However, it is interesting to note that if $f(t)$ and $g(t)$ are obtained by a manual operation—if they are computed by hand from observations of I and O—then they are what has been called "intervening variables." If, on the other hand, $f(t)$ and $g(t)$ are taken directly off the display of a wave analyzer (which is possible with instruments now available), these "intervening variables" become directly observable variables.

The two remaining variables T and S have a somewhat different status from those just discussed. In a certain sense, both are constants rather than variables, but since any constant is a particular value of a variable, they should not be overlooked. (A variable is defined here as a set of mutually exclusive classes, each of which is called a value.) T, the relationship between input and output variables, is asserted to be fixed in any specific application of the theory, i.e., when S, the system and its operating conditions, remains unchanged. T as a variable (an intervening variable?) is a set of sets of mathematical operations and parameters, determined empirically for any given S by analysis of the relationship between $f(t)$ and $g(t)$. S is an empirical variable of a sort which has not been subject to detailed methodological examination. As a single variable representing systems in their environments of operating conditions its individual values (particular systems) are highly complex and qualitative. If we examine in detail any system and its operating conditions which constitute a single value of the qualitative variable S, we find that it can be defined as a configuration, the logical product of a large number of simpler variables, some of which may also be qualitative variables. Because of the complexity of qualitative variables such as S, it is customary in many scientific contexts to solve the problem they pose by treating them, temporarily, at least, as constants. The total complex S is held constant during detailed investigations of relationships among a few special variables such as I and O, or $g(t)$ and $f(t)$. This practice is followed in science generally as well as in systems-engineering research. Once the relationship between input and output has been determined for a given system and a given set of conditions, i.e., once the T associated with a particular S has been found and found to be constant, the next step is to make similar determinations of other values of T associated with other values of S. This is one of the processes involved in the generalization of a law or a theory.

Insofar as S is treated as an undifferentiated qualitative variable, i.e., simply as a set of mutually exclusive classes, its relationship to different values of T can only be expressed as a collection of statements of association between particular values of S and particular values of T. However, as a number of systems are investigated and statements of association between values of T and S accumulate, some order may appear, suggesting the possibility of summarizing a set of relationships between certain subclasses of S and T. For example, as the transforms of a number of pendulums accumulate, it might be noticed that if these pendulums (single values of S) are arranged in an order determined by the weight of the bob, the critical frequency (an aspect of T) increases as weight (an aspect of S) decreases. This analytic process has, of course, already occurred in the past history of frequency theory. In the complete theory, which we have not attempted to present, since it is coextensive with much of general physical theory, S is not treated as a constant, but as a variable or a set of variables. The relationships between many values of S and T have been determined, and it has become obvious that there are systematic relationships between certain aspects of S, such as mass of moving parts, and certain aspects of T, such as critical frequency.

These relationships between subvariables in S and characteristics of T have been summarized mathematically in such a way that the complete frequency theory of systems includes the relationships between O and I or $f(t)$ and $g(t)$ as a function of many specific variables to which the qualitative S can be reduced.

As a result of this process, the art of systems engineering, which required the engineer to memorize or "intuit" the T functions associated with qualitatively described S values, is being supplanted by the science of systems engineering in which relationships between T and many possible characteristics of systems are explicitly stated. Insofar as these characteristics of the system are quantitative variables they make it possible to take maximum advantage of the summarizing power of the quantitative language, mathematics, and permit computational solutions to many concrete problems of systems design. The later stages of this process, the generalization of relationships between quantitative aspects of S and T, have been limited almost exclusively to the machine components of systems. In the investigation of the performance of human components we are in a very early stage. We are collecting particular T values that are associated with particular qualitatively described S's. Linear frequency theory provides a means of organizing the collection procedure.

REFERENCES

1. Anderson, Nancy S. Factors of motor skill learning as related to control loading. Unpublished doctoral dissertation, Ohio State Univer., 1956.

2. Benepe, O. J., Narasimhan, R., & Ellson, D. G. "An experimental evaluation of the application of harmonic analysis to the tracking behavior of the human operator," WADC, Tech. Report No. 53-384, May, 1954.

3. Burke, C. J., Narasimhan, R., & Benepe, O. J. "Some problems in the spectral analysis of human behavior records," Tech. Report No. 53-27, Wright Air Development Center, July, 1953.

4. Elkind, J. I. "Tracking response characteristics of the human operator," Memorandum 40, Human Factors Operational Research Laboratories, Air Research and Development Center, USAF, Washington, D.C., Sept., 1953.

5. Elkind, J. I. "Characteristics of simple manual control systems," Tech. Report No. 111, Massachusetts Institute of Technology, Lincoln Laboratory, April, 1956.

6. Ellson, D. G., & Gilbarg, D. "The application of operational analysis to human motor behavior," Air Materiel Command Memorandum Report MCREXD-694-2J, May, 1948. (Also *Psychol. Rev.*, 1949, 56, 9–17.)

7. Ellson, D. G., & Gray, Florence E. "Frequency response of human operators following a sine wave input," USAF Air Materiel Command Memorandum Report MCREXD-694-2N, Dec., 1948.

8. Ellson, D. G., & Wheeler, L. "Resonance in the human operator," Tech. Report No. 5834, Wright Air Development Center, April, 1951.

9. Fitts, P. M. Engineering psychology and equipment design. In S. S. Stevens (Ed.), *Handbook of experimental psychology.* New York: Wiley, 1951. Pp. 1287–1340.

10. Fitts, P. M., Bennett, W. F., & Bahrick, H. P. Application of autocorrelation analysis to the study of tracking behavior. In G. Finch & F. Cameron (Eds.), *Symposium on Air Force Human Engineering, Personnel, and Training Research.* ARDC Tech. Report No. 56-8, National Research Council, Washington, D.C., Nov., 1955.

11. Fontaine, A. B. A model for human tracking behavior in a closed-loop control system. Unpublished doctoral dissertation, Ohio State Univer., 1954.

12. Krendel, E. S. "A preliminary study of the power spectrum approach to the analysis of perceptual-motor performance," Air Force Tech. Report No. 6723, The Franklin Institute, Oct., 1951.

13. Krendel, E. S. "The spectral density study of tracking performance: Part I, The effect of instructions," Tech. Report No. 52-11, Part I, Wright Air Development Center. The Franklin Institute, Jan., 1952.

14. Krendel, E. S. "The spectral density of tracking performance: Part II, the effect of input, amplitude and practice," Tech. Report No. 52-11, Part II, Wright Air Development Center. The Franklin Institute, Jan., 1952.

15. Krendel, E. S., & Barnes, G. H. "Interim report on human frequency response studies," Tech. Report 54-370, Air Materiel Command, USAF, Wright Air Development Center, June, 1954.

16. MacColl, L. A. *Fundamental theory of servomechanisms.* New York: Van Nostrand, 1945.

17. Mayne, R. Some engineering aspects of the mechanism of body control. *Electrical Engng.,* **70**, 207, March, 1951.

18. McCollum, I. N., & Chapanis, A. "A human engineering bibliography," Tech. Report No. 15, ONR, Project NR145-075, Contract Nonr-1268(01), San Diego State College Foundation, San Diego, Calif., 1956. 128 pp.

19. Narasimhan, R., & Benepe, O. J. "The use of autocorrelation functions in the harmonic analysis of human behavior," Tech. Report No. 6529, Wright Air Development Center, Oct., 1951.

20. North, J. D. The human transfer function in servo systems. In A. Tustin (Ed.), *Automatic and manual control.* New York: Academic Press, 1952. Pp. 473–501.

21. Russell, L. Characteristics of the human as a linear servo element. Unpublished master's thesis, Electrical Engineering Department, Massachusetts Institute of Technology, June, 1951.

22. Tustin, A. The nature of the operator's response in manual control and its implications for controller design. *J. Inst. Electrical Engrs.* (London), 1947, **94**, Part IIA, 190.

23. Tustin, A. (Ed.) *Automatic and manual control.* Cranfield Conference, 1951. New York: Academic Press, 1952.

24. Walston, C. E., & Warren, C. E. "Mathematical analysis of the human operator in a closed loop control system," Research Bulletin, AFPTRC-TR-54-96, Air Force Personnel and Training Command, Lackland Air Force Base, San Antonio, Tex., 1954.

25. Watson, Claude E. A mathematical analysis of the human operator in a closed-loop control system. Unpublished doctoral dissertation, Ohio State Univer., 1953.

APPENDIX: SUGGESTED DISCUSSION TOPICS FOR CONTRIBUTORS OF SYSTEMATIC ANALYSES[1]

INTRODUCTION

We will use the term "systematic formulation" as any set of sentences formulated as a tool for ordering empirical knowledge with respect to some specifiable domain of events, or furthering the discovery of such knowledge. As is evident in science in general and psychology in particular, such formulations may vary in their characteristics over a very wide range. These variations may reflect differences in the intentions of the systematist, limits imposed by the nature of the subject matter, by the status of knowledge about it and related domains, by the availability of techniques for ordering the events in the domain, etc.

Defined in this sense, a "systematic formulation" may vary from one or a few orienting ideas towards the conduct of research, or towards the organization of extant knowledge within a given empirical domain (of any scope), to an explicit, elegant, and quantified systematization. Such highly diverse expressions as "viewpoint," "research philosophy," "Weltanschauung," "exploratory hypothesis" or set of such, "frame of reference," "dimensional system," "systematic (or "theoretical") framework," "explanatory (or "descriptive") system," "hypothetico-deductive system," "theory," "explanatory mechanism" (or set of such), "model," etc., may all be subsumed under "systematic formulation," as we wish to use this phrase.

This study is interested in the "systematic formulations" of present-day psychological science. Comparative analyses of "theory" and discussions of systematic methodology have considered far too narrow a range of formulations during the past few decades. We seek an inventory of current systematic resources which will adequately reflect the diversity and richness of conceptual experimentation of recent and present psychology. Only by the widest possible representation of formulations, with respect both to methodological type and em-

[1] This is a copy of the document concerning the discussion themes and their significance, sent to all Study I contributors at the time of their invitation to participate.

pirical domain, can clear light be shed on problems that cut across various classes of "system." Only in this way can problems which are unique to given classes of "theory" be isolated, and interrelationship issues be treated justly and comprehensively.

This study begins with no value judgments with respect to some preferred mode of systematization, or even with respect to some preferred set of systematic aims or ideals. On the contrary, the only value judgment it makes is that issues of this order have tended, in recent decades, to be prejudged. Nor is it the intention of this study to end with such a set of value judgments. Our intentions are explicative, not evaluative, and our belief is that explication of the current systematic situation on a broadened and less stereotype-bound basis is as valuable to a rational determination of next steps on the part of systematists and research workers as it is to more effective pedagogy.

In this era of second and *n*-order self-study questionnaires and professional nose-counting, investigators whose mode of work is as essentially individualistic and inspirational as that of the systematist may understandably feel that there is a suggestion of the Philistine in any project which requires the answering of questions about their work. To this, we can only reply that among the intentions of this study are not eavesdropping on the creative process, the determination of excellence by ballot, or even the charting of "directions" by consensus. We believe merely that where we can go—no matter in how many different directions—is some function of where we are, and that the assessment of where we are can proceed perhaps a little more efficiently in the light of the information for which this study calls. The type of reflective re-analysis of one's position from a common incidence which this study seeks finds its precedent in such institutionalized channels as symposia, anthologies, handbooks, and the occasional journal issues which are devoted to a common theme.

RATIONALE OF THE DISCUSSION TOPICS

Explicit knowledge about the characteristics of the many and varied systematic formulations put forward in the history of science is in its infancy, but a reasonable amount of information exists about a few of the formulations in natural science (e.g., Newtonian mechanics, relativity theory) particularly distinguished for their generality, explicitness, "elegance," and success in mediating the organization of knowledge. It is highly unlikely that all "successful" systematic formulations in all fields of science exhibit all of the known properties —even in some degree—of the criterion formulations which have so far been studied by methodologists. But it is probable that all formulations which realize in some measure (whether actually or potentially) such scientific objectives as "prediction," "understanding," or "control" exhibit at least some of these properties.

The discussion topics in the following outline have perforce been derived from the specifiable characteristics of the class of scientific systems which has so far received attention from methodologists of science. Nevertheless, we have no great confidence in the adequacy to psychology (and the biological and social sciences) of the generalizations about problems of empirical systematization made by methodologists of science. Whether systematizations of psychological data can be expected to conform to any large number of such characteristics is, of course, an entirely open question. Unfortunately, we do not as yet have a vocabulary, and a set of corresponding distinctions, which permits us to talk with precision about the widely varying characteristics of non-natural science systematic formulations. Given writers will therefore find that not all items will be equally relevant to their own systematic formulations, and some items will probably be entirely irrelevant. Depending on the nature of his system, the systematist must necessarily give differential attention and emphasis to certain of the items. He may also find it necessary to discuss the formulation with respect to characteristics not included in the outline.

Clearly, we are aiming for commensurability of treatment, but not blindly or rigidly so. Not only may individual writers find it necessary to omit certain of the items, but they may wish, in some cases, to re-interpret items in order to bring them to bear more precisely on the nature of the formulation under analysis, and they may wish to alter the order in which the various discussion topics are arranged. Despite such necessary variations of treatment, the procedure should result in a more commensurable airing of issues connected with systematic formulations than has hitherto been the case.

It would be meaningless to suggest any standard length for the manuscripts. Obviously, we should like to have sufficiently sustained consideration of the discussion topics to ensure clarity for a heterogeneous audience, and to derive maximum explicit benefit from the systematist's wisdom with respect to the problems at issue. On the other hand, we do not wish to burden the systematist with an overly laborious or time-consuming task. The purposes of the study will be adequately served by manuscripts which are as brief as is compatible with meaningful discussion of the outline rubrics.

We have tried to formulate the following list of discussion topics explicitly enough to ensure univocality of interpretation, yet at the same time to avoid unconscionable discursiveness in our presentation. For reasons indicated above, we have used certain of the "standard" distinctions and terminological counters of the general methodology of science with a reluctance which has only given way because of the unavailability of any alternate vocabulary for talking, with general intelligibility, about systematic problems. If the authors of such distinctions have, in the past, applied them in such a way as to imply value judgments based on the degree of correspondence between the material under analysis and the analytic distinctions at hand, we can only regard this as a regrettable historical circumstance to which the results of the present study may conceivably supply the proper corrective. Indeed, a useful outcome of the present study might well be the aid it can give towards the development of a more meaningful way of talking about problems of psychological systematization.

THE THEMES OF DISCUSSION

{1} Background factors and orienting attitudes

(a) Background factors which have influenced objectives, methods, and content of system.

(b) Orienting attitudes which have determined systematic objectives, methods, and conceptual content.

Explanation

"Background factors" would include, of course, such matters as education, influence of other theorists, general currents of thought within the field or the culture at large, previous research history, or any other genetic circumstance which the systematist deems noteworthy.

"Orienting attitudes" register those presystematic judgments, values, and beliefs which, in a relatively general and stable way, have determined the aims, inductive basis, conceptual content, or formal organization of the system. Examples might be the systematist's general commitments towards such issues as:

a. the nature and limits of psychological prediction
b. "level of analysis" at which it is fruitful to constitute explanatory constructs, with respect both to "ontological reference" (e.g., "purely behavioral," "physiological," "sociological"), and "coarseness-fineness" of the "causal" or explanatory units
c. utility and role of "models"
d. comprehensiveness of empirical reference (in terms of some such continuum as "unrestricted generality of scope—extreme delimitation") towards which it is fruitful for a system to aim, in the present phase

   e. degree and mode of quantitative and mensurational specificity towards which it is desirable and/or feasible to aim

   f. type of formal organization (on some such continuum as "explicit, hypothetico-deductive axiomatization—informal exposition") considered best suited to requirements for systematization, at the present phase, in the area selected by the systematist.

In order to promote adequate understanding of the systematist's goals and working methods, it would be desirable to make the itemization of "orienting attitudes" reasonably complete.

{2} Structure of the system as thus far developed

   (*a*) Exhaustive itemization of *systematic* independent, intervening, and dependent variables.

   (*b*) Mode of definition of representative variables of each category.

   (*c*) Major interrelations among constructs.

   (*d*) Discussion of order of determinacy and other characteristics of construct linkages.

Explanation

What is sought here is not a discursive summary of the system, so much as a reconstruction of its conceptual structure via the isolation of the chief systematic constructs of all categories, and the exhibition of how they are interrelated within the system. The presentation need not be particularly lengthy, since, for the purpose of the analysis, the systematist need not summarize contents of prior expository publications, to any marked extent.

In order to promote commensurability, we are suggesting that the systematists adhere to the independent-intervening-dependent variable schema which has become more or less conventional in recent methodological discussion. Since many systematic formulations have not been explicitly patterned on such a schema, the recasting of the systematic structure in this way may present difficulties, but, we suspect, not very formidable ones, in most cases.

In cases where a systematist feels that an attempt to recast his material into the independent-intervening-dependent variable schema does violence to his formulation, he may, of course, recapitulate the structure of his system in any way that he considers appropriate.

In certain cases (e.g., "positivistic" systematizations), a system may not contain conceptual components which correspond in functional significance to "intervening variables." In such cases, the systematist's task will obviously reduce to the isolation of systematic independent and dependent variables, and their interrelations.

For purposes of this study, we stipulate the following rather informal definitions of the three classes of systematic variables.

   1. The "independent variables" of a system are the terms referring to the factors available for identification, "measurement," and, when

possible, manipulation, which are discriminated within the system as the antecedent conditions of the events that the system is designed to predict.

2. The "dependent variables" of a system are the terms designating the classes of events that the system is designed to predict.

3. "Intervening variables" are terms interpolated between the independent and dependent variables, having properties such that a class of empirical relationships describable by a given number of statements which directly relate independent and dependent variables can be derived from a substantially smaller number of statements which relate independent to intervening variables and these, in turn, to dependent variables.

Note that the item {2} discussion topics call for the isolation of *"systematic"* independent and dependent variables. In explanation of this, it may be well to note that the expressions "independent variable" and "dependent variable" have become highly ambiguous in discussions of psychological methodology. The independent-intervening-dependent variable schema established (in the first instance) by Tolman for the analysis of theory implies a sense of the expressions "independent variable" and "dependent variable" which overlaps only partly with these expressions as they are used in mathematics and in general scientific methodology. In order to be entirely clear for the purpose of the present study, we present three senses of the expression "independent variable" (analogous definitions may immediately be derived for the expression "dependent variable").

SENSE I. SYSTEMATIC INDEPENDENT VARIABLES

Terms in the *construct language* of a theory denoting the chief classes of empirical events which serve as the operationally identifiable or "measurable," and, wherever possible, manipulable antecedent conditions of the events that the theory is designed to predict. This is precisely the sense in which the present discussion topic calls for the isolation of the "independent variables" of the system under analysis. We may refer to "independent variables," in this sense, as "systematic independent variables."

SENSE II. EMPIRICAL INDEPENDENT VARIABLES

A term or expression denoting any factor in an experimental situation which is systematically varied, or operated upon in some way, with the intent to observe and record a correlated change in another part of the system defined by the experiment. Sense II independent variables may be called *"empirical* independent variables." Sense I and Sense II are very often confused. *Empirical* independent variables *may* be specific, singular "realizations" (operational or reductive "symptoms") of a *systematic* independent variable; they are not, however, to be identified with the systematic independent variable to which they are ordered. Sense I independents are terms in the *construct language;* Sense II independents are expressions in *immediate data language* (cf. "explanation," item {3}). A Sense II independent variable need not be a "realization" of a Sense I independent; empirical relations between experimental variables which are ordered to no extant theory are often investigated.

SENSE III. "MATHEMATICAL" INDEPENDENT VARIABLES

All terms in a statement of functional dependency of which a given term (the dependent variable) is a specified function. This corresponds roughly to the usage of "independent variable" in mathematics. We give this rather obvious usage for purposes of completeness.

It might be added, at this point, that in most instances *systematic* independent and dependent variables are introduced into a system and given empirical meaning by some stipulated linkage(s) to a set of *empirical* independent or dependent variables (this is one way of elucidating what is meant by so-called "empirical" or "operational" *definitions*). Thus, in the present analysis, a systematist may wish to employ some such distinction when discussing such questions as "mode of definition of representative variables" [item {2}(*b*)] and certain other questions introduced in later sections [e.g., items {3}(*c*) and (*d*)].

{3} Initial evidential grounds for assumptions of system

(*a*) Identify the chief classes of experimental and/or empirical data which have served as the initial source of evidence on which the system was based, or have been used in any way to suggest the major assumptions of the system.

(*b*) Why was this material considered "strategic," or in some sense "fundamental," relative to:

(1) other sources or varieties of data within the same empirical area,

(2) data in other empirical areas for which the system is intended to hold?

(*c*) Isolate the chief *empirical* independent and dependent variables (in "theoretically neutral," "immediate data language" terms) in the evidence on which the system is based.

(*d*) Show how empirical independent and dependent variables (as expressed in "immediate data language") are linked to *systematic* independent and dependent variables (construct language).

Explanation

In the discussion of (*a*), it would be interesting for the systematist to consider whether, in general, the system has thus far been based primarily on *extant* empirical data, or whether the systematic program has been contingent on the prior extension, or "opening up," of a field of data by the individual systematist, or group of investigators working within the systematic context.

In (*d*) we have reference to the distinction between *systematic* independent and dependent variables (Sense I) and *empirical* independent and dependent variables (Sense II), precisely as made above (cf. "explanation," item {2}).

For uniform understanding of items (c) and (d), it might be useful to specify what we mean by "immediate data language." One may say that all empirical ("operational") definitions of a system are constructed from a linguistic base that may be called the "data language" of the system in question. *Immediate data language* is the language, presumably univocally intelligible to all competent workers in the field, in which empirical or operational definitions of systematic terms are put forward, and against which primitive and derived statements of the system are compared. In general, then, "immediate data language" tends to appear in two contexts in connection with an empirical system:

1. in statements which are explicitly intended to provide operational definitions of terms in the construct language, and
2. in descriptions of experimental (or general empirical) conditions, observations, and the results of statistical or mathematical transformations of observations which the systematist or investigator is relating in some way to the construct language of the system.

One may distinguish *"immediate* data language" from another sense in which "data language" is often used in methodological discussions—i.e., as the "epistemic reduction basis" of the terms of a system. This involves reduction of the systematic (construct language) terms to the "ultimate" confirmation language to which all proper statements of the system are, in principle, reducible. We are not concerned with "data language" in this latter sense in the present group of discussion topics.

{4} **Construction of function forms**

(a) How are independent-intervening-dependent variable—or, in the case of "positivistic" systems, independent-dependent variable function specifications constructed?

(b) Rationale of, and grounds for confidence in, the procedure.

(c) Contemplated modifications or extensions of the procedure as the theory develops.

(d) Grounds for favoring employment or nonemployment of intervening variables.

Explanation

When thrown into independent-intervening-dependent variable form, any system will contain stipulations, at one level of explicitness or another, with respect to the interrelations among these variables. Such construct linkages will vary from rather general adumbrations of the functional relationships to highly specific descriptions of function forms. Thus, "function specifications" may range from "purely qualitative" verbal descriptions through varying degrees and modes of quantitative explicitness, depending on the systematic intentions, the area under systematization, etc.

Such function-form specifications are, in one sense, free and creative "constructions" on the part of the theorist. In another sense, however, they "come from somewhere," and are "arrived at" on the basis of some set of rules, however implicit. It would be most useful if systematists participating in the present study, would make an attempt to explicate or reconstruct their procedure in arriving at the specification of function forms. In the case of some systems, construct interrelations may register in a relatively *direct* way the interrelations among *empirical* variables, as determined in specific experiments or empirical studies which are believed to have fundamental significance. Such relationships may be "transposed" to the systematic variables in a variety of ways, ranging from empirical "curve-fitting" to verbal descriptions of the trend of the findings. In the case of other systems, the construct linkages may apparently be arrived at by "rational analysis," but in ways which are differentially based on inductive evidence, and which may range in form from the positing of rational equations to the stipulation of verbally formulated, qualitative interrelations. In still other cases, the technique of function construction may be partly "empirical" and partly "rational," as combined into various concrete strategies.

{5} **Mensurational and quantificational procedures**

(*a*) What procedures are either specified or presupposed by the system with respect to the "measurement" (in the broadest sense) of the systematic independent and dependent variables?

How would the "level" or type of mensurability presently characteristic of the systematic independent and dependent variables be located by the systematist within the terms of the logic of measurement?

(*b*) To what extent do the procedures for "measurement" of the systematic independent and dependent variables satisfy the mathematical requirements of whatever quantitative techniques are employed for the description of function forms?

(*c*) What is the systematist's estimate of the principal difficulties in the way of increasing the mensurational and quantitative adequacy of the system? Future plans with respect to the mensurational and quantitative development of the system.

(*d*) Views of the systematist with respect to limitations, *in principle*, on "level" of measurement and degree of quantitative specificity of:

(1) his own system,

(2) systematic efforts in psychological science generally.

Explanation

Obviously, certain of these discussion topics will not be relevant to many of the systematic formulations sampled within the present study. Some formulations will be nonquantitative, in principle. Others will be prequantitative in their current form. In such cases, it would nevertheless be of great interest for the systematist to discuss items (*c*) and (*d*).

{6} **Formal organization of the system**

(*a*) Status of the system with respect to explicitness of axiomatization, and of derivational procedures employed.

(*b*) What factors (e.g., "strategic," "empirical") are responsible for the present mode of formal organization of the system?

(*c*) Views of the systematist about the ultimate level of formal explicitness for which it is desirable, *in principle*, to aim.

Explanation

Explicitness of axiomatization and derivational specificity or rigor can clearly vary over a very wide range, from informal exposition to detailed hypothetico-deductive development within the resources of mathematical notation and symbolic logic. It would be interesting if, in the discussions of the above topics, the systematist would present his views on such questions as the degree of "formalization" which he feels it may be fruitful to aim towards, in areas other than those to which his own systematic work is relevant.

In the discussion of "formal organization" a recapitulation of the definitional techniques employed within the system would be highly useful. Ideally, this would include a reconstruction of the roles of "implicit" (i.e., "postulational") definition, "explicit" definition, empirical or "operational" definition, and, in certain cases, "coordinating" definition, as these are respectively realized within the system.

{7} Scope or range of application of system

(*a*) Actual scope, as the system is currently constituted.

(*b*) Intended, ultimate scope and grounds for this delimitation. Concrete plans and programmatic devices for extension.

(*c*) Interrelations, present and potential, with formulations of other systematists in:

(1) areas coextensive with system, and

(2) other empirical areas.

{8} History of system to date in mediating research

(*a*) Itemization of the chief experimental or empirical research studies, or clusters of such, which the system has directly (i.e., by logical implication) or indirectly (i.e., by suggestive or heuristic guidance) instigated.

(*b*) What specific components of the system—e.g., orienting attitudes, general but incompletely specified "explanatory mechanisms" or constructs, specific lawful assumptions, methods—have been responsible for the research instigated by the system?

{9} Evidence for the system

(*a*) Current status of the "positive" evidence for the system (to the extent that this is not covered in item {8} above).

(*b*) Major extant sources of incompatible or "embarrassing" data.

(*c*) Specification of experimental designs which would be regarded as "critical" or important tests of principal foundation assumptions.

(*d*) Types of data which, in the opinion of the theorist, the theory accounts for more successfully than do alternate formulations. Classes of data which alternate formulations handle more successfully.

{10} Specific methods, concepts, or principles of the system believed valuable outside the context of the system

(*a*) Methods, concepts, or principles deemed fruitful for systematic advance in areas outside the projected range of application of the system.

(*b*) Chief methods, concepts, or principles believed to be of long-term significance, independently of the over-all structure or detailed assumptional content of the system.

{11} Degree of programmaticity

(*a*) Evaluation of the over-all extent to which the systematic program has been realized, at the given time.

(*b*) Estimation of the extent to which the system is tending towards convergence with other coextensive systems, articulation with systems having different empirical domains, subsumption of more limited systems, or subsumability under more general ones.

{12} Intermediate and long-range strategy for the development of the system

(*a*) What classes of empirical relationships does the theory most require knowledge about, and in what priority order?

(*b*) Estimate of the chief conceptual and empirical difficulties working against the development of the system.

(*c*) Estimates, based on the systematist's experience, of the chief barriers blocking *general* theoretical advance in psychology.

NOTE ON THE USE OF DISCUSSION TOPIC INDEX NUMBERS

As a convenience for the reader interested in the relation of essays to the discussion topics and in the cross-comparison of positions on key issues, index numbers corresponding to the twelve discussion themes have been inserted at relevant places in the Table of Contents preceding each of the essays. These numbers are placed in brackets immediately following the germane rubrics of the author's plan of discussion.

By and large, correspondences between authors' organization and the discussion topics are straightforward, and can easily be identified from the author's formulation of headings. Not infrequently, however, an author's system of headings may, in one or another way, be out of phase with the discussion rubrics, even though some or all of the relevant issues are considered. This circumstance has led to the following conventions:

The section designated by a given author-heading may be relevant to two or more themes. In such cases, the brackets will contain the requisite plurality of index numbers, e.g. {3, 8, 9}.

In cases in which a section, or some part of it, is *primarily* relevant to a given theme but includes brief, partial, or implicative consideration of a number of others, that is indicated by a + after the index number of primary relevance, e.g. {2+}.

When a section encompasses a number of discussion topics but gives them markedly different attention or emphasis, it has occasionally seemed worth setting the bracketed numbers in an order which roughly reflects this, e.g. {4, 5, 3}. Since such discriminations of relative emphasis cannot always be clearly made, there is no implication that index numbers are *not* differentially relevant when they are given in consecutive numerical order, e.g. {4, 5, 6}.

We should note, also, certain *general* restrictions on the use of index numbers:

With very few exceptions, they have been used only in conjunction with *major* subdivisions of the papers (i.e., headings of high "value"), the exceptions having been mainly cases in which essays contain a final section specifically for the purpose of bringing aspects of the preceding discussion

674

to bear on the themes. In such cases, index numbers have been inserted to identify the themes dealt with in relevant subsections.

Index numbers uniformly pertain to discussion themes as a whole, and do not separately identify the subitems which invite differentiated discussion under each theme. Once the correspondence with a given theme is identified, the reader will find that, in most instances, the bearing on particular sub-themes is easily discriminated.

In several papers, the author's plan of organization is such as to preclude the insertion of index numbers. In some of these (e.g., Ellson, Skinner) the author has preferred a type of discursive presentation sans headings— or has used so few of them that any use of index numbers would have been nondiscriminating. In a few cases (e.g., Pirenne and Marriott, Kallmann), the author's organization is so markedly out of phase with the discussion themes as to make any use of the numbers either confusing or unnatural. Nevertheless, it will be found in most of these cases that it requires little effort to determine the author's position with respect to many of the thematic issues. There are a few essays, however, to which certain of the suggested themes are not relevant in principle in that the concern is primarily with presystematic issues (e.g., Harlow).

Whatever the explicitness of relation of each paper to the themes, it should be emphasized that each is a self-contained essay, having *sui generis* properties in substance and form. Any cross-comparison or integration of findings which the reader may wish to conduct must depend on his own active discriminations; it will not be provided ready-made by any mechanical device. The present system of indexing is offered merely as a convenient starting point for comparative analysis. It has been kept typographically inconspicuous, and used in conjunction only with molar rubrics, both of author and thematic organization, so as not to interfere with the organic unity of each presentation.

NAME INDEX

SUBJECT INDEX

Topics followed by an asterisk are those treated by all or most authors (often extensively). These pertain mainly to the "crosscutting" systematic and methodic issues raised by the themes of analysis and related editorial proposals. In most instances, page references for such topics are given *only* to basic definitions or explanations. Individual author treatments of many asterisked topics can be located by reference to the tables of contents appearing with each article, in conjunction with the use of discussion topic index numbers (see Note on the Use of Discussion Topic Index Numbers, pp. 674–675).

Abstraction, method of, 48–50
Achievement, drive, 270
    and Zeigarnik effect, 34
Action Potential, Specific, 586
Action research, 47
Activity, and drive, 255–256, 269
    Vacuum and Overflow, 592
Acts, 133, 177, 183–184, 185, 189, 252
    consummatory, 572–577
    pure-stimulus, 302
    receptor-orienting, 316, 339
Adaptation, 524, 525, 530
    (*See also* Practice)
Advertising, 273
Afferent stimulus interaction, 316
Aggression, in contiguity theory, 170
    in Lewinian theory, 55
Agonistic behavior, 577, 586–587, 590–591
Agreement, intersubjective, 164
Alcohol, 225–226
Algebra, of inequalities, 285, 306–308
    matrix, 280
Alien facts of life space, 70–71
All-or-nothing behavior, 232–233
Alternation, spontaneous, 518
Ambiguity, in linear frequency theory, 640
    in nonspatial discrimination, 515–516
    scaled, 435–436
Ambivalence, in conflict of forces, 27–28, 230
    and redirection in behavior, 594–595
American Psychological Association, Policy and Planning Board of, vi
Amnesia, combat, 226–227
Amplification ratio, 645, 646, 650, 654
Amplifying systems, 639, 641–642, 644
Amplitude of response, 313, 327
Analog computer (*see* Servo theory)

Analysis, human motor behavior, in linear frequency theory, 638
    level of (*see* Level, of analysis*)
    mathematical, 470
        (*See also* Algebra; Equations; Experimental design; Graph theory; Learning curves; Method; Models*; Prediction*; Probability; Quantification*; Scaling; Statistics)
    rational, 671
        (*See also* Equations; Learning curves)
    themes of (*see* Themes of analysis)
    of variance, 444, 633
Anchoring, concepts, 309–311
    variables, 554–555
Animal stunt training, 370–371
Animals, rationale of experimental use of, 204
Anthropology, relation of psychology to, 272, 303
Anxiety, nomothetic vs. ideographic study of, 372, 375
    stimulus-response analysis of, 267–269
    studies showing effect of treatment of, 373
    (*See also* Fear)
Apparatus, tracking, 651–652
Apparatus breakdown, 367
Appetitive behavior, 569, 572–577
    (*See also* Orientation)
Applied psychology, 371–372
    (*See also* Linear frequency theory)
Approach-avoidance conflict, 199–238
Approach gradient postulates, 205–206, 228–230
    (*See also* Conflict, theory of)
Approach training, Tolman's conception of, 99–117
Approximation, and correction, 249–250, 469–472

[1] For a detailed statement of aims, design, working methods, history, etc., of *Psychology: A Study of a Science,* see Vol. 1, pp. 1–40. Pages 1–18 comprise the "General Introduction to the Series"; pp. 19–40, the "Introduction to Study I Conceptual and Systematic."